The Psychological Development of Low-Birthweight Children

ANNUAL ADVANCES IN APPLIED DEVELOPMENTAL PSYCHOLOGY VOLUME 6

VOLUME EDITORS:

Sarah L. Friedman
*National Institutes of Child Health
and Human Development
Bethesda, MD*

Marian D. Sigman
*University of California
Los Angeles, CA*

SERIES EDITOR:

Irving E. Sigel
Educational Testing Service

ABLEX PUBLISHING CORPORATION
NORWOOD, NEW JERSEY

Printed in the United States of America.

ISBN: 0-89391-855-5   ISSN: 0748-8572

Ablex Publishing Corporation
355 Chestnut Street
Norwood, New Jersey 07648

This book is dedicated to
Arthur Hawley Parmelee
who has taught us all so much about child development.

Contents

         Birthweight Infants
     Virginia A. Rauh and John Brennan

     Author Index   471
     Subject Index   490

Contributors

Heidelise Als, Ph.D.
Enders Pediatrics Research
The Children's Hospital
300 Longwood Ave.
Boston, MA 02115

Robert F. Asarnow, Ph.D.
Department of Psychiatry NPI
UCLA School of Medicine
760 Westwood Plaza
Los Angeles, CA 90024

Kathryn E. Barnard, R.N., Ph.D.
University of Washington
Mail Stop WJ-10
Seattle, WA 98195

Valerie E. Barsky, M.A.
Dept. of Special Education
OISE
252 Bloor Street West
Toronto, Ontario
Canada M5S 1V6

Leila Beckwith, Ph.D.
Department of Pediatrics
School of Medicine
University of California
Los Angeles, CA 90024

Patricia A. Brandt, Ph.D.
Department of Psychology
George Washington University
2125 G Street, NW
Washington, DC 20052

John L. Brennan, M.B.B.S.
Department of Psychiatry
The University of South Wales
Sidney, Australia

Jeanne Brooks-Gunn, Ph.D.
Education Testing Service
Princeton, NJ 08525

Stephen Buka, Ph.D.
Child Study Center
Brown University
Box 1836
Providence, RI 02912

Heather Carmichael-Olson, Ph.D.
Behavioral Teratolgy Clinic
2707 NE Blakely Street GG-20
University of Washington
Seattle, WA 98105

Sarale E. Cohen, Ph.D.
Department of Pediatrics
School of Medicine
University of California
Los Angeles, CA 90293

Bruce A.B. Cooper, Ph.D.
Harold E. Jones Child Study Center
Institute of Human Development
University of California
2425 Atherton Street
Berkeley, CA 94704

Keith A. Crnic, Ph.D.
612 Moore
Department of Psychology
Penn State University
University Park, PA 16802

Carol O. Eckerman, Ph.D.
Department of Psychology
Duke University
Durham, NC 27706

Sarah L. Friedman, Ph.D.
National Institutes of Child Health and
    Human Development
9000 Rockville Pike
Bethesda, MD

Mark T. Greenberg, Ph.D.
Department of Psychology NI-25
University of Washington
Seattle, WA 98195

Ruth Gross
Infant Health and Development Program
Center for the Study of Youth Development
Bldg 460
Stanford, CA 94305-2135

Mary Hammond, Ph.D.
Parent and Child Nursing
University of Washington
Mail Stop SC74
Seattle, WA 98195

Frances D. Horowitz, Ph.D.
City University Graduate Program
32 West 42nd St.
New York, NY 10036

Jane V. Hunt, Ph.D.
University of California
Harold E. Jones Child Study Center
2425 Atherton St.
Berkeley, CA 94704

Joel Kleinman, Ph.D., deceased
Division of Analysis
National Center for Health Statistics
3700 East West Highway
Hyattsville, MD 20782

Lewis P. Lipsitt, Ph.D.
Hunter Laboratories of Psychology
Brown University
89 Waterman
Providence, RI 02912

Diane Magyary, Ph.D.
Parent and Child Nursing
University of Washington
Mail Stop SC74
Seattle, WA 98195

Marie C. McCormick, M.D., Sc.D.
Joint Program in Neonatology
Brigham and Women Hospital
75 Francis St.
Boston, MA 02115

Klaus K. Minde
Department of Psychiatry
72 Barrie St.
Queen's University
Kingston, Ontario
Canada K7L 3N6

Jerri M. Oehler, Ph.D.
Box 3322
Duke University Medical Center
Durham, NC 27710

Arthur H. Parmelee, Jr., M.D.
764 Ififf Street
Pacific Palisades, CA 90272

Virginia A. Rauh, Ph.D.
Center for Population and Family Health
Columbia University Health Sciences
New York, NY 10027

Carol J. Rodning, Ph.D.
UCLA
Department of Pediatrics/Child
  Development
1000 Veteran Avenue
Rehab 23-10L
Los Angeles, CA 90024

Linda S. Siegel, Ph.D.
Department of Special Education
OISE
252 Bloor Street W.
Toronto, Ontario
Canada M5S 1V6

Marian D. Sigman, Ph.D.
68237 Department of Psychiatry
University of California
School of Medicine
Los Angeles, CA 90024

Anita M. Sostek, Ph.D.
Division of Research Grants
National Institutes of Health
9000 Rockville Pike
Westwood Bldg., Room 203A
Bethesda, MD 20892

Donna K. Spiker, Ph.D.
Infant Health and Development Program
Center for the Study of Youth Development
Stanford University
Building 460
Stanford, CA 94305

William H. Tooley, M.D.
Pediatrics Department
University of California, San Francisco
Box 0734
U-501
San Francisco, CA 94143

Ming T. Tsuang, M.D., Ph.D.
Psychiatry Department
Brockton Roxbury VA Medical Center
940 Belmont Street
Brockton, MA 02401

I
Introduction

Introduction

Irving E. Sigel

The understanding about the sequelae of low-birthweight infants should be one of national interest. With the incidence of preterm low-birthweight infants surviving due to the increased sophistication of medical technology, it becomes imperative that we expand our knowledge about the nature of preterm low-birthweight children so that psychological as well as medical procedures can be developed to optimize their social, psychological, and biological development. I have invited Friedman and Sigman to ask a group of expert practitioners and researchers to address the critical issues, as well as contemporary approaches, used to deal with the developmental social, intellectual, and coping problems of low-birthweight infants and their families.

The editors have organized the volume into five sections which in their totality demonstrate the scope of knowledge relevant to the understanding and study of low-birthweight infants. After a comprehensive introductory overview of the problems attendant on low-birthweight infants and the needs for future research, the remaining chapters fall into four sections beginning with a discussion of epidemiological, methodological, and theoretical considerations for the study of low-birthweight infants. This is followed by drawing attention to the advances in neonatal intensive care, with the aim of increasing the probability of infant survival. A perspective to help organize one's thoughts about this ambiguous concept of *infant-at-risk* follows, enabling the reader to conceptualize about research and intervention with infants at risk. Research reports of social, emotional, and intellectual development follow. Here one reads of the long-term effects of prematurity and low birthweight. These longitudinal studies have much to offer in defining psychological outcomes beyond the early years. The last chapters deal with intervention, the procedures to ameliorate the potential negative effects of low birthweight.

The essays presented in the foregoing sections of the book represent a significant body of work by expert researchers and practitioners to address the psychological problems particular to these populations. Armed with this information, options become available to help optimize the course of development for these children and their families. The mix of basic research studies, complemented by discussions of developmental theory and intervention programs, provides a unique, rational, and coherent whole where knowledge and practice are connected in one place. The whole encompasses what applied developmental psychology is all about.

Perhaps a word about what applied developmental psychology is, at least from my point of view as the series editor. This relatively new field of psychology is a growing professional specialty which can be defined as one that employs a multidisciplinary approach in the service of working on real-life human problems in natural settings. Applying this definition to work with low-birthweight infants, it becomes readily apparent that the editors, Friedman and Sigman, have brought together in one volume a set of articles that fits the definition. Although most of the writers of these chapters are psychologists, they play very different roles in their work places and so have different kinds of expertise which are required to deal with the myriad of complex problems facing the low-birthweight infant and his or her family.

Of particular interest in this volume are the studies describing the long-term effects of low birthweight on intellectual and social functioning of these children in the context of the caregiving approaches of parents. These studies become possible because of the long-term attention researchers have dedicated to the study of these children. We are very fortunate that such data are available, because basically the long-term sequelae are of paramount interest in order to know what the background developmental factors are that must be considered to optimize their development. These follow-up studies should enable practitioners to plan intervention programs early in the lives of the children to prevent adverse psychological outcomes. Since there is every likelihood that the number of surviving low-birthweight infants born in the United States may be higher because of advances in medical technology, such information will be of considerable value to policymakers and practitioners.

To be sure, no single volume can encompass the many topics of interest in this field. All a single volume can do is to present some of the most salient questions, pose some answers, and describe prescriptive methods aimed at solutions.

What Friedman and Sigman have done is to provide an excellent compendium of significant research, basic and applied, as well as conceptual and integrative chapters. In so doing, within one volume they provide the interested researcher or graduate student with a fund of valuable information which will lead to an informed understanding of the state of knowledge in the field.

Not only will the reader have an opportunity to acquire a set of substantiated knowledge, but also come to see how the diverse laboratories have acquired this information. By combining discussions of theory and method, as well as application, the reader becomes a richer and better informed researcher and/or practitioner.

1

Past, Present, and Future Directions in Research on the Development of Low-Birthweight Children

Sarah L. Friedman
Marian D. Sigman

ORIGINS AND NEW DIRECTIONS OF WORK PUBLISHED IN THE 1980s

In 1981 we edited a volume entitled *Preterm Birth and Psychological Development*, with chapters presenting information representative of the research questions, methods, and findings of the 1970s. The present volume contains chapters representative of scientific research conducted in the 1980s and pertaining to all low-birthweight children, the majority of whom are preterm. We undertook the editing of this volume because we wanted to compile in one volume research representative of work conducted in the 1980s. We also wanted to document the directions that research on low-birthweight children has taken over the last 10 years and to reflect on directions that research may take in the future. In general terms the enterprise of studying low-birthweight children still has the same goals as it had in the early 1970s: (a) To evaluate the developmental outcome of children with low birthweight, some of whom would not have survived the neonatal period or whose future development might have been compromised without medical intervention; (b) To discover the conditions that are associated with successful developmental outcome; and (c) To plan and evaluate interventions that are based on scientific knowledge.

There are several reasons why the evaluation of outcomes of low birthweight is still ongoing and is continuously expanding. The overarching reason is that the causes for prematurity are not understood and that, consequently, low birthweight is a condition that has not been eradicated. At the same time, medical technology and expertise are continuously improving and leading to the survival of smaller and smaller infants. These infants experience medical complications that are resolved but which may affect the developmental outcome of the children. Given these circumstances, researchers, and clinicians are called upon to evaluate the success of medical interventions and to devise interventions that will complement the work of physicians by improving the quality of life of the survivors.

As researchers have pursued the goal of evaluating the outcome of low-birthweight children, they have expanded the scope of the evaluation methods they used. In earlier studies of preterm children, investigators looked at neuro-developmental status (i.e., motor function, the presence of visual and auditory impairment, and the presence of cerebral palsy), school performance, and global intellectual function (as measured by I.Q. tests). Only studies of infants included more detailed measures of sensory and cognitive processes. In the past 10 years, however, researchers of the intellectual development of low-birthweight pre-school and school age children have added to their studies finer measures of cognitive processes. The scope of the research about the development of low-birthweight infants and children was also expanded in terms of the domains of psychological function that were investigated. As mentioned earlier, publications appearing in the 1970s emphasized the evaluation of sensory and cognitive function. During the same period, a few investigators compared the aspects of temperament of preterm and full-term infants as well as processes of mother–child interaction. In the 1980s more and more research programs added a focus on the social and emotional development of low-birthweight infants and children.

This expansion in the domains of investigation occurred when it did due to influences from the mainstream of research in the area of child development. Investigators were applying newly developed methods to their investigations of low-birthweight children. This application of new methods led to findings showing that the behavior of low-birthweight children differed from the behavior of full-term children.

Another expansion in the scope of research was made possible by the matura-tion of the children in samples already studied at earlier ages. Investigators were eager to follow their low-birthweight research subjects into middle childhood, adolescence, and early adulthood. They wanted to determine whether some of the effects they discovered when the children were infants or toddlers were maintained and whether new group differences between preterms and full-term children emerged when the children were older. Consequently, evidence has accumulated about many characteristics of children who were born very early and very small and who were followed up to older ages. This volume reflects all the above mentioned aspects of the expansion in the scope of investigations conducted and/or published in the 1980s.

Psychologists and medical researchers who have investigated the develop-ment of low-birthweight children wanted to identify the conditions that place these children at risk. They have investigated relationships between demograph-ic, parental, and infant health variables and the quality of the neurodevelopmen-tal and psychological outcome of low-birthweight infants and children. Research in the 1970s focused on gestational age, birthweight, and medical status as possible predictors of outcome. In general, the medical status of the infants was not found to predict reliably to later developmental outcome. Research findings in the 1980s have revealed that proximal social variables, such as the quality of the mother–child interaction and of the home environment, have a major influ-ence on the outcome of low-birthweight children.

Some of the prediction research literature focuses on the degree to which there is stability from early classification of the children to later classification of these children. Like most of the research that deals with predicting the outcome of low-birthweight infants, such research was designed to make statements about groups (or subgroups) of children. The findings from most studies were not expected to allow prediction in individual cases. One chapter in this volume (by Barsky and Siegel) presents an attempt to evaluate the success of prediction for individual very low-birthweight children based on environmental, perinatal, and reproductive variables, all of which are either believed or known to interact and influence the outcome of low-birthweight children. The conceptually and empirically guided attempt to move from statistical prediction to clinical prediction through knowledge of component variables may prove particularly valuable for prescribing interventions for children who are at risk.

Much of the research concerning the development of low-birthweight children that was conducted before the 1980s was empirical, as described above. However, a major theoretical question that was addressed concerned the role of extrauterine experience versus the role of biological maturation in the development of early sensory and cognitive function. The scientific literature published in the 1970s showed that preterm infants did not benefit from their lengthened extrauterine experience. For the most part, the cognitive and perceptual abilities of the preterm infants tested at corrected ages were either equivalent to or somewhat behind those of full-term infants. This can be interpreted to mean that the capacities of the preterm infants were largely determined by their maturation and/or that the kinds of extrauterine environments available to the infants were ineffective for maintaining their development.

In the 1980s, somewhat different theoretical issues have been addressed by investigators of low-birthweight children. In this volume we have repeated reference to the Transactional Model proposed by Sameroff and Chandler (1975) and a reference to Systems Theory (e.g., Fogel & Thelen, 1987). Both theoretical models describe the development of the child as shaped or moderated by interactions with his or her environment. However, it is worth noting that the conceptual frameworks referred to are not translated into well-articulated research hypotheses or into the details of research design or analysis. As a response to the increasing interest in embedding research about low-birthweight children in a theoretical framework, we have incorporated a theoretical chapter (Horowitz) in this volume. The conceptual framework provided by that chapter builds on and extends the Transactional Model.

The study of the development of low-birthweight children is necessarily a multidisciplinary venture. It calls for expertise in medicine, epidemiology, sociology, and psychology. Many of the chapters in this volume tacitly suggest the need for multidisciplinary contributions in this line of research. This need was recognized by the March of Dimes when, in the mid 1970s, it started its program of support for research concerning preterm children. The foundation's call for research applications required that the principal investigator for a proposed project consist of a team of medical and behavioral scientists. The multi-disciplinary nature of the research questions and the need for cross-disciplinary collaborations have manifested themselves in the fact that some of the more influential research in this field was conducted by teams that included medical and psychological researchers. Yet it is unfortunate that epidemiologists and sociologists who study low birthweight rarely participate in research teams investigating the development of low-birthweight children.

AN OVERVIEW OF THIS VOLUME

Epidemiological, Medical, and Theoretical Considerations

The volume opens with a section on epidemiological, medical, and theoretical considerations. The three chapters in this section provide rationales for the study of low-birthweight children as well as new research ideas. Dr. Kleinman presents survival data for low-birthweight (1,500–2,500 grams) and very low-birthweight (less than 1,500 grams) infants of different racial backgrounds and asks if the factors that are predictive of survival are also the ones that are predictive of the developmental outcome of the survivors. He emphasizes the enigma of racial differences in low birthweight in the U.S.A. and suggests that cultural and intergenerational factors may be responsible for this phenomenon. He also suggests that, in order to make meaningful comparisons between the outcome for black and caucasian infants, the cut-off points for the classification of low birthweight may need to be different for black and caucasian infants.

McCormick discusses the lack of understanding of the mechanisms leading to a premature termination of pregnancy. At the same time, she presents evidence showing that the medical technologies for saving smaller and smaller neonates are improving. While it is doubtful that neonates weighing less than 500 grams or born before 23 weeks of gestation will survive, it is expected that work will continue on improving the outcome for survivors. The resulting medical advances will need to be evaluated in terms of their impact on the development of the children and the functioning of their families. McCormick advocates evaluations that go beyond I.Q. tests and tests of neurodevelopmental status as well as evaluations that continue beyond the period of infancy. She also advocates interventions that rely heavily on the involvement of the family.

Both Kleinman and McCormick make a distinction between low-birthweight and very low-birthweight neonates. That distinction is also made in the developmental follow-up scientific literature. In the last decade, investigators of low-birthweight infants and children have sometimes focused on the very low-birthweight children, to the exclusion of heavier birthweight children. This trend is also reflected in this volume. While the distinction between very low birthweight and low birthweight is meaningful in terms of medical management and survival, it is less clear how meaningful the distinction is from a developmental point of view. It is possible that a continuum of birthweight or other birthweight classifications is more meaningful. The distinction may also be meaningful for some areas of development but not for others. Studies to evaluate the relationship between categories of low birthweight and short- or long-term psychological outcome may be stimulated by the November 1990 publication by McCormick, Gortmaker, and Sobol, who conducted a secondary analysis of the 1981 National Interview Health Survey—Child Health Supplement. They found that 34% of very low-birthweight children could be characterized as having school difficulty, compared with 20% of low-birthweight children and 14% of normal birthweight children. The very low-birthweight children were also more likely to have higher scores on the hyperactivity subscale of an index of behavior problems.

The chapter by Horowitz presents a theoretical framework for the study of children at risk. Many of the investigations reported in the volume are inspired by the Transactional Model proposed by Sameroff and Chandler (1975). The framework by Horowitz elaborates on that model and extends it. For example, organismic and environmental variables are described as being on a continuum. Possible interactions between organismic variables, environmental variables, and different classes of dependent variables are assessed. The framework provides guidance and fresh ideas for (a) the evaluation of the concept of risk, (b) the investigation of developmental processes and developmental outcomes associated with different types or combinations of risk, and (c) research on intervention.

Social and Emotional Development

The second section of the volume includes six chapters with a focus on the social and emotional development of low-birthweight children. This is in contrast to only one chapter dealing with the social domain appearing in the volume we edited in 1981. In two of these chapters, the authors also provide information about the intellectual and/or academic performance of the children. We have decided to include these chapters in this section of the volume because the focus on the social-emotional development of the children is more novel in the context of the history of research on the development of low-birthweight children.

The chapter by Eckerman and Oehler is critical of the way that investigators have been studying low-birthweight infants and their interactions with their social partners. In particular, these authors reject the deficit model that compares low-birthweight infants and full-term infants. They also reject the model that conceptualizes the low-birthweight infant as a responder rather than as a participant in social interchanges. Eckerman and Ohler explain the need to understand low-birthweight infants and their social partners in their own right and in the context of the conditions that shape their mutually interdependent interactions. They present data on the responsiveness of very low-birthweight young infants to the human voice and to stroking. They find that the human voice promotes attention, and that stroking promotes irritability. They also describe goals mothers have when they interact with their very low-birthweight infants.

The longitudinal follow-up research reported by Greenberg, Carmichael-Olson, and Crnic is guided by the Transactional Model. These authors compare the development of low-risk preterms with that of healthy full-term infants during the first 4 years of life. Development was evaluated with cognitive, linguistic, social, and behavioral measures. The predictive usefulness of health, social ecology, and parental variables was assessed. At 4 years of age, most of the preterms appeared to perform within normal limits. There were, however, some subtle skill deficits in nonverbal cognition and in the social domain. The parents of preterms reported more behavioral problems. Boys were more likely to have such problems and they perceived themselves as less accepted by peers. The relation between the cognitive and social measures were different for the two groups. In full-term children, distal variables such as socioeconomic class predicted the developmental outcome, while in preterms early maternal attitudes and the quality of the home environment were better predictors.

The chapter by Minde reviews the scientific literature and reports on a series of studies of very low-birthweight infants and their parents that were undertaken in the last decade. Minde reports findings about the process of parenting a premature infant and about the developmental outcome of low-birthweight infants. Both biological risk factors and parenting factors were considered as possible predictors of parent–child interaction and of the children's emotional and social functioning. Minde and his collaborators found that low-birthweight infants do not have a higher rate of psychiatric disturbances by age 4 than do full-term children. However, they display a significant number of behavior problems such as hyperactive or impulsive behaviors, temper tantrums, and general immaturity that are reported both by parents and teachers. Interestingly, the problems described by teachers are associated with nonresponsive mothering at early infancy, with poorer marital relationships and maternal emotional health, little social support, and little satisfaction in the maternal role.

Buka, Lipsitt, and Tsuang review 17 studies of the emotional and behavioral development of low-birthweight children and report preliminary findings from ongoing analyses of another study. All the studies except one were published in the 1980s. They are all prospective and include longitudinal studies of only low-birthweight children, longitudinal studies of low-birthweight and comparison children, and cohort studies. The age of the subjects ranges from 3 years to adulthood, with most in middle childhood. The studies show that, as a group, low-birthweight children and young adults are at increased risk for the development of emotional and behavioral problems characterized by high activity levels and low attention spans. Infants born small for gestational age are at a particular risk, as are boys born into an adverse social environment who show signs of early neurological and developmental problems. Low-birthweight girls may be at risk for more withdrawn, shy, and passive behavior.

Magyary, Brandt, Hammond, and Barnard sought to identify neonatal and

8-year predictors of behavioral problems and of intellectual outcomes in 68 8-year-old preterms. They used three categories of predictors: Infants' status variables, distal variables describing the family (e.g., demographic characteristics), and proximal variables of the quality of family interactions. Generally, they found that family stress and other family variables are significantly related to the social-emotional development of the children, with specific family variables predicting specific social-emotional outcomes. The intellectual outcomes, the general intelligence, and the academic achievement of the children were predicted by infant mental development, infant readiness to learn, and the home environment.

Cohen, Parmelee, Beckwith, and Sigman examined the antecedents and correlates of social-emotional competence as assessed by ratings of behavior problems and social behavior in a group of early adolescents (12-year-olds) who were born preterm. Their findings support previous research showing a high number of behavioral problems in school children who were born prematurely. In early adolescence, children were more likely to be described as exhibiting problem behavior by their parents than by their teachers. In particular, slow-maturing boys were seen by their parents, but not by their teachers, as more problematic. The children who were identified as having problems were less confident of themselves, less able to focus their attention, and less competent in school than the early adolescents who were perceived as showing normal behavior. This was the case even though no differences were found between these two groups of children in terms of their intelligence. There were few clear antecedent conditions in infancy and early childhood as to problem behavior as perceived by the parents. Parental ratings of low social competence, however, had antecedents in the children's medical condition, early development, and the home environment. Teacher ratings, in contrast, appeared more related to external factors such as the children's social class and school achievement.

The findings reported in the chapters reviewed above suggest that low-birthweight children are at risk in the social and emotional domains. It is clear that the risk is not massive and that they are not predisposed to psychiatric problems. The individual differences that were found in the functioning of the low-birthweight children strongly suggest that it is quite possible that the social and emotional problems of these children can be resolved with interventions directed at their primary social partners and at the children themselves. The fact that the findings are based on parental and teacher reports, and that these reports are not consistent, suggests that there is a need for investigations examining the children in different social contexts (e.g., with siblings, with peers, with parents) and for using observational methodologies as well as self-reports.

Intellectual and Academic Performance

The third section of the volume deals with intellectual and academic performance. Even though this domain of developmental functioning has the longest history of psychological research pertaining to low-birthweight children, the research questions to be asked have not been exhausted, and the chapters in this volume present findings beyond those that were reported in our 1981 volume on the psychological development of preterm children. Overall, the chapters in this section indicate that, even though they have more learning and cognitive problems than full-birthweight children, only a small portion of low-birthweight children suffer serious intellectual deficits. These findings parallel the ones in the social/emotional domain, where low-birthweight children show behavior problems but fewer psychiatric disturbances.

The chapter by Sostek presents an attempt to differentiate between the effects of intraventricular hemorrhage (IVH) and the effects of prematurity on the psychological functioning of children whose age ranges between 4½ and 5½. Routine prospective screening of preterm infants by ultrasonography for intraventricular hemorrhage started approximately in 1980. This has allowed investigators to evaluate the effects of different degrees of bleeding in the brain ventricles of preterm neonates on the development of the affected children as they matured from infancy into the toddler years. Sostek reports that 4½- to 5½-year-old children who suffered from major hemorrhage performed more poorly than children free of hemorrhage on general cognitive functioning, recognition/discrimination, alphabet recitation, and kindergarten readiness. Also, their motor skills were particularly vulnerable. Children who suffered minor hemorrhage were significantly more ready for school than the children with major IVH and had better motor performance. Preterms with no history of hemorrhage performed worse than full-term children in perceptual-motor, memory, and quantitative skills — areas that are associated with learning disabilities.

The chapter by Barsky and Siegel provides a review of studies aimed at predicting the cognitive and school performance outcome of very low-birthweight children. The authors are guided by the Transactional Model mentioned earlier and review studies on the effects of both biological and environmental variables on the development of low-birthweight children. The authors' review is also guided by the conviction that the use of neurodevelopmental and intelligence tests is of limited value when applied to the prospective evaluation of the development of low-birthweight children. They advocate and review studies that examine specific cognitive processes and specific aspects of school performance. Such detailed studies are more interesting and useful, since they reveal the specific areas of difficulty for low-birthweight children and may lead to successful interventions for these children. The chapter ends with a description of a method for predicting the developmental outcome of individual very low-birthweight children. Siegel and her collaborators found that this method correctly classified 93.3% of children on the 2-year Bayley MDI scores. Prediction to ages 6, 7, and 8 was not as good, with error (14%–18%) mainly on the side of false positives.

Sigman, Cohen, Beckwith, Asarnow, and Parmelee are also interested in prediction. Their research investigates what aspects of cognition at 8 and 12 years of age can be predicted from measures of infant responsiveness to visual stimuli, sleep state integration, and infant–caregiver interaction. Cognition at 8 years of age was measured by the three factors of WISC-R I.Q.: verbal comprehension, perceptual organization, and freedom from distractibility. Cognition at 12 years of age was evaluated by measures of accuracy of speeded processing, capacity for sustained attention, and ability to reason with novel information. The research subjects for this investigation were preterms born at the mean gestational age of 32.5 weeks. For this group of children, statistically significant relations were found between measures taken in infancy and those taken at ages 8 and 12.

The research literature shows differences between full-term and preterm groups on measures of infant information processing, infant sleep state organization, childhood cognition, and child–caregiver interaction. The extent to which the relationships between measures taken in infancy and those taken in adolescence as described by Sigman et al. distinguish preterm children from full-term children has yet to be investigated.

Hunt, Tooley, and Cooper describe long-term consequences of low birthweight at 8 years of age and in young adulthood. Outcome at 8 years is described in terms of I.Q., school performance, and need for educational intervention. Performance in early adult life was measured in terms of educational attainment and occupational status. They also describe their method for characterizing neonatal illness and nutritional status which they found to be predictive of long-term outcome as measured by an I.Q. test.

The follow-up of low-birthweight individuals to adult age (also reported in Buka et al., this volume) represents an important extension of the scientific investigation of low birthweight and its consequences. The chapter by Hunt and her collaborators tells us that the 20 young adults that were born between 1964 and 1971 and contacted again between the ages of 18 and 24, present themselves as typical young adults in middle class American society. This is the case even though 8 of them were identified by the investigators as having some psychological-test performance problems in school age, and despite the fact that 6 of the remaining 12 reported educational interventions. The findings show that normal intellectual and occupational outcome is possible for children born at risk. It is possible that the same individuals might have reached higher standards with less effort and less cost if they were born with normal birth weight. Yet, given the fact that they were born with low birthweight, the evaluation of their outcome is measured against a standard of normalcy, not against a standard of highest possible potential. Overall, the results of this pioneering study are very reassuring, and they raise the need to replicate the findings in other samples, in more domains of functioning and with as many objective measures as possible.

The self-report findings described by Hunt are important not only because the subjects were young adults. They are also important because they suggest that, despite difficulties, low-birthweight individuals are pleased with themselves and with the way they have coped. The sense of well-being as well as low-birth-weight individuals' self-esteem are worth exploring longitudinally from early childhood throughout adolescence and young adulthood. An important criterion for evaluating the developmental outcome for low-birthweight individuals should be a subjective criterion: these individuals' satisfaction with the quality of their life. To date, research has been missing such subjective criteria.

Interventions and Their Effects

The last section of this volume presents studies of interventions and their effects. The rationale for many intervention studies grows out of the Transactional Model of development and out of the research literature showing that the quality of life of surviving low-birthweight infants and children is influenced by the quality of the social environment in which they grow. To the extent that intervention studies are successful in improving the developmental outcome of low-birth-weight individuals, they provide further evidence in support of the Transactional Model, according to which the outcome of children at risk is dependent on the continued interaction between biological and environmental factors.

The chapter by Als represents attempts at intervention in the neonatal intensive care unit (NICU). Such attempts include the use of waterbed mattresses (Korner, Lane, Berry, Rho, & Brown, 1990), introducing a "breathing" teddy bear (Thoman & Graham, 1986), and pressure massaging of the infants (Field, 1990).

Als proposes interventions for humanizing the intensive care environment through involving the families very actively in the care of their infants and fitting the social aspects of care to the individual needs of the infants. The intervention calls for "the astute observation of the infant's current behavioral cues" and "the interpretation of the infant's behaviors in a framework of regulatory efforts toward self-set goals." Als presents some data showing that the care she advocates leads to improvement in growth, health, and psychological development. The effects are demonstrated in the neonatal period, throughout infancy and up to 3 years of age.

Beckwith and Rodening show that intervention with mothers who are at social-economic risk may not always translate into improved developmental outcome for their low-birthweight children. These authors provided intervention that was aimed at improving the relationship between the mothers and their infants and at increasing the percentage of infants who show secure attachment to their mothers. The intervention was very successful in terms of its effects on maternal attitudes and behaviors but less successful in terms of the social/emotional or cognitive development of the children. At the termination of intervention, when the children were 13 months old, they did not perform differently from the control children. At 20 months corrected age the intervention group children showed less of a decline than control children on a cognitive scale. Also, at 20 months, the intervention children who were securely attached to their mothers demonstrated more positive affect than securely attached control children even though there were no group differences in the percentage of children who were securely attached. The effects of the intervention on the mothers were related to the relationships between the mothers and their families of origin, with mothers from unstable homes benefitting most during the intervention, but not able to maintain the benefits after the intervention was discontinued. Mothers who came from stable homes maintained the benefits of intervention 7 months after it was discontinued.

The most ambitious study of the effects of intervention on the development of low-birthweight infants and toddlers is reported by Gross, Brooks-Gunn, and Spiker. The intervention group consisted of 377 infants and the control group included 608 infants. The children were from eight sites across the United States. Children in both groups received care and were followed up during the children's first 3 years of life. However, the intervention group was the target of more services and greater personalized care. The intervention was associated with superior cognitive function, as measured by I.Q. tests, fewer behavior problems as reported by mothers, and higher scores on measures of the social and physical home environment.

As mentioned above, the infants and toddlers in the control group were also the target of an intervention: "Infants in both groups participated in the same pediatric follow-up, comprised of medical, developmental, and social assessments, with referrals to existing pediatric care and other community services as needed. These took place at eight clinic visits at 40 weeks conceptional age, 4, 8, 12, 24, 30, and 36 months corrected age." Even though Gross and her collaborators do not provide further detail about the services for the control subjects, it is clear that children in the control group were more privileged in terms of the services provided than many other low-birthweight children. Despite this, the children in the control group had surprisingly low Stanford Binet I.Q. scores (m = 84.5, S.D. = 19.9).

While the follow-up control children were not doing as well as the children in the experimental group, it is worth asking how well they did relative to matched controls who were not provided with the same extent of follow-up, as well as how well they are doing relative to full-term children of the same social and economic background. Such findings may be of particular interest to policy makers who want to know the extent to which increments in developmental outcomes are associated with increments in intervention costs.

The outcomes for the intervention group are impressive and encouraging. Even though the interventions must have been expensive, they are undoubtably much less expensive than the resources that society would have to invest over these children's lifetime if no intervention was provided. Retaining children in grade, providing special classes for the learning disabled, the lost productivity of individuals who could function at higher levels when they reach the work place, and the social problems that are generated by individuals who used to have behavior problems as children — all need to be considered when evaluating the merits of extensive early intervention.

The concluding chapter by Rauh and Brennan discusses the influences of demographic factors, social-contextual factors, parental psychological characteristics, and infant characteristics as moderator variables that influence the success of environmental interventions with low-birthweight children. The authors review pertinent research and present statistical analyses to support the points they are making. They use the Transactional Model in order to guide their evaluation of the conditions that enhance or hamper the success of intervention programs. While others have used the Transactional Model to justify social and educational interventions, Rauh and Brennan use it to explore and highlight the conditions under which interventions may be more or less successful.

Future Directions

The overview of the chapters includes suggestions for future directions pertaining to the work presented in the chapters. Below are future directions not mentioned previously.

Optimally, conceptual frameworks lead to specific research questions and to specific hypotheses. To date, the transactional conceptual frameworks, which are the dominant models in the field, have provided only very general ideas for research design and have guided after-the-fact interpretations of results. One important reason for this is that the authors of the models and those who chose to adopt the models have not developed a detailed description of each component in the model. Likewise, they have not described methods for measuring these components.

The further elaboration and specification of Transactional Models will make it possible for researchers to ask specific research questions that are suggested by the models. The elaboration of the models, and the statement of specific research questions, will also drive the development of methods that will allow measurement of the different components of the models at similar levels of specificity. The choice of the level of detail in the measurement of the different components of the models would need to be tailored to the question asked and the answers that are being sought. At present, it seems that the level of measurement is dictated by the instruments that are available, not by the research questions. For example, consider the fact that most studies investigating the effects of environmental influences on the development of low-birthweight children have not used detailed measures of the proximal physical environment in which the children find themselves. In most studies where the proximal social environment of the child is measured, it is measured by evaluating the mother while ignoring characteristics of the physical environment or the fact that many children spend hours with other important social others. An exception are recent studies using the H.O.M.E. scale (Caldwell, Heider, & Kaplan, 1966), which combines items measuring both the physical and the social aspects of the environment in which young children grow (Siegel & Cunningham, 1984; Bradley, Caldwell, Rock, Casey, & Nelson, 1987).

Most long-term follow-up studies of low-birthweight children have been designed and redesigned as the children matured and as research funds became available. The various follow-up components of the studies have not been planned in all their details before the children were born. In other words, there was no one a priori plan to study the children at all the ages at which they ended up being studied. Within the subplans that encompassed a limited number of years for follow-up, the choice of ages for follow-up was often not determined by knowledge as to when children reach certain developmental milestones. In addition, only a few measures (primarily measures of intelligence) were administered repeatedly. The measures that were not used repeatedly could be used as predictors, or could be correlated with predictor measures, but they could not be used for describing profiles of development over the years. Due to these design limitations, the longitudinal data was frequently analyzed in two general ways: (a) as cross sectional data, comparing the performance of different groups of children at a given age point; and (b) using regression analyses that relate data from a given phase of data collection to data from other phases of the investigation. Both types of analyses have proven very informative. However, they cannot provide information about the course of development or the profile of development of children who vary in terms of their risk status. Only research designs that include repeated measures of the same psychological construct lend themselves to different types of profile analyses (e.g., Appelbaum, Burchinal, & Terry, 1989; Burchinal & Appelbaum, 1991). Such analyses would allow investigators to describe the development of low-birthweight children in ways not previously possible. For example, such analyses would allow investigators to determine the extent to which low-birthweight children manifest developmental lags or developmental deficits — a distinction that is very important theoretically and practically.

Analyses that take advantage of the longitudinal nature of follow-up data could also tell us the extent to which the environment plays an equally important role throughout the development of low-birthweight children. It is possible that there are some developmental periods during which optimal environmental support is more critical than during other periods. Such information would be useful for planners of interventions as well as for parents of low-birthweight children.

At the conceptual level, researchers of low-birthweight infants have been justifiably concerned with those infants who were born early, light, and sick. However, the research samples frequently include a mix of children, some of whom are quite healthy. For example, in the Infant Health and Development Project (described by Gross et al. in this volume), 22% of the 985 infants were released from the hospital during their first 7 days of life and were probably quite healthy (K. Scott, personal communication, September 20, 1990). While various attempts were made to determine the extent to which different levels of developmental outcome (e.g., Sostek, this volume), there are no studies of the healthiest of the preterms and consequently we do not know if the healthiest of the group are more at risk than full-term children.

One issue that will certainly be investigated in the future concerns the effects of exposure to drugs in utero on the development of children. Infants exposed to drugs in utero are more likely to have shortened gestational periods and lower birthweights, be small for gestational age, and have smaller head circumferences than do infants not exposed to drugs (Chasnoff, Griffith, MacGregor, Dirkes, & Burns, 1989; Hingson, Alport, Day, Dooling, Kayne, Morelock, Oppenheimer, & Zuckerman, 1982; Householder, Hatcher, Burns, & Chasnoff, 1982; Livesey, Ehrlich, Ryan, & Finnegan, 1989). Therefore, studies that aim to identify the effects of drugs on children's development will need to follow control groups of infants who are born preterm but are not exposed to drugs. Furthermore, it may be that some of the subjects in the studies reviewed in this volume have been exposed to drugs, but this information was not known to the researchers who conducted these studies. In the future, more attention on the nutritional and drug history of the mother of the infant born small will be expected from researchers of high-risk infants.

The study of the effects of drugs in utero on the development of children will undoubtedly profit from the studies conducted on low-birthweight children. At this point, the typical study of drug effects is rather like the typical study in the early 1970s regarding the effects of low birthweight. Most of the studies that have been conducted are clinical follow-ups of infants in well-baby clinics or infants whose mothers were in methadone treatment programs. The information from these studies is limited because of the subject self-selection, unassessable attrition rates, the absence of control groups and of descriptive data on family and caregiver characteristics, and the use of imprecise behavioral and developmental assessments. The increasing precision of studies of low-birthweight children will be required in investigations of the effects of drug exposure. The research designs and assessment techniques may be applicable to studies of drug exposed children. In addition, the conceptual understanding derived from other high-risk groups may help shape the research studies of drug effects.

With over 50% of mothers of infants in the workforce, investigators are studying the effects of variations in the age of entry, the type, the quality, and the extent of care on the development of infants and toddlers of employed mothers (for a summary of knowledge to date, see Hayes, Palmer, & Zaslow, 1990). Research findings about low-birthweight children suggest that low-birthweight infants are particularly vulnerable to environmental effects. Yet investigators who study the effects of child care on child development have not attended to the effects of child care arrangements on low-birthweight children. This suggests a need to study the placement of low-birthweight infants in alternate care and its effect on their behavioral development. Currently, we do not know what percentage of low-birthweight and very low-birthweight children are placed in alternate care arrangements. We need information as to the ages at which they are placed in alternate care and the number of hours per week that they are in such care. We need to learn about the quality of care in the various arrangements and about the combined effects of the home and the alternate care environments on the development of low-birthweight and of very low-birthweight children. Currently, we do not know under what conditions alternate care supports the healthy development of these children, and under what conditions alternate care interferes with such healthy development. Research addressing these issues will either substantiate or raise questions about existing models of human development.

In summary, the research of the 1980s has had many of the same aims as the research conducted in the 1970s. However, there has been a greater focus on social-emotional development and more opportunity for long-term follow-up. Conceptualizations, based mostly on the Transactional Model, have become somewhat more complex although not always translated into well-articulated research hypotheses. Assessment methods for predictors and outcomes have become more precise, more process oriented, and broader in scope. Major advances have been made in the understanding and implementation of intervention with families of low-birthweight children. We see the need for more conceptually driven research studies as well as for continuing efforts to assess profiles of development, teratogenic and biological factors, and the daily life experiences of these children. We anticipate that the research of the next 10 years will continue the considerable achievements made in studies of low-birthweight children during the past decade.

REFERENCES

Appelbaum, M.I., Burchinal, M.R., & Terry, R.A. (1989). Quantitative models and the search for continuity. In M.H. Bornstein & N.A. Krasnegor (Eds.), *Stability and continuity in mental development.* Hillsdale, NJ: Erlbaum.

Burchinal, M., & Appelbaum, M.I. (1991). Estimating individual developmental functions: Methods and their assumptions. *Child Development, 62,* 23–43.

Bradley, R.H., Caldwell, B.M., Rock, S., Casey, P., & Nelson, J. (1987). The early development of low birthweight infants: Relationships to health, family status, family context, family process and parenting. *International Journal of Behavioral Development, 10,* 1–18.

Caldwell, B.M., Heider, J., & Kaplan, B. (1966, September). *The Inventory of Home Stimulation.* Paper presented at the annual meeting of the American Psychological Association, New York.

Chasnoff, I.J., Griffith, D.R., MacGregor, S., Dirkes, K., & Burns, K.A. (1989). Temporal patterns of cocaine use in pregnancy. *Journal of the American Medical Association, 261*(12), 1741–1744.

Field, T. (1990). Alleviating stress in newborn infants in the intensive care unit. *Clinical Perinatology, 17,* 1–19.

Fogel, A., & Thelen, E. (1987). Development of early expressive and communicative action: Reinterpreting the evidence from a dynamic systems perspective. *Developmental Psychology, 23,* 747–761.

Friedman, S.L., & Sigman, M.D. (Eds.). (1981). *Preterm birth and psychological development.* New York: Academic Press.

Hayes, C.D., Palmer, J.L., & Zaslow, M.J. (Eds.). (1990). *Who cares for America's children?* Washington, DC: National Academy Press.

Hingson, R., Alport, J.J., Day, N., Dooling, E., Kayne, H., Morelock, S., Oppenheimer, E., & Zuckerman, B. (1982). Effects of maternal drinking and marijuana use on fetal growth and development. *Pediatrics, 4,* 539–546.

Householder, J., Hatcher, R., Burns, W., & Chasnoff, I. (1982). Infants born to narcotic-addicted mothers. *Psychological Bulletin, 2,* 453–468.

Korner, A.F., Lane, N.M., Berry, K.L., Rho, J.M., & Brown, B.W., Jr. (1990). Sleep enhanced and irritability reduced in preterm infants: Differential efficacy of three types of waterbeds. *Journal of Developmental and Behavioral Pediatrics, 11,* 240–246.

Livesey, S., Ehrlich, S., Ryan, L., & Finnegan, L.P. (1989). Cocaine and pregnancy: Maternal and infant outcome. *Annals of the New York Academy of Science, 562,* 358–359.

McCormick, M.C., Grotmaker, S.L., & Sobol, A.M. (1990). Very low birth weight children: Behavior problems and school difficulty in a national sample. *The Journal of Pediatrics, 117,* 687–693.

Sameroff, A., & Chandler, M. (1975). Reproductive risk and the continuum of caretaking casualty. In F.D. Horowitz, M. Hetherington, S. Scarr-Salapatek, & G. Siegel (Eds.), *Review of child development research* (Vol. 4, pp. 187–244). Chicago: University of Chicago Press.

Siegel, L.S., & Cunningham, C.E. (1984). Social interaction: A transactional approach with illustrations from children with developmental problems. In A. Doyle & S.D. Markowitz (Eds.), *Children in families under stress* (pp. 85–98). San Francisco: Jossey Bass.

Thoman, E.B., & Graham, S. (1986). Self regulation of stimulation by premature infants. *Pediatrics, 78,* 855–860.

II

Epidemiological, Medical, and Theoretical Considerations

2

The Epidemiology of Low Birthweight*

Joel C. Kleinman

INTRODUCTION

Duration of pregnancy and intrauterine growth are the two most important determinants of infant health. Both these factors are reflected in the infant's birthweight. Many studies have shown that adverse pregnancy outcomes decrease with increasing birthweight until about 3,500–4,000 grams, after which there is a slight increase.

A commonly used classification is to dichotomize births as low birthweight (less than 2,500 grams) vs. others. This dichotomy is crude but provides striking contrasts in outcomes: compared to those 2,500 grams or more, low-birthweight babies are nearly 40 times as likely to die during the neonatal period, and neonatal survivors are five times as likely to die during the postneonatal period (Hogue, Buehler, Strauss, & Smith, 1987). Of those who survive infancy, low-birthweight babies are about 50% more likely to have serious developmental problems or other illness (Shapiro, McCormick, Starfield, Krischer, & Bross, 1980; McCormick, 1985).

Other classification schemes have been used to further identify those at most serious risk. The low-birthweight group is sometimes disaggregated into very low birthweight (less than 1,500 grams) and moderately low birthweight (1,500 to 2,499 grams). The very low-birthweight infants are at much greater risk of death and disability than the moderately low-birthweight group (Kleinman & Kessel, 1987). At the other end of the scale, infants with high birthweight (HBW—4,500 grams or more) are also at higher risk of adverse outcome than those in the "normal" group (but still considerably lower than the moderately low-birthweight group).

Supplementing birthweight with information regarding gestation produces a more detailed classification. Infants with intrauterine growth retardation can be distinguished from those born prematurely. Thus, it is possible to distinguish preterm (gestation less than 37 weeks) and postterm (gestation greater than 42 weeks) from term births, and to classify birthweight as small for gestational age (less than the 10th percentile of birthweight for each gestational age), large for

* The author would like to thank the Missouri Center for Health Statistics for providing vital statistics data used in this chapter.

gestational age (above the 90th percentile) and adequate for gestational age. Very low-birthweight infants are almost all preterm (but could also be small for gestational age) and are at greatest risk of mortality and morbidity. Moderately low-birthweight infants are about equally divided into preterm and term births. Use of the measures dependent upon gestational age is complicated by the difficulty of gestational age measurement. The most commonly used method to determine gestational age is based on date of last menstrual period, but this has been shown to result in substantial misclassification of preterm and postterm births and consequently intrauterine growth retardation (Kramer, McLean, Boyd, & Usher, 1988). Because it can be measured precisely and routinely, the use of birthweight as a composite measure of gestation and intrauterine growth is a reasonable compromise when investigating trends and variations in population-based studies.

TRENDS IN LOW BIRTHWEIGHT

Published data are available showing national trends in low birthweight and very low birthweight for white, black, American Indian, and Asian births since 1970, and for Hispanic births since 1980 (National Center for Health Statistics, 1990). All groups show a flattening of the downward trend in low birthweight during the 1980s. There is little difference in low birthweight among whites, Cubans, Mexicans, Indians, and Asians. However, blacks have by far the highest low-birthweight rate (12.7% in 1987) while Puerto Ricans (9.3%) fall midway between blacks and the other groups (5.7–6.4%).

With respect to very low birthweight, the relative risk among blacks is even higher than for low birthweight, nearly 3 to 1. Puerto Ricans have a very low-birthweight rate about 50% higher than whites, while the rates for Mexican and Cuban mothers are about the same as for whites. Indians have about 15% higher very low-birthweight rates than whites, while Asians have about 10% lower rates. The higher risk groups also appear to be getting worse: during the 1980s blacks, Puerto Ricans, and Indians have all had increases in very low birthweight of about 1.5% per year.

For the entire 1960–1987 period, low birthweight declined on average by 0.8% per year among whites and 0.3% per year among blacks. Some of the initial increase between 1960 and 1970 is probably due to improved reporting (Kleinman, 1986).

Trends in very low birthweight show an even sharper divergence by race. Between 1960 and 1987 very low birthweight decreased by 0.3% per year among whites but increased by 0.7% per year among blacks.

Because there have been large declines in birthweight-specific mortality (Buehler, Kleinman, Hogue, Strauss, & Smith, 1987), the small changes in very low-birthweight births mask a much larger change in very low-birthweight survivors. The proportion of all live births below 1,500 grams decreased by 7% among whites and increased by 17% among blacks between 1960 and 1983. But the proportion of infant survivors below 1,500 grams more than doubled for both whites and blacks over the same time period. Consequently, infant survivors below 1,500 grams account for a larger proportion of low-birthweight survivors. In 1960, 4% of white and 6% of black low-birthweight survivors were very low birthweight; in 1983 the proportions increased to 11% and 14%, respectively. It is of interest to note that Paneth, Kiely, Stein, and Susser (1981) predicted that the increase in very low-birthweight survivors would have a small but noticeable impact on the prevalence of neurodevelopmental handicaps in children.

TRENDS IN MATERNAL CHARACTERISTICS

The role of changes in sociodemographic factors on these trends should be considered. There have been remarkable changes in the age-parity distribution of live births. Let us define *high-parity* as third- or higher order births to mothers under 20 and fourth- or higher order births to mothers 20 and over. In 1960, 27% of the white births and 46% of the black births were high-parity. By 1985, high-parity births accounted for only 9% of white and 15% of black births. Concomitantly, first births increased from 28% of white and 22% of black births in 1960 to 43% of white and 40% of black births in 1985. Young teenagers (under 18) accounted for an increasing proportion of births between 1960 and 1970 but have been decreasing since then (to 4% of white and 10% of black births in 1985). Births to 18- and 19-year-olds followed similar patterns (7% of white and 13% of black births in 1985). The other large relative change in composition was the increasing proportion of first births to mothers aged 30 and over: from 2% in 1960 to 6% in 1985 among whites, and from 1% to 3% among blacks.

Although age and parity are associated with low birthweight, adjustment for the changing age-birth order distribution of births had little effect on the overall low-birthweight trends from 1960 to 1985. There were, however, some differences in trends among the age-birth order groups. The most striking difference was the large decline in low birthweight among white women 30 and over (from 98.8 per 1,000 in 1960 to 70.6 per 1,000 in 1985). This is probably due in part to the changing mix of women in this group; during the 1960s first live births to older mothers probably included a large proportion of women who had prior fetal losses. By 1985, a much larger proportion of women in this group had intentionally postponed childbirth. In addition, the medical management of pregnancies among women with chronic illness may have improved.

Educational attainment has increased substantially: in 1970, 9% of mothers of live births were college graduates, compared to 18% in 1987 (National Center for Health Statistics, 1990). On the other hand, the proportion of births to unmarried mothers has also increased, from 11% in 1970 to 25% in 1987. Large differentials among ethnic groups in the prevalence of adverse maternal characteristics persist: in 1987, 63% of black, 53% of Puerto Rican, and 45% of Indian births were to unmarried mothers, compared to 17% of white and 12% of Asian births. The proportion of births to mothers who were college graduates varied from less than 10% of blacks and Indians to 20% of whites and 32% of Asians.

Among black and white women there have been somewhat more rapid declines in low birthweight among women with higher educational attainment and among married mothers (Kleinman & Kessel, 1987). These changes could be related in part to greater declines in smoking among these groups (Kleinman & Kopstein, 1987).

After a narrowing of the black–white gap in the utilization of prenatal care during the 1970s, there has been essentially no change during the 1980s in the proportion of mothers who began care in the first trimester (Ingram, Makuc, & Kleinman, 1986). By 1987, the proportion ranged from about 60% of black, Mexican, Puerto Rican, and Indian mothers to nearly 80% for white, Asian, and Cuban mothers (National Center for Health Statistics, 1990).

RISK FACTORS FOR LOW BIRTHWEIGHT

Sociodemographic factors have long been associated with low birthweight and infant mortality (e.g., Shapiro, Schlesinger, & Nesbitt, 1968). Nevertheless, the specific causal factors responsible for these differences in pregnancy outcome remain elusive. For example, the adverse effects of maternal cigarette smoking on pregnancy outcome have been documented in many studies conducted over a period of several decades (Lowe, 1959; Meyer, Jonas, & Tonascia, 1976; Kleinman, Pierre, Madans, Land, & Schramm, 1988). Smoking is one of the strongest preventable risk factors for low birthweight: women who smoke are about twice as likely as nonsmokers to have a low-birthweight infant. Furthermore, smoking cessation has been shown in a randomized controlled trial to increase birthweight (Sexton & Hebel, 1984). The effect of smoking on low birthweight is stronger for term than preterm low birthweight (or IUGR compared to prematurity) (Kramer, 1987). However, although the relative odds for smoking is greatest among births weighing 2,000 to 2,499 grams (2.4), the relative odds remains high for births as low as 500–999 grams (1.7) (Malloy, Kleinman, Land, & Schramm, 1988).

Kleinman and Madans (1985) showed that, among white married mothers, smoking accounts for about half the excess incidence of low birthweight among mothers with low education. They also showed that maternal height and prepregnancy weight had strong effects on low birthweight. Data from 1979–1983 Missouri birth certificates were used to investigate further the effects of these maternal risk factors on low birthweight and infant mortality (Kleinman et al., 1988; Malloy et al., 1988). Missouri birth certificates are unique, since they include information on smoking, height, and prepregnancy weight as well as standard sociodemographic risk factors related to low birthweight. Multiple logistic regression analysis (Kleinbaum, Kupper, & Morgenstern, 1982) was used to estimate the effects of marital status, education, age, and parity on low birthweight and very low birthweight before and after adjustment for smoking and maternal prepregnant weight and height. Effects were expressed in terms of odds ratios, which in this situation were very similar to risk ratios or relative risks. For example, an odds ratio of 1.5 for unmarried mothers indicates that after adjusting for all other risk factors in the model, the odds of having a low-birthweight baby is 1.5 times higher among unmarried than married mothers.

Low birthweight decreased steadily with increasing education for both whites and blacks. After adjustment for smoking, however, the excess risk of low birthweight among mothers with less than 12 years education decreased by half. Adjustment for height and weight further narrowed the educational differentials among whites. Both white and black unmarried mothers had a substantially higher risk of low birthweight than their married counterparts. Adjustment for smoking narrowed these differentials to some extent, but little additional narrowing occurred after adjustment for height and weight. Primiparas 30 years of age and over, and multiparas under 18 years of age, had the highest low-birthweight rates. These excess rates were accentuated by adjustment for smoking and stature. Black primiparas under 20 years of age had low rates. For both whites and blacks, smoking doubled the risk of low birthweight. Low birthweight decreased steadily with increasing height and weight.

The education effect was not nearly as strong as for low birthweight, especially among blacks, and adjustment for smoking essentially eliminated the effect. Unmarried women had about the same excess risk of very low birthweight as low birthweight, and adjustment for smoking reduced the excess slightly. Teenagers had higher relative odds of very low birthweight than low birthweight. Among blacks the relative odds for primiparas 30 and over was only 0.92, but the confidence interval was quite wide (0.47 to 1.79), due to small numbers of cases. Smoking, height, and weight had smaller effects on very low birthweight than moderately low birthweight.

Other studies have identified additional risk factors for low birthweight (see Kramer, 1987, for a comprehensive review). With respect to the situation in the United States, three of these warrant special attention. First, there are several articles which document intergenerational effects of low birthweight (Hackman, Emanuel, van Belle, & Daling, 1983; Klebanoff, Graubard, Kessel, & Berendes, 1984; Klebanoff, Meirik, & Berendes, 1989). That is, a woman who was low birthweight herself is more likely to have a low-birthweight baby. Second, unintended pregnancies are more likely to result in low-birthweight babies, and black women are much more likely to have unintended pregnancies than white women (WHO Collaborating Center, 1987; Pamuk & Mosher, 1989). Third, drug abuse, particularly cocaine, has been increasing (Chasnoff, Landress, &

Barrett, 1990) and is a strong risk factor for low birthweight (Zuckerman, 1989; Chasnoff, Griffith, MacGregor, Dirkes, & Burns, 1989). These factors could account for a substantial portion of the black–white differential in low birthweight.

RISK FACTORS FOR SURVIVAL

Because low-birthweight infants are much more likely to die than normal-birthweight infants, many of the risk factors for low birthweight also exert an effect on mortality. However, the effects of these risk factors on mortality within the low-birthweight group appear counterintuitive. The best example is the long-documented survival advantage of black infants over white infants in the low-birthweight range (e.g., Chase, 1972). It is important to understand this phenomenon within the context of developmental problems of low-birthweight infants, because many of the principles underlying the mortality differential may also apply to other health and developmental indices.

The data from the 1983 United States birth cohort was used to illustrate this issue. Maternal sociodemographic risk factors were summarized into three categories. *Low-risk* consisted of married mothers with at least 13 years of education who were either primiparas 20–29 years or low-parity multiparas 20 years of age and older. *High-risk* mothers included unmarried mothers with less than 12 years of education who were either teenagers, primiparas 30 years of age or older, or high-parity multiparas. The *moderate risk* group included all other combinations of maternal characteristics.

Among whites, high-risk mothers had 2.7 times the IMR of low-risk mothers while among blacks the ratio was 2.0. Within each risk group, blacks had a higher IMR than whites, but the ratio declined from 1.9 among low-risk to 1.4 among high-risk mothers. However, when we limited attention to the low-birthweight group, the differentials by maternal race and risk almost disappeared. Moreover, the racial comparisons were confounded by the birthweight distribution within the low-birthweight group: black mothers had a greater proportion of very low-birthweight births within the low-birthweight group. When we adjusted mortality among low-birthweight infants for birthweight (using a quadratic model), blacks had about 30% lower mortality than whites at each level of maternal risk.

This apparent paradox has led to the suggestion that population-specific standards should be used to compare birthweight-specific infant mortality rates (Wilcox & Russell, 1990; David, 1990; Kleinman, 1991). That is, the fairest way to compare birthweight-specific mortality among populations with different birthweight distributions is to express birthweight in terms of its distance from the mean rather than its absolute value. The first step in understanding this approach is to characterize the birthweight distribution. Wilcox and Russell

(1990) note that the birthweight distribution is a mixture of two distributions: a predominant Gaussian (*normal*) distribution, with a small but important excess at the lower birthweights (the *residual* distribution).

Three parameters can be used to characterize this birthweight distribution: the mean and standard deviation of the predominant distribution, and the proportion of births in the residual distribution. The methods used to estimate these parameters were given by Kleinman (1991). There was a 223-gram difference in birthweight means between infants of high- and low-risk white mothers, and a 177-gram difference for infants of black mothers. The black–white differences were 214 grams among low-risk and 168 grams among high-risk mothers. The differences in standard deviations were relatively small and showed no consistent pattern. The proportion of births in the residual distribution showed a 2 to 1 ratio between high and low risk and between black and white mothers (although the black–white ratio declined to 1.5 at the highest level of maternal risk).

The next step in understanding the approach is to recognize that birthweight-specific mortality follows a consistent pattern in all populations: mortality is nearly one at the lowest birthweight, decreases rapidly with increasing birthweight, reaches a minimum, and then increases. Furthermore, the minimum mortality occurs at lower birthweights among populations with lower mean birthweights, typically at a point about 1.5 standard deviations above the mean. Thus, given differences in birthweight distribution, birthweight-specific mortality in different populations should be compared by how far a particular birthweight is from its population mean. A convenient way to do this is to express birthweight as a standardized "z-score," that is, the distance of a particular birthweight from the mean in standard deviation units, (bw-mean)/sd. In order to compare mortality rates among the low-birthweight group by maternal race and risk in our example, we adjusted using birthweight z-scores (again using a quadratic model). With this adjustment, the risk of death was 2.5 times as high among high-risk white mothers and 66% higher among high-risk black mothers, compared to their low-risk counterparts. The black–white ratio ranged from 1.4 among low-risk mothers to 1.0 among high-risk mothers.

Thus, the use of population-specific standards results in rather different interpretations of the mortality experience among low-birthweight infants. This approach to comparing mortality outcomes among low-birthweight infants provides a useful perspective for further understanding differences in other health and developmental outcomes. For example, it would be extremely useful to assess risk factors for these outcomes using a standardized birthweight measure. Even individual assessment of prognosis could be influenced by considering the degree to which an infant's birthweight departs from its distribution. For example, by analogy to the mortality results, expectations for developmental markers in a black infant weighing 1,800 grams should be comparable to white infants of 2,000 grams. Further work in this area could lead to a better understanding of risk factors and intervention effectiveness.

DISCUSSION

In the United States, race remains one of the strongest risk factors for adverse pregnancy outcome: black mothers are more than twice as likely as white mothers to have a wide variety of adverse pregnancy outcomes, including fetal and infant death, preterm births, and IUGR. Although black mothers have a greater proportion of births with high-risk characteristics, this difference does not account for their higher rates of adverse outcomes. At every level of maternal risk, black mothers have higher rates of adverse outcomes than white mothers. Furthermore, the black–white ratio is highest among mothers with the most favorable risk factors (e.g., married, college-educated mothers ages 20–29) (Kessel, Kleinman, Koontz, Hogue, & Berendes, 1988).

It is important to note that, even within apparently similar groups, large black–white differences remain. For example, data from the 1983 National Health Interview Survey show that, among married women 20–44 years of age who graduated from college, 23% of whites, as compared to 35% of blacks, had an annual family income below $25,000 (Kleinman & Kessel, 1987). Newer research on the role of intergenerational effects (Hackman et al., 1983; Klebanoff et al., 1984, 1989) indicates that birth outcomes may depend upon the grandmother's socioeconomic status as well as the mother's current socio-economic status. The cumulative intergenerational effects of racism and social deprivation undoubtedly contribute to the racial disparity in pregnancy outcome, but it has been difficult to identify the specific factors involved or develop effective intervention strategies to reduce the disparity.

The role of prenatal care in reducing low birthweight has received a great deal of attention (Institute of Medicine, 1985; U.S. Congress, Office of Technology Assessment, 1988). Although studies of the effectiveness of prenatal care in reducing low birthweight have not been definitive (e.g., Harris, 1982; Peoples, Grimson, & Daughtry, 1984; Strobino et al., 1986; Kleinman, 1991), it is quite clear that women at highest risk of low birthweight are least likely to receive early prenatal care. In addition, after substantial progress during the 1970s in narrowing such inequities, there has been little change in the utilization of prenatal care during the 1980s (Ingram et al., 1986). Changes in the content of prenatal care (Public Health Service Expert Panel on the Content of Prenatal Care, 1989), as well as increases in the utilization of care, are needed to reduce the incidence of low birthweight and improve the health of low-birthweight babies.

The differences among ethnic groups within the United States raise several questions about the role of traditional risk factors and the need to identify cultural or social factors that may be beneficial. Mexican-Americans and American Indians are two interesting examples. Both these groups have relatively low education, high poverty, and low use of prenatal care. Yet the incidence of low and very low birthweight in these groups is about the same as for white mothers.

New approaches to comparison of birthweight-specific mortality suggest that the prognostic significance of an infant's birthweight could vary among populations with different birthweight distributions. For example, with adequate and appropriate interventions, black infants weighing 1,800 grams might be expected to have rates of neurological impairments similar to those of white infants weighing 2,000 grams. This conjecture would depend upon whether neurological and behavioral development follow the same patterns as mortality. Comparing the extent to which variations in mortality, morbidity, and neuropsychological development are related to variations in birthweight per se or population-specific birthweight standards could lead to a better understanding of the potential for intervention.

Finally, for those who deal with the health and development of infants, it should be reemphasized that, although there has been little change in the incidence of live births below 1,500 grams (those at highest risk of neurologic sequelae and developmental problems), reduced mortality among these infants has led to a doubling over the past 25 years in the proportion of infant survivors with birthweight below 1,500 grams. Many of these survivors have only relatively minor developmental problems (McCormick, 1989). However, the lower limit of survival has been decreasing in the last decade and the cocaine epidemic has been increasing, raising the possibility of a new set of potential problems to those who care for these vulnerable infants.

REFERENCES

Buehler, J.W., Kleinman, J.C., Hogue, C.J.R., Strauss, L.T., & Smith, J.C. (1987). Birth weight-specific infant mortality, United States, 1960 and 1980. *Public Health Reports, 102*(2), 151–161.

Chase, H.C. (1972). *Comparison of neonatal mortality from two cohorts studies, United States, January–March 1950–1960.* (National Center for Health Statistics: Series 20, Number 13. DHEW Pub. No. (PHS) 72-1056.) Rockville, MD: Public Health Service.

Chasnoff, I.J., Griffith, D.R., MacGregor, S., Dirkes, K., & Burns, K.A. (1989). Temporal patterns of cocaine use in pregnancy. *Journal of the American Medical Association, 261,* 1741–1744.

Chasnoff, I.J., Landress, H.J., & Barrett, M.E. (1990). The prevalence of illicit-drug or alcohol use during pregnancy and discrepancies in mandatory reporting in Pinellas County, Florida. *New England Journal of Medicine, 322,* 1202–1206.

David, R. (1990). Race, birth weight, and mortality rates. *Journal of Pediatrics, 116,* 101–102.

Hackman, E., Emanuel, I., van Belle, G., & Daling, J. (1983). Maternal birth weight and subsequent pregnancy outcomes. *Journal of the American Medical Association, 250,* 2016–2019.

Harris, J.E. (1982). Prenatal care and infant mortality. In V.R. Fuchs (Ed.), *Economic aspects of health.* Chicago: The University of Chicago Press.

Hogue, C.J.R., Buehler, J.W., Strauss, L.T., & Smith, J.C. (1987). Overview of the National Infant Mortality Surveillance (NIMS) Project—design, methods, results. *Public Health Reports, 102,* 126–138.

Ingram, D.D., Makuc, D., & Kleinman, J.C. (1986). National and state trends in use of prenatal care, 1970–83. *American Journal of Public Health*, 76(4), 415–423.

Institute of Medicine, Committee to Study the Prevention of Low Birthweight. (1985). *Preventing low birthweight*. Washington, DC: National Academy Press.

Kessel, S.S., Kleinman, J.C., Koontz, A.M., Hogue, C.J.R., & Berendes, H.W. (1988). Racial differences in pregnancy outcomes. *Clinics in Perinatology*, 15, 745–754.

Klebanoff, M.A., Graubard, B.I., Kessel, S.S., & Bernedes, H.W. (1984). Low birth weight across generations. *Journal of the American Medical Association*, 252, 2423–2427.

Klebanoff, M.A., Meirik, O., & Berendes, H.W. (1989). Second-generation consequences of small-for-dates birth. *Pediatrics*, 84(2), 343–347.

Kleinbaum, D.G., Kupper, L.L., & Morgenstern, H. (1982). *Epidemiologic research*. New York: Von Nostrand Reinhold Publishers.

Kleinman, J.C. (1986). Underreporting of infant deaths: Then and now (invited editorial). *American Journal of Public Health*, 76(4), 365–366.

Kleinman, J.C. (1991). Methodologic issues in the analysis of vital statistics. In M. Kiely (Ed.), *Reproductive and perinatal epidemiology* (pp. 447–468). Boca Raton, FL: CRC Press.

Kleinman, J.C., & Kessel, S.S. (1987). Racial differences in low birth weight: Trends and risk factors. *New England Journal of Medicine*, 317, 749–753.

Kleinman, J.C., & Kopstein, A. (1987). Smoking during pregnancy, 1967–80. *American Journal of Public Health*, 77, 823–825.

Kleinman, J.C., & Madans, J. (1985). The effects of maternal smoking, physical stature, and educational attainment on the incidence of low birth weight. *American Journal of Epidemiology*, 121(6), 843–855.

Kleinman, J.C., Pierre, M., Madans, J., Land, G., & Schramm, W. (1988). The effects of maternal smoking on fetal and infant mortality. *American Journal of Epidemiology*, 127, 274–282.

Kramer, M.S. (1987). Determinants of low birth weight: Methodological assessment and meta-analysis. *Bulletin of the World Health Organization*, 65, 663–737.

Kramer, M.S., McLean, L.H., Boyd, M.E., & Usher, R.H. (1988). The validity of gestational age estimation by menstrual dating in term, preterm, and postterm gestations. *Journal of the American Medical Association*, 260, 3306–3308.

Lowe C.R. (1959). Effect of mothers' smoking habits on birth weight of their children. *British Medical Journal*, 2, 673–676.

Malloy, M.H., Kleinman, J.C., Land, G.H., & Schramm, W.F. (1988). Association of maternal smoking with age and cause of infant death. *American Journal of Epidemiology*, 128, 46–55.

McCormick, M.C. (1985). The contribution of low birthweight to infant mortality and childhood morbidity. *New England Journal of Medicine*, 312, 82–90.

McCormick, M.C. (1989). Long-term followup of infant discharged from neonatal intensive care units. *Journal of the American Medical Association*, 261, 1767–1772.

Meyer, M.B., Jonas, B.S., & Tonascia, J.A. (1976). Perinatal events associated with maternal smoking during pregnancy. *American Journal of Epidemiology*, 103, 464–476.

National Center for Health Statistics. (1990). *Health, United States, 1989*. Hyattsville, MD: Public Health Service.

National Center for Health Statistics. (1989). Public Use Data Tape Documentation. *Linked Birth/ Infant Death Data Set: 1983 Birth Cohort*. Hyattsville, MD: Public Health Service.

Pamuk, E.R., & Mosher, W.D. (1988). *Health aspects of pregnancy and childbirth: United States, 1982. Vital and Health Statistics*. (Series 23, No. 16. DHHS Pub. No. (PHS) 89-1992. Public Health Service.) Washington, DC: U.S. Government Printing Office.

Paneth, N., Kiely, J., Stein, Z.A., & Susser, M.W. (1981). Cerebral palsy and newborn care: III. Estimated prevalence rates of cerebral palsy under differing rates of mortality and impairment of low birthweight infants. *Developmental Medicine and Child Neurology*, 23, 801–806.

Peoples, M.D., Grimson, R.C., & Daughtry, G.L. (1984). Evaluation of the effects of the North Carolina improved pregnancy outcome project: Implications for State-level decision making. *American Journal of Public Health*, 74, 549–554.

Public Health Service Expert Panel on the Content of Prenatal Care. (1989). *Caring for our future: The content of prenatal care*. (NIH Publication No. 90-3182. Reprinted August 1990). Washington, DC: Public Health Service, Department of Health and Human Services.

Sexton, M., & Hebel, J.R. (1984). A clinical trial of change in maternal smoking and its effect on birth weight. *Journal of the American Medical Association, 251*, 911–915.

Shapiro, S., McCormick, M.C., Starfield, B.H., Krischer, J.P., & Bross, D. (1980). Relevance of correlates of infant deaths for significant morbidity at 1 year of age. *American Journal of Obstetrics and Gynecology, 136*, 363–373.

Shapiro, S., Schlesinger, E.R., & Nesbitt, R.E.L., Jr. (1968). *Infant, perinatal, maternal, and childhood mortality in the United States* (American Public Health Association, Vital and Health Statistics Monographs). Cambridge, MA: Harvard University Press.

Strobino, D.M., Chase, G.A., & Kim, Y.J. (1986). The impact of the Mississippi Improved Child Health Project on prenatal care and low birth weight. *American Journal of Public Health, 76*, 274–278.

U.S. Congress, Office of Technology Assessment. (1988). *Healthy children: Investing in the future* (OTA-H-345). Washington, DC: U.S. Government Printing Office.

WHO Collaborating Center in Perinatal Care. (1987). Unintended pregnancy and infant mortality/morbidity. In R.W. Amler & H.B. Dull (Eds.), *Closing the gap: The burden of unnecessary illness*. New York: Oxford University Press.

Wilcox, A., & Russell, I. (1990). Why small black infants have a lower mortality rate than small white infants: The case for population-specific standards for birth weight. *Journal of Pediatrics, 116*, 7–10.

Zuckerman, B. (1989). Effects of maternal marijuana and cocaine use on fetal growth. *New England Journal of Medicine, 320*, 762–768.

3

Advances in Neonatal Intensive Care Technology and Their Possible Impact on the Development of Low-Birthweight Infants*

Marie C. McCormick

INTRODUCTION

Neonatal intensive care technology encompasses a wide range of potential topics from complex equipment such as infant ventilators and monitors, through medications of various types, to more mundane but no less important items such as appropriate infant formulae or tubes of the correct size and composition for tiny airways or blood vessels. In addition, such technology includes less evident but equally important support services such as blood banks, nutrition services, and laboratories capable of dealing with tiny infants and their needs. Finally, organizational and financial arrangements that assure access to appropriate levels of services are also intrinsic to such care. Insofar as each contributes to the survival and well-being of low-birthweight (LBW) infants, there is a potential effect on future development. To attempt to review specific changes in all these areas, however, would be a daunting task well beyond the scope of a single report. Indeed, a recent bibliography of controlled trials in perinatal medicine (National Perinatal Epidemiology Unit, 1985) achieved book length with a substantial portion of the articles reflecting neonatal technologies and outcomes. Thus, the approach taken in this chapter will be to select recent changes in intensive care to illustrate effects on development.

The importance of the role of neonatal technology, however, cannot be understood outside the context of the factors influencing infant mortality in the United States. Thus, this chapter will begin with a brief review of these changes in mortality, and the evidence for the general contribution of technology to increased infant survival. This discussion will be followed by more detailed presentations of topics selected to illustrate specific issues raised by neonatal intensive care techniques that are designed to affect the survival and development of LBW infants, and to highlight the role that developmentalists may play in enhancing development. These topics include (a) new management approaches

* The thoughtful comments of Dr. Mary Ellen Avery and an anonymous reviewer have been extremely helpful. This chapter was supported in part by a contract from the NICHD (NO1-HD-5-2928) and a grant from the Robert Wood Johnson Foundation (9104).

to respiratory problems of the preterm infant illustrated by high-frequency ventilation, surfactant replacement therapy, and the use of highly invasive technologies like extracorporeal membrane oxygenation; and (b) the implications of the high costs of care and cost-containment efforts. The chapter will conclude with some speculations about the future.

CHANGES IN INFANT MORTALITY AND THE ROLE OF NEONATAL TECHNOLOGY

The infant mortality rate in the United States is about 10 per 1,000 live births. In other words, about 1% of infants die before the first birthday, or a total of about 40,000 deaths. As will be demonstrated in more detail later, the majority of these deaths occur shortly after birth among infants born too small. This level of mortality is higher than for any age group in the U.S. under the age of 65. It is also higher than the rates experienced by most industrialized countries, including substantially poorer countries like Ireland and Spain. Despite this relatively poor international ranking, the U.S. has made great strides in reducing its infant mortality rate; the infant mortality rate is less than half what it was 20 years ago. Understanding the importance of this trend and the role of technology, both in the past and in the future, requires a brief review of the causes of infant mortality and potential sources of change.

Definitions

The *infant mortality rate* is defined as the number of infant deaths less than one year of age per 1,000 live births in one year. There are two ways this rate can be calculated, either by dividing all the infant deaths in a calendar year by the births in the same calendar year, or by tracking the deaths in a cohort of births, occurring in a single calendar year, with some of the deaths occurring in the following year. The latter is preferred, but the former is more timely. The two methods will only differ, however, when marked year-to-year variations in births occur—as might be encountered in small areas such as cities. An additional advantage of the cohort approach can be realized if infant death and birth certificates are linked, in that much of the information on maternal characteristics, such as age and education, prior reproductive experience of the mother, and infant characteristics such as gestational age and birthweight, is on the birth certificate. Without such linkage, examination of mortality specific to these characteristics is not possible. Because it is a time-consuming and costly process, not all U.S. jurisdictions perform this linkage, so that national data on infant mortality are available only by race (which appears on the death certificate), and data on other factors are restricted to subsets of the states. Thus, those whose research involves interpreting changes in infant mortality and in the identification of at-risk groups should be aware of how the rates are calculated and the potential of linked birth/death certificate files. In the absence of such linkage, time trends for outcomes among subsets of the population will not be available, and are generally unavailable for the U.S. as a whole. The absence of this information leads to difficulties in assessing the potential role of medical and other interventions in improving outcomes.

Traditionally, infant mortality is partitioned into two time periods: neonatal mortality or infant deaths <28 days of life, and postneonatal mortality or infant deaths in the remainder of the first year. The significance of this partition lies in the fact that changes in neonatal and postneonatal mortality tend to correspond to two different sets of events affecting infant health. Neonatal mortality generally reflects events in pregnancy, delivery, and the period immediately after birth, and includes factors that influence the rates of congenital malformations, immaturity, birth injury and asphyxia, and the acute problems of the newborn. In contrast, postneonatal mortality is influenced by environmental factors affecting rates of common infectious conditions (pneumonia, gastroenteritis), injuries, and sudden infant death syndrome—most notably, poverty. Clearly, individual children with malformations may survive long enough to die in the postneonatal period, and likewise individual neonates may die of infectious processes. The overall rates, however, have proven to be sensitive indicators of changes in these two major sets of events (Shapiro, Schlesinger, & Nesbitt, 1968; Pharoah & Morris, 1979; Shapiro, McCormick, Starfield, Krischer, & Bross, 1980).

Trends in Infant Mortality and Its Causes

At the beginning of the century, infant mortality rates in the United States were as high as in many developing countries today. The rates approached 100/1,000 live births; in other words, 10% of all infants born died before their first birthday. The causes of mortality were also very similar to the pattern characterizing current developing countries in that a high proportion of deaths were due to infectious diseases of the respiratory and gastrointestinal tracts, for example, pneumonia, and vomiting and diarrhea. To a great extent these deaths occurred in the postneonatal period. During the first half of the century, infant mortality rates declined by well over 50%, largely as a reflection of a decline in postneonatal mortality. Much of this change was due to mprovements in living conditions such as increased access to pasteurized milk, clean water supplies, more adequate housing, and better sewage disposal. In addition, immunizations against several common childhood diseases and the first antibiotic effective against bacterial illnesses also became available during that period (Shapiro et al., 1968).

After World War II, the majority of infant deaths were occurring in the neonatal period, with a neonatal mortality rate of 25.9 per 1,000 in 1959–1961. Causes of early neonatal demise (i.e., in the first week of life) were dominated by events related to pregnancy and delivery: immaturity (26% of all deaths), asphyxia (26%), congenital malformations (14%), birth injuries (11%), and other nonspecific conditions of the newborn (10%). Later in the neonatal period, the risk of infection became greater with an increase in the percentage of neonatal deaths attributed to pneumonia (Shapiro et al., 1968).

With adjustments for changes in coding conventions, current causes for neonatal mortality appear similar, and, with the addition of hyaline membrane disease (HMD) or respiratory distress syndrome (RDS) of the newborn, account for 80% of neonatal and close to half of all infant deaths (Manniello & Farrell, 1988; Wegman, 1976, 1988). In the most recent period, when the infant mortality rate is 10.4 per 1,000, the underlying causes of all infant deaths (not just neonatal) are: RDS (10%), congenital malformations (21%), short gestation/LBW (formerly "immaturity") (9%), asphyxia (2%), and birth trauma (2%) (Wegman, 1988).

In summary, although infant and neonatal mortality rates have declined to the present, conditions relating to the newborn period continue to predominate as causes of mortality, and, as will be illustrated presently, to lead to substantial morbidity. It should be noted, however, that distributions of causes of death present only partial pictures of the problems underlying neonatal mortality. The causes, as reported, indicate what the clinician considers to be the event that underlies the death of the infant and results in the other problems the infant experienced. Thus, considerable overlap and areas of confusion could occur in coding the cause of death of a preterm infant with RDS who also had a congenital malformation—all of which are related. In particular, the role of shortened gestation/inadequate fetal growth is not well captured by such information.

When birthweight-specific mortality rates are examined, a somewhat different picture of the contribution of LBW/prematurity emerges. LBW (<2,500 grams) infants account for about 6%–7% of all live births; VLBW (<1,500 grams), for about 1%. Among infants dying in the neonatal period, however, two-thirds are LBW; half are VLBW (Shapiro et al., 1980; Buehler, Kleinman, Hogue, Strauss, & Smith, 1987). Thus, the majority of neonatal deaths are associated with inadequate fetal growth, even if the underlying cause of death is recorded as RDS, immaturity, or congenital malformation. Moreover, infant mortality increases exponentially with decreasing birthweight, from a low of 3.5 per 1,000 live births at 3,500–3,999 grams to 695.2 per 1,000 for infant born weighing 1,000 grams or less (Buehler et al., 1987). Rarely does an infant weighing 500 grams or less survive (Buehler et al., 1987; Wilcox & Russell, 1983).

Role of the Neonatal Technology in Changes in Neonatal Mortality

Since 1950, the infant mortality rate has declined from 29.2 per 1,000 live births to 11.0 in 1980 for the U.S. as a whole (Shapiro et al., 1968; Buehler et al., 1987), and most of this change has occurred among neonatal deaths. However, that decline has not been a steady one. Three periods in which the rates of change exhibit different patterns can be considered: (a) 1950 to the late 1960s, when neonatal mortality rates were relatively stable from year to year; (b) the late 1960s to the early 1980s, when mortality rates dropped dramatically, averaging decreases of 4% per year; and (c) the current period, when infant mortality rates are continuing to decrease but at a slower rate (2% per year). Identifying the factors influencing the transitions in these periods provides insight into the role of technology in infant survival.

When the infant mortality rate began to decrease in the second period, several major advances were considered sources of the improvement:

1. The availability of reliable means of contraception and access to thera-peutic abortion for the regulation of fertility were increasing during this period (Cates, 1982; Rosenfield, 1989). Hence, one possibility was that the declines in mortality could be attributed to decreases in the number of births to high-risk women.
2. Major federal programs, the Great Society programs, were also initiated. These programs dramatically increased the access of the poor to medical care, including prenatal care, and to other social services (Aday & Andersen, 1984; Davis & Schoen, 1978), offering the opportunity to improve pregnancy outcome among those high-risk women who did become pregnant.
3. Substantial changes in the content of perinatal and neonatal care also occurred particularly with more effective approaches to the management of RDS and other problems of the neonate (Cone, 1985; Malloy, Hart-ford, & Kleinman, 1987).

Although the first two advances have played a role, most evidence suggests that the major factor in the decline in infant (and neonatal) mortality throughout the 1970s was the increased survival of high-risk infants, that is, those of LBW and VLBW, largely through intensive care techniques. The evidence for this assertion comes from several types of studies or observations, summarized below:

1. The sharp decrease in neonatal mortality occurred in the context of only modest decreases in the proportion of LBW infants and no change in the proportion of VLBW infants (DHHS, 1989; Kleinman, Kovar, Feldman & Young, 1978; Lee, Paneth, Gartner, Pearlman, & Gruss, 1980; Wil-liams & Chen, 1982; David & Siegel, 1983). These observations sug-gested that neither of the first two sources of change had been effective in altering the level of risk in the population of live-born infants. Thus, decreases in mortality must have occurred through increased survival, a conclusion reinforced by other studies.

2. Decreases in neonatal mortality were seen in geographically defined populations when access to neonatal care was improved by the introduction of a new unit (Usher, 1971; Schlesinger, 1973; Horwood, Boyle, Torrance, & Sinclair, 1982), or, more recently, by organizational arrangements which facilitated the transfer of the care of high-risk pregnancies or infants to tertiary care centers (Harris, Isaman, & Giles, 1978; McCormick, Shapiro, & Starfield, 1985; Hein & Lathrop, 1986; Gortmaker, Clark, Graven, Sobol, & Geronimus, 1987; Walker, Vohr, & Oh, 1985).

3. Other studies documented the association between lower mortality rates in hospitals with NICUs controlling for other risk factors known to alter mortality rates (Williams & Hawes, 1979; Hein & Brown, 1981; Paneth, Kiely, Wallenstein, Marcus, Pakter, & Susser, 1982; Verloove-Van Loreck, Verwey, Ebeling, Brand, & Ruys, 1988).

4. Repeated studies noted improvements in birthweight-specific survival among infants provided intensive care (Hack & Fanaroff, 1986; Office of Technology Assessment, 1987).

Consistent with this empirical evidence was the rapid expansion of technological approaches to the newborn that began to emerge in the late 1960s (Cone, 1985). Early approaches to management, based on limited observations and understanding of neonatal physiology, gave way to techniques grounded in basic research and assessed by more rigorous clinical methods. This expanding range of technology included improved management of respiratory distress with special ventilators and techniques of monitoring, better understanding of the nutritional needs of premature infants and the development of special formulae, a broader range of noninvasive diagnostic tests like ultrasound and echocardiography that permitted more accurate assessments in fragile newborns, and less invasive methods of managing common complications of prematurity like bilirubin lights for jaundice and pharmacologic approaches to the patent ductus arteriosus. In addition, prenatal management of high-risk pregnancies improved, with a broader range of assessment approaches to monitor fetal development, and approaches to complications of pregnancy such as better glucose control for maternal diabetes and tocolysis for preterm labor. While not all of these interventions enjoyed the same level of empirical support for efficacy, the total package of services proved to be effective in reducing neonatal loss.

The effect of these technologic innovations is reflected in a report from the Congressional Office of Technology Assessment, which has recently updated its assessment of neonatal intensive care (Office of Technology Assessment). The report reviews studies relating to the neonatal intensive care experience in three periods: 1960, 1971–1975, and 1980–1985. Mortality declined from 72.2% of infants born weighing <1,500 grams in the first period to 27.2% in the most recent period. For even smaller infants, those born weighing <1,000 grams, the risk of mortality declined from virtual certainty to 42.6%. The review concludes that neonatal intensive care continues to be effective in increasing survival of VLBW infants.

In summary, the U.S. continues to experience a relatively high rate of infant mortality, in large part because of relatively high rates of LBW and VLBW births. The persistence of such high rates indicates that current prepregnancy and prenatal interventions have not been successful in markedly reducing the risk of such births (which is not to argue their ineffectiveness, as the rates that might be encountered without current interventions is difficult to estimate). Thus, much of the current evidence converges to the conclusion that the current declines in neonatal mortality are due to increased survival through intensive-care technology. In the following section of this chapter, some recent changes in neonatal intensive care are used to illustrate the issues that are believed to pertain to the current low levels of infant mortality, as well as the research still needed to understand their use. It will be followed by a section exploring the implications of these and other technologies, in particular to try to understand the recent slowing in the rate of decline in infant mortality rates.

SOME RECENT INNOVATIONS IN NEONATAL INTENSIVE CARE

As noted earlier, the changes to be discussed in this section have been selected to illustrate some of the issues affecting neonatal care. The first section will deal with newly emerging techniques for management of respiratory distress in the premature and term infant. Then, the discussion will proceed to the costs of care to address some of the organizational issues affecting the delivery of care to neonates.

Management of RDS in the Premature: Surfactant Replacement and High Frequency Ventilation

As noted earlier, hyaline membrane disease/respiratory distress syndrome (HMD/RDS) is a major cause of mortality among premature infants. An underlying problem is that the cells in the lungs of infants born prematurely may be too immature to produce substances called pulmonary surfactants. The role of these substances is to help keep open the small air sacs where gas transfer occurs (i.e., the alveoli). Without surfactants, the sacs collapse, causing the infant to exert more effort to keep the remaining sacs open and to effect gas exchange (Avery & Mead, 1959).

The initial breakthrough in management occurred in the late 1960s with the realization that increasing the pressure of the air mixture being breathed helped to keep the lungs extended (Gregory, Kitterman, Phibbs, Tooley, & Hamilton, 1971). Much of the activity in the ensuing decade was dedicated to refining this approach to achieve adequate ventilation. This was done by balancing the intensity of the pressure required, the concentration of oxygen, and the rate at which the ventilators cycled to maintain appropriate concentrations of oxygen and carbon dioxide in the blood (Carlo & Martin, 1986). Although these techniques have proven successful in many cases, not all infants respond. Often very high pressures and/or levels of oxygen are required to achieve adequate blood gas concentrations in severe cases of HMD/RDS. In this clinical context, the risks are increased for the recognized complications of prematurity such as bronchopulmonary dysplasia (BPD or chronic lung disease of the newborn), intraventricular hemorrhage, and retinopathy of prematurity (ROP, formerly retrolental fibroplasia) (Lucey, 1988; Bancalari & Flynn, 1988; Bancalari & Gerhardt, 1986). The more severe forms of all these complications are associated with developmental problems (Saigal & O'Brodovich, 1987). Thus, improvements in pulmonary management would offer the potential of improving developmental outcomes. Conversely, assessment of development should play a salient role in establishing the efficacy of new procedures. To illustrate this point, two different innovations will be described.

The first is a modification of artificial ventilatory support to provide high-frequency ventilation. The principle is to supply amounts of inspired gas at very high frequency or, in other words, a rapid ventilatory cycle rate (150–3,000 cycles/minute, depending on the type of ventilatory, compared to 20–40 with conventional ventilation, which provides ventilation rates more in the physiological range). These high-frequency approaches have been shown to provide adequate gas exchange at much lower airway pressures, and offer an alternative in infants with severe disease who would be at risk of bronchopulmonary dysplasia or who have already developed air leaks in the lung due to high pressures on conventional ventilation (Carlo & Martin, 1986; Bancalari & Goldberg, 1987).

While the early work supports the use of high-frequency ventilation, several questions remain. First, in some studies, tracheal damage in the infants dying after the exposure to high-frequency ventilation has been reported, raising the question of pulmonary complications of a sort other than bronchopulmonary dysplasia. Secondly, the strategies for its use remain to be established; that is, should it be used as a primary mode of management or only in infants who cannot be treated conventionally? Finally, the potential for other side effects, especially intracranial bleeding, require evaluation, as the use of high-frequency modes of ventilation results in fragile prematures being vibrated for long periods of time.

Combining the experience of several centers proves to be impossible in that the rates of bronchopulmonary dysplasia vary widely among different centers (Avery, et al., 1987; Horbar, et al., 1988). To address this issue, multicenter trials are required. Despite early successes, however, a multicenter trial of one form of high-frequency ventilation shows no evidence of an advantage over conventional therapy in terms of major outcomes such as bronchopulmonary dysplasia and mortality. Disconcertingly, significant differences are reported for intracranial complications such as hemorrhage (including the more severe grades) (The HIFI Study Group, 1989). However, since the latter is not a designated end point of the trial (sample sizes are based on the rate of bronchopulmonary dysplasia), this finding may represent a chance outcome of multiple testing. Further, the trial does not explore various combinations of ventilatory support and, therefore, cannot address issues of more complex strategies, including the use of other high-frequency techniques. Finally, it is too early to assess the developmental outcomes of infants in the trial. However, it does suggest that developmentalists interested in the outcomes of very premature infants ought to take into account the types of ventilatory support such infants received in the neonatal period.

In contrast to the uncertainty about high-frequency techniques, another technique, surfactant replacement, appears to be effective, although many questions remain. As noted earlier, one of the basic defects underlying the pathogenesis of hyaline membrane disease/respiratory distress syndrome has been known since the 1950s. However, early attempts at introducing surfactant-like substances into the lungs of premature infants met with little success, and the availability of more efficacious interventions occurred only after two decades of research, which allowed better characterization of the components of surfactants (Jobe & Ikegami, 1987; Notter & Shapiro, 1987). While substantial experience is accumulating about the use of surfactant replacement therapy, it should be noted that this experience encompasses a great deal of heterogeneity. Among the sources of this heterogeneity are: (a) variations in study design with not all studies involving controls and/or randomization, (b) variations in indications for the use of surfactant as either prophylaxis or "rescue" (i.e., the treatment of established respiratory distress syndrome), (c) the source of surfactant (animal lung lavage extract, human amniotic fluid, and synthetic preparations), (d) the potential strategies for its use such as one-time vs. repeated administration and variations in dosage, and (e) the selection of outcomes reported in various studies (Soll, 1988; Merritt & Hallman, 1988).

With these caveats in mind, most available studies, but not all, indicate early improvements in ventilatory function with rapid decreases in the pressure required for ventilation and in oxygen concentrations, but not all report decreases in mortality, bronchopulmonary dysplasia, and other complications of prematurity (Soll, 1988; Merritt & Hallman, 1988). At least one study (Maniscalco, Kendig, & Shapiro, 1989) reports that surfactant may lower costs of neonatal hospitalization, but not total costs, in part because, in the sample population examined, surfactant led to increased survival, which incurs greater costs than early death. While data on longer term outcomes of survivors of these trials is accumulating (Dunn, Shennan, Hoskins, & Einhorning, 1988; Vaucher, Merritt, Hallman, Jarvenpaa, & Telsy, 1988; Jain, Vidysagar, & Raju, 1989; Msall,

Rogers, Catanzaro, Kwong, & Bach, 1989; Ware, Taeusch, Soll, & McCormick, 1990), most are too small to provide adequate statistical power individually, and even in combination, about overall developmental outcomes, let alone stratified by the various sources of heterogeneity noted above. Nonetheless, a summary of the currently available results (Ware et al., 1990) does not indicate a statistically significant increase in developmental handicap among infants who have received surfactant. It should be noted, in addition, that most of these results pertain to outcomes in children under 2 years of age, and information on later outcomes is just becoming available. Thus, although the preliminary results of surfactant replacement therapy have been positive enough to support release by the Federal Drug Administration (FDA) ("Wellcome drug set," 1989), much remains to be done in characterizing the most efficacious use of this therapy, and developmentalists must play a role in this process.

Management of Respiratory Distress in the Term Infant: Extracorporeal Membrane Oxygenation (ECMO)

Generally, the use of ECMO has been reserved primarily for term infants, in large part because of the risk of intraventricular hemorrhage. However, selection criteria in some programs (Glass, Miller, & Short, 1989) would include the larger LBW infants now. Further, as more experience is gained with ECMO, the indications may be extended. Thus, developmentalists involved with LBW populations may be involved in assessing and intervening with children who may have experienced this intervention.

Respiratory distress is also encountered in the full-term infant, although more rarely and for different reasons. One situation in which severe, life-threatening respiratory failure may occur is characterized by some degree of asphyxia during the perinatal period, with or without aspiration of meconium into the lungs of the infant during the first breath. The infant develops very high vascular pressures in the lung bed, making it difficult to circulate blood through the lungs, thus increasing the work load on the heart to the point of failure, and little or no gas exchange. If the infant can be supported through this acute phase, however, the process is reversible, although in severe cases traditional reports indicted relatively high mortality rates, often over 50%, due to the inability of conventional ventilatory approaches to provide this degree of support (Fox, Gewitz, Dinwiddie, Drummond, & Peckham, 1977; Fox & Duara, 1987).

In view of this high degree of mortality in a potentially reversible condition, a relatively dramatic technique based on the heart-lung bypass in cardiac surgery has been used: extracorporeal membrane oxygenation (ECMO). The principal component of this approach consists of a pump that takes the blood from the infant and pushes it through a container with an extensive membrane across which oxygen enters the blood and carbon dioxide leaves. The blood continues through a heater and reenters the infant (Short, Miller, & Anderson, 1987). By providing an ancillary pump, the work load of the heart is reduced, and by providing an alternative to the lungs, oxygenation is improved. Most infants respond within days with dramatic improvements in ventilatory function. It should be noted, however, that the use of ECMO requires heparinization (anticoagulation) of the blood to reduce the risk of clotting, and the ligation (tying off) of the right internal jugular vein and carotid artery to allow access to the circulatory system through large vessels. As one might expect, then, complications may involve bleeding, including intracranial bleeding, and the sequelae of ligation of major vessels in cerebral circulation. Indeed, the presence of intraventricular hemorrhage is considered a contraindication to the procedure in many centers (Short et al., 1987).

Early results indicating improvement rely on historical comparisons. With criteria associated with 70%–80% mortality historically, ECMO provides 70%–80% survival in infants with meconium aspiration syndrome and persistent pulmonary hypertension (Short et al., 1987; Kirkpatrick, Krammel, Mueller, Ormazabal, Greenfield, & Salzberg, 1983). However, since other methods of ventilation therapy were also changing, as noted above, two randomized trials of ECMO (Bartlett, Roloff, Cornell, Andrews, Dillon, & Zwischenberger, 1985; O'Rourke et al., 1989) have been conducted. Both studies present ethical dilemmas in that, with such high a priori mortality rates, the failure to provide a promising therapy might present a real disadvantage to any infants randomized to the control group. The conclusion of both studies is that ECMO achieves better survival than conventional ventilatory management, but the studies illustrate the difficulties of assessing new technologies in such a situation. Both studies rely on allocation procedures weighted towards whichever therapy emerges as more successful. In the first study, however, this weighting is so extreme that little information on the outcomes of conventional therapy can be gleaned. The second study relies on a controversial approach to obtaining informed consent (Zelen, 1979). In this approach, subjects are first randomized, and informed consent is obtained only for those receiving the experimental procedure, with the reasoning that the other group is receiving what would be the standard of care. While reducing the difficulty of conducting such trials, this approach raises questions about uninformed participation in an experiment and incurs the pragmatic difficulty of complicating the follow-up, since those in the conventional arm are unaware of their study status.

The other result from this second trial is a lower than expected mortality in the conventional treatment arm, a finding reinforced by other work on improved survival of infants with conventional treatment techniques (Dworetz, Moya, Sabo, Gladstone, & Gross, 1989). These results challenge the need for such highly invasive approaches, even if efficacious.

The developmental outcomes of infants treated with ECMO are just emerging. For developmentalists, children surviving this procedure should present an interesting situation in which to examine the effects of ligation of major vessels supplying blood to the head early in infancy. Moreover, comparisons of outcomes of infants managed in different ways should also be conducted. An issue of particular interest is the extent to which variations in outcome reflect underlying processes of asphyxia in the newborn versus the management of asphyxia and related syndromes.

Reports (Andrews, Nixon, Cilley, Roloff, & Bartlett, 1986; Schumacher et al., 1988) from two of the more active ECMO centers provide some indication of the outcomes of these children. Of the 56 surviving children reported in both studies, 7 are reported as experiencing delays in motor development, and 6, mental delay. Other findings include 5 with microcephaly and 6 with failure to thrive with or without severe lung disease, although some of these children also are in the delayed group. While one (Glass et al., 1989) of these studies reports transient and/or mild asymmetries in right–left motor functioning, more severe forms have been reported in 14% of one series (Schumacher et al., 1988), with most of these children also experiencing mental and motor delay. As noted above, however, these outcomes most likely represent sequelae of a combination of the underlying problem and the use of ECMO.

The technologies above have been selected to illustrate several points. The first is that the management of very tiny infants is an evolving process and may limit the comparability of outcomes among different units and over time. The information on how technological interventions influence outcomes is limited, and even less certain is the influence of the various combinations of interventions that constitute the practices of individual units. Unlike the studies concerning bronchopulmonary dysplasia (Avery et al., 1987; Horbar et al., 1988), comparisons of units for developmental outcomes have not been published.

The second issue is that, while developmental outcomes are a critical aspect of assessing the effect of neonatal care, more comprehensive conceptualizations of outcomes are needed to assure more adequate information on the factors influencing development. The focus on developmental quotients and neuro-developmental diagnoses requires expansion to include other aspects of child and family functioning. Such broader conceptualizations have been developed (Eisen, Donald, Ware, & Brook, 1980) and applied to longer term outcomes of VLBW infants (McCormick, 1989). The application of these conceptualizations of outcome within the context of broad theories of development should lead to clearer definition of those children and families who may require further intervention for optional development.

Finally, the information on other types of interventions which may influence outcomes is extremely limited. As will be discussed in a later chapter, some developmental interventions in the intensive care unit appear successful in promoting some aspects of development. The range of postdischarge interventions that have been assessed is very limited, and tailoring interventions to families and infants with different needs remains an underdeveloped area. The successful experience in fostering the development of disadvantaged children needs to be extended to children with physical health problems (Brooks-Gunn, McCormick, & Heagarty, 1988).

Implications of Innovations: Costs of Care

When recent changes in neonatal intensive care are considered, the issue of costs does not usually leap to mind in the same way as thoughts of ventilators or sophisticated monitoring equipment. Yet neonatal care remains a very expensive service and therefore cannot be immune to the more general cost-containment pressures occurring throughout the American medical care system. Moreover, both the costs and the processes in place to affect costs may challenge the implementation of services aimed at enhancing the developmental outcome of high-risk survivors.

Costs of neonatal care. In general, VLBW survivors average 45–50 days in the hospital before coming home for the first time, with an average cost of $27,000 to $60,000 (Office of Technology Assessment, 1987). The average cost may mask skewed distributions with substantially higher costs for the smallest and sickest infants, who may accrue up to 90 days of hospitalization at the cost of $150,000. Concerns about the total amount of costs of care are reinforced in a recent publication from the Guttmacher Institute (The Alan Guttmacher Institute, 1989) on the costs of maternity care. This report provides comparable data on the total amount, but points out the substantial gaps in insurance coverage for the costs of maternity and neonatal care, even among those with health insurance policies. Thus, much of the care falls to the hospital (self-pay, bad debt) or to the public sector (Medicaid and other public programs). Both private and public payors are seeking to reduce the burden of payment for the services they do cover by techniques that encourage early discharge from the hospital such as per-case or prospective reimbursement (Resnick et al., 1986; Phibbs, Phibbs, Pomerance, & Williams, 1986; Poland, Bollinger, Bedard, & Cohen, 1985; Berki & Scheier, 1987) and/or retrotransport to a lower cost community hospital (Bose, Lapine, & Jung, 1987).

Both the lack of third party coverage for medical care, and the pressures of cost-containment to reduce length of stay, have several implications for the care of neonatal intensive care graduates. First, the burdens of paying for care may be shifted to parents, affecting their ability to participate in services designed to foster their child's development. Despite the fact that only 4% of neonatal care is ultimately borne by the parents (McCarthy, Koops, Honeyfield, & Butterfield, 1979), the stress of interacting with various financial counsellors and completion of multiple applications for financial assistance, as well as the anxiety about ability to pay, may interfere with the parents' relation to the child. The mother may return to work temporarily when the baby has stabilized but is not ready for discharge in order to contribute to payments for care. Working hours may limit her hours of visiting and raise concerns among staff about the quality of early mother–infant interactions. Moreover, regular and prolonged visiting to tertiary centers may itself increase the economic burden on the family. Although one British study (Smith & Bourn, 1983) has examined this question, the relevance of this study to the American situation is limited.

Less well appreciated than the costs of the initial hospitalization are the ongoing costs of medical care during infancy. One-third to one-half of these children will incur one or more rehospitalizations over the first 3 years of life (McCormick, Shapiro, & Starfield, 1980; Hack, De Monterice, Merkatz, Jones, & Fanaroff, 1980; Hack, Rivers, & Fanaroff, 1983). More recent reports (Shankaran, Cohen, Linver, & Zonia, 1988; McCormick, Bernbaum, Eisenberg, Kustra, & Finnegan, 1991) indicate that the costs of ambulatory care may also be substantially higher than for normal birthweight children, and these costs are more likely to represent out-of-pocket costs to the family not covered by other resources. One estimate (Shankaran et al., 1988) is that the average monthly costs for direct medical care over the first 3 years of life of a neonatal intensive care graduate ranged from $60 to $1,200, depending on health status, compared to about $22 to $26 nationally for children of a similar age. It should be noted that this estimate does not include costs of transportation for medical care, special child care, or equipment rental, as well as other potentially related expenditures. Among the latter may well be time costs to the parents as they obtain all this additional care and follow through on the recommendations. The pressures of cost containment may only increase this burden, as the infant is discharged earlier to require more frequent ambulatory visits early in infancy.

Implications for early intervention programs. These high costs and measures introduced to reduce costs may influence the implementation of intervention programs for LBW infants. Shortened lengths of stay and/or retrotransport also decrease the opportunity for developmental programs delivered in the intensive care unit, and suggest the need for programs directed toward community hospitals and families. That intervention programs can be successful in fostering child development even when mothers have quite limited resources is attested to by the success of a variety efforts among healthy disadvantaged children (Olds, Henderson, Chamberlin, & Tatelbaum, 1986; Brooks-Gunn & Hearn, 1982). Fewer studies have been conducted with neonatal intensive care graduates who may be characterized by some combination of socioeconomic and biological vulnerability. Brooten and her colleagues (Brooten, et al., 1986) have conducted a randomized, controlled trial of early discharge of stable infants weighing <1,500 grams. In comparison to the control group, infants discharge early and supported with nursing home visits and telephone access had lower neonatal intensive care costs with no differences in subsequent growth, health care use or development (as measured by a Bayley score) at 18 months.

That interventions may actually improve outcomes is argued by a multisite, randomized trial (Infant Health and Development Program, 1990) of an intervention consisting of regular home visits, educational day care, and intensive medical surveillance during the first 3 years of life, as compared to intensive medical surveillance alone. The intervention group had substantially better developmental outcomes (as measured by the Stanford-Binet), and somewhat fewer behavioral problems as reported by the mother. An increase in reported morbidity was seen in the intervention group consistent with other studies of the early exposure of infants to congregate care, but this morbidity reflected primarily relatively brief illnesses, as measures of more severe conditions were similar between the two groups.

The limited studies available suggest that earlier discharge is possible providing adequate professional guidance and support is available to the parents. The nature of this support still requires further definition and empirical examination. Brooten's (1986) work suggests that a relatively modest degree of nursing support can achieve similar results to continued hospitalization, but she still encountered substantial morbidity. The larger multisite study results offer the goal of improvement but require intensive maneuvers well beyond the scope of many communities or families to provide. The addition of more developmentally oriented services to the nursing model might prove useful, but the nature of such services is not clear.

That further empirical examination of different combinations of developmental services is needed is suggested by another set of literature which indicates that not all postdischarge interventions have proven unequivocally successful. A recent summary (Tirosh & Rabino, 1989) of trials of the efficacy of interventions based on physical therapy services revealed mixed results, in part because the trials lack sufficient statistical power to support firm conclusions.

While the evidence currently suggests that the type of educational interventions based on developmental theories and research may help in improving outcomes, some caveats are in order. The first is that the outcomes being measured are heavily dependent on changes in IQ scores. The latter may not be sensitive to qualitative differences in performance such as the neuromuscular strategies used by children with less severe forms of impairment in attaining developmental milestones, strategies which might be improved with physical therapy input. Likewise, such scores may not tap many domains relevant to functioning such as behavior. Secondly, children with complex medical problems such as extreme prematurity, and major congenital anomalies or severe sequelae of prematurity such as bronchopulmonary dysplasia or necrotizing enterocolitis, have not been included in the current trials so that the generalizability to such children is not certain. Finally, longer term outcomes, either benefits or adverse events, remain to be established. Thus, the definition of an economical and efficacious set of services for fostering the development of these infants presents a challenge to both pediatricians and developmentalists, a challenge which has assumed greater urgency since the passage of PL 99-457 with its mandate to provide early intervention services for such children as neonatal intensive care graduates (DeGraw et al., 1988).

The extent to which early interventions affect the total costs of care for LBW infants remains to be established. In Brooten's (1986) study early discharge from the nursery, even with more intensive nursing surveillance, proved to be less costly than remaining in the hospital and achieved comparable outcomes. In the short term, additional early intervention services represent additional costs of care, sometimes substantial, which may be justified in the longer term by decreases in special education services and other support of individuals with preventable disabilities. Little empirical data are currently available to address this issue for any group.

However, the consideration of costs does raise a specific issue of importance. In designing such programs, developmentalists should also be sensitive to cost shifting to the parents. The studies already cited indicate the substantial burden of medical care these infants require, which imposes both monetary and non-monetary costs on the family (McCormick, & Richardson, 1991). Prescriptions for regular activities to foster development may be added to special feeding needs, regular medicine administration and physical therapy for pulmonary and other conditions, as well as visits to multiple medical providers. Moreover, the burden of providing these services may limit parental (especially maternal) work-force participation, thus reducing the financial resources for additional care, as well as vacation opportunities and interactions with siblings. While this caveat is not to argue against such early intervention programs, it does suggest the importance of overt attention to the monetary and nonmonetary burden on the family, and coordination of care with other providers as an element of the planning and evaluation of such programs.

POTENTIAL IMPLICATIONS OF MOST RECENT CHANGES IN INFANT MORTALITY

The extent to which such improvements as illustrated earlier in this chapter can sustain a continuation of the rapid decline in infant mortality of the 1970s remains to be established. The recent slowing of the rates of decline in infant mortality raises questions that represent the converse of the questions of the early 1970s. As the answers unfold, developmentalists must play a role in assessing the impact of various changes on the developmental outcomes of infants and children individually and as a group. In parallel with the discussion above of infant mortality trends, sources for the recent changes in mortality can be summarized as follows.

Alterations in Availability of Methods to Regulate Fertility Especially Among Low-Income (High-Risk) Women

Many changes in the 1980s have reduced access to methods of regulating fertility, especially for poor women or women with difficulty in complying with regular medical regimens. Such factors include the risk of malpractice to com-panies manufacturing contraceptive drugs and devices (Djerassi, 1980), non-monetary barriers to care (Radicki & Bernstein, 1989), limitations in funding of publicly supported contraceptive services (Dryfoos, 1989; Aries, 1987), legally mandated fragmentation of reproductive services (Aries, 1987), and the furor over abortion. While overall pregnancy rates are not increasing, both induced abortion and live birth rates remain substantial among women at increased risk of adverse outcomes (Ventura, Taffel, & Mosher, 1988). The implications of these changes may be an increase in the number of infants requiring neonatal care among women unprepared and/or ill equipped to take on the role of parent.

Alterations in Access to Prenatal Services

Likewise, support for publicly funded programs for medical care, including prenatal care, has eroded. Currently, median eligibility for Medicaid, the federal–state program for the poor, is at less than half of the federal poverty level (Burwell & Rymer, 1987; Davidson, Cromwell, & Schurman, 1986), and, in many states, the eligibility levels are lower. Moreover, many states have established limits to care through variations in payment mechanisms such as "gate-keeper" approaches (Harley & Freund, 1988), which place primary care providers at financial risk for referral services like developmental assessment. Less well appreciated, however, is the fact that shifts in employment patterns and cost-containment efforts of private insurers have also led to reductions in coverage for working couples with private insurance (Renner & Navarro, 1989). An additional factor may be the effect of malpractice litigation (Weisman, Teitelbaum, & Morlock, 1988). However, the full impact of this threat is currently difficult to disentangle from other factors.

Whatever the major influence, one indicator of the potential impact of these and other barriers to primary care is the slowing in the rate of women who start care in the first trimester, which has plateaued at 79% for white women and 61% for black women since 1980 (Ingram, Makuc, & Kleinman, 1986). Another is the persistence of the rate of low-birthweight births at about 7%; of very low-birthweight births for all births at 1%. These overall numbers mask an increase in the very low-birthweight rate among blacks from 2.37% in 1975 to 2.66% in 1986 (DHHS, 1989). The extent to which the latter finding represents a worsening of the conditions of black women vs. an improvement in reporting of live births of very immature infants among black women remains to be established.

Besides access to care, recent information also raises questions about the adequacy of current prenatal care to deal with the problems of prematurity. While the overall data support an important effect of prenatal care in reducing the risk of low birth weight (Institute of Medicine, 1985), the specific package of services appropriate to various types of women remains to be established. Further, the reasons and risk factors for premature termination of pregnancy remain unresolved in a large proportion of the cases (Kramer, 1987; Berendes, Kessel, & Yaffe, 1991), and, partially as a result, preventive strategies have not proven universally successful (Berendes et al., 1991). These findings suggest the need for more investigation into the basic pathogenesis of premature delivery, as well as more comprehensive approaches to intervention. We have previously suggested that social scientists have a role to play in the design and assessment of preventive strategies, in part based on the experiences of early childhood intervention studies (Brooks-Gunn et al., 1988). The social scientist perspective should prove helpful in developing more sophisticated models of risk factors and behavior. Such models would include a broader array of risk factors derived from coherent theoretical frameworks linked to plausible biological mechanisms of labor and fetal development, as well as to later parent–infant interactions. Such models, in turn, should lead to more successful intervention strategies.

Limits to the Effect of Neonatal Technology

While technology innovation continues, some investigators are beginning to present information which suggests that there is a limit to what can be achieved. This evidence is derived from quite disparate sources, such as anatomic information pertaining to the ability of the fetal lung to sustain respiration (Di Maio, Gil, Ciurea, & Katlan, 1989), the lack of improvement in survival rates below a certain birthweight/gestational age over the immediate past (Heinonen, Hakulineu, & Jokela, 1988; Hack & Fanaroff, 1989), and questions about the futility of certain intensive procedures for some very immature infants (Lantos, Miles, Silverstein, & Stocking,1988; Guillemin & Holmshorn, 1983). The results of the studies vary, as do their intent, but they begin to suggest that survival under 500 grams and 23 weeks of gestation is extremely rare, in part because we may be approaching biological limits on viability. Thus, in the absence of a reduction in rates of births of very premature infants, the infant mortality may not continue to decline as quickly.

Each of these changes has implications for changes in developmental outcomes. If, indeed, restrictions in access to family planning services are contributing to the slowing in the rate of decline in infant mortality, then the proportion of children at risk for developmental problems will increase. The risk, however, will not be restricted to those just at medical risk since it is likely that the proportion of women ill prepared for parenting due to age (e.g., adolescents) or timing of pregnancy will increase. Thus, developmental outcomes of neonatal intensive care graduates may be worse but less as a reflection of intensive care technology than of the ability of their parents to provide support.

Decreased access to prenatal care incurs the risk, not only of higher numbers of LBW and VLBW infants, but also of the longer term effects of maternal conditions and health habits inadequately managed during pregnancy. The persistence of poor maternal health and adverse behaviors, and the potential for prenatal interventions to improve child outcomes has received little attention. Clearly, however, maternal morbidity resulting from complications of pregnancy, and failure to alter health habits like smoking have clear implications for the child. The most dramatic example in some inner city areas can be drawn from the combination of maternal substance abuse and AIDS, but other less dramatic problems can be cited.

Finally, any limits of current technology to improve survival focus sharp attention on improving the functional outcomes of those children who can respond to current techniques in the least costly fashion. Such improvements require identification of the most efficacious interventions both during and after the neonatal hospitalization.

For the foreseeable future, neonatal intensive care will continue to change, and to be an important intervention in the survival of at least some portion of neonates, both preterm and term. The short-term and long-term implications of these changes require careful assessment. Such assessments require an understanding of the biological processes underlying both the indication for intensive care and the management techniques, so that appropriate evaluation approaches can be used. In addition, however, developmentalists should also be cognizant of other processes affecting the need for and access to neonatal care in order to understand the potential changes in environmental influences on outcome, as well as the technological influences. As this discussion indicates, both technological and organizational innovations require assessment and should be considered in evaluation approaches. Clearly, developmentalists have a key role in defining the questions and identifying assessment techniques for this process.

REFERENCES

Aday, L.A., & Andersen, R.M. (1984). The national profile of access to medical care: Where do we stand? *American Journal of Public Health, 74*, 1331–1339.

The Alan Guttmacher Institute. (1989). *Blessed events and the bottom line*. New York: Author.

Andrews, A.R., Nixon, C.A., Cilley, R.E., Roloff, D.W., & Bartlett, R.H. (1986). One-to-three year outcome for 14 neonatal survivors of extracorporeal membrane oxygenation. *Pediatrics, 78*, 692–698.

Aries, N. (1987). Fragmentation and reproductive freedom: Federally subsidized family planning services, 1960–80. *American Journal of Public Health, 77*, 1393–1395.

Avery, M.E., & Mead. J. (1959). Surface properties in relation to atelectasis and hyaline membrane disease. *American Journal of Diseases of Children, 97*, 517–523.

Avery, M.E., Tooley, W.H., Keeler, J.B., Hurd, S.S., Bryan, H., Cotton, R.B., Epstein, M.F., Fitzhardinge, P.M., Hansen, C.B., Hansen, T.N., Hodson, W.A., James L.S., Kitterman, J.A., Nielsen, H.C., Poirier, T.A., Truog, W.E., & Wung, J-T. (1987). Is chronic lung disease in low birth weight infants preventable? *Pediatrics, 79*, 26–30.

Bancalari, E., & Flynn, J.T. (1988). Respiratory physiology, oxygen therapy and monitoring: A report of a clinical trial of constant monitoring. In J.T. Flynn & D.L. Phelps (Eds.) *Retinopathy of prematurity: Problems and challenges* (March of Dimes Birth Defect Original Article Series, Vol. 24, No. 1.) New York: Alan R. Liss.

Bancalari, E., & Gerhardt, T. (1986) Bronchopulmonary dysplasia. *Pediatric Clinics of North America, 33*, 1–23.

Bancalari, E., & Goldberg, R.N. (1987). High-frequency ventilation in the neonate. *Clinical Perinatology, 14*, 581–597.

Bartlett, R.H., Roloff, D.W., Cornell, R.G., Andrews, A.F., Dillon, P.W., & Zwischenberger, J.B. (1985). Extracorporeal circulatory support in neonatal respiratory failure: A prospective randomized study. *Pediatrics*, *76*, 479–487.

Berendes, H.W., Kessel, S., & Yaffe, S. (Eds). (1991). *Advances in the prevention of low birthweight: An International Symposium*. Washington, DC: National Center for Education in Maternal and Child Health.

Berki, S.E., & Scheier, N.B. (1987). Frequency and cost of diagnosis-related group outliers among newborns. *Pediatrics*, *79*, 874–881.

Bose, C.L., Lapine, T.R., & Jung, A.L. (1987). Neonatal back-transport cost effectiveness. *Medical Care*, *23*, 14–19.

Brooks-Gunn, J., & Hearn, R. (1982). Early intervention and developmental dysfunction: Implications for pediatrics. *Advances in Pediatrics*, *29*, 497–527.

Brooks-Gunn, J., McCormick, M.C., & Heagarty, M.C. (1988). Preventing infant mortality and morbidity: Developmental perspectives. *American Journal of Orthopsychiatry*, *58*, 288–296.

Brooten, D., Kumar, S., Brown, L.P., Butts, P., Finkler, S.A., Bakewell-Sachs, S., Gibbson, A., & Delivoria-Papadopoulos, M. (1986). A randomized clinical trial of early hospital discharge and home follow-up of very-low-birth-weight infants. *New England Journal of Medicine*, *315*, 934–993.

Buehler, J.W., Kleinman, J.C., Hogue, C.J.R., Strauss, L.T., & Smith, J.C. (1987). Birthweight-specific infant mortality, United States, 1960 and 1980. *Public Health Reports*, *102*, 151–161.

Burwell, B.O., & Rymer, M.P. (1987). Trends in Medicaid eligibility: 1975 to 1985. *Health Affairs*, *6*, 30–45.

Carlo, W.A., & Martin, R.J. (1986). Principles of neonatal assisted ventilation. *Pediatric Clinics of North America*, *33*, 221–237.

Cates, W. (1982). Legal abortion: The public health record. *Science*, *215*, 1586.

Cone, T.E. (1985). *History of the care and feeding of the premature infant*. Boston: Little, Brown & Co.

David, R.J., & Siegel, E. (1983). Decline in neonatal mortality, 1968 to 1977: Better babies or better care? *Pediatrics*, *71*, 531–540.

Davidson, S.M., Cromwell, J., & Schurman, R. (1986). Medicaid myths: Trends in Medicaid expenditures and prospects for reform. *Journal of Health Politics, Policy & Law*, *10*, 699–728.

Davis, K., & Schoen, C. (1978). *Health and the war on poverty. A ten year appraisal*. Washington, DC: The Brookings Institution.

DeGraw, C., Edell, D., Ellers, B., Hillemeir, M., Liebman, J., Perry, C., & Palfrey, J.S. (1988). Public Law 99-457: New opportunities to serve young children with special needs. *Journal of Pediatrics*, *113*, 971–974.

Department of Health and Human Services (DHHS). (1989). *Health United States, 1988* (DHHS Pub. No. (PHS) 89-1232). Hyattsville, MD: U.S. Government Printing Office.

Di Maio, M., Gil, J., Ciurea, D., & Katlan, M. (1989). Structural maturation of the human fetal lung: A morphometric study of the development of air-blood barriers. *Pediatric Research*, *26*, 88–93.

Djerassi, C. (1989). The bitter pill. *Science*, *245*, 356–361.

Dryfoos, J.G. (1989). What President Bush can do about family planning. *American Journal of Public Health*, *79*, 689–90.

Dunn, M.S., Shennan, A.T., Hoskins, E.M., & Einhorning, G. (1988). Two-year follow-up of infants enrolled in a randomized trial of surfactant replacement therapy for prevention of neonatal respiratory distress syndrome. *Pediatrics*, *82*, 543–47.

Dworetz, A.R., Moya, F.R., Sabo, B., Gladstone, I., & Gross, I. (1989). Survival of infants with persistent pulmonary hypertension without extra- corporeal membrane oxygenation. *Pediatrics*, *84*, 1–6.

Eisen, M., Donald, C.A., Ware, J.E., & Brook, R.H. (1980). *Conceptualization and measurement of health of children in the health insurance study*. Santa Monica: CA: The Rand Corporation.

Fox, W.W., Gewitz, M.H., Dinwiddie, R., Drummond, W.H., & Peckham, G.J. (1977). Pulmonary hypertension in perinatal aspiration syndrome. *Pediatrics, 59*, 205.

Fox, W.W., & Duara, S. (1987). Persistent pulmonary hypertension in the neonate: Diagnosis and management. *Journal of Pediatrics, 103*, 505–514.

Glass, G., Miller, M., & Short, B. (1989). Morbidity for survivors of extracorporeal membrane oxygenation: Neurodevelopmental outcome at 1 year of age. *Pediatrics, 83*, 72–78.

Gortmaker, S.L., Clark, C.J.G., Graven, S.N., Sobol, A.M., & Geronimus, A. (1987). Reducing infant mortality in rural America. Evaluation of the rural infant care program. *Health Services Research, 22*, 91–116.

Gregory, G.A., Kitterman, J.A., Phibbs, R.H., Tooley, W.H., & Hamilton, W.K. (1971). Treatment of idiopathic respiratory distress syndrome with continuous positive airway pressure. *New England Journal of Medicine, 284*, 1333–1340.

Guillemin, J.H., & Holmshorn, L.L. (1983). Legal cases, government regulations, and clinical realities in newborn intensive care. *American Journal of Perinatology, 1*, 89–97.

Hack, M., DeMonterice, D., Merkatz, I.R., Jones, P., & Fanaroff, A.A. (1980). Rehospitalization of the very-low-birth-weight infant: A continuum of perinatal and environmental morbidity. *American Journal of Diseases of Children, 135*, 262–266.

Hack, M., & Fanaroff, A.A. (1986). Changes in the delivery room care of the extremely small infant (<750 g.). Effects on morbidity and outcome. *New England Journal of Medicine, 314*, 660–664.

Hack, M., & Fanaroff, A.A. (1989). Outcomes of extremely-low-birth-weight infants between 1982 and 1988. *New England Journal of Medicine, 321*, 1642–1647.

Hack, M., Rivers, A., & Fanaroff, A.A. (1983). The very low birth weight infant: The broader spectrum of morbidity during infancy and early childhood. *Journal of Behavioral and Developmental Pediatrics, 4*, 243–249.

Harley, R.E., & Freund, D.A. (1988). A typology of Medicaid managed care. *Medical Care, 26*, 764–774.

Harris, T.R., Isaman, J., & Giles, H.R. (1978). Improved neonatal survival through maternal transport. *Obstetrics and Gynecology, 52*, 294–300.

Hein, H.A., & Brown, C.J. (1981). Neonatal mortality review: a basis for improving care. *Pediatrics, 6*, 504–509.

Hein, H.A., & Lathrop, S.S. (1986). The changing pattern of neonatal mortality in a regionalized system of perinatal care. *American Journal of Diseases of Children, 140*, 989–993.

Heinonen, K., Hakulineu, A., & Jokela, V. (1988). Survival of the smallest. Time trends and determinants fo mortality in a very preterm population during the 1980s. *Lancet, 2*, 204–207.

The HIFI Study Group. (1989). High-frequency oscillatory ventilation compared with conventional mechanical ventilation in the treatment of respiratory failure in preterm infants. *New England Journal of Medicine, 320*, 88–93.

Horbar, J.D., McAuliffe, T.L., Adler, T.M., Albersheim, S., Cassady, G., Edwards, W., Jones, R., Kattwinkel, J., Kraybill, E.N., Krishnan, V., Raschko, P., & Wilkinson, A.R. (1988). Variability in 28-day outcomes for very low birth weight infants: An analysis of 11 neonatal intensive care units. *Pediatrics, 82*, 554–559.

Horwood, S.P., Boyle, M.H., Torrance, G.W., & Sinclair, J.C. (1982). Mortality and morbidity of 500-1499-gram birth weight infants live-born to residents of a defined geographic region before and after neonatal intensive care. *Pediatrics, 69*, 613–620.

Infant Health and Development Program. (1990). Enhancing the outcomes of low birth weight, premature infants: A multi-site randomized trial. *Journal of the American Medical Association, 2630*, 3035–3042.

Ingram, D.D., Makuc, D., & Kleinman, J.C. (1986). National and state trends in the use of prenatal care, 1970–1983. *American Journal of Public Health, 76*, 415–423.

Institute of Medicine. (1985). *Preventing low birthweight*. Washington, DC: National Academy Press.

Jain, L., Vidysagar, D., & Raju, T.N.K. (1989). Developmental outcomes of infants from surfactant trials. *Pediatric Research, 25*, 255A (abs).

Jobe, A., & Ikegami, M. (1987). Surfactant for the treatment of respiratory distress syndrome. *American Review of Respiratory Disease, 136*, 1256–1275.

Kirkpatrick, B.V., Krammel, T.M., Mueller, D.G., Ormazabal, M.A., Greenfield, L.J., & Salzberg, A.M. (1983). Use of extracorporeal membrane oxygenation for respiratory failure in term infants. *Pediatrics, 72*, 872–876.

Kleinman, J.C., Kovar, M.G., Feldman, J.J., & Young, C.A. (1978). A comparison of 1960 and 1973–74 early neonatal mortality in selected states. *American Journal of Epidemiology, 108*, 454–459.

Kramer, M.S. (1987). Intrauterine growth and gestational duration determinants. *Pediatrics, 80*, 502–511.

Lantos, J.D., Miles, S.H., Silverstein, M.D., & Stocking, C.B. (1988). Survival after cardio-pulmonary resuscitation in babies of very low birthweight. Is CPR futile therapy? *New England Journal of Medicine, 318*, 91–95.

Lee, K-S., Paneth, N., Gartner, L.M., Pearlman, M.A., & Gruss, L. (1980). Neonatal mortality: An analysis of the improvement in the United States. *American Journal of Public Health, 70*, 15–21.

Lucey, J.F. (1988). Perinatal intracranial hemorrhage and retinopathy of prematurity: Currently non-preventable complications of premature birth: In J.T. Flynn & D.L. Phelps (Eds.), *Retinopathy of prematurity: Problems and challenges* (March of Dimes Birth Defect Original Article Series, Vol. 24, No. 1). New York: Alan R. Liss.

Malloy, M.H., Hartford, R.B., & Kleinman, J.C. (1987). Trends in mortality caused by respiratory distress syndrome in the United States, 1969–83. *American Journal of Public Health, 77*, 1511–1514.

Maniscalco, W.M., Kendig, J.W., & Shapiro, D.L. (1989). Surfactant replacement therapy: Impact on hospital charges for premature infants with respiratory distress syndrome. *Pediatrics, 83*, 1–6.

Manniello, R.L., & Farrell, P.M. (1977). Analysis of United States neonatal mortality statistics from 1968–1974 with specific reference to changing trends in major causalities. *American Journal of Obstetrics and Gynecology, 129*, 667–674.

McCarthy, J.T., Koops, B.L., Honeyfield, P.R., & Butterfield, L.J. (1979). Who pays the bill for neonatal intensive care? *Journal of Pediatrics, 95*, 755–761.

McCormick, M.C. (1989). Long-term follow-up of infants discharged from neonatal intensive care units. *Journal of the American Medical Association, 261*, 1767–1772.

McCormick, M.C., Bernbaum, J.C., Eisenberg, J.M., Kustra, S.L., & Finnegan, E. (1991). Costs incurred by parents of very low birth weight infants after initial neonatal hospitalization. *Pediatrics*.

McCormick, M.C., & Richardson, D. (1991). Long-term costs of perinatal disabilities. In H.W. Taeusch, R.A. Ballard, & M.E. Avery (Eds.), *Schaffer and Avery's diseases of the newborn* (6th ed.). Philadelphia: Saunders.

McCormick, M.C., Shapiro, S., & Starfield, B.H. (1980). Rehospitalization in the first year of life for high-risk survivors. *Pediatrics, 66*, 991–999.

McCormick, M.C., Shapiro, S., & Starfield, B.H. (1985). The regionalization of perinatal services: Summary of the evaluation of a national demonstration program. *Journal of the American Medical Association, 252*, 799–804.

Merritt, T.A., & Hallman, M. (1988). Surfactant replacement. A new era with many challenges for neonatal medicine. *American Journal of Diseases of Children, 142*, 1333–1339.

Msall, M.E., Rogers, B.T., Catanzaro, N., Kwong, M.A., & Bach, G. (1989). Five year neuro-developmental outcomes of infants less than 28 weeks gestational age enrolled in a surfactant randomized clinical trial. *Pediatric Research, 25*, 284A (abs).

National Perinatal Epidemiology Unit. (1985). *A classified bibliography of controlled trials in perinatal medicine, 1940–1984*. Oxford: Oxford University Press.

Notter, R.H., & Shapiro, D.L. (1987). Lung surfactants for replacement therapy: Biochemical, biophysical and clinical aspects. *Clinics in Perinatology, 14*, 433–479.

Office of Technology Assessment. (1987). *Neonatal intensive care for low birthweight infants: Costs and effectiveness* (Health Technology Case Study 38, OTA-HCS-38). Washington, DC: U.S. Congress.

Olds, D.L., Henderson, C.R., Chamberlin, R., & Tatelbaum, R. (1986). Preventing child abuse and neglect: A randomized trial of nurse home visitation. *Pediatrics, 78*, 65–78.

O'Rourke, P.P., Crone, R.K., Vacanti, J.P., Ware, J.H., Lillihei, C.W., Parad, R.B., & Epstein, M.F. (1989). Extracorporeal membrane oxygenation and conventional medical therapy in neonates with persistent pulmonary hypertension of the newborn: A prospective randomized study. *Pediatrics, 84*, 957–963.

Paneth, N., Kiely, J.L., Wallenstein, S., Marcus, M., Pakter, J., & Susser, M. (1982). Newborn intensive care and neonatal mortality in low-birth-weight infants: A population study. *New England Journal of Medicine, 307*, 149–155.

Pharoah, P.O.D., & Morris, J.N., (1979). Post-neonatal mortality. *Epidemiologic Review, 1*, 170–183.

Phibbs, C.S., Phibbs, R.H., Pomerance, J.J., & Williams, R.L. (1986). Alternative to diagnosis-related groups for newborn intensive care. *Pediatrics, 78*, 829–836.

Poland, R.L., Bollinger, R.O., Bedard, M.P., & Cohen, S.N. (1985). Analysis of the effects of applying federal diagnosis-related grouping (DRG) guidelines to a population of high-risk newborn infants. *Pediatrics, 76*, 104–109.

Radicki, S.E., & Bernstein, G.S. (1989). Use of clinic versus private family planning care by low-income women: Access, cost and patient satisfaction. *American Journal of Public Health, 79*, 692–697.

Renner, C., & Navarro, V. (1989). Why is our population of uninsured and underinsured persons growing? The consequences of "deindustrialization" of America. *Annual Review of Public Health, 79*, 85–94.

Resnick, M.B., Ariet, M., Carter, R.L., Fletcher, J.W., Evans, J.H., Furlough, R.R., Ausbon, W.W., & Curran, J.S. (1986). Prospective pricing system for tertiary neonatal intensive care. *Pediatrics, 78*, 820–828.

Rosenfield, A. (1989). Modern contraception: A 1989 update. *Annual Review of Public Health, 10*, 385–401.

Saigal, S., & O'Brodovich, H. (1987). Long-term outcomes of preterm infants with respiratory disease. *Clinics in Perinatology, 14*, 635–650.

Schlesinger, E.R. (1973). Neonatal intensive care: Planning for services and outcome following care. *Journal of Pediatrics, 82*, 916–920.

Schumacher, R.E., Barks, J.D.E., Johnston, M.V., Donn, S.M., Scher, M.S., Roloff, D.W., & Bartlett, R.H. (1988). Right-sided brain lesions in infants following extracorporeal membrane oxygenation. *Pediatrics, 82*, 155–161.

Shankaran, S., Cohen, S.N., Linver, M., & Zonia, S. (1988). Medical care costs of high-risk infants after neonatal intensive care: A controlled study. *Pediatrics, 81*, 372–378.

Shapiro, S., McCormick, M.C., Starfield, B.H., Krischer, J.P., & Bross, D. (1980). Relevance of correlates of infant deaths for significant morbidity at 1 year of age. *American Journal of Obstetrics and Gynecology, 136*, 363–373.

Shapiro, S., Schlesinger, E.R., & Nesbitt, R.E.L. (1968). *Infant, perinatal, maternal and childhood mortality in the United States*. Cambridge, MA: Harvard University Press.

Short, B.L., Miller, M.K., & Anderson, K.D. (1987). Extra-corporeal membrane oxygenation in the management of respiratory failure in the newborn. *Clinics in Perinatology, 14*, 737–758.

Smith, M.A., & Bourn, J.D. (1983). Costs of visiting babies in special care baby units. *Archives of Diseases of Childhood, 58*, 56–59.

Soll, R.F. (1988). Clinical controlled trials: What do they tell us? In A.H. Jobe & H.W. Taeusch

(Eds.), *Surfactant treatment of lung diseases* (Report of the 96th Ross Conference on Pediatric Research). Columbus, OH: Ross Laboratories.

Tirosh, E., & Rabino, S. (1989). Physiotherapy for children with cerebral palsy. Evidence for its efficacy. *American Journal of Diseases of Children, 143*, 552–555.

Usher, R.H. (1971). Clinical implications of perinatal mortality statistics. *Clinical Obstetrics and Gynecology, 14*, 885–925.

Vaucher, Y.E., Merritt, T.A., Hallman, M., Jarvenpaa, A.L., Telsey, A.M., & Jones, B.L. (1988). Neurodevelopmental and respiratory outcome in early childhood after human surfactant treatment. *American Journal of Diseases of Children, 142*, 927–930.

Ventura, S.J., Taffel, S.M., & Mosher, W.D. (1988). Estimates of pregnancies and pregnancy rates for the United States, 1976–85. *American Journal of Public Health, 78*, 504–511.

Verloove-Van Loreck, S.P., Verwey, R.A., Ebeling, M.C.A., Brand, R., & Ruys, J.H. (1988). Mortality in very preterm and very low birth weight infants according to place of birth and level of care: Results of a national collaborative survey of preterm and very low birth weight infants in the Netherlands. *Pediatrics, 81*, 404–411.

Walker, D-J.B., Vohr, B.R., & Oh, W. (1985). Economic analysis of regionalized neonatal care for very low-birth-weight infants in the state of Rhode Island. *Pediatrics, 76*, 69–74.

Ware, J., Taeusch, H.W., Soll, R.F., & McCormick, M.C. (1990). Health and developmental outcomes of a randomized trial of bovine surfactant treatment of respiratory distress syndrome: Follow-up at 2 years. *Pediatrics, 85*, 1103–1107.

Wegman, M.E. (1976). Annual summary of vital statistics—1975. *Pediatrics, 58*, 793–799.

Wegman, M.E. (1988). Annual summary of vital statistics—1987. *Pediatrics, 82*, 817–827.

Weisman, C.S., Teitelbaum, M.A., & Morlock, L.L. (1988). Malpractice claims experience associated with fertility-control services among young obstetricians-gynecologists. *Medical Care, 26*, 298–306.

Wellcome drug set for limited use in US. (1989, July 28). *Wall Street Journal/Europe*, p. 5.

Wilcox, A.J., & Russell, I.T. (1983). Birthweight and perinatal mortality. II. On weight-specific mortality. *International Journal of Epidemiology, 12*, 319–325.

Williams, R.L., & Chen, P.M. (1982). Identifying the sources of the recent decline in perinatal mortality in California. *New England Journal of Medicine, 306*, 207–214.

Williams, R.L., & Hawes, W.E. (1979). Caesarean section, fetal monitoring and perinatal mortality in California. *American Journal of Public Health, 69*, 864–870.

Zelen, M. (1979). A new design for randomized clinical trials. *New England Journal of Medicine, 300*, 1242–1245.

4

The Concept of Risk: A Reevaluation*

Frances Degen Horowitz
The Graduate School and University Center
The City University of New York

Risk, at-risk, high risk, vulnerable, resilient, developmentally delayed, stress, coping, adaptive, biological risk, social risk, premature birth, low birthweight, small for dates, small for gestational age, disadvantaged, low SES. These are terms that describe the focus of interest of large numbers of psychologists, pediatricians, psychiatrists, social workers, and therapists of all kinds. These are the rubrics under which we do research and the populations for which numerous services and interventions are devised—not the least of which are a variety of early stimulation programs designed to prevent subsequent developmental problems.

Are the terms synonymous, overlapping, mutually exclusive? Are these terms that foreshadow developmental prognosis? Do these terms, or some subset of them, reflect consistency with respect to an underlying theoretical orientation? The answer is yes and no to all of the above. Sometimes the terms are synonymous, sometimes overlapping, and sometimes mutually exclusive. They do and do not foreshadow developmental prognosis. Subsets are used consistently sometimes, other times not. Such is the condition of risk research; such is the result of a relatively productive period of research fueled by concerns for risk conditions and subsequent developmental outcome.

There is now a substantial body of data and a number of reviews and evaluations of the literature on risk (e.g., Kopp, 1983, 1987; Rutter, 1987; Kazdin, 1989; Newcomb & Bentler, 1989). This permits us to take stock, to assess, and to attempt a theoretically consistent approach to research on risk and developmental outcome.

CURRENT PERSPECTIVES ON RISK

Sameroff and Chandler published their seminal article delineating the "continuum of reproductive casualty" in 1975. After reviewing the literature, they

* An earlier version of this chapter was originally presented as an invited address at the 1989 meetings of the Society for Research in Child Development in Kansas City, Missouri. Herbert Gingold provided invaluable aid in preparing for that paper by helping to review some of the recent relevant literature on risk. I am indebted to the editors of this volume for their suggestions and criticisms that influenced the revision of the original SRCD paper.

concluded that there is an interaction of biological/medical conditions and the environment, such that the environment serves to mediate the effects of adverse prenatal and perinatal conditions on subsequent developmental outcome. Lubchenco published her seminal volume on *The High Risk Infant* in 1976, giving form to the basic classification of newborn infants into risk groups. These two publications, however, were not de novo attempts to address infants at risk. Rather, they can be seen as important punctuation marks in a corpus of work pertaining to the at-risk or high-risk infant, work that goes back more than 100 years (see Kopp, 1983, 1990; Kopp & Krakow, 1983; Kopp & Kaler, 1989).

Part of what has driven the different epochs of interest in the high-risk infant has been changing technologies and medical practices, pushing back the point of viability for the prematurely born infant, and increasing survival rates for infants that would not have, in the past, survived. We now have categories for the very low-birthweight infant (VLBW) born at 1,500 grams or below and the low-birthweight infant (LBW) born at 2,500 grams or below down to 1,500 grams. With the survival of smaller and smaller babies there has been increased concern for the implications for morbidity. While mortality rates are easily documented, this is not the case for morbidity, since the definition and identification of morbidity ranges from clear-cut cases of profound and severe retardation or cerebral palsy or handicap to more subtle sequelae in the areas of motor control, learning, minimal brain dysfunction, and developmental delay.

Morbidity rates, however, are only one of several problems in sorting out this area of risk and high risk. Risk, as many in the field have noted, is, in its essence, a probabilistic concept. For example, Kopp and Kaler characterized developmental risk as a "statistical probability that ongoing development will be compromised" (Kopp & Kaler, 1989, p. 224). Much of risk research can be seen as attempts to estimate that probability for different groups of infants born under and into different circumstances using a variety of markers or indices that will enable better prediction of subsequent developmental compromise.

Single events, unless resulting in massive and irreversible organic damage and dysfunction, are rarely predictive of developmental outcome. In recognition of this a variety of cumulative risk score schemes have been attempted. When they have included only the number and severity of prenatal, perinatal, and postnatal medical factors, they have not been particularly successful. Adding socioeconomic variables and performance on early infant tests has increased their utility (Holmes, Reich, & Pasternak, 1984), but not all that much. In fact, in most studies with significant results the predictive power typically involves significant correlations in the range of .30 to .50. Correlations such as these have been called "nature's favorite correlation coefficient" (Clarke & Clarke, 1988), indicating some consistency or continuity over time but leaving more than half the variance unaccounted for and therefore considerable inconsistency. In other words, more changes than stays the same.

Few would maintain any longer that it is possible to make a useful linear prediction on developmental outcome using early measures. We learned a number of years ago that infant IQ was not predictive of later IQ. The recent developments in infant visual preference are considered by some to offer a new infant intelligence test predictive of later child intelligence. However, the correlation coefficients for this assessment are, on the average, generally no higher than those obtained between parental education and child IQ (McCall, 1990), though it appears that parental education and visual preference measures may be accounting for different parts of the variance. Nevertheless, the techniques for evaluating infant visual information-processing behavior have the potential for telling us about process in the development of intelligence and cognition and the role of individual differences in these systems. These techniques can be used as very important windows into the information-processing behavior thought to be critical in early intellectual and cognitive development.

Eschewing linear models, the most widely adopted substitute candidate for a model system is the transactional model. Sameroff and Chandler sounded this as a clarion call in their 1975 article, and many others have followed suit. It is now widely used to guide the choice of measures in research on infants born at risk and often provides the basis of graphic representations. One such, used by Holmes et al. (1984), is shown in Figure 1. The Kansas Infant Development Project (KID) on the development of normal and preterm infants, healthy and sick, has employed a slightly more complex form, as shown in Figure 2.

The transactional model, however diagrammed, involves the set of assumptions originally described by Sameroff and Chandler (1975), namely, that the organism affects the environment and the environment affects the organism, and that, out of these mutual influences, development proceeds. Variations on the theme represent more or less refinements of this basic premise. For example, observations that the child's effect on the environment may be stronger at the extremes of the distribution of child intellect or temperament (Clarke & Clarke, 1988)—a not unreasonable proposal.

Models and theories of development are only as useful as the testable hypotheses they permit us to derive. Has the transactional model been a source of such hypotheses? There has probably been more talk and discussion of the efficacy of such a model for molding our thinking about development than direct tests of hypotheses derived from the model. On the other hand, the ideas inherent in a transactional model have had a significant impact on shaping developmental and risk research to encompass interacting sets of variables (e.g., Garmezy, Masten, & Tellegen, 1984; Belsky, 1984). The environmental contributions of variables associated with family and extrafamily support systems have become important in the discussion of risk, especially with respect to programs of intervention (e.g., Schorr, 1988). The popularity of multiple regression techniques to evaluate large data sets involving numerous variables can be seen as a direct outgrowth of the influence of the transactional model, as well as the result of the development and availability of the appropriate statistical tools—not to mention, in addition, the technological advances in computational resources and online data entry capabilities.

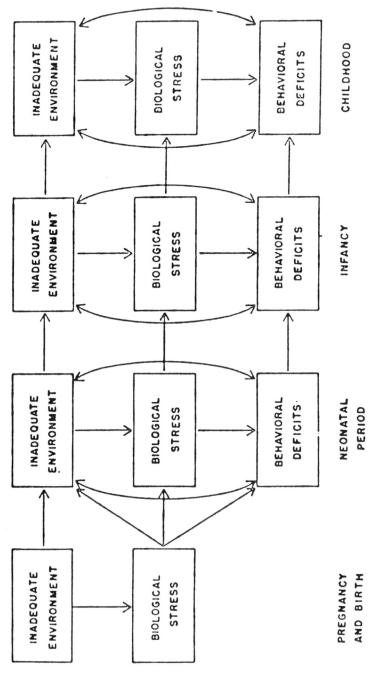

Figure 1. A transactional model of development. (From Holmes, Reich, & Pasternak, 1984, p. 195. Reprinted with permission.)

64

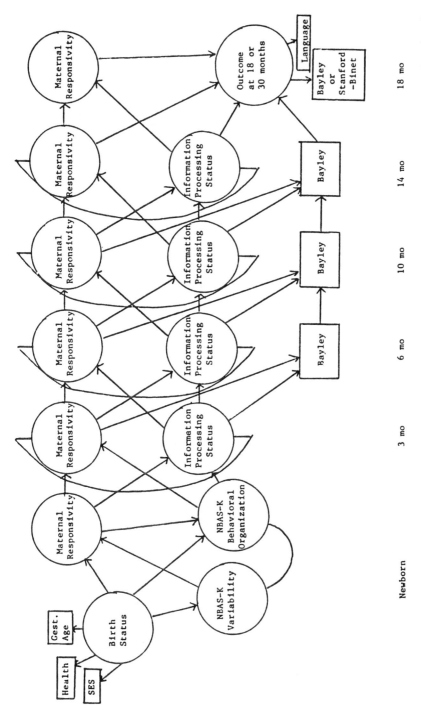

Figure 2. A diagrammatic representation of the process model to be tested in the proposed research. (From Kid Project, University of Kansas.)

65

There has also been an increased focus upon organism/environment inter-actions—especially mother–infant, mother–child, and adult–child interactions (e.g., Bornstein & Tamis-LeMonda, 1990; Emde, Kligman, Reich, & Wade, 1978; Field, 1987; Parrinello & Ruff, 1988; Rogoff, 1991; Wahler & Dumas, 1989). Most of the efforts, however, fall far short of fully encompassing a transactional approach—partly because getting a handle on the totality of a transactional system is expensive. In the meantime, considerable research has also been done looking at single risk variables and studying the effect of a given variable on specific behavior (e.g., Bettes, 1988). This has been quite useful even if not in a transactional framework. There are many complex and fruitful hypotheses that can be formulated using a transactional model, but significant progress beyond the kind of tests we can now make will require us to know more about, and measure better, the constituent components of a transactional system.

Nevertheless, when it comes to understanding developmental outcome in at-risk children, everyone suspects that much of the variance is tied up in the transactional dynamics that result in some children overcoming the risk factors and showing good or excellent development while others succumb to lower levels of developmental achievements. It is useful, at this point in the history of research on children born at risk, to try to explore the dynamics and elements in the currently unaccounted-for portion of the variance in developmental outcome. Are there some approaches to risk research that would enable us to make significant gains in our current understanding of what determines whether or not infants born at risk for normal development attain normal development? Can the concept of risk be usefully applied to each major nodal point of developmental change? Might we broaden the notion that being *at risk* is a concept that should not only encompass risk for downside development but should also encompass risk for not achieving the significant upside of development? This would enable us to include in our risk population those individuals who have the potential for developmental outcomes regarded as gifted and talented but whose achievement of that potential may be placed at risk by some of the same factors that function in those cases we have traditionally associated with the concept of risk. Such children have been referred to as *at promise*. All these questions form the basis for exploring how we might sophisticate our theory or models of development given the advances in our knowledge base.

A THEORETICAL ORIENTATION

In reevaluating the concept of risk and how we employ it in developmentally oriented research, it is clear, as has been noted here, that the most widely used theoretical orientation among risk researchers is the transactional model pro-posed by Sameroff and Chandler (1975). In the years since 1975, the transaction-al model has served as a very useful heuristic in stimulating extensive research on both organismic and environmental variables and their impact on developmental outcome singly and in various combinations. Few formal efforts to modify, refine, or extend this model have been undertaken.

We now have a significant amount of information about many variables that appear to influence organismic functioning, that help better define the environment, and that·determine the interactive/transactive nature of the relationships between organism and environment. We also have a much stronger set of facts that describe normal and nonnormal behavioral development across the childhood years, along with recent renewed studies of development during adolescence. In addition, there has been a growth in research in the areas of developmental psychopathology and deviance and an increased interest in life-span perspectives. It may well be useful to take the heuristic of the transactional model and see if further qualifications can be identified that would refine, extend, and shape the model such that the result would be a developmental model that could serve as a framework for reevaluating the concept of risk, for predicting developmental outcome, and for guiding intervention efforts.

The Human Behavioral Repertoire

Advances in our knowledge of the development of the human behavioral repertoire have been particularly dramatic since the 1960s. The normal human newborn, once thought to be a "tabula rasa," is now known to respond discriminatively in all sensory modalities. Much has been made of the significance of this, not only for how it has changed how we think about the human newborn but for the possible predictive value of assessments of the newborn infant's behavior (Self & Horowitz, 1979; Francis, Self, & Horowitz, 1987). While such assessments are unlikely to provide long-term predictions of developmental outcome by themselves, some aspects of neonatal functioning appear to be particularly informative. Among these, the newborn's ability to regulate state and state transitions appears to be particularly promising (Colombo & Horowitz, 1987; Moss, Colombo, Mitchell, & Horowitz, 1988; Thoman, Denenberg, Sievel, Zeidner, & Becker, 1981).

Efforts to chart the normal course of behavioral development of children are among the longest standing traditions in the field of child development. Motor development was well mapped by Gesell and his colleagues in the 1920s and 1930s (Gesell, 1928, 1933). The research stimulated by Piaget's description of cognitive development has resulted in validation of some of the general sequences he proposed and some of the very interesting behaviors he first described (Gelman & Baillargeon, 1983; Harris, 1983). Recent data and analyses, however, have broadened considerably the discussion of the social and contextual influences on cognitive behavior and cognitive development (Belmont, 1989; Feldman, 1980; Rogoff, 1990).

In other domains of development—social and emotional development and language development—early work in the 1920s and 1930s provided some basic normative information. In the last 20 years in language development and more recently in social and emotional development, major strides have occurred, not only in describing normative sequences, but in identifying the environmental contributions to behavior and development in these domains. (Golinkoff & Hirsh-Pasek, 1990; Hartup, 1989; Lewis, 1987, 1990; Rice, 1989; Tronick, 1989).

What now appears to be the case is that, for the normal human organism, there is a basic template of normal behavioral developmental characteristics and, to some extent, broad developmental progression across the childhood years. However, all of these basic "blueprints" appear to be strongly qualified by both organismic and environmental variables. For this reason, it is reasonable to suggest that a developmental model or a developmental theory ought to distinguish between the development of behaviors that are the universal behaviors in the repertoire and the development of behaviors that are not part of the universal behavioral repertoire (Horowitz, 1987). This distinction between universal and nonuniversal behaviors may be particularly relevant to the consideration of the concept of risk as it is applied to development and developmental outcome.

An attempt to describe the essential differences between the Universal and non-Universal aspects of the human behavioral repertoire in different domains is shown in Table 1.

The identification of those behaviors that are Universal and those that are non-Universal is not difficult. For example, many of the behaviors in the motor domain, such as walking, running, skipping, jumping, are required in the course of development for all normal organisms in all varieties of normal environments. They, therefore, can be designated as among the Universal behaviors in the motor domain. Many non-Universal behaviors can be acquired on the base of the Universal behaviors. Riding a bicycle, dancing, and pole vaulting are examples of behaviors that are highly dependent upon specific learning opportunities that some but not all environments may provide.

Similar examples can be found in each of the behavioral domains shown in Table 1, though the degree to which the Universals have been identified in each of the domains differs. In the cognitive domain any of the behaviors that are described by Piaget appear to be Universal. For example, the acquisition of the understanding that objects continue to exist even when not perceptually present begins to develop in infancy in all children in all environments. The basic cognitive understandings necessary for the acquisition of reading are Universal, though reading itself is not a Universal behavior and its acquisition requires specific instruction.

In the social domain, smiling is a Universal behavior, and the ability to form emotional bonds also appears to be Universal. On the other hand, the individuals with whom such bonds are formed, and even the conditions under which children and adults smile, are highly dependent upon specific environmental factors. In the language domain some of the generic aspects of language and communication appear to be Universal such as negation, singular and plural signifiers, and the

Table 1. Universal and Non-Universal Behaviors and Developmental Risk

Behavioral System	Motor	Cognition/Language	Social/Emotional	Determinants of Risk
UNIVERSAL				
Probability of acquisition high, conditions for learning minimal; basic disturbance organic in origin; rate more likely affected than form	Basic forms highly determined Evolutionarily the oldest system Strong genetic basis	Basic forms range from highly to Moderate genetic components with exceptions Cultural transmission important for relative sculpting of this system	Fewer basic forms and more moderately determined Moderate genetic components with exceptions Cultural transmission critical Evolutionary the youngest system(?)	Initially determined by compromise in biological/ organismic factors
NON-UNIVERSAL				
Probability of acquisition strongly determined by conditions for learning Interference with acquisition can be organic in origin, environmental in origin, or both	Highly determined by environment— including cultural transmission Universal repertoire unconditional basis for acquisition of non-Universal repertoire	Strong reliance on environmental— cultural transmission Multiple paths to same end points Many optional end points Organismic contributions moderate(?)	Critical reliance on environmental social factors Cultural transmission critical Organismic contributions strong(?)	Initially determined by organism interacting with environmental/ social factors unless critical element of the Universal repertoire is biologically compromised

existence of words as a unit of linguistic acquisition. The specific language acquired and the grammar of that language are, on the other hand, a function of the particular language environment in which a child is developing.

There are some aspects of the dichotomization of the Universal and non-Universal behaviors in the different domains (as shown in Table 1) that are speculative. Nevertheless, these distinctions may be particularly useful in helping to frame a stronger model of development than we have had heretofore. They can be used to some important advantage to provide a framework for studying development in populations of children thought to be at risk and for guiding our interventions with such children.

In fact, it is in the risk literature that we find the strongest rationale for suggesting that there is utility in thinking about the human behavioral repertoire in terms of its Universal and non-Universal components. In discussing the research on the development of high-risk infants, Kopp (1987, p. 882) noted that: "With the exception of the most severe risks, fundamental forms and sequences of early infancy behavior are not modified by adverse influences," although, she says, the rate of development may be affected. The notion of "fundamental forms" is analogous to the suggestion that some aspects of the human behavioral repertoire are "universal." The behaviors identified as Universals have a very high probability of acquisition in all normal human organisms and in many with some abnormalities and problems. While these behaviors may be "learned," the conditions that account for the learning are so ubiquitous and in overabundance everywhere in the environment—unless the environment is severely abnormal—that the acquisition of these "basic forms" is inevitable.

There are, however, a number of qualifications that must be made to this kind of general statement about Universal behaviors, and some are included in Table 1. The extent of the Universal elements in the behavioral repertoire depends upon whether one is focusing upon the motor system, cognition and language, or the social/emotional/personality system. The degree to which there are basic universal forms in each of these systems differs, as does the controlling strength of genetic determinants and the role of cultural transmission. As Feldman (1980) has suggested, some currently universal behaviors such as the concept of number may well be in the human repertoire as a function of universal cultural transmission. Further, cultural transmission may well help to "sculpt" the relative strength of behaviors in the universal repertoire—some cultures emphasizing some of the basic forms over others.

It is also likely that the older the behavioral system, in evolutionary terms, the more rigid the basic forms of the system. Thus, the motor system is depicted as the oldest behavioral system of the species, with the social/emotional system as the youngest, though one might argue about some elements of the emotional system as perhaps being among the older parts of the species in evolutionary terms.

The organization of the human behavioral repertoire in terms of the three systems shown—motor, cognition and language, and the constellation of social/ emotional/personality—is somewhat arbitrary, since not all aspects of each of these systems are discrete. Recent evidence from animal research suggests that there are separate sensory pathways involved in the affective and cognitive systems, but that these pathways can also be interactive. From a developmental point of view, however, there is some indication that, during the earliest periods of postnatal development, differential rates of neural maturation may prevent interaction of the cognitive and affective systems. One possible interesting result is that earliest emotional/affective experiences may not be available for cognitive processing (LeDoux, 1989; LeDoux, Romanski, & Xagoraris, 1989).

If subsequent research validates this information and if there is reason to believe that it holds for the human organism, the traditional Freudian view of the primacy of early emotional experiences will receive important support. Further, in populations of high-risk infants, where the normal differences in maturational rates may be amplified for longer periods of time, it is possible that the period when emotional/affective experiences are isolated from cognitive accessibility will be lengthened with subsequent developmental consequences for cognitive control of emotional responses. The Universals of the early emotional response repertoire remain to be determined. However, the basic responses of rage and crying, of fear, anger, and pleasure, would appear to be likely candidates, though they obviously get "sculpted" by the environment. An interesting question is whether genetic and/or biological insult factors make some of the Universal aspects of the emotional system more or less resistant to environmental influence. In populations of risk children the cognitive control of the emotional components of responses may be particularly affected.

The last column on Table 1 lists the determinants of risk. The Universal behavioral repertoire is shown as subject to developmental risk due to organic compromise. This can be the result of genetic factors and also a result of internal or external agents that affect biological function. Such effects are most likely seen in slowing the rate of development of the basic forms of the Universal behaviors rather than altering the basic forms themselves, though there are genetic, biochemical, and structural conditions that can affect the basic forms. Further, different critical factors, including genes, can turn on at different points in time for different domains. There do not appear to be many constant sources of genetic influence (Thompson, 1990) across time and across domains.

The Universal behavioral repertoire in each system provides the basis upon which the non-Universal repertoire can be acquired. The non-Universal behaviors are heavily dependent upon environmental facilitation and conditions that permit learning to occur. These learning conditions are less ubiquitous and more under the control of the particular social and physical constellations of different environments. They are relatively more reliant upon mechanisms of cultural transmission and more easily influenced by variations in environment. However, this is different in different domains. For example, as Field (1987) has noted, it may be easier for an individual to compensate for lack of socially provided stimulation in the cognitive domain than in the social/affective domain. Behavioral domains are not independent in their functioning, and this is probably more particularly the case with the non-Universal behaviors where social/cognitive/linguistic/affective interactions are standard. Indeed, the degree of interaction and separation of domains may well be one of the particularly defining characteristics of individual differences—some of which have organismic origins, and some of which are influenced by environmental experience.

The non-Universal behavioral repertoires in each of the systems have few final end points, evolve across the life span, and involve a large variety of forms. The influence of genetic components is weaker in the non-Universal repertoires as compared to the Universal repertoires, though the degree of organismic predispositions, partially influenced by genetic inheritance, may differ across the behavioral systems.

Risk is more culturally defined with respect to the non-Universal behavioral repertoire than is true for the Universal behavioral repertoire. For example, the inability to learn to read and write will never surface as a predicted consequence of risk conditions in a nonliterate society. The initial determinants of risk in affecting the non-Universal behavioral repertoire involve the organism interacting with environmental factors. This assumes the critical forms of the Universal repertoire are not biologically compromised. However, organismically based individual differences are strong contributors to the interaction with the environment.

Some concrete examples will be useful in seeing the kinds of clarifications that are possible if we use the matrix shown in Table 1 for thinking about developmental risk. A child born prematurely without obvious organic compromise, and who traverses the postnatal period without complication, is probably not highly at risk in the developmental aspects of the Universal behavioral repertoire. Depending upon the nature of the socially mediated environment that provides the infant's care, the non-Universal behavioral repertoire may or may not be at risk. If the infant is ''difficult'' in the sense of crying a lot, less responsive to social initiatives, and hard to console, the nature of the environment may become critical. If the caregivers cannot adjust effectively to these characteristics, the result may be an environment that becomes a risk factor because it does not provide the conditions necessary for the acquisition of the non-Universal behavioral repertoire as fully or as well as expected according to the cultural norms of the environment in which that child will have to function.

The notion of *double disadvantage* has been advanced by a number of investigators in the high-risk research area (Rutter, 1987; Bateson & Hinde, 1987; Escalona, 1982). The presence of biological risk *and* social risk factors compounds the situation for developmental outcome. However, I believe we will find that double disadvantaged does not operate evenly across the behavioral repertoire. The optimal threshold of organism/environment conditions, especially with respect to the non-Universal behavioral repertoire, is particular to the behavioral system as well as to the period of development during which these conditions operate. Initially, some high-risk infants may have a generalized abnormally high or abnormally low threshold to stimulation in the cognitive and affective domains (Field, 1987), but often these general characteristics will settle out to affect some domains more than others.

In many instances of biological, and for most instances of social, risk conditions, the Universal aspects of gross motor development in infancy will not be affected except perhaps in rate of development. Most of what develops in the motor system during infancy involves the Universal behavioral repertoire of sitting, standing, walking, and so on. The non-Universal aspects of gross motor behavior are not prevalent during this period and therefore not likely to be affected by conditions that obtain during the earliest years. This is not the case in the areas of cognition and language. There is a strong developmental trajectory involving the basic Universal forms in language and cognition during infancy. But there is also the development of the non-Universal aspects as a function of particular environments and cultures. Some components of cognitive and linguistic behavior are more strongly valued in some cultures and environments than others. These will be responded to and with greater or lesser elaboration on the basic forms. The claim, therefore, that the infancy period is "buffered" and unlikely to be perturbed, especially by social risk factors (Scarr-Salapatek, 1976), may only be relevant to the Universal components of the behavioral repertoire and not the non-Universal ones, many of which have their initiation during infancy. In particular, the sensorimotor behaviors described by Piaget will develop in almost all environments, though environment may affect their rate of development. What will not develop equally in all environments, however, are the qualitative aspects of these behaviors that ultimately serve as a foundation upon which some of the non-Universal repertoire is built. Evolutionarily, the protected, buffered aspect may be largely in the Universal motor and cognitive aspects that develop during the period described by Piaget as the sensorimotor period.

In the social/emotional system the nature of the Universal repertoire may be less extensive than for the other systems, though the initial organizing element of state control may be quite pervasive and may significantly influence early development in cognition and language. The early Universal forms of social and emotional behavior can be compromised by organic factors but this compromise may work its effect largely through state and state modulation. State factors may also affect cognition and language development—especially as they introduce individual difference elements that affect information processing (e.g., see Moss et al., 1988). Thoman's identification of state inconsistency as a risk indicator for later developmental dysfunction lends support to considering early state organization as an important individual difference variable in the developmental process (Thoman et al., 1981). Large portions of the social repertoire are non-Universal. The degree of risk for the social repertoire may be heavily determined by environmental factors interacting with organismic dispositions. In this area state organization may be an early indicator of some of those dispositions. The relevance of the concept of temperament here is clearly obvious.

Individual/Environment Interactions

Further qualifications related to organism/environment interaction must be considered. This is at the heart of the *transactional* model. The organism and environment are depicted as mutually influencing systems whereby the organism modifies the environment and the environment modifies the organism. The transactional model may actually be more particularly useful to thinking about the development of the non-Universal behavioral repertoire than to thinking about the development of the Universal behavioral repertoire except with respect to the rate of development of the Universal behavioral repertoire. An essential feature of the transactional model is the notion of mutual influence of child and environment. An important refinement, in light of our present state of knowledge, requires consideration that organismic and environmental variables range along a continuum. The model shown in Figure 3 can be used for this purpose.

This model was first developed as a heuristic for thinking about individual differences (Horowitz, 1978). Subsequently, it was used to elaborate the nature of the interactions that determine developmental outcome in high-risk infants (Horowitz, 1984). More recently, referred to as a Structural/Behavioral model of development, it has been used as the basis for showing that both organismic and behavioristic theories of development need to be used in accounting for behavioral development and behavioral outcome (Horowitz, 1987).

In this model risk can be a function of either organismic or environmental characteristics or both. It incorporates the notion of degree of physical impairment as well as a continuum of organismic vulnerability or resilience. The physical impairment can have a genetic basis and/or an environmental basis as a function of accident, infection, or insult with a resulting biological compromise. Similarly, resilience and vulnerability can also have a genetic basis and/or an experiential basis affecting learning that influences coping strategies, information-processing behaviors, and so on.

The environment is ranged on a theoretical continuum of facilitative of development to nonfacilitative, but the mutual influence of environment and organism may be attenuated at various interactive combinations. The facilitative environment can enhance the rate of development of Universal behaviors in a child who is organismically compromised. For example, early stimulation programs for Down syndrome infants have been demonstrated as affecting developmental rate in the areas of motor, cognitive, and language development. It is the non-Universal behavioral repertoire that is most dependent upon the degree to

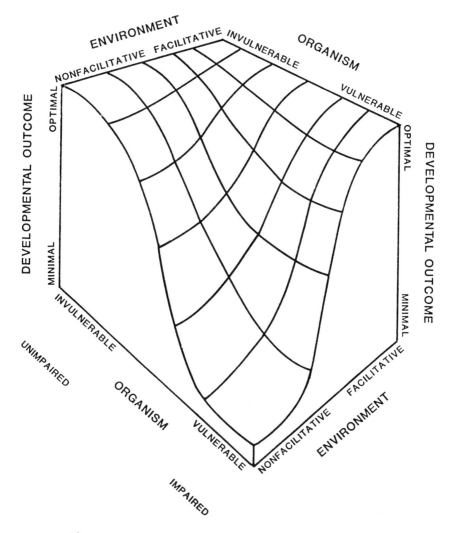

Figure 3.   (From Horowitz, 1987. Reprinted by permission.)

which the environment is facilitative. However, in the situation where organic impairment is present, given the limits of our present technologies for intervention, organic factors can impose a ceiling on the possibilities of acquisition of the non-Universal behavioral repertoire.

The combination and permutations possible using the Structural/Behavioral model are extensive. The individual differences that the organism brings to the interaction with the environment may modify or not modify the environment, and vice versa. Environmental modification will be less critical for the development of the Universal behavioral repertoire. The surface of the model is a graphic representation of developmental risk, assuming the middle portion of the sloping surface represents normal development, the upper far quadrant excellent development, and the lower near quadrant very poor development.

In risk populations we normally focus upon movement from the normal range downward to the model's lower quadrant of the developmental outcome surface. However, the notion of risk is equally applicable to lack of movement in the opposite direction wherein conditions could obtain to produce a very high level of developmental outcome but do not. Admittedly, we know less about this kind of "loss of potential" than when developmental progress is below normal. Still, the loss of human resources is no less serious. From society's point of view the loss of gifted development may be a more critical loss than the loss of potential in retardation. Giftedness is, almost by definition, a realization of advanced or different functioning in the non-Universal behavioral repertoire. This advanced or different function is more likely to be put at risk by environmental and social factors, though biological elements could contribute to compromising gifted levels of functioning or make more difficult the attainment of gifted functioning. An example would be the case of learning disabled gifted children.

The Structural/Behavioral model represents an attempt to refine the transactional model so as to delineate the sources of influence on developmental outcome and to permit hypotheses about mutually influencing variables on both the organismic and the environmental dimensions. The Structural/Behavioral model is a generic model with applicability to normal as well as high-risk populations. The identification of an infant as at risk can occur because of the nature of the environment into which the child has been born (a nonfacilitative environment) or because of particular organismically based variables that reflect physical impairment and/or relative vulnerability to the environmental dimension or because of both organismic and environmental factors.

Using the model, it becomes possible to shape a more specific research agenda for studying the effect of different variables and their interaction on developmental outcome than is true with the more undifferentiated transactional model. Further, the Structural/Behavioral model explicitly recognizes that the influence of variables may be quite different on the development of Universal behaviors than on the development of non-Universal behaviors. For example, organically insulted infants being raised in developmental facilitative environments can be expected to show slower development of the Universal behaviors than is true of normal infants or a blunting of the development of those behaviors, though the nature of the organic problem will determine which of the Universal behaviors might be particularly impacted. The development of behaviors in the non-Universal repertoire will require a relatively more facilitative environment. However, depending upon the nature of the organic insult, some of the non-Universal behaviors that might be shaped in that child's environment may not be developmentally possible even in the most developmentally facilitative environment.

Infants who appear to have no organic involvement will begin life with individual differences in the level of environmental stimulation most suited to fostering their development. Such infants will exhibit few problems in the development of the Universal behavioral repertoire unless they are being raised in an environment that is particularly developmentally nonfacilitative. In such an instance the rate will be slowed, but the basic behavioral repertoire will eventually develop. The development of most of the non-Universal behaviors expected in the environment in which the child is being raised will occur depending upon how effective the environment is in facilitating the acquisition of those behaviors and depending upon the degree to which the individual differences make the child more or less dependent upon the facilitative nature of the environment.

The Structural/Behavioral model can be applied specifically to the development of the low-birthweight (LBW) infant. For example, in the case of LBW infants who are basically without organic complications and considered healthy, we would expect to see the rate of the development of the Universal behaviors and the repertoire of non-Universal behaviors acquired to be entirely a function of the interaction of infant and environment, and the nature of the infant/environment interaction not to be essentially different than one would find for infants not low in birthweight.

The infant/environment interaction for the LBW or normal infant may be described as follows. Infant A demonstrates a high level of vocalization; infant B has a relatively low level. Both infants will show the basic forms of language acquisition of the language community in which they are being reared. But infant A's rate of language acquisition may be relatively rapid whether or not, in the first year, the infant's caregivers are highly responsive to the vocalizations. For infant B, however, the Structural/Behavioral model would predict that with caregivers highly responsive to the infant's vocalizations there would be a normal and perhaps advanced rate of early language acquisition. Under conditions where the caregivers exhibited little responsiveness, early language acquisition would be predicted to be slow to delayed.

While the generic aspects of the language being acquired would not vary greatly for the two infants, the quality and extensivity of the language being acquired would be influenced strongly by the caregivers. The size of vocabulary, for example, for both infants will be a function of the opportunities provided by the environment, though the rate of acquisition will be a joint function of infant individual differences and environmental responsiveness.

If there are organic complications such as impaired hearing, then, depending upon the nature of the hearing impairment, acquisition of the basic universal aspects of language may be slowed considerably, and some may be distorted with the importance of environmental facilitation amplified in its interaction with individual differences in the infant. Infant C may be very responsive and compensate for the hearing impairment by more focused attentiveness and greater involvement of the visual system in the early acquisition of language. Infant D may be relatively unresponsive, have poorly focused attention patterns, and resort less to the compensatory use of the visual modality. Infant C, in an environment that does not pick up on or reinforce the compensatory behaviors, may show poorer early language acquisition than Infant D, whose caregivers may be particularly skilled in helping the infant to focus attention and to learn to use compensatory avenues for accessing linguistically relevant information.

For LBW infants with and without organic impairments, state organization may be a particularly critical individual difference with respect to environmental interaction. Some LBW infants can exhibit highly organized state characteristics and appear to negotiate state transitions smoothly. Others can show poor state organization and be particularly vulnerable to disorganization at state transition points. It was a recognition of just this kind of complexity in the interaction between individual differences in state organization, physiological parameters, and environmental stimulation that led to a set of guidelines for early stimulation of the preterm infant (Gunzenhauser, 1987). In these guidelines reference is made to matching environmental stimulation with respect to "amount, type, timing, patterning and quality" (Gunzenhauser, 1987, p. 181), as well as modality to individually assessed differences in responsivity in the infant and with respect to particular organic conditions. A recent report (Duffy, Als, & McAnulty, 1990) implicated inappropriate early sensorimotor stimulation for preterm infants in individual negative assessments of early behavioral status.

Use of the Structural/Behavioral model leads to suggesting that the power of early environmental interventions could be amplified by better matching of the intervention with individual infant characteristics. For example, it was reported that massaging preterm infants improved weight gain and some behavioral measures (Scafidi et al., 1990). The massage treatment was standardized across infants. From the point of view of the Structural/Behavioral model, a next step in this research would be to explore whether an individual matching of the duration of the treatment or its patterning (perhaps using differences in state organization as a guide for varying duration and/or patterning) would increase the effectiveness of the massage intervention.

There are many candidates for the infant individual differences that are important in affecting the influence of the environment on behavioral development. Those that currently appear to have the most promise include early state organization, information-processing behaviors, and social/emotional responsiveness. In the Kansas Infant Development (KID) project, the Structural/Behavioral model was used to formulate the basic hypothesis: For infants showing relatively robust early behavioral state organization and information-processing behaviors, the level of maternal responsiveness would be less critical than for those infants where behavioral organization was more fragile and early information-processing behaviors less efficient. Measures of term and preterm infants on these characteristics were made beginning at birth and through 30 months of age.

Preliminary analyses of KID project data are supportive of the general hypothesis. It appears that with infants whose information-processing behaviors are less efficient (as measured in visual information-processing tasks at 3 and 10 months of age) their mothers worked harder in eliciting responses from the infant. This matching of maternal effort and infant information-processing characteristics resulted in better developmental outcome at 14 and 18 months of age as measured by the Bayley Scale. In those cases where the mothers did not amplify their stimulation and responsiveness with their less efficient infants, developmental outcome was poorer. Infants whose behaviors were initially strong were not affected by whether or not their mothers were particularly responsive. Further validation of the model in the KID project awaits completion of data collection when these infants all reach 30 months of age, additional data analysis, and specific analyses in the term and preterm sample.

It is interesting to note that in the KID project data so far analyzed the standard socioeconomic status (SES) variable only works in a LISRL model analysis when it is taken through the mother's behavior. That is what would be expected from the Structural/Behavioral model because SES is a summary variable and not a functional variable. That is, SES by itself does not specify the behaviors that affect the functioning of the interaction of organism and environment. The relation of SES to behavior will vary across cultures. In another culture or in another time the role of the function variables associated with socioeconomic status could operate quite differently. Similarly, cultural variables and the processes of cultural transmission across generations can be expected to be particular to specific cultures (e.g., Frankel & Roer-Bornstein, 1982). Thus, we should expect that in some cultures the power of the variables typically associated with socioeconomic status will be much stronger than in other cultures and the definition of what constitutes and does not constitute a developmentally facilitative environment will be culture specific. How the variables of birth status function in interaction with the environment will be qualified by the nature of the cultural milieu in which the functional environment is operating. (See, particularly, discussion of culture in Horowitz, 1987.)

THE DEVELOPMENTAL FOCUS OF THE RISK LITERATURES

One might ask whether or not it is possible to consider the matter of the developmental outcome of LBW infants in a larger context of the issues related to risk factors and developmental outcome. This question raises a number of other relevant topics. First, developmentalists interested in infant behavior and development are being asked, increasingly, to consider the issues that concern them—such as birth status and environmental interactions—in a larger, life-span perspective. What are the long-term developmental outcome implications of LBW or slowed development during the period of infancy? How do the qualitative differences in behavioral acquisition in LBW and normal infants affect or not affect subsequent development either of specific behaviors or of the quality of those behaviors. This, of course, is the basic focus of the issues that surround the controversy over continuity and discontinuity in development.

Second, are there generic issues related to risk and development that cross different kinds of studies of developmental outcome and risk. There are at least five bodies of risk literatures relevant to this discussion. Table 2 identifies them: the high-risk infant literature; the conduct disorder literature; the literature on the effects of behavioral teratogens; the research on developmental psychopathology; and, finally, the sensitive periods literature.

The high-risk infant literature uses the terms *risk*, *high-risk*, and *at risk*. More recently the distinction between infants at biological risk and infants at social risk has been emphasized. LBW infants can be at risk biologically, or socially, or both (double disadvantage). The outcome indices have been heavily dominated by cognitive and intellectual measures (e.g., Bradley et al., 1989; Escalona, 1982; Kopp, 1983, 1990; Kopp & Kaler, 1989; Kopp & Krakow, 1983; Horowitz, 1984; Hoy, Bill, & Sykes, 1988; Korner, 1987; Streissguth, Barr, Sampon, Darby, & Martin, 1989). In this literature there has been a strong concentration of research on infants born prematurely as well as infants born following a variety of risk conditions associated with the prenatal period (e.g., Greenberg & Crnic, 1988; Rose, Feldman, & Wallace, 1988). There has also been a particular interest in infants with known handicapping conditions and in

Table 2.

Risk Literatures	Terms	Ages
1. High-Risk Infant	At risk Biological risk Social risk	Prenatal Neonate Infants
2. Conduct Disorder	Deviant Delinquent Aggressive	Middle childhood Adolescent
3. Behavioral Tetratogenesis	Specific risk elements: lead methylmercury alcohol, etc.	Animal analogs Infants Preschool Middle childhood
4. Developmental Psychopathology	Emotionally disturbed Specific syndromes Vulnerable/resilient Protective factors	Middle childhood Adolescent
5. Sensitive Periods	Critical, optimal sensitive epochs for environmental events	Animal analogs Infants Adolescents

the efficacy of intervention programs for these children (Ramey & Trohanis, 1982).

The second literature relates to what has been variously called *delinquency, social-conduct disorder*, and *social deviance*. In this literature the focus tends to be upon the period of middle childhood and adolescence dealing largely with behavioral disorders and the conditions that dispose toward them (e.g., Patterson, DeBaryshe, & Ramsey, 1989). More recently the social deviance risk literature has included such topics as substance abuse (Newcomb & Bentler, 1989) and teenage pregnancy (Furstenberg, Brooks-Gunn, & Chase-Linsdale, 1989). The deviance, social-conduct disorder research areas employ the terms *vulnerability* and *invulnerability*, invoke notions of protective agents and buffers, and deal largely with social environmental stressors as important variables interacting with constitutional factors.

The third literature is somewhat more circumscribed to an area referred to as *behavioral teratogenesis* (Vorhees & Mollnow, 1987; Streissguth et al., 1989), where the focus is on infancy and the effect of exposure to environmental agents such as lead, methylmercury, and alcohol prenatally or in the early postnatal years. The risk referents here are largely to the environment though organismic and developmental susceptibility introduce concepts of relative vulnerability. For obvious reasons, the experimental literature is based almost entirely on animal work, though there are some important exceptions (e.g., Streissguth et al., 1989).

The fourth literature relates to developmental psychopathology, focusing largely on the emotional/social domain. This literature overlaps the social-conduct disorder literature but the emphasis is more upon psychological dysfunction that involves labels such as *emotionally disturbed* in a range of deviance requiring individual clinical intervention. The age range of interest is typically middle childhood and adolescence. The terms *vulnerable, at risk, stress*, and *resilience*, along with notions of protective factors and competence, reflect acknowledgment of the role of constitutional variables interacting with environmental factors (Kazdin, 1989; Richters & Weintraub, 1990; Garmezy et al., 1984).

Finally, a fifth literature, not typically referenced in the risk literature, is that which deals with sensitive periods (Almli & Finger, 1987; Bateson & Hinde, 1987; Bornstein, 1989). Much of the literature is based on nonhuman animals with the analogs to human development variously described. The terms *critical period, optimal period, sensitive period* are used in conjunction with environmental stimulation matched to organismic receptivity at a particular time during development—most often early development. However, sensitive periods for animals can occur at multiple points across the life span. Thus, there may be a continual renewal of points during development when the absence of particular experiences or particular facilitating environments puts the organism at risk.

These literatures are as obviously diverse as they are conceptually overlapping. Nevertheless, they share in common a focus on variables that has the power to adversely affect development progress, behavioral functioning, and developmental outcome.

A DEVELOPMENTAL FRAMEWORK FOR THE CONCEPT OF RISK

The current evidence on the developmental prognosis of the LBW infant points strongly in the direction of needing to involve a complex of variables whose form of functional interaction is only imperfectly understood. The Structural/Behavioral model offers a theoretical heuristic for framing developmentally oriented research questions that attempt to focus upon greater specificity in the nature of interaction and transaction of organismic and environmental variables and the continua on which they range. The LBW infant develops in an environmental context that is complex and changing across time. Similarly, the LBW infant contributes a variety of characteristics that are associated with LBW but that also include individual differences associated with a particular infant. As such, the LBW infant is a particular instance of a more generic situation of an organism at risk.

Recognizing a general concept of risk and using the general focus of the Structural/Behavioral model permits one to entertain the possibility that there may be a useful set of principles set in a developmental framework for helping to frame the research agenda. Table 3 presents such a list of principles. Principles 2 and 3 have already been discussed, and aspects of Principle 4 have also been addressed. Principle 1 is critical for a developmental perspective. As noted above, the different risk literatures tend to concentrate either on the infant or on middle childhood and adolescence. Until recently the infant literature has tended to be concerned more with cognitive and intellectual development, the middle childhood and adolescent literature with social/emotional development (see Buka et al., this volume).

Table 3. A Developmental Framework for the Concept of Risk

Principles
Principle 1: Risk conditions should be specific in terms of developmental periods.
Principle 2: Risk conditions should be specified with reference to behavioral systems.
Principle 3: Risk conditions should be specified with reference to the Universal and non-Universal behavioral repertoires.
Principle 4: Risk variables should be specified as residing in the organism or in the environment or both with different degrees of mutual influence recognized as a possibility for different behavioral repertoires, different behavioral systems, and in different development periods.

The emphasis upon infancy stems in part from the influence of Hebb's (1949) assertions about the role of early experience on brain development, and from the notions of greater plasticity early in life. Other orientations, however, have been suggested (Clarke & Clarke, 1976). The focus upon middle childhood and adolescence is, in part, driven by the incidence of developmental problems and aberrant behavior during these years.

On the other side of the early experience issue is the argument made by several that the period of infancy is so buffered and overdetermined that environmental variations are of little basic import (Kagan, 1984; Scarr-Salapatek, 1976). As has been suggested previously, this analysis is probably correct with respect to the Universal behavioral repertoire but not correct with respect to the non-Universal behavioral repertoire. And, in the case of LBW infants and other infants born at risk, it may not even be totally valid for the Universal behaviors.

An alternative approach may be more reasonable—especially in light of the advances in knowledge in many areas related to development. This alternative approach views each developmental period as having its own matrix of conditions necessary for development with risk factors ever potentially affecting development. Included in that matrix are the "entrance" conditions or legacy conditions that carry over from one period of development to another. Further, the change in the matrix of conditions can become the definition of the nodal points that segment the developmental course—thus a chance for an empirical definition of stage or developmental period. It is assumed, in this approach, that these nodal points do not occur at the same time across behavioral systems nor even for various subsystems within a larger behavioral system. Table 4 summarizes the implications of this perspective for research. One involves the matter of how the results of nondevelopmental studies of risk variables and risk populations are reviewed. Others include the need for multiple assessment of both the organism and the environment, the notion that risk variables exist in the context of a matrix of variables, the importance of individual differences, the way in which continuity and discontinuity in development are viewed, and, finally, the importance of making a distinction between the Universal and non-Universal behavioral repertoire.

With respect to the issue of continuity and discontinuity in development, the point of view adopted here requires that we seek to understand continuity and discontinuity in the context of the processes that produce one or the other rather than in the developmental phenomena themselves. Adopting this kind of process strategy has the potential for going beyond "nature's favorite correlations" toward a significant advance in accounting for the unaccounted variance in developmental outcome.

Such a viewpoint has further implications for putting risk and risk conditions into a consistent framework of developmental dynamics wherein the potential for the individual to be at risk occurs at each nodal point of change in the matrix of conditions affecting development within each behavioral system or subsystem.

Table 4. Implications for Research

1. Nondevelopmental study of risk variables and their relation to behavior is important but *relevance to developmental outcome requires short- and long-term longitudinal research.*

2. Risk research aimed at understanding developmental outcome across developmental epochs requires *assessment of both the organism and the environment at multiple points in time.*

3. Risk factors are embedded in a matrix of variables that affect development. Research needs to be focused on the *risk factors in the context of the matrix* to understand when and how the risk factors operate to affect development.

4. *Individual differences* in the context of environments are key variables in whether or not risk factors have adverse effects. Individual differences need to be studied as variables in developmental process.

5. *Risk factors can exist and operate at any period of development* to affect or change the developmental trajectory of an individual. Continuities and discontinuities in development do not reside in the phenomena of development. They are determined by the processes affecting development. Research on continuities and discontinuities in development needs to focus on the processes that result in continuities and discontinuities.

6. Applied research aimed at prevention and intervention needs to be guided by *distinctions related to the Universal and non-Universal behavioral repertoires* and to *organic and/or environmental sources of risk.*

Such nodal points may be of the nature of *biobehavioral shifts* (Emde, Gaensbauer, & Harmon, 1976) or may reflect developmental periods defined by environmental task demands within a particular society or culture. Individual differences and how they function in process may be different during different periods and in different domains. Development is, therefore, not assumed to be either essentially continuous or discontinuous. Instead of continuity/discontinuity having the status of an assumption, it becomes a set of empirical questions. The answers to the questions will have to come from short- and long-term longitudinal research investigations that are framed in the context of the effect of risk conditions in a dynamic interplay of process and condition matrices. Or, put more simply, the notion of being at risk is related to probabilities that are specific to behavioral domains, to developmental period, and to the matrix of organism/environment conditions that are relevant to the behavioral domain at a particular period in developmental time.

This reevaluation of the concept of risk does not nullify much of the current research on risk. It does suggest, however, that we need to change how we talk about the results of research, how we prognosticate about long-term outcome, and how we frame our questions about developmental outcome so that they are truly informed by a developmental context that tries to approximate the complexity of the processes responsible for development. This reevaluation of the concept of risk has implications for the ways in which we frame questions about specific risk populations, the LBW infant among them. Ultimately, as our knowledge base expands, all of this has further implications for how we design programs of intervention for children determined to be at risk with respect to developmental outcome.

REFERENCES

Almli, C.R., & Finger, S. (1987). Neural insult and critical period concepts. In M. Bornstein (Ed.), *Sensitive periods in development: Interdisciplinary perspectives* (pp. 123–143). Hillsdale, NJ: Erlbaum.

Bateson, P., & Hinde, R.A. (1987). Developmental changes in sensitivity to experience. In M. Bornstein (Ed.), *Sensitive periods in development: Interdisciplinary perspectives* (pp. 19–37). Hillsdale, NJ: Erlbaum.

Belmont, J.M. (1989). Cognitive strategies and strategic learning. *American Psychologist, 44,* 142–148.

Belsky, J. (1984). The determinants of parenting: A process model. *Child Development, 55,* 83–96.

Bettes, B.A. (1988). Maternal depression and motherese: Temporal and intonational features. *Child Development, 59,* 1089–1096.

Bornstein, M.H. (1989). Sensitive periods in development. *Psychological Bulletin, 105,* 179–197.

Bornstein, M.H., & Tamis-LeMonda, C.S. (1990). Activities and interactions of mothers and their firstborn infants in the first six months of life: Covariation, stability, continuity, correspondence and prediction. *Child Development, 61,* 1206–1217.

Bradley, R.H., Caldwell, B.M., Rock, S.L., Ramey, C.T., Barnard, K.E., Gray, C., Hammond, M.A., Mitchell, S., Gottfried, A.W., Seigel, L., & Johnson, D. (1989). Home environment and cognitive development in the first 3 years of life: A collaborative study involving six sites and three ethnic groups in North America. *Developmental Psychology, 25,* 217–235.

Clarke, A.M., & Clarke, A.D.B. (1976). *Early experience: Myth and evidence.* New York: The Free Press.

Clarke, A., & Clarke, A.D.B. (1988). The adult outcome of early behavioral abnormalities. *International Journal of Behavior Development, 11,* 3–20.

Colombo, J., & Horowitz, F.D. (1987). Behavioral state as a lead variable in neonatal research. *Merrill-Palmer Quarterly, 33,* 423–437.

Duffy, F.H., Als, H., & McAnulty, G.B. (1990). Behavioral and electrophysiological evidence for gestational age effects in healthy preterm and fullterm infants studied two weeks after expected due date. *Child Development, 61,* 1271–1286.

Emde, R.N., Gaensbauer, T.J., & Harmon, R.J. (1976). Emotional expression in infancy. A bio-behavioral study. *Psychological Issues, Monographs,* Series 10 (37).

Emde, R.N., Kligman, D., Reich, J., & Wade, T. (1978). Emotional expression in infancy: I. Initial studies of social signaling and an emergent model. In M. Lewis & L. Rosenblum (Eds.), *The development of affect* (pp. 125–148). New York: Plenum.

Escalona, S.K. (1982). Babies at double hazard: Early development of infants at biological and social risk. *Pediatrics, 70,* 670–676.

Feldman, D.H. (1980). *Beyond universals in cognitive development.* Norwood, NJ: Ablex Publishing Corp.

Field, T. (1987). Affective and interactive disturbances in infants. In J.D. Osofsky (Ed.), *Handbook of infant development* (2nd ed., pp. 972–1005). New York: Wiley.

Francis, P.L., Self, P.A., & Horowitz, F.D. (1987). The behavioral assessment of the neonate: An overview. In J.D. Osofsky (Ed.), *Handbook of infant development* (2nd ed., pp. 780–817). New York: Wiley.

Frankel, D.G., & Roer-Bornstein, D. (1982). Traditional and modern contributions to changing infant-rearing ideologies of two ethnic communities. *Monographs of the Society for Research in Child Development, 47* (Serial No. 196).

Furstenberg, F.F., Brooks-Gunn, J., & Chase-Linsdale, L. (1989). Teenaged pregnancy and child-bearing. *American Psychologist, 44,* 313–320.

Garmezy, N., Masten, A.S., & Tellegen, A. (1984). The study of stress and competence in children: A building block for developmental psychopathology. *Child Development, 55,* 97–111.

Gelman, R., & Baillargeon, R. (1983). A review of some Piagetian concepts. In P.H. Mussen (Ed.), *Handbook of child psychology* (4th ed., Vol. 3), J.H. Flavell & E.M. Markman (Eds.), *Cognitive development* (pp. 167–230). New York: Wiley.

Gesell, A.L. (1928). *Infancy and human growth.* New York: Macmillan.

Gesell, A.L. (1933). Maturation and the patterning of behavior. In C. Murchinson (Ed.), *A handbook of child psychology.* Worcester, MA: Clark University Press.

Golinkoff, R.M., & Hirsh-Pasek, K. (1990). Let the mute speak: What infants can tell us about language acquisition. *Merrill-Palmer Quarterly, 36,* 67–92.

Greenberg, N.T., & Crnic, K. (1988). Longitudinal predictors of developmental status and social interaction in premature and full-term infants at age two. *Child Development, 59,* 554–570.

Gunzenhauser, N. (Ed.). (1987). *Infant stimulation: For whom, what kind, when, and how much?* (Johnson & Johnson Pediatric Round Table Series, 13.)

Harris, P.L. (1983). Infant cognition. In P.H. Mussen (Ed.), *Handbook of child psychology* (4th ed., Vol. 2), M.M. Haith & J.J. Campos (Eds.), *Infancy and developmental psychobiology* (pp. 689–782). New York: Wiley.

Hartup, W. (1989). Social relationships and their developmental significance. *American Psychologist, 44,* 120–126.

Hebb, D.O. (1949). *The organization of behavior.* New York: Wiley.

Holmes, D.L., Reich, J.N., & Pasternak, J.F. (1984). *The development of infants born at risk.* Hillsdale, NJ: Erlbaum.

Horowitz, F.D. (1978, September). *Toward a functional analysis of individual differences.* Presidential address to the Division of Developmental Psychology, American Psychological Association Meeting, Toronto.

Horowitz, F.D. (1984). The psychobiology of parent-offspring relations in high-risk situations. In L.P. Lipsitt & C. Rovee-Collier (Eds.), *Advances in infancy research* (Vol. 3, pp. 1–22). Norwood, NJ: Ablex Publishing Corp.

Horowitz, F.D. (1987). *Exploring developmental theories: Toward a structural/behavioral model of development.* Hillsdale, NJ: Erlbaum.

Hoy, E.A., Bill, J.M., & Sykes, D.H. (1988). Very low birthweight: A long term development impairment? *International Journal of Behavioral Development, 11,* 37–68.

Kagan, J. (1984). *The nature of the child.* New York: Basic Books.

Kazdin, A.E. (1989). Developmental psychopathology: Current research, issues and directions. *American Psychologist, 44,* 180–187.

Kopp, C.B. (1983). Risk factors in development. In P.H. Mussen (Series Ed.), *Handbook of child psychology* (4th ed., Vol. 2), M.M. Haith & J.J. Campos (Vol. Eds.), *Infancy and developmental psychobiology* (pp. 1081–1188). New York: Wiley.

Kopp, C.B. (1987). Developmental risk: Historical reflections. In J.D. Osofsky (Ed.), *Handbook of infant development* (2nd ed., pp. 881–912). New York: Wiley.

Kopp, C.B. (1990). Risks in infancy: Appraising our research. *Merrill-Palmer Quarterly, 36,* 117–139.

Kopp, C.B., & Kaler, S.R. (1989). Risk in infancy: Origins and implications. *American Psychologist, 44,* 224–230.

Kopp, C., & Krakow, J.B. (1983). The developmentalist and the study of biological risk: A view of the past with an eye toward the future. *Child Development, 54,* 1086–1108.

Korner, A.F. (1987). Preventive intervention with high-risk newborns: Theoretical, conceptual, and methodological perspectives. In J.D. Osofsky (Ed.), *Handbook of infant development* (2nd ed., pp. 1006–1036). New York: Wiley.

LeDoux, J.E. (1989). Cognitive-emotional interactions in the brain. *Cognition and Emotion, 3,* 267–289.

LeDoux, J.E., Romanski, L., & Xagoraris, A. (1989). Indelibility of subcortical emotional memories. *Journal of Cognitive Neuroscience, 1,* 238–243.

Lewis, M. (1987). Social development in infancy and early childhood. In J.D. Osofsky (Ed.), *Handbook of infant development* (2nd ed., pp. 419–493). New York: Wiley.

Lewis, M. (1990). Social knowledge and social development. *Merrill-Palmer Quarterly, 36,* 93–116.

Lubchenco, L.O (1976). *The high risk infant.* Philadelphia: W.B. Saunders.

McCall, R.B. (1990). Infancy research: Individual differences. *Merrill-Palmer Quarterly, 36,* 141–158.

Moss, M., Colombo, J., Mitchell, D.W., & Horowitz, F.D. (1988). Neonatal behavioral organization and visual processing at three months. *Child Development, 59,* 1211–1220.

Newcomb, M.D., & Bentler, P.M. (1989). Substance use and abuse among children and teenagers. *American Psychologist, 44,* 242–248.

Parrinello, R.M., & Ruff, H.A. (1988). The influence of adult intervention on infants' level of attention. *Child Development, 59,* 1125–1135.

Patterson, G.R., DeBaryshe, B.D., & Ramsey, E. (1989). A developmental perspective on antisocial behavior. *American Psychologist, 44,* 329–335.

Ramey, C., & Trohanis, P.L. (1982). *Finding and educating high-risk and handicapped infants.* Baltimore: University Park Press.

Rice, M.L. (1989). Children's language acquisition. *American Psychologist, 44,* 149–156.

Richters, J., & Weintraub, S. (1990). Beyond diathesis: Toward an understanding of high risk environments. In J.E. Rolf, A. Basten, D. Cicchetti, D. Neuchterlein, & S. Weintraub (Eds.), *Risk and protective factors in the development of psychopathology.* New York: Cambridge University Press.

Rogoff, B. (1990). *Apprenticeship in thinking.* Oxford: Oxford University Press.

Rogoff, B. (1991). The joint socialization of development by young children and adults. In M. Lewis & S. Feinman (Eds.), *Social influences and behavior.* New York: Plenum Press.

Rose, S.A., Feldman, J.F., & Wallace, J.F. (1988). Individual differences in infants' information processing: Reliability, stability and prediction. *Child Development, 59,* 1177–1197.

Rutter, M. (1987). Continuities and discontinuities from infancy. In J.D. Osofsky (Ed.), *Handbook of infant development* (2nd ed., pp. 1256–1296). New York: Wiley.

Sameroff, A.J., & Chandler, M.J. (1975). Reproductive risk and the continuum of caretaking casualty. In F.D. Horowitz (Ed.), *Review of child development research* (Vol. 4, pp. 187–244). Chicago: University of Chicago Press.

Scafidi, F.A., Field, T.M., Schanberg, S.M., Bauer, C.R., Tucci, K., Roberts, J., Morrow, C., & Kuhn, C.M. (1990). Massage stimulates growth in preterm infants: A replication. *Infant Behavior & Development, 13,* 167–188.

Scarr-Salapatek, S. (1976). An evolutionary perspective on infant intelligence. In M. Lewis (Ed.), *Origins of intelligence: Infancy and early childhood* (pp. 165–197). New York: Plenum.

Schorr, L.B. (1988). *Within our reach.* New York: Anchor Press, Doubleday.

Self, P.A., & Horowitz, F.D. (1979). Neonatal assessment: An overview. In J.D. Osofsky (Ed.), *Handbook of infant development* (2nd ed., pp. 126–164). New York: Wiley.

Streissguth, A.P., Barr, H., Sampon, P.D., Darby, B.L., & Martin, D.C. (1989). IQ at age 4 in relation to maternal alcohol use and smoking during pregnancy. *Developmental Psychology, 25,* 3–11.

Thoman, E., Denenberg, V., Sievel, J., Zeidner, L., & Becker, P. (1981). State organization in neonates: Developmental inconsistency indicates risk for developmental dysfunction. *Neuropediatrica, 12,* 45–54.

Thompson, L.A. (1990). Genetic contributions to early individual differences. In J. Colombo & J. Fagen (Eds.), *Individual differences in infancy: Reliability, stability and prediction* (pp. 45–76). Hillsdale, NJ: Erlbaum.

Tronick, E.Z. (1989). Emotions and emotional communication in infants. *American Psychologist, 44*, 112–119.

Vorhees, C.V., & Mollnow, E. (1987). Behavioral teratogeneses: Long-term influences on behavior from early exposure to environmental agents. In J.D. Osofsky (Ed.), *Handbook of infant development* (2nd ed., pp. 913–971). New York: Wiley.

Wahler, R.G., & Dumas, J. (1989). Attentional problems in dysfunctional mother-child interactions: An interbehavioral model. *Psychological Bulletin, 105*, 116–130.

III
Social and Emotional Development

5
Very-Low-Birthweight Newborns and Parents as Early Social Partners*

Carol O. Eckerman
Jerri M. Oehler

At any point in development, a child's social functioning is the product of numerous diverse elements, some of which are typically thought of as residing within the child (e.g., neural maturation, cognitions, learned behaviors, affects, arousal states) and others of which reside outside the child—in the social partner, the task demands of the social encounter, and the broader animate and inanimate environment. These elements interrelate with one another, constraining each other's actions and thus enabling the system of elements to self-organize into one or a few recognizable forms of behavior (see Fogel & Thelen, 1987; Thelen, 1989, for a fuller explication of a dynamic systems perspective on behavioral organization and development). Social development consists of a succession of changes in these contributing elements and their interrelationships, and hence in the ways they self-organize. The result is a progression of distinctive forms of social functioning. Each change in form is built upon the prior form—upon the contributing elements and the changes in these elements as well as the experience facilitated by the prior form. We can take snapshots of a child's social functioning at particular points in time in specific contexts, and string these snapshots together to provide one kind of account of social development. But when we seek to understand development itself, we must relate earlier ways the multiple elements contributing to social functioning organize into a behavioral form to changes in the contributing elements and the resultant way they reorganize into a new form.

In this chapter, we focus upon one early transition in social functioning—the beginning of the postnatal social partnership forged between newborn infants and their parents. Further, we seek to understand this transition for a high-risk, newly surviving group of human newborns—infants born at very low birthweights (<1,500 grams), who develop in the extrauterine environment during most if not

* This research and chapter preparation were supported in part by National Institute of Child Health and Human Development Grants HD21530 and HD213554 to Carol O. Eckerman, and research grants from the National Association of Neonatal Nurses and the Duke University Research Council to Jerri M. Oehler. We gratefully acknowledge the assistance of Mandy B. Medvin, Thomas E. Hannan, Marta Gay, Evelyn Shaw, and Duke Medical Center's Intensive Care Nursery staff in the conduct of the studies of infant behavior.

all of the usual last trimester of pregnancy. What are the multiple elements contributing to their "premature" postnatal interactions with their parents? How do these elements interrelate and constrain each other's actions? How does the parent–infant system self-organize into one or more relatively stable forms of social interaction? Do these forms differ from those for full-term newborns and their parents? What are the contemporaneous and developmental consequences of the forms of social interaction found for very-low-birthweight infants?

Although the study of each developmental transition is of intrinsic value, given the conceptualization of development just articulated, the study of beginnings can be of special importance. An understanding of beginnings can (a) serve as an anchor point for subsequent developmental analysis, (b) effectively open our eyes to the multitude of contributing elements and their interrelationships, and (c) yield clear evidence of basic principles of developmental process. Earlier forms of social functioning often seem more understandable given the prevalent view of earlier as simpler. We are more inclined to seek out a full accounting of the elements involved and study their interrelationships. Hence, the complexity to be found in early forms of social organization sets a minimum level of expected complexity for our subsequent analyses; and the processes found responsible for these early forms provide us with a set of guiding principles about the nature of developmental process.

A second source of inherent value in the study of social beginnings lies in the importance of these beginnings for both parent and infant at the time they are occurring. New parents seek out the experience of making contact with their infant, and from the resultant experiences draw attributions about themselves as parents and about their babies as individuals with distinctive characteristics and needs. These processes are likely to hold special importance for parents of high-risk infants. We have heard, for example, parents of very-low-birthweight infants remark that their infants looked at them for a few moments and then draw the conclusion that "she knows I'm here" or "she's saying she loves me." Or parents may observe vigorous limb activity in response to their stroking and conclude that their baby is a fighter, that he or she will make it! Very-low-birthweight newborns, too, like all newborns, depend on these early postnatal interactions with others for their very survival. Premature birth, however, by disrupting the usual intrauterine communication between mother and developing child, necessarily thrusts both newborn and parent into new modes of interaction, perhaps before either is well equipped for the interactions customary after birth. Just as breathing, eating, blood circulation, and digestion after birth pose substantial challenges for the very immature newborn, so too may postnatal social interactions. The routine administrations of others can contribute to both the organization and disorganization of very-low-birthweight newborns' functioning (Als, Lawhon, Brown, Gibes, & Duffy, 1986; Oehler, Eckerman & Wilson, 1988). We urgently need a better understanding of how to tailor these interactions in ways facilitative of healthy development for such immature infants.

This chapter presents our orientation to the study of the beginnings of postnatal social interactions for very-low-birthweight infants and their parents. By *beginnings* we mean from the birth of these infants 2 to 4 months before term age to around 1 month after term age, the customary ending to the newborn period for full-term infants. We first discuss current views on beginnings for healthy full-term infants and their parents, and then detail the multiple reasons why these beginnings may differ for very-low-birthweight infants and their parents. Next, we evaluate the current state of knowledge about these beginnings for premature infants, noting the need to study premature infants and their parents in their own right, and not just as perturbations from healthy full-term infants and their parents. Further, we detail the need to study variations in social functioning within the premature population, and even within the considerably more restricted very-low-birthweight population. Then, we present two illustrative studies examining specific elements contributing to the beginnings of social interaction for very-low-birthweight infants and their parents. The first focuses upon elements contributed by the infants—their behavioral responsiveness to human speech and touch; the second, upon elements contributed by their parents—how they attend to and process their infants' behavioral cues and their goals in these early interactions. Finally, we integrate these findings with others and suggest how they can lead to productive next steps in research on the forms of social interaction occurring between very-low-birthweight infants and their parents.

A FULL-TERM MODEL OF BEGINNINGS

Over the past 15 years, an explosion of studies on young full-term infants and their parents has markedly changed our ideas about the beginnings of social interaction. Today we view both full-term newborns and their parents as "preadapted" for these encounters. Each brings elements conducive to social interaction; and, most importantly, the elements contributed by each appear to intermesh, or fit together, to produce social interactions that are both orderly and complex and that address important developmental tasks. Although this model has been developed on a limited database (e.g., mostly healthy full-terms, mostly white and middle-class, mostly American or Western European), it warrants scrutiny because (a) it is a rich source of hypotheses about the elements and processes contributing to the beginnings of social interaction among low-birthweight infants and their parents within Western culture, and (b) it has in fact guided most existing inquiries into such beginnings for different populations of infants and parents.

Six claims can be extracted from the extensive literature on full-terms infants and their parents and expressed in terms of complementary contributions of infants and parents (Table 1). These claims overlap in several ways but are

Table 1. Six Claims About Complementary Contributions to the Beginnings of Social Interaction Between Full-Term Newborns and Their Parents

Full-Term Newborn	Parent
Has organized states	Helps regulate infant's states
Attends selectively to certain stimuli	Provides these stimuli
Behaves in ways interpretable as specific communicative intent	Searches for communicative intent
Responds systematically to parent's acts	Wants to influence newborn, feel effective
Acts in temporally predictable ways	Adjusts actions to newborn's temporal rhythms
Learns from, adapts to parent's behavior	Acts repetitively and predictably

sufficiently distinctive to warrant separate scrutiny. Together they form a model of the beginnings of social interaction for full-term newborns and their parents.

The first claim is that newborns show multiple, quite different states of arousal, and that their parents behave in ways that help regularize their newborns' states. Multiple states of arousal are detectable well before birth, and they develop from states of higher and lower activity to the emergence by term age of quiet and active sleep states as well as different awake states (e.g., Hofer, 1981). After an initial disruption of states at birth, cycling among these states quickly resumes in the newborn; and these states affect the occurrence and nature of the newborns' responses to stimulation. Among the earliest developmental tasks for newborn and parent is the regularizing of the newborn's physiological processes, including these states of arousal (Als, 1979; Schaffer, 1984). Although newborns cycle among these states irrespective of external stimulation, these states become quickly entrained to stimuli provided by parents (e.g., Sander, Stechler, Burns, & Lee, 1979); and a variety of activities of parents function to maintain these states or facilitate transitions from state to state. Rhythmic rocking of the newborn, for example, appears to aid the newborn in achieving and maintaining sleep states, and the picking up and putting of a crying infant to the shoulder facilitates the infant's transition from a crying state to an alert attentive state (Korner & Thoman, 1972).

The second claim is that in the awake alert state newborns are perceptually predisposed to attend to the sensory/perceptual characteristics their parents customarily provide. Infants look more at visual stimuli that are bilaterally symmetrical and moving and that fall within certain ranges of contour change, brightness, and size; and these visual predispositions match well the types of visual stimuli customarily presented by a parent's face (see Sherrod, 1981, for a useful review). Infants, too, appear to find speech-like auditory stimuli particularly salient (Eisenberg, 1976). Newborns turn their head to orient to the source of speech (Alegria & Noirot, 1978) and, in experimental paradigms, even learn to modify their sucking to produce their own mother's voice (DeCasper & Fifer, 1980). Parents and others talk to infants from birth and modify their speech in a number of ways (*motherese*) that appear designed to make their speech even more salient to infants (Fernald, 1984). Further, the usual combination of the sight of the human face with the sounds of speech may be especially perceptually salient: Infants at least as young as 10 weeks of age look longer at a speaking face when the speech is appropriately synchronized with lip movements (Dodd, 1979; Spelke & Cortelyou, 1981), and the addition of sound to a visual stimulus appears to prompt infants' use of the more mature visual strategy of scanning the central aspects of a stimulus rather than focusing upon the external contour (Haith, Bergman, & Moore, 1977; Sherrod, 1981).

The third claim is that parents expect and search for evidence of recognizable communicative intent in their infants (e.g., Snow, 1984, Stern, 1977), and that even newborns exhibit behaviors easily interpretable as indicating specific communicative intents. For example, the facial expressions customarily associated with happiness, sadness, surprise, interest, and disgust are recognizable in the newborn (Field, Woodson, Greenberg, & Cohen, 1982; Fox & Davidson, 1986); visual orienting to, and tracking of, the human face are detectable (Brazelton, 1973; Goren, Sarty, & Wu, 1975) and interpretable as interest in or approach to the parent; movements of the mouth and tongue (e.g., the "prespeech movements" of Trevathen, 1979), and such motoric bursts of activity as raising arms outward and toward the midline or yawning are interpretable as talking to, reaching for the parent, or being tired.

The fourth claim involves parents' desire to have an influence upon their baby—to be responded to and to feel effective in dealing with their baby. Newborns, in turn, respond systematically to their parents' behavior. When parents pick up a crying baby and put the baby to their shoulder, babies tend to quiet and become visually alert (Korner & Thoman, 1972). The behavior patterns we call *orientation*, or attention to the sight of a face or the sound of a voice, also yield ready evidence to a parent of their babies' responsiveness to them. The phenomenon of newborn imitation of an adult's facial expressions or mouth movements (Bjorklund, 1987; Field et al., 1982; Meltzoff & Moore, 1983) holds the same potential.

The fifth claim involves the temporal regularities found repeatedly in interactions between full-term infants and their parents. Infants are viewed as behaving in temporally regular bursts of activity separated by pauses; their parents, as sensing these regularities and adapting their behavior so as to produce both turn-taking patterns of interaction and coaction patterns (Brazelton, Kowlawski & Main, 1974; Schaffer, 1984; Stern, Jaffe, Beebe, & Bennett, 1975). Perhaps the most rigorously studied of these early temporal rhythms is the feeding rhythm (Kaye & Wells, 1980). Newborns suck in bursts during their feedings, and mothers tend to be quiet while their infant is sucking and to become active in the pauses between successive bursts of sucking (e.g., they jiggle their baby). The cessation of parents' jiggling seems to stimulate the baby to begin sucking again. This turn-taking rhythm is discernible in the earliest feeding encounters and becomes even smoother and more regular over the first few days of life as the parent comes to jiggle in short bursts and some infants come to "wait" more reliably for the jiggle before resuming sucking. Although the details of the processes contributing to rhythms may well differ from one rhythm to another, what is stressed is the presence of temporal regularities that parents can detect and use as a pacer for their own activities in interaction.

The final claim is that parents behave repetitively and predictably in their early interactions with their infant and that their infants learn or adapt to these specific experiences. Evidence of full-term newborns' learning abilities is by now abundant (e.g., Rovee-Collier & Lipsitt, 1982). Less clear are specific examples of young infants' learning in their social encounters, although the above examples of the burst-pause rhythm of sucking and of newborns' learning to adjust their sucking to produce their own mother's voice lend credence to this possibility. Other potential evidence of early adaptation to specific social experiences includes the entrainment of infants' sleep cycles under specific rearing circumstances (Sander et al., 1979), the increased efficiency of feeding with one's own mother over the first few days of life (Thoman, Barnett, & Lederman, 1971), and avoidance of the breast when a prior breast feeding has led to occlusion of the infant's nostrils (Gunther, 1961).

THE POTENTIAL FOR QUITE DIFFERENT BEGINNINGS FOR VERY-LOW-BIRTHWEIGHT INFANTS AND PARENTS

The circumstances of the beginnings of postnatal social interaction differ dramatically for very-low-birthweight infants and their parents in at least four ways that hold implications for the elements contributing to their early interactions (see Table 2). First, postnatal social interactions begin at a much earlier point in the development of the infant. Most very-low-birthweight infants are born at least 10 weeks early, some as many as 16 weeks early. We have made substantial progress in recent years in understanding better how their immature lungs, heart, liver, and so on are not well equipped for the tasks of postnatal life and in developing special ways to compensate at least partially for these immaturities so as to support their survival and healthier development. Similarly, we must entertain the possibility that such immature organisms may not be well prepared to deal with the social stimulation typically provided a newborn, and that they may need special forms of social stimulation or special assistance in dealing with this stimulation. Very-low-birthweight newborns may or may not be perceptually predisposed to the postnatal sounds and sights of their parents. They may

Table 2.   Four Sources of Potential Differences for Very-Low-Birthweight Newborns and Their Parents as Early Social Partners

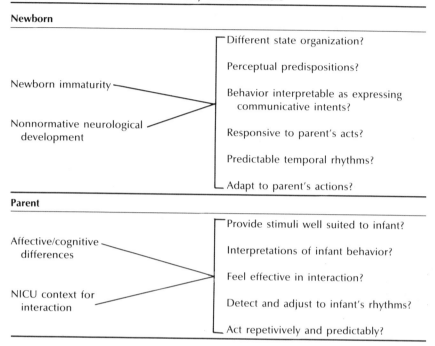

respond in a disorganized, even avoidant manner to stimulation sought out by full-term newborns. They may respond to their parents' stimulation, but with a complex of behavioral cues less easily interpretable as responsiveness or recognizable communicative intents. They may less quickly adapt their responses to the specific stimulation they receive. Further, their immature state at birth means that they differ markedly in physical appearance from healthy full-term newborns; their appearance may be far from attractive to their parents and may alter the impact of their behavioral cues.

Second, social interaction begins, not only with an immature infant, but in many instances with a sick infant at high risk for nonnormative neurological development. A variety of medical conditions frequently experienced by very-low-birthweight infants (e.g., respiratory distress syndrome, heart failure, necrotizing entercolitis, apnea, bradycardia, hyperbilirubinemia, hypoxia), as well as the treatments used for these conditions, place the developing nervous system at risk. Differences in nervous system development may result in very-low-birthweight infants of the same postconceptional age who differ markedly in their characteristics as early social partners. For example, higher perinatal biological risk may be associated with greater heterochronicity of neural development, resulting in newborns who show unexpected, not easily interpretable patterns of behavioral responsiveness and differences in the temporal regularities of their behavior. The various elements of their behavior may be organized in quite different ways than customary for the full-term or less high-risk premature infant. Or differences in neural development may affect infants' abilities to adapt to their specific social experiences. Further, such extreme results of their illnesses as blindness or deafness alter dramatically the elements contributing to their social interactions.

Third, postnatal social interactions begin in a context of different and often intense affects for the parents of very-low-birthweight infants. Their babies' birth occurs most usually as an unanticipated emergency—before they had expected and before they are "ready." We have premature parents, as well as premature babies. Further, such unexpected early births with high risks to the baby are often accompanied by feelings of grief for "a normal baby," guilt and blame about possible reasons for the early birth, anxiety about their baby's survival, an emotional roller-coaster ride as their baby's condition takes dramatic swings for both the better and worse, and intense concern for the future normality of their baby (e.g., Pederson, Bento, Chance, Evans, & Fox, 1987). As a result, this often is a period of intense stress for the parent, and that stress may be exacerbated by such factors as the transfer of the baby to a referral hospital far from one's own home, separation from customary sources of social support, monetary concerns, and the competing demands of caring for the newborn and one's other children. Such affective contexts may alter what parents bring to their interactions with their newborns. Parents may, for example, disengage from the baby, seeking to protect themselves against a possible loss; or they may even more intensely seek evidence of their infant's communicative intent and responsiveness to them. Different behavioral cues may be salient to them in contrast to full-term parents: For example, motor activity may be especially important for some parents as an indicator of their baby's being a "fighter." Further, the same behavioral cues may lead to different attributions, reflecting the quite different issues these parents bring to their interactions. For example, fussing or crying may lead more readily to attributions of tiredness, and needing to sleep, for the sick very-low-birthweight infant.

Finally, their social interactions proceed under quite different constraints than for the full-term infant. First, they occur under the physical and social constraints of the intensive care nursery environment; parents, for example, may become acquainted with their infant in brief periods widely separated in time, in periods not related to the feeding of their infant, and in a noisy, bright environment in the presence of strangers. Second, our conversations with parents suggest that they often approach these interactions believing that others know better how to care for their baby; others feed their baby, clean their baby, tell them when and how to contact their baby, and decide what is or is not an emergency. The belief that others know better may well alter parents' view of their role in caring for and interacting with their baby.

LIMITATIONS ON OUR UNDERSTANDING OF SOCIAL BEGINNINGS FOR PREMATURE INFANTS

Despite such compelling reasons for expecting both very-low-birthweight infants and their parents to bring different elements to their early social interactions, we still know little about the specific characteristics of each partner and even less about how these characteristics complement or fail to complement one another during the first few months of postnatal life. We are far from having generated a model of the beginnings of their social interaction comparable in detail to that already outlined for full-term infants.

Much of our existing empirical knowledge about these social beginnings comes from three sources: (a) a handful of studies of naturally occurring interactions between premature infants and their parents during their hospital stay and/ or the first month or two after hospital discharge; (b) a much larger group of studies of premature infants' performance during neonatal behavioral and neurological assessments; and (c) a few interview/questionnaire studies of the parents of premature infants around the time of their infants' births. In this literature, the premature infant near term age has often been described as less alert and responsive to social stimulation, as emitting less clear behavioral cues, and as showing poorer state and motor control (e.g., Alfasi et al., 1985; Bakeman & Brown, 1980; Field et al., 1978; Goldberg, Brachfield, & DiVitto, 1980; Minde, Perotta, & Marton, 1985). Some describe premature infants' responsiveness as "all-or-nothing": The infants are more difficult to bring to an alert or responsive state; and once there, they are more easily overaroused or overstimulated (e.g., Aylward, 1982; Field, 1981; Telzrow, Kang, Mitchell, Ashworth, & Barnard, 1982). Als (1983 pp. 370–371) has been especially articulate about her impressions of the premature infant near term age, whom she describes as "more poorly organized," "more highly sensitive and easily overreactive to environmental inputs, more easily stressed and over-stimulated, necessitating more finely tuned, sensitive environmental structuring and support."

The impact of the premature birth on the parent has also received some attention. In interactions with their infants of around term age, mothers have been described as touching and talking to their infants less and holding them at a greater distance during feeding (DiVitto & Goldberg, 1979; Goldberg et al., 1980; Minde et al., 1985), as trying harder to get their infants to feed and assuming a more active role in structuring interactions (Bakeman & Brown, 1980), and as being less responsive to their infants' cues (Alfasi et al., 1985). Interviews and questionnaires, too, have been used to assess parents' affective experiences around the birth of a premature infant (e.g., Pederson et al., 1987), mothers' perceived sources of social support, life stress, general life satisfaction and satisfaction with parenting (Crnic, Greenberg, Ragozin, Robinson, & Basham, 1983), and individual differences among mothers in psychological functioning and experienced stress associated with their infants' birth (Minde et al., 1985).

There are, however, several important limitations of this knowledge base for generating a model of the beginnings of social interaction for premature infants and their parents. Six will be discussed in turn.

Conflicting descriptions of the behavior of premature infants. Upon close examination, statements about premature infants' behavioral characteristics are often conflicting. For example, at least two studies of mother–infant interactions around term age found no differences in looking behavior between full-term and premature infants (Censullo, Lester, & Hoffman, 1985; Goldberg et al., 1980). In contrast, one other study found that premature infants had their eyes open as much as full-term infants but that premature infants looked less often to the mother (Bakeman & Brown, 1980), and another study found that premature infants had their eyes open less (Minde et al., 1985). Similarly, premature newborns have been described as both less irritable than full-term newborns (Riese, 1987) and as more irritable (Aylward, 1982). Even when the same examination procedure has been used across studies (the Brazelton Neonatal Behavioral Assessment Scale), premature infants have been described as scoring poorer on the orientation items (Field et al., 1978; Holmes et al., 1982), scoring more poorly on the visual items but not on those requiring orientation to sound alone (DiVitto & Goldberg, 1979), or scoring equivalently to full-term neonates (Sostek, Quinn, & Davitt, 1979; Telzrow et al., 1982).

Paucity of behavioral detail. There is a paucity of behavioral detail about how premature infants respond to social stimulation. Instead of describing how eye opening, different facial expressions, and limb movements co-occur, researchers have most often relied upon ratings of behavior (e.g., Alfasi et al., 1985; and studies using the Brazelton exam), frequency counts of selected infant behaviors (e.g., Bakeman & Brown, 1980; DiVitto & Goldberg, 1979), global factors derived by factor analysis (Beckwith, Cohen, Kopp, Parmelee, & Marcy, 1976), or summaries of dyadic states (e.g., Bakeman & Brown, 1980; Censullo et al., 1985).

Seldom, too, are we able to link specific behavioral responses to well-specified forms of social stimulation. Indeed, in the studies of mother–infant interaction, infant behavioral differences are confounded with maternal behavioral differences (Bakeman & Brown, 1980; DiVitto & Golberg, , 1979; Minde et al., 1985); even in such standardized exams as the Brazelton, the examiner's behavior varies across infants, in line with the goal of bringing out the infant's optimal performance. As a result, we have very little understanding about how premature infants respond to being talked to in *motherese* versus being stroked, cradled, or jiggled; and we have not specified what forms of social stimulation lead to alert attentive responses versus disorganized or avoidance responses.

Period prior to term age largely unexamined. Premature infants' responsiveness to social stimulation prior to term age remains largely unexamined, even though parent–infant postnatal interactions may begin long before term age. Descriptions of infants at the time of their discharge from the hospital or at term age have been treated as if they were adequate reflections of what the infants bring to their postnatal interactions. Yet it certainly seems plausible that, at 30 weeks' postconceptional age, infants may show quite different behavioral characteristics than they will 10 weeks later, and that parent–infant interactions at term age may be influenced by the interactions transpiring during the prior 10 weeks (cf. Minde, Whitelaw, Brown, & Fitzhardinge, 1983).

Differences in social functioning among premature infants. Our understanding of differences in social functioning among prematurely born infants remains quite limited. Many studies either treat heterogeneous populations of premature infants as if they were a single population to be contrasted to a full-term population, or deal only with the larger, relatively healthy premature infants. Some studies have attempted to tease out the effects of neonatal illness from those of immaturity at birth (e.g., Goldberg et al., 1980; Green, Fox, & Lewis, 1983; Krafchuk, Tronick, & Clifton, 1983; Minde et al., 1983; Sostek et al., 1979) and have shown differences in behavioral characteristics as a function of illness as well as of prematurity. Nevertheless, we have few studies of the more immature and sicker premature infants whom we believe to be at highest risk for adverse developmental outcomes—for example, very-low-birthweight infants. Even among very-low-birthweight infants, there are major differences in perinatal biological status that relate to subsequent courses of development (e.g., Eckerman, Sturm, & Gross, 1985; Gross & Eckerman, 1983; Gross, Oehler, & Eckerman, 1983). We have little understanding of the impact of such differences in perinatal biological status upon newborn social functioning, and hence upon the role such behavioral characteristics may play in subsequent paths of both normative and nonnormative development.

Attempts to capture important differences within the premature population have been hindered by the difficulties inherent in assessing variations in perinatal central nervous system development. Specific illnesses (e.g., respiratory distress syndrome) or counts of number of medical complications have been most often used to define different groups of premature infants in studies of early social functioning, yet we know that such illness states are only indirectly linked to the differences in nervous system development or biological risk that we wish to assess. Recently, we have been exploring new strategies for assessing variations in perinatal biological risk related to subsequent courses of behavioral development among very-low-birthweight infants. One is a neurobiologic risk scoring system applied to infants' medical records, which assesses the severity and duration of 13 factors related to brain injury caused by hypoxia, hypoperfusion, insufficient substrate or direct damage to brain tissue (Brazy, Eckerman, Oehler, Goldstein, & O'Rand, 1991). A second strategy assesses the adequacy of head growth both prenatally and during the first 6 weeks of life—periods of known rapid brain growth during which head growth may reflect such important aspects of brain development as the multiplication of neural and glial cells, myelination, and growth in dendritic complexity and the establishment of synaptic connections (Eckerman, et al., 1985; Gross & Eckerman, 1983; Gross et al., 1983). We will illustrate shortly the utility of this latter strategy for capturing differences in social functioning within the very-low-birthweight population.

Limited knowledge of parents. Our knowledge of the characteristics of premature infants' parents is even more limited than our knowledge of premature infants. The studies of how parents behave in early social interactions are limited by reliance on summary characterizations of parental behavior and the already mentioned difficulties in (a) capturing important variations among premature infants, and (b) disentangling infant differences from parent differences. We know little about how parents respond to infant behaviors and very little about parents' interpretations of their infants' behaviors (Helm, 1988). The handful of existing interview and questionnaire studies with parents close to the time of their premature infant's birth are necessarily restricted in the parental characteristics they tap, leaving many important characteristics yet to be examined. For example, we know of no study asking parents of premature infants about their early interactions with their baby—what they are trying to do, what infant cues they attend to and how they use them, how these interactions feel, or what conclusions they draw about their baby and themselves. For reasons detailed earlier it seems probable that parents behave differently, not only because of their infants' different behavior, but also because of their own sources of difference prompted by the premature birth. What many of these differences are and how they complement or fail to complement their infants' characteristics have yet to be addressed.

Overreliance on the full-term model of beginnings. Finally, there is the pervasive limitation to our understanding of premature infants and parents arising from our having studied these infants and parents almost exclusively in terms of a full-term model of beginnings, rather than in terms of their own modes of functioning. Typically, they are described in such terms as *more, less, poorer, better, hypo-,* or *hyper-,* where the reference point is the organization of behavior for healthy full-term infants and their parents. An implicit assumption here is that the full-term model is appropriate for describing the functioning of quite different populations, specifically premature infants and their parents—that one can capture the functioning of premature infants and parents in terms of quantitative differences in measures based upon a full-term model.

Unfortunately, this is largely an unexamined assumption, and there exist multiple reasons to question it. First, we have already pointed out reasons to expect very-low-birthweight infants and their parents to bring different elements to their earliest interactions. Second, the existing research literature documents the existence of differences and adds to quantitative contrasts descriptive terms suggesting qualitative differences—for example, *all-or-nothing* response, or *disorganized.* Finally, studies of the forms shown by complex systems have documented how even the smallest of changes in a single element of a system can so change the nature of the interrelationships among elements that the system reorganizes into a new form (e.g., Gleick, 1987; Thelen, 1989). Surely, we should entertain this possibility for such a complex biological system as parent–infant interaction. Instead of relying on assumptions, we must address the critical empirical question of whether the differences in elements found for very-low-birthweight infants and their parents lead to qualitatively different forms of social functioning.

Given these limitations, we have embarked upon a series of studies designed to contribute to the building of a model of beginnings for very-low-birthweight infants and their parents. We have used the full-term model as a guide but attempted to study very-low-birthweight infants and their parents in their own right, rather than only as perturbations from a full-term model. In this chapter we present two early steps in this endeavor: Illustrative studies of very-low-birthweight infants' responsiveness to human speech and touch; and a first study of what infant behavioral cues the parents of very-low-birthweight infants respond to, some of their attributions about their babies, and what they are trying to accomplish in their interactions during the first 2 postnatal months of life. Obviously, a complete account of their beginnings is not our goal; rather, we hope these examples will illustrate a promising strategy for understanding these beginnings.

VERY-LOW-BIRTHWEIGHT INFANTS' BEHAVIORAL RESPONSIVENESS TO HUMAN SPEECH AND TOUCH PRIOR TO TERM AGE

Our examination of the elements contributing to the beginnings of postnatal social interaction between very-low-birthweight infants and their parents began with the infants. We asked whether, long before term age, they could respond to the social stimulation their parents provided and, if so, what form their behavioral responsiveness took. Further, we asked whether infants of higher perinatal biological risk showed different forms of behavioral responsiveness than those at lower risk. Rather than starting with the complex and variable forms of social stimulation parents customarily provide, we began more simply and presented the infants with standardized episodes of social stimulation that mimicked some of this naturally occurring stimulation. In this way, we hoped to learn (a) whether some forms of social stimulation elicited attentive orienting responses in such immature infants and others, distress, disorganization, or avoidance, and (b) how very-low-birthweight infants at higher perinatal biological risk differ from those at lower risk in their responses to the same forms of stimulation.

A first study: Social stimulation and the regulation of infant state. In our first study of infants' behavioral responsiveness long before term age (Oehler et al., 1988), we used those forms of social stimulation parents in our nursery were being encouraged to provide such immature infants (talking to them and lightly stroking their limbs and trunk). Further, we mimicked the situation in which parents most often interacted with their infants at these early ages: We simply entered the nursery at a specified time, approached the infant's bed, briefly watched the infant, and then began to talk and/or stroke the infant. Thus, the stimulation was provided in whatever state of arousal the infant happened to be at the start of our exams. Their responsiveness then was assessed as a function of their state at the beginning of the interaction.

We enlisted the aid of 10 experienced intensive care nurses in providing the social stimulation. Each followed a standard protocol that consisted of simply standing beside the infant's bed for a baseline period of 80 seconds, followed by three 80-second periods of different forms of social stimulation in counterbalanced order. The three forms of stimulation were speaking in a low, "soothing" voice near the infant's head, quietly stroking each body part of the infant in turn, and the combination of these two forms of stimulation (talking to and stroking the infant simultaneously). Exams were conducted midway between feedings, avoiding times following closely upon painful procedures. An observer, standing beside the bed, recorded at 10-second intervals the infant's eye opening, limb movements, and what we called "avoidance cues" (facial grimaces, tongue protrusions, yawning, and fussing/crying).

Fifteen very-low-birthweight infants were studied intensively; each was born at least 10 weeks early, appropriately grown at birth, and free of major congenital abnormalities. Exams began as soon after birth as the infant was judged medically stable, and three exams per week were scheduled until the infant was discharged from the hospital. The data reported derive from the three exams per week obtained for all infants for the 4 weeks corresponding to 30 to 34 weeks' postconceptional age.

To assess variations in perinatal biological risk, we relied on the measures of early head growth we had previously studied in collaboration with Steven Gross (Eckerman et al., 1985; Gross & Eckerman, 1983; Gross et al., 1983). The 15 subjects of the present study, all of whom were normocephalic at birth, were divided into a higher- versus a lower-biological-risk group on the basis of their head growth during their first 6 postnatal weeks (high risk: <3.5 cm change in head circumference; low risk: ≥3.5 cm change). Our prior work had shown that groups of very-low-birthweight infants defined in this way had both markedly different incidences of medical complications during their intensive care nursery stay and markedly different developmental courses through 2 years of age, indicating that these head growth measures were useful markers of important differences in perinatal biological status. Less postnatal head growth, for example, was associated with requiring mechanical ventilation, sepsis, congestive heart failure, and long delays in achieving adequate enteral caloric intake. In terms of subsequent development, infants normocephalic at birth with more postnatal head growth were indistinguishable in outcome (physical growth, neurological exam, and Bayley Scales of Infant Development) from a comparison group of healthy full-term infants from similar family backgrounds at 6, 15, and 24 months corrected ages. Infants with less postnatal head growth, in contrast, showed a variety of problems of development: Increased incidences of growth failure and abnormal neurological exams; increased incidences of continuing severe delays on the Bayley Scales and late-appearing delays on these scales after earlier normative performance; and normal development trajectories but with significantly lower scores within the normal range on the Bayley Scales.

Irrespective of their biological risk status, these very-low-birthweight infants clearly responded to our social stimulation long before term age. What is more, their response differed depending on the form of stimulation and, with a given form of stimulation, depending upon their state at the start of the exam. Further, infants at higher biological risk differed in the details of their behavioral responsiveness from those at lower risk.

Consider first the behavioral responsiveness found when infants began as they most often did (70%) in a low activity, presumed sleep state. When in this state, talking led to significant increases over the baseline condition in the amount of time with their eyes open, whereas stroking and the combination of stroking and talking led to significantly increased limb movement. These findings held for both higher risk and lower risk infants; higher risk infants, however, showed significantly greater increases in limb movement in response to stroking, and unlike the lower risk infants, they showed significantly more avoidance cues in response to the combination of talking and stroking (see Figure 1).

A quite different picture of behavioral responsiveness emerged for the next most frequent initial state (20%), a state we called *high activity*. This state, marked by much body movement and little eye opening, corresponds roughly to Als's (1984) states of active awake and crying. In this state, no significant differences were found between higher and lower risk infants; both groups responded to talking with significantly decreased body movement and an increase in eyes open that approached significance. Stroking, or the combination of stroking and talking, in contrast, led to no significant changes in behavior; infants continued to show much movement and avoidance cues, suggestive of agitation, avoidance, or distress.

Finally, the infants were very seldom in a quiet, visually attentive state at the start of our stimulation (10%); but when they were, some marked differences in responsiveness occurred for the higher versus lower risk infants. Stroking, or both stroking or talking, produced marked increases in body movement for the higher risk infants, but not for those at lower risk. Talking, in contrast, led to no significant changes in behavior for either group; infants remained quiet and visually attentive. Throughout all conditions, however, the higher risk infants showed significantly more avoidance cues, thus providing quite a different behavioral picture for their social partner even when they were awake and motorically quiet.

In summary, from long before term age, it appears that human speech is a salient stimulus for very-low-birthweight infants that has the potential to aid

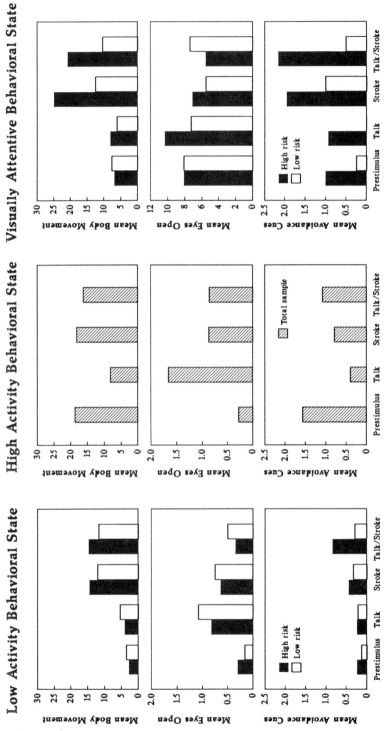

Figure 1. Behavioral responsiveness to talking and stroking in premature newborns of 30 to 34 weeks' postconceptional age as a function of newborn state and degree of biological risk.

106

these infants in maintaining or achieving a motorically quiet, visually attentive behavioral state. Talking quieted already aroused infants and aroused sleeping infants to an awake or drowsy state. Human speech had this effect, however, only in the absence of stroking; talking in combination with light stroking led to a quite different response, similar to that for stroking alone. These latter forms of social stimulation either maintained or produced a motorically active state suggestive of agitation and motoric disorganization, with these effects being more pronounced for the higher risk very-low-birthweight infants.

An ongoing study: Responsiveness in the awake, nonagitated state. In ongoing work, we are looking more closely at very-low-birthweight infants' responsiveness to talk and different forms of tactile contact when they are initially in an awake, nonagitated state, the state most often studied for full-term infants' contributions to early face-to-face interactions. The limited data about this state from our first study had suggested (a) that talk may help maintain or prolong this visually attentive state for both higher and lower risk infants, and (b) that stroking either alone or in combination with talking seemed to easily disrupt this state for the higher risk infants leading to a motorically active state punctuated with avoidance cues. We set out now to study responsiveness in this state thought so important for early social interactions and to do so with (a) a much larger sample of very-low-birthweight infants, and (b) videorecords of their behavior that would enable us to more closely examine the temporal organization of their behavior.

To increase our chances of observing infants in an awake, nonagitated state, we manipulate the infants prior to the exam, changing and dressing them and putting them in a specially designed infant seat reclined at a 40-degree angle (see Figure 2). The positioning in the infant seat increases both the infant's ability to orient to the stimulation we provide and our ability to observe and code the infant's behavior, now from high-quality videotaped records. Booties and fleece-lined "jogging suits" maintain the temperatures of even our most immature infants during the 6 to 7 minutes they are outside their bed, while still enabling us to detect their limb movements. Exams take place immediately beside the infants' bed with all the infants' monitors remaining in place. Currently our exams occur 30 minutes before the next scheduled feeding in medically stable infants who may be as young as 29 weeks' postconceptional age and still on oxygen support.

We now use trained female examiners to standardize our social stimulation further. To begin an exam, the examiner positions the infant's head in the midline, places her face about 10 inches in front of the infant's, and then proceeds to follow instructions delivered through small headphones. The instructions consist of a taped record that tells the examiner when to start and stop talking to or touching the infant; for talking, it provides the actual phrases and intonation patterns for the examiner to mimic. Four different stimulation protocols, each 4.5 minutes in length, are used for each infant during different exams;

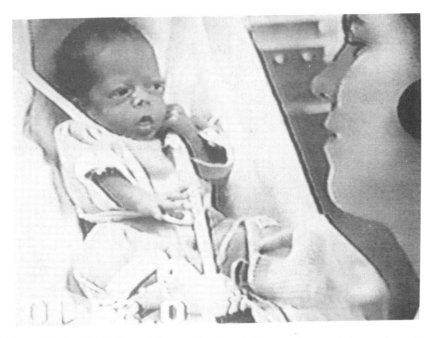

Figure 2.   An illustration of the positioning of the examiner and the newborn in our ongoing studies of premature newborns' behavioral responsiveness to human talk and touch.

two (Quiet and Talk) are involved in the present report. In the Quiet protocol, viewed as a baseline condition, the examiner simply remained quiet in front of the infant, maintaining a pleasant facial expression. The other protocols added further stimulation to this basic condition. In the Talk protocol, after 30 seconds of quiet, the adult talked to the infant in *motherese* during repeated 10-second bursts of speech separated by 5-second pauses, using the set phrases and intonation patterns of the taped instructions.

All very-low-birthweight infants at Duke Hospital who are inborn and from a five-county area are being recruited to this study and a companion 4-year follow-up study. Depending upon the infant's gestational age at birth, time of hospital discharge, and when he or she is medically stable, exams with the different protocols are done on successive days in counterbalanced order at 29–30, 31–32, 33–34, and 35–36 weeks' postconceptional age. Only a few preliminary findings can be presented at this point. These findings are based on a single behavioral measure (eyes open) and the first 50 infants tested with all protocols between 33 and 36 weeks' postconceptional age (the age range during which the highest proportion of subjects was examinable). Only the Talk and Quiet protocols are contrasted here since the other protocols require additional behavioral measures before meaningful contrasts can be made.

With our various manipulations prior to an exam, these infants began our exams in the desired awake, nonagitated state about half the time (53%). Within-subjects comparisons between the Quiet and Talk protocols were possible for 16 infants who were in the desired state at the start of both protocols. Between-subjects comparisons were possible for an additional 21 infants (8 who were in the desired state for the Quiet and 13 for the Talk protocol). For present purposes, an awake nonagitated state was defined as having the eyes open during at least 30% of the first 30-second period of the exam (during which the examiner remains silent), being judged to be predominantly awake or drowsy during this period, and the absence of fussing/crying or extensive facial grimacing during this period. All coding of behavior is done from videotaped records using a computer-based system that records the time of onset and offset of each behavior code.

Given that the infants began in an awake, nonagitated state, the Quiet and Talk protocols led to markedly different amounts of time with the infants' eyes open. For both within- and between-subjects comparisons the average amount of eye opening at the start of the exam was high (around 80%) and not significantly different for the two protocols (Figure 3). During the Talk protocol, infants maintained their eye opening virtually through the entire 4.5 minute exam. During the Quiet protocol, in contrast, they spent progressively less time with their eyes open as the exam proceeded. As a result, talking led on average to infants' spending 46 seconds more with their eyes open during the last 4 minutes of the exam, $t(15) = 2.547$, $p<.025$, two-tailed, for the within-subjects comparison, and 74 seconds more for the between-subjects comparison, $t(19) = 2.327$, $p< .025$.

Even with only a single behavioral measure to work with, we can get some clues about how talking leads to more total eye opening and hence what this increased eye opening might look like to parents. Talking led to more prolonged individual episodes for eye opening. The protocols did not differ significantly in their overall number of bouts of eyes open, but they differ markedly in the average duration of a bout of eyes open: 54 seconds for the Talk protocol versus 18 seconds for the Quiet protocol in the within-subjects comparison, $t(15) = 1.830$, $p <.05$; 38 versus 15 seconds for the between-subject comparison, $t(19) = 1.800$, $p< .05$. The possibility that the progressive decrease in eye opening for the Quiet protocol may simply reflect progressively more infants falling asleep as the exam proceeded was also explored. This, however, appears not to be the case. In fact, during the last minute of the exam the number of infants who had their eyes closed most of the time was equivalent for both the Quiet and Talk protocols—12% for the within-subjects and around 30% for the between-subjects comparisons.

Strong contrasts between how higher versus lower biological risk infants respond to these two protocols cannot be made yet: Final designations of risk status based on head growth have not been made for some infants and the n's for

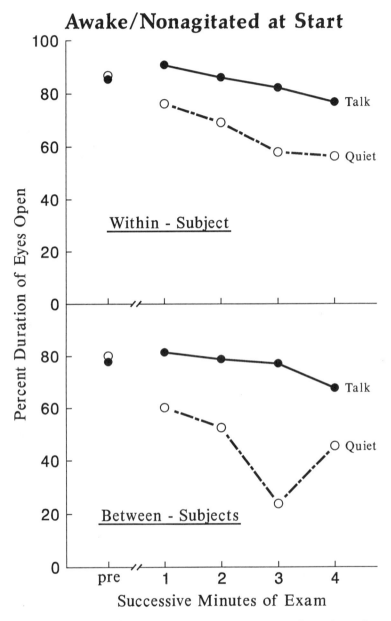

Awake/Nonagitated at Start

Figure 3. Contrasts in the amount of time premature newborns have their eyes open during the course of exams in which the examiner either remains quiet in front of the newborn (Quiet) or talks in *motherese* (Talk). The top panel presents a within-subject contrast for the 16 newborns successfully tested with both types of exams; the bottom panel, a between-subjects contrast for those newborns successfully tested with only one type of exam, either Quiet ($n = 8$) or Talk ($n = 13$).

these analyses are still quite small. Nevertheless, preliminary examination of the data suggests that the conclusions stated for the entire sample hold for each risk group considered separately. If anything, the reported differences between the protocols are accentuated for the higher risk infants.

Ongoing coding is capturing several further aspects of the infants' behavior, especially their facial expressions and limb movements. When these codings are completed, we can begin to describe very-low-birthweight infants' behavioral responsiveness to social stimulation further and explore the meaning of these responses for both the infant and parent. For example, we can ask about the behavioral accompaniments of longer bouts of eyes open. Are longer bouts accompanied by limb inactivity and relaxed or attentive facial expressions? Or, do we find increased limb activity and progressively more facial grimacing as these bouts continue? And so on. It is our strategy to explore empirically the organization of these infants' behavioral responsiveness in the face of social stimulation in order to understand better these infants' characteristics as early social partners for their parents and to reason about the effects of different types of stimulation upon the current functioning of these infants.

Despite the preliminary nature of the data presented, we can draw some conclusions about very-low-birthweight infants' responsiveness to human speech as an element contributing to their early postnatal interactions with others. First, the present findings confirm those of the earlier study in documenting the salience of human speech to these infants from long before term age. Second, these findings go beyond the earlier findings to document clearly the ability of human speech to maintain or prolong an awake, visually attentive state presumed conducive to social interaction. Finally, both the size of the effect of talking upon eye opening (almost 20% more time with eyes open in a 4-minute period) and the form of the effect (longer individual bouts of eyes open) suggest that this aspect of infant responsiveness to parental action is potentially perceptually salient to parents. It remains, however, to understand what infant behavioral cues are salient to their parents, how these cues are interpreted, how parents attempt to get their babies to respond to them, and their goals in these early interactions. A second line of research has sought beginning answers to these questions.

HOW PARENTS OF VERY-LOW-BIRTHWEIGHT INFANTS TALK ABOUT THEIR EARLY ATTEMPTS TO INTERACT WITH THEIR INFANTS

To discover elements parents of very-low-birthweight infants bring to their early interactions with their infants, we have begun to systematically talk to mothers about these interactions. The data reported here come from interviews with mothers 3 to 5 weeks after their very-low-birthweight infant's birth, while their infants were still hospitalized but after the mothers had had a number of opportunities to interact with their infants in the hospital. Mothers were selected only on the basis of their having given birth to a very-low-birthweight infant meeting the requirements for enrollment in our studies of infant behavior and developmental outcome. The sample of 24 mothers reported upon here was quite heterogeneous. Mothers ranged in age from 17 to 37 years (mean = 26) and in education from failure to complete high school to college degrees (mean = 13 years). Half were white and 59% were first-time mothers. Two mothers had given birth to triplets and one, to twins. Their infants, too, were heterogeneous. They averaged 28.5 weeks' gestational age (range: 24 to 33) and 32 weeks' postconceptional age at the time of the interview; they were about equally divided between males and females.

Mothers were interviewed during a return visit to the nursery by a single interviewer (JMO), who is both a developmental psychologist and a psychiatric clinical nurse specialist experienced in neonatal intensive care. She was familiar to the mothers at the time of this interview as a result of several prior contacts, including an interview during the first 10 days after birth. Upon the interview at 3 to 5 weeks after their infant's birth, mothers were told that we wished to learn more about the mother's experience of having a premature infant and her thoughts about interacting with her baby. The semi-structured interview consisted of 28 questions that addressed in turn the mother's feelings about the premature birth, her perception of her infant's medical condition, how she compared her infant to a full-term infant and what she saw as her infant's special needs, and her experiences in interacting with her baby. Only the final topic is considered here; relevant questions are listed in Table 3. Interviews averaged about 40 minutes in length, with a few as short as 20 minutes and some lasting as long as 90 minutes. Interviews were audiotaped, transcribed verbatim, and entered into a computer program that could sort responses by mother, by question, and by designated key words. Commonalities in mothers' responses will be stressed here in an effort to capture some of the elements mothers of very-low-birthweight infants typically bring to their very early interactions with their babies. Three topics are examined in turn: (a) mothers' perceptions of their infants' responsiveness to them, (b) infant behavioral cues mothers may use in regulating their interactions, and (c) mothers' goals in these early interactions.

Mothers' perceptions of infant responsiveness. All mothers viewed themselves as trying to get their newborn infants to respond to them and most (92%) felt that their infants did respond: 19 claimed such responsiveness without reservation, 3 said they thought their infants responded, and 2 said that their infants were really too young or little to tell. Mothers quantified their babies' responsiveness in terms of how frequently their visits led to some indication of response, not in terms of how often their babies responded to their attempts during a visit. Roughly equal numbers thought their infants responded (a) every time they visited, (b) during most or a lot of their visits but not all, or (c) during fewer of their visits. Half of those in the latter two categories spontaneously described visits when their baby did not respond no matter what they or anyone

Table 3. Questions About Mother's Interactions with Her Baby

1. I am also interested in knowing more about what it is like to try to get a premature baby to respond to you. What do you do to try to get him/her to respond to you?

2. Do you think your baby tries to respond to you?

3. What does he/she do?

4. How often do you think these things (named above) happen?

5. Do you try to get your baby to respond to you first, or do you wait for him/her to respond to you?

6. How long do you think your baby responds to you at one time?

7. What does your baby do that tells you to keep on or stop playing with him/her?

8. Sometimes it is difficult to get a premature baby to respond to you. Are there things your baby does that make it hard for you?

9. What do you think is the benefit of playing with your baby at this time? How do you see yourself as helping your baby?

10. Mothers have also told me that sometimes when they are playing with their baby, he/she looks away from them at things in the room for a while and then looks back to them. Does your baby ever do this? What do you think is happening at those times? What do you do?

11. Does your baby ever fuss when you are trying to get his/her attention? What do you think is going on? What do you usually do?

12. On the other hand, babies at this age may sometimes get very quiet, or still, and stare at their mothers. Are there times when your baby does this? What do you do?

13. How would you describe your baby's personality at this age? What stands out in your mind about how he acts with you?

else did. Regardless of the frequency of their infants' responsiveness, mothers agreed that the usual duration of bouts of responsiveness was brief; 68% described them as lasting only a few minutes (2–5 minutes), 5% as "little" or "brief," and 18% as measured in seconds.

The mothers also described specific behaviors of their infants that they interpreted as responsiveness. Answers to Questions 1 through 6 were examined for such descriptions. The greatest number of mothers mentioned opening their eyes (86%), followed by reaching for or grabbing onto their clothes or hand (36%), smiling or grinning (27%), some other general form of body movement such as "moves" or "stretches" (27%), calming down if fussing or crying (18%), and movements suggestive of agitation such as squirms, goes rigid, or jumps (14%). Only the first three (eyes open, reach/grab, and smile) were mentioned by multiple mothers as their first description of how their infants showed their responsiveness. Of these, infants' eye opening seemed an especially salient cue: Almost all mothers mentioned eye opening either first or second (86%), over half (59%) mentioned it more than once, and well over a third (41%) went beyond talking about eye opening to describe their infants as looking at them or orienting toward them.

Most mothers, too, were able to articulate links between specific actions on their part and specific responses on their infant's part. The entire interaction segment of the interview was searched for articulations of such contingencies. Eighteen of the 22 mothers claiming responsiveness (82%) provided them at least once: 15 for their talking to their infant, 11 for some form of touching their infant, and 4 for some combination of their talking to and touching their infant. Clear commonalities in the links expressed occurred only for their talking to their infants, where 87% of the mothers articulated a link between their talking to their infant and their infants' eyes. Most expressed this link as simply their infant's eyes opening or widening (67%), but 47% talked about their infants' looking directly at them or trying to look toward the source of the sound in response to their talking. Many fewer mothers (29%) mentioned their infant's eyes when expressing links to their touching of their baby or their talking and touching together.

The infant responses expressed for touching or both talking and touching were strikingly diverse (jerks as if ticklish, jumps, squirms, wiggles around, body relaxes, calms down, gets real upset, smiles, frowns, wakes up, goes asleep, screams, eyes open, reaches toward me, grabs my finger, clings to my hand). Only four of these infant responses other than eye opening were mentioned by more than a single mother: wakes up, by two mothers; squirms, wiggles, jerks, or jumps, by three; smiles, by two; and grabs on or holds hand, by three. Attempts to relate type of infant response to type of touching did not reveal any clear commonalities. In part this may be due to the mothers' lack of specificity in describing their physical contacts with their infants (e.g., "touch"); but even when the form of touching was more explicitly described, quite different infant responses were mentioned. For example, rubbing was described as leading to both waking up and going to sleep; and tickling, as producing smiles, eye opening, and squirming.

Potential infant cues mothers use. The interview data also provide insights into what infant behaviors mothers use as cues as to how they should behave in interaction with their infant. First, we looked for clearly articulated links between their infants' behavior and their own subsequent actions in two ways: (a) by collecting all such links mentioned spontaneously throughout the interview, and (b) by examining the links mentioned in Questions 10–12, which explicitly prompted their expression for infants' looking away from the mother, fussing or crying, and staring at the mother (prompted links). Few mothers (25%) gave spontaneous links of this nature; but two specific links were mentioned more than once. The opening of the infants' eyes was seen as prompting mothers' talking by three mothers; the infants' sleeping, as prompting tactile stimulation (touch, stroke, rub) also by three mothers. Even when explicitly prompted to express such links, relatively few mothers did so—41% for the infant looks away, 40% for the infant fusses, and 43% for the infant stares at mother. Those links most frequently mentioned were staring at the mother prompting talking (38%), looking away prompting talking (23%), fussing prompting holding baby tightly (15%), fussing prompting talking (15%), and staring at the mother prompting smiling (14%).

Second, we examined all responses to Question 7 about what their infant does to tell them to keep on or stop playing with them. Most (88%) could articulate something that told them to stop; fewer (60%) could articulate what told them to keep on. For stopping, the most frequently mentioned cues were a frown or mean, serious, wrinkled, or ugly face (33%); fussing or crying (21%); falling asleep or acting sleepy (17%); moving a lot as described by jerking, squirms, wiggles, keeps moving (17%); and closes eyes (17%). For keeping on, these cues were eyes open (33%), a pleasant facial expression or smile (12%), lying still (8%), and moving their arms or legs (8%).

Finally, we gathered all descriptions of their infant's behavior given in response to the first 10 questions, whether or not the mother linked the infant's behavior to her behavior. These descriptions provide a measure of what infant behaviors were salient or noteworthy to these mothers, and hence were potential cues for regulating their interactions. As shown in Table 4, mothers most frequently talked about their infants' eyes, whether frequency was measured as percentage of mothers mentioning a particular behavior, percentage of mothers mentioning this behavior among the first three behavioral descriptions they gave, or the percentage of mothers who mentioned a behavior in response to more than one question. Virtually all mothers mentioned eye opening; over a third mentioned their infant looking at them, and fewer mentioned eye closing. The next most frequently mentioned aspect of infant behavior was the sleep/awake state of the infant, with sleep being mentioned somewhat more frequently than awake. Descriptions of body movements and facial expression followed closely as the third and fourth most often mentioned aspects of infant behavior. Most descriptions of body activity were fairly nonspecific (e.g., "moves," "stretches"). Among the more specific descriptions, descriptions suggesting the quieting of body activity or being motorically quiet occurred somewhat more often than those suggesting jerky or agitated movements. "Positive" facial expression (smile/grin) and "negative" ones were mentioned roughly equally often. Interestingly, several mothers seemed to have no ready conventional terms to describe faces they viewed as negatively toned; such faces were described as "making a face," "wrinkled up," "mean," or "ugly." Only two mothers mentioned infant yawning. Specific activities of the arm or hand and vocal sounds were less often mentioned and less frequently repeated. Finally, descriptions of physiological cues (changes in color and drops in oxygen saturation level) were quite

Table 4. Relative Frequency with Which Various Infant Behaviors Were
Mentioned by Their Mothers

Infant Behavior	Percentage Who Mention	Percentage Who Mention Early	Percentage Who Mention Repeatedly
Eyes	96	92	75
Open	96	83	58
Look at me	42	29	12
Close	25	4	8
State	75	50	58
Asleep	75	42	29
Awake	54	17	17
Body Movement	71	42	38
Quiet/relaxed	38	8	8
Moving	50	33	25
Jerks/startles	21	8	4
Facial Expression	67	33	25
"Positive"	42	21	12
"Negative"	38	17	8
Yawn	8	0	4
Arms/Hands	42	25	8
Grab onto me	25	21	4
Reach to me	12	12	4
Other	8	0	4
Cry/Fret/Scream	33	4	12

infrequent (21% mentioned at some point), and never included among the first three descriptions of infant's behavior or responsiveness.

When these three analyses are summarized, it is apparent that infants' eye activity is an especially salient cue to mothers. It was most frequently mentioned in the specific links mothers articulated between their infant's behaviors and their own subsequent responses. It, too, was most frequently mentioned as a cue that told mothers to continue playing with their infant; and it occurred most often among all the ways mothers described their infants' behavior.

Mothers' goals in early interactions. Implicit in the prior analyses was the mothers' goal of trying to get their infants to respond to them: All mothers could articulate ways they "tried to get their baby to respond to them." We examined further goals, however, by explicitly asking mothers about what they saw as the benefits of these early interactions for their infants. All except three mothers (88%) readily described at least one specific benefit they saw in these early interactions. The benefits fell into three categories: (a) helping the infant know the parent; (b) letting the infant know he or she is loved or giving the infant comfort; and (c) stimulating the infant in ways facilitative of their development or learning.

The most frequently cited benefit was that of helping the infant know the parent; such statements occurred almost twice as often as statements falling in either of the latter two categories. Half the mothers clearly articulated this benefit first; one other clearly mentioned it later, and four others made less clear statements that nevertheless talked about the infant learning something about them (e.g., "tells her that I love her"). Altogether 71% of the mothers seemed to view their interactions with their newborn infants as somehow helping the baby get to know them. Of those mothers clearly articulating this benefit, half also explicitly talked about the infant coming to know them in distinction from the many other people around them. As one mother expressed it: "I hope he'll learn my voice and learn to recognize it and know not to be afraid of me. I'm not coming to do what the nurses do, just to touch him and make him feel good. He'll know that somebody comes just to touch me and make me feel good."

The other two categories of benefit were mentioned about equally often and by roughly a quarter of the mothers. In the second category were such statements as "It gives her comfort," "It makes her feel happy," and "It helps her to feel special." Statements concerning stimulation included "It helps him learn," "It stimulates her . . . talking to her helps her develop her hearing," and "Whatever you can do to help them grow, whether it's making them look toward a certain noise or whatever."

FROM DISCOVERING ELEMENTS TO UNDERSTANDING FORMS OF SOCIAL INTERACTION

The findings presented here are a start on understanding the elements contributing to the earliest postnatal interactions of very-low-birthweight infants and their parents. They show that even the very immature and high-risk very-low-birthweight infant is behaviorally responsive to postnatal forms of social stimulation—and differentially responsive to talking, forms of touching, and the combination of talking and touching. Further, some aspects of their responsiveness are similar to those discussed for healthy, full-term newborns. Talking, for example, can elicit an awake state in infants who are asleep, maintain and prolong a visually attentive state in infants who are already awake, and calm motorically aroused, agitated infants. These are all phenomena mentioned for full-term infants. In contrast, however, adding light stroking to talking often does not support this visually attentive state in very-low-birthweight infants; rather, it can lead to a motorically aroused state marked with avoidance cues, especially in higher risk infants. Although comparable studies have not yet been done with full-term newborns, we would expect differences based on our own observations and the reports of the touching and talking typically engaged in by mothers of full-terms.

We have caught hints, too, of some of the elements contributed by the parents of very-low-birthweight infants. First, they bring both a desire to obtain from their newborns signs of responsiveness to them and the belief that their infants respond to them and somehow know them—elements similar in broad strokes to our full-term model. The frequency and duration of their experience of such responsiveness, however, seems of another order of magnitude than for full-term parents; responsiveness is measured by its occurrence at some point during an often extended visit with their babies rather than by how often it occurs per maternal attempt to elicit responsiveness. Second, both full-term and very-low-birthweight parents seem to emphasize their infants' eye opening and the importance of eye contact, although it remains unclear whether this cue of responsiveness holds different meanings or salience for these different groups of parents. Too, it appears likely that the very-low-birthweight infants' eye openings may be accompanied by different behavioral cues than for full-terms (e.g., McGehee & Eckerman, 1983), altering parents' perceptions of and perhaps attributions about their infants' eye opening. Third, parents of very-low-birthweight infants report talking to and touching their newborns in a variety of ways; but it remains unclear how often talking and touching are presented together. We can speculate that parents' tendency to provide active touching along with their talking fails to complement their infants' tendency to show more eye opening when talked to alone. Finally, it seems clear that parents of very-low-birthweight infants have at least one different goal in their early interactions with their infants—to have their infants not only know them but distinguish them from the many other people caring for them and often hurting them.

Our increasing understanding of the elements very-low-birthweight infants and their parents contribute to their early interactions naturally prompts questions about the forms of social interactions to be found between them. How do these elements and others still to be discovered act together to generate relatively stable and recognizable forms of social interaction? What are these forms, and how do they compare to those of full-term newborns and their parents? What are the consequences of these forms of social interaction both for the contemporaneous functioning of very-low-birthweight infants and their subsequent development? Our research increasingly moves to address these questions.

In searching for answers to such questions, we have found our thinking congruent with the dynamic systems model of behavioral organization and development briefly outlined at the start of this chapter (cf. Eckerman & Stein, 1990; Fogel & Thelen, 1987; Thelen, 1989). This perspective, which emphasizes that the source of form is to be found in the interrelationships among the multiple contributing elements, is a radical departure from the more usual positing of central regulators within the individual as the source of order (e.g., neural maturation, cognitions, or affective states). Others have posited that the source of order comes from outside the individual (e.g., cultural expectations, socialization pressures). Either way, these traditional approaches have focused upon one element, or one set of elements, among many, assuming this set of elements to be critical both for the generation of orderly developmental change and for the order existing in an individual's behavior at any one developmental point.

In contrast, in the dynamic systems model no one contributing element is given precedence over others in the generation of form in behavior, and no distinction is made between elements existing within versus outside the individual. Form arises from the ways in which multiple elements act together; it arises in the process of interaction, rather than being the result of some preexisting information or plan. With development, individual elements change in their properties, and new elements come into play; some of these changes so alter the constraints operating among the diverse elements that the system reorganizes into a new stable form of behavior. Thus, this perspective emphasizes the importance of discovering the multiple contributing elements, their interrelationships, and the stable forms of behavior resulting from these elements and their interrelationships. At this point, we can only sketch the next two steps in our efforts to move from the discovery of contributing elements to understanding early forms of social interaction for very-low-birthweight newborns.

Our first step seeks to understand how the multiple contributing elements relate to one another, for it is these interrelationships that enable the complex system of elements to self-organize into one or a few stable forms of social interaction. We have begun this study of interrelationships. Our planned analyses of the temporal relationships existing between different aspects of very-low-birthweight infants' behavior, for example the opening of their eyes and their body movements and facial expressions, illustrate one type of interrelationship— interrelationships within the individual. We expect different interrelationships among behavior for very-low-birthweight infants versus full-term newborns (cf. McGehee & Eckerman, 1983), as well as for very-low-birthweight infants varying in perinatal biological risk (Oehler et al., 1988). Also begun is the task of empirically assessing how specific elements in the partner's behavior interrelate with specific elements within the infant. For example, in our ongoing work we are presenting different standardized episodes of social stimulation to the infant and assessing the differential impacts of these elements upon the behavioral organization of the infant. Only envisioned are various manipulations of the infants' behaviors in order to assess their impact upon parents. Selected aspects of our videotaped infant behavior, for example, could be presented to parents to probe which behaviors they key in on and remember and their attributions about these behaviors.

In our second step, armed with greater knowledge of the contributing elements and their interrelationships, we will plunge into the core task of searching for the stable recognizable forms of interaction. In seeking these forms, our focus will be upon discovering the patterns existing for very-low-birthweight infants and their parents, rather than solely upon assessing the extent to which their interactions match or diverge from the forms of behavior typical of full-term infants. As argued earlier, the stable behavior patterns to be found in the interactions of very-low-birthweight infants and their parents may differ qualitatively from those of full-term infants. Within a complex system, even a slight change in a single contributing element can lead to the system of elements self-organizing into a quite different form. Thus, we will seek the stable interaction patterns of the very-low-birthweight population through detailed study of the interactions of individual dyads within this population. We plan to begin this task by tracing the interactions of individual dyads from the hospital period through the first 3 or 4 months in the home, using contrasts to help us detect the forms that exist. First, we will contrast interactions at different points in the development of the infant, covering a span of development expected to yield different forms of interaction. Second, we will contrast the interactions for groups of very-low-birthweight infants chosen for their very different behavioral characteristics during their intensive care nursery stay; again, we expect contrasts in the forms of parent–infant interaction that emerge.

Beyond these two next steps, many further steps remain. Are the forms of social interaction discovered facilitative of very-low-birthweight infants' functioning? How do they enable the infant and parent to address such major developmental tasks of the newborn period as the regulation of emotional arousal or the regularization of physiological processes? Can they be altered in ways more facilitative of very-low-birthweight infants' current functioning and subsequent development? How do the details of such interaction patterns impact upon developmental change in the elements involved and hence upon subsequent patterns of interaction?

The challenges are immense, yet the promised rewards are great. Clinically, we expect our inquiry to provide sorely needed information about the behavioral organization of very-low-birthweight infants of varying degrees of perinatal biological risk and about how postnatal forms of social stimulation can facilitate both the development of these high-risk newborns and the partnership emerging between the parent and infant. Theoretically, we expect new insights into general principles of behavioral organization and developmental change, parental scaffolding, the impact of an infant's own functioning on contemporaneous social interactions, and the processes by which perinatal biological risk is translated into later problems of behavioral development.

REFERENCES

Alegria, J., & Noirot, E. (1978). Neonate orientation behavior towards human voice. *International Journal of Behavioral Development, 1,* 291–312.

Alfasi, G., Schwartz, F.A., Brake, S.C., Fifer, W.P., Fleischman, A.R., & Hofer, M.A. (1985). Mother–infant feeding interactions in preterm and full-term infants. *Infant Behavior and Development, 8,* 167–180.

Als, H. (1979). Social interaction: Dynamic matrix for developing behavioral organization. *New Directions for Child Development*, *4*, 21–39.

Als, H. (1983). Infant individuality: Assessing patterns of very early development. In J.D. Call, E. Galenson, & R.L. Tyson (Eds.), *Frontiers of infant psychiatry* (pp. 363–387). New York: Basic Books.

Als, H. (1984). *Manual for the naturalistic observation of newborn behavior (preterm and fullterm infants).* (Rev. ed.). Boston: The Children's Hospital.

Als, H., Lawhon, G., Brown, E., Gibes, R., & Duffy, F.H. (1986). Individualized behavioral and environmental care for the VLBW preterm infant at high risk for bronchopulmonary dysplasia. *Pediatrics*, *78*, 1123–1132.

Aylward, G.P. (1982). Forty-week full-term and preterm neurologic differences. In L.P. Lipsitt & T.M. Field (Eds.), *Infant behavior and development: Perinatal risk and newborn behavior* (pp. 67–83). Norwood, NJ: Ablex Publishing Corp.

Bakeman, R., & Brown, J. (1980). Analyzing behavioral sequences: Differences between preterm and full-term infant-mother dyads during the first months of life. In D.B. Sawin, R.C. Hawkins, L.O. Walker, & J.H. Penticuff (Eds.), *Exceptional infant* (Vol. 4, pp. 271–299). New York: Brunner/Mazel.

Beckwith, L., Cohen, S.E., Kopp, C.B., Parmelee, A.H., & Marcy, T.G. (1976). Caregiver-infant interaction and early cognitive development in preterm infants. *Child Development*, *47*, 579–587.

Bjorklund, D.F. (1987). A note on neonatal imitation. *Developmental Review*, *7*, 86–92.

Brazelton, T.B. (1973). *Neonatal Behavioral Assessment Scale*. Philadelphia: Spastics International Medical Publications, Lippincott.

Brazelton, T.B., Koslowski, B., & Main, M. (1974). The origins of reciprocity: The early mother-infant interaction. In M. Lewis & L.A. Rosenblum (Eds.), *The effect of the infant on its caregiver* (pp. 49–76). New York: Wiley.

Brazy, J.E., Eckerman, C.O., Oehler, J.M., Goldstein, R.F., & O'Rand, A.M. (1991). Nursery neurobiologic risk score: Important factors in predicting outcome in very-low-birthweight infants. *Journal of Pediatrics*, *118*, 783–792.

Censullo, M., Lester, B., & Hoffman, J. (1985). Rhythmic patterning in mother-newborn interaction. *Nursing Research*, *34*, 342–346.

Crnic, K.A., Greenberg, M.T., Ragozin, A.S., Robinson, N.M., & Basham, R.B. (1983). Effects of stress and social support on mothers and premature and full-term infants. *Child Development*, *54*, 209–217.

DeCasper, A.J., & Fifer, W.P. (1980). Of human bonding: Newborns prefer their mothers' voices. *Science*, *208*, 1174–1176.

DiVitto, B., & Goldberg, S. (1979). The effects of newborn medical status on early parent-infant interaction. In T.M. Field, A.M. Sostek, S. Goldberg, & H. H. Shuman (Eds.), *Infants born at risk* (pp. 311–331). New York: Spectrum.

Dodd, B. (1979). Lip reading in infants: Attention to speech presented in- and out-of-sychrony. *Cognitive Psychology*, *11*, 478–484.

Eckerman, C.O., & Stein, M.R. (1990). How imitation begets imitation and toddlers' generation of games. *Developmental Psychology*, *26*, 370–378.

Eckerman, C.O., Sturm, L.A., & Gross, S.J. (1985). Different developmental courses for very-low-birthweight infants differing in early head growth. *Developmental Psychology*, *21*, 813–827.

Eisenberg, R.B. (1976). *Auditory competence in early life*. Baltimore: University Park Press.

Fernald, A. (1984). The perceptual and affective salience of mothers' speech to infants. In L. Feagans, C. Garvey, & R. Golinkoff (Eds.), *The origins and growth of communication* (pp. 5–29). Norwood, NJ: Ablex Publishing Corp.

Field, T. (1981). Infant arousal, attention and affect during early interactions. In L.P. Lipsitt & C.K. Rovee-Collier (Eds.), *Advances in Infancy Research* (Vol. 1, pp. 57–100). Norwood, NJ: Ablex Publishing Corp.

Field, T., Hallock, N., Ting, G., Dempsey, J., Dabiri, C., & Shuman, H.H. (1978). A first-year follow-up of high-risk infants: Formulating a cumulative risk index. *Child Development, 49*, 119–131.

Field, T.M., Woodson, R., Greenberg, R., & Cohen, D. (1982). Discrimination and imitation of facial expressions by neonates. *Science, 218*, 179–181.

Fogel, A., & Thelen, E. (1987). Development of early expressive and communicative action: Reinterpretng the evidence from a dynamic systems perspective. *Developmental Psychology, 23*, 747–761.

Fox, N.A., & Davidson, R.J. (1986). Taste-elicited changes in facial signs of emotion and the asymmetry of brain electrical activity in human newborns. *Neuropsychologia, 24*, 417–422.

Gleick, J. (1987). *Chaos*. New York: Penguin Books.

Goldberg, S., Brachfeld, S., & DiVitto, B. (1980). Feeding, fussing, and play: Parent-infant interaction in the first year as a function of prematurity and perinatal medical problems. In T.M. Field, S. Goldberg, D. Stern, & A.M. Sostek (Eds.), *High-risk infants and children: Adult and peer interactions* (pp. 133–153). New York: Academic Press.

Goren, C.C., Sarty, M., & Wu, P.Y.K. (1975). Visual following and pattern discrimination of face-like stimuli by newborn infants. *Pediatrics, 56*, 544–549.

Green, J.G., Fox, N.A., & Lewis, M. (1983). The relationship between neonatal characteristics and three-month mother-infant interaction in high-risk infants. *Child Development, 54*, 1286–1296.

Gross, S.J., & Eckerman, C.O. (1983). Normative early head growth in very-low-birthweight infants. *Journal of Pediatrics, 103*, 946–949.

Gross, S.J., Oehler, J.M., & Eckerman, C.O. (1983). Head growth and developmental outcome in very-low-birthweight infants. *Pediatrics, 71*, 70–75.

Gunther, M. (1961). Infant behavior at the breast. In B.M. Foss (Ed.), *Determinants of infant behavior* (Vol. 1). London: Methuen.

Haith, M.M., Bergman, T., & Moore, M.J. (1977). Eye contact and face scanning in early infancy. *Science, 198*, 853–855.

Helm, J.M. (1988, April). *Maternal interpretations of preterm infant behaviors*. Paper presented at the International Conference on Infant Studies, Washington, DC.

Hofer, M.A. (1981). *The roots of human behavior*. San Francisco: W.H. Freeman.

Holmes, D.L., Nagy, J.N., Slaymaker, F., Sosnowski, R.J., Prinz, S.M., & Pasternak, J.F. (1982). Early influences of prematurity, illness, and prolonged hospitalization on infant behavior. *Developmental Psychology, 18*, 744–750.

Kaye, K., & Wells, A.J. (1980). Mothers' jiggling and the burst-pause pattern in neonatal feeding. *Infant Behavior and Development, 3*, 29–46.

Korner, A.F., & Thoman, E.B. (1972). The relative efficacy of contact and verstibular-proprioceptive stimulation in soothing neonates. *Child Development, 43*, 443–453.

Krafchuk, E.E., Tronick, E.Z., & Clifton, R.K. (1983). Behavioral and cardiac responses to sound in preterm neonates varying in risk status: A hypothesis of their paradoxical reactivity. In T. Field & A. Sostek (Eds.), *Infants born at risk: Physiological, perceptual, and cognitive processing*. New York: Grune and Stratton.

McGehee, L.J., & Eckerman, C.O. (1983). The preterm infant as a social partner: Responsive but unreadable. *Infant Behavior and Development, 6*, 461–470.

Meltzoff, A.N., & Moore, M.K. (1983). Newborn infants imitate adult facial gestures. *Child Development, 54*, 702–709.

Minde, K., Perrotta, M., & Marton, P. (1985). Maternal caretaking and play with full-term and premature infants. *Journal of Child Psychology and Psychiatry, 26*, 231–244.

Minde, K. Whitelaw, A., Brown, J., & Fitzhardinge, P. (1983). Effect of neonatal complications in premature infants on early parent-infant interactions. *Developmental Medicine and Child Neurology, 25*, 763–775.

Oehler, J.M., Eckerman, C.O., & Wilson, W.H. (1988). Social stimulation and the regulation of premature infants' state prior to term age. *Infant Behavior and Development, 11,* 333–351.

Pederson, D.R., Bento, S., Chance, G.W., Evans, B., & Fox, A.M. (1987). Maternal emotional responses to preterm birth. *American Journal of Orthopsychiatry, 57,* 15–21.

Riese, M.L. (1987). Longitudinal assessment of temperament from birth to 2 years: A comparison of full-term and preterm infants. *Infant Behavior and Development, 10,* 347–363.

Rovee-Collier, C.K., & Lipsitt, L.P. (1982). Learning, adaptation, and memory in the newborn. In P. Stratton (Ed.), *Psychobiology of the human newborn* (pp. 147–190). New York: Wiley.

Sander, L.W., Stechler, G., Burns, P., & Lee, A. (1979). Change in infant and caregiver variables over the first two months of life: Integration of action in early development. In E.B. Thoman (Ed.), *Origins of the infant's social responsiveness* (pp. 349–407). Hillsdale, NJ: Erlbaum.

Schaffer, H.R. (1984). *The child's entry into a social world.* London: Academic Press.

Sherrod, L.R. (1981). Issues in cognitive perceptual development: The special case of social stimuli. In M.E. Lamb, & L.R. Sherrod (Eds.), *Infant social cognition: Empirical and theoretical considerations.* Hillsdale, NJ: Erlbaum.

Snow, C.E. (1984). Parent-child interaction and the development of communicative ability. In R.L. Schiefelbusch, & J. Pickar (Eds.), *The acquisition of communicative competence* (pp. 71–107). Baltimore: University Park Press.

Sostek, A.M., Quinn, P.O., & Davitt, M.K. (1979). Behavior, development and neurologic status of premature and full-term infants with varying medical complications. In T.M. Field, A.M. Sostek, S. Goldberg, & H.H. Shuman (Eds.), *Infants born at risk* (pp. 281–300). New York: SP Medical and Scientific Books.

Spelke, E.S., Cortelyou, A. (1981). Perceptual aspects of social knowing: Looking and listening in infancy. In M.E. Lamb & L.R. Sherrod (Eds.), *Infant social cognition: Empirical and theoretical considerations* (pp. 61–84). Hillsdale, NJ: Erlbaum.

Stern, D. (1977). *The first relationship.* Cambridge, MA: Harvard University Press.

Stern, D.N., Jaffe, J., Beebe, B., & Bennett, S.I. (1975). Vocalizing in unison and in alternation: Two modes of communication within the mother-infant dyad. *Annals of the New York Academy of Sciences, 263,* 89–100.

Telzrow, R.W., Kang, R.R., Mitchell, S.K., Ashworth, C.D., & Barnard, K.E. (1982). An assessment of the behavior of the preterm infant at 40 weeks conceptional age. In L.P. Lipsitt & T.M. Field (Eds.), *Infant behavior and development: Perinatal risk and newborn behavior.* Norwood, NJ: Ablex Publishing Corp.

Thelen, E. (1989). Self-organization in developmental processes: Can systems approaches work? In M. Gunnar (Ed.), *Systems and development: The Minnesota symposium in child psychology* (Vol. 22). Hillsdale, NJ: Erlbaum.

Thoman, E.B., Barnett, C.R., & Leiderman, P.H. (1971). Feeding behaviors of newborn infants as a function of parity of the mother. *Child Development, 42,* 1471–1483.

Trevarthen, C. (1979). Communication and cooperation in early infancy: A description of primary intersubjectivity. In M. Bullowa (Ed.), *Before speech: The beginning of interpersonal communication.* Cambridge, UK: Cambridge University Press.

6

The Development and Social Competence of a Preterm Sample at Age 4: Prediction and Transactional Outcomes*

Mark T. Greenberg
Heather Carmichael-Olson
Keith Crnic

Preterm birth is believed to be a significant risk factor for a variety of social and cognitive delays, or deficiencies, in early childhood. During the first 2 years, much evidence shows that preterm generally display processing and developmental deficits, both mental and motor, as compared to fullterms (Bennett, 1984).

A considerable amount is also known about mother–infant interaction. Early in life, preterm mother–infant dyads often strike an atypical equilibrium in interaction compared to full-term dyads. They show proportionately more maternal activity and lower infant social responsiveness than do full-term dyads, and their interaction partners are usually less contingently responsive and more stereotyped (Bakeman & Brown, 1980; Barnard, Bee, & Hammond, 1984; Crnic, Greenberg, Ragozin, Robinson, & Basham, 1983; Field, 1977, 1979; McGhee & Eckerman, 1983). Further, the interactions of preterm dyads do not appear to be as satisfying as those of full-term pairs; mothers show less positive affect, as well as lower sensitivity, and the preterm infant shows more negative affect in interaction than does a full-term baby (Crnic et al., 1983; Field, 1980; Goldberg, 1979). High levels of maternal activity and stimulation usually continue throughout the first year (Crnic, Ragozin, Greenberg, Robinson, & Basham, 1983).

In spite of early differences, by the second year of life the effects of prematurity appear to attenuate, at least for healthy children born in recent cohorts (Kitchen, Ryan, Rickards, Astbury, Ford, Lissenden, Keith, & Keir, 1982; Drillien, Thomson, & Burgoyne, 1980; Bennett, 1984). In the cognitive domain,

* This study was supported by continuing research grant support from DHHS, Maternal and Child Health Services (MC-R-530431 and 530517). We are grateful to the mothers and children who participated in the study. We also wish to acknowledge the excellence of our research staff members: Kathy Sullivan, Shannon Meyer, Maura Costello, Emily Farrell, Sally Stuart, Debbie Preller, Joni Padur, Chris Akutsu, Debbie Campanella, Stella Chow, Monica Galloway, Robin Lacy, Lee Merrill, Chris Montagne, Chris Sanders, and Nora Stern. We are especially indebted to Dr. Nancy Slough for her work in conceptualization and analysis.

preterms born more recently score within the normal range according to test norms (Cohen & Beckwith, 1979; Jacob, Benedict, Roach, & Blackledge, 1984; Wallace, 1984). Yet their scores are often somewhat lower than matched full-term controls (Field, Dempsey, & Shuman, 1983; Kitchen, Rickards, Ryan, Ford, Lissenden, & Boyle, 1986). However, in earlier cohorts, weaknesses among preterms have been uncovered in verbal and nonverbal cognition, language development, visuomotor skills, and school achievement. This suggests that preterms may be at risk for learning disabilities (Bennett, 1984; Blackman, Lindgren, Hien, & Harper, 1987; Drillien et al., 1980; Eilers, Desai, Wilson, & Cunningham, 1986; Hunt, 1981; Klein, Hack, Gallagher, & Fanaroff, 1986; Nickel, Bennett, & Lamson, 1982; Ungerer & Sigman, 1983).

In general, there appears to be wide heterogeneity in preterm samples, and it is likely that factors such as biological integrity (Blackman et al., 1987; Crisafi & Driscoll, 1989; Hunt, Cooper, & Tooley, 1988; Janowsky & Nass, 1977; Landry, Fletcher, Zarling, Chapieski, & Francis, 1984; Lloyd, Wheldall, & Perks, 1988; Meisels, Plunkett, Roloff, Pasik, & Steifel, 1986), medical intervention (Kitchen et al., 1986), and family environment (Siegel, 1984) all play a role in cognitive and linquistic outcomes. During the past few decades, there have also been important changes in medical and clinical intervention that have led to greater effectiveness and higher survival rates for very-low-birthweight infants. Due to these cohort effects, it is difficult to generalize from past findings to the current cohort of preterm infants (Kitchen et al., 1986; Kopp, 1983).

Far less is known about cognitive and, especially, social outcomes as preterms move into their childhood years. This is particularly true among recent birth cohorts who have received more advanced medical care and show higher rates of survival, but were often smaller and more vulnerable at birth. The existing data seem to indicate that ill or neurologically impaired preterms demonstrate social deficits (Astbury, Orgill, & Bajuk, 1987; Escalona, 1982; Field et al., 1983; Landry et al., 1984; Lloyd et al., 1988; Ross, Lipper, & Auld, 1985). However, among relatively healthy preterms, social behavior and parent–child interaction may approach normalcy at least after the first year (Bakeman & Brown, 1980; Greenberg & Crnic, 1988; Jacob et al., 1984; Rauh, Achenbach, Nurcombe, Howell, & Teti, 1988; Ungerer & Sigman, 1983).

Given the early preterm biological difficulties, as well as the psychological trauma, often experienced by parents (Jeffcoate, Humphrey, & Lloyd, 1979; Pedersen, Bento, Chance, Evans, & Fox, 1987), the cognitive and social outcome for preterms are not as poor as might be expected. Such findings have prompted researchers to investigate systematically the multivariate and interactive influences of biological, social/ecological, and interactional variables on infants at biological risk (Greenberg & Crnic, 1988; McCormick, 1989; Siegel, 1982, 1984; Sigman, Cohen, Beckwith, & Parmelee, 1981). In the present project, we investigated what factors mediate developmental outcomes of preterms in the first four years of life.

A transactional model. From the outset of the project, the developmental process of preterm children was conceptualized within a transactional framework (Sameroff & Chandler, 1975). A transactional framework suggests developmental models that involve complex feedback systems involving continual interplay between the developing child and changing environment (Sameroff & Seifer, 1983). In this view, multiple factors must be assessed to explain development, and different factors may assert their importance at different points in ontogeny (Hoy, Bill, & Sykes, 1988). Given this assumption, we attempted to assess the child and aspects of the child's environment frequently during the first 4 years of life.

The transactional view may be considered as one developmental model of general systems theory (Sameroff, 1982). As such, a relevant systems principle pertaining to the question of biological risk is that of *equifinality,* which states that dissimilar starting conditions may lead to similar end results. From this principle emerges the notion of *self-righting,* suggesting that, in some instances, the developmental process is characterized by a tendency to compensate for traumatic, nonnormative influences and can thus protect the organism (McCall, 1981; Sameroff, 1982).

Previous research attempting to identify salient self-righting influences in preterms suggested that the influence of biological variables, such as birth status and illness, declines as the child grows older. However, the quality of direct parent–infant interactions and the nature of the home environment appeared to maintain or grow in influence in infancy and early childhood.

The Mother–Infant Project

In this report, we examine cognitive, linguistic, and social outcomes of preterm and full-term children at 4 years of age. The present report consists of the fifth follow-up of a longitudinal study contrasting outcomes and patterns of development between preterm and full-term children, beginning at birth (Carmichael-Olson, 1986; Crnic et al., 1983; Crnic & Greenberg, 1987; Greenberg & Crnic, 1988). Throughout the project we have attempted to examine how variables assessing the domains of child biological status, family demographics, family support systems and stresses, the quality of the family environment, parental attitudes, and the nature of mother–child interaction impact on the social, cognitive, and linguistic development of the growing child. We first review findings from the first 2 years of life.

During the first year of life, the preterms in this project scored significantly lower on measures of mental, communicative, and motor development (corrected for gestational age). Preterm dyads engaged in fewer reciprocal interactions, and the infants were less responsive and displayed more negative affect. The mothers of preterms displayed less sensitivity and satisfaction during face-to-face interactions. However, no group differences were found in the quality of the home environment (Crnic et al., 1983) or in the quality of attachment relations at one year of age (Crnic, Greenberg, & Slough, 1986). By age 2, these premature children no longer differed significantly from their full-term controls on measures of mental or linguistic development, though the preterms received lower developmental motor scores. Differences in the quality of mother–child interaction and affect were no longer apparent (Greenberg & Crnic, 1988).

Although preterm and full-term dyads had reached similar developmental outcomes by 2 years of age, longitudinal analyses revealed that ecological, maternal, and interactional factors differentially accounted for preterm and fullterm outcomes. In general, more variance was explained among the preterms in both developmental and, especially, interactional outcomes. Notably, different aspects of the environment influenced the two groups. Among the preterms, early maternal attitudes and the quality of the home environment were significantly related to outcome. In contrast, full-term outcomes were influenced by more distal demographic variables, such as socioeconomic, welfare, and marital status. Counterintuitively, the preterm infant's degree of biological risk was negatively related to outcome (Greenberg & Crnic, 1988).

The fourth-year phase is reported here and discussed in detail by Carmichael-Olson (1986). Of particular interest at this phase of the study was the investigation of differential transactions leading to social outcomes, as well as the structure of social behavior in these children at age 4. We were particularly interested in the child's social outcomes at age 4, because at this point the child faces two important developmental tasks: (a) the regulation of affect, and (b) the establishment of peer relations in the preschool. Further, at approximately age 4 it is possible to reliably assess risk for childhood externalizing behavior problems (Campbell, Ewing, Breaux, & Szumowski, 1986).

In the 4-year phase we examined three major outcomes. First, we examined cognitive and linguistic development. Between the ages of 2 and 4 years there is significant subskill differentiation, and it thus becomes possible to assess how preterm birth might differentially affect aspects of verbal and nonverbal forms of cognition. Second, we examined the child's social competence by assessing multiple perspectives, including: (a) parental report of behavior problems, positive social skills, temperament, and ego control and resilience; (b) child report of perceived competence; and (c) observer report of the child's behavior under moderate stress. Third, we continued to collect information on social/ecological and interactional factors that we presumed would affect these child outcomes.

METHODS

Sample and Data Collection Procedures

The sample was composed of relatively healthy, low-birthweight and very-low-birthweight preterm children and their mothers, along with a case-matched sample of full-term mother–child pairs. Child subjects were born in 1979–1980.

Preterm children had birthweights less than 1,801 grams, and gestational ages under 38 weeks. Full-terms weighed more than 2,500 grams, with gestational ages of 39–42 weeks. Full-terms were matched according to race, maternal education, and family structure. Groups were balanced for infant's sex, birth order, and type of delivery. Demographic characteristics for the original sample are given in Crnic et al. (1983).

Data were collected at 1, 4, 8, 12, 18, and 24 months (corrected age), and at 48 months (chronological age). The corrected age score served as the data collection criterion during infancy, since it is thought that maturational characteristics are most significant during early development. At age 4, chronological age was used as the scheduling and scoring criterion, since experiential characteristics increasingly assert their importance over time.

At 1 month, the sample included 52 preterm and 53 full-term mother–child dyads. There was variable sample attrition. For the entire sample attrition ranged from 12.4% at 4 months; 33.3% at 24 months; 21% at 48 months. There was somewhat less attrition in the full-term group at 48 months: 26.9% for preterms and 15.1% for full-terms.

The fourth-year phase, the focus of this report, involved 38 preterm and 45 full-term dyads from the original group. The fourth-year sample showed only two differences from the original sample when the two groups were compared on 14 biological and demographic characteristics. Those who dropped out at 48 months had mothers who were somewhat less educated, $t(104) = -2.18$, $p < .05$, and had children with shorter gestational ages (younger at birth), $t(104) = -1.95$, $p = .05$. Sample characteristics are presented in Table 1.

Comparing the preterm and fullterm groups on 12 biological and demographic characteristics, there were three significant differences. The preterm group had a lower corrected age score ($t(81) = -5.15$, $p < .001$), an artifact of the decision to use chronological age as the data collection criterion. As was true in the original sample, mothers of preterms were slightly older (1.6 years) than their full-term counterparts $t(80) = 2.03$, $p < .05$. This difference, along with the discrepancy in age according to environmental status, required use of maternal age as a covariate in all between-group statistical analyses. There was no difference between preterms and fullterms on maternal education, but the preterms did show a somewhat higher socioeconomic status (mean difference of 6.1 units, though both groups had middle class means, $t(80) = 2.11$, $p = .05$. This difference suggested the use of environmental status, along with birth status, in a two-factor examination of group differences.

The sample followed at 48 months continued to be largely middle class, but with a full range of socioeconomic scores. The sample was divided into low, medium, and high environmental status subgroups according to socioeconomic status (SES), as measured by the Four-Factor Hollingshead index. Two major differences were found between the three SES subgroups: the lower the socioeconomic status, the more optimal the child's overall biological status, and thus the healthier the child. In addition, the lower the social status, the more likely the

Table 1.   Characteristics of Preterms and Full-Terms

Variable	Preterms (n = 38)			Full-terms (n = 45)		
	M or n	low–high	%	M or n	low–high	%
Child Characteristics:						
Corrected C.A. (months)	47.26	44–51	—	49.02	47–52	—
Sex (male)	22	—	57.9%	21	—	46.7%
Firstborn	22	—	57.9%	27	—	60%
Birthweight (grams)	1388.2	840–1800	—	3488.7	2600–4500	—
Gestation (weeks)	31.37	26–36	—	40.62	39–42	—
Days in hospital from 1m data	34.29	5–106	—	2.84	1–11	—
Presence of IRDS	19	—	50%	0	—	0%
Postnatal health factors score (higher = better health)	71.94	50–160	—	149.80	87–160	—
Childhood health (higher = better health)	2.29	1–3	—	2.67	1–3	—
Family Characteristics:						
Maternal age (years)	30.43	21–46	—	28.09	21–41	—
48-month maternal educational level (years of school)	13.00	10–18	—	13.24	9–19	—
4-Factor Family Hollingshead Score	38.32	14–66	—	32.33	12–66	—
Ethnicity (white)	32	—	84.2%	33	—	73.3%
Presence of income supplement	12	—	31.6%	9	—	20.0%

mother to be younger, on welfare, living alone, and of minority status (Carmichael-Olson, 1986).

Longitudinal data collection. To examine transactions, both child and environment were assessed with multiple measures over time. Data were gathered at several ecological levels. Table 2 presents information on the measures at each time period.

At 1 and 48 months, the mother–child pairs were visited in their homes. At 4, 8, 12, and 24 months, data collection occurred at The Child Development and Mental Retardation Center (CDMRC) at the University of Washington. Demographic and attitudinal information was collected from the mothers through structured interviews (at 1, 8 and 48 months) and questionnaires (at all time periods). The children were tested at 4, 12, 24, and 48 months to obtain developmental data. At the 4, 8, 12, and 24 month time periods, interactional

Table 2. Measures Utilized at Each Time Period

Date and Location	Child Biological Information	Child Developmental Information	Child Social Behavior	Mother–Child Interaction	Global Environmental Information	Maternal Attitudes
1 month (Home)	BIOSUM (see Text) SGA				Maternal Age, Education, Ethnicity, Marital Status	(IPE) Inventory of Parent Experiences Maternal Satisfaction
4 Months (Lab)		Bayley Scales		Quality of Mother–Infant Interaction in Free Play		
8 Months (Lab)			Infant Temperament	Same as above at 4 Months	Modified HOME Inventory	Same as 1 Month
12 Months (Lab)		Bayley Scales		Same as above at 4 Months added book-reading task		
24 Months (Lab)		Bayley Scales PPVT SICD		Same as above at 12 months		Same as 1 Month
48 Months (Home)	Child Health 1–4 Years	WPPSI subtest Information Block Design PPVT VMI	5 measures listed in Table 3 (from factor analysis)	Quality of Mother–child interaction in "Waiting Task"	Hollingshead 4-Factor SES Index	Same as 1 Month

131

data were gathered in a laboratory playroom. In each of these videotaped sessions, the pairs engaged in a 10-minute unstructured free play episode, followed by a semistructured episode that varied in length and content at each age. At the 48-month session, the dyads were observed during a 10-minute semistructured interaction in their homes.

MEASURES

Child Biological Status

Data obtained from hospital records included the child's birthweight, gestational age (Dubowitz, Dubowitz, & Goldberg, 1970), sex, presence of IRDS (infant respiratory distress syndrome), and SGA (small for gestational age), number of days in the hospital, and infant postnatal health complications. A postnatal factor score (PNHEALTH) was created according to a procedure developed by Littman and Parmelee (1978). The child's health from age 1½ to 4 years (KIDHEALTH) was measured by a 3-point severity rating of maternal descriptions of the child's illnesses, accidents, and developmental problems over that time period (interrater reliability calculated as percentage of agreement was 95%).

A summary score for biological risk status, BIORISK, was computed for the preterm sample by summing the z-scores of the following variables: birthweight, gestational age, IRDS (present or not present), and number of days in hospital prior to discharge (alpha = .69).

Earlier and Concurrent Child Developmental Status

Early. At 4, 12, and 24 months, developmental mental and motor status was assessed via the Bayley Scales of Infant Development (Bayley, 1969). Receptive language development was assessed at 24 months, using a combination of the Peabody Picture Vocabulary Test (PPVT) (Dunn, 1959) and the Sequenced Inventory of Communicative Development (Hedrick, Prather, & Tobin, 1975). The original version of the PPVT was used at age 4 to maintain comparability with the same measure which had been given at 2 years of age.

Concurrent. At age 4, three measures of developmental status were utilized. To assess general cognitive ability the Information and Block Design subtests of the Wechsler Preschool and Primary Scales of Intelligence (WPPSI) were administered. These two subtests were chosen because they correlate most highly with the WPPSI Verbal IQ and Performance IQ scores, respectively. Receptive language was again evaluated using the PPVT. Visuomotor skills were assessed using the Developmental Test of Visuomotor Integration (VMI) (Beery, 1967). For the VMI, age equivalent scores were calculated according to their chronological age (age from their actual birthdate) and using their conceptual age (age calculated from expected date of birth).

Earlier and Concurrent Child Social Behavior and Temperament

Early. During the early phases of the project, aspects of temperament were examined. Temperament measures included factors from the Sostek and Anders's (1977) instrument, used at 1 month, and the three subscales (mood, intensity, and distractibility) from the Carey Infant Temperament Scale (Carey & McDevitt, 1977), which was used at 8 months.

Concurrent. At 48 months, multiple measures of social behavior were chosen to assess this multidimensional construct. The five instruments, all with acceptable reliability and validity, and the summary measures derived from them, are listed in Table 3. Multiple viewpoints were tapped (e.g., parent, observer, and child self-report). *Product* vs. *process* definitions of child social behavior were evaluated. A *product* measure indicates how the rater (and the culture) label the child's behavior (e.g., internalizing problems, sociable), while a *process* measures yields a theoretical profile of the child's approach to the world (e.g., degree of emotional control). Measures were also chosen to assess the three domains of positive aspects of competence, behavior problems, and temperamental characteristics.

Table 3.   48-Month Measures of Child Social Behavior

Measure	Summary Variables Utilized
California Child Q-Set (Block & Block, 1969)	Ego control Ego resiliency
Child Behavior Checklist (CBCL) (Achenbach & Edelbrock, 1983)	Externalizing T-score Internalizing T-score Social Competence Score
Health Resources Inventory (HRI) (Gesten, 1976)	Frustration tolerance Good student Gutsy Peer sociability Rule-following
Perceived Competence Scale (Harter & Pike, 1981)	Peer Acceptance Maternal Acceptance
Dimensions of Temperament Scale (DOTS) (Lerner et al., 1982)	Activity Adaptability Attention span Reactivity Rhythmicity
Observer's Assessment of Child During Waiting Task	Sum of: 1. Child Affect 2. Child Style

"Proximal" Environmental Status: Mother–Child Interaction

Early. Interaction between mother and child was assessed in developmentally appropriate situations from 4 months to age 4. Unstructured free play was observed at each time period through 24 months. A semistructured observational episode was included at each visit, with different tasks used at different developmental periods.

At each time of assessment, interaction quality was rated separately for mother and child during the unstructured and semistructured episodes. Each measure represented the sum of three 5-point scales: mother gratification from interaction (degree of enjoyment), general affective tone (angry/irritated to happy), and sensitivity to infant cues (intrusiveness to synchrony), as well as infant gratification from interaction, general affective tone, and responsiveness to mother (avoidant to active involvement). Interrater reliability was calculated as percentage of exact agreement (4–12 months: 76%) and agreement within one scale point (4–12 months: 97%), and reliability from 4–24 months was similar. See Crnic et al. (1983) for further details regarding the rating scales and their psychometric properties.

Concurrent. Mother–child interaction at 48 months was coded live during a brief, semistructured observational situation, called the "Waiting Task," designed for this study. This task was conceived from an attachment theoretical viewpoint (Bowlby, 1969/1982; Marvin, 1977) and is described further in Carmichael-Olson (1986). It was designed to assess the "partnership" between a parent and preschooler engaged in a developmentally salient task. During the task the mother and child must wait for 10 minutes to open a gift that is in plain sight and that the child has been told is for him or her. To accomplish this task, the dyad must cooperate, setting up and carrying out a plan for waiting. For the child, waiting requires impulse control and attempts at cooperation, and the child was classified positively or negatively on his or her style during the waiting period. Maternal and child affect were rated on a 5-point scale of affective tone, from negative through flat/mixed to positive. Dyadic satisfaction was rated from 1 (low) to 5 (high). Interrater reliability was 92% for child style, 97% for maternal affect, and 92% for dyadic satisfaction. Eighty-four percent of the mothers noted that their child's behavior during this task was somewhat or very typical.

"Proximal" Environmental Status: Maternal Attitudes Toward the Child, Parenting and the Family

At 1, 8, and 48 months, maternal attitudes were assessed with the Inventory of Parenting Experiences (Crnic et al., 1983). The IPE includes two separate factors related to satisfaction with parenting: the mother's degree of pleasure in her child and in her parenting role. Summary variables at 1 and 8 months were formed by combining the measures of satisfaction with parenting, marital relations, and general life satisfaction. These summary variables, MOMATT1 and MOMATT8, showed acceptable internal consistency at both ages and for both groups (Greenberg & Crnic, 1988).

An interview adaptation of the HOME scale (Elardo, Bradley, & Caldwell, 1975) developed by Barnard and Bee (1983) was also administered at 8 months. A summary variable (HOMESUM) consisted of the sum of two of the HOME subscales; Provision of Appropriate Play Materials and Variety of Opportunities for Stimulation (the correlation between these two scales was .78).

RESULTS

Preterm–Full-term Analyses

Preterm–full-term group differences at 48 months were examined through a series of 2-factor ANCOVAs. Between-groups factors included birth status (preterm vs. full-term) and global environmental status (low, medium, and high socioeconomic status), while maternal age was used as a covariate (due to initial group differences previously described). Measures of 4-year cognition, language, visuomotor skill, and social behavior comprised the set of outcome variables.

Developmental skills. In contrast to the single group difference in motor skills at age 2, there were differences between preterms and fullterms in varied developmental domains, as can be seen in Table 4. Compared to full-terms, preterm children received lower scores on measures of nonverbal cognition, $F(6,72) = 9.8$, $p < .01$. For visuomotor performance, preterms were significantly poorer when chronological age (age since date of birth) was utilized, $F(6,70) = 7.2$, $p < .01$; however, there was no significant group difference when preterm corrected age was utilized. The preterms' lower mean scores still fell within normal limits. No differences were found in verbal abilities (PPVT or Information subtest of WPPSI).

Factor structure of social competence. As presented in Table 3, there were 17 scales derived from instruments that assessed social competence, and two child indices derived from the "Waiting Task" observations. All these scores were summarized in five factors, defined by a principal components analysis. The five factors accounted for 69% of the variance and were correlated less than .30 with each other. Five estimated factor scores were created for the entire sample (see Table 5). The reliability of the factors were acceptable, ranging from .62 to .91. The five factors represented parent (three separate factors), child and observer views of social behavior. Note that several of the individual scales from the 48-month temperament measure showed considerable unique variability, and were sometimes analyzed as separate outcome variables. There were no signifi-

Table 4. Preterm/Full-term Findings on Child Developmental and Social Outcomes at 4 Years

Measures	Preterm M (SD)	Full-term M (SD)
Developmental Skills:		
Receptive Language (PPVT)	100.6	106.6
	(15.7)	(17.8)
Verbal Cognition		
(WPPSI Information Scale Score)	11.1	12.0
	(3.0)	(2.8)
Nonverbal Cognition		
(WPPSI Block Design)	10.6**	12.6
	(2.5)	(2.8)
Visuomotor Skill		
(VMI—chronological age)	88.5*	99.1
	(15.5)	(17.2)
Visuomotor Skill		
(VMI—corrected age)	92.2	99.1
	(15.4)	(17.2)
Summary Social Outcomes:		
Summary Social Competence[a]	−3.4**	2.9
	(2.8)	(2.7)
Positive Social Skill (Parent View)	−0.9*	0.7
	(5.3)	(6.8)
Self-Control (Parent View)	−0.8*	0.6
	(3.5)	(4.0)
Absence of Behavior Problems		
(Parent View)	−0.8*	0.6
	(0.6)	(0.5)
Component Social Outcomes:		
Activity (Parent View)	1.3*	0.7
	(1.4)	(1.2)
Attention (Parent View)	4.6***	6.2
	(3.4)	(2.8)
Reactivity (Parent View)	3.3*	4.4
	(1.4)	(1.6)
Ego Resilience (Parent View)	0.4*	0.5
	(0.2)	(0.2)

[a]The summary social competence score combined the scores for all five factors assessing social competence.
*$p < .05$
**$p < .01$
***$p < .001$

Table 5.   Child Social Behavior Factor Scores

Label and Name of Factor	Definition of Factor (unstandardized alpha)	Reliability
PSOCSKILL: Parent View of Child Positive Social Skills	High scores reflect high scores on: CBCL Social Competence HRI Factors DOTS Adaptability Ego Resilience	.908
PCONTROL: Parent View of Child Self-Control	High Scores reflect low CBCL Externalizing scores DOTS Reactivity and high scores on: DOTS Attention Span Ego Control (balanced)	.731
PBEHWELL: Parent View of Absence of Behavior Problems	High scores reflect low: CBCL Externalizing CBCL Internalizing DOTS Activity	.703
OCONTROL: Observer View of Child Self-Control in Waiting Task	High scores reflects high: Child facilitation Child affect	.683
KDACCEPT: Child View of Social Acceptance	High Scores on: Maternal acceptance Peer acceptance	.620

cant differences in the relationship of the five factors when examined separately for the preterm and full-term samples.

Social competence findings. Mothers rated preterms lower than full terms on the social competence factors of positive social skills, $F(6,72) = 4.0$ $p < .05$, self-control, $F(6,72) = 4.4$, $p < .05$, and behavior problems $F(6,72) = 8.4$, $p < .01$ (see Table 4). More specifically, within the self-control factor, the mothers of preterms gave their children less optimal temperament ratings, reporting shorter attention span ($p < .001$), overactivity ($p < .05$) and overreaction to stimuli ($p < .05$). Within the positive social skills factor, preterms showed lower ego resiliency ($p < .05$).

There was no overall difference on the factor assessing child self-report. However, preterms did perceive lowered peer acceptance ($p < .05$), although this finding appeared to be true only in preterm boys. There was no difference in perception of maternal acceptance. Finally, the factor assessing observations of child coping (both affect and coping style) during the waiting task indicated no group differences.

Preterm–full-term differences in maternal attitudes and interaction measures. A factorial MANCOVA was used to examine the effects of birth status and socioeconomic status on the set of maternal attitude variables (life stress, social support, satisfaction with parenting, childrearing attitudes, and perceptions of the family environment). As at previous times of assessment, maternal attitudes remained similar in the preterm and full-term groups.

Group differences in 48-month mother–child interaction also were examined with a set of two-factor ANCOVAs. No significant preterm–full-term differences appeared on measures of dyadic satisfaction or maternal affect during the Waiting Task.

Social class differences. There were a number of significant main effects for socioeconomic status. All differences were in the expected direction, with children from higher SES backgrounds showing more optimal scores. Differences were found on receptive language (PPVT), $F(6,72) = 3.6, p < .05$, as well as the parents' view of positive social skills, $F(6,72) = 5.4, p < .01$, self-control, $F(6,72) = 6.3, p < .01$, and behavior problems, $F(6,72) = 8.0, p < .001$. No SES differences were found on either measure from the WPPSI (Block Design or Information), the VMI, or either the child or observer's view of social competence.

Percentage of cases delayed. A comparison was made of the percentage of preterm and full-term children achieving test scores below a cutoff point representing significant delay defined as either less than a scale score of 8 or a developmental quotient of less than 80. The results are presented in Table 6. These individual difference data confirmed the group difference findings. When compared to full-terms, data showed a greater percentage of preterms falling below the cutoff on academic measures, social competence, as well as a combined measure of overall delay.

Sex differences. Using Hotelling's T^2, the effect of child gender was examined across the total sample in three groups of dependent variables: child outcome, mother–child interaction, and maternal attitudes. There were no significant effects. Sex differences were then examined separately for preterms and fullterms. Significant differences emerged for preterms on the factors of parental view of positive social skills ($p < .01$), parent view of behavior problems ($p < .01$), and on the child's view of peer acceptance ($p < .01$). In all cases, preterm boys had lower scores than preterm girls. It should be noted that, although there were no significant differences on postnatal health among preterms, preterm males tended to have more frequent illness during childhood. In contrast, there were no sex differences on social outcomes within the full-term sample.

Table 6. Percentage Delayed on 4-Year Outcome Measures

	Percentage Delayed	
Measure	Preterm	Full-term
PPVT IQ Equivalent less than 90	24.3%	11.1%
WPPSI Information Scale Score < 9	18.9	13.3
WPPSI Block Design Scale Score < 9	19.4	8.9
VMI Developmental Quotient		
less than 90	51.4	31.8
less than 80	42.9	22.7
Summary Social Competence[a]		
1 S.D. below the mean	25.8	15.5
General Delay[b]	13.5	5.7

[a]The summary Social Competence score combined the scores for all five factors assessing social competence.
[b]To be included in "General delay" a subject had to score less than 8 (scale score), less than 80 (developmental quotient), or 1 s.d. below the mean on at least 3 of the above outcome scores.

Relations of Early Factors to 48-month Outcomes

Selected correlations between summary variables from the first two years and 48-month outcomes are shown in Tables 8 and 9. Table 7 provides descriptions of the abbreviations used in the following tables. As seen in earlier reports, patterns in the two groups were different. In both, however, there were many more findings for social and interactional outcomes than there were for developmental outcomes.

Cognitive outcomes. Among preterms, there were few significant relationships between early factors and later "academic" outcomes. Surprisingly, but consistent with findings at 2 years, neither biological risk or socioeconomic status were predictive of 4-year cognitive outcomes. Further, no 1- or 4-month variables (parent or child) predicted verbal or cognitive outcomes. However, at 8 months, parental ratings of child distractibility (8-month temperament factor), and baby affect during interaction were related to later verbal and language outcomes. Although 12-month MDI showed little continuity to 4 years, at 24 months both MDI and PDI scores predicted such outcomes.

In contrast, for full-terms, a host of variables including maternal early attitudes, maternal interaction, aspects of the global environment (SESRISK), and early infant mental development (12- and 24-month MDI) predicted language and verbal/cognitive performance. As expected, SES was most related to outcomes; however, maternal affect also consistently predicted outcomes.

Social outcomes. For preterms, more optimal biological status was related to

Table 7.   Legend for Abbreviated Variable Names

SESRISK	Socioeconomic Risk at 1-Month Combination of: 1. Marital Status 2. Maternal Education 3. Welfare Status
BIORISK	Biological risk Combination of: 1. Birthweight 2. Gestational Age 3. IRDS 4. Number of Days in Hospital
BDISTRACT8	Subscale of Carey Infant Temperament Scale (at 8 months)
HOMESUM	Sum of Two HOME Subscales: 1. Provision of Appropriate Play Materials 2. Variety of Opportunities for Stimulation
MOMATT1	Maternal Attitudes from the Inventory of Parent Experiences (at 1 month)
MOMATT8	Maternal Attitudes from the Inventory of Parent Experiences (at 8 month)
MAFFECT4	Summary ratings of Maternal Affect (4 months)
MAFFECT8	Summary ratings of Maternal Affect (8 months)
MAFFECT12	Summary ratings of Maternal Affect (12 months)
BAFFECT4	Summary ratings of Baby Affect (4 months)
BAFFECT8	Summary ratings of Baby Affect (8 months)
BAFFECT12	Summary ratings of Baby Affect (12 months)
MDI-12	Bayley Scale of Mental Development (12 Months)
PDI-12	Bayley Scale of Physical Development (12 Months)
MDI-24	Bayley Scale of Mental Development (24 Months)
PDI-24	Bayley Scale of Physical Development (24 Months)

higher scores on self-control, as well as the child's perception of acceptance by others. However, there was no relationship between BIORISK and parent ratings of positive skills or behavior problems, or a self-control rating by an outside observer during the Waiting Task. Sex strongly related to outcome in preterms with boys showing significantly lower social competence on four of the five factors.

Maternal attitudes and the quality of the home environment at 8 months, both "proximal" environmental measures, were significantly related to later social outcomes. However, the more "global" measure of socioeconomic status was not significantly associated with social skills.

Table 8. Correlations between Measures in the First 2 Years of Life and 48-Month Cognitive Outcomes in Preterm (PT) and Full-term (FT) Groups

	Cognitive/Developmental Outcomes			
	PPVT	WPPSI Information	WPPSI Block Design	VMI
1 month:				
BIORISK				
PT	NS	NS	NS	NS
SEX				
PT	− .32*	NS	NS	NS
FT	.00	NS	NS	NS
SESRISK				
PT	.09[a]	.16	NS	NS
FT	.58***	.42**	NS	NS
MOMATT1				
PT	.23	NS	NS	− .11[a]
FT	.50***	NS	NS	.39**
4 months:				
MAFFECT4				
PT	.08	NS	NS	− .14[a]
FT	.31*	NS	NS	.32*
BAFFECT4				
PT	NS	NS	NS	NS
FT	NS	NS	NS	NS
8 months:				
MOMATT8				
PT	.05	.03	NS	NS
FT	.27*	.31*	NS	NS
HOMESUM				
PT	.04	NS	NS	NS
FT	.29*	NS	NS	NS
BDISTRACT8				
PT	− .30*	− .47**[a]	− .48**[a]	− .33*
FT	.02	.09	− .06	.00
MAFFECT8				
PT	.05	.03	NS	NS
FT	.27*	.31*	NS	NS
BAFFECT8				
PT	.25	.33*	NS	NS
FT	.13	.21	NS	NS
12 months:				
MAFFECT12				
PT	.29	.22	NS	NS
FT	.40**	.35*	NS	NS
BAFFECT12				
PT	NS	NS	NS	NS
FT	NS	NS	NS	NS
MDI-12				
PT	.26	.22	.12	.19
FT	.22	.37**	.41***	.36**
PDI-12				
PT	NS	NS	NS	NS
FT	NS	NS	NS	NS

Table 8. (*Continued*)

	Cognitive/Developmental Outcomes			
	PPVT	WPPSI Information	WPPSI Block Design	VMI
24 months:				
MDI-24				
PT	.60***	.63***	.62***	.47**
FT	.44**	.61***	.39**	.32*
PDI-24				
PT	.37*[a]	.31*	NS	.30
FT	−.06	.16	NS	.14

*p < .05
**p < .01
***p < .001
[a]Correlations between preterm and full-term samples are significantly different.

Despite differences in patterning, for both groups maternal and child affect during the first year predicted later social outcomes. For full-terms, maternal affect at all three times was consistently predictive of later outcomes; in contrast, for preterms, maternal behavior only began to predict at 8 months of age. A similar pattern is shown for child affect, with full-terms' affect predicting at an earlier age. Although both 12- and 24-month MDI scores showed some predic-

Table 9. Correlations between Measures in the First 2 Years of Life and 48-Month Social Outcomes in Preterm (PT) and Full-term (FT) Groups

	Social Competence Factors				
	Positive Social Skills	Self-Control	Absence of Behavior Problems	Observer Control	Child Acceptance
1 month:					
BIORISK					
PT	NS	.33*	NS	NS	.43*
SEX					
PT	.38**	.43**[a]	.45***[a]	NS	.61***[a]
FT	.12	−.20	−.21	NS	.17
SESRISK					
PT	.23	.30*	.10[a]	NS	NS
FT	.44**	.43**	.53***	NS	NS
MOMATT1					
PT	.11[a]	.00	.12[a]	−.30	NS
FT	.64***	.34*	.58***	.04	NS
4 months:					
MAFFECT4					
PT	.25	.01[a]	.23	−.09	NS
FT	.37**	.42**	.35**	.33*	NS

Table 9.   (*Continued*)

	Social Competence Factors				
	Positive Social Skills	Self-Control	Absence of Behavior Problems	Observer Control	Child Acceptance
BAFFECT4					
PT	.17	.24	.20	.16	NS
FT	.34*	.31*	.29*	.36**	NS
8 months:					
MOMATT8					
PT	.32*	NS	.43**	NS	.30*
FT	.36**	NS	.38**	NS	.00
HOMESUM					
PT	.43**	NS	.30*	.31*	NS
FT	.08	NS	.32*	.09	NS
BDISTRACT8					
PT	NS	NS	NS	NS	.25
FT	NS	NS	NS	NS	.45**
MAFFECT8					
PT	.38**	.39**	.46**	NS	NS
FT	.43**	.44**	.40**	NS	NS
BAFFECT8					
PT	.40**	.12	.42**	NS	NS
FT	.37*	.45**	.28*	NS	NS
12 months:					
MAFFECT12					
PT	.46**	.22	.32*	.31*	NS
FT	.31*	.33**	.29*	.20	NS
BAFFECT12					
PT	.29	.30	.33*	.39*	.34*
FT	.10	−.10	−.08	.31*	.16
MDI-12					
PT	.38*	.27	.40**	NS	NS
FT	.30*	.29*	.29*	NS	NS
PDI-12					
PT	NS	NS	.33*a	NS	NS
FT	NS	NS	−.22	NS	NS
24 months:					
MDI-24					
PT	.55***	NS	.50**	.19	.11
FT	.34*	NS	.25	.38*	.42**
PDI-24					
PT	.34*a	NS	.42*a	NS	NS
FT	−.24	NS	−.10	NS	NS

*p < .05
**p < .01
***p < .001
aCorrelations between preterm and full-term samples are significantly different.

tion for both groups, 24-month MDI was a particularly strong predictor for both positive and negative social behavior in preterms.

There were a number of predictors that were unique to a single group. Being male, and 24-month physical development, only predicted positive and negative social behaviors for preterms. SES and maternal attitudes at 1 month only predicted social outcomes for fullterms.

Regression analyses. In order to examine more fully the relations between measures in the first year of life and 48-month outcomes, a series of regressions equations were computed. In all cases, 48-month outcomes were the criterion variables, and equations were conducted separately for preterms and full terms. It was hypothesized that significantly more variance in 48-month outcomes would be accounted for in the preterm group. Given both the sample size and collinearity of variables both within and between times of measurement, these analyses were conducted only for purposes of prediction, not explanation (Pedazur, 1982). The analyses combined hierarchical and stepwise procedures. Groups of predictor variables were entered hierarchically in steps; within each step a stepwise procedure was utilized to determine the order and significance of entry. Variables were entered in the following order: (a) SESRISK, BIORISK, and Sex; (b) MOMATT1; (c) 8-month variables, including maternal behavior ratings (MAFFECT8), child behavior ratings (BAFFECT8), and HOMESUM; (d) 12-month variables of maternal behavior (MAFFECT12), child behavior (BAFFECT12), and child mental (MDI12), and physical development (PDI12). Thus, the ordering was created in relation to developmental priority and maximizes the importance of demographic and 1-month variables. In order to maximize the number of degrees of freedom and thus limit the number of variables used in the equation, a variable did not enter the final equation unless it accounted for at least 5% of the variance. As the sample size was different between the two groups the F to enter was 1.8 for the preterm sample and 2.2 for the full-terms. Eighteen- and 24-month variables were not entered into the equation due to the sample size. Because only cases with no missing data at any time point were utilized for the regression analyses, relationships are somewhat different than shown in the preceding correlations.

Cognitive outcomes. The regressions for 48-month criteria involving child developmental outcomes are shown in Table 10. Similar amounts of variance in developmental outcome were accounted for in both groups. For receptive language outcomes, 36% of the variance was accounted for in preterms, with more positive maternal attitudes at 1 month being the only variable to significantly enter the equation. However, the preterms' behavior at 12 months and MDI score at 12 months contributed more than 5% of variance to the outcome. For the full-terms, SESRISK strongly predicted language outcomes, while early maternal attitudes tended also to do so.

For the WPPSI scales, only the preterms MDI at 12 months predicted later scores on the Information subtest; in contrast, only SESRISK predicted for full-

Table 10.   Results of Regressions for Prematures and Full-terms on Cognitive Outcomes at 48 Months

48-Month Outcome	Preterm			Full-term		
	Predictor	F	R^2 Change	Predictor	F	R^2 Change
PPVT	MOMATT1	4.5*	.18	SESRISK	18.0***	.36
	BAFFECT12	2.7	.10	MOMATT1	3.8*	.07
	MDI-12	3.2	.10	SEX	2.7	.05
$F(3,19) = 4.0*$, adjusted $R^2 = .36$				$F(3,30) = 7.2***$, adjusted $R^2 = .48$		
WPPSI-Information	MOMATT1	2.3	.09	SESRISK	5.0*	.14
	BAFFECT12	2.6	.10	PDI-12	3.0	.08
	MDI-12	6.7**	.21			
$F(3,19) = 4.3*$, adjusted $R^2 = .32$				$F(2,31) = 4.2*$, adjusted $R^2 = .21$		
WPPSI Block Design	SEX	2.1	.09	PDI-12	8.0**	.20
	HOMESUM	2.7	.11			
	MAFFECT12	3.5	.12			
$F(3,19) = 3.3*$, adjusted $R^2 = .22$				$F(1,32) = 8.0**$, adjusted $R^2 = .17$		
VMI	SEX	4.3*	.17	None Significant		
$F(1,21) = 4.3*$, adjusted $R^2 = .13$						

  * = $p < .05$
 ** = $p < .01$
*** = $p < .001$

terms. For the Block Design subtest, no variables significantly predicted for preterms and 12-month PDI predicted for full-terms. Thus, as indicated in Table 8, it is not until 24 months that developmental status begins to be predictive for the preterm sample.

Social outcomes. The regression equations for 48 month social competence outcomes are shown in Table 11. Sex was highly significant across all outcomes for preterms but had little predictive value in the full-term samples. In all cases, preterm boys were rated significantly less positive in social outcome. For the full-term sample, the two variables representing parental social risk and maternal early attitudes were predictive of both positive social skills/resilience, a *process* measure, and of behavior problems, a *product* measure. In the preterms, positive skills were predicted from being female, having low social risk, and lower biological vulnerability. Behavior problems were only predicted in preterms by being male, and lower maternal affect at the 8-month interaction. In the pre-terms, the rating of child self-control/temperament was predicted by being female, lower social risk, and more positive maternal affect at 12 months; only social risk mildly predicted this outcome in fullterms. Similarly, in the preterms, the child's self-report of social acceptance was predicted by being female, having less biological vulnerability; no variables predicted this outcome in the full terms.

Table 11. Results of Regressions for Prematures and Full-terms on Social Outcomes at 48 Months

48-Month Outcome	Preterm			Full-term		
	Predictor	F	R^2 Change	Predictor	F	R^2 Change
Positive Social	SEX	9.8**	.32	SESRISK	7.3**	.19
Skills	SESRISK	9.2**	.21	MOMATT1	19.4***	.31
	MAFFECT12	3.1	.07	BAFFECT8	5.0*	.07
	BIORISK	5.3*	.09			
$F_{(4,18)} = 10.0***$, adjusted $R^2 = .62$				$F_{(3,30)} = 13.3***$, adjusted $R^2 = .53$		
Self-Control	SEX	4.9*	.19	SESRISK	5.0*	.14
	SESRISK	5.4*	.17	MAFFECT8	3.1	.08
	BIORISK	2.8	.08			
	MAFFECT12	4.2*	.10			
$F_{(4,18)} = 5.0**$, adjusted $R^2 = .46$				$F_{(2,31)} = 3.3*$, adjusted $R^2 = .20$		
Absence of	SEX	6.8*	.24	SESRISK	10.2**	.24
Behavior	MAFFECT8	6.0*	.18	MOMATT1	11.0**	.20
Problems				HOMESUM	3.1	.05
$F_{(2,20)} = 5.0*$, adjusted $R^2 = .34$				$F_{(3,30)} = 9.7***$, adjusted $R^2 = .44$		
Observer Rating of Control	None Significant			None Significant		
Child Rating of	SEX	21.5***	.51	None Significant		
Social	BIORISK	6.4*	.12			
Acceptance						
$F_{(2,20)} = 12.0***$, adjusted $R^2 = .58$						

*$p < .05$
**$p < .01$
***$p < .001$

DISCUSSION

Though placed at risk by their very low birthweight, the prematurely born children in this study were relatively healthy and were recipients of the optimal medical care of Neonatal Intensive Care Units (NICU) in the early 1980s. After the first year, although the preterms were delayed in their cognitive and physical development, they appeared to be developing towards normalcy, suggesting that self-righting influences were at work. At age 2, both cognitive and linguistic development appeared normal and there were no marked differences in interactional skills. However, their physical development still lagged behind.

At age 4, most of these preterm children appeared to be on a fairly normal developmental trajectory, and their cognitive and social development was generally within normal limits. We once again found no differences in either receptive language or verbal development. But at age 4 the preterm group showed subtle skill deficits in the preacademic domains of nonverbal cognition (Block Design) and perceptual-motor skills. Further, two to three times as many preterms were showing mild delays across a number of different developmental domains. This pattern of differences in nonverbal skills and no differences in verbal skills are consonant with a number of recent reports (Breslau, Klein, & Allen, 1988; Jacob et al., 1984; Sostek, Katz, Valvano, & Smith, 1988).

Findings on social competence. Examined in depth, *subtle* social deficits were apparent as these preterm children reached preschool age and confronted a new set of developmental tasks. Compared to full-terms, parents of preterms reported their children to have a shorter attention span, to be overreactive, and to have a higher activity level, as well as less positive social skills and more behavior problems. These findings were especially true of preterm boys, and these boys, themselves, reported less acceptance by peers.

Findings from the present study extend the literature on social outcome among recently born preterms. Early on, temperamental differences have been found in ill preterm infants (Field et al., 1983; Goldberg, Brachfeld, & DiVitto, 1980), and personal-social delays have been reported in relatively unimpaired infants (Ungerer & Sigman, 1983). Other investigators have reported persistent social problems in ill preterms during the toddler and preschool years (Astbury et al., 1987; Escalona, 1982; Field et al., 1983). However, previous reports from this study and others have suggested that social behavior approaches normalcy among relatively healthy preterms, at least after the first year (Bakeman & Brown, 1980; Blackman et al., 1987; Ungerer & Sigman, 1983). The present data may indicate the reemergence of subtle social difficulties in *some* relatively healthy preterms during the preschool years.

Implications of 4-year findings. At present, it is unclear what these subtle differences portend for later development. However, even subtle deficits can be significant for a 4-year-old who is entering a preschool environment (Klein et al., 1986; McCormick, 1989). When placed in a preschool, an overreactive, active child with a short attention span might well be considered "difficult," a construct that predicts later behavior problems in middle class, nonproblem samples (Lee & Bates, 1985). A child with visuomotor problems may have later school difficulties. Siegel (1985) found that 4-year VMI scores showed the highest correlation of any measure at this age with 6-year school achievement scores. Recently, four other studies have also been reported to show a similar pattern of nonverbal, LD-type problems among preterms at ages 5 and 6 (Blackman et al., 1987; Klein et al., 1986; Saigal, Szatmari, Rosenbaum, Campbell, & King, 1990; Sostek et al., 1988)

Early factors and prediction of 4-year outcomes. In addition to group differences at 4 years in both the cognitive and social domain, differences also occurred in the *relationship* between these domains. In the full-term group, at 4 years, verbal and non-verbal cognitive abilities were significantly related to measures of social competence. In the preterms this was not so; that is, preterm children who were low in cognitive achievements might be high in social competence. As a result, one might expect that predictive factors would have domain-specific impacts on preterm outcomes. Our findings indicated that this was so. Thus, although early parent attitudes and infant distractability, as well as 24-month mental development, were related to the preterm's cognitive outcome at 4 years, different factors such as sex, parental social risk status, and maternal and infant social interactions predicted preterm social competence. Among full-terms, in contrast, not only were 4-year cognitive and social outcomes more interrelated, but similar factors (parental social risk and parent attitudes during infancy) predicted both domains of outcome.

The role early factors play in predicting 4-year outcomes is similar, in many ways, to those we have previously reported at 2 years of age for this same sample. First, biological risk within relatively healthy preterms plays a relatively small role; it does not predict cognitive outcomes, and it does not have a pervasive influence on development (Beckwith & Cohen, 1984). However, in the present analyses it did show some relationship to social outcomes. Second, it appears that global environmental factors that are included in the measure of social risk (maternal education, marital and welfare status) are much more predictive of full-term than of preterm outcomes. This finding is supported by a recent report that maternal education was more highly related to verbal skills in fullterm than in preterm children at 5 years of age (Blackman et al., 1987).

There were also important differences from our 2-year findings. At 2 years of age, preterm cognitive and social outcomes were related to maternal attitudes at 1 and 8 months, the baby's interactional skills and temperamental characteristics at 8 months, and the early quality of the home environment. However, at 4 years, the direct influence of early maternal attitudes and the quality of the home environment had declined. Do these findings mean that earlier findings at 2 years were either unstable or unimportant?

Transactional processes. We believe that it may be critical to apply a transactional model in interpreting these results. Within a transactional frame-work, it may be of little import to find that variables that were predictive of 2-year outcomes are no longer showing direct relationships to 4-year outcomes. This would be especially true if either discontinuity or a new stability occurs during this period. Such a condition holds in the present sample, as it is not until 24 months that the preterm's own cognitive status shows stability or begins to predict 4-year outcomes. Instead, one might consider that some variables such as early attitudes and the home environment may have had important short-term effects (i.e., they relate to 2-year cognitive outcomes); however, their importance begins to wane as the preterm begins to stabilize. Thus, these variables show an important and direct short-term effect, but an indirect long-term effect via their influence on 2-year outcomes. Other variables, such as biological or social risk status, may demonstrate a different pattern of influence showing little or no effects at one point and yet show significant prediction at other points in time.

Further, transactions may be quite different between preterm and full-term samples, even when the same outcome is reached (principle of equifinality). In this regard, maternal attitudes are a particularly interesting variable to contrast between the preterm and full-term groups. There were no differences between preterm and full-term mothers in their perceived satisfaction with their life, parenting, and their infant when they were home with the babies for 1 month. However, maternal satisfaction at 1 month was more highly related to low social risk in the full-term sample (Greenberg & Crnic, 1988). This association with social risk in the full-term sample might explain why these early attitudes/affects continue to show predictions to outcome at 4 years of age, as the role of global environmental variables is quite predictive of fullterm outcomes. In the preterm sample, however, one might expect that a variety of events during the preterm's hospital stay, maternal expectations regarding infant survival, and emotional and instrumental support from friends and extended family might have important short-term effects on the preterm mother's perceived satisfaction. Thus, global indicators of social risk may have less influence on the preterm mother's well-being (Parke & Tinsley, 1982; Pedersen et al., 1987). In the preterms, maternal attitudes at 1 month were related to quality of affect with the baby at 4 and 8 months as well as the quality of the home environment, and thus began a series of transactions that assisted the adaptation of both parent and infant. However, by the preschool years how mothers felt during the early time of crisis might no longer influence their child's current developmental course. Thus, the same factor might have widely different short-term and long-term effects in these two samples.

Compensatory mechanisms. The absence of direct, clearly identifiable long-term biological effects (i.e, those variable tied directly to the premature condition) may be related to compensatory mechanisms that are mediated through the parent's attitudes and behavior toward the very small and vulnerable infant. Specifically, when their infants had been home for 1 month, mothers who had the most vulnerable preterms reported significantly more positive attitudes toward their parenting role, more pleasure with and positive feelings towards their infant, greater satisfaction with their marital relationship, and greater general life satisfaction. Thus, there may be a sensitive period in the weeks following the preterm's arrival in the home that influences the mother's subsequent affective involvement with the infant.

It is not surprising to find some preterms with less than optimal development. What was surprising was the subtlety of these developmental problems, considering the preterm's early biological and interactional struggles. This prompted further examination of what factors might explain these self-righting influences. Of particular interest was the hypothesis that preterms who were raised in environment of high social risk would have the worst outcomes, for example, poor environmental circumstances would amplify the risk of premature birth (the "double whammy" hypothesis). However, while main effects were found for both prematurity and social risk/class, no such interaction effects were found.

Thus, although the biological characteristics of the infant (birthweight, gestational age, IRDS, days in the hospital) do not themselves predict outcomes, prematurity itself appears to impact interactional processes in such a way that the "expected" effects of SES do not as strongly influence outcomes. Maternal behavior appeared to act as a self-righting process, apparently independent of SES, becoming a particularly important influence for the preterms. Our speculations regarding the process notwithstanding, it is clear that environmental conditions operated differently to influence the outcomes of the two groups. It should be noted that our findings on the relative lack of impact of SES run counter to a number of recent studies of preterm children (Escalona, 1982; Ross et al., 1985).

Subgroup findings. It is clear that the preterm population is quite heterogeneous. Further, even within a healthy preterm sample there is considerable variability. An individual preterm child was more at risk for outcome problems, perhaps multiple problems, than was his or her fullterm peer. However, those with multiple difficulties were more likely to have experienced physiological sequelae such as mild cerebral palsy and hearing loss, as well as growth or communication disorders. There was one subgroup of preterm children who were consistently ill, an enduring influence, and these children were more often Caucasian and male. As few sex differences have been reported in the preterm literature, it may be wise not to overinterpret such a finding. However, the fact that males were perceived as less socially competent, were perceived as having characteristics more related to "difficult" temperament, and scored lower on visuomotor skills may indicate that they were neurologically immature. Such an interpretation would fit with previous findings in literature that both males and preterms are more likely to be disabled, to show difficulties in behavioral control, and higher rates of learning disabilities. These findings are in accord with those of Breslau and colleagues (1988), who report that only preterm males, and not females, show significantly higher rates of behavior problems and lower social competence at age 9 in comparison to matched controls. Regardless of the sex-linked nature of these specific findings, it appears clear that a subgroup of relatively healthy preterms are at risk for Attention Deficit Disorders and learning disorders (Astbury et al., 1986; Sostek et al., 1988; Saigal et al., 1990).

CONCLUSION

Clearly, many findings concerning the preterm developmental process fit a complex transactional model in which there is reciprocal causation between child, family, and environment. Multiple developmental factors were significant, salient factors changed over time, and self-righting seemed to be occurring. Developmental factors different from those that affected full-terms emerged as important, and influences were not always direct. Further, both continuity and discontinuity were manifest in these processes.

While we have attempted to isolate the effects of variables from different domains in explaining preterm development, it is clear that multiple causation is ubiquitous and reciprocal effects abound. As the assessment of such domains as child characteristics, parent attitudes and affects, the family system, and the social ecology improve, we will be better able to delineate the joint and independent effects such domains produce in concert with the infant's capabilities. We believe our investigation points to the need for more refined, multivariate longitudinal models to further unravel these developmental processes. Our findings point to a number of predictions. The manner in which the family and their ecology mobilize in response to the preterm birth will significantly impact the cognitions (attributions and expectations) and emotional outlook of the parents. Further, these cognitions and emotions will directly impact the child via parent–child interactions and indirectly through the environmental stimulation provided to the infant. However, we suggest that only in some cases will a positive social ecology serve to buffer the effects of biological risk. In order to delineate under what conditions buffering and moderating effects of the social environment might obtain, future studies will need to provide a more fine-grained analysis of homogeneous subgroups of preterms who are classified by a matrix of medical indicators in infancy.

REFERENCES

Achenbach, T.M., & Edelbrock, C. (1983). *Manual for the Child Behavior Checklist and Revised Child Behavior Profile*. Burlington, VT: University of Vermont.

Astbury, J., Orgill, A., & Bajuk, B. (1987). Relationship between two-year behaviour and neuro-developmental outcome at five years of very low-birthweight survivors. *Developmental Medicine and Child Neurology, 29*, 370–379.

Bakeman, R., & Brown, J.V. (1980). Early interaction: Consequences for social and mental development at three years. *Child Development, 51*(2), 437–447.

Barnard, K.E., & Bee, H.L. (1983). The impact of temporally patterned stimulation on the development of preterm infants. *Child Development, 54*(5), 1156–1167.

Barnard, K.E., Bee, H.L., & Hammond, M.A. (1984). Developmental changes in maternal interactions with term and preterm infants. *Infant Behavior and Development, 7*, 101–113.

Bayley, N. (1969). *The Bayley Scales of Mental and Motor Development*. New York: Psychological Corporation.

Beckwith, L., & Cohen, S.E. (1984). Home environment and cognitive competence in preterm children during the first 5 years. In A.W. Gottfried (Ed.), *Home environment and early cognitive development* (pp. 235–271). New York: Academic Press.

Beery, K.E. (1967). *Visual-motor integration: A monograph*. Chicago: Follett Publishing.

Bennett, F.C. (1984). Neurodevelopmental outcome of low-birth-weight infants. In V.C. Kelley (Ed.), *The practice of pediatrics* (Vol. 2, pp. 1–24). Philadelphia: Harper and Row.

Blackman, J.A., Lindgren, S.D., Hein, H.A. & Harper, D.C. (1987). Long-term surveillance of high-risk children. *American Journal of Diseases in Children, 141*, 1293–1299.

Block, J.H., & Block, J. (1969). *The California Child Q-Set*. Unpublished manuscript, University of California, Berkeley.

Bowlby, J. (1982). *Attachment and loss: (Vol. 1). Attachment* (2nd ed.). New York: Basic Books. (Original work published 1969)

Breslau, N., Klein, N., & Allen, L. (1988). Very low birthweight: Behavioral sequelae at nine years of age. *Journal of the American Academy of Child and Adolescent Psychiatry, 27*(5), 605–612.

Campbell, S.B., Ewing, L.J., Breaux, A.M., & Szumowski, E.K. (1986). Parent-referred problem three year olds: Followup at school entry. *Journal of Child Psychology and Psychiatry, 25*, 473–488.

Carey, W.B., & McDevitt, S.C. (1977). *Infant Temperament Questionnaire (for 4 to 8 month old infants).* Unpublished manuscript. (Available from the senior author, 319 West Front St., Media, PA, 19063.)

Carmichael-Olson, H. (1986). *Developmental process and outcome in preterm children: A transactional study.* Unpublished doctoral dissertation, University of Washington, Seattle.

Cohen, S.A., & Beckwith, L. (1979). Preterm infant interaction with the caregiver in the first year of life and competence at age two. *Child Development, 50,* 767–776.

Crisafi, M., & Driscoll, J. (1989, April). *Intellectual development at 3 years of age in very low birth weight infants.* Poster presented at the biennial meeting of the Society for Research in Child Development, Kansas City.

Crnic, K.A., & Greenberg, M.T. (1987). Transactional relationships between family style, risk status, and mother-child interactions with two-year-olds. *Journal of Pediatric Psychology, 12,* 343–362.

Crnic, K.A., Greenberg, M.T., Ragozin, A.S., Robinson, N.M., & Basham, R.B. (1983). Effects of stress and social support on mothers and premature and full-term infants. *Child Development, 54,* 209–217.

Crnic, K.A., Greenberg, M.T., & Slough, N.M. (1986). Early stress and social support influences on mothers' and high-risk infants' functioning in late infancy. *Infant Mental Health Journal, 7,* 19–33.

Crnic, K.A., Ragozin, A.S., Greenberg, M.T., Robinson, N.M., & Basham, R.B. (1983). Social interaction and developmental competence of preterm and full-term infants during the first year of life. *Child Development, 54,* 1199–1210.

Drillien, C.M., Thomson, A.J.M., & Burgoyne, K. (1980). Low-birthweight children at early school-age: A longitudinal study. *Developmental Medicine and Child Neurology, 22,* 26–47.

Dubowitz, L.M.S., Dubowitz, V., & Goldberg, C. (1970). Clinical assessment of gestational age in the newborn infant. *Journal of Pediatrics, 77*(1), 1–10.

Dunn, L.M. (1959). *Peabody Picture Vocabulary Test.* Circle Pines, MN: American Guidance Service.

Eilers, B.L., Desai, N.S., Wilson, M.A., & Cunningham, M.D. (1986). Classroom performance and social factors of children with birth weights of 1,250 grams or less: Follow-up at 5 to 8 years of age. *Pediatrics, 77,* 203–208.

Elardo, R., Bradley, R., & Caldwell, B. (1975). The relation of infants' home environments to mental test performance from six to thirty-six months: A longitudinal analysis. *Child Development, 46,* 71–76.

Escalona, S.K. (1982). Babies at double hazard: Early development of infants at biological and social risk. *Pediatrics, 70*(5), 670–676.

Field, T.M. (1977). Effects of early separation, interactive deficits, and experimental manipulations on infant-mother face-to-face interaction. *Child Development, 48,* 763–771.

Field, T. (1979). Games parents play with normal and high-risk infants. *Child Psychiatry and Human Development, 10*(1), 41–48.

Field, T.M. (1980). Interactions of preterm and term infants with their lower- and middle-class teenage and adult mothers. In T.M. Field, S. Goldberg, D. Stern, & A.M. Sostek (Eds.),

High-risk infants and children: Adult and peer interactions (pp. 113–132). New York: Academic Press.

Field, T., Dempsey, J., & Shuman, H.H. (1983). Five-year follow-up of preterm respiratory distress syndrome and post-term postmaturity syndrome. In T. Field & A. Sostek (Eds.), *Infants born at risk: Physiological, perceptual and cognitive processes* (pp. 317–336). New York: Grune & Stratton.

Gesten, E.L. (1976). A health resources inventory: The development of a measure of the personal and social competence of primary-grade children. *Journal of Consulting and Clinical Psychology, 44*(5), 775–786.

Goldberg, S. (1979). Prematurity: Effects on parent-infant interaction. *Journal of Pediatric Psychology, 3*(3), 137–144.

Goldberg, S., Brachfeld, S., & DiVitto, B. (1980). Feeding, fussing, and play: Parent-infant interaction in the first year as a function of prematurity and perinatal medical problems. In T.M. Field, S. Goldberg, D. Stern, & A.M. Sostek (Eds.), *High risk infants and children: Adult and peer interactions* (pp. 133–154). New York: Academic Press.

Greenberg, M.T., & Crnic, K.A. (1988). Longitudinal predictors of developmental status and social interaction in premature and full-term infants at age two. *Child Development, 59*, 554–570.

Harter, S. & Pike, R. (1981). *The Pictorial Scale of Perceived Competence and Acceptance for Young Children: A manual*. Unpublished manuscript, University of Denver.

Hedrick, D.L., Prather, E.M., & Tobin, A.R. (1975). *Sequenced inventory of communication development*. Seattle: University of Washington Press.

Hoy, E.A., Bill, J.M., & Sykes, D.H. (1988). Very low birthweight: A long-term developmental impairment? *International Journal of Behavioral Development, 11*, 37–67.

Hunt, J.V. (1981). Predicting intellectual disorders in childhood for preterm infants with birth-weights below 1501 grams. In S.L. Friedman & M. Sigman (Eds.), *Preterm birth and psychological development* (pp. 329–352). New York: Academic Press.

Hunt, J.V., Cooper, B.A.B., & Tooley, W.H. (1988). Very low birth weight infants at 8 and 11 years of age: Role of neonatal illness and family status. *Pediatrics, 82*, 596–603.

Jacob, S., Benedict, H.E., Roach, J., & Blackledge, G.L. (1984). Cognitive, perceptual, and personal-social development of prematurely born preschoolers. *Perceptual and Motor Skills, 58*, 551–562.

Janowsky, J.S., & Nass, R. (1987). Early language development in infants with cortical and subcortical perinatal brain injury. *Developmental and Behavioral Pediatrics, 8*(1), 3–7.

Jeffcoate, J.A., Humphrey, M.E., & Lloyd, J.K. (1979). Disturbance in parent-child relationship following preterm delivery. *Developmental Medicine and Child Neurology, 21*, 344–352.

Kitchen, W.H., Rickards, A.L., Ryan, M.M., Ford, G.W., Lissenden, J.V., & Boyle, L.W. (1986). Improved outcome to two years of very low-birthweight infants: fact or artifact? *Developmental Medicine and Child Neurology, 28*, 479–588.

Kitchen, W.H., Ryan, M.M., Rickards, A., Astbury, J., Ford, G., Lissenden, J.V., Keith, C.G., & Keir, E.H. (1982). Changing outcome over 13 years of very low birth weight infants. *Seminars in Perinatology, 6*(4), 373–389.

Klein, N., Hack, M., Gallagher, J., & Fanaroff, A.A. (1986). Preschool performance of children with normal intelligence who were very low-birth-weight infants. *Pediatrics, 75*, 531–537.

Kopp, C.B. (1983). Risk factors in development. In P.H. Mussen (Ed.), *Handbook of child psychology* (4th ed., Vol. 2). *Infancy and developmental psychobiology*. New York: Wiley.

Landry, S.H., Fletcher, J.M., Zarling, C.L., Chapieski, L., & Francis, D.J. (1984). Differential outcomes associated with early medical complications in premature infants. *Journal of Pediatric Psychology, 9*(3), 385–401.

Lee, C.L., Bates, J.E. (1985). Mother–child interaction at age two years and perceived difficult temperament. *Child Development, 56*(5), 1314–1325.

Lerner, R., Palermo, M., Spiro, A., & Nesselroade, J. (1982). Assessing the dimensions of temperamental individuality across the life span: The dimensions of temperament survey (DOTS). *Child Development, 53*(1), 149–159.

Littman, B., & Parmelee, A.H. (1978). Medical correlates of infant development. *Pediatrics, 61,* 470–474.

Lloyd, B.W., Wheldall, K., & Perks, D. (1988). Controlled study of intelligence and school performance of very low-birthweight children from a defined geographical area. *Developmental Medicine and Child Neurology, 30,* 36–42.

Marvin, R.S. (1977). An ethological-cognitive model for the attenuation of mother–child attachment behavior. In T.M. Alloway & L. Krames (Eds.), *Advances in the study of communication and affect (Vol. 3.): The development of social attachments.* New York: Plenum.

McCall, R.B. (1981). Nature–nurture and the two realms of development: A proposed integration with respect to mental development. *Child Development, 52*(1), 1–12.

McCormick, M.C. (1989). Long-term follow-up of infants discharged from neonatal intensive care units. *Journal of the American Medical Association, 261,* 1767–1772.

McGhee, L.J., & Eckerman, C.O. (1983). The preterm infant as a social partner: Responsive but unreadable. *Infant Behavior and Development, 6,* 461–470.

Meisels, S.J., Plunkett, J.W., Roloff, D.W., Pasick, P.L., & Stiefel, G.S. (1986). Growth and development of preterm infants with respiratory distress syndrome and bronchopulmonary dysplasia. *Pediatrics, 77*(3), 345–352.

Nickel, R.E., Bennett, F.C., & Lamson, F.N. (1982). School performance of children with birth weights of 1,000 grams or less. *American Journal of Diseases in Childhood, 136,* 105–110.

Parke, R.D., & Tinsley, B.R. (1982). The early environment of the at-risk infant: Expanding the social context. In D.D. Bricker (Ed.), *Intervention with at-risk and handicapped infants: From research to application* (pp. 153–177). Baltimore: University Park Press.

Pedazur, E.J. (1982). *Multiple regression in behavioral research* (2nd ed.). New York: Holt, Rinehart & Winston.

Pederson, D.R., Bento, S., Chance, G.W., Evans, B., & Fox, A.M. (1987). Maternal emotional responses to preterm birth. *American Journal of Orthopsychiatry, 57*(1), 15–21.

Rauh, V.A., Achenbach, T.M., Nurcombe, B., Howell, C.T., & Teti, D.M. (1988). Minimizing adverse effects of low birthweight: Four-year results of an early intervention program. *Child Development, 59,* 544–553.

Ross, G., Lipper, E.G., & Auld, P.A.M. (1985). Consistency and change in the development of premature infants weighing less than 1,501 grams at birth. *Pediatrics, 76,* 885–891.

Saigal, S., Szatmari, P., Rosenbaum, P., Campbell, D., & King, S. (1990). Intellectual and functional status at school entry of children who weighed 1000 grams or less at birth: A regional perspective of births in the 1980s. *Journal of Pediatrics, 116(3),* 409–16.

Sameroff, A.J. (1982). The environmental context of developmental disabilities. In D.D. Bricker (Ed.), *Intervention with at-risk and handicapped infants: From research to application* (pp. 141–152). Baltimore: University Park Press.

Sameroff, A.J., & Chandler, M. (1975). Reproductive risk and the continuum of caretaking casualty. *Review of child development research* (Vol. 12, pp. 187–244). New York: Russell Sage Foundation.

Sameroff, A.J., & Seifer, R. (1983). Familial risk and child competence. *Child Development, 54*(5), 1254–1268.

Siegel, L.S. (1982). Reproductive, perinatal and environmental factors as predictors of the cognitive and language development of preterm and full-term infants. *Child Development, 53*(4), 963–973.

Siegel, L.S. (1984). Home environmental influences on cognitive development in preterm and full-term children during the first 5 years. In A.W. Gottfried (Ed.), *Home environment and early mental development* (pp. 197–233). New York: Academic Press.

Siegel, L.S. (1985, April). *Linguistic, visual-spatial and attentional processes in school-age, prematurely-born children.* Paper presented at the meetings of the Society for Research in Child Development, Toronto, Canada.

Sigman, M., Cohen, S.E., Beckwith, L., & Parmalee, A.H. (1981). Social and familial influences on the development of preterm infants. *Journal of Pediatric Psychology, 6*(1), 1–13.

Sostek, A.M., & Anders, T.F. (1977). Relationships among the Brazelton Neonatal Scale, Bayley Infant Scales and early temperament. *Child Development, 48*, 320–323.

Sostek, A.M., Katz, K.S., Valvano, J., & Smith, V.F. (1988, April). *School readiness: Effects of prematurity independent of intraventricular hemorrhage.* Paper presented at the International Conference on Infant Studies, Washington, DC.

Ungerer, J.A., & Sigman, M. (1983). Developmental lags in preterm infants from one to three years of age. *Child Development, 54*(5), 1217–1228.

Wallace, I. (1984, April). *Indicators of cognitive functioning in school-aged low birthweight children.* Paper presented at the International Conference on Infant Studies, New York.

7

The Social and Emotional Development of Low-Birthweight Infants and Their Families Up To Age 4

Klaus Minde

INTRODUCTION

Prematurity has long been recognized as a condition that provides an opportunity to assess the potential role biological adversities and parenting behaviors have in the development of children. At the same time, it is a very complex variable that can affect the quality of an infant's life in many ways. Defined by the objective criteria of low birthweight and low gestational age, prematurity is generally associated with several other factors such as multiple births, lower socioeconomic status, and particular parental emotional responses. Finally, prematurity is a changing variable, since the outcome varies with the technology available in different settings, and with whether a baby is cared for in a perinatal unit with the hospital of birth or had to be transported from one institution to another.

In 1978, a number of basic scientists and clinicians met for 2 days in Bethesda, Maryland, to exchange ideas and experiences about the complexities of prematurity and its effects on children's psychological development. Their deliberations were published in a book in 1981 (Friedman & Sigman, 1981). Among other things this book dealt with the impact prematurity can have on specific cognitive factors, and discussed possible associations.

At that time our own group suggested ways to measure early mother–infant interactions and provided preliminary data on the influence the mothers' own experiences had on their initial reaction to their very small premature infants (Marton, Minde, & Ogilvie, 1981a).

More than 10 years have passed since then, and those of us who have continued to study prematurely born infants have followed our samples beyond early infancy. These studies have taught us a great deal about the interdependence of the physical condition prematurity and social aspects of development. They have also demonstrated the advantages and disadvantages of specific interactional, social, and biological measures in the early assessment of the premature infant's developmental capacities. Finally, these follow-up studies have also provided an opportunity to examine and validate specific developmental hypotheses.

In the present chapter I will summarize the data from our studies as they relate to the emotional functioning of premature infants and their families during the first 4 years of their lives and will compare our results with those of other recent studies which have dealt with this subject. As there now exists a very extensive literature on this topic, I will select only studies which have focussed on small premature infants (less than 1,500 gms) and used validated measuring instruments. To eliminate potentially transient findings, only studies that have followed children for at least 3 years will be included in this review.

WHY SHOULD PREMATURE INFANTS BE AT RISK FOR LATER EMOTIONAL DISTURBANCE?

There are many factors surrounding the birth of a low-birthweight infant which can potentially influence the quality of this infant's later life. Two groups are especially important. (a) A premature infant may have characteristics which can elicit parenting responses leading to later caretaking difficulties, and/or show behaviors which are independently associated with behavioral dysfunction. An example of the latter would be the comparatively high incidence of brain damage (at least 15% according to Hoy, Bill, & Sykes, 1988) these children suffer even in present day high-technology nurseries, and which may lead to later behavioral difficulties. (b) Particular responses of caretakers to the early birth of an infant may affect this infant's later life. Parental anxieties, delayed mother/infant bonding, and subsequent decreased caregiving competence are seen as some of the mediating factors responsible for subsequent behavioral abnormalities.

Biological risk factors. There is continuing evidence that small premature infants suffer more often from cerebral disorders than do full-term infants (Kopp, 1987). While the overall incidence of major neurodevelopmental disorders in this population has decreased in recent years, some 10%–15% of these infants still show intellectual and/or cognitive abnormalities (Kopp, 1983; Grigoroiu-Serbanescu, 1984; Hoy et al., 1988; Minde, Perrotta, & Hellmann, 1988).

Given that, generally, the incidence of behavior disorders in brain-damaged children is two to three times higher than in control populations (Rutter, 1981; Seidel, Chadwick, & Rutter, 1975), one would expect the overall incidence of behavioral difficulties to be raised in this population (Minde, 1984). However, as this review will repeatedly show, the long-term outcome of prematurity and associated factors is to a significant degree also influenced by the developing child's transactions with his or her family (Sameroff & Chandler, 1975; Sigman & Parmelee, 1979; Minde, Marton, Manning, & Hines, 1980a). This means that the long-term implications of biological difficulties and handicaps can best be understood within the total psychosocial context of the infant.

While this is generally accepted today, there is still little known about the actual pathways in which insults to the brain are translated into later emotional difficulties (Cohen, Velez, Brook, & Smith, 1989). The work I shall discuss in this chapter may provide some tentative answers in this area.

Psychological risk factors. There is a substantial body of descriptive research that demonstrates that mothers of premature infants show continuing anxiety and less confidence in caregiving competence at least during the first year of their infants' life (Jeffcoate, Humphrey, & Lloyd, 1979; Gennaro, 1985; Brooten, Gennaro, Brown, Butts, Gibbons, Bakewill-Sachs, & Kumar, 1988). These parental concerns are thought to be related to specific interaction patterns that have been observed between these infants and their caretakers. In short, it has been suggested that preterm infants have problems with information processing and are therefore easily disorganized in their overall behavior (Brazelton, Koslowski, & Main, 1974; Field, 1977). As this disorganization often makes them appear hyporeactive to everyday stimuli of handling, mothers initially tend to compensate for this perceived deficit through excessive stimulation. This often has the unintended effect of derailing the infant's behavior even further. Consequently, they may abruptly shift from hypo- to hyperreactivity, leaving the caretaker at a loss of how to appropriately stimulate such an infant (Beckwith & Cohen, 1983; Barnard, Bee, & Hammond, 1984).

Another suggested pathway to compromised parenting has been the generally lower socioeconomic status of premature infants (Crnic, Greenberg, Ragozin, Robinson, & Basham, 1983a). Poverty, among other things, is associated with limited emotional support services for mothers and subsequent maternal insensitivity (Sameroff, 1986).

As can be seen from this brief review, there is evidence that both premature infants and their caretakers are exposed to biological and psychosocial risks that are often associated with later behavioral deviance. However, since much still needs to be learned about the process by which specific biological infant characteristics may influence parenting competence as well as later cognitive and emotional outcome of premature infants, a more detailed review of relevant empirical data is indicated.

WHAT IS THE EVIDENCE FOR BEHAVIOR DIFFICULTIES IN PREMATURE INFANTS?

Follow-up studies of very low-birthweight (VLBW) infants have long claimed that these children are at an increased risk for a variety of behavioral difficulties, including major and minor psychiatric disorders (Drillien, 1964). Benton (1940), half a century ago, already described prematurely born children as suffering from "restlessness, nervousness, fatigability which resulted in distractibility and disturbed concentration" (p. 737). However, as Kopp stated in 1983, "studies of this population have created an unsystematic, uncohesive and decidedly atheoretical research literature" (Kopp, 1983, p. 1110). Too often investigators have used poorly defined sample populations or applied nonstandardized assessment measures in describing the outcome of these children.

While such factors make comparisons of studies difficult, one can nevertheless distinguish between two general types of investigations, best labeled the *outcome* and the *process* approaches.

Researchers using the outcome approach have been concerned with short- or long-term benefits of newly developed NICU techniques. They have tabulated the percentages of disturbed children, categorized them according to the particular neonatal complications they suffered or the specific treatments they received. Most studies of premature infants use this methodology. In the process approach, investigators focus on VLBW infants as a prototype for studying the effects of normal or compromised early developmental abilities and/or experiences on later functioning.

Outcome studies. Recent studies using the *outcome approach* have come from Field and her group (Field, Dempsey, & Shuman, 1983). Field followed 57 premature infants who had an average birthweight of 1,597 grams and compared them to a group of normal full-term and postmature infants. On average her preterms had experienced 3 days of mechanical ventilation. At 2 and 5 years of age, the premature children scored significantly worse on the Behavior Problem Check List devised by Quay and Peterson (1975). However, as this scale was designed for and validated on school-age children, these results must be interpreted with caution. Silva, McGee, and Williams (1984), in a follow-up study of all 31 preterm, 71 SGA, and 750 full-term infants born in one New Zealand hospital, found the preterm group to have been rated by their parents and teachers as showing significantly more symptoms on the Rutter Child Scale (Rutter, 1967) than did the normal controls. Scores reported by Silva and his colleagues, while statistically higher than those for children of the control group, were nevertheless only between 7.1 at age 5 and 9.7 at age 9 and hence still well within the normal range (cut-off point, suggesting psychological disorder = 13.0).

In a study of premature infants born in the 1960s, Dunn, Ho, Crichton, Robertson, McBurney, Grunau, and Penfold (1986) followed 40 out of 61 preterm survivors who had shown signs of "Minimal Brain Dysfunction" at 6 ½ years. Of these children, 40.5% were given a psychiatric diagnosis by a child psychiatrist at age 12 to 15. This diagnosis was based on a report from a social worker who had made a home visit and seen each child, together with his or her parents. The parents had also filled in a questionnaire and the Devreux Adolescent Behavior Rating Scale. However, since no information is given about these data, and since the 40 children of this study made up a particularly high-risk subsample of the 335 low-birthweight children enrolled in this follow-up study, this percentage figure is of little direct value. It merely confirms the well-established finding that children who show signs of cerebral dysfunction often also tend to fail in their social relationships.

Another study dealing with the emotional outcome of prematurity was reported by Escalona (1984). This author observed psychological maladjustment in 33% of her low-birthweight infant sample at the age of 3½ years (Escalona, 1987). She defined maladjustment as prolonged behavior problems reported by the family and judged significant by psychiatric criteria. However, this author never operationalized her criteria of maladjustment, leaving her data open to various interpretations. She also clearly stated that her definition of *maladjustment* did not imply a psychiatric disorder, since transient sleeping and eating difficulties, to take just one example, qualified a child as maladjusted.

In summary then, there is some evidence from outcome studies that a substantial number of premature infants score high on various behavior checklists, primarily on symptoms denoting attentional factors and impulsivity. However, there is no convincing evidence that these children have a higher rate of psychiatric disturbances.

Process studies. Process studies of the development of preterms attempt to discover the pathways which lead to a particular behavioral or cognitive outcome by delineating in detail the complex network of interacting variables. The premise here is that a variety of interrelated risk factors may produce either a good or poor outcome, depending on built-in compensatory biological or environmental support structures. Unfortunately, work using this approach has lagged behind the more traditional outcome studies. Possible reasons for this are the complexity of variables which can affect the development of an individual infant, the multitude of outcomes which have been described in this population, as well as the lack of a theory or conceptual model that is detailed enough to allow the testing of specific hypotheses regarding processes of development.

There are two ways in which investigators have tried to tackle these issues. Some have stayed away from medically or otherwise compromised children but concentrated on describing the pathways of psychosocially deprived populations so as to explain, e.g., the later vulnerability to depression or parenting disorders of specific segments of our population. A good example here is the work by Rutter (1989) on children who were raised in institutions. He could document some important way stations which could either compromise or ameliorate the behavior of these individuals up to age 25. Others have tried to harness the complexity inherent in medically compromised populations and have devised studies that considered the bio-psychosocial factors determining the social outcome of prematurity at specific ages. These investigations have found that VLBW children are generally more lethargic, unresponsive or else more irritable than controls and more difficult to soothe (DiVitto & Goldberg, 1979). Such infants are also found to be slower in processing novel stimuli (O'Connor, Cohen, & Parmelee, 1984; Sigman, 1976; Sigman, Kopp, Littman, & Parmelee, 1977; Sigman & Parmelee, 1974), which may lead caretakers either to withdraw from these infants (Field et al., 1983) or to become increasingly intrusive (Crnic et al., 1983b; Patterson & Barnard, 1990). Such poorly organized children, as

Hoy et al. (1988) suggest in a recent review of this area, may receive insensitive mothering, which may in turn effect their ability to benefit from potentially compensatory interactions with teachers and peers later on (Sroufe, 1983) and compromise their long-term outcome.

These approaches raise questions regarding the nature of the relationship between characteristics specific to preterm infants and particular caretaking patterns, which in turn may lead to later emotional difficulties. This has become a major theme of our own studies.

THE TORONTO STUDIES

Work with premature infants at the Hospital for Sick Children in Toronto began in 1975. This hospital had, at that time, the largest neonatal intensive care unit in North America (75 beds), and provided an opportunity to involve in the study a multidisciplinary group of professionals consisting of pediatricians, nurses, psychologists, and psychiatrists. While the overall objective of this work was to provide better care to preterm infants, a major thrust was our interest in the impact of prematurity on the social and emotional development of these infants and on family systems.

OBJECTIVES

The aim of our early work was to describe the overall ecology of the premature infant in the NICU and observe how both fathers and mothers come to grips with parenting such a small infant. This was done by direct observation of parent/child interactions in the nursery and up to 3 months after discharge. Some 70 infants were involved in these studies (Minde, Trehub, Corter, Boukydis, Celhoffer, & Marton, 1978; Minde et al., 1980a; Hines, Minde, Marton, & Trehub, 1980; Marton et al., 1981a).

We next examined the impact specific medical complications of the infant and/or social conditions of the family had both on the behavior of premature infants in the nursery and during the first three months at home, and on their parents. In particular, we examined the association between the number of medical complications as well as the general preterm versus full-term status and parent/child interactions. Fifty-seven preterms and 20 full-term infants were involved in these studies (Minde, Whitelaw, Brown, & Fitzhardinge, 1983; Minde et al., 1988; Washington, Minde, & Goldberg, 1986).

These early studies led to an intervention program in which parents met regularly with each other and a "veteran" parent for a limited time right after the birth of their infant. Twenty-eight families participated in the program, and its effect on their parenting ability was assessed and compared with that of a matched nontreatment control group of 29 families. Follow-up extended to 12 months corrected age (Minde, Shosenberg, Marton, Thompson, Ripley, & Burns, 1980b; Minde, Shosenberg, & Marton, 1981).

During this final phase of our work, which began in 1980, we followed 77 infants, 42 of whom were twins, for 48 months. The aim in this work was to trace the longer term bio-psychosocial development of these infants in the context of their families. Research design made use of recently developed methodologies to examine the attachment between these children and their parents. We were especially interested in the effect specific biological risk factors within the infant and the potentially unusual early relationship between these infants and their parents may have on the children's early attachment status and later development of psychopathology (Goldberg, Perrotta, Minde, & Corter, 1986; Minde, Perrotta, & Corter, 1982; Minde, 1986; Minde, Goldberg, Perrotta, Washington, Lojkasek, Corter, & Parker, 1989; Minde, Corter, Goldberg, & Jeffers, 1990; Goldberg, Corter, Lojkasek, & Minde, 1990).

Description of Samples

All participants of our various studies were recruited from consecutive admissions to the tertiary care neonatal unit at the Hospital for Sick Children. In order to be eligible for the study, infants had to weight less than 1,501 grams at birth, to have weight appropriate for gestational age, survive the first 72 hours, and have no known congenital abnormalities. Parents had to live within commuting distance of the hospital, be fluent in English, and agree to participate.

There were a total of 203 premature infants who participated in our investigations. These infants represented the sum total of 4 subsamples (A–D).

Subsample A: This sample consisted of 32 infants who provided data on early mother–infant interactions. All infants were followed for 3 months after their expected date of birth.

Subsample B: This group consisted of 40 infants. Twenty were considered to have had a comparatively uncomplicated neonatal course and 20 had suffered serious and long-lasting complications (more than 35 days).

Later on, a third group of 17 infants was added who had experienced serious but rather brief medical complications in the NICU (less than 17 days). These infants were followed 3 months after their expected date of birth.

Subsample C: This sample consisted of 57 infants and their families. Twenty-eight families were provided with a prevention program while the infants were hospitalized, and 29 participated as matched controls. Children were observed in the nursery and followed for 12 months after discharge home.

Subsample D: This group included 77 infants. Of these, 26 were singletons, 46 were twins, and 5 made up a subgroup where only 1 twin had survived. These were the infants who were most intensively studied by our group. They were all followed to 48 months after their expected date of birth.

Evaluations. Three types of evaluations were used: direct and nonstructured observations of parent/child interactions; interviews and newly devised assessment measures; standardized tests or questionnaires.

Table 1 provides a summary of all the evaluations derived from the four subsamples.

Table 1.   Assessment Procedures

	Time of Procedure (month)						
	Neonatal Period	6 wks	3m	6m	9m	12m	48m
Subsample A & B							
Psychiatric Interview	X						
Mother–Child Observation							
hospital	X						
home		X	X				
Illness Rating	X						
Subsample C							
Psychiatric Interview	X					X	
Discharge Interview	X						
Mother–Child Observation							
hospital	X						
home		X	X			X	
Illness ratings	X						
Child Developmental Status						BS	
Subsample D							
Psychiatric Interview	X					X	X
Malaise Inventory Mother							X
Mother–Child Observation							
hospital	X						
home		X	X	X	X		
laboratory						SST	PTT
Temperament		RITQ				TTS	TTS
Child Developmental Status				BS			SB
Behavior Problems							
Mother reports							BCL
Teachers reports							PBQ
Illness Rating	X						
Family Ratings						X	X

SST   = Strange Situation Task
PTT   = Puzzle and Teaching Task
TTS   = Toddler Temperament Scales
RITQ = Revised Infant Temperament Questionnaire
BS   = Bayley Scales
SB   = Stanford Binet Intelligence Test
BCL   = Behavior Checklist (Richman-Graham)
PBQ   = Preschool Behavior Questionnaire (Behar)

DESCRIPTION OF MEASURES

Psychiatric Interviews

When the infants were 4 weeks old, all parents were given a semistructured psychiatric interview by a child psychiatrist (KM) assessing their social background; their experiences during the pregnancy, delivery, and postnatal course of their infants; their attitudes; and their expectations towards the future, and available support structures. Parents' responses to 46 areas of information were quantified and recorded. At 12 and 48 months, the same format was used to obtain follow-up information on the same areas of the children's and families' medical, psychological and social functioning. From these data we obtained an overall *Family Rating Scale*, which consisted of six dimensions: marital discord, adequacy of housing, financial status, the support mothers perceived to have outside the nuclear families, mother's emotional health, and mother's satisfaction with the maternal role. Each dimension was rated on a Likert Scale, which varied in range from 3 (e.g., type of housing) to 5 (e.g., marital relationship) with a possible score of 20. Two raters scored each file retrospectively, approximately 1 year after the 4-year data collection. Since both raters had known the families, they were rated without identifying information, and the two protocols for a given family were not rated in sequence. Interrater reliability, based on a subset of 20 protocols, ranged from 0.84 (mother's emotional health) to 0.95 (housing) with a mean of 0.89.

At 48 months of age, each child was also given a DSM-III-based diagnosis, if this was appropriate.

Direct and Nonstructured Observations of Parent/Child Interactions

All infants who fulfilled the selection criteria were observed (a) in the hospital, together with their mothers, during two parental visits per week, provided the parents visited that often; and (b) at home, together with their mothers, during two standard feeding situations 6 weeks and 3 months after discharge from hospital. In subsample C, there was also an additional home observation at 12 months, and in subsample D at 6 and 9 months after discharge.

These observations lasted up to 40 minutes. Two observers continuously recorded a total of 9 infant and 10 maternal behaviors. Infant behaviors included: arm, head, leg, and hand to mouth movement; eyes open; cry; vocalize; smile; and yawn. Maternal behaviors included: look; look *en face;* verbalize to baby and others; instrumental and noninstrumental touch; hold; feed; smile; and standing further than one meter away from the baby.

A digital event recorder activated by pressing telephone-style touch buttons was used to enter the behavior on a cassette tape, from which they were transferred to a minicomputer for storage and analysis. Each observation could last up to 14 minutes. Observations were made by two research assistants with a minimum of 2 months' training. Reliability checks were done on 20% of all observations and indicated average interobserver reliability of 85% and greater than 70% in all categories.

During the home visits at 6 weeks and at 3, 6, and 9 months corrected age, in addition to the direct mother–infant observations, our research assistants also rated the overall maternal caretaking style as well as the baby's style of response. The rating was done using a scale developed by Egeland, Taraldson, and Brunquell (1977) that has 33 ratings. Thus, there are scales assessing mother's facility in caretaking, appropriateness of interventions, accessibility, supportiveness in play and sensitivity, and such infant variables as responsivity to mother's interaction, social behavior, temperament, satisfaction with the play situation, and amount of looking at mother's face during feeding. These scales are adaptations from Ainsworth's categories of attachment (Ainsworth, Blehar, Waters, & Wall, 1978). Interrater reliability for these ratings was calculated for percentage agreement for the two observers for the same observation. Agreements ranged from 0.72 to 1.00 with an average agreement of .90. For the purpose of our studies, we focused on Ainsworth's four "summary" scores for sensitivity, acceptance, accessibility, and cooperation (Ainsworth et al., 1978), which have been most widely used to characterize maternal responsiveness. In our work with out latest cohort of 77 infants, we reduced these four summary scores to a single score, that is, all ratings during the first year were summed and averaged to yield a single "maternal responsiveness score" for the first year.

Standardized Tests and Questionnaires

Developmental assessment. The Bayley Scale of Infant Development (Bayley, 1969) was administered when the infant was approximately 6 months corrected age. This test yields scores for mental development (MDI) and psychomotor development (PDI). At 48 months all children received the Stanford Binet Intelligence Test.

Temperament ratings. These were obtained from both parents when the children were 6, 12, and 48 months old. At 6 months, mothers and fathers were asked to complete the Revised Infant Temperament Questionnaire (RITQ) (Carey & McDevitt, 1978). At 12 months, parents completed the Toddler Temperament Scale (TTS) (Fullard, McDevitt, & Carey, 1984). This 97-item questionnaire groups children into five temperamental clusters ranging from "easy" through "slow to warm up" to "difficult" temperament. It also yields scores on nine dimensions of temperament.

Child behavior. This was measured using the Behaviour Checklist (BCL) developed by Richman and Graham (1971) and Richman (1977). This 12-item questionnaire allows the parent to rate the presence or absence of specific behavioral symptoms in their children on a 3-point ordinal scale (absent, mildly, and very much present). A score of 10 or more indicates a child to be at risk for emotional or behavioral problems. This checklist was chosen because recent local norms of 4-year-old children were available (Minde & Minde, 1981).

Teacher reports. Teachers of children who attended junior kindergarten filled in the Pre-school Behavior Questionnaire (PBQ) (Behar & Stringfield, 1974). This 30-item questionnaire is based on concepts similar to the Behavior Checklist (BCL). A score of 13 or above is considered to identify children at risk for psychopathology.

Malaise inventory. This symptom checklist, developed by Rutter, Tizard, and Whitmore (1970), consists of 24 items referring to maternal emotions and aspects of the physical state which have an important psychological component. The total number of "yes" responses is scored.

Attachment status. This was assessed by using the methodology and categories developed by Ainsworth et al. (1978). This includes three major types: secure (B), avoidant (A), and ambivalent (C). Within major types, there are subgroups: secure (4 groups), avoidant (2), ambivalent (2). All ratings were done by Dr. S. Goldberg and a senior research assistant who had been especially trained in the scoring method of this procedure. More recently, all tapes were rescored and the D-category added (Main & Solomon, 1986). Dr. M. Main reviewed all the D-categories in conjunction with Dr. S. Goldberg.

Morbidity scale. This scale, described in detail elsewhere (Minde et al., 1983), is based on daily ratings of 20 diseases or pathophysiological states most commonly encountered in infants weighing <1,500 grams in our neonatal intensive care unit. Each medical condition was rated daily from 0 (absent) to 3 (life-threatening), and these ratings were summed to yield a total global score of each infant's hospital stay. These ratings were done by a specially trained nurse. Initial reliability checks showed a 92% concordance between the nurse and the neonatologist who participated in the development of this scale.

THE PROCESS OF PARENTING A PREMATURE INFANT

When we began our studies of premature infants and their parents, there was much discussion in the literature about the anguish and alienation experienced by parents who were routinely denied contact with their infants in the NICU. This lack of contact was thought to inhibit bonding, a concept first described by Klaus and Kennell (1976), which in turn could lead to "disorders of mothering" (Fanaroff, Kennel, & Klaus, 1972) or even to abuse (Hunter, Kilstrom, Kraybill, & Loda, 1978). The literature also suggested that a substantial number of these parents were either ambivalent towards their premature infants or so depressed that normal caretaking could not be expected (Kaplan & Mason, 1960).

However, a careful review of this literature (Minde, 1980; Corter & Minde, 1987) suggested that some of these alarming assertions were based on a questionable interpretation of specific data, or the use of nonrandom populations, and required further investigation. Since the literature suggested that the initial weeks of interactions between infant and caretaker were of great importance, we chose to explore individual differences in the visiting behavior of parents with their premature infants in the NICU (Minde et al., 1978, 1980a; Marton, Minde, & Perrotta, 1981b). As indicated above, we objectively recorded the interactions between parents and their infants by using two observers. One continuously recorded 10 discrete behaviors of the parent (such as looking *en face*, smiling, feeding, touching, verbalizing, etc.), and the other, 8 behaviors of the infant (such as eyes open, crying, arm movement, smiling, etc.). We recorded all first visits, and subsequently tried to record interactions twice a week if the parents visited that often.

Our observations of maternal visiting revealed that mothers generally became more engaged with their infant during each successive visit. However, some mothers were consistently more engaged than others. In order to examine the factors associated with these differences in engagement with the infant, we divided our sample into high-, medium-, and low-activity groups (Minde et al., 1978, 1980a). Not unexpectedly, we found that the quantity of interaction a mother showed during her visits was related to the frequency of her visits. Mothers who showed little activity with their children visited infrequently. More significantly, we also found that the level of engagement with the infant in the hospital predicted the numbers of interactions mothers showed towards these infants in the home at 3 months corrected age.

To determine what might contribute to these relatively stable differences in engagement, we examined background data taken from the psychiatric interview during the hospital period. These measures ranged from complications during pregnancy or delivery to SES of the family, but the factors that most distinguished between the high and low engagement groups involved the strength of the relationships the mother reported with her own mother and with her husband. Factors such as the length of time before mother could first see her infant after birth, or the initial prognosis given her by the physician, did not correlate with her later style of interaction. This strongly suggests that early maternal behavior with a premature infant is subject to second-order effects of other relationships the mother had in the past and does not reflect events occurring at the time of delivery. This is confirmed by later work of Main and her group, who reported strong intergenerational continuities in the transmission of attachment patterns (George, Caplan, & Main, 1984; Crowell, & Feldman, 1988) and caretaking abnormalities (Egeland, Jacobvitz, & Sroufe, 1988).

Having established that the family system affects the infant's social environment in the early days of life, we considered the infant's contribution to parental behavior. This was done by examining sequences of mother/infant interaction for evidence of mutual influence in which one partner responds to the immediately preceding behavior of the other (Minde et al., 1980a; Marton et al., 1981a). Among low engagement mothers and their infants, there was little evidence that either partner was responding to the other. In contrast, there was strong evidence that mothers in the high engagement group often responded to their infants: for example, "infant stretches" was followed by "mother smiles." The potential importance of this difference in sequencing of interactions between mother/infant dyads in the high- and low-engagement groups is seen in a more recent study that suggests that later language difficulties of premature infants may reflect deficient patterns of sequencing during earlier mother/infant interaction (Lester, Hoffman, & Brazelton, 1985). A preliminary report also states that differences in mother/infant synchrony provided better prediction of 2-year Bayley MDI scores than previously used predictors such as social status or state regulation as assessed by the Brazelton Scale (Booth, 1985).

In our work with these highly compromised infants and their families, we soon recognized that the medical complications of such infants can have a substantial impact on the parental perception of the infant. We also recognized that much of the neonatal literature differentiated only between healthy and sick premature infants and failed to recognize the enormous range and degree of seriousness of medical complications experienced by them. In addition, because most other studies did not take into account the variability of complications from week to week, they tended to provide a far less differentiated picture of the infant's life in the NICU. For this reason, we developed an objective scale for measuring a range of medical problems and came up with a Morbidity Scale which identified the twenty most common diseases or pathophysiological states encountered in premature infants (Minde et al., 1983). Subsequently, this scale was used to examine 184 infants differing in degrees and duration of illness during the hospital period. In one study, we reported on 20 infants who had very few complications during their hospital stay and compared them with 20 infants who showed serious complications (morbidity scores: M 19.9, SD 12.7 versus M 161.4, SD 44.2) but who did not differ in terms of other potentially important variables such as weight, gestational age, or socioeconomic status. Comparisons of these groups revealed a clear association between illness and mother/infant interaction. In dyads with a sicker baby, the baby's levels of motor activity and alertness, and the mother's levels of smiling and touching both during nursery visits and during observation 6 and 12 weeks after discharge home, were consistently lower. In a companion study, which involved 14 infants with a long perinatal illness (more than 35 days) and 17 with a short perinatal illness (less than 17 days), we also found significant differences in infant and parental behaviors. In the case of infants who were sick for less than 17 days, both motor and social behaviors of the infant and mother rebounded quickly following recovery from the illness. However, in the case of infants who were sick for more than 35 days, the recovery of maternal behavior lagged behind the infant's recovery and could still be noted 3 months after discharge home.

In other words, even after the sick infant had recovered physically and reached healthy levels of activity with no sign of CNS damage, maternal behavior remained at a lower level. These associations permit a variety of interpretations:

1. Illness may act on maternal behavior via the infant's behavior. This interpretation requires some additional features to account for effects that persist after the infant's behavior has recovered.
2. Illness may act independently on the infant's behavior and on the mother's behavior, for example, by causing mother to view the infant as fragile. Support for this possibility is provided by observations of mothers with newborns undergoing phototherapy for hyperbilirubinemia (Brazelton, 1981). Depressed behavior in these sick babies was matched by depressed interaction on the part of the mothers. We therefore interpreted the low levels of maternal interaction following the apparent recovery of the infant to reflect maternal worries about possible brain damage and later difficulties of the infant.

Having examined the beginning relationship of mothers with premature infants, we were very conscious of the special role fathers had in our NICU. The Hospital for Sick Children does not have an obstetrical unit, so that all the infants were transported there from somewhere else. Fathers, therefore, often visited their infants several times before the mother was able to come and see her baby. In a study which described fathers' visiting patterns and interactions with 20 premature infants (Marton et al., 1981b) we found that fathers maintained their high interest in these infants throughout the hospital period and, on average, visited as much as the mothers did. Furthermore, there was no difference in the engagement levels of mothers and fathers, and very little difference in the particular way they interacted with the baby. The only difference was that mothers talked to their infants more than the fathers did. Even following discharge home, fathers remained active and involved with their infants. For example, during seven continuous 24-hour periods, 3 months after discharge, fathers fed their infants in 17% of the feeding instances, changed diapers in 13% of the instances, and gave a bath in 10% of the observed bathing episodes. This was three times higher than had been reported for fathers of full-term infants (Marton et al., 1981b).

Our finding of similarities in mothers' and fathers' interactions with their infants in the hospital and following discharge is supported by Park's research on fathers (Tinsley & Park, 1983). In addition to demonstrating that both parents do the same sorts of things with a baby, Park showed that mothers as well as fathers explored more and smiled more at the baby when the other parent was present as compared to times when the parent visited the baby alone. In the terminology of the family ecologist, this suggests that the presence of the other parent has a second order effect on the parent/infant dyad and that parents draw support from one another while interacting with their baby.

Parental Support Systems During The Infant's Stay In the NICU

The abovementioned studies have documented some of the factors that go into the parenting of low-birthweight infants. Even more importantly, they also showed us that some variables that generally are considered to be important for the emotional development of children did not contribute to the early caretaking competence of the parents of the preterm infants. For example, neither socio-economic class nor family size influenced the caretaking behavior in our sample. Neither did the experience the mother had with her obstetrician during her pregnancy and delivery, the degree of trauma associated with the birth process, or the amount of immediate contact the mother had with her infant. While the latter finding confirmed the work of others (Leiderman, 1981), the failure to find an association between SES and caretaking competence suggested that the impact of prematurity per se may be more powerful than that commonly identified predictor.

As we had also experienced the challenge which the birth of such an infant provided to the overall coping abilities of many parents, and as crisis intervention theory would suggest this to be a potentially useful time to assist this high-risk population (Caplan, 1964), we designed a specific intervention program. The program consisted of peer oriented self-help groups which took in six to eight parents at one time in an attempt to help them in coping with the biological and ecological stresses associated with prematurity (Minde et al., 1980b, 1981). In particular, the group discussions aimed to allow mothers and fathers to:

1. Share the concerns they had about their infants with each other and with a "veteran" mother who had given birth to a premature infant within the past year,
2. Learn how to negotiate the administrative complexities associated with an NICU and thus increase their sense of effectiveness,
3. Obtain practical information about the care premature infants require after discharge, and
4. Provide practical and emotional support to each other.

In this study, 28 families (the experimental group) who met for seven to ten weeks with a nurse coordinator and a "veteran" mother were compared to 29 control families. The families were matched on SES, ethnicity, and family size, and the infants were matched on sex, and perinatal complications. It was of interest that initial group meetings tended to focus on feelings of depression, fear, and guilt about having produced a small, frail baby. It was our impression that this initial emotional sharing left the parents in a better state to assimilate information on the treatment and care of their infants during later meetings. At that time, specific resource people spoke on infant stimulation and the general philosophy of neonatal intensive care. Films and slides highlighting the developmental needs of premature infants were also shown. In addition, attempts were made to help parents with concrete problems such as getting babysitters, a better apartment, or improved unemployment benefits.

The comparison of the intervention and control groups revealed a number of differences. The families who participated in the self-help groups visited their infants in the hospital significantly more than did the control parents. They also touched, talked to, and looked at their infants *en face* more during their visits, and rated themselves as more confident in taking care of the infants at the time of discharge. They also evaluated the hospital atmosphere as more positive than the controls. Three months after the discharge of the infants, mothers who had received intervention continued to show more involvement with their babies.

In a follow-up study 1 year later, which included all but 2 of the original sample of 57 families, we again found significant differences between the mothers who had participated in the group meetings and their controls. For example, a statistically significant 69% of the mothers in the experimental group perceived the development of their infants at an age corrected for gestation and adjusted their expectations accordingly. Only 37% of the control mothers did so. The intervention group mothers at one year also gave their infants significantly more floor space to play, disciplined them less, and in general, were more open in expressing concerns they had about them. When observed during routine feedings, the mothers who had received intervention were found to spend less time feeding their children, instead allowing them to feed themselves more. During the play periods, these mothers also vocalized and played more with their infants. We interpreted these findings to mean that the mothers who received intervention generally gave their infants more autonomy and stimulation, and had a more appropriate understanding of their competence. At the same time, the infants of the intervention families were observed to spend significantly more time sharing food with their mothers during their meals, and to play more and touch their mothers more frequently during their play sessions. When the infants were reunited with their mothers after a 5-minute separation, the intervention mothers hugged and kissed their infants significantly more. In contrast, the control mothers showed their joy at the reunion by doing instrumental tasks, such as changing their babies diapers or combing their hair. In other words, the intervention mothers were more socially stimulating with their infants and shared their feelings with them more easily. Their children reciprocated by showing more social and independent behavior such as general playing, food sharing, and self-feeding. The most interesting results, from a family system's point of view, came from analyses in which we examined maternal engagement levels (high, medium, or low) in terms of associated variables identified in our previous work. Among mothers in the control group, relationships with husband and the mother's own mother, and severity of the infant's illness, were again shown to correlate with engagement level. This correlation replicated previous findings in families who did not have the support of a self-help group. However, among mothers who had participated in the group interventions, we found no correlations between the mother's past relationship with her own mother or spouse and her present level of engagement with her infant. This suggests that the mothers who were helped the most by the intervention were those who had the most problematic relationships with their own mothers and would normally have been most at risk for a low involvement with their infants.

We can only speculate about how such positive effects were achieved. One possibility is that fears and anxiety aroused by the infant's illness were dispelled somewhat by the educational aspects of the support group. Lack of support from husbands or grandmothers may have been offset by the emotional support from peers. Alternatively, the fact that husbands and wives generally attended the meetings together may have increased the husband's involvement with the baby and strengthened the marital relationship.

Unfortunately, we did not examine this group of infants with Ainsworth's Attachment Paradigm. However, looking at these data within the framework of attachment theory, it appears that infants from the support group families exhibited more behaviors typically seen in securely attached infants.

FOUR-YEAR FOLLOW-UP

Most recently, we examined the emotional and cognitive outcome of a group of low-birthweight twins and singleton infants up to age 48 months.

This work included 77 children. Of these, 26 were singletons, 46 were twins, and 5 made up a subgroup where only one twin had survived. At age 48 months, 7 of these children could not be followed up because the family had left the country (one twin pair), refused to be seen again (one twin pair), or could not be traced (three children). Six more children were not included because they were significantly delayed in their development. This left us with 22 singletons and 42 twins.

At 48 months, all these children and their families had an evaluation (see also Table 1), which included a clinical psychiatric interview as well as information on psychological and cognitive functioning obtained from teachers, parents, and clinicians. The results showed these children generally did well physically and cognitively. Thus, these infants had experienced few hospitalizations ($M = 0.6$), showed a normal I.Q. ($M = 101$, $SD = 14.8$), and had a normal height and weight ($M = 102.4$ cm.; 15.9 kg.). Psychologically, however, the results were more mixed. While no child had been brought to the attention of the authorities because of physical abuse, two infants had been placed with relatives by the mother for about 1 year. Six families had experienced a divorce. In addition, 43% of the children scored within the abnormal range on the Richman-Graham Behavior Checklist (BCL), indicating a likelihood of a behavior disorder. This was four times higher than among a nonclinical preschool group examined by us earlier (Minde & Minde, 1981). The high-scoring children did not differ in their sex distribution, neonatal illness score, and intellectual assessment at 12 and 48 months. However, the high scorers were reported by their mothers to have an intermediate high or difficult temperament more often than children with low BCL scores both at 1 year (55% versus 14%) and at 4 years (42% versus 7%). This suggests that, of the distribution of temperament ratings that comprise the categories easy, intermediate low, intermediate high, slow to warm up, and difficult, our children scored more frequently in the three most difficult categories.

Attachment ratings at 12 months did not differentiate between high- and low-scoring children on the Richman Graham Behavior Checklist, as about 20% of the children showing an insecure attachment. However, when we reviewed the videotapes again, using Mary Main's more recent D-category (Main & Solomon, 1986), we found that three of the previously secure infants as well as one A infant were also given a high-D rating. This attachment dimension, according to Main and her colleagues, assesses the coherence of the strategies which children use in coping with separations and reunions. Children with a D score above 5 show a disorganized and noncoherent approach towards the stress engendered by a short separation from their mothers. The D dimension has also been associated with the way mothers have dealt with previous losses of their own attachment figures (Main, Caplan, & Cassidy, 1985). Three of the four children with a high D score also scored within the abnormal range on the Richman Graham Behavior Checklist.

The age of the mothers, their socioeconomic status, and the Malaise scores also did not differentiate children with low and high BCL scores (Minde et al., 1989). However, abnormal scores on the Family Rating Scale, which dealt with the emotional functioning of the family both at 12 months and 48 months, most consistently predicted those children who had an abnormally high score on the BCL.

The next step was to see how the parental measures compared to the behavior ratings of the teachers on the Pre-school Behavior Questionnaire (PBQ) (Behar, 1977). Teachers rated only 24% of the children as abnormal, which was higher than reported in previous investigations of nonclinical samples but did not reach statistical significance. Correlations between maternal and teacher ratings were nonsignificant ($r = .17$).

Teacher ratings did not correlate with temperament assessments at 12 months ($r = .19$) and 48 months ($r = .22$), nor were they related to attachment ratings at 12 months. However, the four children who obtained a D category were all rated as abnormal by the teachers. In addition, teacher ratings correlated significantly with the items of the Family Rating Scale which dealt with the emotional climate of the family ($r = .57$) as well as with the items denoting housing and income ($r = .48$). Socioeconomic status was not related to any of our other measures.

In an attempt to establish the relative contributions of specific types of background variables made to behavior problems at 4 years, we combined some of our data into four factors: perinatal medical complications, infant temperament, mother/child relationship, and family ratings (Goldberg et al., 1990). We then looked at behavior problems as rated by the mother (BCL) and the teacher (PBQ) as outcome criteria. Using stepwise regression analyses we found that the two behavioral outcome measures had different predictors. As can be seen in Figure 1, mothers' reports of behavior disorders at age 4 were predicted only by temperament ratings at 1 (22% of the variance) and 4 years (32% of the variance). Together the summary scores accounted for a significant total of 38% of the variance. In contrast, for teacher reports of behavior problems on the PBQ, temperament and observed mother/child relationship significantly entered the initial regression equation, both accounting for 31% of the variance. In year 4, aspects of the mother/child relationship and family ratings significantly entered the equation accounting for 55% of the variance. Together the summary scores accounted for a significant total of 56% of the variance. This means that maternal reports of behavioral problems at age 4 were predicted only by other characteristics rated by mothers (in this case the children's temperament at ages 1 and 4). In contrast, teacher reports were predicted by observed mother–child interactions, especially the category of negative maternal responsiveness, and certain items on the Family Rating Scale, such as negative maternal well-being (see Figure 1).

These findings confirm the observations of others (e.g., Field et al., 1983; Hoy et al., 1988) who report that low-birthweight children do have a high rate of behavior problems during their preschool years. However, there are some important qualifications to our data as well as those by the other authors. First, we must realize that behavior problems as reported on a behavior checklist or screening instrument are not synonymous with psychological disorders identified through a psychiatric interview. Thus both the BCL and PBQ are only screening instruments and were not meant to measure psychiatric or behavior disorders. An individual high total score therefore cannot say anything about a child's need for mental health services. Therefore, results on these instruments cannot answer questions regarding the psychiatric morbidity of low birthweight infants.

An item analysis of the BCL suggested one possible reason for the limited usefulness of this instrument as an indicator of psychiatric morbidity in our study population. It showed that the most frequently appearing problems (those occurring in more than 40% of all the children) were associated with eating difficulties, settling, and overactivity, as well as with temper tantrums, demanding attention, and general difficulties of control. On these symptoms, an average of 52.1% of children received a score of 1 (moderate problem) while only 9.6% scored 2 (severe problem). Likewise, the PBQ items that were noted to be present in more than 40% of the children were "being restless, solitary, inattentive, and showing poor concentration." Here again, 46.2% of the children were given a score of 1 and only 8.5% a score of 2. This means that in most cases the

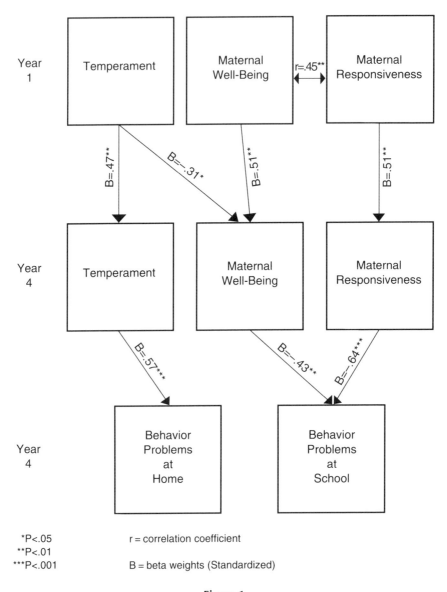

Figure 1

total scores of the ''difficult'' children were made up of many ''moderately severe'' problems. In addition, most of these problems centered around attentional difficulties.

Furthermore, and possibly more importantly, children who scored ''high'' on the checklist filled out by the mother (BCL) formed a narrow cluster of cases just above the conventional cut-off point of 10, with only one child scoring higher than 14 out of a possible 38 on the BCL. This was in contrast to the much more even distribution of the scores given to children on the teacher questionnaire (PBQ). Children who obtained high scores on both instruments tended to have a behavioral profile best described as "problems of behavioral organization"; i.e., they displayed symptoms of overactivity, restlessness, poor concentration, problems of settling and waiting, demanding attention, and temper tantrums. This could be seen to represent general immaturity, possible hyperactivity or an overall poor behavioral organization. Furthermore, the cluster of "cases" scoring between 10 and 13 on the BCL could indicate that this particular cut-off point may be inappropriate for this population, since even at 48 months, these children have not quite caught up with their agemates in their overall behavioral organization and may be penalized by a scoring system based on different standardization populations.

This interpretation is supported by the results of our psychiatric evaluation of the children and their families. Here only 7 children (10.9%) warranted a psychiatric diagnosis, using criteria of DSM-III. This is compatible with findings in other nonclinical populations (Offord, Boyle, Szatmari, Rae-Grant, Links, Cadman, Byles, Crawford, Munroe-Blum, Bynne, Thomas, & Woodward, 1987). The psychiatric diagnoses were: reactive attachment disorder (2); oppositional disorder (2); attention deficit disorder (1); adjustment disorders (2). Using the criteria developed by Earls, Jacobs, Goldfield, Gilbert, Beardslee, and Rivins (1982), four of these children had moderate, and three marked, problems. Thus the latter three youngsters were seriously disruptive to family life and seriously emotionally disturbed. Of six psychiatrically diagnosed children who attended school, teachers identified only two on the PBQ, while parents identified only one of the seven children on the BCL. This means that a mere 15% of the psychiatrically disturbed children were given an "abnormal" rating on the maternal screening instrument, while teachers identified about 33% of these cases on their symptom checklist.

It is of interest that all of the psychiatrically disturbed preschoolers were given easy or intermediate temperament ratings at 48 months. This was in contrast to the children who scored high on the BCL, most of whom had also been rated as showing a difficult temperament. The attachment ratings of these seven children showed four of them at 1 year to be securely attached (i.e., they received a B rating); one could not be scored and two were given a rating of A and C, implying anxious or avoidant attachment. However, when we reviewed the videotapes again using Mary Main's more recent D-category (Main & Solomon, 1986), we found that two of the previously secure infants, as well as the A infant, were now given a high-D rating. In terms of our study this means that, of the seven children who were thought to have a psychiatric diagnosis at age 4, five either had been insecurely attached or had received a high-D rating 3 years earlier.

WHAT DO THESE DATA SUGGEST TO THE PRACTICING CLINICIAN?

A number of points from this work seem relevant for the practitioner. Most important may be that neither the behavior status of low-birthweight infants up to 48 months, as rated by mothers and teachers, nor the assessment of their psychiatric status by a child psychiatrist, is in any way related to the early medical history of the child. As we had excluded from our study infants who showed signs of a congenital abnormality at birth and eliminated six children in the follow-up evaluations because of severe mental and/or physical delay, this finding may not be true for all low-birthweight infants. However, it does support the notion that later development is more dependent on the child's psychosocial circumstances than on the presence or absence of specific neonatal complications (Sameroff, 1986).

Another finding was that, by age 4, mothers and teachers were concerned about the behavior of different children, while a child psychiatrist identified yet another group of youngsters as psychiatrically disturbed. In our sample there was virtually no overlap between children identified by their mothers and by the psychiatrist. Teachers, on the other hand, rated about 30% of the psychiatrically diagnosed children as symptomatic. This discrepancy may be explained in part by the predictors of these ratings at earlier ages. Thus mothers appeared to base their judgment of the children's behavior to a significant degree on their assessment of their children's temperament. They may also have used both the behavior and temperament questionnaire to express their feelings and sentiments about their children. In contrast, teacher ratings could be predicted from early mother–child interactions as well as from the psychiatrist's clinical judgment, which took into account the overall family environment.

The psychiatrically disturbed children at age 4, on the other hand, could be identified by abnormal family relationships and by the quality of their attachment 3 years earlier. Thus six of the seven disturbed children were assessed to have been either insecurely attached at 12 months or to have a secure attachment rating in combination with a D rating. The latter ratings were quite specific as only one child without a psychiatric diagnosis had a D rating. This suggests that psychiatric abnormalities, at least in our sample, were predicted by some of the measures which predicted school problems (e.g., abnormal family ratings) as well as by special attachment patterns. Why this should be so is not clear, as there is no particular reason to assume that an infant with prematurity would afflict families with particular attachment histories. One possibility is that these infants' behavioral disorganization disrupts the parents predominant attachment status stirring up previous experiences with loss. There is some suggestion from other studies of our research group that this may indeed be the case. For example, Goldberg and her colleagues found that children with specific chronic medical conditions had a high incidence of high D-ratings (Goldberg et al., 1989b). The somewhat disorganized behavior of low-birthweight infants, as shown on the maternal checklist ratings, could be one trigger for eliciting negative maternal internal representations. These, together with specific environmental risk factors, could lead to psychiatric abnormalities as we have observed them.

We have no knowledge that the connection between D ratings and possible psychiatric disorders has previously been reported. It will therefore require replication by others. However, the practitioner may nevertheless be prudent to watch out for premature infants who live in discordant families and show disorganized features during separation from their parents. Such children may be highly vulnerable for future psychiatric disorders and may profit from referral to a mental health specialist.

SUMMARY

The present chapter gives a detailed review of investigations which have examined the impact prematurity has on the emotional development and behavior of children up to school age. It furthermore summarizes a number of studies which have come out of the neonatal intensive care unit in Toronto's Sick Children's Hospital between 1980 and 1990.

These data document that the parenting of very small premature infants is a highly complex process that defies easy generalization. However, they also suggest that these infants pass through specific way-stations that may serve as important markers for their later development. For example, premature infants do show specific behavioral characteristics during their first year of life that make parenting more difficult and stressful. Mothers who rapidly engage themselves with their newborn infants in the hospital nursery also seem to be more sensitive to their behavioral cues and, during the ensuing 4 years, have better relationships with these children. There is also good evidence that interventions during the first months of life can modify the interactional patterns of the mother–child dyad quite significantly. Such interventions seem especially useful when they combine a supportive and educational component and include other parents who have lived through the experience of having a premature infant in the recent past.

A further important theme of the reviewed studies is the repeated finding that, during their toddler years, a substantial number of prematurely born children display a significant number of behavior problems best summarized as signs of behavioral disorganization. The described problems are hyperactive or impulsive behaviors, temper tantrums, and general immaturity, and are reported both at home and at school in up to 40% of these children. The behaviors, when described by teachers, occur 3.8 times more often in children whose mothers were described as nonresponsive to their children's emotional signals 3 years earlier. These same mothers had also been identified by a psychiatrist as having a poorer marital relationship and emotional health, little social support, and little satisfaction with their maternal role. When abnormal behaviors were described by the mother, they do not relate to any family or previous mother–infant interaction pattern but only to the temperament of the child as assessed by the mother. This suggests that the behavior ratings by the teachers of these children which are based more on traditionally described transactions may give a more reliable estimate of behavioral abnormalities in these youngsters.

The reviewed data furthermore suggest that interpersonal and family influences that affect the mental health of physically normal children are equally relevant in the development of potentially compromised infants. Thus, low-birthweight infants do not have a higher rate of psychiatric disturbance by age 4 than do full-term babies, although they show the previously mentioned high incidence of individual abnormal symptoms on specific screening instruments. Those who do become psychiatrically disturbed show many of the traditionally accepted stress factors in their background, such as marital discord in the parents and a poor relationship between the mother and her own mother (Rutter, 1989). Their disturbance is not related to their initial medical condition.

Conventional attachment ratings predicted neither later psychiatric disorders nor abnormal ratings on maternal and teacher behavior screening instruments. On the other hand, a difficult temperament as reported by the mother predicted an abnormal score on the parent behavior questionnaire. However, as both ratings were obtained from the mother, it appears that this correlation is more a reflection of her perceptions than of the actual behavior of the child.

The final issue discussed in this chapter is the degree previous internal representations of the mother, as evidenced by her assessment of her relationships with her father and mother, may contribute to distorted perceptions of, and behavior towards, her own child. The work reviewed here suggests that at least the D category of attachment predicts later maladjustment of the youngster. This is a most interesting finding which may bridge the conceptual gap between traditional attachment research and psychopathology. Because of the small number of psychiatrically disturbed children in the sample, it clearly requires replication in a larger sample of psychiatrically disturbed children. In light of the suggestion that changes in maternal and infant behavior can be brought about with relative ease by specific early interventions, that is, support groups, in such a population, it would seem to be of great interest to assess in future work whether clinical interventions also affect the internal representations of the child's caretakers. For example, using theoretical concepts developed by Main and her colleagues about the intergenerational continuity of attachment patterns, one could examine whether support groups for parents of premature infants can help mothers to resolve past losses and hence help them to raise fewer children who receive a D rating in their attachment assessment at 12 months.

It would also be necessary to examine the fate of the abnormal behavioral symptoms which were observed in about 40% of the toddlers at age 4. If these children indeed show a syndrome best described as general behavioral disorganization, one would like to know if such a syndrome persists into later childhood and if so, how it presents clinically. For example, one could imagine that children who at age 4 show poor fine-motor coordination or a high degree of impulsivity, later on exhibit difficulties in pursuing specific subjects in school and/or in negotiating disputes with peers and families. Finally, the present review clearly shows that the work of establishing the developmental pathways which guide the growth and development of these special infants has only begun and will provide many challenges for another generation of researchers.

REFERENCES

Ainsworth, M.D., Blehar, M.C., Waters, E., & Walker, C. (1982). Bonding as perceived by mothers of twins. *Pediatric Nursing, 8,* 411–413.

Ainsworth, M.D., Bell, S.M., & Stayton, D.J. (1971). Individual differences in strange situation behaviors of one- year-olds. In H.R. Schaffer (Ed.), *The origins of human social relations.* London: Academic Press.

Barnard, K., Bee, H., & Hammond, M. (1984). Developmental changes in maternal interactions with term and preterm infants. *Infant Behavior and Development, 7,* 101–113.

Bayley, N. (1969). *Bayley Scales of Infant Development.* Berkeley, CA: Institute of Human Development, University of California.

Beckwith, L., & Cohen, S. (1983, April). *Continuity of caregiving with preterm infants.* Paper presented at the Society for Research in Child Development, Detroit, MI.

Behar, L. (1977). The preschool behavior questionnaire. *Journal of Abnormal Child Psychology, 5,* 265–275.

Benton, A.L. (1940). Mental development of prematurely born children. *American Journal of Orthopsychiatry, 10,* 719–746.

Booth, C. (1985, April). *New and old predictors of cognitive and social outcomes in high-social-risk toddlers.* Paper presented at the biennial meeting of the Society for Research in Child Development, Toronto.

Brazelton, T.B. (1981). Parental perception of infant manipulation: Effects on parents of inclusion in our research. In V.L. Smeriglio (Ed.), *Newborns and parents.* Hillsdale, NJ: Erlbaum.

Brazelton, T.B., Koslowski, B., & Main, M. (1974). The origins of reciprocity: The early mother-infant interaction. In M. Lewis & L. Rosenblum (Eds.), *The effect of the infant on its caregiver.* New York: John Wiley.

Brooten, D., Gennaro, S., Brown, L., Butts, P., Gibbons, A., Bakewill-Sachs, S., & Kumar, S. (1988). Anxiety, depression, and hostility in mothers of preterm infants. *Nursing Research, 37,* 213–216.

Caplan, G. (1964). *Principles of preventive psychiatry.* New York: Basic Books.

Carey, W.B., & McDevitt, S.C. (1978). Revision of the Infant Temperament Questionnaire. *Pediatrics, 61,* 735–739.

Cohen, P., Velez, C.N., Brook, J., & Smith, J. (1989). Mechanisms of the relation between perinatal problems, early childhood illness and psychopathology in late childhood and adolescence. *Child Development, 60,* 701–709.

Corter, C., & Minde, K. (1987). Impact of infant prematurity on family systems. In M. Wolraich (Ed.), *Advances in developmental behavioral pediatrics* (Vol. 8). Greenwich, CT: JAI Press.

Crnic, K.A., Greenberg, M.T., Ragozin, A.S., Robinson, N.M., & Basham, R.B. (1983a). Effects of stress and social support on mothers and premature and full-term infants. *Child Development, 54,* 209–217.

182   MINDE

Crnic, K.A., Ragozin, A.S., Greenberg, M.T., Robinson, N.M., & Basham, R.B. (1983b). Social interaction and developmental competence of preterm and full-term infants during the first year of life. *Child Development, 54,* 1199–1210.

Crowell, J.A., & Feldman, S.S. (1988). Mothers' internal models of relationships and children's behavioral and developmental status: A study of mother-child interaction. *Child Development, 59,* 1273–1285.

DiVitto, B., Goldberg, S. (1979). The effects of newborn medical status on early parent-infant interaction. In T.M. Field, A.M. Sostek, S. Goldberg, & H.H. Shuman (Eds.), *Infants born at risk.* Jamaica, NY: Spectrum.

Drillien, C.M. (1964). *The growth and development of the prematurely born infant.* Edinburgh: Livingstone.

Dunn, H.G., Ho, H.H., Crichton, J.U., Robertson, A.M., McBurney, A.K., Grunau, R.V., & Penfold, P.S (1986). Evolution of minimal brain dysfunctions to the age of 12 to 15 years. In H.G. Dunn (Ed.), *Sequelae of low birthweight: The Vancouver Study. Clinics in Developmental Medicine No. 95/96.* Oxford: MacKeith Press.

Earls, F., Jacobs, G., Goldfield, D., Gilbert, A., Beardslee, W., & Rivinns, T. (1982). Concurrent validation of behavior problem scale for use with 3 year-olds. *Journal of the American Academy of Child Psychiatry, 21,* 57–67.

Egeland, B., Jacobvitz, D., & Sroufe, L.A. (1988). Breaking the cycle of abuse. *Child Development, 59,* 1080–1088.

Egeland, B., Taraldson, B., & Brunquell, D. (1977). *Observations of waiting room and feeding situations.* Unpublished manual, University of Minnesota.

Escalona, S.K. (1984). Social and other environmental influences on the cognitive and personality development of low birthweight infants. *American Journal of Mental Deficiency, 88,* 508–512.

Escalona, S.K. (1987). *Critical issues in the early development of premature infants.* New Haven: Yale University Press.

Fanaroff, A., Kennell, J., & Klaus, M. (1972). Follow-up of low birth-weight infants—the predictive value of maternal visiting patterns. *Pediatrics, 49,* 288–290.

Field, T.M. (1977). Effects of early separation, interactive deficits and experimental manipulations on mother-infant face-to-face interaction. *Child Development, 48,* 763–771.

Field, T., Dempsey, J., & Shuman, H.H. (1983). Five-year follow-up of preterm respiratory distress syndrome and post-term postmaturity syndrome infants. In T. Field & A. Sostek (Eds.), *Infants born at risk: Physiological, perceptual and cognitive processes.* New York: Grune and Stratton.

Friedman, S., & Sigman, M. (1981). *Preterm birth and psychological development.* New York: Academic Press.

Fullard, W., McDevitt, S., & Carey, W. (1984). Toddlers temperament scale for 1–3 year old children. *Pediatric Psychology, 9,* 205–217.

Genarro, S. (1985). Anxiety and problem solving ability in mothers of premature infants. *Pediatric Nursing, 11,* 343–348.

George, C., Kaplan, N., & Main, M. (1984). *The adult attachment interview.* Unpublished manuscript, University of California, Berkeley.

Goldberg, S., Corter, C., Lojkasek, M., & Minde, K. (1990). Prediction of behavior problems in 4-year-olds born prematurely. *Development and Psychopathology, 2,* 15–30.

Goldberg, S., Fischer-Faye, A., Simmons R.J., Fowler, R.S., & Levison, H. (1989b, April). *Effects of chronic illness on infant-mother attachment.* Paper presented at SRCD meeting, Kansas.

Goldberg, S., Perrotta, M. Minde, K., & Corter, C. (1986). Maternal behavior and attachment in low birthweight twins and singletons. *Child Development, 57,* 34–46.

Grigoroiu-Sebanescu, M. (1984). Intellectual and emotional development and school adjustment in preterm children at 6 and 7 years of age. *International Journal of Behavior Development, 7,* 307–320.

Hines, R.B., Minde, K., Marton, P., & Trehub, S. (1980). Behavioral development of premature infants. *Developmental Medicine in Child Neurology, 22*, 623–632.

Hoy, E.A., Bill, J.M., & Sykes, D.H. (1988). Very low birthweight: A long term developmental impairment? *International Journal Behavior Development, 11*, 37–67.

Hunter, R.S., Kilstrom, N., Kraybill, E.N., & Loda, F. (1978). Antecedents of child abuse and neglect in premature infants: A prospective study in a newborn intensive care unit. *Pediatrics, 61*, 629–635.

Jeffcoate, J., Humphrey, M., & Lloyd, J. (1979). Disturbance in parent-child relationship following preterm delivery. *Developmental Medicine in Child Neurology, 21*, 344–352.

Kaplan, P.M., & Mason, E.A. (1960). Maternal reactions to premature birth viewed as an acute emotional disorder. *American Journal of Orthopsychiatry, 69*, 539–547.

Klaus, M., & Kennell, J. (1976). *Maternal-infant bonding.* St. Louis: C.V. Mosby.

Kopp, C.B. (1983). Risk factors in development. In J.J. Campos & M. Haith (Eds.), *Handbook of child psychology* (Vol. 2). New York: Wiley.

Kopp, C.B. (1987). Developmental risk historical reflections. In J. Doniger Osofsky (Ed.), *Handbook of infant development* (Vol. 2). New York: Wiley.

Leiderman, P.H. (1981). Human mother to infant social bonding: Is there a senstive phase? In K. Immelman, G., Barlow, L., Petrinovich, & M. Main (Eds.), *Behavioral development.* New York: Cambridge University Press.

Lester, B.M., Hoffman, J., & Brazelton, T.B. (1985). The rhythmic structure of mother-infant interaction in term and preterm infants. *Child Development, 56*, 15–27.

Main, M., Kaplan, N., & Cassidy, J. (1985). Security in infancy, childhood and adulthood: A move to the level of representation. In I. Bretherton & E. Waters (Eds.), *Growing points of attachment theory and research, Monographs of the Society for Research in Child Development, 50* (1–2, Serial No. 209).

Main, M., & Solomon, J. (1986). Discovery of an insecure-disorganized/disoriented attachment pattern. In T.B. Brazelton & M.W. Yogman (Eds.), *Affective development in infancy,* Norwood, NJ: Ablex Publishing Corp.

Marton, P., Minde, K., & Ogilvie, J. (1981a). Mother-infant interactions in the premature nursery: a sequential analysis. In S. Friedman & M. Sigman (Eds.), *Birth and psychological development.* New York: Academic Press.

Marton, P., Minde, K., & Perrotta, M. (1981b). The role of father for the infant at risk. *American Journal of Orthopsychiatry, 51*, 672–679.

Minde, K., (1980). Bonding of parents to premature infants: Theory and practice. In P. Taylor (Ed.), *Monographs in neonatology series.* New York: Grune & Stratton.

Minde, K. (1984). The impact of prematurity on the later behavior of children and on their families. *Clinics in Perinatology, 11*, 227–244.

Minde, K. (1986). Attachment and bonding: Some theoretical and practical implications for the treatment of high-risk caretaker-infant dyads. In *The prevention of mental-emotional disabilities. Report National Mental Health Association Commission on the Prevention of Mental-Emotional Disabilities.* Alexandria, VA: National Mental Health Association.

Minde, K., Corter, C., Goldberg, S., & Jeffers, D. (1990). Maternal preference toward premature twins up to age four. *Journal of the American Academy of Child and Adolescent Psychiatry, 29*, 367–374.

Minde, K., Goldberg, S., Perrotta, M., Washington, J., Lojkasek, M., Corter, C., & Parker, K. (1989). Continuities and discontinuities in the developmnent of 64 very small premature infants to 4 years of age. *Journal of Child Psychology and Psychiatry, 30*, 391–404.

Minde, K., Marton, P., Manning, P., & Hines, B. (1980a). Some determinants of mother-infant interaction in the premature nursery. *Journal of the American Academy of Child Psychiatry, 19*, 139–164.

Minde, K., & Minde, R. (1981). Behavioural screening of preschool children: a new approach to mental health? In P.J. Graham (Ed.), *Epidemiological approaches in child psychiatry.* London: Academic Press.

Minde, K., Perrotta, M., & Corter, C. (1982). The effect of neonatal complication in same-sexed premature twins on their mothers' preference. *Journal of the American Academy of Child Psychiatry, 21*, 446–452.

Minde, K., Perrotta, M., & Hellmann, J. (1988). The impact of delayed development in premature infants on mother-infant interaction: a prospective investigation. *Journal of Pediatrics, 112*, 136–142.

Minde, K., Shosenberg, N., Marton, P., Thompson, J., Ripley, J., & Burns, S. (1980b). Self-help groups in a premature nursery—a controlled evaluation. *Journal of Pediatrics, 96*, 933–940.

Minde, K., Shosenberg, N., & Marton, P. (1981). The effects of self-help groups in a premature nursery on maternal autonomy and caretaking style 1 year later. In L. Bond & J. Joffe (Eds.), *Facilitating infant and early child development*. Hanover, NH: University Press of New England.

Minde, K., Trehub, S., Corter, C., Boukydis, C., Celhoffer, L., & Marton, P. (1978). Mother-child relationships in the premature nursery: an observational study. *Pediatrics, 61*, 373–379.

Minde, K., Whitelaw, H., Brown, J., & Fitzhardinge, P. (1983). Effect of neonatal complications in premature infants on early parent-infant interaction. *Developmental Medicine and Child Neurology, 25*, 763–777.

O'Connor, M.J., Cohen, S., & Parmelee, A.H. (1984). Infant auditory discrimination in preterm and full-term infants as a predictor of 5-year intelligence. *Developmental Psychology, 20*, 159–165.

Offord, D.R., Boyle, M.H., Szatmari, P., Rae-Grant, N., Links, P., Cadman, D.T., Byles, J.A., Crawford, J.W., Munroe-Blum, H., Bynne, C., Thomas, H., & Woodward, C.A. (1987). The Ontario Child Health Study: Prevalence of disorder and rates of service utilization. *Archives of General Psychiatry, 44*, 832–836.

Patterson, D.M., & Barnard, K. (1990). Parenting of low birthweight infants: a review of issues and interventions. *Infant Mental Health Journal, 11*, 37–56.

Quay, H., & Peterson, D.W. (1975). *Manual for the behavior checklist*. Unpublished manuscript.

Richman, N., & Graham, P. (1971). A behavioural screening questionnaire for use with three-year-old children: Preliminary findings. *Journal of Child Psychology and Psychiatry, 16*, 277–287.

Rutter, M. (1967). A childrens' behaviour questionnaire for completion by teachers: preliminary findings. *Journal Child Psychology and Psychiatry, 8*, 1–11.

Rutter, M. (1981). Psychological sequelae of brain damage in children. *American Journal of Psychiatry, 138*, 1533–1544.

Rutter, M. (1989). Pathways from childhood to adult life. *Journal of Child Psychology and Psychiatry, 30*, 23–51.

Sameroff, A.J. (1986). Environmental context of child development. *Journal of Pediatrics, 109*, 192–200.

Sameroff, A., & Chandler, M. (1975). Reproductive risk and the continuum of caretaking casualty. In F.D. Horowitz, M. Hetherington, S. Scarr-Salapatek, & G. Siegel (Eds.), *Review of child developmental research* (Vol. 4). Chicago: University of Chicago Press.

Seidel, U.P., Chadwick, O., & Rutter, M. (1975). Psychological disorder in crippled children: A comparative study of children with and without brain damage. *Developmental Medical Child Neurology, 17*, 563–573.

Sigman, M. (1976). Early development of preterm and full-term infants: Exploratory behavior in eight-month-olds. *Child Development, 47*, 606–612.

Sigman, M., Kopp, C.B., Littman, B. & Parmelee, A.H. (1977). Infant visual attentiveness in relation to birth condition. *Developmental Psychology, 13*, 431–437.

Sigman, M. & Parmelee, A.H. (1974). Visual preferences of four-month-old preterm and full-term infants. *Child Development, 45*, 959–965.

Sigman, M., & Parmelee, A.H. (1979). Longitudinal evaluation of the preterm infant. In T.M. Field, A.M. Sostek, S. Goldberg, & H.H. Shuman (Eds.), *Infants born at risk: Behavior and development*. Jamaica, NY: Spectrum.

Silva, P.A., MaGee, R., & Williams, S. (1984). A longitudinal study of the intelligence and behavior of preterm and small for gestational age children. *Journal of Developmental Behavioral Psychiatry*, *5*, 1–5.

Sroufe, L.A. (1983). Infant-caregiver attachment and patterns of adaptation in preschool: The roots of maladaptation and competence. In M. Perlmutter (Ed.), *Development and policy concerning children with special needs. Minnesota Symposia on Child Psychology*, *16*, 41–83.

Tinsley, B., & Parke, R. (1983). The person-environment relationship: lessons from families with preterm infants. In D. Magnusson & V. Allen (Eds.), *Human development: An interactional perspective*. New York: Academic Press.

Washington, J., Minde, K., & Goldberg, S. (1986). Temperament in preterm infants: style and stability. *Journal of the American Academy of Child Psychiatry*, *25*, 493–502.

8
Emotional and Behavioral Development of Low-Birthweight Infants

Stephen L. Buka
Lewis P. Lipsitt
Ming T. Tsuang

INTRODUCTION

Current interest in the emotional and behavioral development of low-birthweight children stems from two major research traditions. Both originate with the historic work of Pasamanick, Lilienfeld and their associates in Baltimore in the 1950s (Lilienfeld & Pasamanick, 1955; Lilienfield, Pasamanick, & Rogers, 1955; Pasamanick & Kawi, 1956; Pasamanick & Lilienfield, 1955). These authors undertook a series of large-scale epidemiologic investigations, identifying children with various functional disorders (cerebral palsy, epilepsy, speech defects, etc.), selecting matched control groups, and comparing maternal pregnancy experiences as coded on birth certificates and hospital obstetric records. These studies generally reported significant associations between the clinical disorders and complications of pregnancy and delivery (Pasamanick & Knobloch, 1961). Pasamanick et al. (1956, p. 613) postulated that complications of pregnancy and delivery might produce ''a continuum of reproductive casualty extending from death . . . through cerebral palsy, epilepsy, mental deficiency, and perhaps even to behavior disorder.''

This suggestion of a dose–response relationship between the severity of perinatal trauma and the degree of neuropsychiatric damage generated a flurry of research activity in pediatrics, psychology, psychiatry, and related disciplines. One line of research employed case/control designs similar to those of the Baltimore group. The psychiatric literature includes numerous investigations examining the perinatal antecedents of a host of childhood and adult neuropsychiatric disorders, such as infantile autism, schizophrenia, and behavior problems. A second line of research focused on prospective investigations of the survival and developmental course of at-risk infant groups (including low-birthweight and preterm infants). These longitudinal studies were reported mostly in the pediatric and psychology literature and primarily focused on neurological and cognitive outcomes during the early years of life. However, as these study subjects age and enter the school years, investigators have begun to report on their emotional, behavioral, and scholastic functioning.

Several recent publications have reviewed the case-control studies of the relationships between various forms of child and adult psychopathology and conditions of pregnancy and delivery. McNeil (1988) provides a summary of the extensive literature on childhood and adult schizophrenia. Buka (1990a,b) reviews the literature on infantile autism and antisocial behavior. McCurry, Silverton, and Mednick (1990) have reviewed this entire literature. In summation, the literature indicates a clear association between adverse perinatal events and organic brain disorders (McCurry et al., 1990), autism, childhood schizophrenia, and adult schizophrenia (McNeil, 1988), and a questionable association with antisocial behavior (Buka, 1990b). There is no literature available that focuses specifically on adult affective or anxiety disorders.

While compelling, these case-control studies have several serious methodologic features that limit their interpretation. Case-control designs are of limited utility for the detection of specific and relatively rare perinatal events. Although these studies suggest a relationship between certain psychiatric conditions and "complications of pregnancy and delivery," it is unclear which perinatal events are implicated and through what mechanisms they exert an influence on the development of psychopathology. Finally, although these studies permit us to judge the relative rates of perinatal difficulties among cases and controls, they are unable to address the more critical question: Given a particular pregnancy or birth condition, what is the probability that various disorders will develop?

Accordingly, developmental scientists interested in testing whether Pasamanick's "continuum of reproductive causality" truly does extend into the behavioral and emotional domains have focused on the second line of research— prospective studies of specially selected samples of infants. The literature prior to 1960 has been reviewed in detail (Alm, 1953; Benton, 1940; Caputo & Mandell, 1970; Harper & Weiner, 1965; Wiener, 1962). However, since 1960 improved medical technologies leading to the establishment of the modern neonatal intensive care unit have dramatically altered the population of surviving low-birthweight infants (Hack, Fanaroff, & Merkatz, 1979; OTA, 1987). McCormick (1989) reviews this recent literature and summarizes the results regarding pulmonary function, physical growth, neurological status, and psychosocial development (intelligence quotient scores, academic achievement, and school failure). She notes the lack of studies examining behavioral/emotional outcomes of infants born in the modern era of neonatal care.

This chapter summarizes the recent world literature on the emotional and behavioral development of low-birthweight infants. Included are published reports of longitudinal studies of low-birthweight (or preterm) infants, born since 1960, which include any information on emotional or behavioral functioning, as reported either by formal measures or by parent/clinical reports. We are aware of the excellent discussions that indicate the predictive value of subtyping low-birthweight infants according to gestational age, evidence of intrauterine growth retardation, and the presence of perinatal complications (Francis-Williams & Davies, 1974; Harvey, Prince, Bunton, Parkinson, & Campbell, 1982; Rubin & Balow, 1977, Westwood, Kramer, Munz, Lovett, & Watters, 1983). Yet we have intentionally established broad inclusion criteria for this review to generate comprehensive summary of the published literature on this topic. The many studies which report scholastic functioning alone, however, are not included. The studies reviewed are discussed under three headings: (a) studies that include low-birthweight subjects only; (b) studies that include low-birthweight and comparison subjects; and (c) studies of entire birth or community cohorts.

The key questions that we will consider through this review and that were prompted by the earlier volume in this series (Sameroff, 1981) include:

1. Are low-birthweight infants, as a group, at increased risk for the development of emotional and behavioral problems during childhood, adolescence, or early adulthood?

2. Are there subpopulations of low-birthweight infants that are at higher risk of emotional and behavioral problems than the low-birthweight population as a whole?
   a. Are low-birthweight males a subpopulation at particular risk?
   b. Are smaller low-birthweight infants a subpopulation at particular risk?
   c. Are low-birthweight infants who show signs of early neurological or developmental problems a subpopulation at particular risk?
   d. Are low-birthweight infants from poor families a subpopulation at particular risk?

3. What forms of emotional and behavioral disorder (if any) are displayed by low-birthweight children?

LONGITUDINAL STUDIES OF LOW-BIRTHWEIGHT SUBJECTS

The six studies of low-birthweight infants only (without comparison subjects) are summarized in alphabetical order in Table 1. For each study identified we list the first author and year of publication, the selection criteria for the low-birthweight sample ("index series"), the sample birth years and location, the total number of surviving infants who were eligible for follow-up assessment, the number seen at follow-up, the age at follow-up, the measures of behavioral or emotional outcome used, and the principal study findings regarding behavioral and emotional functioning.

Only two of these studies used standardized behavioral measures. At age 3, Smith, Somner, and Von Tetzchener (1982) administered the Behavioral Problems Questionnaire (Richman & Graham, 1971) to the mothers of 33 low birthweight infants born in Oslo, Norway in 1976–1977. The proportion of

Table 1. Longitudinal Studies of Low-Birthweight Infants, Only

Author	Year	Index Series Selection*	Birth Year(s)	Location	Eligible Sample	Follow-Up: Number (m/f)	Age
Astbury	1987	< 1,501 g	1979	Melbourne, Australia	79	62	5
Escalona	1984	< 2,250 g & 4 wks pre-term or SGA	1975–76	Bronx, NY	127	114	3
Hertzig	1981	< 1,750 g	1962–65	New York, U.S.	71	66	8
Rickards	1987	< 1,000 g	1977–80	Melbourne, Australia	60	58	5
Smith	1982	< 2,000 g	1976–77	Oslo, Norway	48	33	3
Steiner	1980	< 1,501 g	1963–71	Mansfield, England	137	131	6–16

Behavioral Measure	Findings*
Maternal Reports	Only those children that showed abnormal behavior at age 2 (inattention, impulsivity, and hyperactivity) were reported by their mothers to have had problems in adjusting to kindergarten (26% vs. 0%). These early "attention deficit disorder" children were rated as significantly more aggressive, difficult to manage, and less able to cope with frustration. (33% rated as having behavioral problems; 43% "ADD" vs. 26% non-"ADD").
Family Interviews, Standardized Assessments and Observations	Of 97 nonretarded infants, 27 were clinically rated as overtly maladjusted (28%). Incidence of maladjustment was unrelated to social class. Both SES and maladjustment have a significant and independent effect upon IQ scores.
Social & Behavioral Histories from Parents	Children with neurological "soft" signs were significantly more likely ot have been referred for psychiatric consultation than were children who were neurologically normal (50% vs. 15%). Both severity and chronicity tended to be less pronounced in the neurologically normal children. Clinical features vary greatly.
Examiner Observations, Parent Reports (two or more abnormal behavior traits).	Behavior during the assessment was rated abnormal for 50% of the children, and the parents considered there to be behavioral problems in 29% of the sample. Abnormal behavior was equally common in both disabled and nondisabled children.
Parent: Behavioral Problems Questionnaire (Richman & Graham, 1971)	SES (and not BWT or Prechtl, 1968, pregnancy, delivery or postnatal complications scores) was the only variable that accounted for a significant part of the variance in behavioral problems at age 3; the mulitple correlation was 0.45. The Prechtl optimality index did not discriminate children with low scores on the behavioral questionnaire. Behavioral problems were not significantly related to any home environment measures (at 6 months).
Teacher: Rutter Behavior Questionnaire	No specific undesirable pattern of behavior, emotional disturbance or neurosis was apparent. Maladjustment was not reported. Teachers indicated that poor concentration and attention span were present in 36% and distinctive features in 27% of 130 children. This is perhaps 9 times more common than in British children of all birthweights.

*Abbreviations used: BWT = birthweight
IQ = intelligence quotient
SES = socioeconomic status
SGA = small for gestational age

190

infants receiving extreme ratings is not reported. Within this sample, however, socioeconomic status was the only variable examined that was significantly related to the number of behavioral problems reported at age 3. The degree of complications associated with either pregnancy, delivery, or neonatal status (Prechtl, 1968) were not associated with behavioral problems, nor were any measures of the home environment as assessed at 6 months of age. Steiner, Sanders, Phillips, and Maddock (1980) obtained teacher reports on the Rutter Behavior Questionnaire (Rutter, 1967) for a sample of 131 very low-birthweight (VLBW) infants born in Mansfield, England, between 1963 and 1971. The sample varied in age from 6 to 16 at the time of assessment. These investigators report that no specific undesirable pattern of behavior, emotional disturbance, or neurosis was apparent among these children, and that there were no reports of general maladjustment. However, the teachers did indicate that poor concentration and attention span were present in 36% of the children and distinctive features in 27%. Poor concentration and attention span among this VLBW sample is reported to be nine times more common than in British children of all birthweights, based on national figures.

The remaining four studies use unstructured parent reports and examiner observations to determine the presence and severity of emotional and behavioral disturbance. Although the samples vary substantially in terms of location (New York and Australia), birth years (1962 to 1980), and birthweight (1,000–2,250 g), the findings are quite consistent. Approximately one-third of the low-birthweight samples are rated as "overtly maladjusted," exhibiting "abnormal behavior," or having been referred for psychiatric consultation. Each study examines different features which might distinguish those low birthweight children who also exhibit behavioral abnormalities. Astbury, Orgill, and Bajuk (1987) report that very low-birthweight infants ($<$ 1,501 g) who at age 2 showed behaviors associated with *attention deficit disorder* (ADD; inattention, impulsivity, and hyperactivity) were 1.6 times more likely to be rated by mothers as having behavioral problems at age 5 (more aggressive, difficult to manage, and less able to cope with frustration). These ADD children were the only ones reported to have had difficulty in adjusting to kindergarten; none of the non-ADD low-birthweight children evidenced such difficulties. Rickards et al. (1987) report on an extremely low-birthweight sample ($<$ 1,000 g) born at the same time and location, also followed until age 5. Of this sample, 29% were considered by their parents to have behavioral problems, in comparison to the 33% reported by Astbury. There were no particular features which differentiated those ELBW children who went on to develop behavioral problems from the remainder of the sample. Of the two studies from the United States, Hertzig (1981) reports that the severity, chronicity, and form of behavioral disturbance among low-birthweight infants is associated with the presence of neurological "soft" signs: 50% of low-birthweight infants with "soft" signs were referred for psychiatric consultation, vs. 15% of the neurologically normal subjects. Escalona (1984) focused on the role of social class in the developmental course of low birthweight infants. Among this sample of urban infants, social class was unrelated to the development of behavioral maladjustment at age 3, but both social class and maladjustment were shown to have a significant and independent effect upon intelligence scores.

In total these six studies suggest that low-birthweight infants as a group are apparently at elevated risk for the development of emotional and behavioral difficulties. Little information is provided regarding the specific forms of disturbance that emerge among these samples. Attempts to identify the distinguishing features of those low-birthweight infants who go on to exhibit emotional and behavioral problems are inconsistent. The findings are divided concerning the contributing role of social class (Escalona, 1984; Smith et al., 1982) and neurological impairment (Hertzig, 1981; Rickards et al., 1987; Smith et al., 1982). These inconsistent results may well result from the different samples and measures used across studies.

LONGITUDINAL STUDIES OF LOW BIRTHWEIGHT AND COMPARISON SUBJECTS

The 11 longitudinal studies summarized in this section differ considerably from those discussed above. Most notably, these all contain a comparison group and thereby partially control for some of the confounding factors associated with both low-birthweight and emotional/behavioral problems (most notably gender, age and socioeconomic status). The criteria for selecting the comparison group varies considerably between studies. Most (but not all) studies match for gender and age. Many match for social class using a variety of measures, such as hospital of birth, classroom, parental occupation, and other indices. In addition, the majority of these studies include standardized measures of behavioral functioning, including structured clinical interviews and observations of the child, and parent or teacher questionnaires. Finally, these studies represent a more heterogeneous population of ''low-birthweight'' infants than those reviewed above, which were selected solely on the basis of birthweight. Subjects in this section are selected on the basis of birthweight alone, gestational age alone, a combination of birthweight and gestational age, and receipt of neonatal intensive care. However, all may be considered to be low-birthweight with or without additional features. The studies in this section are summarized in Table 2, which includes the same information as Table 1. In addition we note the number of male and female subjects included in the follow-up assessment and the criteria for selecting the comparison group.

The study by Simonds, Silva, and Aston (1981) is notable as the only investigation to include psychiatric interviews of the study children. Employing a 45-minute semistructured psychiatric interview with satisfactory psychometric properties and maternal reports, these authors rated 51 low-birthweight (LBW)

Table 2. Summary of Controlled Longitudinal Studies

Author	Year	Index Series Selection*	Birth Year(s)	Location	Eligible Sample	Follow-Up: Number (m/f)	Age
Bjerre	1976	< 2,501 g	1966	Malmo, Sweden	156	144 (71/73)	7
Breslau	1988	< 1,500 g	1976	Cleveland, OH	112	65 (40/25)	9
Calame	1986	< 1,500 g	1972–76	Lausanne, Switzerland	101	83 (?)	8
Dunn	1980	< 2,500 g	1959–77	Vancouver, Canada	419	335 (163/172)	6
Grigoroiu-Serbanescu	1984	< 37 wks	?	Bucharest, Romania	540	282 (132/150)	7
Hertzig	1984	< 1,750 g	1962–65	New York	71	66 (31/35)	3
Noble-Jamieson	1982	NICU graduates	1968–75	London, England	60	23 (12/11)	9

Comparison Group	Behavioral Measure	Findings*
144 matched for age, sex, & classroom	Parent & Teacher Questionnaires	Teachers rate LBW children as less active, shyer with classmates & maintaining more contact with adults; teachers rate parents of LBW children as more overprotective.
65 full-term, matched for age, race, sex, & classroom	Parent & Teacher Achenbach Child Behavior Checklist	VLBW boys manifested more behavioral disturbance and poorer social competence than matched full-term boys. VLBW girls same as control girl subjects. A broad range of problems, including emotional distress and conduct problems were identified. Not a function of IQ.
41 AGA, term, normal pregs., matched for sex, nationality, & SES.	Parent Questionnaire, "Behavioral Assessment"	34% of VLBW presented behavioral problems, including mainly contact and emotional disorders, hyperactivity, and short attention span, vs. 22% behavioral problems in the control gruop (not statistically significant). (Different disorders among the controls—mainly parent-child relationship disturbances.)
1) 139 NBW 2) 670 classroom controls, matched for age & sex	Teacher: Haggerty-Olson-Wickman Behavior Rating Scale	"Clinically these children may present with language disorders, reading disability, hyperactivity, clumsiness and various other problems" (no data presented).
74 full-term, NBW matched for sex, age, site of maternity care.	Examiner: "Emotional Maturity Inventory" Teacher/Parent Behavior Reports	Emotional maturity was dependent on the degree of prematurity during the first 2 years of life, not ages 3 to 6. At age 7, the mean levels are lower in the two most premature groups (G.Age < 34 wks, Bwt < 2,000g) than among the full-term children. No sex differences evident. All behavior problems more common in extreme preterm groups, particularly boys (not statistically significant).
107 NBW, normal pregnancies, singleton births (NYLS sample)	Parent Temperament Interviews	LBW differed from NBW on 4 of 9 temperament categories; less distractible, less adaptable, more intense, and having higher thresholds to sensory stimuli. LBW were no more likely to fit the "difficult child" constellation than NBW.
23 term "selected randomly from the local population"	Rutter Children's Behavior Questionnaire: Parents & Teachers	No significant differences on either parents' or teachers' reports. No consistent pattern of either neurotic or antisocial behavior in the index group. Twice as many index children received scores in the "abnormal" range (not statistically significant).

Table 2.   Summary of Controlled Longitudinal Studies (cont.)

						Follow-Up:	
Author	Year	Index Series Selection*	Birth Year(s)	Location	Eligible Sample	Number (m/f)	Age
Parkinson	1981	< 36 wks, SFD	?	London, England	60	45 (17/28)	7
Portnoy	1988	< 1,001 g, no major handicap at age 2	1980–81	London, England	18	15 (9/6)	5
Simonds	1981	< 37 wks or < 2,501 g	1967–68	Missouri	62	54 (30/24)	10
Szatmari	1989	< 1,001 g	1980–82	Ontario, Canada	90	84 (?)	5

Comparison Group	Behavioral Measure	Findings*
19 normal births matched for age, sex, birth order, social class, & race	Teachers Behavior Rating Scale	Noted a variety of behavioral problems of SFD sample. Severity of problems associated with gender, social class, and the stage of pregnancy at which slow head-growth began. Boys more extreme ratings for being clumsy, worried, fidegty, unhappy and upset by new situations. Girls more extreme for crying, irritability, and bullying.
NBW, term, group matched for age, sex, IUGR previous births, birth order, marital status, ethnic origin, father's SES, maternal age	Temperament: Behavioral Style Questionnaire Behavioural Screening Questionnaire Parent Interview Maternal Over-Protectiveness Parental Opinion Form	ELBW children have significantly higher mean scores on the activity and intensity variables, only. No mean differences between ELBW and control children. No children (ELBW or control) rated at extreme levels. No differences between parent groups on maternal over-protectiveness. (Most data not presented.)
52 full-term, NBW, matched for sex.	Semi-structured psychiatric interview of child, Conners Questionnaire, Rutter Child Scale, Devereux Child Behavior Scale	No significant differences in the frequency of psychiatric diagnosis between the index group (21.6%) and the controls (17.3%). No differences in behavior rating scores. Above average maternal protectiveness at some point reported for 48% of preterm, 39% of LBW-term, and 33% of controls (not statistically significant).
Age-matched stratified random community sample	Parent Reports: Survey Diagnostic Instrument from the Ontario Health Study	16% ELBW vs. 6.9% controls diagnosed with attention deficit disorder with hyperactivity (ADDH). Rates of other diagnoses (conduct disorder and emotional disorders) not raised in the ELBW group. No sex differences observed.

*Abbreviations used: AGA   = appropriate for gestational age; BWT = birthweight
    G.AGE = gestational age; IUGR = intrauterine growth retardation
    LBW   = low birthweight, · 2,501 g
    NBW   = normal birthweight, · 2,500 g;
    VLBW = very low birthweigh · 1,501 g
    ELBW = extremely low birthweigh · 1,001 g
    SFD   = small for dates; NICU = neonatal intensive care unit

and 52 normal birthweight (NBW) children at ages 9 to 11 for the presence or absence of a psychiatric diagnosis according to prespecified criteria (Guy, 1976). They reported no differences in the frequency of psychiatric disorder between the LBW and NBW groups (21.6% vs. 17.3%). In addition, this study found no difference between the LBW and NBW groups on three well-validated child behavior rating scales completed by study mothers (Conners, Goyette, & Southwick, 1976; Rutter, Tizard, & Whitmore, 1970; Spivack & Spotts, 1966). They conclude that preterm birth or low birthweight, alone or combined, do not necessarily predispose a child to psychiatric or emotional disorders at a later age. There was a slight but nonsignificant relationship between birth status and self-reports of maternal protectiveness. Above-average maternal protectiveness at some point during the subjects' lives was reported for 48% of the preterm and 39% of the full-term LBW groups and 33% of the NBW controls.

Two other investigations rated children based in part upon clinical assessments. Calame et al. (1986) combined parental questionnaire data and an unspecified "behavioral assessment" to rate 83 very low-birthweight (VLBW) infants and 41 normal birthweight controls for the presence of behavioral disorders at age 8. They report a nonsignificant difference where 34% of the VLBW versus 22% of the NBW subjects presented behavioral disorders. They note differences in the forms of disorder evidenced in the two groups. Among the VLBW sample there was a common pattern of severe disorders with similar features, i.e., anxiety, phobia, irritability, short attention span, and hyperdependency. The disorders among the NBW controls were less severe and of a different form, consisting mainly in parent–child relationship disturbances. Grigoroiu-Serbanescu (1984) rated 282 preterm infants and 74 full-term controls on an Emotional Maturity Inventory involving clinical assessment (Grigoroiu, 1978). She reports a relationship between the degree of prematurity and ratings of emotional maturity, where girls less than 1,500 g and boys less than 2,000 g scored significantly lower than the full-term controls.

Most studies included parent reports of behavioral problems. Of the five which used established child behavior rating scales, two reported statistically significant differences indicating more behavioral problems among the low birthweight samples. Both of these positive reports used items from the Achenbach Child Behavior Checklist (Achenbach & Edelbrock, 1983). Szatmari, Saigal, Rosenbaum, and Campbell (1989) compared parent ratings of 84 extremely low-birthweight ($< 1,001$ g) children at age 5 with those of an age-matched stratified random sample from the community. Sixteen percent of the VLBW cohort were diagnosed as having an attention deficit disorder with hyperactivity, compared to 6.9% of controls ($p < .05$). Rates of conduct disorder and emotional disorder were not elevated among the VLBW sample. No sex differences in the rates of psychiatric disorder were observed. Additional analyses showed that the association between ADDH and VLBW was mediated by the presence of developmental delay in the child.

Breslau, Klein, and Allen (1988) administered the Achenbach instrument to parents and teachers of 65 very-low-birthweight infants ($< 1,500$ g) and 65 full-term controls, individually matched by school, race, sex, and age, at age 9. VLBW boys were rated as manifesting significantly more psychiatric symptoms and significantly lower social adjustment that their controls, whereas VLBW girls were indistinguishable from other controls. Behavior ratings for the boys were elevated for all of the domains assessed, including emotional distress as well as conduct problems, and statistically significant for all but two. Additional analyses showed that the association between VLBW and behavioral disturbance in boys was not a function of IQ.

Three studies did not detect significant differences in parent reports of behavioral problems on established instruments. As described earlier, Simonds et al. (1981) reported no differences in maternal ratings on the Rutter, Conners and Devereux behavioral rating scales. Portnoy, Callias, Wolke, and Gamsu (1988) administered a Behavioral Screening Questionnaire (Richman & Graham, 1971) to the parents of 14 extremely low-birthweight infants (< 1,001 g) and 14 closely matched controls at age 5. There were no significant differences on the mean behavioral ratings for the two groups, and no children were rated as having scores at the extreme range (> 10 points). Noble-Jamieson, Lukeman, Silverman, and Davies (1982) administered a Children's Behaviour Questionnaire (Rutter et al., 1970) to the parents of 23 survivors of a neonatal intensive care unit (NICU) and 23 randomly selected controls. There were no differences on the mean scores for the two groups; however, twice as many of the NICU graduates received scores in the "abnormal" range.

Three studies obtained parent ratings on measures of infant temperament or maternal overprotectiveness. Hertzig and Mittleman (1984) collected information on infant temperament for 66 low-birthweight infants and 107 term infants, through parent interviews throughout the first 3 years of life. At age 3, the low-birthweight sample showed significant differences on four of nine categories of temperament. These children were less distractible, exhibited higher sensory thresholds, and were more intense and less adaptable. The LBW sample as a whole was no more likely to fit the "difficult child" constellation of temperamental features; however, those who were found to exhibit signs of central nervous system dysfunction or disorder were. Portnoy et al. (1988) obtained temperament ratings through the use of a Behavioral Style Questionnaire (McDevitt & Carey, 1978). Their sample of extremely low-birthweight infants (< 1,001 g) received significantly higher scores than the control group on the activity and intensity variables. None of the other temperament scales reached significance. These authors also report no differences in maternal ratings of overprotectiveness.

Teachers tended to report more behavioral problems among the low-birthweight children than did the parents. This is demonstrated most clearly by Bjerre and Hansen (1976), who compared parents' and teachers' evaluations of 144 low-birthweight children at age 7 on a self-designated questionnaire. Compared to the parents, teachers rated the low-birthweight children as shyer, having poorer contact with schoolmates, being more dependent on contact with adults, less active, and more compliant. Compared to the normal weight controls, teachers rated the low-birthweight children as significantly less active and more compliant. This is the only study to report *lower* activity levels among a low-birthweight sample. Teachers in this study also reported significantly more parents in the low birthweight group as having an overprotective attitude towards their children.

All of the studies using teacher ratings reported some evidence of increased behavioral problems in the school setting among low-birthweight samples. This is consistent with the reports of poorer school adjustment and scholastic attainment, which are not discussed here. Teacher ratings from Breslau et al. (1988) parallel the parent ratings: more behavior problems among the male very low-birthweight sample than controls, across a range of emotional and conduct domains. Teachers also rated the very low-birthweight girls as having higher scores than their controls, unlike the parents, who rated each group similarly. Teacher ratings on the Anxious and Self-destructive scales reached statistical significance. Grigoroiu-Serbanescu (1984) reported a significant association between the child's degree of prematurity and teacher ratings of fatigability, emotional immaturity in school events, and social behavior troubles. Rates of attention deficit were elevated among the most premature subjects (particularly the boys) but did not reach statistical significance. The teacher results of Dunn et al. (1980) and Parkinson, Wallis, and Harvey (1981) are difficult to interpret, yet also indicate that the low-birthweight samples are rated as demonstrating more behavioral abnormalities than the control groups. As in the parent ratings, Noble-Jamieson et al. (1982) find no mean differences on teachers' behavioral ratings. However, twice as many NICU graduates as normal control subjects were rated at the ''abnormal'' behavior level.

Taken as a whole, these 11 controlled studies tend to support the hypothesis that low-birthweight children display more emotional and behavioral problems and extreme temperamental qualities. The well-designed study of Simonds et al. (1981) is one notable exception. The negative findings reported by Noble-Jamieson et al. (1982) and Portnoy et al. (1988) may be attributed to their particularly small sample sizes (46 and 28 total subjects, respectively). The key finding of the Breslau et al. study that behavioral problems were particularly pronounced among low birthweight boys is supported by the results of Grigoroiu-Serbanescu (1984) and Parkinson et al. (1981) but not those of Szatmari et al. (1989) or Simonds et al. (1981). Other variables which were reported in association with the development of behavioral problems were socioeconomic status and the stage of pregnancy at which growth retardation began (Parkinson et al., 1981), the degree of prematurity (Grigoroiu-Serbanescu, 1984), central nervous system problems (Hertzig & Mittleman, 1984) and developmental delay (Szatmari et al., 1989). Thus, a consistent pattern of results is suggested, in which those low-birthweight infants (particularly boys) who show the greatest prenatal growth retardation, central nervous system problems, and signs of developmental delay are at greatest risk for the development of behavioral abnormalities.

Although a broad range of behavioral and emotional problems was reported some consistent patterns emerge. The behavioral problem reported most often concerns the child's activity level. Five studies reported elevated activity ratings among the low-birthweight sample; one rated the low-birthweight children as less active. In a well-designed study, Szatmari et al. (1989) report that extremely low-birthweight children at age 5 are 2.8 times more likely to be diagnosed with attention deficit disorder with hyperactivity (ADDH) than a representative community sample. Short attention span is reported in four studies; one study reports low birthweight children as less distractible. Emotional immaturity, anxiety, and sadness/depression are other emotional and behavioral features reported across studies.

COHORT STUDIES

Although the controlled longitudinal studies summarized in the preceding section have distinct methodologic advantages over both the uncontrolled studies of Section 1 and case-control designs, they are still limited by the size and quality of the comparison group. Whereas the size of the comparison group limits the statistical "power" of the investigators' analyses, the quality of appropriateness of the comparison group limits the scientific validity of those analyses. All of the studies in Section 2 may be questioned regarding which variables associated with low birthweight were or were not "controlled" for and the adequacy of the control procedures.

One solution to this problem is to recruit large birth cohorts from a prescribed geographic region and contrast the emotional and behavioral development of the low-birthweight subset of these cohorts with the normal weight members (or some portion). This procedure ensures large numbers of comparison subjects, permits statistical as well as design (matching) procedures for the "control" of confounding variables, and limits differential selection forces between the index and comparison samples. This design strategy has been used in several informative studies of low-birthweight infants born prior to 1960. These include the 1946 and 1958 British birth cohorts (Davie, Butler, & Goldstein, 1972; Douglas, 1960) the Edinburgh sample of Drillien, Thomson, and Burgoyne (1980), and, in the U.S., the Baltimore (Wiener, Rider, Oppel, & Harper, 1968) and Kauai (Werner & Smith 1982) cohorts. This section will summarize six behavioral outcome studies of large cohorts born since 1960, culminating in our own recent work.

Neligan, Kolvin, Scott, and Garside (1976) assessed two index series and a randomly selected comparison group from the Newcastle Survey of Child Development at ages 5 and 7. This survey enrolled all of the survivors of the first month of life who were born to Newcastle mothers between 1960 and 1962. The investigators followed those children born between June 1, 1961, and May 31, 1962, who were: (a) "born too small" (below the 10th percentile of birthweight for gestational age); (b) "born too soon" (before 255 days gestation); and (c) a randomly selected one-in-seven sample of the entire birth cohort, stratified by school. This design allows the investigators to generalize to the entire birth cohort without following excessive numbers of control subjects and also ensures that the index and comparison groups are selected from the same underlying population, thereby reducing study biases resulting from the sample selection procedures.

Four types of behavioral data were collected: (a) mothers' ratings by a technique described as "focussed interviewing" (Wolff, 1967); (b) teachers' ratings on the Rutter Behavioral Rating Scale (Rutter, 1967); (c) examiners' ratings; and (d) psychiatrists' assessments by a standard interview of the child (Rutter et al., 1970). Temperament data were gathered from maternal interviews. Their analyses showed "a clear excess of abnormalities among the children in both extreme abnormal groups [very light-for-dates and short gestation] as compared with the controls. . . . The general picture is that of a hyperactive pattern in both the extreme abnormal groups, but particularly in the very light-for-dates" (Neligan et al., p. 44). This association was more pronounced for boys than for girls. "Clearly the boys appear to be more vulnerable to the effects of abnormalities of intra-uterine growth" (p. 45). Social class was also found to be related to both birth status and behavioral outcome. These authors conclude that "the abnormalities of intra-uterine growth produce more adverse effects in children from an unfavourable social background than in those from a favourable background" (p. 47).

McGee, Silva, and Williams (1983) reached similar conclusions with a birth cohort from Dunedin, New Zealand. These investigators examined the prevalence of parent- and teacher-reported behavior problems at ages 5 and 7 among 949 children enrolled in the Dunedin Multidisciplinary Child Development Study and who had been rated on the Rutter Child Scales A and B (Rutter et al., 1970). Children who were rated at an extreme level by either parents or teachers at both ages 5 and 7 were classified as having "stable behavior problems." This classification procedure identified 52 boys and 32 girls with IQs above 70 who were compared with the remainder of the sample. Among a variety of perinatal variables examined, being small for gestational age (below the 10th percentile of birthweight for gestational age) was the only variable which was significantly associated with stable behavior problems. Neither birthweight nor gestational age alone were significantly related to behavior problems. The relative risk of stable problem behavior associated with being small for gestational age (SGA) was 2.44; SGA children were 2.44 times more likely to develop stable ybehavior problems than were AGA children. This relative risk rose to 4.86 among children residing in high family-adversity environments, compared to 2.04 for low family-adversity environments. Although not statistically significant, these results suggest an interaction between perinatal and environmental stress in the development of behavioral problems. This study failed to demonstrate a significant association between socioeconomic status and stable behavior problems.

Also, the relationship between SGA and behavior did not differ by gender. Finally, although the children in the stable problem group did not show early developmental delays in walking and talking, by age 7 they did show delays on measures of cognitive, primarily verbal, functioning.

Nichols and Chen (1981) analyzed the age 7 psychological and neurological data of 28,889 children born between 1959 and 1965 and enrolled in the NINCDS Collaborative Perinatal Project (NCPP); 2,356 children (8.2%) were classified by factor analysis methods as extreme on "hyperkinetic-impulsive behavior" (HI). The relative rates of HI in relation to low gestational age (36 weeks or less) and low birthweight (various criteria) were determined for white and black, males and females. The short gestation children were 1.16 times more likely to be classified as HI as were the normal gestation children. This relative rate was significant only among white boys. Low-birthweight children were 1.5 times more likely to be classified as HI that the normal birthweight sample. This association held for all race-sex groups except for white girls. Subjects who were low birthweight and low gestational age were at the greatest relative risk for HI. Birthweight continued to have a small but significant association with HI once all other known correlates (including SES) were included in a discriminant function analysis.

McCormick, Gortmaker, and Sobol (1989) also examined the relationship between birthweight and behavioral problems in a large cohort. These investigators conducted a secondary analysis of the 1981 National Health Interview Child Health Supplement, a representative sample of the civilian noninstitutionalized population of the United States. Parents of 11,699 children ages 4–17 completed the Behavior Problem Index (BPI), which is designed to encompass domains of behavior similar to those covered by the Achenbach Child Behavior Checklist (Achenbach & Edelbrock, 1983). Very low-birthweight children (< 1,500 g) were significantly more likely to receive higher scores on the hyperactivity subscale than were normal birthweight children. No significant differences were detected for the additional five subscales (Antisocial, Depression/Anxiety, Headstrong, Immature, and Peer Conflict) or for the total behavior scale. Multivariate analyses indicated that socioeconomic disadvantage, very low birthweight, and hyperactivity were independent risks for school failure among this sample. They conclude that the poor, VLBW child who develops a behavior problem is at greatest risk of school failure.

Cohen, Velez, Brook, and Smith (1989) reported on a psychiatric follow-up of a random sample of 976 families living in upstate New York in 1975. A total of 725 children between ages 9 to 18 and their parents were assessed by both the parent and youth versions of the NIMH Diagnostic Interview Schedule for Children (Costello, Edelbrock, Dulcan, & Kalas, 1984). These authors included birthweight in a combined index of pregnancy problems which also included maternal illness during pregnancy, complications of the pregnancy or of the delivery, and so on. This pregnancy problems index was significantly related to two of six psychiatric syndromes (conduct problems and separation anxiety), and one of six diagnosable disorders (overanxious disorder). Somatic events of early childhood were as predictive of symptoms of psychopathology as were pregnancy and birth problems. The study results did not support any simple model of matching the form of psychopathology with the kind of early risk.

Finally, we have recently completed a variety of record linkage, record review, and personal interview follow-up studies with the 4,000 children enrolled in the Providence cohort of the NINCDS Collaborative Perinatal Project (NCPP) (Buka, Lipsitt, & Tsuang, 1988). The NCPP entailed a single study design which called for the systematic collection of data through the prospective observation and examination of approximately 60,000 pregnancies nationwide, through the first 7 years of life. Obstetrical intake occurred between January 1959 and December 1965. The members of the Providence cohort include 3,475 pregnancies enrolled through the prenatal clinic of a large maternity hospital, plus 665 pregnancies enrolled through a private obstetrician affiliated with the study, providing considerable socioeconomic diversity within this sample. Major findings from the NCPP have been summarized by Niswander and Gordon (1972) and Broman, Nichols, and Kennedy (1975).

We have examined the behavioral development of the low-birthweight members of this cohort at four different ages: 4, 7, 18, and 25 (Buka, Tsuang, & Lipsitt, 1990). For ages 4 and 7 we have reanalyzed the behavioral ratings which were assigned as part of the original NCPP protocol. For age 18 we have obtained data on delinquent offending and examined the relationship of delinquency to low birthweight and other measures of fetal growth. At ages 18 to 28 we have conducted structured psychiatric interviews and analyzed the relative rates of psychiatric disorder among low birthweight and normal birthweight subjects. Each of these analyses are discussed below.

Major psychological assessments of the NCPP subjects took place at 8 months, 4 years, and 7 years. As part of the 4-year and 7-year assessments the children were rated by psychological examiners on a number of behavioral dimensions (10 and 15 items, respectively). Items such as "degree of dependency," "duration of attention span," and "level of activity" were scored on a five-point scale, ranging from one extreme to the opposite extreme. For instance, "duration of attention span" could be rated as (a) very brief, (b) short, (c) adequate, (d) more than average, or (e) highly perseverative. In addition, the psychological examiners assigned a global behavioral rating for each child (normal/suspect/abnormal), based upon the item ratings and clinical impressions.

Comparisons of the global behavioral ratings at ages 4 and 7 are summarized in Table 3. For males and females separately, the frequency of each rating (normal/suspect/abnormal) is listed by birthweight group. Logistic regression methods were employed to determine whether the frequency of deviant ratings were elevated among the low-birthweight groups (Kleinbaum, Kupper, & Morgenstern, 1982). Control variables in these analyses included race (white versus

Table 3. Frequency and Adjusted Relative Risk of Abnormal/Suspect Behavioral Ratings at Ages 4 & 7—Providence Cohort of the National Collaborative Perinatal Project

	Age 4					
	Male			Female		
Behavioral Rating	NBW (1312)	LBW (115)	§OR	NBW (1316)	LBW (156)	§OR
Normal	67.8%	69.6%		78.0%	68.0%	
Suspect	25.5%	20.9%	0.7	17.4%	26.3%	1.6*
Abnormal	6.7%	9.6%	1.3	4.6%	5.8%	1.3
Suspect/Abnormal	32.2%	30.5%	0.9	22.0%	32.1%	1.6*

	Age 7					
	Male			Female		
Behavioral Rating	NBW (1434)	LBW (124)	§OR	NBW (1406)	LBW (170)	§OR
Normal	81.2%	79.5%		86.1%	84.1%	
Suspect	15.6%	16.1%	1.0	11.9%	12.9%	1.0
Abnormal	3.3%	4.0%	1.3	2.0%	2.9%	1.4
Suspect/Abnormal	18.9%	20.1%	1.0	13.9%	15.8%	1.1

§OR = estimated odds of particular behavioral ratings, relative to rating of "normal," adjusted for race and socioeconomic level.
*one-sided p value < .01

non-white) and socioeconomic status (using a five-point composite index derived from the U.S. Bureau of the Census for use in the Collaborative Project) (Myrianthopoulos & French, 1968). The results of these logistic regression models provide a race- and SES-adjusted estimate of the relative odds of a deviant behavioral rating (suspect, abnormal, or both) relative to a rating of "normal," for low-birthweight subjects in comparison with normal birthweight subjects. For example, at age 4, low-birthweight males were 0.7 times as likely to be rated "suspect" as were normal birthweight males. Low-birthweight females were 1.6 times as likely to be rated "suspect" than were normal birthweight females, both adjusted for race and socioeconomic status. The results presented in Table 3 fail to support the hypothesis that low-birthweight children are more likely to be rated as deviant on a global behavioral index. The sole exception is for low-birthweight females at age 4, who were 1.6 times more likely to receive a suspect rating than were their normal birthweight counterparts.

This same analytic approach was used to examine whether low-birthweight children were more likely to receive deviant ratings on the individual behavior items assigned at ages 4 and 7. The results of these analyses are summarized in Tables 4 and 5 (for ages 4 and 7, respectively). For each behavioral item where there was a significant difference between the ratings assigned to low-

Table 4.   Frequency and Adjusted Relative Risk of Abnormal/Suspect Ratings on 10 Behavioral Items at Age 4—Providence Cohort of the National Collaborative Perinatal Project

	Male			Female		
Behavioral Items	NBW (1312)	LBW (115)	§OR	NBW (1316)	LBW (156)	§OR
Emotional Reactivity						
Extremely flat	1.4%	3.5%	2.6*	1.5%	0.6%	0.4
Degree of Irritability						
Extremely phlegmatic	1.0%	0.9%	0.8	0.6%	1.9%	4.1*
Degree of Dependency						
Demands more attention/ constant demand	25.5%	23.5%	1.0	19.5%	26.3%	1.6**
Duration of Attention Span						
Short/brief	24.3%	27.0%	0.9	20.0%	27.6%	1.4*
Goal Orientation						
Brief/no effort	24.5%	27.0%	1.0	18.2%	27.6%	1.6**
Response to Directions						
Completely dependent upon directions	0.2	1.7	8.3**	0.3	0.6	1.9

No differences noted for the following variables: *Degree of Cooperation, Level of Activity, Nature of Activity, Nature of Communication.*

§OR = estimated odds of particular behavioral rating, relative to rating of "normal," adjusted for race and socioeconomic level.
*one-sided p value < .05; **one-sided p value < .01.

birthweight and normal birthweight subjects (either among the males or the females) the frequency, adjusted odds ratio, and significance level are shown. For instance, the first line of Table 4 indicates that, at age 4, the male low-birthweight subjects were 2.6 times more likely to be rated as "extremely flat" for the item Emotional Reactivity than were normal birthweight males (one-sided p value < .05); female low birthweight subjects were unlikely to receive this rating (odds ratio = 0.4, n.s.). Males were also more likely to be rated as "completely dependent upon directions." Low birthweight girls were deviant on a number of items, including "degree of irritability" (extremely phlegmatic), "degree of dependency" (demands more attention or constant attention), "duration of attention span" (short or brief), and "goal orientation" (brief or no effort).

At age 7 (Table 5) the male low-birthweight subjects were more likely to be rated as showing no or very little fear, as very or extremely friendly, and as very self-confident than were the normal birthweight males. The low-birthweight

Table 5. Frequency and Adjusted Relative Risk of Abnormal/Suspect Ratings on 15 Behavioral Items at Age 7—Providence Cohort of the National Collaborative Perinatal Project

Behavioral Items	Male			Female		
	NBW (1434)	LBW (124)	§OR	NBW (1406)	LBW (170)	§OR
Fearfulness						
No/very little fear	9.8%	17.7%	1.7*	8.4%	7.1%	0.8
Rapport with Examiner						
Shy/exceptionally shy	20.9%	18.6%	0.9	21.4%	29.4%	1.6**
Very/extremely friendly	9.4%	19.4%	2.3***	9.0%	8.2%	1.2
Self-Confidence						
More than usually/ very self-confident	3.2%	6.5%	2.1*	3.4%	0.6%	0.2*
Emotional Reactivity						
Somewhat/extremely flat	13.1%	16.9%	1.4	12.2%	21.8%	1.9***
Duration of Attention Span						
More than average/ highly perseverative	9.4%	7.3%	0.8	6.3%	3.5%	0.4*
Level of Activity						
Extreme inactivity	0.8%	0.8%	1.2	0.2%	1.2%	9.2**
Assertiveness						
Passive acceptance/ extreme passivity	15.2%	12.9%	0.9	16.1%	23.5%	1.5**

No differences noted for the following variables: *Degree of Cooperation, Goal Orientation; Level of Frustration Tolerance; Degree of Dependency; Nature of Activity; Nature of Communication; Separation from Mother;* or *Hostility.*

§OR = estimated odds of particular behavioral rating, relative to rating of "normal," adjusted for race and socioeconomic level.
*one-sided *p* value < .05; **one-sided *p* value < .01; ***one-sided *p* value < .001

females showed a different behavioral profile. As a group, they were less likely to be rated as very self-confident or to have a prolonged attention span than were the normal birthweight females. In addition, they were more often rated as shy or exceptionally shy, of somewhat or extremely flat emotional reactivity, of extreme inactivity, and as passive or extremely passive.

In summary, the results of these analyses suggest that, although the global behavioral ratings are similar for the low-birthweight and normal birthweight subjects, the groups do differ on particular behavioral dimensions. At age 4, both male and female low-birthweight children are described as having flat affect, being extremely phlegmatic, highly dependent, and with a brief attention span.

Table 6. Adjusted Relative Risk of Delinquent Offending
in Relation to Fetal Growth Measures

Condition	Number	One Offense		Two + Offenses	
		mOR*	p-value	mOR*	p-value
Premature Delivery (< 38 weeks gestation)	253	1.0	.98	1.2	.41
Postmature Delivery (> 42 weeks gestation)	278	1.1	.80	1.2	.37
Very Low Birthweight (< 2000 grams)	65	0.5	.35	0.2	.15
Low Birthweight (< 2500 grams)	252	0.8	.52	0.8	.41
High Birthweight (> 4000 grams)	165	1.1	.78	1.2	.43
Small-for-Gestational-Age (bottom 10%)	244	0.5	.04	0.6	.13
Large-for-Gestational-Age (top 10%)	237	1.2	.52	1.6	.04

*mOR = Mantel-Haenszel odds ratio, stratified by race, sex, and socioeconomic level.

The particular items differ between males and females, but the general constellation of items is similar for each gender. At age 7, however, the low-birthweight boys are rated as significantly more confident and friendly, and less fearful than their normal birthweight counterparts. The low-birthweight girls, on the other hand, continue to be described as having a brief attention span, flat affect, and being inactive, passive, and shy. Further analyses of these suggested gender effects, which capitalize on the longitudinal nature of these data, are warranted.

The next behavioral outcome for the Providence cohort concerned antisocial behavior as defined by court-recorded delinquent activity. By January 1, 1985, all members of the Providence cohort of the NCPP had reached age 18 and were no longer under the jurisdiction of the juvenile court system. With permission from the Family Court of Rhode Island, subjects from the Providence cohort of the NCPP with court records were identified by linking names and birthdates with computerized court listings. Mothers' names, siblings' names and in some cases home address and fathers' name were used for verification when possible. Seven hundred and twenty subjects were identified as having juvenile court records. These records were then reviewed and coded according to the age, nature, and disposition of each offense petition. Each adjudicated offense was classified by us as "dependency" (child care violations by the subject's parents), "status," or true "delinquent offenses," according to Rhode Island statutes.

Table 7. Subject Location and Interview Rates by Birthweight—
Providence Cohort of the National Collaborative Perinatal Project

	NBW*		LBW*	
	#	%	#	%
Initial Sample	870	—	195	—
Deceased/Adopted	92	—	44	—
Eligible Sample	778	100.0	151	100.0
Dead End	57	7.3	16	10.6
Still Tracing	74	9.5	11	7.3
Located	647	83.2	124	82.1
interviewed	577	89.2	113	91.1
refused	58	9.0	10	8.1
unavailable	12	1.8	1	0.8

*Abbreviations used: NBW = normal birth weight
                      LBW = low birthweight (< 2500 g)

To assess the reliability of the juvenile offense data obtained through this process a random 5% sample of the entire cohort was reclassified by the same process 1 year later. There was a 100% concordance for classification as having a court record or not. For the 31 subjects with court records, there was a 85% agreement on the number of petitions filed, with 97% of the comparisons agreeing within one petition. There was a 90% concordance for specific petition classification categories, with less than 1% varying by two or more offenses. These findings suggest that the coded petition data serve as a sufficiently reliable measure of the arrest data recorded by the Family Court System.

Subjects with any recorded delinquent offenses were further classified as having only one ("single") or more than one ("repeat") offenses. We are particularly interested in the group with recorded repeat offenses, for the following reasons. First, from the vantage of the juvenile court system, subjects with recorded repeat offenses are of special concern as they place a particular burden on the legal system. Second, assuming that recorded offenses are an accurate index of actual offenses, recurrent offenders are of greater public concern than the single offender. Finally, given that arrest data are imprecise indicators of true offense rates (as many delinquent offenses go unprosecuted), the contrast between repeat offenders and nonoffenders is particularly informative. Persons with more than one delinquent arrest are clearly "repeat offenders." Persons with no arrests may quite likely be infrequent offenders ("single offenders") but are less likely to be "repeat offenders" (under the assumption that most instances of repeated delinquency will result in at least one arrest).

We examined the association of these behavioral outcomes to several indices of fetal growth, derived from measures of birthweight and gestational age. These include prematurity (less than 38 weeks gestation), low birthweight (less than 2,500 grams), and small- and large-for-gestational-age (bottom and top decile of the birthweight distributions for each gestational age in weeks). Each prenatal and perinatal condition examined was converted into a dichotomous variable (0 = absent, 1 = present). Control variables included gender, race, and socioeconomic level (again using the composite index described by Myrianthopoulos & French, 1968). Subjects below the median composite index value for their race and sex group were classified as "low-SES" and the remainder as "high-SES." The association between each dichotomous exposure variable and both delinquency outcomes (single offense or repeat offense) was assessed by calculating the Mantel-Haenszel (MH) test statistic and corresponding probability value and odds ratio (mOR), stratified for race, sex, and socioeconomic level (low/high) (Mantel & Haenszel, 1959). The probability value associated with each MH test statistic and the point estimate for the mOR are reported. These analyses were limited to a sample of 2,608 black and white children enrolled from the public clinic sample (only) who completed the final (age 7) study assessment, and excludes all subjects known to have died before age 18.

Table 6 presents test statistics for seven measures of fetal growth. Shown for each condition are the number of subjects positive for the condition, the MH odds ratio (mOR) comparing single offenders versus nonoffenders, the MH test statistic probability value and the mOR and probability value comparing repeat offenders versus nonoffenders. Following the discussion above, we reason that these last two statistics (for repeat offenders) should provide the most valid estimate of the relationship between the fetal growth variables analyzed and delinquent activity. We expect that particularly strong effects would also be evident in the statistics for the single offender group.

Among the measures of fetal growth shown in Table 6, in general, conditions reflecting smaller size at birth (low-birthweight, small-for-gestational-age) are associated with diminished risk of repeat offending, and conditions reflecting larger size at birth (high-birthweight and large-for-gestational-age) are associated with increased risk of repeat offending. Of these conditions, only large-for-gestational-age is statistically significant at the 0.5 level. Low-birthweight children are slightly less likely to be arrested for delinquent behavior than are normal birthweight children (nonsignificant). Premature and postmature delivery are both associated with slightly increased rates of repeat offending (mOR = 1.2, p = 0.41). The magnitude of the association between all of the measures of fetal growth and single offending is less than for repeat offending, with one exception. Small-for-gestational-age infants are half as likely to become single offenders (mOR = 0.5, p. = 0.04) but only 40% less likely to become repeat offenders (mOR = 0.6, p = .13).

The apparent direct association between birthweight and risk of single and repeat offending suggested by these results was examined further by logistic regression methods (Kleinbaum et al., 1982). We regressed single and repeat offending on each of the birthweight measures, along with height and weight measurements of the children at age 7. After adjusting for differences in size at age 7, the effect sizes shown in Table 6 remained virtually unchanged. Apparently, other features of large-for-gestational-age children than their size later in life account for their increased likelihood of delinquent activity. Similarly, the diminished rate of delinquent activity among low-birthweight children is not associated with their size.

Finally, we are presently completing a 25-year psychiatric follow-up study of approximately 1,000 children selected from this cohort (Buka et al., 1990). The background, rationale, and design for this study has been described previously (Buka et al., 1988). A sample of 500 index subjects were selected on the basis of a combination of perinatal complications (prolonged fetal hypoxia or ''other'' complications) and prematurity (gestational age of 36 weeks or less). A sample of 500 comparison subjects matched for sex, race, parity, date of birth, maternal age, and maternal education was also selected.

Subjects were recontacted between ages 18 and 28 and administered a battery of instruments designed to assess psychiatric diagnosis, cognitive and psychosocial functioning, and family history of mental disorders. Lifetime psychiatric symptomatology was assessed through administration of Version III of the NIMH Diagnostic Interview Schedule (DIS). The DIS is a completely structured interview form constructed to gather information about current and lifetime psychiatric symptoms. This information is organized for computer diagnostic assessment using DSM-III, Research Diagnostic Criteria or Feighner criteria (Robins, Helzer, & Croughan, 1981a). The DIS has satisfactory psychometric and administrative properties for the ascertainment of psychiatric diagnoses within large community samples (Robins, Helzer, & Croughan, 1981b). Although the DIS may be used to differentiate between current and previous symptoms, our analyses have focused on lifetime events, that is, whether a person has ever experienced a particular form of psychiatric disorder.

As with all longitudinal studies, differential attrition may bias the study results. Table 7 shows the subject location and interview rates for the study to date, by birthweight group. The subject location and interview completion rates are quite comparable between the low and normal birthweight groups. Approximately 83% of the sample have been located at the time of this analysis. Of those located, approximately 90% have been interviewed, for an overall completion rate of 74% of the eligible sample. Although males were slightly harder to locate and recruit than were females, within each gender there is no evidence of differential attrition in relation to birthweight.

A preliminary analysis of the rates of psychiatric disorder in association with gender and birthweight is shown in Table 8 for the first 690 subjects interviewed. This table shows for males and females the proportion of normal birthweight and low-birthweight ($< 2,500$ g) subjects meeting DSM-III criteria for each of six psychiatric disorders. Also shown are the race- and SES-adjusted odds ratios estimated by logistic regression models. None of the differences in the rates of psychiatric disorders by age 28 for the normal and low birthweight samples reach

Table 8.   Lifetime Prevalence (%) of DIS/DSM-III Psychiatric Disorders at Ages 18–28 for 690 Subjects from the Providence NCPP Sample, by Sex, and Birthweight

	Males			Females		
Psychiatric Disorder	NBW* (255)	LBW* (48)	§OR	NBW* (322)	LBW* (65)	§OR
Alcohol Dependence	17.6	12.5	0.8	6.8	6.2	0.7
Antisocial Personality	13.7	14.6	0.9	4.3	4.6	1.2
Anxiety Disorders	14.9	14.6	1.0	24.2	24.6	0.9
Affective Disorders	14.1	10.4	0.8	17.1	15.4	0.7
Drug Dependence	12.2	14.6	1.0	10.6	9.2	0.8
Schizophrenia/ Schizophreniform	0.8	0.0	—	1.9	0.0	—

*Abbreviations used: NBW = normal birth weight
LBW = low birthweight (< 2500 g)
§OR = estimated odds of psychiatric disorder, adjusted for race and socioeconomic level.

statistical significance. None of the LBW subjects received a diagnosis of schizophrenia/schiozphreniform disorder, whereas 0.8% of the NBW males (2 subjects) and 1.9% of the NBW females (6 subjects) did. As with the delinquency data, these results do not support the hypothesis that low-birthweight children are at increased risk for the development of behavioral and emotional problems later on in life. Further analyses of these data are ongoing, and will address some of the selective risk conditions which have been suggested in the discussion above.

As a whole, however, the cohort studies in this section tend to support the general findings of the controlled longitudinal studies reported in Section 2, and also suggest one new result. Among the general population of low-birthweight infants, those subjects classified as small-for-gestational-age (as a result of intrauterine growth retardation) are at particular risk for the development of emotional and behavioral problems. This conclusion is supported by the results of Neligan et al. (1976) and McGee et al. (1983) and partially by those of Nichols and Chen (1981)—the only studies that directly addressed this issue. The Neligan study reported an increased vulnerability among males, which was not found in the New Zealand study. Socioeconomic status was found to have both an independent relationship to behavior problems and to interact with birth status, where poorer low-birthweight (or SGA) infants are at particular risk. Both the Neligan and the McCormick studies again confirm that a pattern of hyperactivity is the distinguishing behavioral feature among these low-birthweight samples. Although preliminary, the study by Buka et al. (1990) provides the only published results regarding psychiatric status in adulthood of low-birthweight infants. These results fail to support the hypothesis that low-birthweight children are at increased risk for the development of behavioral and emotional problems later on in life. However, as with the results at ages 4 and 7 for this cohort, although the low-birthweight subjects may not appear deviant for global conditions (such as DSM-III diagnoses), more subtle behavioral tendencies may develop. Further analyses addressing this issue and the selective risk associated with being born small-for-gestational-age are ongoing.

CONCLUSION

This review indicates that the published literature concerning the school-age-through-adult behavioral and emotional functioning of low-birthweight infants is sufficient to address several of the questions noted at the outset. As all of the studies reviewed were prospective investigations of low-birthweight samples, they overcome many of the methodologic problems associated with the earlier case/control studies of child and adult psychopathology discussed in the Introduction section, and provide a better test of the hypothesis of a "continuum of reproductive casualty" (Pasmanick, Rogers, & Lilienfeld, 1956). Results from all three categories of studies generally indicate that low-birthweight infants, as a group, are at increased risk for the development of emotional and behavioral problems.

Within the low-birthweight population, infants who are small-for-gestational-age appear to be at particular risk. Ultrasound information regarding the time of onset of intrauterine growth retardation has been suggested as a potential diagnostic variable for detecting the at-risk low-birthweight infant. Being male, born into an adverse social environment, and showing signs of early neurological or developmental problems are also significant features of the at-risk low-birthweight infant. The few available studies suggest, however, that both constitutional and environmental conditions associated with low-birthweight births are independent and interactive risk factors for the development of emotional and behavioral problems.

A general profile of behavioral abnormality emerges from these studies, characterized by high activity levels and low attention spans, thus approximating the clinical diagnosis of attention deficit disorder with hyperactivity (ADDH). Some of the known correlates of low-birthweight births, including subtle neurological damage ("soft" signs), poor visual–motor integration, verbal deficits, and motor difficulties, and which have been suggested risk factors for ADDH, may account for this relationship. The results from the Providence NCPP sample also suggest that low-birthweight girls may be at risk for more withdrawn, shy, and passive behavior.

We regard the findings of this review with optimism. Recognition that certain subpopulations of low-birthweight infants are at risk for emotional and behavioral problems and that these relationships have both constitutional and environmental bases provides opportunities for early detection and intervention. Recent evidence from a large multisite randomized trial indicates that a family-based educational curriculum and family support program is effective in reducing behavioral problems among low-birthweight children (Infant Health and Development Program, 1990). Targeted application of successful interventions of this type could result in substantial improvements in the developmental course of low-birthweight infants and an overall reduction of the incidence of severe emotional and behavioral disorder in the population at large.

REFERENCES

Achenbach, T.M., & Edelbrock, C. (1983). *Manual for the Child Behavior Checklist and Revised Child Behavior Profile.* Queen City, VT: Queen City Printers.
Alm, I. (1953). The long-term prognosis for prematurely born children. *Acta Paediatrica Stockholm, 42* (Suppl. 94).
Astbury, J., Orgill, A., & Bajuk, B. (1987). Relationship between two-year behavior and neuro-developmental outcome at five years of very low-birthweight survivors. *Developmental Medicine and Child Neurology, 29,* 370–379.
Benton, A.L. (1940). Mental development of prematurely born children. *American Journal of Orthopsychiatry, 10,* 719–746.
Bjerre, I., & Hansen, E. (1976). Psychomotor development and school-adjustment of 7-year-old children with low birthweight. *Acta Paediatrica Scandinavia, 65,* 88–96.
Breslau, N., Klein, N., & Allen, L. (1988). Very low birthweight: Behavioral sequelae at nine years of age. *Journal of the American Academy of Child and Adolescent Psychiatry, 27,* 605–612.
Broman, S.H., Nichols, P.I., & Kennedy, W.A. (1975). *Preschool IQ: Prenatal and early developmental correlates.* New York: Halstead Press.
Buka, S.L. (1988). *Perinatal complications and psychiatric disorder.* Unpublished doctoral dissertation, Harvard School of Public Health.
Buka, S.L. (1990a). *Prenatal and perinatal antecedents of delinquent offending.* Unpublished manuscript.
Buka, S.L. (1990b). *The relationship between complications of pregnancy and delivery and infantile autism.* Unpublished manuscript.
Buka, S.L., Lipsitt, L.P., & Tsuang, M.T. (1988). Birth complications and psychological deviancy: A twenty-five year prospective inquiry. *Acta Paediatrica Japonica, 30,* 537–546.
Buka, S.L., Tsuang, M.T., & Lipsitt, L.P. (1990). *Preterm birth and psychiatric disorder: A longitudinal study.* Unpublished manuscript.
Calame, A., Fawer, C.L., Claeys, V., Arrazola, L., Ducret, S., & Jaunin, L. (1986). Neurodevelopmental outcome and school performance of very-low-birth-weight infants at 8 years of age. *European Journal of Pediatrics, 145,* 461–466.
Caputo, D.V., & Mandell, W. (1970). Consequences of low birth weight. *Developmental Psychology, 3,* 363–383.
Cohen, P., Velez, C.N., Brook, J., & Smith, J. (1989). Mechanisms of the relation between perinatal problems, early childhood illness, and psychopathology in late childhood and adolescence. *Child Development, 60,* 701–709.
Conners, C.K., Goyette, C.H., & Southwick, D. (1976). Food additives and hyperkinesis: A controlled double blind experiment. *Pediatrics, 58,* 154–166.
Costello, A.J., Edelbrock, C.S., Dulcan, M.K., & Kalas, R. (1984). *Testing of the NIMH Diagnostic Interview Schedule for Children (DISC) in a clinical population: Final report to the Center for Epidemiological Studies. NIMH.* Pittsburgh: University of Pittsburgh.

Davie, R., Butler, N., & Goldstein, H. (1972). *From birth to seven: The second report of the National Child Development Study.* London: Longman Group.

Douglas, J.W.B. (1960). "Premature" children at primary schools. *British Medical Journal 1,* 1008–1013.

Drillien, C.M., Thomson, A.J.M., & Burgoyne, K. (1980). Low-birthweight children at early school-age: A longitudinal study. *Developmental Medicine and Child Neurology, 22,* 26–47.

Dunn, H.G., Crichton, J.U., Grunau, R.V.E., McBurney, A.K., McCormick, A.Q., Robertson, A.M., & Schulzer, M. (1980). Neurological, psychological and educational sequelae of low birth weight. *Brain Development, 2,* 57–67.

Escalona, S.K. (1984). Social and other environmental influences on the cognitive and personality development of low birthweight infants. *American Journal of Mental Deficiency, 88,* 508–512.

Francis-Williams, J., & Davies, P.A. (1974). Very low birthweight and later intelligence. *Developmental Medicine and Child Neurology, 16,* 709–728.

Grigoroiu, M. (1978). Un instrument de mesure de la maturite emotionelle de l'enfant de 5 a 7 ans. *Enfance, 1,* 53–65.

Grigoroiu-Serbanescu, M. (1984). Intellectual and emotional development and school adjustment in preterm children at 6 and 7 years of age: Continuation of a follow-up study. *International Journal of Behavioral Development, 7,* 307–320.

Guy, W. (1976). *ECDEU assessment manual for psychopharmacology, revised edition.* Washington, DC: U.S. Dept. of Health, Education, and Welfare.

Hack, M., Fanaroff, A.A., & Merkatz, I.R. (1979). The low-birth-weight infant—evolution of a changing outlook. *New England Journal of Medicine, 301,* 1162–1165.

Harper, P.A., & Wiener, G. (1965). Sequelae of low birth weight. *Annual Review of Medicine, 16,* 405–420.

Harvey, D., Prince, J., Bunton, J., Parkinson, C., & Campbell, S. (1982). Abilities of children who were small-for-gestational-age babies. *Pediatrics, 69,* 296–300.

Hertzig, M.E., & Mittleman, M. (1984). Temperament in low birthweight children. *Merrill-Palmer Quarterly, 30,* 201–211.

Hertzig, M.E. (1981). Neurologic "soft" signs in low-birthweight children. *Developmental Medicine and Child Neurology, 23,* 778–791.

Infant Health and Development Program. (1990). Enhancing the outcomes of low-birth-weight, premature infants. a multisite randomized trial. *Journal of the American Medical Association, 263,* 3035–3042.

Kleinbaum, D.G., Kupper, L.L., & Morgenstern, H. (1982). *Epidemiologic research: Principles and quantitative methods.* Belmont, CA: Lifetime Learning Publications.

Lilienfeld, A.M., & Pasamanick, B. (1955). The association of maternal and fetal factors with the development of cerebral palsy and epilepsy. *American Journal of Obstetrics and Gynecology, 70,* 93–101.

Lilienfeld, A.M., Pasamanick, B., & Rogers, M. (1955). Relationship between pregnancy experiences and the development of certain neuropsychiatric disorders in childhood. *American Journal of Public Health, 45,* 637–643.

Mantel, N., & Haenszel, W. (1959). Statistical aspects of the analysis of data from retrospective studies of disease. *Journal of the National Cancer Institute, 22,* 719–748.

McCormick, M.C. (1989). Long-term follow-up of infants discharged from neonatal intensive care units. *Journal of the American Medical Association, 261,* 1767–1772.

McCormick, M.C., Gortmaker, S.L., & Sobol, A.M. (1989). Very low birth weight children: Behavior problems and school failure in a national sample. *Journal of Developmental and Behavioral Pediatrics, 10,* 266. (Abstract)

McCurry, C., Silverton, L., & Mednick, S.A. (1990). Psychiatric consequences of pregnancy and birth complications. In J.W. Gray & R.S. Dean (Eds.), *Neuropsychology of perinatal complications.* New York: Springer Publishing.

McDevitt, S.C., & Carey, W.B. (1978). The measurement of temperament in 3-7 year old children. *Journal of Child Psychology and Psychiatry, 19*, 245–253.

McGee, R., Silva, P.A., & Williams, S. (1983). Perinatal, neurological, environmental and developmental characteristics of seven-year-old children with stable behavior problems. *Journal of Child Psychology and Psychiatry, 25*, 573–586.

McNeil, T.F. (1988). Obstetric factors and perinatal injuries. In M.T. Tsuang & J.C. Simpson (Eds.), *Handbook of schizophrenia: Nosology, epidemiology and genetics* (Vol. 3). B.V.: Elsevier Science Publishers.

Myrianthopoulos, N.C., & French, K.S. (1968). An application of the U.S. Bureau of the Census socioeconomic index to a large, diversified patient population. *Social Science and Medicine, 2*, 283–299.

Neligan, G.A., Kolvin, I., Scott, D.M., & Garside, R.F. (1976). *Born too soon or born too small.* London: Spastics International Medical Publications (Clinics in Developmental Medicine, No. 61).

Nichols, P.L., & Chen, T.C. (1981). *Minimal brain dysfunction: A prospective study.* Hillsdale, NJ: Erlbaum.

Niswander, K.R., & Gordon, M. (1972). *The women and their pregnancies.* Washington, DC: U.S. Government Printing Office.

Noble-Jamieson, C.M., Lukeman, D., Silverman, M., & Davies, P.A. (1982). Low birth weight children at school age: Neurological, psychological, and pulmonary function. *Seminars in Perinatology, 6*, 266–273.

Office of Technology Assessment. (OTA). (1987). *Neonatal care for low birthweight infants: Costs and effectiveness* (Publication No. OTA-HCS-38). Washington, DC: U.S. Government Printing Office.

Parkinson, C.E., Wallis, S., & Harvey, D. (1981). School achievement and behavior of children who were small-for-dates at birth. *Developmental Medicine and Child Neurology, 23*, 41–50.

Pasamanick, B., & Kawi, A. (1956). A study of the association of prenatal and paranatal factors with the development of tics in children. *Journal of Pediatrics, 48*, 596–601.

Pasamanick, B., & Knobloch, H. (1961). Epidemiologic studies on the complications of pregnancy and the birth process. In G. Caplan (Ed.), *Prevention of mental disorders in children.* New York: Basic Books.

Pasamanick, B., & Lilienfeld, A.M. (1955). Association of maternal and fetal factors with development of mental deficiency: Abnormalities in the prenatal and paranatal periods. *Journals of the American Medical Association, 159*, 155–160.

Pasamanick, B., Rogers, M.E., & Lilienfeld, A.M. (1956). Pregnancy experience and the development of behavior disorder in children. *American Journal of Psychiatry, 112* 613–618.

Portnoy, S., Callias, M., Wolke, D., & Gamsu, H. (1988). Five-year follow-up study of extremely low-birthweight infants. *Developmental Medicine and Child Neurology, 30*, 590–598.

Prechtl, H.F.R. (1968). Neurological findings in newborn infants after pre- and paranatal complications. In J.G.P. Jonxis, H.K.A. Visser, & J.A. Troelstra (Eds.), *Aspects of praematurity and dysmaturity: Proceedings of nutricia symposium.* Leiden: Stenfert Kroese.

Richman, N., & Graham, P.J. (1971). A behavioral screening questionnaire for use with three-year-old children: Preliminary findings. *Journal of Child Psychology and Psychiatry, 12*, 5–33.

Rickards, A.L., Ford, G.W., Kitchen, W.H., Doyle, L.W., Lissenden, J.V., & Keith, C.G. (1987). Extremely-low-birthweight infants: Neurological, psychological, growth and health status beyond five years of age. *Medical Journal of Australia, 147*, 476–481.

Robins, L.N., Helzer, J.E., & Croughan, J. (1981a). *The NIMH Diagnostic Interview Schedule. Version III* (Public Health Service Publication No. ADM-T-42-3). Washington, DC: U.S. Government Printing Office.

Robins, L.N., Helzer, J.E., Croughan, J., & Ratcliff, K.S. (1981b). The NIMH Diagnostic Interview Schedule: Its history, characteristics, and validity. *Archives of General Psychiatry, 3*, 381–389.

Rubin, A.R., & Balow, B. (1977). Perinatal influences on the behavior and learning problems of children. In B.B. Lahey & A.E. Kazdin (Eds.), *Advances in clinical child psychology* (Vol. 1). New York: Plenum Press.

Rutter, M. (1967). A children's behaviour questionnaire for completion by teachers. *Journal of Child Psychology and Psychiatry, 8*, 1–11.

Rutter, M., Tizard, J., & Whitmore, K. (1970). *Education, health and behavior.* New York: John Wiley & Sons, 1970.

Sameroff, A.J. (1981). Longitudinal studies of preterm infants. In S.L. Friedman & M. Sigman (Eds.), *Preterm birth and psychological development.* New York: Academic Press.

Simonds, J.F., Silva, P., & Aston, L. (1981). Behavioral and psychiatric assessment of preterm and full-term low birth weight children at 9–11 years of age. *Developmental and Behavioral Pediatrics, 2*, 82–88.

Smith, L., Somner, F.F., & Von Tetzchner, S. (1982). A longitudinal study of low birthweight children: Reproductive, perinatal, and environmental precursors of developmental status at three years of age. *Seminars in Perinatology, 6*, 294–304.

Spivack, G., & Spotts, J. (1966). *Devereux Child Behavior Rating Scale Manual.* Devon, PA: Devereux Foundation.

Steiner, E.S., Sanders, E.M., Phillips, E.C.K., & Maddock, C.R. (1980). Very low birthweight children at school age: Comparison of neonatal management methods. *British Medical Journal, 281*, 1237–1240.

Szatmari, P., Saigal, S., Rosenbaum, P., & Campbell, D. (1989). Psychiatric disorders in infants <1000 g born in the 1980's: A regional perspective. *Pediatric Research, 25*, 19A. (Abstract)

Werner, E.E., & Smith, R.S. (1982). *Vulnerable but invincible.* New York: McGraw-Hill.

Westwood, M., Kramer, M.S., Munz, D., Lovett, J.M., & Watters, G.V. (1983). Growth and development of full-term nonasphyxiated small-for-gestational-age newborns: Follow-up through adolescence. *Pediatrics, 71*, 376–382.

Wiener, G. (1962). Psychologic correlates of premature birth: A review. *Journal of Nervous and Mental Disease, 134*, 129–144.

Wiener, G., Rider, R.V., Oppel, W.C., & Harper, P.A. (1968). Correlates of low birth weight: Psychological status at eight to ten years of age. *Pediatric Research, 2*, 110–118.

Wolff, S. (1967). Behavioral characteristics of primary school children referred to a psychiatric department. *British Journal of Psychiatry, 113*, 885.

9

School Age Follow-up of the Development of Preterm Infants: Infant and Family Predictors*

Diane Magyary
Patricia A. Brandt
Mary Hammond
Kathryn Barnard

INTRODUCTION

School age functioning of children born preterm is a relevant social and health issue. Abilities to attend regularly, maintain attention, complete assignments with minimal supervision and interact appropriately are needed for school as well as adult work behaviors. For children to function effectively in these areas, intellectual and social-emotional competencies are needed.

Few longitudinal studies have followed preterms into the school age years. The individual difference question, ''Why do some infants born preterm do well at school age and others do not?'' has been primarily studied in respect to intellectual competencies. The purpose of the study reported in this chapter was to complete a longitudinal follow-up of a relatively healthy preterm infant sample and to examine the early correlates of intellectual and social-emotional outcomes at 8 years of age.

The design of this study permitted us to ask the question, ''What early and concurrent variables best predict intellectual and social-emotional outcomes at school age?'' The investigators believed that individual differences among preterms could best be understood when intellectual and social-emotional dimensions of school age functioning are examined with respect to both infant status and family predictors. It was hypothesized that intellectual outcomes would be best predicted by infant developmental variables and family interactive quality variables that reflect the learning environment of the infant, whereas social-emotional outcomes would be best predicted by family context variables that reflect stress, and the family interactive quality variables that reflect relational and organizational patterns.

* This study was supported by the Robert Wood Johnson Foundation.

REVIEW OF LITERATURE

Previous results of longitudinal studies of children born preterm are summarized in two ways. First, variables that best predict development from infancy to school age are examined. These predictors are typically categorized as biophysical or environmental. Second, school age functioning is examined with respect to intellectual and social-emotional outcomes.

Biophysical and Environmental Predictors

In the search for relevant explanations of later functioning, biophysical and environmental categories of predictors have been inconsistently used with respect to indicators, age periods, and analyses. Highlights of selected studies are summarized to portray evolving patterns.

Studies that follow preterms from birth to 3 years indicate that biophysical factors are better predictors for neurologic and motor outcomes than environmental factors. Intellectual outcomes are best predicted by environmental factors (Aylward, 1988). The child's environment appears to be particularly critical for preterms during early childhood, as environmental predictors have been found to have more predictive power for preterms than full terms in relation to language, intellectual, and parent—child interactions (Greenberg & Crnic, 1988).

Proximal influences in the child's environment, such as caregiving interactions (Beckwith & Cohen, 1984) and the provision of play and stimulation by the parent (Greenberg & Crnic, 1988) have been found to be good predictors of intellectual outcomes during the early childhood years. When studies include global environmental indicators such as socioeconomic status and maternal education, as well as proximal indicators, the global indicator is less effective as a predictor of intellectual outcomes (Greenberg & Crnic, 1988). If global indicators of the child's environment are used without proximal indicators, the infant's biophysical status has been found to be a better predictor than a global environmental measure. In a longitudinal follow-up of preterms at age 8 years, biological status at birth was a better predictor of intellectual functioning for the Spanish speaking subgroup than the global environmental factor, maternal education (Cohen, Parmelee, Beckwith, & Sigman, 1986). Global indicators of the environment may not consistently prove to be the best predictors of preterm's intellectual functioning at school age, but inclusion of these influences in analyses is important. Cohen et al. (1986) found that for the LBW children whose mothers were English speaking and had a higher education level than the Spanish speaking subgroup, maternal education accounted for more variance in the intellectual outcome than did the infant's biophysical status at birth.

Due to the limited study of biophysical and environmental predictors in respect to social-emotional competence during the preterm's school age years, the significance of environmental or biophysical indicators on social-emotional outcomes is undetermined. There is also a paucity of longitudinal research in which the ''family as a unit'' variables are used as indicators of the proximal environment of the child. When family unit variables are included, they are likely to be global indicators of the child's environment and measure maternal education and/or family socioeconomic status. Proximal measures which reflect family unit functioning such as family interactions need to be included in studies to determine their usefulness for predicting school age outcomes of preterms.

Intellectual and Social-emotional Outcomes During School Age

Intellectual outcomes of preterms during school age indicate that scores on intelligence tests are not necessarily indicative of actual school performance. Preterms' school failure or placement in special services range from 8% to 58% depending on the study (McCormick, 1989). Using standardized intelligence tests, preterms tend to have scores in the normal range but slightly lower in comparison to controls of normal birth weight (McCormick, 1989).

Test performance on academic achievement measures is a useful way to understand difficulties the children may have in school. In one of the few studies in which academic achievement was used as an outcome, preterm children at 9 years of age were found to have significantly lower scores on math achievement than controls who were born at term (Klein, Hack, & Breslau, 1989). Lower scores in the math test were not a function of IQ in this particular study. Reading scores did not differ between preterms and controls. The researchers hypothesized that math difficulties may be related to deficits in visually mediated tasks. A minor neurological difficulty that is found most often in the preterm during preschool and school age years is perceptual-motor difficulty (Hunt, Cooper, & Tooley, 1988; Klein, 1988).

Analysis of subgroups within samples of preterms may also be helpful for determining factors that influence school performance. When comparisons are made among subgroups of school age children who are either low birthweight (LBW), or small for gestational age (SGA), only the SGA children obtained significantly lower IQ scores and higher social-emotional problem scores (Silva, McGee, & Williams, 1984). IQ scores in the McGee study were within normal range and socioeconomic status did not differ among groups. As school performance may be particularly influenced by the child's neurologic competencies, further study is needed (Klein, 1988; Lloyd, Wheldall, & Perks, 1988).

Social-emotional outcomes of LBW children during the school years are just beginning to be addressed. Prematurity as well as other high-risk birth conditions coupled with a stressful caregiving context during infancy substantially increases the risk of adjustment problems later in childhood (O'Grady & Metz, 1987; Lindgren, Harper, & Blackman, 1986). Although psychiatric diagnoses for children age 9–11 years and born preterm do not differ from controls, adjustment problems of LBW children during school years are a concern of parents (Simonds, Silva, & Aston, 1981).

Classroom behaviors of preterms are beginning to be measured and recognized as important indicators of social-emotional adjustment. The demands of the classroom appear to contribute to social-emotional responses that may not be apparent in the home, but are needed for classroom learning and performance. Klein (1988) reported that 5-year-old children born preterm, in comparison to children born full term, matched by race and sex were more passive and withdrawn in classroom activities and had more difficulty in following directions and attending to tasks.

Further study of the interplay among social-emotional, intellectual, environmental, and biophysical factors as children progress through the school years is needed. Given the dynamic changes that occur and the influence of biophysical and environmental factors on school age functioning, a transactional perspective as defined by Sameroff and Chandler (1975) influenced the design, analyses, and interpretation of the study presented in this chapter. Environmental experiences of vulnerable children over time were viewed as enabling individual differences in social-emotional and intellectual outcomes during the school age period. Measurement of environmental predictors included proximal variables of family interactive quality, as well as, global variables that reflect the family context. The inclusion of both proximal and global environmental variables would enable identification of the contextual processes that contribute to the resilience of children born preterm. Having a variety of predictor and outcomes variables in this study allowed us to ask a question about preterm infants that has not been thoroughly addressed, namely, "What is the relative importance of infant versus family environmental variables in predicting intellectual and social-emotional school age outcomes?"

METHODS

Subjects

Subjects of this longitudinal study were 68 preterm infants and their families, selected from the University of Washington Hospital Neonatal Intensive Care Unit (NICU) in Seattle, Washington between 1975 and 1978. These 68 preterms account for 77% of the original sample. They were followed from newborn through 8 years of age through a research grant which was not part of a routine follow-up evaluation of NICU graduates. The highest attrition rate occurred between the hospital and four month period. Given the selection criteria, the infants represented a group of relatively "healthy" preterm infants who displayed a variety of mild to moderately severe physiological complications. See Table 1 for a description of the subjects.

Table 1.   Sample Characteristics

Children	
Exclusion Criteria	Identifiable handicaps at birth and assisted respiration
Conceptual Age: (weeks)	$M = 31$, SD = 1.41, Range = 27–34 (Dubowitz score)
Age of Enrollment in Study	Within 5 days of birth
Birth Weight	69% weighed 840 to 1,500 grams, 31% weighed 1,501 to 2,340 grams
Physical Complications	Majority had mild to moderately severe conditions such as respiratory distress, infections, metabolic or temperature disturbance, or convulsions
Ethnicity	Caucasians
Birth Order	62% were first born, 38% second or later born
Mothers	
Exclusion Criteria	Substance addiction in late pregnancy and diagnosed mental illness or mental retardation
Marital Status at Child's 8th Year	81% married or living with partner, 19% single parent
Work Status at Child's 8th Year	70% worked outside the home

The infants were part of an experimental intervention study in which variations of a rocking bed with heartbeat stimulation were provided while in the neonatal intensive care unit (Barnard & Bee, 1981, 1983). Because the experimental and control groups did not differ on any of the outcome or predictor measures reported in this chapter, the experimental and control groups were combined into a single sample for the present analyses.

Data Collection Procedures

Observation and assessment of the children and their mothers occurred during the child's hospital stay, at 4, 8, and 24 months, and at 8 years of age (second grade). All assessments after hospital discharge were completed in a university based child development clinical setting. To reduce the number of variables included in the analyses, the 4-month data collection was not included in the present report, as findings were similar to the 8-month data. In addition, a subset of the newborn and 8-month variables were selected for the analyses reported in this chapter. The selection included those variables that proved to be most reliable and valid, as well as, had minimal missing data. Table 2 summarizes the predictor and outcome variables included in the present report.

Table 2. Summary of All Variables Included in the Analysis

Predictor Variable	Instrument or Data Source	Times of Assessment (in relation to infant's age)	M	SD
Infant Status:				
Birthweight (grams)	Hospital Records	Birth	1398.60	298.02
Days in Hospital	Hospital Records	Hospital Discharge	38.50	16.50
Postnatal Complication Score	Hospital Records	Hospital Discharge	72.06	9.90
Mental Development	Bayley MDI	24 Months	106.91	17.04
Psychomotor Development	Bayley PDI	24 Months	103.52	16.96
Sex	Hospital Records: Percent Male	Birth	(53%)	
Family Interactive Quality				
Maternal Teaching Style	Observation: mother–infant teaching interaction Maternal total score	8 months	3.49	.30
Infant Readiness to Learn	Observation: mother–infant teaching interaction Infant total score	8 Months	3.40	.47
Home Environment	Modified Version of HOME Inventory Total score	24 Months	37.45	3.20
Mother–Child Relationship*	Parental Acceptance–Rejection Questionnaire Total score	8 Years	93.52	15.53
Family Relationships	Family Environmental Scale: Factor score	8 Years	6.40	.97
Family Organization*	Family Environmental Scale: Factor score	8 Years	5.69	1.16

Family Context	Instrument or Data Source	Times of Assessment	M	SD
Maternal Education	Questionnaire Item	Birth	12.75	1.96
Maternal Caregiving Experience	Questionnaire Item: Percent Yes	Birth	(26%)	
Family Stress	Social Readjustment Rating Scale Total weighted score	Pregnancy	226.21	110.70
Family Stress	Social Readjustment Rating Scale Total weighted score	8 Months	87.98	77.94
Family Stress	Life Experience Survey Total number of negative events score	8 Years	4.47	7.72
Family Social Status	Hollingshead Four Factor Index	8 Years	38.37	11.56
Outcome Variables	**Instrument or Data Source**	**Times of Assessment**	**M**	**SD**
Intellectual: General Intelligence	Wechsler Intelligence Scale for Children-Revised Full scale IQ	8 Years	103.18	13.36
Intellectual: Academic Achievement	Peabody Individual Achievement Test (PIAT) Total standard age score	8 Years	102.54	11.46
Social-Emotional Competence in Classroom	Classroom Behavior Inventory (CBI) Subscale score	8 Years	50.67	13.18
Social-Emotional Adjustment Problems	Child Behavior Checklist (CBCL) Normalized T scores for total behavioral problems	8 Years	54.18	11.66

*The higher the score, the less positive quality.

Predictor Variables

The predictor variables used in the analyses were grouped into three categories to determine the relative predictive power of each category for each outcome variable. The three categories of predictor variables were: (a) infant status variables, (b) family interactive quality variables, and (c) family context variables.

The *Infant Status Variables* included six measures that reflected the infant's physical and developmental status during the early years of life. The infant's physical status during the newborn period was measured using birth weight, number of days stayed in the hospital, sex, and a postnatal complication score (Parmelee & Littman, 1974). The Postnatal Complication Score was obtained on the day the infant was discharged from the hospital and was a composite score reflecting the infant's physiological complications. The infant's developmental status was measured using the Bayley Scales of Infant Development (Bayley, 1969) at 24 months chronological age, adjusting the scoring for gestational age. Two developmental variables from the Bayley were used as predictors, mental development (MDI), and psychomotor development (PDI).

The *Family Interactive Quality Variables* refers to those aspects of the family environment that directly involve the child and reflects a proximal caregiving environment. Two types of family interactive quality variables were measured. The first type primarily reflects interactive patterns related to the infant's learning environment during the first two years. These variables were (a) maternal teaching style, (b) infant readiness to learn, and (c) the home environment. The second type of variables primarily reflects interactive patterns within the family during the school age period. These variables were (a) mother–child relationship, (b) family relationship, and (c) family organization.

The maternal teaching style and infant readiness to learn variables were derived from a mother–infant teaching interaction observed at 8 months. Both variables, maternal teaching style and infant readiness to learn, are interactive measures that reflect how the mother and infant respond to each other's behaviors. The mother was asked to teach the infant a task taken from the Bayley Scales that was several months above the child's age. The mother's behaviors during the teaching episode were rated on 15 five-point scales that reflected the extent to which the mother provided positive messages, negative feedback, teaching techniques, and facilitation of infant's learning. The higher the maternal score, the more positive was the mother's teaching style. The infant's readiness to learn variable provided an indication of the infant's contribution to the quality of family interactions as measured within the context of a maternal teaching and infant learning interactive episode. The infant's behaviors during the teaching episode were rated on 9 five-point scales that indicated the extent the infant exhibited responsiveness to the mother's help during the teaching interaction, the intensity and duration of involvement with the task materials, and alertness during the teaching episode. The higher the infant score, the more positive was the infant's readiness to learn. Interobserver reliability coefficients for the maternal and infant interactive scores ranged from .64 to .86, with a median value of .80 (Barnard & Eyres, 1979). The rating scale for the maternal and infant interactive measures were later developed into the Nursing Child Assessment Teaching Scale (Barnard, 1978).

The variable home environment was measured at 24 months. Since all measurements for this study were completed in the clinic rather than at home, a modified version of Caldwell and Bradley's (1978) HOME was used. This modified version of the HOME (Barnard & Eyres, 1979) resulted in the subscales emotional and verbal responsivity and avoidance of restriction and punishment being observed by an interviewer. Questionnaire items were used to obtain subscale information on the organization of the physical and temporal environment, provision of appropriate play materials, maternal involvement with child, and opportunities for variety in daily stimulation. The observation and questionnaire items were summarized for a total score. A higher score indicated a higher quality of stimulation and relational qualities experienced by the infant.

The mother–child relationship variable was based on the mother's perception of her relationship with her school age child using the Parental Acceptance Rejection Questionnaire (PARQ) (Rohner, 1984). The questionnaire consists of 60 items with a four-point rating scale from "almost never true" to "almost always true." Four dimensions of maternal relationships behaviors displayed toward her child were measured: warmth–affection, aggression–hostility, neglect–indifference, and rejection. A high score indicated a problematic mother–child relationship.

The family's relational and organizational variables were measured at eight years using the Family Environment Scale, FES (Moos, 1974). The FES is a 90-item self-administered questionnaire completed by the mother and measures two dimensions of the family's interactive quality: family relationships and the family organization. These two dimensions were obtained through factor analysis by varimax-rotated solution on the study sample. The results were similar to Fowler's (1981) and Boake and Salmon's (1983) factor structures. A higher score on the family relationship factor reflected more interpersonal growth, closeness, acceptance and activities together. A higher score on the family organization factor reflected more control, rules and rigidity in the daily maintenance properties of the family. The standardized item alpha was .62 for the family relationship dimension and .51 for the family organization dimension. These two dimensions were not correlated significantly ($r = -.06, p < .31$).

The *Family Context* variables referred to aspects of the family environment that could potentially influence parenting and the caregiving environment. The family context variables included three demographic measures and three measures of family stress. The demographic information collected at the time of the infant's birth included the mother's educational level (number of years of schooling) and the mother's previous caregiving experience (yes vs. no). The Hollingshead Four-Factor Index of Family Social Status (Hollingshead, 1975) was obtained at the 8-year time point.

Family stress was assessed at three time points: intake, 8 months and 8 years. The Social Readjustment Rating Scale (SRE) (Holmes & Rahe, 1967) is a 42-item questionnaire and was used to measure life changes encountered by a mother during her pregnancy and during the first 8 to 9 months after delivery. The SRE yields a total weighted score based on normative assigned item weights and indicates average readjustment required. The Life Experience Survey (LES) (Sarason, Johnson, & Siegel, 1978) was used to measure the level of family stress at the 8-year time point. The 47-item questionnaire allowed for individualized ratings of the event to be negative or positive. A total score for negative life events was obtained.

Child Outcome Variables

The child outcome variables used in the analyses reflected the child's intellectual and social-emotional functioning. The school age intellectual variables were general intelligence and academic achievement. The school age social-emotional variables were the child's social-emotional competence to maximize learning in the classroom and the child's social-emotional adjustment problems.

For *intellectual outcomes*, general intelligence was measured using the full scale IQ standard score derived from the Wechsler Intelligence Scale for Children Revised (WISC-R) (Wechsler, 1974). Academic achievement was assessed using the Peabody Individual Achievement Test (PIAT) (Dunn & Markwardt, 1970). The PIAT examines five areas of performance: reading recognition, reading comprehension, spelling, mathematics, and general information. The total standard score for age was used in the analyses.

For *social-emotional outcomes*, the child's social-emotional competence to maximize learning in the classroom was assessed by the teacher using the Classroom Behavior Inventory (CBI) (Schaefer & Edgerton, 1978). The CBI is a 42-item questionnaire with a five point rating scale from "very much like" to "not at all like" the identified child. Several studies of normal and clinical samples have indicated that the CBI had respectable validity and reliability (Schaefer & Edgerton, 1978). For the purpose of data reduction, a factor termed social-emotional competence in the classroom was used for analysis. This factor consisted of items from three subscales of the CBI and reflected behaviors such as (a) initiates and participates in classroom dialogue and activities in interesting and creative ways, (b) independently engages in activities and demonstrates resourcefulness, and (c) expresses self and comprehends complex ideas using a large and varied vocabulary. Previous work by Schaefer (1986) indicated that these items had substantially loaded on the same factor. In the present study, the standardized item alpha obtained for the social-emotional competence factor was

.895. A higher score indicated higher social-emotional competence in the classroom.

The variable, social-emotional adjustment problems, was assessed by the mother using a questionnaire, the Child Behavior Checklist (CBCL) (Achenbach & Edelbrock, 1983). Normalized T scores were derived from the behavioral problems total scores and entered into the analyses. A high score indicated more social-emotional problems.

Plan of Analysis

Pearson correlation coefficients were computed to examine the relationship patterns among predictor variables, among child school age outcome variables, and between predictor and school-age outcome variables. In addition to computing simple correlations between two variables, multiple regression analysis was used to examine the relationship between a set of independent variables and a single outcome variable. To identify the best linear prediction equation for each outcome variable and to evaluate its prediction accuracy, a sequence of stepwise multiple regression was computed to determine the independent variables' order and significance of entry. For each outcome variable, the sequence of regressions included two steps. For the first step, a *separate* regression was computed using each category of independent variables in order to determine which independent variables *within* each category added significantly to prediction accuracy. For the second step, a *single* regression was completed using the "best significant predictors" from each category of independent variables in order to determine which independent variables *across* each category added significantly to prediction accuracy.

This type of analysis has benefits conceptually and methodologically. Conceptually, the analysis isolated an optimal prediction equation with as few variables as possible for each outcome variable. The relative predictive power of three categories of independent variables are examined in relation to each outcome variable. Methodologically, the basic rule of thumb of at least 10 subjects for each variable entered into a multiple regression was met. The concept of prediction was broadly used to foretell the child's school age development by analyzing past and present information about the family, and past information about the infant's physical and developmental status.

RESULTS

Descriptive Statistics

The means and standard deviations for all variables in the study are given in Table 2. In examining the mean scores, the sample as a group exhibited average performance on the school age outcome measures of intellectual and social-emotional functioning, as well as average performance on the two year mental and psychomotor developmental measures. The mean scores obtained on the environmental measures depict the sample, as a group, growing up in an overall positive supportive environment. However, the average family stress level was moderate to high at all three time points—pregnancy, and at 1 and 8 years of life.

Variability in the scores of outcome and predictor variables was sufficient to examine questions about individual differences with correlational procedures. The children exhibited a wide distribution in their school age developmental scores. On standardized instruments, the standard deviation scores approximated normative values. Twenty-two percent of the children had "high average to superior" IQ scores on the WISC-R, and 5% were in an advanced class for academic achievement on the PIAT. Sixteen percent of the children had "low average to borderline" IQ scores. Twenty-three percent were identified by the teacher as having a learning disability. Thirty-five percent of the children received some type of remedial or special school services. Child social-emotional adjustment problems on the CBCL were identified by parents in 26% of the sample. A T score greater than 63 (90th percentile), was used to distinguish between "normal" and "adjustment problems" on the CBCL. Twenty-one percent of the children were identified by teachers as having a behavioral problem in the classroom. Teachers were asked a single question, "Has the child been a behavior problem in the classroom?"

Regression Analyses

Table 3 depicts the results of the first set of regression equations. Prediction accuracy was examined within each category of prediction variables for each dependent measure. Table 4 depicts the results of the second set of regression equations. Prediction accuracy across categories of predictor variables was examined for each dependent variable. For the second set of regressions, only the significant variables identified in the first set of regressions were entered into the analyses.

As expected, the pattern of regression results were consistent with the pattern and strength of the intercorrelations among predictor and outcome variables.[1] On the predictor variables, a few subjects obtained an isolated extreme score, often referred to as an outlier. There were no outliers found on the outcome variables. Essentially, the pattern of regression results were the same when the analyses were completed with or without the outliers.

The prediction equations for the *intellectual outcomes, general intelligence and academic achievement,* shared common predictors. In the first set of regressions, the common predictors were infant mental development, infant readiness

---

[1] Tables that depict simple correlations among predictors and outcome variables can be obtained from the first author.

to learn and the home environment. The second set of regressions narrowed the common predictors to infant mental development, which accounted for 26% of the variance in general intelligence and 19% of the variance for academic achievement. The variables that entered into the regression equation after infant mental development differed for general intelligence and academic achievement. An additional 14% of the variance in general intelligence was accounted for by maternal education and infant readiness to learn. An additional 15% of the variance in academic achievement was accounted for by infant psychomotor development, birth weight, and home environment.

The regression results for the two school age intellectual outcome variables were generally consistent with the hypothesis, the "best of the best predictors" would include information on infant development and the family interactive quality variables that reflected the child's proximal learning environment. Although family interactive quality variables significantly contributed information for each intellectual outcome, only 4% of the variance for each intellectual outcome was explained. Infant developmental variables, however, contributed 25% to 26% of the variance for academic achievement and general intelligence respectively. The data suggest that information about the infant's development at 2 years was relatively more useful for predicting school age intellectual functioning than the learning environment of the family during the child's first 2 years.

In respect to the intellectual outcomes, the results revealed two exceptions to the hypothesis. Maternal education explained 10% of the variance in general intelligence. Infant birth weight explained 5% of the variance in academic achievement.

The prediction equations for the two *social-emotional outcomes, social-emotional adjustment problems* and *social-emotional competence in the class-room,* had little in common. The only common predictor was family stress in the first set of regressions when prediction accuracy was examined within each category of predictor variables for each dependent measure. When only the significant variables identified in the first set of regressions were entered into analyses for the second set of regressions, no common predictors were found for the social-emotional outcomes. Each outcome had different significant predictors. Forty-six percent of the variance in social-emotional adjustment problems was accounted for by the family's stress measured at 8 months and 8 years. Twenty-eight percent of the variance in social-emotional competence in the classroom was accounted for by the mother–child relationship at 8 years, with an additional 6% accounted for by the 24 month home environment.

The regression results predicting school age social-emotional functioning were consistent with the stated hypothesis. The best predictors did include information from the family context category pertaining to stress and the family interactive quality category pertaining to relational patterns. The "best of the best predictors" proved to be very specific, depending on the type of social-emotional outcome. Family stress best predicted social-emotional adjustment,

Table 3. First Set of Multiple Regression Analyses: Predicting Developmental 8 Year Outcomes Using Variables within Each Category in Separate Regressions

Developmental 8-Year Outcome Variables	Category of Predictors	Significant Predictors Within Each Category	Beta	Multiple R	R^2	R^2 Change	F to Enter
1. Intellectual: General Intelligence (WISC-R full-scale IQ)	Infant Status	Bayley MDI (24 Months)	.51	.51	.26	.26	22.93***
		$F_{(1,66)} = 22.93, p < .001$					
	Family Interactive Quality	Infant Readiness to Learn (8 months)	.32	.34	.12	.12	8.91**
		Home Environment (24 Months)	.24	.45	.21	.09	7.20**
		Family Relationship (8 Years)	.22	.50	.26	.05	4.04*
		$F_{(3,64)} = 7.26, p < .001$					
	Family Context	Maternal Education (Infant birth)	.37	.37	.14	.14	10.72**
		$F_{(1,66)} = 10.72, p < .01$					
2. Intellectual: Academic Achievement (PIAT total standard score for age)	Infant Status	Bayley MDI (24 Months)	.31	.43	.19	.19	15.38***
		Bayley PDI (24 Months)	.27	.50	.25	.06	5.01*
		Birth Weight	.23	.55	.30	.05	4.69*
		$F_{(3,64)} = 9.08, p < .001$					
	Family Interactive Quality	Infant Readiness to Learn (8 Months)	.33	.34	.12	.12	8.47**
		Home Environment (24 Months)	.31	.46	.22	.10	8.10**
		$F_{(2,65)} = 8.74, p < .001$					
	Family Context	None					

3. Social-Emotional Competence in Classroom (CBI subscale score)	Infant Status	None				
	Family Interactive Quality	Mother–Child Relationship (8 Years)	−.48	.52	.28	.28	22.02***
		Home Environment (24 Months)	.25	.58	.34	.06	5.06*
		$F_{(2,57)} = 14.31, p < .001$				
	Family Context	Family Stress (8 Years)	−.30	.30	.09	.09	5.57*
		$F_{(1,58)} = 5.57, p < .05$				
4. Social-Emotional Adjustment Problems (CBCL T score for total)	Infant Status	None				
	Family Interactive Quality	Family Relationship (8 Years)	−.48	.48	.23	.23	18.74***
		$F_{(1,63)} = 18.74, p < .001$				
	Family Context	Family Stress (8 Years)	.52	.60	.36	.36	35.53***
		Family Stress (8 Months)	.33	.68	.46	.10	11.39**
		$F_{(2,62)} = 26.39, p < .001$				

$*p < .05$, $**p < .01$, $***p < .001$ two-tailed test

Table 4. Second Set of Multiple Regression Analyses:
Predicting Developmental 8-Year Outcomes Using the Significant Predictors Across Categories in One Regression

Developmental 8-Year Outcome Variables	Significant Predictors Across Categories	Beta	Multiple R	R^2	R^2 Change	F to Enter
1. Intellectual: General Intelligence (WISC-R full-scale IQ)	Bayley MDI (24 Months)	.41	.51	.26	.26	22.93***
	Maternal Education (infant birth)	.31	.60	.36	.10	10.19**
	Infant Readiness to Learn (8 Months)	.21	.63	.40	.04	4.19*
		$F_{(3,64)} = 14.10, p < .001$				
2. Intellectual: Academic Achievement (PIAT total standard score for age)	Bayley MDI (24 Months)	.26	.43	.19	.19	15.38***
	Bayley PDI (24 Months)	.26	.50	.25	.06	5.01*
	Birth Weight	.22	.55	.30	.05	4.69*
	Home Environment (24 Months)	.22	.59	.34	.04	4.19*
		$F_{(4,63)} = 8.20, p < .001$				
3. Social-Emotional Competence in Classroom (CBI subscale score)	Mother–Child Relationship (8 years)	−.48	.52	.28	.28	22.02***
	Home Environment (24 Months)	.25	.58	.34	.06	5.06*
		$F_{(2,57)} = 14.31, p < .001$				
4. Social-Emotional Adjustment Problems (CBCL T score for total)	Family Stress (8 Years)	.52	.60	.36	.36	35.53***
	Family Stress (8 Months)	.33	.68	.46	.10	11.39**
		$F_{(2,62)} = 26.39, p < .001$				

$*p < .05$, $**p < .01$, $***p < .001$ two-tailed test

whereas, the mother–child relationship best predicted social-emotional competence in the classroom. The family unit measures family relationship and family organization did not prove to be the "best of the best predictors." Another unexpected finding was that the home environment variable measured at 24 months of age was a significant predictor for the outcome, social-emotional competence in the classroom, contributing 6% of the variance.

When comparing the prediction equations for intellectual versus the social-emotional type outcomes, few similarities were found. In the first set of regressions, general intelligence, academic achievement, and social-emotional competence in the classroom had a common predictor, the home environment. Another similarity found in the first set of regressions was that family relationships significantly predicted social-emotional adjustment problems as well as general intelligence. For the second set of regressions when only the significant predictor variables from the first set of regressions were entered into the analyses, the home environment contributed significantly to academic achievement and to social-emotional competence in the classroom.

DISCUSSION

A combination of diverse information about the child and family is needed to predict intellectual and social-emotional school-age functioning of children born preterm. Certain types of information were relatively more useful in predicting certain functions. The amount and type of information required for prediction varied, depending on the outcome. Overall, infant development as measured by a standardized test best predicted intellectual outcomes, whereas, family environmental variables best predicted social-emotional outcomes. Similar to other research, these results are influenced by the type of measures selected to represent the constructs. Given the sample size and collinearity of variables both within and across categories of predictor variables, these analyses must be interpreted with caution. Findings are discussed with respect to prediction, not causal explanation.

The assumption that diversity of information yields the best prediction equation proved to be more true for intellectual outcomes than social-emotional outcomes. The extent that diversity of information is needed for prediction is an interesting question. Theoretically, the more diverse the information, the better prediction could be expected. Empirically, the prediction of social-emotional outcomes in this study was not based on diverse information. Future research needs to explore what variables in addition to family stress and the mother–child relationship could add significantly to the prediction equation for social-emotional functioning during school age. The identification of early predictors during infancy may become more apparent as measurement of the social-emotional climate shared between the parent and infant is advanced. Variables which reflect attachment and emotional availability and responsiveness during infancy may be particularly valuable to include in future studies.

The general magnitude of the predictive relationships obtained for this follow-up study of preterm infants over an 8-year time period is consistent with the results of studies that follow term and preterm infants for two to four years after birth (Bee et al., 1982; Bradley & Caldwell, 1976; Greenberg & Crnic, 1988; Ramey, Farran, & Campbell, 1979) and an 8-year follow-up study of term infants (Hammond, Bee, Barnard, & Eyres, 1983). In our study, multiple correlations were obtained in the range of .58 to .68. These correlations are particularly striking, especially for general intelligence and academic achievement outcomes as prediction was based on information collected during the infants' first 2 years of life. The idea that "later measures are better than earlier measures" did not hold true for the intellectual outcomes in this study. This finding highlights the critical need of monitoring the infant's developmental trajectory and family environment during the very early years of life.

The usefulness of infant standardized developmental tests for long-term prediction of intellectual functions has been disputed in the literature. Studies of full-term infants suggest that standardized infant tests do not provide long-term prediction until the infant is approximately 24 months of age (McCall, 1979; Bee et al., 1982). In our sample of preterm infants, the 24-month standardized measure of infant development proved to be a useful predictor of school age intellectual functioning.

Infant's physical status at birth and during hospitalization proved to be information that was least useful for predicting either intellectual or social-emotional school age outcomes. This finding supports previous LBW longitudinal studies. Perhaps different results would have been obtained if other dimensions of school age functioning were measured as outcomes, such as physical health status or perceptual-motor performance. Another possible reason why the infant's physical status at birth was not a good predictor of later development may be the relatively healthy preterm infant sample in this study. Study samples in which it is possible to classify infants across the full range of health status, mild to serious illness, would be useful to determine how infant status variables at birth add to long-term prediction accuracy.

In this study, infant physical status was measured by traditional indices, birth weight and gestational age. An expansion of how infant status variables are conceptualized may enhance a better understanding of how the child and environment interact. Within the past 10 years, a renewed interest in infant temperament has emerged. Prediction of later social-emotional problems may be improved if early infant status variables such as self-regulation, reactivity level, emotionality, and sleep–wake activity patterns are measured. Indications of problematic behaviors may appear early in childhood. Mothers of preschool-age children with social-emotional adjustment problems reported that their concerns about the child's behavior began during the child's first 2 years (Webster-Stratton, 1989).

Family interactive and family context variables contributed significantly to the regression equations of all four outcomes, although the extent of contribution ranged from substantial to minimal depending on the outcome measure. Of all the outcome measures, the variance in academic achievement was least explained by family variables. This finding is perplexing, because children who have normal intelligence may exhibit poor academic achievement for many different reasons, including the existing family environment.

General intelligence, academic achievement, and social-emotional competence in the classroom did contain a common significant predictor—a proximal measure of the child's early environment, the 24-month Home scale. Although the HOME scale entered into the regression only after other variables, the results are still striking in view of the 6-year interim between the predictor variable and the 8-year outcome. The quality of the infant's proximal learning environment appears to have some relevance for long-term developmental functioning. Perhaps the linkages between early environment and later developmental functioning would become more apparent if conceptualized within a path analysis model. The infant's proximal learning environment may relate to infant development, which in turn may directly relate to developmental functioning during school age.

The family context variable, maternal education, seems to be a marker for a whole range of differences in environments and had some importance for predicting one outcome in this study, general intelligence. However, for other longitudinal studies of preterms, global indicators of the child's environment have not consistently been significant predictors of 24-month intellectual outcomes when proximal measures such as caregiving interactions are also included in the prediction equations (Greenberg & Crnic, 1988).

In this study, other aspects of the family environment proved to be important for prediction of school age outcomes, especially for social-emotional functioning. Stress, a family context variable measured at early and concurrent time points had strikingly important prediction power. Sameroff and Seifer (1983) identified the importance of understanding child development within the context of enduring organizational aspects of the environment. Within our sample, the family stress measures were significantly related across time and may represent that consistent context the child develops and interacts within over time.

Families of low-birthweight children have been described as being vulnerable to stresses related to parenting (Crnic, Ragozin, Greenberg, Robinson, & Basham, 1983) and financial problems due to the multiple services needed by preterms (McCormick, Stemmler, Bernbaum, & Farran, 1986). In addition to the stresses associated with prematurity, these families may also experience major life stresses such as unemployment, divorce, or death. Knowing these families are at risk for high stress levels, the mechanisms that influence child outcomes are important to understand.

One of the few studies that examined the interplay between family stress and child social-emotional functioning indicated that mothers with higher stress reported significantly more behavioral problems for children aged 3 through 7 years (Webster-Stratton, 1989). Verbal interactions between the higher stressed mothers and their children demonstrated that the mothers were more critical and the children displayed more problematic and noncompliant behaviors in response to their mothers than did the mothers and children with fewer family stresses.

Other studies have examined the relationship between family stress and school age functioning in samples of children with chronic health conditions. Children classified at birth as developmentally at risk who also experience stress throughout childhood are more likely to have adjustment problems during school age (O'Grady & Metz, 1987). Studies of families and children who face adaptation over time in response to a child's chronic illness have affirmed the relevance of family stress. Families who have children with asthma or diabetes in association with family stress and conflict have been found to have children with increased difficulties in managing the respective health condition (Brand, Johnson, & Johnson, 1986; Wikran, Fateide, & Blaker, 1978).

The family and child's vulnerability to stress depends not only on the experiencing of a particular stress or a continuum of stressful events, but the availability of family resources for handling these stresses and the family's interpretation of the events (McCubbin & Patterson, 1983). In the few studies of LBW children that investigated family stresses and resources, families whose children (aged 1 through 4 years) had more limitations in daily living activities had more difficulties in coping and family relationships (McCormick et al., 1986). The child's physical limitations may have increased the demands on the family and, thus, impacted upon the family's functioning.

In our study, family organization and family relationship were the two family interactive variables that obtained information about family ''unit'' functioning. Family organization showed no usefulness, whereas family relationship showed limited usefulness as a predictor variable. Pearson correlations indicated that family relationship was significantly related to many of the other family predictor variables, whereas, family organization was not.

The family relationship variable showed limited usefulness as a predictor, probably due to its multicollinearity pattern with the other family predictor variables. If family unit variables are introduced in studies, unique information must be gained. Issues regarding the usefulness of family unit measures for predicting schoolage functioning of children born preterm need to be addressed. First, would a ''purer'' measure of family relationships enhance the prediction? The family relationships variable was a factor score that included a combination of concepts: interpersonal growth, closeness, acceptance, and activities together. Second, would a different methodology and/or multiple sources improve the prediction? An observation of family relationships during situations in which family members discuss and problem solve may be more relevant than a questionnaire about family relationships with only mothers as the source of information. Third, do family unit measures serve better as interactive rather than predictive variables? Fourth, are family unit indicators more predictive if other concepts of family functioning are used such as family coping or family role expectations?

No single family factor accounted for the effects of family environment on school age functioning of preterms. This finding held true when comparing the prediction equations for the broad domains of development, intellectual and social-emotional competencies, as well as when comparing single developmental dimensions within the broad domains: general intelligence versus academic achievement in the intellectual domain, or social-emotional competence in the classroom versus social-emotional adjustment problems in the social-emotional domain. If intervention programs are designed to enhance the child's functioning across intellectual and social-emotional domains, then a broad array of family factors needs to be considered, as well as ongoing monitoring of the infant's own developmental processes.

Early intervention and community service programs have begun to broaden their assessment and intervention focus to include not only the child, but the child within the context of the family, and the family within the context of the larger community. Children living in families that experience high ongoing stress levels may be particularly vulnerable to social-emotional adjustment problems. Parents who experience high levels of stress may need community support services to enable management of the stress and mitigate the impact on the child's social-emotional development. Early intervention programs become especially critical for parents who need support in parenting and management of life stresses.

REFERENCES

Achenbach, T., & Edelbrock, C. (1983). *Manual for the child behavior checklist*. Burlington, VT: Department of Psychiatry, University of Vermont.

Aylward, G.P. (1988). Issues in prediction and developmental follow-up. *Developmental and Behavioral Pediatrics*, 9(5), 307–309.

Barnard, K. (1978). *NCAST teaching scale manual*. Seattle, WA: NCAST Publications.

Barnard, K.E., & Eyres, S.J. (1979). *Child health assessment Part II: The first year of life* (DHEW Publication No. HRA79-25). Hyattsville, MD: U.S. Department of Health, Education and Welfare, Public Health Service, HRA Bureau of Health, Manpower Division of Nursing.

Barnard, K.E., & Bee, H.L. (1981). *Premature infant refocus* (Final report, Grant #MC-R-530348). Submitted to the Maternal and Child Health and Crippled Children's Services, Bureau of Community Health Services, HSA, PHS, DHHS. Published by the National Technical Information Service, U.S. Department of Commerce, Springfield, Virginia.

Barnard, K.E., & Bee, H.L. (1983). The impact of temporally patterned stimulation on the development of preterm infants. *Child Development, 54,* 1156–1167.

Bayley, N. (1969). *Bayley scales of infant development.* New York: Psychological Corp.

Beckwith, L., & Cohen, S. (1984). Home environment and cognitive competence in preterm child during the first 5 years. In A.W. Gottfried (Ed.), *Home environment and early cognitive development: Longitudinal research* (pp. 235–271). Orlando, FL: Academic Press.

Bee, H.L., Barnard, K.E., Eyres, S.J., Gray, C.A., Hammond, M.A., Spietz, A.L., Snyder, C., & Clark, B. (1982). Prediction of IQ and language skill from perinatal status, child performance, family characteristics and mother-infant interaction. *Child Development, 53,* 1134–1156.

Boake, C., & Salmon, P. (1983). Demographic correlates and factor structure of the Family Environment Scale. *Journal of Clinical Psychology, 39,* 95–100.

Bradley, R.H., & Caldwell, B.M. (1976). The relation of infants' home environment to mental test performance at fifty-four months: A follow-up study. *Child Development, 47,* 1172–1174.

Brand, A., Johnson, J., & Johnson, S. (1986). Life stress and diabetic control in children and adolescents with insulin-dependent diabetes. *Journal of Pediatric Psychology, 11,* 481–495.

Caldwell, B.M., & Bradley, R.H. (1978). *Manual for the HOME observation for measurement of the environment.* Unpublished manuscript, University of Arkansas, Little Rock.

Cohen, S., Parmelee, A., Beckwith, L., & Sigman, M. (1986). Cognitive development in preterm infants: Birth to 8 years. *Developmental and Behavioral Pediatrics, 7*(2), 102–110.

Crnic, K.A., Ragozin, A.S., Greenberg, M.T., Robinson, N., & Basham, R. (1983). Social interaction and developmental competence of preterm and full term infants during the first year of life. *Child Development, 54,* 1199–1210.

Dunn, L., & Markwardt, F. (1970). *Peabody individual achievement test manual (PIAT).* Circle Pines, MN: American Guidance Service, Inc.

Fowler, P. (1981). Maximum likelihood factor structure of the family environment scale. *Journal of Clinical Psychology, 37,* 160–164.

Greenberg, M., & Crnic, K. (1988). Longitudinal predictors of developmental status and social interaction in premature and full term infants at age two. *Child Development, 59,* 554–570.

Hammond, M.A., Bee, H.L., Barnard, K.E., & Eyres, S.J. (1983). *Child health assessment part IV: Follow-up at second grade.* Seattle: University of Washington, Parent and Child Nursing.

Hollingshead, A.B. (1975). *Four factor index of social status.* New Haven, CT: Yale University Press.

Holmes, J.H., & Rahe, R.H. (1967). The social adjustment rating scale. *Journal of Psychosomatic Research, 11,* 213–218.

Hunt, J.V., Cooper, B., & Tooley, A. (1988). Very low birth weight infants at eight and eleven years of age: The role of neonatal illness and family status. *Paediatrics, 82*(4), 596–603.

Klein, N.K. (1988). Children who were very low birth weight: Cognitive abilities and classroom behavior at five years of age. *Journal of Special Education, 22*(1), 41–52.

Klein, N., Hack, M., & Breslau, N. (1989). Children who are very low birth weight: Development and academic achievement at nine years of age. *Developmental and Behavioral Pediatrics, 10*(1), 32–37.

Lindgren, S., Harper, D., & Blackman, J. (1986). Environmental influences and perinatal risk factors in high-risk children. *Journal of Pediatric Psychology, 11*(4), 531–547.

Lloyd, B.W., Wheldall, K., & Perks, D. (1988). Controlled study of intelligence and school performance of very low birth weight children from a defined geographical area. *Developmental Medicine and Child Neurology, 30,* 36–42.

McCall, R.B. (1979). The development of intellectual functioning in infancy and the prediction of later IQ. In J.D. Osofsky (Ed.), *Handbook of infant development* (pp. 707–741). New York: Wiley.

McCormick, M. (1989). Long term follow-up of infants discharged from neonatal intensive care units. *JAMA, 261*(12), 1767–1772.

McCormick, M., Stemmler, M., Bernbaum, J., & Farran, H. (1986). The very low birth weight transport goes home: Impact on the family. *Developmental and Behavioral Pediatrics, 7*(4), 217–223.

McCubbin, H., & Patterson, J. (1983). The family stress process: The double ABCX model of adjustment and adaptation. *Marriage and Family Review, 6,* 7–37.

Moos, R. (1974). *Family environment scale manual.* Palo Alto, CA: Consulting Psychologists Press.

O'Grady, D., & Metz, J.R. (1987). Resilience in children at high risk for psychological disorder. *Journal of Pediatric Psychology, 12*(1), 3–20.

Parmelee, A., & Littman, B. (1974). *Perinatal factor scores.* Unpublished manuscript, University of California, Los Angeles, Department of Pediatrics.

Ramey, C.T., Farran, D.C., & Campbell, F.A. (1979). Predicting IQ from mother-infant interactions. *Child Development, 50,* 804–814.

Rohner, R. (1984). *Handbook for the study of parental acceptance and rejection.* Storrs, CT: University of Connecticut Center for the Study of Parental Acceptance-Rejection.

Sameroff, A.J., & Chandler, M.J. (1975). Reproductive risk and the continuum of caretaking casualty. In F.D. Horowitz, M. Hetherington, S. Scarr-Salapotek, & G. Siegel (Eds.), *Review of child development research* (Vol. 4, pp. 177–244). Chicago: University of Chicago Press.

Sameroff, A.J., & Seifer, R. (1983). Familial risk and child competence. *Child Development, 54,* 1254–1268.

Sarason, I., Johnson, J., & Siegel, J. (1978). Assessing the impact of life changes: Development of the life experiences survey. *Journal of Consulting and Clinical Psychology, 46,* 932–946.

Schaefer, E. (1986). *Personal communication on the factor structure of CBI.* Chapel Hill, NC: The Frank Porter Graham Child Development Center.

Schaefer, E., & Edgerton, M. (1978). *Classroom behavior inventory (CBI).* Chapel Hill, NC: The Frank Porter Graham Child Development Center.

Silva, P., McGee, R., & Williams, S. (1984). A longitudinal study of the intelligence and behavior of preterm and small for gestational age children. *Developmental and Behavioral Pediatrics, 5*(1), 1–5.

Simonds, J., Silva, P., & Aston, L. (1981). Behavioral and psychiatric assessment of preterm and full term low birth weight children at 9–11 years of age. *Developmental and Behavioral Pediatrics, 2*(3), 82–88.

Webster-Stratton, C. (1989). The relationship of marital support, conflict and divorce to parent perceptions, behaviors and childhood conduct problems. *Journal of Marriage and the Family, 51,* 417–430.

Wechsler, D. (1974). *Manual for the Wechsler intelligence scale for children-revised.* New York: Psychological Corp.

Wikran, R., Fateide, A., & Blaker, R. (1978). Communication in the family of the asthmatic child. *Acta Psychiatrica Scandinavica, 57,* 11–26.

10
Behavior Problems and Social Competence During Early Adolescence in Children Born Preterm*

Sarale E. Cohen
Arthur H. Parmelee
Leila Beckwith
Marian Sigman

Preterm birth and the hazardous perinatal events that may accompany it have been associated with a variety of deleterious outcomes (Cohen, 1986; Kopp, 1983). A number of studies have examined behavior problems in preschool and school-aged children who were born preterm, and found an increased incidence of various behavior problems (Breslau, Klein, & Allen, 1988; Caputo, Goldstein, & Taub, 1981; Drillien, Thompson, & Burgoyne, 1980; Escalona, 1982; Mitchell, Bee, Hammond, & Barnard, 1985; Wiener, Rider, Oppel, Fischer, & Harper, 1965). Though the evidence seems to indicate that, as a group, the preterm infant is at risk for behavior problems, the agreement is not unanimous (Baker, Mednick, & Hunt, 1987; Noble-Jameson, Lukeman, Silverman, & Davis, 1982; Simonds, Silva, & Aston, 1981).

Little is known as to the impact of the preterm birth on problems in early adolescence, as few of the studies have measured behavior problems past childhood. Early adolescence is a critical period to evaluate social-emotional development, as it is a time of biological, psychological, and social challenges (Powers, Hauser, & Kilner, 1989). For many years the view prevailed that turmoil during adolescence was normal and consequently the investigation of psychological problems was minimal. More recent research has pointed out the absence of significant psychological problems among the majority of adolescents (Offer & Offer, 1975) and has attempted to examine a variety of influences on psychological adjustment (Petersen, 1988).

The focus of much of the research with children born preterm has been on comparing the incidence of behavior problems in preterm and control samples and little attention has been paid to the identification of antecedent conditions. It is recognized that little is known about risk factors in infancy for later pathology (Lewis, Feiring, McGuffog, & Jaskir, 1984), and that there is a need for longitudinal studies that assess biological and family influences (Quay, Routh, &

* This work was supported by a contract from NICHD (#1-HD-3-2776), grants from the William T. Grant Foundation (#B771121, G801203), and a grant from NICHD (#HD 18621).

Shapiro, 1987). The prospective longitudinal study that we have conducted following preterm infants from birth to 12 years of age provides an ideal base for examining a number of infancy and childhood risk factors.

A multiaxial approach using data from different informants has been proposed as an important approach to maladjustment (Achenbach, 1985). A recent meta-nalysis of behavioral and emotional problems (Achenbach, McConaughy, & Howell, 1987) found the mean correlation between parent and teacher ratings of behavioral and emotional problems to be modest ($r = .27$), indicating the need for multiinformants to get a comprehensive picture of problem behavior. Cross situational assessment was used in the longitudinal study reported in this chapter and behavioral problems were rated by both parents and teachers.

Even less is known about the social competence of children who were born preterm than is known about behavior problems, as few studies have examined this aspect of behavior. Although it is agreed that social competence is an important aspect of behavioral assessment, the measurement of social competence has been difficult. Frequently measures of social competence have been found to be highly related to general cognitive ability (Ford, 1982). A standardized measure has been developed as part of the Child Behavior Checklist (Achenbach & Edelbrock, 1983), requiring the parent or teacher to rate the child's quality and quantity of involvement in activities and interpersonal relationships as well as performance in school. These social competence scores from the Child Behavior Checklist are relatively independent of IQ. The social competence scores are more than a mirror image of behavior problems but their relationship to measures other than behavior problems and IQ is largely unknown. A comparison of the antecedents and correlates of social competence and behavior problems may elucidate the similarities and differences between social competence and behavior problems.

The purpose of this chapter is to examine the antecedents and correlates of social-emotional competence as assessed by ratings of behavior problems and social behavior in a group of early adolescents who were born preterm.

METHOD

Subjects

The subjects in this study consist of a group of children all born preterm who have been studied intensively since birth in a prospective longitudinal study (Cohen, Parmelee, Beckwith, & Sigman, 1986, 1992; Sigman & Parmelee, 1979). The data reported in this chapter are from all of the children seen at age 12 years who had both parent and teacher ratings of their behavior and who were from homes where English was the primary language.

The sample consisted of 56 children, 34 boys and 22 girls. The four-factor

Hollingshead index indicated that, on the average, the group was middle class, with a range of social class backgrounds. The occupations of the parents varied from unskilled laborer to professional ($M = 43.9$; $r = 19$–66). The children differed as to the number of medical complications that they had experienced as neonates. There were some children who had few complications other than their low birthweight, whereas other children had suffered a number of complications and were hospitalized for some time. Fifty percent of the sample had respiratory distress syndrome as neonates. The average birthweight of the sample was 1,832 grams, range 800 to 2,495, and the average gestational age was 32.7 weeks, range 25 to 37. The average length of hospitalization was 26.2 days, range 2 to 88.

Of the group of 77 children from English speaking homes who were followed intensively to age 2 years, 81%, or 62 of the children, were seen at age 12, and of this group 56 children had both teacher and parent ratings. Ten of this group of 56 were children who lived out of state or some distance from Los Angeles and were tested by trained local examiners. The group that was not included in the analyses for this chapter, as they did not participate in the 12-year testing or did not have both teacher and parent ratings, did not differ significantly from the group of 56 children as to birthweight, gestational age, length of hospitalization, or years of maternal education. However, the group that was not included was lower in SES ($t = 2.20$, df $= 75$, $p < .05$) than the group with complete data.

Procedure

In addition to the parent and teacher's ratings of the child's behavior, a wide range of assessments was administered at age 12, consisting of cognitive tests, school achievement, and the child's self-perception ratings. As the 12-year follow-up was part of a prospective longitudinal study since birth, many assessments during infancy and toddlerhood, early childhood, and 8 years were also available for analysis. These assessments covered the domains of neurobehavior, medical status, cognitive development, and the social environment. The measures and their summary scores have been described thoroughly in previous publications (Cohen et al., 1986; Parmelee, Kopp, & Sigman, 1976) and will be mentioned only briefly here.

Infancy measures. Demographic information was available from parental interview. Obstetrical history, birth information, and medical history were available from the medical records and from the Postnatal Complication Scale (Littman & Parmelee, 1978), which described the early medical status of the infant and yielded an optimality score. Neurobehavioral measures in infancy included infant visual attention (Sigman, Kopp, Parmelee, & Jeffrey, 1973) and sleep state organization and EEG activation (Beckwith & Parmelee, 1986). Cognitive assessments (Gesell Developmental Schedules) were administered at 4, 9, and 24 months. The responsiveness of the caregiving parent was measured at 1, 8, 21, and 24 months (Beckwith & Cohen, 1984, 1989) and yielded a responsiveness score and also a parental control factor score in the second year.

Childhood measures at 5 and 8 years. Included in the analyses in this chapter are the following measures of problematic behavior filled out by the parent: the Child Behavior Checklist (Achenbach & Edelbrock, 1983) was given at age 8; and the Conners abbreviated scale (Conners, 1973) of 10 items to measure hyperkinesis was given at 5 and 8 years. The Child Behavior Checklist is designed to identify deficient social competence and excessive behavioral problems. The social competence section contains 40 questions about the child's activities, social involvement, and school performance, and yields a total social competence T score. The behavior problems section contains 113 items that are rated as being not like, somewhat like, or very like the characteristics of the child. Three global scales are obtained yielding internalizing, externalizing, and total problem T scores. The classroom teacher-rated problem behavior on the Child Behavior Scale (Rutter, Tizard, Yule, Graham, & Whitmore, 1976) at 8 years. The scale consists of 26 items that are rated as to certainly applies (2), applies somewhat (1), or doesn't apply (0). Problem score cutoff points have been established for each of these measures.

12-year measures. Social-emotional development was assessed by parental and teacher ratings as at year 8. One parent (in 79% of the cases, the mother) filled out the Child Behavior Checklist (Achenbach & Edelbrock, 1983) in order to identify behavior problems and social competence and the abbreviated Conners scale (Conners, 1973). The mathematics teacher or the general teacher filled out the Child Behavior Scale (Rutter et al., 1976) and the abbreviated Conners scale.

Other assessments that were administered at 12 years and that are included in this chapter are as follows: the Wechsler Intelligence Scale for Children, Revised (Wechsler, 1974); the Wide Range Achievement Test, Revised (Jastak & Wilkerson, 1984); self-report questionnaires filled out by the early adolescent, namely the Perceived Competence scale (Harter, 1982) and two subscales, family relationships and emotional tone, from the Self-Image Questionnaire for Adolescents (Offer, Ostrov, & Howard, 1982). The parent filled out the California Psychological Inventory (Gough, 1975) and three summary scores were used to describe parental adjustment: interpersonal effectiveness, intrapersonal control, and achievement motivation (Vaughn, Bradley, Joffe, Seifer, & Barglow, 1987). The parent also completed the Family Environment Scale (Moos & Moss, 1981), which comprises 10 subscales that measure the social-environmental characteristics of the family. Two underlying domains were scored: the Relationship dimensions and the System Maintenance dimensions. Parent–child interaction was assessed in the laboratory (Beckwith, Rodning, & Cohen, in press), and a responsiveness score was derived using a Q sort procedure derived from the work of Gjerde (1986). Additionally, a physical examination by a pediatrician provided a measure of the Tanner (1962) stage of pubertal development.

Table 1.   Distribution of Behavior Problems
Rated by Parent and Teacher

Problem Behavior	No. of Children
P behavior, T behavior	7
P behavior only	13
T behavior only	7
No behavior problems	29

P = parent-rated behavior problem,
T = teacher-rated behavior problem

RESULTS

Statistical analyses focused on group comparisons of problem versus normal groups rather than correlations across the range of scores as the primary interest was in identifying children with excessive problems, not in describing variations around normal scores. Three types of problem groups were established on the basis of the established cutoff scores: Parent report of behavior problems, parent report of low social competence, and teacher report of behavior problems. Standard scores on the Child Behavior Checklist suggested by Achenbach and Edelbrock (1983) as discriminating between clinic and nonclinic samples were used to constitute the parent report behavior problem group (scores above the 90th percentile of the normative group) and the problem social competence group (scores below the 10th percentile of the normative group). The cutoff point for problems as perceived by the teacher was a score of 9 or more on the Child Behavior Scale, as suggested by Rutter and colleagues (1976), since this cutoff has been shown to discriminate between clinic and nonclinic samples. The three problem groups were not mutually exclusive. Table 1 presents the distribution of children with behavior problem ratings.

Behavior Problems Reported by the Parent

The mean behavior problem score was 57.9 (SD = 10.2). Thirty-six percent of the preterm group scored within the clinical range, as compared to 10% of the normative group. The internalizing and externalizing behavior problem scores ($M = 57.4$, SD = 8.8 and $M = 54.9$, SD = 9.9, respectively) were highly related, $r = .76$, $p < .001$. Thus, for the data analyses in this chapter the total behavior problem score was used to establish problem and normal groups.

Table 2 compares the behavior problem and normal groups by gender on the narrow band scales of the Child Behavior Checklist. The girls in the problem group differed from the normal group on all of the narrow band subscales except schizoid, aggressive, and cruel. The biggest difference between the problem girls

Table 2. Comparison of Mean Scores on Narrow Band Scales
for Parent-Rated Behavior Problem and Normal Groups

	Behavior Problem		Behavior Normal	Clinical Range[a]
Girls	N = 6		N = 16	
Anxious/obsessive	66.0	***	57.9	0
Somatic	65.7	*	60.4	5
Schizoid	64.0		59.3	5
Depressed/withdrawn	65.2	***	58.6	0
Immature/hyperactive	72.3	***	58.9	14
Delinquent	65.5	***	57.8	5
Aggressive	63.8		56.3	5
Cruel	64.7		59.8	5
Boys	N = 14		N = 20	
Somatic	66.5	***	59.0	12
Schizoid	63.5	*	57.8	9
Uncommunicative	64.7	***	55.6	3
Immature	70.3	***	60.1	21
Obsessive/compulsive	63.9	***	56.2	9
Hostile/withdrawn	68.6	***	56.4	15
Delinquent	67.4	***	56.0	18
Aggressive	65.9	***	55.3	3
Hyperactive	71.3	***	56.1	16

*$p < .05$, ***$p < .001$
[a]percent in clinical range in behavior problem group

and the normal group girls was on the immature/hyperactive scale. Fourteen percent of the scores of the problem group were in the clinical range (a T score above 70), as compared to 0% in the normal group in this study and 2% in the normative group.

The boys in the behavior problem group differed on every individual narrow band scale from the behavior normal rating group. They differed significantly from the normative group as to the percentage of children scoring in the clinical range on the following subscales: immature, somatic, hyperactive, delinquent, and hostile/withdrawn.

Social Competence as Perceived by the Parent

Social competence was not the same as the converse of behavior problems, although social competence was significantly correlated ($r = -.56$) with behavior problems as reported by the parent. The mean social competence score was 46.2 (SD = 11.6). The scores for the three components of social competence were as follows: Activities M = 48.2 (SD = 8.4); Social relationships M = 45.4 (SD = 10.0); and School M = 43.1 (SD = 11.1). Twenty-nine percent of the sample scored within the clinical range on the total social competence score.

If a child were rated as socially incompetent by the parent, it was likely that the child was also rated as having behavior problems. Only 4 (7%) of the children had social competence problems without having behavior problems according to the parent. In contrast, of the 20 children who were described by the parent as having behavior problems, 8 children were described as socially competent. Of the 16 children the parents rated as low in social competence 9 (56%) were rated by their teachers as not showing behavior problems.

Teacher Ratings of Problem Behavior

In terms of teacher ratings of problem behavior, 25% of the sample scored above the cutoff range of normal behavior problems. The mean score was 5.4 (SD = 6.8). The teacher ratings correlated positively ($r = .32$) with parent ratings of behavior problems and negatively ($r = -.35$) with the social competence rating. The modest size of the correlation indicates that there were many children classified differently by parents and teachers.

Concurrent Performance

There were a number of ways in which problem and normal groups differed at 12 years (see Table 3). The differences are summarized below. Prior to examining differences it is worthwhile to note that none of the problem groups studied in this chapter differed from the comparison normal groups as to their overall

Table 3. Significant Differences in Concurrent Behaviors for 12-Year Behavior Problem and Social Competence Groups

	Parent Rating				Teacher Rating	
	Behavior		Social Competence		Behavior	
	Problem N = 20	Normal N = 36	Problem N = 16	Normal N = 40	Problem N = 14	Normal N = 42
Tanner stage	2.4 *	3.3	1.8 ***	3.4		
Freedom from distract.			94.0 **	104.7	93.7 *	104.3
Achievement						
Reading					96.9 *	107.8
Arithmetic			88.2 *	100.6	84.5 **	101.3
Self-Perception						
Cognitive	2.6 *	3.0	2.4 **	3.0	2.5 *	2.9
Self-esteem			2.8 *	3.2	2.8 *	3.1
Family relationships	50.5 *	62.3	49.5 *	61.5		
Emotional tone	48.8 **	60.4	45.6 ***	59.8		
Parent responsiveness					109 **	143
Parent perception— relationship dimensions	16.3 **	21.1	16.1 **	20.8		

*p < .05, **p < .01, ***p < .001

intelligence at 12 years. In terms of their cognitive development, children in both problem and normal groups were functioning well. The average IQ score on the Wechsler Intelligence Scale for Children was 110.2 (SD $=$ 14.6, r $=$ 78-139).

Parent reported behavior problems. The parent rated behavior problem group was less mature in pubertal development as measured by the Tanner (1962) stages. Children who were seen by their parents as showing behavior problems at age 12 did not differ from the normal group in school achievement; however, they did have some problems in maintaining and focusing their attention as shown by the distractibility factor of the WISC-R.

The parents who described their children as showing problem behavior were not different from the parents who described their children as not having behavior problems in their actual interaction with their early adolescents in a semistructured laboratory situation. However, the two groups differed in terms of the parent perception of the Relationship dimensions on the Family Environment Scale (Moos & Moos, 1981). Parents of ''problem'' children described their family environment as lower in commitment, help, and support, and higher in conflict.

In order to specify group differences as to the number of families seeking help from mental health professionals, interview questions that were part of the social history obtained from the parent were examined. It was noted that the parent perceived behavior problem group differed from the normal group in that more of the problem group children had received psychiatric help in the past than the normal group children (5 versus 1 respectively, Fishers exact probability test, p $=$ .02). None of the children in either group was currently receiving psychiatric help and one child in each group was receiving counseling at the time of the 12 year testing. More fathers in the problem group were currently receiving counseling than in the normal group (3 fathers in the problem group and no fathers in the normal group, Fishers exact probability test p $=$ .04).

Parent reported social competence. Social competence groups showed a broad range of concurrent performance differences, similar to those of behavior problems, but somewhat more extensive (see Table 2). As a group children rated low in social competence were less physically mature, showed attentional problems, were lower in arithmetic achievement, saw themselves as less cognitively competent, had lower self-esteem, perceived their family relationships as less satisfactory, and were themselves less happy. Additionally their parents described the Relationship dimensions of the Family Environment Scale as less satisfactory.

Interview questions indicated that children described as showing problems in their social competence as compared to children rated as normal in social competence were more likely to have received psychiatric help in the past and their mothers were also more likely to have had psychiatric help (Fishers exact probability test p $=$ .03 and p $=$ .02 respectively).

Teacher reported behavior problems. Children that the teachers saw as presenting a behavior problem were less competent in their reading and arithmetic achievement scores on the Wide Range Achievement Test (see Table 3). They also had some difficulty in focusing their attention. The children saw themselves as less cognitively competent and had a lower general self-esteem score. Responsive family interaction was lower in the problem group as measured in the laboratory situation. Children that the teachers saw as showing problem behavior were more likely to have had mothers who had received psychiatric help in the past than the normal group (Fishers exact probability test, $p = .002$).

Antecedents

Are there antecedents of problem behavior that may be identified in infancy or early childhood? A series of t tests were run comparing the problem and no problem groups on background variables, medical history, developmental history, and neurobehavioral measures. (See Table 4 for a summary of the significant mean differences.) The results indicated a paucity of early antecedents of later behavior problems. In contrast to the many concurrent behaviors showing differences between problem groups there were few antecedents of behavior problems or social competence.

Demographic. Lower social class and fewer years of maternal education were associated with behavior problems rated by the teacher, but not by the parents. However, parents who saw their children as low in social competence were lower in maternal education, as a group.

Medical status. Early hazardous medical events were not associated with behavior problems, but children who were seen as less socially competent were more likely to be of a younger gestational age, to have spent more time in the hospital, and to have had more postnatal complications in the neonatal period.

Neurobehavioral measures. The infant's own characteristics as shown in neurobehavioral measures (neonatal visual attention, state regulation, and EEG organization), which have been shown in our previous work (Cohen & Parmelee, 1983; Cohen, Parmelee, Sigman, & Beckwith, 1988; Sigman, Beckwith, Cohen, & Parmelee, 1989) to be so important for cognitive development were not associated with behavior problems or with social competence.

Developmental tasks. Developmental status in the first year of life was not associated with parental or teacher perception of behavior problems but was with parental perception of social competence. Those children whose social competence was reported as problematic at age 12 years had lower mean scores on developmental tests in both the first and second year of life than those children whose social competence was normal.

Home environment. The home environment in the first 2 years of life was not related to parental perception of behavior problems at age 12. However,

Table 4. Significant Differences in Antecedents for Behavior Problem and Social Competence Groups

	Parent Rating				Teacher Rating	
	Behavior	Behavior	Social Competence		Behavior	Behavior
	Problem N = 20	Normal N = 36	Problem N = 16	Normal N = 40	Problem N = 14	Normal N = 42
Demographic						
Maternal education			11.9 *	13.4	12.1 *	13.2
SES					38.3 *	46.9
Medical						
Gestational age			31.0 *	33.0		
Birthweight			1631 *	1912		
Length of hospitalization			39.7 *	23.3		
Postnatal complications[a]			72.9 *	91.8		
Cognitive Scores						
Gesell—9 mos			96.0 *	101.3		
Gesell—24 mos			96.2 *	104.7		
Receptive language—24 mos			87.5 *	103.4		
Home Environment						
Responsiveness—21 mos			76 *	132	59 **	134
Control—24 mos					153 *	80
Consistent responsiveness			1.1 *	1.8		
Parent Rating—Connors—5 yr.	22.1 **	15.7	20.7 *	17.1		

*$p < .05$, **$p < .01$,
[a]optimal score

those children that were described by the parents as low in social competence and those children the teacher reported as showing problem behavior had less responsive caregiving as toddlers. Additionally, children in the teacher problem group had parents who were more controlling in the toddler period.

Parental personality dimensions on the California Psychological Inventory were not significantly different between any of the problem and normal groups.

Pervasiveness of behavior problems. Children with behavior problem ratings from both parent and teacher (N = 7) were compared to children with problem ratings in only one setting ($N = 20$). As the majority of the multiple setting problem children were boys (86%) versus 60% boys in the problem group in only one setting, the comparisons were made only for boys. The results are tentative due to the small number of cases in each group. The multiple setting problem behavior boys, as compared to single settings problem boys, were very similar on concurrent behavior. They differed only two antecedent conditions: the multiple setting boys were hospitalized longer and received less parental responsiveness at 21 months than the single setting problem boys.

Relationship Across Time

At 8 years, using the same measure (the CBCL) 30% of the parents reported behavior problems and 11% rated their children low social competence. Parent ratings were highly related across the two time periods (see Table 5). The ratings of two different teachers 4 years apart, one when the child was 8 years and one when the child was 12 years, correlated slightly higher (but not significantly so) with each other, $r = .49$, $p < .001$ than the concurrent rating of the parent and teacher, $r = .32$, $p < .05$.

In spite of the high correlations across the range of scores, an examination of the categorical analysis shows shifts for individual children. The least shifting was in terms of parental ratings of behavior problems. There were 2 children who were categorized by their parents as having behavior problems at age 8 but not at age 12; 15 children who were categorized as showing problem behavior at both ages; and 5 children (all boys) who emerged with behavior problems at 12 years. Low social competence showed a somewhat different pattern as only 6 children were rated as low in social competence at 8 years. Of these 6 children, 4 remained low at age 12, whereas 12 children were newly rated as low in social competence. Teacher ratings, on the other hand, showed a slight decrease in problems over time for those children who received teacher ratings at both 8 and 12 years. Of the 42 children rated at both ages by their teachers, more children showed problems at age 8 ($N = 12$) than at age 12 ($N = 8$); 7 children had problems at age 8 only; 5 children at both ages; and 3 children had problems emerging only at age 12 years. Six children who were not rated at age 8 by their teachers had problem teacher ratings at age 12.

Table 5. Relationships Between Parent and Teacher Ratings

	Parent Rating				Teacher Rating	
	Behavior Problems		Social Competence		Behavior Problems	
	8	12	8	12	8	12
Parent						
Connors—5 yrs.	.56***	.49***	−.28	−.38**	.22	.14
Connors—8 yrs.	.72***	.70***	−.23	−.39**	.35*	.27
Connors—12 yrs.	.62***	.79***	−.28*	−.55***	.51***	.47***
CBCL—8 yrs.						
Behavior problems		.78***	−.26	−.38**	.28	.20
Social competence	−.26	−.29*		.76***	−.37**	−.35**
Teacher						
CBS—8 yrs	.28*	.34*	−.37**	−.43**		.48**
12 yrs	.20	.32*	−.34**	−.35**	.48***	
Connors—12 yrs	.24	.37**	−.31*	−.37**	.56***	.80***

$N = 42–56$
*$p < .05$, **$p < .01$, ***$p < .001$

Children with persistent behavior problems as rated by the parent ($N = 15$) were compared to those children who were rated as having behavior problems only at age 8 or age 12 years ($N = 7$). As the number of cases is small, the findings are tentative. Actual differences between the persistent and not persistent groups were few. There were no concurrent differences at age 12 on any of the measures reported in Table 3. An examination of antecedent conditions was also similar for the groups except that the one time behavior problem group (mostly newly emerging) had a lower social class than the persistent group ($M = 33.9$ and 47.4 respectively) and was not rated as low at age 5 or age 8 on the Conners scale.

Gender Differences

Boys and girls did not differ in their mean total problem score on the CBCL or in the internalizing and externalizing scores. Girls were higher than boys in their social competence score ($M = 50.0$ and 43.8 respectively, $t = 2.07$, $p < .05$) but did not differ significantly in terms of the percentage who scored in the problem range. The teacher rating score was not significantly different for boys and girls.

In order to test for behavior problem differences that might be related to the child's gender a series of 2 (behavior problems as described by the parent) x 2 (gender) analyses of variance were done. Only selected behaviors were analyzed to reduce the possibility of capitalizing on chance differences. The behaviors selected to be analyzed were the five behaviors that were shown to be statistically different for the problem versus normal groups (see Table 3) and the full scale IQ score. Of the six ANOVAs, two behaviors were significantly different between boys and girls. These two behaviors, pubertal development and the parental perception of the Relationship dimensions, also showed a significant gender x behavior problem interaction. In each of these analyses Scheffe post hoc analyses indicated that the male problem group was significantly lower than any other group. There were no significant gender differences or interaction of gender and behavior problems in the child's self-perception, IQ, or parent behavior.

There were too few girls in the social competence problem group (3 girls, or 19%) and in the teacher problem group (4, or 29%) to conduct similar analyses of a gender x problem group interaction. In spite of the low percentage of girls in the social competence and teacher-rated problem categories, statistical tests indicated that differences in the distribution of boys and girls were not statistically significant.

The relationship of antecedent conditions to parent perceived behavior problems was tested for each gender. First the correlations between the behavior problem score and the potential antecedent conditions were examined by gender. Next, multiple regressions were done by gender, selecting the set of three antecedent variables that were most highly related to the problem score for each gender. The variables were then used to predict to a problem or normal group. For boys, the parent's achievement motivation, the child's birthweight, and maternal responsiveness at 21 months yielded a significant multiple R, F (3, 14) = 13.12 p < 0002, adjusted R^2 = .68. For girls, the antecedent independent variables that individually related to the behavior problem score did not enter the regression equation predicting to problem or normal group categories.

DISCUSSION

Our results support previous research as to finding a high number of behavioral problems in school children who were born prematurely. The children were more likely to be described as showing problem behavior by their parents than by their teachers, at least using the measures administered in this study. As the parents and teachers used different instruments to rate problem behavior this finding may be questioned. However, when the two groups of informants used the identical measure (Conners abbreviated scale), describing a more circumscribed problem behavior (hyperkinesis), the parents were almost twice as likely as the teachers to describe the child as high in the problem behavior. In spite of the parents categorically rating more children as problematic, the ratings of parents and teachers were significantly correlated. That is, teachers and parents ranked the children in a very similar fashion.

As the children matured and became early adolescents, parents saw more problems emerging particularly in terms of social competence, whereas teachers tended to see fewer behavior problems. It was the slow-maturing boy that was seen as more problematic by the parent but not by the teacher. Parental ratings corroborate the classic research by Eichorn (1963) that late-maturing boys have psychological disadvantages. Recent research as to the relationship between pubertal change and psychological status indicates that the disadvantages may be of short duration (Petersen, 1988).

There were few clear antecedent conditions in infancy and early childhood as to problematic behavior as perceived by the parent. As there has been little study of the antecedents of behavior problems, the lack of antecedents found in this study is an important result. A number of reliable and valid infancy and childhood measures were tested as potential antecedents and were unrelated to behavior problems. These same measures have been identified in our work as antecedents of cognitive functioning and school achievement (Cohen et al., 1986, 1988) but were not antecedents of parent reported behavior problems. Parental beliefs about behavior problems in their children were independent of social background, maternal personality, infant characteristics, early maternal responsiveness, and the child's intellectual development. It was not until 5 years that an antecedent could be identified. Those parents who saw their early adolescents as showing overall behavior problems began to view the behavior as more problematic when the children were 5 years of age. The negative perception that was established at 5 years showed stability to early adolescence. It may be that a good time to identify potential persisting parent–child conflicts is when the child is ready to enter school. On the other hand, it may be that had the parent been asked to rate the child's temperament or behavior at an age younger than 5 years, that earlier antecedents would have been identified.

Parental ratings of low social competence, on the other hand, had antecedents in maternal background, the child's medical condition, early development and the home environment. Infants who were smaller, sicker, and less competent in infancy and toddlerhood were more likely to be rated as showing low social competence at 12 years. Further, they were more likely to have less responsive caregiving in the toddler period and have mothers who were less educated. The reasons for the difference in antecedents to behavior problems and social competence is not clear and merits further investigation.

Teacher ratings, in contrast to parent ratings, appeared more related to external factors such as the child's social class background and school achievement. The fact that teacher ratings were related to actual observations of parent–toddler interaction, suggests that early parental responsivity and control altered the child's behavior such that the impact was long lasting and was perceived by the teacher.

The child's level of cognitive development in infancy was not related to behavior problem ratings but it was related to ratings of social competence. Infants who were less competent were more apt to be perceived as low in social competence in early adolescence. The importance of this lower level of early cognitive functioning did not persist in terms of cognitive differences as there were no IQ differences at age 12 between any of the problem and normal groups. These findings suggest that perhaps the parents established a tendency to be critical of the child's abilities in the infancy period, and that it was this negative attitude that persisted. This hypothesis is supported by the lower parental responsiveness and the greater control shown in toddlerhood by those parents whose children were later rated as showing behavior problems by the teacher. The deleterious effects of a negative affective climate in the family and of parental criticism has been documented in research on the family and psychopathology (Goldstein, 1988).

Issues such as the pervasiness versus situational aspects of behavior problems (Klein & Mannuzza, 1989) and the persistence of behavior problems across time (Loeber, 1982) are important questions that could not be addressed sufficiently in this study due to the sample size. Nonetheless, the data from this study suggest that the early family environment plays a significant role in determining both the extent and persistence of behavior problems.

Few gender differences were found. Girls were rated more socially competent than boys and prediction of problems was better for boys than for girls. Our finding that low birthweight was related to problems in boys, but not girls, corroborates results reported in very low-birthweight children (Breslau et al., 1988). The boys also seemed to be more susceptible to unfavorable environments, as indicated by lower maternal responsiveness being a significant predictor for boys but not for girls.

The impact of being perceived negatively was reflected in the early adolescent's self perception and school performance. The children identified as having problems were less confident of themselves, less able to focus their attention, and less competent in school than the adolescents who were perceived as showing normal behavior, in spite of no differences between the groups in their intelligence.

The results of this study confirm others (Mitchell et al., 1985) that a simple model of early detection of later behavior problems is not supported by current data. Yet the impact on the early adolescent of being perceived as a problem is significant and it is hoped that further investigation will elucidate areas that may serve as targets for intervention. Currently, the long-term consequences of behavior problems and low social competence, as examined in this study, are largely unknown. Other research (Rutter, 1984) and our own findings at ages 8 and 12 years suggest that many behavior problems persist. The meaning of these problems for development in late adolescence and early adulthood is an important question to be answered by future research.

REFERENCES

Achenbach, T.M. (1985). *Assessment and taxonomy of child and adolescent psychopathology.* Beverly Hills, CA: Sage Publications.

Achenbach, T.M., & Edelbrock, C. (1983). *Manual for the child behavior checklist and revised child behavior profile.* Queen City, VT: Queen City Printers.

Achenbach, T.M., McConaughy, S.H., & Howell, C.T. (1987). Child/adolescent behavioral and emotional problems: Implications of cross-informant correlations for situational specificity. *Psychological Bulletin, 101,* 213–232.

Baker, R.L., Mednick, & Hunt, N. (1987). Academic and psychosocial characteristics of low-birthweight adolescents. *Social Biology, 34,* 94–109.

Beckwith, L., & Cohen, S.E. (1984). Home environment and cognitive competence in preterm children in the first five years. In A.W. Gottfried (Ed.), *Home environment and early cognitive development: Longitudinal research* (pp. 235–271). New York: Academic Press.

Beckwith, L., & Cohen, S.E. (1989). Maternal responsiveness with preterm infants and later competency. In M.H. Bornstein (Ed.), *Maternal responsiveness: Characteristics and consequences* (pp. 75–87). *New Directions for Child Development, 43.* San Francisco: Jossey-Bass.

Beckwith, L., & Parmelee, A.H. (1986). EEG patterns of preterm infants, home environment, and later IQ. *Child Development, 57,* 777–789.

Beckwith, L., Rodning, C., & Cohen, S.E. (in press). Preterm children at early adolescence and continuity and discontinuity in maternal responsiveness from infancy. *Child Development, 63.*

Breslau, N., Klein, N., & Allen, L. (1988). Very low birthweight: Behavioral sequelae at nine years of age. *Journal of American Academy of Child and Adolescent Psychiatry, 27,* 605–612.

Caputo, D.V., Goldstein, K.M., & Taub, H.B. (1981). Neonatal compromise and later psychological development: A 10-year longitudinal study. In S.L. Friedman & M. Sigman (Eds.), *Preterm birth and psychological development.* New York: Academic Press.

Cohen, S.E. (1986). The low-birthweight infant and learning disabilities. In M. Lewis (Ed.), *Prenatal and perinatal factors relevant to learning disabilities* (pp. 153–193). Urbana, IL: University of Illinois Press.

Cohen, S.E., & Parmelee, A.H., Jr. (1983). Prediction of five year Stanford-Binet scores in preterm infants. *Child Development, 54,* 1242–1253.

Cohen, S.E., Parmelee, A.H., Beckwith, L., & Sigman, M. (1986) Cognitive development in preterm infants: Birth to 8 years. *Developmental and Behavioral Pediatrics, 7,* 102–110.

Cohen, S.E., Parmelee, A.H., Sigman, M., & Beckwith, L. Antecedents of school problems in children born preterm. (1988). *Journal of Pediatric Psychology, 13,* 493–508.

Cohen, S.E., Parmelee, A.H., Beckwith, L., & Sigman, M. (1992). Biological and social precursors of 12-year competence in children born preterm. In C. Greenbaum & J. Auerbach (Eds.), *Longitudinal studies of children born at psychosocial risk: Cross-national perspectives* (pp. 65-78). Norwood, NJ: Ablex Publishing.

Conners, C.K. (1973). Rating scale for use in drug studies with children. *Psychopharmacology Bulletin* (Special issue: *Pharmacotherapy of Children*), pp. 24–29.

Drillien, C.M., Thompson, A.J.M., & Burgoyne, K. (1980). Low-birthweight children at early school-age: A longitudinal study. *Developmental Medicine and Child Neurology, 22,* 26–47.

Eichorn, D.H. (1963). Biological correlates of behavior. In H.W. Stevenson (Ed.), *Child psychology, part 1, 63rd yearbook of national social study education* (pp. 4–61). Chicago: University of Chicago Press.

Escalona, S.K. (1982). Babies at double hazard: Early development of infants at biologic and social risk. *Pediatrics, 70,* 670–676.

Ford, M.E. (1982). Social cognition and social competence in adolescence. *Developmental Psychology, 18,* 323–340.

Gjerde, P.F. (1986). The interpersonal structure of family interaction settings: Parent-adolescent relations in dyads and triads. *Developmental Psychology, 22,* 297–304.

Goldstein, M.J. (1988). The family and psychopathology. *Annual Review of Psychology, 39,* 283–299.

Gough, H.G. (1975). *Manual for the California Psychological Inventory.* Palo Alto, CA: Consulting Psychologists Press.

Harter, S. (1982). The Perceived Competence Scale for Children. *Child Development, 53,* 87–97.

Jastak, S., & Wilkerson, G. (1984). *Wide Range Achievement Test.* Wilmington, DE: Jastak Associates.

Klein, R.G., & Mannuzza, S. (1989). The long-term outcome of the attention deficit disorder/hyperkinetic syndrome. In T. Sagvolden & T. Archer (Eds.), *Attention deficit disorder* (pp. 71–91). Hillsdale, NJ: Erlbaum.

Kopp, C.B. (1983). Risk factors in development. In M. Haith & J. Campos (Eds.), *Infancy and the biology of development* (Vol. 2), in P. Mussen (Ed.), *Manual of child psychology* (pp. 1081–1188). New York: Wiley.

Lewis, M., Feiring, C., McGuffog, C., & Jaskir, J. (1984). Predicting psychopathology in six-year-olds from early relations. *Child Development, 55,* 123–136.

Littman, B., & Parmelee, A.H. (1978). Medical correlates of infant development. *Pediatrics, 61,* 470–474.

Loeber, R. (1982). The stability of antisocial and delinquent child behavior: A review. *Child Development, 53,* 1431–1446.

Mitchell, S.K., Bee, H.L., Hammond, M.A., & Barnard, K.E. (1985). Prediction of school and behavior problems in children followed from birth to age eight. In W.K. Frankenburg, R.N. Emde, & J.W. Sullivan (Eds.), *Early identification of children at risk: An international perspective* (pp. 117–132). New York: Plenum Press.

Moos, R.H., & Moos, B.S. (1981). *Family Environment Scale manual*. Palo Alto, CA: Consulting Psychologist Press.

Noble-Jameson, C.M., Lukeman, D., Silverman, M., & Davies, P. (1982). Low birthweight children at school age: Neurological, psychological, and pulmonary function. *Seminars in Perinatology, 6*, 266–273.

Offer, D., & Offer, J. (1975). *From teenage to young manhood: A psychological study*. New York: Basic Books.

Offer, D., Ostrov, E., & Howard, K.I. (1982). *The Offer Self-Image Questionnaire for Adolescents*. Chicago: Michael Reese Hospital and Medical Center.

Parmelee, A.H., Kopp, C.B., & Sigman, M. (1976). Selection of developmental assessment techniques for infants at risk. *Merrill Palmer Quarterly, 22*, 177–199.

Petersen, A.C. (1988). Adolescent development. *Annual Review of Psychology, 39*, 583–607.

Powers, S.I., Hauser, S.T., & Kilner, L.A. (1989). Adolescent mental health. *American Psychologist, 44*, 200–208.

Quay, H.C., Routh, D.K., & Shapiro, S.K. (1987). Psychopathology of childhood: From description to validation. *Annual Review of Psychology, 38*, 491–523.

Rutter, M. (1984). The family, the child, and the school. In M.D. Levine & P. Satz (Eds.), *Middle childhood: Development and dysfunction* (pp. 293–343). Baltimore: University Park Press.

Rutter, M., Tizard, J., Yule, W., Graham, P., & Whitmore, K. (1976). Research report: The Isle of Wight studies, 1964–1974. *Psychological Medicine, 6*, 313–332.

Sigman, M., Beckwith, L., Cohen, S.E., & Parmelee, A.H. (1989). Stability in the biosocial development of the child born preterm. In M.H. Bornstein & N.A. Krasnegor (Eds.), *Stability and continuity in mental development: Behavioral and biological perspectives* (pp. 29–42). Hillsdale, NJ: Erlbaum.

Sigman, M., Kopp, C.B., Parmelee, A.H., & Jeffrey, W.E. (1973). Visual attention and neurological organization in neonates. *Child Development, 44*, 461–466.

Sigman, M., & Parmelee, A.H., Jr. (1979). Longitudinal follow-up of premature infants. In T.M. Field, A.M. Sostek, S. Goldberg, & H.H. Shuman (Eds.), *Infants born at risk* (pp. 193–217). New York: Spectrum.

Simonds, J.F., Silva, P., & Aston, L. (1981). Behavioral and psychiatric assessment of preterm and full-term low birth weight children at 9–11 years of age. *Developmental and Behavioral Pediatrics, 2*, 82–88.

Tanner, J.M. (1962). *Growth at adolescence*. Springfield, IL: Thomas.

Vaughn, B.E., Bradley, C.F., Joffe, L.S., Seifer, R., & Barglow, P. (1987). Maternal characteristics measured prenatally are predictive of ratings of temperamental "difficulty" on the Carey Infant Temperament Questionnaire. *Developmental Psychology, 23*, 152–161.

Wechsler, D. (1974). *Manual for the Wechsler Intelligence Scale for Children-Revised*. New York: Psychological Corporation.

Weiner, G.R., Rider, V., Oppell, W.C., Fisher, L.K., & Harper, P.A. (1965). Correlates of low birthweight: Psychological status at six to seven years of age. *Pediatrics, 35*, 434–444.

IV
Intellectual and Academic Competence

11
Prematurity as well as Intraventricular Hemorrhage Influence Developmental Outcome at 5 Years*

Anita Miller Sostek

Attempts to understand the medical factors contributing to developmental delay and disability have had a long history. There is a continuing trend for preterm infants of earlier gestational ages and smaller birthweights to survive, and developmental outcome studies can hardly keep pace with medical advances. In the past decade, significant attention has been paid to the effects of *intraventricular hemorrhage* (IVH) because it relates directly to the brain of the preterm infants. Use of prospective sonography has revealed that approximately 43%–58% of infants less than 1,500 grams and/or 32 weeks gestational age have some degree of IVH. The incidence declines after 32 weeks and again at 35 weeks (Allan, Dransfield, & Tito, 1984; Dubowitz, Levene, Morante, Palmer, & Dubowitz, 1981).

Knowledge of the pervasiveness of IVH in the preterm infant raises a number of intriguing research questions. Clearly, it is of theoretical as well as clinical interest to understand the effects of different degrees of IVH on the cognitive, language, and motor development of preterm infants. It is also known that preterm infants as a group have rates of developmental delay and disability that are substantially higher than those of children born at fullterm. Even in the absence of obvious handicap, children born preterm have been widely reported at increased risk for learning disabilities (Caputo, Goldstein, & Taub, 1979; Nelson & Broman, 1977; Siegel, 1982, 1983; Taub, Goldstein, & Caputo, 1977). It is not known from these early studies, done prior to sonographic screening, however, whether IVH is responsible for that risk. Finally, knowledge of direct insult to the brain in preterm infants raises questions of developmental capabilities over time and general issues of vulnerability and recovery.

Since approximately 1980, most perinatal centers screen prospectively preterm infants for IVH using ultrasonography at periodic intervals during the first months of life (Papile, Burstein, Burstein, & Koffler, 1978). IVH can be classified according to severity and is typically graded as minor (without ventricular dilatation) or major (with ventricular dilatation).

---

* This research was supported in part by the March of Dimes Birth Defects Foundation Grant #12-160. I thank Kathy S. Katz, Yolande F. Smith, Joanne M. Valvano, and Edward G. Grant for their continued collaboration.

Outcome studies of preterm infants with IVH have been reported through 3 years of age. The infant development studies typically find that outcome relates to the presence and severity of IVH with poor performance on the Bayley Scales of Infant Development most often associated with IVH of Grades III and IV (Papile, Munsick-Bruno, & Shaefer, 1983). In an early follow-up study, Papile and her associates followed a large sample of infants weighing less than 1,500 grams who were prospectively screened for IVH. They were later tested at 12 or 24 months corrected age with the Bayley Scales and a neuromotor evaluation. The neuromotor examination focused on posture, movement, and tone. Degree of handicap related to severity of IVH with the majority of impairments in Grades III and IV.

It is notable that infants with minor hemorrhages (Grades I and II) did not differ in outcome from those with no hemorrhages. Papile and her colleagues conclude, however, that these infants may still be at risk for sensory or perceptual deficits and disorders of learning attention, coordination, and behavior. Studies on visual information processing and IVH support these concerns (Glass & Sostek, 1986; Landry, Leslie, Fletcher, & Francis, 1985).

Studies that have been conducted on 3-year-olds support these findings in the areas of cognitive, language, and motor skills (Bendersky & Lewis, 1990; Landry, Fletcher, Zarling, Chapieski, Francis, & Denson, 1984; Lewis & Bendersky, 1989). Since 1980, our research group has been interested in the effects of intraventricular hemorrhage in the preterm infant up to school age (Glass & Sostek, 1986; Sostek & Glass, 1986; Sostek, Smith, Katz, & Grant, 1987). The basic follow-up study at 2 years of age utilized traditional measures of developmental functioning and neurologic status to investigate the effects of IVH. Related studies examined IVH and visual information processing abilities.

Our work on early IVH outcome generated several hypotheses concerning school readiness and longer term follow-up. At school entry age (4½–5½ years), outcome was measured in terms of general and specific cognitive abilities as well as language abilities, motor skills, and behavior. After comparing IVH groups at 5 years, however, we were still concerned about the general issue of the effects of prematurity on developmental functioning. A related comparison using the same outcome measures was carried out between preterms without IVH and a fullterm group at school entry age.

IVH SCREENING PROCEDURE

All premature infants under 1,750 grams born at Georgetown University Hospital or transferred in during the first 24 hours were included in the sample. Of the infants under 1,750 grams born during the years of 1980–1983, approximately three-quarters survived and most were screened for serial sonography to detect evidence of intraventricular hemorrhage. *Real-time ultrasonography* (RTUS) through the anterior fontanelle was performed at the time of birth (after stabilization), on days 1 and 7, and at discharge. This schedule allowed for determination of the incidence and timing of intraventricular hemorrhage and the progressive course of the hemorrhage. All examinations were performed with an ATL Mark III real-time sector scanner and a 5-MHz transducer with a 90-degree field of vision. No sedation is necessary for this procedure, and examinations were performed in the nursery without removing the infants from their Isolettes.

RTUS was performed according to the following procedure: after palpation of the anterior fontanelle, the transducer was oriented in the coronal plane using the circle of Willis as a landmark. The transducer was gradually angled forward (directing the ultrasound beam toward the back of the head) until the plane of vision almost approached an axial orientation. The transducer was then turned in the reverse direction, reorienting in the coronal plane and examining the frontal portions of the brain. A similar method was used in the sagittal and parasagittal planes. Each portion of the brain was examined by directional angling of the transducer (Grant, Borts, Schellinger, McCullough, Siva Subramanian, & Smith, 1981). Intraventricular hemorrhage was graded by a modified Papile classification (Papile et al., 1978):

Grade 1: Hemorrhage confined to the germinal matrix without ventricular blood
Grade 2: IVH in the lateral ventricles without ventricular distention
Grade 3: IVH with ventricular distention
Grade 4: IVH extending into the brain parenchyma.

SUBJECTS AT 1 AND 2 YEARS

The 1- and 2-year follow-up focuses on the developmental status of 113 preterm infants born at 34 weeks or less and weighing less than 1750 grams who returned for follow-up at 11 months or later (Sostek et al., 1987). All of the infants were appropriate size for gestational age. Because some infants have hemorrhages that enlarge gradually, each infant was classified for hemorrhage grade by the highest degree of hemorrhage observed during the hospitalization. Nine additional infants who were diagnosed sonographically as having *periventricular leukomalacia* (PVL) were eliminated from the data analysis because of the markedly poor outcome that has been found following PVL (de Vries, Dubowitz, Dubowitz, Kaiser, Lary, Silverman, Whitelaw, & Wigglesworth, 1985; Smith, Sostek, Kate, & Grant, 1987; Smith, Young, Sostek, & Grant, 1985). Three of the infants with PVL had no IVH, and six had hemorrhages (one Grade 3 and five Grade 4). Rates of other serious medical complications, such as bronchopulmonary dysplasia and necrotizing enterocolitis, were similar among the groups.

INFANT DEVELOPMENT FOLLOW-UP

The infants were seen in the Georgetown University Child Development Center's High-Risk Infant Follow-up Clinic as closely as possible to 4, 8, 12, 18, and 24 months of chronologic age. At each visit, they were tested on the Bayley Scales of Infant Development (Bayley, 1969), and mental and motor scale scores were corrected for prematurity. An extensive neurologic examination adapted from Amiel-Tison was conducted by the physical therapist or developmental pediatrician to evaluate muscle tone, primitive reflexes, deep tendon reflexes, protective and equilibrium reactions, and range of motion (Amiel-Tison & Grenier, 1980; DeGangi, Berk, & Valvano, 1983). The neurologic findings were rated normal, suspect, or abnormal at each age on the basis of the presence and extent of deviations in muscle tone, reflex development, and equilibrium and protective reactions.

ONE- AND 2-YEAR RESULTS

For the purpose of data analysis, four groups were compared: no IVH, minor IVH (Grades 1 and 2), IVH Grade 3, IVH Grade 4. One-way ANOVAS were applied to the data. For each of the analyses, the total number of subjects was close to 90. Analysis of 1-year developmental scores (mean age = 12.7 months) revealed significantly lower mental and motor scores in the group with major hemorrhages. At 2 years of age (mean age = 21.8 months), mental and motor differences were no longer significantly lower in the group with major hemorrhages, although the direction of effects paralleled the earlier findings (Sostek et al., 1987) (see Figure 1).

VISUAL INFORMATION PROCESSING

A subset of the infants were tested on visual information processing tasks at 8–10 months corrected age (Glass & Sostek, 1986; Sostek & Glass, 1986). Using a standard habituation/dishabituation paradigm, two tasks were administered to each infant: a configuration task and a facial-expression task. The stimuli were presented sequentially using a fixed number of trials. The length of the trial was under infant control. The infants were presented a series of seven redundant stimuli (smiling faces) followed by two novel stimuli (surprised faces), according to a standard familiarization/novelty paradigm. The preferred response was a decrement in attention from the first pair to the last pair of the redundant stimuli, followed by an increase in attention to the novel test pair.

All sessions were videotaped for later scoring without knowledge of sonographic findings. Length of fixation rounded to the nearest second was scored

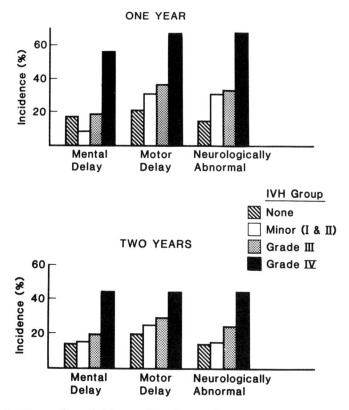

Figure 1. Proportion of delay and/or abnormality among preterm groups with varying degrees of IVH (from Sostek et al., 1987, reprinted by permission).

using a chronometer. Attention, habituation (amount and rate), and response to novelty were scored. Response to redundancy and novelty related to the presence and severity of IVH. There was a significant difference between Grade 1 and Grade 2 hemorrhages as well as the more predictable difference among no hemorrhage, minor hemorrhage, and major hemorrhage groups.

IMPLICATIONS FOR LATER DEVELOPMENTAL OUTCOME

The findings on intraventricular hemorrhage up to 2 years of age suggest four major trends:

1. Developmental functioning and incidence of impairment relate to the presence and severity of IVH. Lewis and Bendersky (1989) found similar differences between IVH groups in mental and motor performance on the

Bayley Scales. These differences were independent of SES and other medical complications.

2. The performance of many infants in our sample suggests improvement between 1 and 2 years.
3. Motor delays are more prevalent than mental delays.
4. Minor hemorrhages are similar in prognosis to no hemorrhages on traditional developmental measures, although response to novelty and recovery on visual information processing tasks suggest intermediate-level deficits in the infants with minor hemorrhages. These findings confirm differences in visual information processing abilities reported by Landry and associates (Landry et al., 1985).

The school entry age follow-up study was designed to examine the developmental functioning of a sizable group of children born prematurely with varying degrees of IVH. The assessments focus on kindergarten readiness, general cognitive functioning, specific cognitive areas, detailed motor skills, and language development. We hypothesized that, at ages 4½–5½, the children will demonstrate the following trends:

1. Delays in cognitive and motor skills at 4½–5½ will relate to severity and presence of IVH. Motor effects will remain more severe.
2. Differences between children who experienced minor hemorrhages and children with no hemorrhages will be in subtle, well-defined areas of development.

It was not clear, however, whether the effects of IVH would continue to decrease as they seemed to do between 1 and 2 years, or whether the effects would increase with the more complex task demands at school entry age.

SUBJECTS

The preterm sample includes 85 children born between late 1979 and 1983. Racial composition among the preterm infants was 60.5% white, 33.3% black, and 6.1% other. Males comprised 60.6% of the sample. Children with a history of echodense lesions in the periventricular area were excluded from the study because of their generally poorer outcome (Smith et al., 1987). The preterm infants were divided into groups based on their history of IVH with the following breakdown: no IVH ($n = 31$), minor IVH ($n = 24$) and major IVH ($n = 30$). Every attempt was made to keep the groups consistent as to birthweight, gestational age, and age at testing (see Table 1). The no-hemorrhage preterm group tended to be slightly larger and less premature than the minor and major hemorrhage groups, however. In order to equate the groups as much as possible,

Table 1. Subject Characteristics: Intraventricular Hemorrhage Groups

	IVH Group		
	None	Minor	Major
Number	31	24	30
Percent Male	41.9	37.5	53.3
Percent White	64.5	58.3	60.0
Percent Black	22.6	33.3	30.0
Percent Twins[a]	6.5	8.3	13.3
Birthweight	1247.3	1211.3	1140.5
Gestational Age*	30.1	29.6	28.5
Months of Age	57.7	57.9	58.7

*$p < .05$

[a]Includes two members of a set of triplets; the third triplet did not survive to 5 years of age. Twins were often not in the same hemorrhage group, and in one case only one twin met the criteria for the study (the other was too large at birth).

the largest of the no-hemorrhage preterm infants were omitted from the data analysis of the effects of IVH. The remaining groups did not differ significantly by birthweight, although gestational age was different among the IVH groups ($F(2,82 = 4.53, p < .05$). The larger no-hemorrhage infants who were eliminated from the preterm comparisons were included in the no-hemorrhage preterm sample when it was compared to the fullterms.

PROCEDURE

Parents were contacted when the child was between 4½–5½ years of age and asked to participate in the preschool follow-up project. Age at testing averaged 59.5 months. Parking or tax fare was offered to the parents.

The following assessments were performed in a test session lasting 2 hours by testers blind to the neonatal history of the child. Reliability was checked periodically and maintained at .90 or better. A 15-minute stretch-and-snack break was included between the cognitive and the motor testing.

- *McCarthy Scales of Child's Abilities (McCarthy, 1972)* Scale indices for general cognitive index (GCI), verbal and quantitative skills, perceptual/ performance, memory, and motor performance were analyzed.
- *DeGangi-Berk Test of Sensory Integration (DeGangi, Berk & Valvano, 1983)*. The DeGangi-Berk evaluates sensory and motor integration for preschool children ages 3 to 5, measuring postural control, bilateral motor integration, reflex integration (often referred to as vestibular-based function), and symmetry. Problems in these areas of development may relate to learning disabilities (DeQueros, 1976). The DeGangi-Berk yields a more

refined examination of fine and gross motor skills than the McCarthy.
*   *The Beery Developmental Test of Visual-Motor Integration (VMI) (Beery, 1967)*. Poor visual motor integration is often associated with learning difficulties in children born preterm (Siegel, 1983).
*   *The Peabody Vocabulary Test (Revised-Form L) (Dunn & Dunn, 1981)*. The child selects one of four pictures to illustrate the word presented by the tester. The PPVT-R is thus a test of receptive vocabulary.
*   *Recognition discrimination*. The child selects which of four alternatives matches the target stimuli which becomes increasingly complex as the test proceeds. The number of correct matches are scored.
*   *Alphabet recitation*. The child is asked to recite the alphabet and the number of letters named correctly is tallied.
*   *The Florida Kindergarten Screening Battery* (Satz & Fletcher, 1982) includes the last four measures. The Florida Battery has been found to relate to prematurity and to predict reading level at the end of grade 1 for 5-year-olds (Satz, Friel, & Goebel, 1975; Siegel, 1983).

Finally *activity* and *distractibility* during testing were rated on five-point scales for each child.

RESULTS

The dependent variables yielding continuous data are the McCarthy GCI and subscales, the DeGangi-Berk total and subscales, the Beery VMI, the PPVT, the Alphabet Recitation, recognition discrimination task, and Florida Kindergarten Readiness Screening. They were analyzed for the effects of IVH using one-way ANOVA's with three levels of IVH group (none, minor [1 and 2], and major [3 and 4]) followed by posthoc comparisons using Scheffe's test. For the 5-year data analysis, the numbers are not sufficient to analyze the Grades 3 and 4 separately.

Degree of intraventricular hemorrhage related extensively to developmental functioning (see Table 2a). Intraventricular hemorrhage related in the expected direction to performance on the McCarthy GCI ($F(2,82) = 10.42, p < .001$); quantitative subscale $F(2,82) = 5.88, p < .01$; memory subscale $F(2,82) = 6.81, p < .01$; verbal subscale $F(2,82) = 6.95, p < .01$; and perceptual subscale $F(2,82) = 8.69, p < .001$). Other measures that related to hemorrhage were recognition/discrimination ($F(2,82) = 4.70, p < .05$); alphabet recitation ($F(2,82) = 5.47, p < .01$); receptive vocabulary (PPVT-Revised ($F(2,82) = 6.01, p < .01$)); Florida Kindergarten Readiness ($F(2,82) = 10.55, p < .001$). Post-hoc analyses indicated that the major hemorrhage group differed significantly from the no-hemorrhage group. For the alphabet recitation and the Florida

Table 2a. McCarthy GCI, School Readiness, Language, and Perceptual-Motor Skills: Effects of Intraventricular Hemorrhage at 5 Years

	IVH Group		
	None	Minor	Major
General Cognitive Index**	109.81	100.29	88.70
Verbal*	57.58	53.67	46.23
Perceptual/Performance**	52.94	47.13	41.07
Quantitative*	53.61	49.00	44.33
Memory*	54.58	50.75	43.93
Motor**	47.70	39.83	33.67
Beery Visual-Motor	43.84	31.25	27.27
Recognition Discrimination*	10.10	8.75	7.21
Peabody Picture Vocabulary**	105.68	95.96	87.80
Alphabet Recitation**	21.58	22.25	15.97
Kindergarten Screening***	−0.30	−0.77	−1.87

*$p < .05$
**$p < .01$
***$p < .001$

screening, the minor hemorrhage group also differed significantly from the major hemorrhage group. The Beery VMI and activity and distractibility during testing did not differ among the groups.

The DeGangi-Berk sensory-motor scores are reported in Table 2b. Motor abilities were significantly poorer in the major hemorrhage group than in the no

Table 2b. Motor Skills and Behavior Ratings: Effects of Intraventricular Hemorrhage at 5 Years

	IVH Group		
	None	Minor	Major
DeGangi-Berk Test			
Total Score***	69.77	66.71	54.86
Postural Control*	24.42	23.24	20.17
Bilateral Motor***	32.07	31.47	23.83
Symmetry***	7.77	7.43	6.10
One-foot balance	6.17	4.67	4.33
Behavior Ratings			
Activity	2.62	2.57	2.75
Distractibility	2.69	2.66	3.13

*$p < .05$
**$p < .01$
***$p < .001$

IVH or minor hemorrhage groups (total $(F(2,82) = 7.91, p < .001)$; postural control $(F(2,82) = 4.66, p < .05)$; bilateral motor control $(F(2,82) = 8.56, p < .001)$ and symmetry $(F(2,82) = 10.43, p < .001)$. The DeGangi motor results were paralleled by the McCarthy motor subscale $(F(2,82) = 10.87, p < .001)$.

DISCUSSION OF THE IVH FINDINGS

These data indicate several preliminary trends. In line with our findings at 1 and 2 years, the motor system is particularly vulnerable to the effects of major hemorrhage (Sostek et al., 1987). The major hemorrhage children also performed more poorly than the children with no hemorrhage on general cognitive functioning, recognition/discrimination, alphabet recitation, and kindergarten readiness. Children who experienced minor hemorrhage were significantly more ready for school than the children with major IVH and had better motor performance.

It was surprising, however, that IVH did not influence perceptual-motor integration or behavior during testing to a greater degree. The Beery Test of Visual-Motor Integration and the activity and distractibility ratings did not differ significantly between the groups. When data from a full-term sample was compared to the performance of the preterms without IVH on these three measures, it was clear that all of the preterm groups performed relatively poorly. IVH therefore did not account for a significant further deficit in visual-motor integration or behavior during testing.

The data that we reported at 1 and 2 years of age suggested that IVH affects developmental functioning to a lesser degree as time proceeds. At 2 years, the severity of hemorrhage did not significantly affect Bayley mental scale scores, although it did at 1 year of age. The fact that 5-year follow-up reveals extensive cognitive, motor, language, and school readiness differences among IVH groups may have several implications. First, the issue of the adequacy of global developmental measures in infancy arises. The Bayley scales may simply not be sensitive or specific enough to pick up the effects of IVH. Data on visual information processing in relation to IVH would support this possibility (Glass & Sostek, 1986; Landry et al., 1985). The second interpretation of the presence of more extensive effects at 5 years centers on the more complex developmental demands at the time of school entry. It may in fact be the case that the challenges of the 5-year-old yield "sleeper effects" which are not evident at 2 years of age. Finally, issues of insult, vulnerability, recovery, and potential plasticity of the brain may relate to the extent of effects of IVH at different ages. Little correspondence between the location of brain insult and the type of effect has been demonstrated in such young children, however, and these questions remain unresolved.

EFFECTS OF PREMATURITY WITHOUT IVH

It has long been reported that children born preterm are at increased risk of learning disabilities even in the absence of more severe developmental sequelae (Caputo et al., 1979; Nelson & Broman, 1977; Siegel, 1982, 1983; Taub et al., 1977). Previous studies on the outcome of preterm infants did not differentiate between prematurity and IVH. Since IVH is so prevalent and has significant implications for school entry skills, it is important to examine the developmental effects of prematurity independent of IVH to determine whether it increases risk of learning disabilities.

Compared to normative data, our 2-year global developmental findings did not suggest that the preterms without IVH performed more poorly than normal fullterms. The mean Bayley scores for both groups were within the normal range and less than one-half standard deviation apart. However, the literature strongly indicates that there are functional deficits even in preterms of normal intelligence (Coolman, Bennett, Sells, Swanson, Andrews, & Robinson, 1985; Hunt, Cooper, & Tooley, 1988; Klein, Hack, & Breslau, 1989; Williams, Lewandowski, Coplan, & D'Eugenio, 1987). School readiness in preterm infants without IVH was therefore compared to the performance of a fullterm group. It was hypothesized that preterm infants without IVH would perform similarly to a comparable sample of children born at term except in the area of perceptual-motor skills (Sostek, Katz, Valvano, & Smith, 1988, 1989).

Is it just this?

SUBJECTS

The subjects include 38 preterm and 42 full-term children born between 1980 and 1983. The preterm infants averaged 30.4 ($\pm$1.91) weeks gestation (range = 26 to 33 weeks) and had a mean birthweight of 1,358.82 ($\pm$298.01) grams (range 780 to 1,980 grams); six were products of multiple gestations. Predominant neonatal medical complications were mild to moderate respiratory distress syndrome, hyperbilirubinemia and hypocalcemia. Subject characteristics are represented in Table 3 and indicate that racial composition and gender did not differ between the preterm and fullterm groups. All of the preterms were screened prospectively for intraventricular hemorrhage using serial portable ultrasonography in the newborn period. Children with a history of intraventricular hemorrhage or echodense lesions in the periventricular area were excluded from the prematurity study. As indicated above, this sample overlaps to a great extent with the no-IVH children included in the comparisons of hemorrhage groups, although it includes additional children who were born at slightly larger birthweights (compare Tables 1 and 3).

All of the children in the study were in regular public or private kindergarten

Table 3. Subject Characteristics:
Preterm and Full-Term Groups[a]

	Preterm	Full-term
Number	38	42
Percent Male	55.3	59.5
Percent White	65.8	69.1
Percent Black	26.3	23.8
Percent Twins[b]	13.2	4.8
Birthweight*	1326.5	3313.1
Gestational Age*	30.4	39.9
Months of Age	58.7	60.2

*$p < .001$
[a]Preterm infants were screened prospectively for intraventricular hemorrhage using serial portable sonography. None were diagnosed as having IVH.
[b]In one case only one twin was free of IVH. This figure is substantially higher than the no-IVH preterm group figure in Table 1, because two sets of twins were too large to be included in the comparisons between hemorrhage groups.

school or in preschool, and none had obvious sensory or motor handicaps. The full-term contrast group was matched for age and racial characteristics (see Table 3). The full-term children were recruited from a local day care center and public school. They therefore come from a different subject pool from the preterms who were enrolled in a high-risk infant follow-up program. The full-term infants averaged 39.9 (± 0.64) weeks gestation and had a mean birthweight of 3,313.10 (± 512.98) grams; two were products of multiple gestations. They were free of neonatal medical complications except that the pair of twins was small for gestational age and required brief intensive care hospitalization. The intention was to recruit a random group of fullterms, and a rate of growth retardation under 5% is representative of the larger population. The sample was recruited in an attempt to represent SES and other medical complications broadly. The neonatal screening of the preterm infants for IVH and the assessment procedures at 5 years of age were identical to those described above.

RESULTS

The full-term and preterm no-hemorrhage groups were compared by t-tests. These data are particularly valuable for examining whether preterm infants are at increased risk for learning disabilities even in the absence of IVH. It is important to note that none of the children born preterm was mentally retarded or had obvious motor impairment.

Table 4a.   McCarthy GCI, School Readiness, Language,
and Perceptual-Motor Skills: Effects of Prematurity at 5 Years

	Preterm	Full-term
McCarthy Scales		
General Cognitive Index	105.79	112.29
Verbal	55.92	57.64
Perceptual/Performance*	50.08	55.17
Quantitative*	51.53	56.55
Memory*	52.89	58.07
Motor	45.86	48.61
Perceptual-Motor, Language and School Readiness		
Beery Visual-Motor*	40.26	54.26
Recognition Discrimination*	10.08	11.60
Peabody Picture Vocab	102.82	105.35
Alphabet Recitation	22.63	24.76
Kindergarten Screening**	−0.34	+0.37

*$p < .05$
**$p < .01$

As indicated in Table 4a, the McCarthy GCI did not differ between the groups. Scores for the preterms range from 69 to 150 and scores for the full terms ranged from 87 to 141, and the mean GCI was within the normal range (105.79). The mean GCI for the fullterms was 112.29. The significant differences between the preterms and full terms centered on a number of McCarthy subscales: perceptual/performance ($t(78) = 2.27$, $p < .05$), quantitative ($t(78) = 2.55$, $p < .05$) and memory ($t(78) = 2.51$, $p < .05$). School readiness, language and perceptual-motor skills are reported in Table 4a. The premature group had poorer performance on the Beery Test of Visual-Motor Integration ($t(78) = 2.22$, $p <$

Table 4b.   Motor Skills and Behavior Ratings:
Effects of Prematurity at 5 Years

	Preterm	Full-term
DeGangi-Berk Test		
Total Score	70.35	72.90
Postural Control	24.55	25.24
Bilateral Motor	32.27	33.49
Symmetry	7.55	7.73
One-foot balance**	5.97	8.18
Behavior Ratings		
Activity*	2.53	2.09
Distractibility*	2.65	2.12

*$p < .05$
**$p < .01$

.05, recognition/discrimination ($t(78) = 2.32, p < .05$) and the Florida Kindergarten Readiness Screening ($t(78) = 2.99, p < .01$). There were no differences relating to prematurity on any of the measures of language skills.

Interestingly, qualitative ratings of behavior during the testing also differed between the full-term and no hemorrhage preterm groups: activity ($t(78) = 1.99$, $p = .05$) and distractibility ($t(78) = 2.38, p < .05$) (see Table 4b). Although there were no differences in any motor skills, subtle differences in equilibrium were suggested by a significant effect for one-foot balance (number of seconds up to 10 that the child can balance on one foot) ($t(78) = 4.06, p < .001$).

DISCUSSION OF THE PREMATURITY FINDINGS

Comparisons between the full-terms and the preterms without hemorrhage indicated that the children born preterm performed more poorly in the areas of perceptual-motor, memory, and quantitative skills, one-foot balance, and overall kindergarten readiness. These results support the classic findings that preterm infants are at risk for learning disabilities (Caputo et al., 1979; Nelson & Broman, 1977; Siegel, 1982, 1983; Taub et al., 1977). These early studies were performed before preterm infants were screened by prospective cranial sonography, however, and it was impossible to know whether the observed developmental effects derived from prematurity or direct brain insult.

Our data confirm that children born preterm, even when free of IVH and severe cognitive delay, are at risk for learning disabilities and/or attentional deficits. Prematurity clearly seems to compromise perceptual-motor integration as measured by the McCarthy, the Beery Test of Visual-Motor Integration, and the recognition discrimination task. Furthermore, activity and distractibility during testing were significantly higher among the preterms than among the fullterms. Perceptual-motor integration and attentional behaviors remain problematic areas of functioning for children born preterm. The results of the Florida Kindergarten Screening indicate that prematurity in fact reduces general readiness for school entry.

The challenges of managing the preterm infants during the immediate postnatal period include oxygen regulation, adequate nutrition, maintaining metabolic balance, and avoiding the typical medical complications such as respiratory compromise. It is rarely possible to achieve a completely smooth medical course for the preterm infant. The specific medical as well as psychobiological aspects of preterm birth that contribute to increased risk for learning disabilities are not as yet fully understood.

REFERENCES

Allan, W.C., Dransfield, D.A., & Tito, A.M. (1984). Ventricular dilatation following periventricular-intraventricular hemorrhage: Outcome at one year. *Pediatrics, 73*, 158–162.

Amiel-Tison, C., & Grenier, A. (1980). *Evaluation neurologique du nouveau-né et du nourrison.* Paris: Masson.

Bayley, N. (1969). *The Bayley Scales of Infant Development.* New York: Psychological Corp.

Beery, K.E. (1967). *Developmental test of visual motor integration.* Chicago: Follett.

Bendersky, M., & Lewis, M. (1990). Early language ability as a function of ventricular dilatation associated with intraventricular hemorrhage. *Developmental and Behavioral Pediatrics, 11,* 17–21.

Caputo, D., Goldstein, K., & Taub, H. (1979). The development of prematurely born children through middle childhood. In T.M. Field, A. Sostek, S. Goldberg, & H.H. Shuman (Eds.), *Infants born at risk: Behavior and Development.* Jamaica, NY: Spectrum Books.

Coolman, R.B., Bennett, F.C., Sells, C.J., Swanson, M.W., Andrews, M.S., & Robinson, N. (1985). Neuromotor development of graduates of the neonatal intensive care unit: Patterns encountered in the first two years of life. *Journal of Developmental and Behavioral Pediatrics, 6,* 327–333.

DeGangi, G., Berk, R., & Valvano, J. (1983). Assessment of motor and neurological functions in high risk infants. *Journal of Behavioral Pediatrics, 4,* 182–187.

DeQueros, J.B. (1976). Diagnosis of vestibular disorders in the learning disabled. *Journal of Learning Disabilities, 9,* 50–58.

de Vries, L.S., Dubowitz, L.M.S., Dubowitz, V., Kaiser, A., Lary, S., Silverman, M., Whitelaw, A., & Wigglesworth, J.S. (1985, July 20). Predictive value of cranial ultrasound in the newborn baby: A reappraisal. *The Lancet,* pp. 137–140.

Dubowitz, L.M.S., Levene, M.I., Morante, A., Palmer, P., & Dubowitz, V. (1981). Neurologic signs in neonatal intraventricular hemorrhage: A correlation with real-time ultrasound. *The Journal of Pediatrics, 99,* 127–133.

Dunn, L., & Dunn, L. (1981). *The Peabody Picture Vocabulary Test-Revised.* Circle Pines, MN: American Guidance Service.

Glass, P., & Sostek, A.M. (1986). Information processing and intraventricular hemorrhage. *Infant Behavior and Development, 9,* 142.

Grant, E., Borts, F., Schellinger, D., McCullough, D., Siva Subramanian, K.N., & Smith, Y. (1981). Real-time ultrasonography of neonatal intraventricular hemorrhage and comparison with computerized ultrasonography. *Radiology, 139,* 687–691.

Hunt, J.V., Cooper, B.A., & Tooley, W.H. (1988). Very low birthweight infants at 8 and 11 years of age: Role of neonatal illness and family status. *Pediatrics, 82,* 596–603.

Klein, N., Hack, M., & Breslau, N. (1989). Children who were very low birthweight: Development and academic achievement at nine years of age. *Developmental and Behavioral Pediatrics, 10,* 32–37.

Landry, S.H., Fletcher, J.M., Zarling, C.L., Chapieski, L., Francis, D.J., & Denson, S. (1984). Differential outcomes associated with early medical complications in premature infants. *Journal of Pediatric Psychology, 9,* 385–401.

Landry, S.H., Leslie, N.A., Fletcher, J.M., & Francis, D.J. (1985). Visual attention skills of premature infants with and without intraventricular hemorrhage. *Infant Behavior and Development, 8,* 309–321.

Lewis, M., & Bendersky, M. (1989). Cognitive and motor differences among low birthweight infants: Impact of intraventricular hemorrhage, medical risk, and social class. *Pediatrics, 83,* 187–191.

McCarthy, D. (1972). *The McCarthy Scales of Children's Abilities.* New York: The Psychological Corporation.

Nelson, K.B., & Broman, S.H. (1977). Perinatal risk factors in children with serious motor and mental handicaps. *Annals of Neurology, 2,* 371–377.

Papile, L., Burstein, J., Burstein, R., & Koffler, H. (1978). Incidence and evolution of subependymal and intraventricular hemorrhage: A study of infants with birthweights less than 1500g. *The Journal of Pediatrics, 92,* 529–534.

Papile, L., Munsick-Bruno, G., & Shaefer, A. (1983). Relationship of cerebral intraventricular hemorrhage and early childhood neurologic handicaps. The Journal of Pediatrics, 103, 273–277.

Satz, P., & Fletcher, J. (1982). The Florida Kindergarten Screening Battery. Odessa, FL: Psychological Assessment Resources.

Satz, P., Friel, J., & Goebel, R. (1975). Some predictive antecedents of specific reading disability: A three-year follow-up. Bulletin of the Orton Society, 25, 91–110.

Siegel, L.S. (1982). Reproductive, perinatal, and environmental factors as predictors of cognitive and language development of preterm and fullterm infants. Child Development, 53, 963–973.

Siegel, L.S. (1983). The prediction of possible learning disabilities in preterm and full-term children. In T.M. Field & A. Sostek (Eds.), Infants born at risk: Physiological, perceptual, and cognitive processes (pp. 295–315). New York: Grune & Stratton.

Smith, Y.F., Sostek, A.M., Katz, K.S., & Grant, E.G. (1987). Echodense lesions of the cerebral parenchyma in the preterm infant: Diagnostic localization and developmental outcome. Pediatric Research, 21, 403A.

Smith, Y.F., Young, M.A., Sostek, A.M., & Grant, E.G. (1985). Periventricular leukomalacia: Incidence and significance in premature infants. Pediatric Research, 19, 395A.

Sostek, A.M. (1988). The utility of risk indices: Intraventricular hemorrhage as a model. In P.M. Vietze & H. Vaughan (Eds.), Early identification of infants with developmental disabilities (pp. 53–67). Philadelphia: Grune & Stratton.

Sostek, A.M., & Glass, P. (1986, August). Relationship of visual information processing and traditional developmental measures with severity of intraventricular hemorrhage (IVH). Poster presented at the annual meetings of the American Psychological Association, Washington, DC.

Sostek, A.M., Katz, K.S., Valvano, J., & Smith, Y.F. (1988). School readiness: Effects of prematurity independent of intraventricular hemorrhage. Infant Behavior and Development, 11, 294.

Sostek, A.M., Katz, K.S., Valvano, J., & Smith, Y.S. (1989). Prematurity affects development and kindergarten readiness in the absence of IVH. Pediatric Research, 25, 264A.

Sostek, A.M., Smith, Y.F., Katz, K.S., & Grant, E.G. (1987). Developmental outcome of preterm infants with intaventricular hemorrhage at one and two years of age. Child Development, 58, 779–786.

Taub, H.B., Goldstein, K.M., & Caputo, D.V. (1977). Indices of neonatal prematurity as discriminators of development in middle childhood. Child Development, 48, 797–805.

Williams, M.L., Lewandowski, K.J., Coplan, J., & D'Eugenio, D.B. (1987). Neurodevelopmental outcome of preschool children born preterm with and without intracranial hemorrhage. Developmental Medicine and Child Neurology, 29, 243–248.

12

Predicting Future Cognitive, Academic, and Behavioral Outcomes for Very-Low-Birthweight (<1,500 grams) Infants*

Valerie E. Barsky and Linda S. Siegel

Jonathan's scrawny, jaundiced body, all 1,392 grams of it, lay in the isolette. One or the other of his legs would occasionally kick out, and then you could see that the soles of his feet were bruised from the blood samples that had been taken. He was only as big as his father's hand, but that did not deter the various gadgets that were taped to his body, such as the fetal heart monitor attachments and the tube in his nose that provided a steady flow of oxygen. Jonathan's parents watched him with a mixture of love and apprehension. In many ways this was not the baby they had awaited. At this point, the doctors thought that Jonathan would survive. Now, on Jonathan's fourteenth day of life, his parents silently wondered, "Will Jonathan be o.k.?"

Very low-birthweight infants (VLBW) of 1,500 grams or less may have a myriad of medical obstacles to surmount (i.e., asphyxia, apnea, respiratory distress syndrome, intraventricular hemorrhage, hyaline membrane disease, bronchopulmonary dysplasia, hyperbilirubinemia) to maintain their survival. However, medical technology and the proper use of it during neonatal care have advanced sufficiently to substantially decrease the mortality rate for these VLBW infants (Hack, Fanaroff, & Merkatz, 1979; McCormick, this volume; Rawlings, Reynolds, Stewart, & Strang, 1971; Stewart, Reynolds, & Lipscomb, 1981). The above vignette sums up the stage at which we presently find ourselves. The previous struggle for maintaining the survival of VLBW infants is giving way to determining what are the possible sequelae for these infants in terms of long-range functioning. The subsequent development of the VLBW infant is a question that concerns both parents and the professionals who work with them.

The majority of past research has focussed on the prediction of group outcomes versus the more clinically relevant prediction of individual infant outcome. The present chapter will serve to illustrate the need to develop and utilize

* The preparation of this chapter was supported by a Medical Research Council Studentship to Valerie Barsky, and a Natural Sciences and Engineering Research Council of Canada Grant to Linda S. Siegel. The authors wish to thank Susan Hall and Letty Guirnela for secretarial assistance.

cumulative risk indices that are cost efficient and provide a high degree of accuracy in predicting outcome for the individual VLBW infant. These indices require the incorporation of both biological and environmental factors in order to predict cognitive, academic, and behavioral outcomes, but must be simple enough to be easily used by the practitioners who work with at-risk infants and their families. The goals of the successful development and use of cumulative risk indices are to identify, as early as possible, the need to monitor the progress of a particular VLBW infant, and, if necessary, to provide intervention. Such sensitive care may potentially help to ameliorate long-term effects of the less than optimal neonatal experience that the individual VLBW infant has endured.

Therefore, the purpose of this chapter will be to review the literature of outcome studies pertaining to VLBW infants. Neurodevelopmental outcomes and their relationship to global measures of intelligence will be briefly examined. The chapter will specifically address the more recent research that has investigated specific cognitive, academic, and behavioral outcomes and the prediction of learning disabilities for the VLBW infants. The perinatal, reproductive, and environmental factors that appear to influence these outcomes will be discussed. A system of risk index variables that predicts the range of outcome for the individual VLBW infant will be presented. Finally, directions for future research will be suggested.

NEURODEVELOPMENTAL OUTCOME STUDIES

It is necessary to review briefly the kind of group outcome studies that have contributed largely to the existing literature and to the major advances that have been made in medical technology. Typically, these studies have adopted a medical model approach and have investigated the neurodevelopmental outcome of groups of VLBW infants.

Determining the integrity of central nervous system functioning appears to be the basic premise of neurodevelopmental outcome studies for VLBW infants. Neurodevelopmental examinations are used by the pediatricians during the VLBW infants' first few years of life to assess motor functioning, and the presence or absence of *cerebral palsy* (CP). Visual and auditory impairment are also ascertained. On the basis of these ratings and global measures of intelligence, the VLBW infants are generally assigned to one of three categories: normal, suspect, or abnormal (Ross, Lipper, & Auld, 1985, 1986; Vohr & Garcia Coll, 1985) or to the comparable categories of minor neurobehavioural abnormalities, mild to moderate impairment, or severe sensorineural or intellectual impairments (Kitchen, Ford, Rickards, Lissenden, & Ryan, 1987). Generally, the infants in the normal category lack neurological or developmental handicap and have an IQ greater than or equal to 80. The suspect and abnormal categories are defined primarily by the presence of neurological deficit. The infants in the suspect category may have mild CP or fine and gross motor inefficiencies, and the infants in the abnormal category may have moderate to severe CP, visual or auditory impairment. The IQ scores of the infants in these groups could range from the average to the delayed categories.

These early neurodevelopmental categories are then related to later neurodevelopmental and cognitive outcomes. These studies indirectly investigate the efficacy of early identification for VLBW infants. The ability to predict from this form of initial examination which infants may be in need of early intervention programs has an obvious appeal to it, but such a classification method is not without inherent problems. The transient nature of some neurological states (e.g., hypotonia) and the reliance on global neurological and intellectual measures for prediction purposes are two of these difficulties.

Transient Neurological Status

For those children classified into the abnormal category, neurological status remains relatively stable. Therefore, VLBW infants classified as meeting the criteria for the abnormal category on the basis of neurodevelopmental screening appear to be the best able to benefit from this system of identification. The infants initially classified as belonging to the abnormal category may show improvement over time, but usually remain within their original classification.

It could be argued that VLBW infants in the suspect category would also benefit from early intervention. However, with the progression of time there appear to be changes in the classification of certain children between the suspect and normal categories. For example, in Vohr and Garcia Coll's (1985) longitudinal study of neurodevelopmental and school performance outcome for VLBW 7-year-old children, there were "soft" neurological findings (fine and gross motor inefficiencies) present in 5 of 22 (23%) children who had previously been classified as normal at 1 year of age. As well, 41% of the suspect group in this study met criteria at 7 years of age for the normal category (Vohr & Garcia Coll, 1985).

The apparent transient nature of belonging to the suspect category, in Vohr and Garcia Coll's (1985) study, may be partially explainable in terms of the different measures of neurological status that were used at different ages. At the first-year examination, the neurological assessment "was based on the combined methods of Prechtel and those used in the *Collaborative Perinatal Study*" (Vohr & Garcia Coll, 1985, p. 346). At 7 years of age, Vohr and Garcia Coll (1985) noted that standard neurological examination, which consists of assessing tone, reflexes, and motor, sensory, and verbal performance was administered, but "in conjunction with the Riley motor examination, which consists of specific oral, motor, fine motor, and gross motor components" (p. 346). Thus, the use of a less global instrument that measures specific motor processes may be contributing to the perceived change in performance.

Ross et al. (1986) also reported that of the three categories, prediction was the least accurate for the suspect group on neurological functioning. Specifically, Ross et al.'s (1986) study of neurodevelopmental outcome of VLBW infants found that, of the children classified as suspect at 12 months, 60% were still within the suspect category at 3 years of age, but the remaining 40% of those children were classified as meeting criteria for the normal category at 3 years of age. Ross et al. (1986) proposed that these findings confirm other reports that, "early minor abnormalities of muscle tone or mild developmental delays may be transient or diminished with time" (p. 176). Kitchen et al. (1987) noted that 33% of their VLBW infants (500 to 999 grams) were less severely handicapped in terms of the presence and/or severity of CP at 5 years of age compared to their 2-year-old evaluation.

The present categorization studies of neurodevelopmental outcome are not capable of accurately predicting for the individual VLBW infant. Although the infants in the suspect category who were no longer suspect at 3 (Ross et al., 1986) and 7 years old (Vohr & Garcia Coll, 1985) belonged to the normal category later, a small proportion of the infants originally in the normal category changed to the suspect category at an older age (Vohr & Garcia Coll, 1985). However, initial abnormal classification is usually indicative of abnormal classification later in development, although the degree of severity within that category may decrease over time. As a result, it appears that only abnormal classification is clinically useful when considering neurological functioning. It may be argued that neurological status is not a reliable predictor variable of neurological outcome, except when the severity of the insult is quite marked. Future studies that are designed to determine some of the variables that may predict the transient nature of neurodevelopmental outcome between the suspect and normal categories for the individual VLBW child are required.

Neurodevelopmental Outcome and Global Measures of Intelligence

The transient nature of neurological findings is only one inherent problem with neurodevelopmental outcome studies. The other major problem stems from confounding in the classification between neurodevelopmental outcomes and global measures of IQ. There tends to be an unwarranted assumption that normal, suspect, and abnormal neurodevelopmental or neurological outcomes correspond to similar levels of intellectual functioning. However, while neurodevelopmental outcome does not map directly on to outcome as measured by IQ tests, the two types of tests are not entirely independent either. For example, some infants will have normal intelligence levels but will be classified as suspect on neurodevelopmental assessment, and some infants will be in the suspect range of intelligence but will be classified as abnormal on the neurodevelopmental assessment. Conversely, some infants will be classified as suspect or abnormal based on agreement between both intellectual and neurodevelopmental assessments.

Ross et al. (1986), to obtain an overall outcome for VLBW children at 3 years, classified children as normal if they had IQ scores on the Stanford-Binet Intelligence Scale (Form L-M) equal to or greater than 85 and were neurologically normal; as suspect if their IQ scores were between 71 and 84 and/or they were neurologically suspect; and as abnormal if their IQ scores were equal to or less than 70 and/or they were abnormal on neurodevelopmental assessment (Ross et al., 1986). The neurodevelopmental assessment used incorporated neurological items similar to those of Amiel-Tison, behavioral items, and motor milestones as determined by the Bayley Scales of Motor Development (Ross et al., 1986). Ross et al. (1986) found that 39% of the children were classified differently for IQ than they were for neurological status at three years. This was a significant difference, but there was a high rate of accurate prediction (i.e., 82%) between the 12-month neurodevelopmental assessment and IQ score outcome at 3 years of age. In this particular study the prediction rate of neurological and intellectual outcome based on a neurodevelopmental assessment was very high, but the practice of classification on neurological and/or intellectual measures is still an issue that needs to be addressed, particularly for the 39% of the children who were classified differently on two global measures.

Ross et al. (1986) also classified the VLBW infants into normal, suspect and abnormal categories on the basis of IQ scores only. Ross et al. (1986) reported that 90% of the children predicted to be of normal intelligence were so, whereas only two-thirds of those predicted to be suspect were so, with the remaining third falling into the normal category. In this particular study, only 64% of the children in the abnormal category were correctly predicted on the basis of IQ, while 36% were classified as suspect. It appears that only the normal classification on the basis of IQ scores is useful when predicting intellectual outcome. However, the neurological predictions were 100% accurate for the abnormal category, which is reflective of the stability of the neurological functioning outcome for this group. Ross et al. (1986) noted that these differences in accuracy rates for the prediction of IQ scores as compared to neurological status may be explained on the basis that IQ appears to be influenced more by environmental factors, whereas neurological status tends to be more stable.

To summarize, a review of the literature for neurodevelopmental outcome of VLBW infants revealed the practice of classification of VLBW infants into normal (without neurological deficit), suspect (mild CP or fine and gross motor inefficiencies) and abnormal (moderate to severe CP, visual or auditory impairment) categories that were frequently related to global measures of intelligence. The intellectual and neurological outcomes did not always correspond exactly with each other. For example, classification into the abnormal neurodevelopmental outcome group did not necessarily mean having a lower IQ level.

For the neurological functioning, the outcome of the suspect category was found to be the most variable due to possible transient neurological effects. Change in classification over time occurred largely between the normal and suspect categories. The most clinically relevant classification appears to be the abnormal category when considering neurological outcome. Children in the abnormal group classification may show improvement over time, but do not usually change categories. However, when considering intellectual outcome, the normal category appears to be the most stable.

INTELLECTUAL OUTCOME STUDIES

Intellectual outcome for VLBW infants may appear to be best considered in terms of perinatal insult and environmental factors rather than neurodevelopmental assessment. At the very least, intellectual outcome and neurological status should be treated as two distinct variables in order to pinpoint specific areas of difficulties that can then be addressed through remediation. Studies that consider intellectual outcome separately from neurological status will next be reviewed.

Environmental Factors

Sameroff and Chandler's (1975) seminal work on reproductive risk and the continuum of caretaking causality supported the notion that environmental influences played a pivotal role in minimizing or maximizing the effects of perinatal difficulties over the course of the child's later development. Socioeconomic status and parenting skills were considered to be two major contributors towards determining the intellectual outcome of children who had experienced early perinatal insults. Sameroff and Chandler (1975) reported that high socioeconomic status tended to minimize the effects of low-birthweight or anoxia, but poor social environmental conditions tended to maximize the effects of low-birthweight or anoxia.

More recent research has provided further support for Sameroff and Chandler's (1975) position regarding the importance of environmental factors. For example, Siegel (1979, 1981, 1984) was one of those who proposed that the use of both cognitive test scores and measures of environment provide for more accurate prediction of subsequent development. Siegel (1984) studied home environment influences on cognitive development in preterm and full-term children during the first 5 years of postnatal life. Her sample consisted of two cohorts of preterm infants and two cohorts of full-term children matched on SES (Hollingshead two factor), sex, parity, and maternal age at time of birth. In addition to other developmental measures, the children were assessed on the Bayley Scales of Infant Development, the Stanford-Binet Intelligence Scale (Form L-M), the McCarthy Scales of Children's Abilities and the Home Observation for Measurement in the Environment (HOME). Siegel (1984) found that "there was evidence of environmental influences in that children who showed early developmental delay, but at 3 years functioned normally came from more stimulating environments, as measured by the HOME. Conversely, infants who appeared to be developing normally at 1 year, but who were delayed at 3 years, came from less stimulating environments as measured by the HOME" (p. 231).

Ross et al. (1985) found a significant effect of SES on change in mental ability as measured by the Stanford-Binet Intelligence Scale (Form L-M) in their 3-year outcome study. Children in the lower income group showed a mean decline of seven points, while children in the higher income group experienced a mean increase of 5 points. Kitchen, Ford, Rickards, Lissenden, and Ryan (1987) found that "children with lower MDI scores and better educated mothers were more likely to improve" (p. 286). Other studies that investigated premature infants who were below 2,500 grams provided further support for the influence of environmental factors on intellectual outcome (Cohen & Parmelee, 1983; Cohen, Parmelee, Sigman, & Beckwith, 1988; Escalona, 1982).

The Transactional Model of Development

Parents' responses to their children's level of ability are an important predictor of outcome, in addition to the nature and severity of any biological insult. Wallace (1988) provides a comprehensive review of the literature regarding the socioenvironmental issues in longitudinal research of high-risk infants. The transactional model of development points to factors related to the individual child, which may contribute towards developmental outcome for that particular child. The transactional model proposes that the child's own characteristics or behavior elicit differential responses from the environment (e.g., parents), which ultimately affect the development of the child.

For example, Siegel and Cunningham (1984) found that, although there were no significant differences between preterm and full-term children on the HOME scale scores at any age, there were significant differences on that scale between children delayed at a particular point in time compared to those who were not delayed. Siegel and Cunningham (1984) reported that the differences in HOME scores between the delayed and non-delayed groups increased over time. At 3 and 5 years of age, the HOME scores of the delayed children were lower than those of the nondelayed children, and there were many more significant differences with increasing age. It appears that parents who were not initially responding differentially to the developmental delay began to respond differently as time progressed (Siegel & Cunningham, 1984).

In Siegel and Cunningham's (1984) study, a similar trend between mental functioning and HOME scores was also reported. There was not a significant relationship between the mental test scores and the environment at 1 year of age, but the relationship at both 3 and 5 years of age was significant. Siegel and

Cunningham (1984) hypothesized that, although directional causality cannot be inferred from the findings, perhaps early test scores reflect the child's developmental level independent of environmental influences. Early test scores may be more of a reflection of the effects of the perinatal insult, which may or may not prove to be transient in nature during the child's first year or two of life. The items that are part of the Bayley scales at one year are mostly fine motor, manipulation, perception, and simple cognition and do not involve language. These items do not seem to be sensitive to environmental influences. After this time, the items appear to depend more on language and specific experiences so environmental effects would become more significant.

Siegel and Cunningham (1984) explained how the child's behavior could potentially be influencing the parents' responses through the operation of a positive feedback loop. The positive feedback loop occurs when the delayed child does not provide adequate cues for the parent behavior. The parent then responds with inadequate stimulation, and the child's development becomes more delayed, which consequently makes it even more difficult for the parent to provide an appropriate environment. Siegel and Cunningham (1984) proposed that, if this model is correct, then the cycle must be broken by early detection of developmental delay and the parent–child interaction difficulties.

Thus, environmental factors such as socioeconomic status and parenting skills appear to influence the developmental outcome of VLBW infants. Socioeconomic status, as determined by parent educational level and occupation, tends to significantly affect the outcome of the VLBW infant. The intellectual outcome of a VLBW infant from a higher socioeconomic status may be enhanced, while the intellectual outcome of a VLBW infant from a lower socioeconomic status may be adversely affected. Lack of appropriate stimulation, in part determined by parenting skills as measured by the HOME, may also adversely affect the VLBW infant's development. However, more appropriate stimulation may significantly improve the VLBW infant's intellectual outcome.

Biological Factors

Of course, environmental factors do not operate in isolation of other constitutional conditions of the child. Specific biological variables have been related to intellectual outcome. Growth parameters and the type of perinatal insult are two examples of the kinds of biological factors considered when predicting intellectual outcome for the VLBW infant.

Growth parameters, such as weight, height, and head circumference, are sometimes related to outcome. Height and weight variables are supposed to reflect the optimal development of the nutritional needs of the child. The head circumference variable is believed to be indicative of the optimal development of brain growth. Perinatal insult, which may be the result of specific medical conditions, is believed to determine partially the subsequent level of integrity of central nervous system functioning. The growth parameter of head circumference may also be an indirect indicator of central nervous system functioning. In a broad sense, the less damage sustained to central nervous system functioning, the more likely it is that intellectual ability will remain intact. Recent studies provide evidence to support that environmental and biological factors appear to be operating together to minimize or maximize the future development of the VLBW infant.

For example, Hack and Breslau (1986), in addition to reporting that lower intellectual outcome was associated with lower SES in their study of VLBW infants, also found that head circumference at eight months of age, as a measure of brain growth, "was the best growth parameter for predicting IQ at 3 years" (p. 196). Hack and Breslau (1986) categorized head circumference as a binary variable because previous analyses indicated that abnormal growth was related to extreme deviations and was not linear. Children's head circumferences were measured at the expected term date and at 8, 20, and 33 months corrected age and classified as normal or subnormal ($< -2SD$). Further analyses revealed that children who had a normal 8-month head circumference had a normal IQ at 3 years of age, but children who had a subnormal head circumference at 8 months had low IQ scores at 3 years of age, irrespective of their head circumference status at 2 years of age.

Hack and Breslau (1986) argued that this indicates there is a critical time period for brain growth during the first year of life and concluded that there are multiple implications for these findings. Improved medical technology has the potential to decrease brain growth failure and avert cognitive delay, but, at the same time, these efforts must be sustained by optimizing "the social milieu during the critical period of infancy" (Hack & Breslau, 1986, p. 201).

As with growth parameters, the type of perinatal insult that has occurred operates in conjunction with the environmental factors. In addition to the type of perinatal insult (e.g., hyperbilirubinemia, respiratory distress syndrome, intraventricular hemorrhage), the severity, the time of onset and the duration of the perinatal insult must be included in the examination of biological factors contributing towards intellectual outcome. In Siegel and Cunningham's (1984) study, prematurity alone did not differentiate between the groups on the HOME scale scores, perhaps indicating the importance of the severity of perinatal insult variables when predicting outcome for VLBW infants. The integrity of central nervous system functioning for a particular child appears to play a significant role in the prediction of cognitive outcome.

Effects of biological insult on intellectual outcome have been recently studied by using well controlled subgroups of common medical conditions associated with prematurity (Landry, Chapieski, Fletcher, & Denson, 1988; Landry, Fletcher, Zarling, Chapieski, & Francis, 1984; Meisels, Plunkett, Roloff, Pasick, & Stiefel, 1986). Infants in the Meisels et al. (1986) study were assessed at either 12 or 18 months time post hospital discharge. Meisels et al. (1986) found that the group of less than 2,500-gram infants with bronchopulmonary dysplasia performed in the low average to delayed range (i.e., 35% below 1 sd) on the Bayley MDI when compared to the group of infants with respiratory distress syndrome (only 5% below 1 sd), whose performance more closely resembled healthy full-term infants of the same age.

Landry et al. (1988), using uncorrected age scores, found that the subgroups of intraventricular hemorrhage (IVH) and respiratory distress syndrome infants (RDS) of less than or equal to 1,801 grams had significantly higher Stanford-Binet IQ scores at 36 months than the subgroup of bronchopulmonary dysplasia (BPD) infants. This finding corresponded to the 2-year intellectual outcome for VLBW subgroups using the Bayley MDI (Landry et al., 1984). Both the IVH with RDS, and RDS only infants demonstrated an average level of performance at the chronological age of 24 months, whereas the BPD and the hydrocephalus secondary to IVH (HYD) subgroups had generally lower scores in the delayed range. Length of hospitalization appeared to be significantly correlated with the BPD infants' intellectual outcome. The BPD infants' intellectual outcome, as measured by the Bayley scores, was more delayed the longer they had stayed in the hospital. The type and severity of the perinatal insult appears to have influenced subsequent environmental conditions for these VLBW infants such as a hospital environment versus a home environment for the first few months of their lives, and this may have affected their intellectual outcomes. Landry et al. (1984) concluded that "this study shows that VLBW infants are not at equal risk for developmental problems. The need for early intervention is determined in part by specific medical complications at birth" (p. 399).

Thus, when predicting intellectual outcome, both biological and environmental factors must be considered to increase the degree of predictive accuracy. Biological variables include constitutional factors of the child such as the physical variable of head circumference, which is related to brain growth. Other biological factors are the level of perinatal insult incurred from specific medical conditions, such as intraventricular hemorrhage, bronchopulmonary dysplasia, and respiratory distress syndrome. The type, severity, time of onset, and duration of the perinatal insult appears to influence not only the intellectual outcome of the VLBW infant due to the possible affect on central nervous system functioning, but also appears to influence the succeeding environmental conditions that will be experienced. According to the transactional model of development, biological and environmental factors appear to be mutually dependent on each other in the prediction of the VLBW infant's intellectual outcome.

Relevance of Intellectual Functioning in the Prediction of Outcome

The previously reported findings related to intellectual outcome for VLBW infants did not explain what the specific problems may be for the individual child because only global IQ scores were used. Obviously, if a child is found to be developmentally delayed as measured by an IQ score, there will be certain repercussions in the areas of academic achievement and the level of independence attained. For these children, early identification can provide appropriate intervention for the child and coping strategies for their families. As discussed earlier, the status of a VLBW infant being classified into the "normal" category on the basis of IQ scores only is less likely to change than being classified into the suspect or abnormal category on the basis of IQ scores. However, there are cases where normal IQ level as an outcome measure will not explain the difficulties a child may be experiencing with early language skills or with academic skills in school.

Previous studies have shown that average outcome does not prevent the appearance of difficulties in specific cognitive processes from occurring for VLBW school-aged children (Hunt, Tooley, & Harvin, 1982; Klein, Hack, Gallagher, & Fanaroff, 1985; Siegel, 1985). For instance, Eilers, Desai, Wilson, and Cunningham (1986) found that although 90.9% of the 33 children in their sample (less than or equal to 1,205 grams at birth) were in regular classes, 47% received remedial instruction. In fact, global IQ scores have relatively little significance in the diagnosis of specific learning disabilities. For a comprehensive discussion of the irrelevance of IQ scores to the diagnosis of learning disabilities see Siegel (1988b, 1989b) and Siegel and Heaven (1986). Therefore, as the cohorts of VLBW children enter the school system, it becomes necessary to study specific cognitive processes as well as academic and behavioral functioning to determine if specific learning disabilities exist. The biological and environmental variables that may be related to these outcomes also need to be examined.

SPECIFIC COGNITIVE PROCESSES

To date, there is relatively little research that studies specific cognitive processes of VLBW children. Siegel (1985) reported findings regarding lower performance in specific cognitive processes for VLBW school-aged children. Visual-spatial, linguistic, and attentional processes were affected. A selective review of the findings of studies that investigated specific cognitive processes will be presented next. We suggest that measures of specific cognitive processes be viewed as alternative outcome measures in the prediction of cognitive, academic and behavioral outcome for VLBW infants. We and others (Friedman, Chipman, Segal, & Cocking, 1982) would argue that specific cognitive process outcome measures, rather than global intellectual outcome measures, are more relevant for ascertaining the type of intervention that may be required. Visual-spatial/ perceptual/motor, language, academic, and attention and behavior outcome studies that address four major categories of specific cognitive processes will be reviewed.

Visual-Spatial/Perceptual/Motor Outcome Studies

Previous premature infant outcome studies (Hunt et al., 1982; Taub, Goldstein, & Caputo, 1977; Wiener, Rider, Oppel, & Harper 1968) documented that these children experience difficulties performing visual/motor tasks. As more VLBW infants survive, it has become possible to investigate whether they also experience similar visual/motor difficulties. The findings of four recent studies that include many different measures believed to tap visual/motor abilities are presented.

Klein et al. (1985) studied a 1976 cohort of VLBW 5-year-old children and administered the Beery Developmental Test of Visual-Motor Integration (VMI), which is a measure of eye-hand (fine motor) coordination. Their subjects were matched by race, sex, and family background with classmates who had been born at full term. The VLBW 5-year-old children performed significantly more poorly than the control children on the Beery VMI. Significant correlations were found between the Beery VMI and maternal education, social class and the antepartum risk score. Klein et al. (1985) also found that the VLBW children in their sample performed significantly lower on the Woodcock Johnson Psycho-Educational Battery Spatial Relations subtest.

Lindgren, Harper, and Blackman (1986) assessed high-risk 5-year-old children (mean birth weight 2,811.08 grams) on a variety of measures of specific cognitive processes including the Beery VMI. The children were included in the sample if they met any one of the following criteria: respiratory distress syndrome ($n = 6$), signs of asphyxia ($n = 8$), birthweight less than 1,500 grams ($n = 4$), hypoglycemia ($n = 9$), seizures ($n = 2$), lengthy ventilatory assistance ($n = 10$), or other problems such as sepsis of hyperbilirubinemia ($n = 6$) (Lindgren et al., 1986). The small sample size ($n = 35$) that included a variety of perinatal insults not common to all the children and a wide range of birth weights (from 1,040 to 4,819 grams) may have confounded their findings. The Beery VMI standard scores were not analyzed separately, but were included in obtaining an average for the standard scores of other perceptual-motor measures (i.e., Florida Kindergarten Screening Battery Recognition-Discrimination subtest, Hiskey Nebraska Test of Learning Aptitude Block Patterns subtest, and Corsi Cubes). Although Lindgren et al. (1986) found this average perceptual-motor score to be significantly lower for the high-risk group compared to their normal control group, the finding lacks clarity due to the five measures being treated as a common factor and the heterogeneous nature of the risk group.

Siegel (1985) assessed 44 full-term and 42 VLBW preterm children from a 1975–1976 cohort when they were 5, 6, and 7 years old. The preterm and full-term infants had been matched on socioeconomic level, parity, sex, and age of the mother at the birth of the infant. On the Beery VMI, the preterm children had significantly lower scores at each age. Siegel (1985) found that preterm children at age five performed significantly lower than the full-term controls on the McCarthy Perceptual Performance and Motor Scales. The preterm children at age 6 also performed significantly lower than the control group on the WISC-R Performance IQ and the WISC-R Block Design, Object Assembly, Coding, and Mazes subtests. At age 7, 55.2% of the preterm children were delayed on this Beery VMI as compared to 27.2% of the full-term children.

Vohr and Garcia Coll (1985) assessed a group of VLBW 7-year-old children on the Beery VMI without using a specific comparison group. They reported that 10 out of 22 of the children in their normal group, 9 out of 12 of the children in the suspect group, and all 5 of the children in the abnormal group had VMI scores below the 50th percentile. Indeed, examination of the figure presented appears to indicate the severity of these children's difficulties. The majority of the children had VMI percentiles that were actually below the 30th percentile, that is, in the below average range.

Nickel, Bennett, and Lamson (1982) reported for their sample of 25 VLBW survivors, who had birth weights less than 1,000 grams, that fine and gross motor skills were impaired as measured by the Test of Motor Impairment, and the Motor Accuracy subtest of the Southern California Sensory Integration Tests. A very small sample of the children was administered the Bender-Gestalt Test, and there was a ceiling effect as the mean age of the sample was 10.6 years. However, the findings indicated that perceptual abilities were impaired to a lesser extent than the fine and gross motor skills. Generalizability is limited due to the fact that this was a 1960–1972 cohort, and medical intervention changed during that time span. In addition, generalizability is also limited due to the small sample size and ceiling effects of the measures.

It appears from the studies reviewed that VLBW children do perform significantly lower on measures which tap visual/motor abilities. Specifically, difficulties have been reported with eye-hand (fine motor) coordination skills (e.g., Beery VMI), visual-spatial skills that require motor manipulation ability (e.g., WISC-R Block Design subtest), and spatial or perceptual skills (e.g., Woodcock Johnson Psychoeducational Battery Spatial Relations test).

Language Outcome Studies

There have been very few studies conducted that examine language outcome for the preschool or school-aged VLBW children. Lindgren et al. (1986) averaged the standard scores of several language measures that assessed vocabulary, expressive and receptive language, immediate memory, and verbal association (i.e., Boston Naming Test, Token Test, WPPSI Vocabulary and Sentences subtests, ITPA Auditory Association subtest). They found this score of verbal ability to be significantly lower for the high-risk children compared to the control children. Separate analyses of each test would have been more beneficial perhaps in determining the specific areas of weaknesses in language outcome for this group of preterm children, although the purpose of this study was to determine if there were differences in the expected outcome based on environmental influences.

Klein et al. (1985) found no significant differences on the Woodcock-Johnson Psycho-Educational Battery Picture Vocabulary, Memory for Sentences or Visual Auditory Learning subtests for their sample of 5-year-old preterm children and full-term control children. Siegel (1985) assessed specific language processing outcomes for the VLBW children at 5, 6, and 7 years of age. On measures of general language functioning, such as the McCarthy Verbal Scale and the Peabody Picture Vocabulary Test (PPVT) IQ scores, there were no significant differences between the preterm and full-term children. Receptive vocabulary skills appeared to be relatively intact. The percentage of preterm children and full term children with PPVT IQ scores less than 90 was not significantly different.

Language expression, however, appeared to be affected. At 6 years of age, the preterm children had significantly lower scores than the full-terms on the WISC-R Verbal IQ, and the WISC-R Vocabulary, Similarities, and Comprehension subtests. Syntax skills as measured by the Illinois Test of Psycholinguistic Abilities (ITPA) Grammatic Closure subtest, and an Error Correction test, at ages 6 and 7, respectively, were also significantly lower for the preterm children. On the Sentence Repetition task, which measures memory for language, the 7-year-old preterm children performed significantly lower than the full-term children. It should be noted that the majority of the mean scores were still within the average range for the preterm children.

Siegel (1985) found that the preterm children performed significantly lower than the full-term children on the Sentence Repetition task. The Sentence Repetition task may be comparable in nature to the Memory for Sentences subtest used in Klein et al.'s (1985) study with younger children, where there were no significant differences between the preterm and full-term children. However, the PPVT (Siegel, 1985) and Picture Vocabulary Test (Klein et al., 1985), which both measure receptive vocabulary skills, did not distinguish between the premature and full-term children in both studies.

Very little appears to be known regarding language outcome for VLBW children past the age of 8 or 9 years. It appears as though receptive vocabulary skills (e.g., PPVT) are intact for 5-year-old VLBW children. Relative difficulties with language expression in syntax skills (e.g, ITPA Grammatic Closure subtest) and tasks involving both expressive language and short-term memory skills (Sentence Repetition task) have been reported. However, the evidence is not conclusive and much remains to be investigated in this area, particularly with older VLBW children. Possible directions for future exploration would be to examine the VLBW children's articulation skills, their ability to follow oral directions, and their ability to organize thoughts into words.

Academic Outcome Studies

It is hypothesized that measures of academic achievement are also tapping specific cognitive processes. For example, the Woodcock Johnson Word Attack

subtest may be thought of as a relatively pure measure of phonological processing ability, because the child must rely on phonetic decoding skills to read the
nonword. The Wide Range Achievement Test (WRAT) Arithmetic test, which is
a timed, paper-and-pencil test of written calculation ability, may be tapping the
specific cognitive processes of short-term memory, visual-spatial, and eye-hand
coordination skills.

If this is the case, then the poor performance by VLBW children on certain
achievement tests will also help to determine which cognitive processes are
affected. The underlying assumption is that different achievement tests measure
different kinds of cognitive processes. However, achievement tests are usually
not pure measures of cognitive-processing skills. For instance, a reading comprehension test may be tapping more than one cognitive processing skill, such as
short-term memory, syntax awareness, and phonological processing. Consistent
findings of strengths and weaknesses for VLBW children on certain achievement
tests will only point us in the direction of which cognitive processes to examine
further. More importantly, it will provide us with information regarding which
areas require remediation and compensation strategies. For a detailed discussion,
please see Siegel and Heaven (1986). Three studies will be briefly reviewed to
illustrate this point.

Siegel (1985) found no significant differences between the VLBW preterm
children and the 6-year-old full-term children on the WRAT Reading test, which
is a measure of word recognition, or on the Spache regular word reading test.
However, on an experimental reading test of words that have irregular or
unpredictable letter sound correspondences, the Spache Word Recognition test,
the Gilmore Oral Reading Test, which measures reading comprehension and oral
accuracy, and the Reading of Symbols subtest of the Goldman-Fristoe-Wood-
cock Sound-Symbol Test (nonword reading, a measure of phonics), the premature children had significantly lower scores. Their scores on the WRAT Spelling
and Arithmetic tests were also significantly lower than the full-term children at
ages 6 and 7 years old. Siegel (1985) noted that the WRAT Spelling test is
partially a measure of eye-hand coordination at these ages because it involves the
rapid copying of shapes as well as the spelling of words.

The mean scores of extremely low-birthweight (less than 1,000 grams)
school-aged children in Nickel et al.'s (1982) study indicated that there were
areas of weakness on the WRAT Arithmetic test, WISC-R Arithmetic subtest,
and the Gilmore Oral Reading Test. The performance of these children on the
WRAT Reading test was within the average range. In this case, the similar
findings to Siegel's (1985) study are interesting, given the difference in the mean
birthweight of the children and the time of the cohorts (i.e., Siegel's 1975–1978
cohort and Nickel's 1960–1972 cohort). However, Nickel et al.'s (1982) study
does not have a comparison group of children, and the mean scores in Siegel's
(1985) study were higher. The higher mean scores in Siegel's (1985) study could
be a reflection of both the higher mean birthweight and the reduction in severity
of perinatal insult through medical intervention.

Vohr and Garcia Coll (1985) found that 7 out of 12 of the VLBW children in the neurodevelopmental suspect category, and 4 out of 5 of the children in the abnormal category, were reading below the 50th percentile on the WRAT-R reading test. In fact, from the accompanying figure for this data (Vohr & Garcia Coll, 1985), it appears as if the children in both the suspect and abnormal groups were reading in the below average range. The neurodevelopmental normal category children were reading above the 50th percentile, except for two of the children, who appear to be reading below the 25th percentile. The lower reading ability of the suspect and abnormal groups compared to a group of children in the normal category leads one to speculate that biological insult played a large role in this particular performance difference.

In conclusion, there is some evidence to suggest that outcome for sight word recognition skill is dependent on the severity of the perinatal insult (Vohr & Garcia Coll, 1985). Consistent findings in two studies of poor performance by VLBW children on the same reading comprehension, arithmetic, and spelling achievement tests were reported (Nickel, 1982; Siegel, 1985). In Siegel's (1985) study, premature children also experienced difficulty on a phonetic decoding task in comparison to the performance of full-term children. According to our hypothesis that these measures tap specific cognitive processes, we would view this as documenting further support for eye-hand coordination, short-term memory processing, and phonetic decoding difficulties for some VLBW children, and that perhaps these are the areas that remediation and compensation strategies should address. These potential difficulties for the individual VLBW child are influenced by biological and environmental factors as previously described. We would argue that there is a need for future studies to investigate these specific cognitive processes as outcome measures.

Attention, Memory, and Behavioral Problems

Attention and memory difficulties may have implications for the behavioral outcome of VLBW children. It is only recently that studies have focused specifically on behavioral outcomes.

Astbury, Orgill, Bajuk, and Yu (1983) found that, for their sample of VLBW infants, there was a significant decrease on Bayley MDI scores from corrected ages of 1 to 2 years. Further analyses determined that this finding was explainable on the basis of a hyperactive behavior pattern derived from a rating in the excessive range "on at least four of the following items from the Bayley Infant Behaviour Record: object orientation, goal directedness, attention span, endurance, activity, reactivity and response to sensory areas of interest" (Astbury et al., 1983, p. 712). The subgroup of children who demonstrated this 'hyperactive' behavior tended to have a lower MDI score at both 1 and 2 years of age, and more physical disabilities such as cerebral palsy, and visual and hearing impairments of varying degrees. At the 1-year testing, Astbury et al. (1983) found significant main effects for both disability and behavior. However, at the 2-year testing only behavior influenced the MDI performance.

A follow-up study (Astbury, Orgill, & Bajuk, 1987) found that these 5-year-old children, who had been diagnosed as ADD at 2 years, largely continued to differ from the remainder of the sample. They had lower WPPSI IQ scores and a higher degree of minor physical disabilities. As well, Astbury et al. (1987) noted that mothers of the ADD children reported more minor, chronic illnesses for these children, who also demonstrated poorer visual acuity and gross motor abilities.

Siegel (1985) reported significantly lower scores for the preterm children on all the memory tasks (phonological coding in short-term memory, McCarthy Memory Scale, WISC-R Digit Span and Arithmetic subtests), and on the two measures of attention (Florida Screening Kindergarten Battery Recognition-Discrimination Test and Matching Faces Attention Test).

Breslau, Klein, and Allen (1988) studied 65 9-year-old VLBW children compared to a group of full-term children matched by age, sex, race, and school. On the basis of parents' ratings on the Child Behavior Checklist and teachers' ratings on the Teacher Report Form, it was found that VLBW boys were rated higher on the presence of behavioral problems and lower on social adjustment than the matched controls. There were no significant differences on behavioral problems, however, reported for VLBW girls and their matched controls.

Evidence from the review of these studies suggests that for VLBW children the specific cognitive processing skills of attention and short-term memory are sometimes adversely affected. What needs to be determined is which individual VLBW infant may be at risk for these difficulties. Possible biological and environmental factors can be hypothesized to contribute to behavioral outcomes. Astbury et al.'s (1983, 1987) studies appear to demonstrate that the severity of perinatal insult is very important in determining the outcome of these specific cognitive processing skills. Breslau et al.'s (1988) findings of behavioral difficulties and lower social adjustment for the 9-year-old VLBW boys in their study may perhaps be partly explained by the transactional model of development. It would be interesting to know if there was a significant difference in degree of perinatal insult or central nervous system functioning between the VLBW boys and girls in the sample. If the 9-year-old VLBW girls experienced a significantly lesser degree of perinatal insult, this may have contributed to the lack of behavioral problem findings for them. Breslau et al. (1988) commented that an association between behavioral disturbance and neurological dysfunction could not be drawn, as neurological tests were not included in the study. The influence of biological and environmental factors on determining outcome for VLBW children appears throughout this discussion of specific cognitive processes as alternative outcome measures. Further studies are required to clarify which variables contribute towards predicting outcome for the individual VLBW infant.

A Possible Developmental Pattern of Specific Learning Disabilities

A potential pattern that emerges and is indicative of learning disabilities for at least some of the VLBW children includes visual-spatial and eye-hand coordination difficulties. These may be present when the child is young and are apparent in lower Bayley PDI scores (Ross, 1985; Siegel et al., 1982). In the preschool VLBW child, clumsiness, poor printing legibility or difficulty copying figures may be noticed. Attentional difficulties related to hyperactive behavior, short-term memory-processing deficits and behavioural problems may also occur. Specific problems in language expression such as syntax difficulties or poor memory for sentences (which may later affect ability to understand and follow instructions) have been found for some of the VLBW children at 5 to 7 years of age. Early academic difficulties may be manifested by below average performance in arithmetic and reading-comprehension skills, although word-recognition skills appear to remain intact. It will become possible to investigate if these specific cognitive processes continue to be affected, and if other difficulties arise as the school curriculum changes when the cohorts of VLBW children, who have been treated with comparable medical intervention, enter the middle school years. For example, will more of the VLBW children experience difficulty as there are increased demands for written work in their educational programs? Examination of these specific cognitive processes for the present cohort should result in the early identification of difficulties and the necessary appropriate remediation for these children.

The pattern of performance described above resembles Rourke and Finlayson's (1978) Group 3 (i.e, children whose arithmetic performance was relatively deficient to their average or above average reading performance), or Levine, Oberklaid, and Meltzer's (1981) description of ''developmental output failure,'' or Siegel and Feldman's (1983) writing/arithmetic learning disabilities subtype. However, whether it is accurate to use these terms to describe the cognitive, academic, and behavioral outcomes for VLBW children has yet to be determined. Specific cognitive processes that are affected must be more thoroughly defined and related to a system of risk index variables to address this issue.

A SYSTEM OF RISK INDEX VARIABLES

A major advantage to the conceptualization of the cumulative risk index is that it brings us back to ''Jonathan'' and to predicting individual as opposed to group outcomes. By reviewing the literature, we have shown that a large proportion of the existing VLBW outcomes data is based on comparing group results and does not predict outcome for the individual child. These neurodevelopmental group outcome studies have been criticized for the use of global assessment measures that only incorporated biological factors. For a review of some of the more typically used neurodevelopmental screening measures, see Molfese (1989).

Others studies have attempted to develop a system of risk index variables to predict outcome for infants born at risk (Field, Dempsey, & Shuman, 1983; Field et al., 1978; Parmelee, Sigman, Kopp, & Haber, 1975; Smith, Flick, Ferriss, & Sellman, 1972). However, none of these studies specifically addressed the VLBW infant population. Only some of the studies included both biological and environmental factors and attempted to predict outcome for the individual infant. In addition, those studies that included a complex system of risk variables were often time consuming to implement and were not cost efficient.

Siegel et al. (1982) have developed a relatively simple risk index system with a high degree of accuracy that helps to predict which infants experience subsequent problems. Siegel et al.'s (1982) multivariate model incorporates environmental-demographic, perinatal, and reproductive variables. The demographic variables are the Hollingshead socioeconomic status, sex, and maternal and paternal education levels. The perinatal variables are birth weight, 1-minute and 5-minute Apgar scores, gestational age, severity of respiratory distress, birth asphyxia, and apnea for the preterm infants. Reproductive variables are gravidity, amount of maternal smoking during pregnancy, and number of previous abortions. Siegel et al. (1982) found that this cumulative risk index correctly classified 93.3% of the children on the 2-year Bayley MDI scores.

This multivariate model, which includes both biological and environmental factors, allows for the tabulation of the "truth table" through discriminant function analyses. The "truth table" is capable of classifying an individual child or a group of children into one of the following categories: "*true negatives* who have a score in the normal range in childhood and had a normal average score in infancy; *false negatives* who have a low score in childhood but who had an average score in infancy; *true positives* who were selected as having low scores in both infancy and childhood; and *false positives* who had lower scores in infancy but not in childhood" (Siegel, 1989a, p. 88). Siegel (1983, 1988a) found in the prediction of possible learning disabilities for preterm and full-term children that the rate of false positives was frequently high, ranging from 14% to 18% at the 6-, 7-, and 8-year outcome on the Wide Range Achievement Test. In practical terms, this rate of false positives is not extreme as intervention for these children would not likely be harmful. However, a high number of false negatives would render the risk index to be of little value.

Siegel (1985) also found that perinatal and reproductive variables correlated more highly with the visual-spatial and attentional outcome measures, whereas the environmental-demographic variables such as SES and maternal education were more highly correlated with language outcome measures. Generally, for the preterm infants the performance on these tasks was related to severity of perinatal complications, SES, maternal education, and maternal smoking during pregnancy. For the full-term children outcome performance was related to birth order, SES, maternal education, sex, parity, Apgar scores, and maternal smoking. Therefore, difficulties for VLBW infants appear to be influenced by the nature and severity of the biological insult, and the cumulative effect of the environmental-demographic variables.

"WILL JONATHAN BE O.K.?"

It is interesting to note that Siegel et al.'s (1982) cumulative risk index and statistical analysis provide a means of examining the relationships between specific environmental/biological variables and specific cognitive processes. Professionals working with VLBW infants and their families need to be aware of the perinatal and reproductive variables that appear to predict potential developmental delay or learning disabilities. They must also take into account how the environmental-demographic variables for a particular VLBW child will affect that child's outcome. Although such prediction will not always be accurate, the cost and benefits indicate that it is a worthwhile system. Sharing such information with parents may be useful in order to provide the best comprehensive plan for follow-up. Appropriate intervention could then be recommended. Parents could be made aware of how the child's environment appears to influence later developmental outcome. Programs to help ameliorate environmental conditions could then be implemented (i.e., language stimulation activities, appropriate toys). At the same time, we must acknowledge the limitations of the existing findings and the need for further research.

Future research that incorporate subgroups based on medical conditions of the VLBW infants (Landry et al., 1984, 1988) and restricted ranges of birth weights (Kitchen et al.'s 1987 studies) may provide more salient information for eventual outcome. There are actually very few cognitive, behavioral and academic outcome studies confined to infants who are less than 1,500 grams or who are classified as between 1,000 grams and 1,500 grams. A system of risk index variables needs to be further explored and replicated with other samples. Studies designed to evaluate the effectiveness of intervention with identified at-risk VLBW children are required. Finally, more studies that incorporate examination of specific cognitive processes rather than only global measures of intelligence are needed, especially when considering the possibility of learning disabilities as an outcome. Assessing specific cognitive processing skills is important in order to provide remediation for VLBW children that compensates for their areas of weakness and builds on their areas of strength. Continued long-term follow-up through adolescence and adulthood is recommended, including studying the effects of learning problems on self-concept.

A Hypothetical Answer for Jonathan's Parents

To conclude this chapter, we return to Jonathan's hypothetical case and attempt to provide an answer regarding his possible outcome.

Jonathan had several demographic and reproductive variables from the risk index that were in his favor. He was the first-born child of parents' with college and university levels of education from a middle-class SES. His mother had not smoked during the pregnancy and had no previous spontaneous abortions or pregnancies. Jonathan, however, encountered some of the perinatal high-risk variables. Although he was relatively large at birth, being closer to the 1,500-gram range, he experienced intraventricular hemorrhage with mild respiratory distress syndrome that was treated with oxygen less than 40%. He also had hyperbilirubinemia.

We might be able to predict on the basis of the risk index variables that Jonathan's language development will not be seriously affected, as this outcome is usually related to severity of apnea (Siegel et al., 1982) and level of socio-economic status (Siegel, 1984). The IVH-RDS and hyperbilirubinemia biological insults may place him at risk for motor difficulties as a result of possible central nervous system damage. Stimulation and close monitoring in this area would likely be advisable, although, at present, the effectiveness of many forms of treatment are not clear.

Hypothetically, Jonathan might be described at 8 years of age as being of above average intelligence. He may perform poorly on eye-hand coordination tasks such as the Beery VMI, and may be a slightly clumsy child. He may tend to be somewhat distractible and have difficulty remembering his multiplication tables. Sometimes he may not seem to understand or follow complex instructions. He may be an avid reader. However, his expressive language may be marked by difficulty organizing his thoughts, even though his content is rich and his vocabulary impressive. Jonathan is likely to be in a regular grade 3 class. Evidence from the literature of VLBW children in the last decade does not allow us to speculate much further about Jonathan than to this particular age and grade level.

SUMMARY

The preceding chapter has attempted to demonstrate that group outcome studies are not as clinically relevant as developing cumulative risk indices to predict outcome for the individual VLBW infant. The successful development of a cumulative risk index would be defined by the early identification of any special needs of a particular VLBW infant and the monitoring of that infant's progress. Evidence to support the inclusion of both biological (e.g., type and severity of perinatal insult, growth parameters) and environmental factors (e.g., socio-economic status and parenting skills) as risk index variables to increase the degree of predictive accuracy of a cumulative risk index was presented. Biological and environmental risk index variables can either minimize or maximize the effects of the less than optimal neonatal experience for the individual VLBW infant.

Group outcome studies were criticized for the use of global outcome measures of intellectual functioning and neurodevelopmental status. Alternative outcome measures that are believed to tap specific cognitive processes, such as the visual-spatial, eye-hand coordination, syntax, attention, and short-term memory skills in which VLBW individuals appear to experience difficulties, were recommended. By using these alternative outcome measures, specific areas of weakness for the individual VLBW child may be identified and addressed.

In conclusion, the development of a system of perinatal, reproductive and demographic risk index variables to predict the outcome for individual VLBW infants was advocated. Suggestions for directions in future research included: (a) the use of a system of risk index variables, (b) measuring specific cognitive processes as alternative outcome measures, (c) subgrouping children by perinatal insult and restricted birth weight ranges, (d) studying the effect of intervention for identified at-risk VLBW infants, and (e) long-term follow-up through adolescence and adulthood.

REFERENCES

Astbury, J., Orgill, A., & Bajuk, B. (1987). Relationship between two-year behaviour and neuro-developmental outcome at five years of very low-birthweight survivors. *Developmental Medicine and Child Neurology, 29*, 370–379.
Astbury, J., Orgill, A., Bajuk, B., & Yu, V.Y.H. (1983). Determinants of developmental performance of very low-birthweight survivors at one and two years of age. *Developmental Medicine and Child Neurology, 25*, 709–716.
Breslau, N., Klein, N., & Allen, L. (1988). Very low birthweight: Behavioral sequelae at nine years of age. *Journal of the American Academy of Child and Adolescent Psychiatry, 27*, 605–612.
Cohen, S.E., & Parmelee, A.H. (1983). Prediction of five-year Stanford-Binet scores in preterm infants. *Child Development, 54*, 1242–1253.
Cohen, S.E., Parmelee, A.H., Sigman, M., & Beckwith, L. (1988). Antecedents of school problems in children born preterm. *Journal of Pediatric Psychology, 13*, 493–508.
Eilers, B.C., Desai, N.S., Wilson, M.A., & Cunningham, M.D. (1986). Classroom performance and social factors of children with birthweights of 1,250 grams or less: Follow-up at 5 to 8 years of age. *Pediatrics, 77*, 203–208.
Escalona, S.K. (1982). Babies at double hazard: Early development of infants at biologic and social risk. *Pediatrics, 70*, 670–676.
Field, T., Dempsey, J., & Shuman, H.H. (1983). Five-year follow-up of preterm respiratory distress syndrome and post-term postmaturity syndrome. In T. Field & A. Sostek (Eds.), *Infants born at risk: Physiological, perceptual and cognitive processes* (pp. 317–335). New York: Grune & Stratton.
Field, T., Hallock, N., Ting, G., Dempsey, J., Dabiri, C., & Shuman, H.H. (1978). A first year follow up of high risk infants: Formulating a cumulative risk index. *Child Development, 49*, 119–131.
Friedman, S.L., Chipman, S.F., Segal, J.W., & Cocking, R.R. (1982). Complementing the success of medical intervention. *Seminars in Perinatology, 6*, 365–372.
Hack, M., & Breslau, N. (1986). Very low birth weight infants: Effects of brain growth during infancy on intelligence quotient at 3 years of age. *Pediatrics, 22*, 196–202.
Hack, M., Fanaroff, A.A., & Merkatz, I.R. (1979). The low-birth-weight infant—Evaluation of a changing outlook. *The New England Journal of Medicine, 301*, 1162–1165.

Hunt, J.V., Tooley, W.H., & Harvin, D. (1982). Learning disabilities in children with birth weights ≦1500 grams. *Seminars in Perinatology, 6*, 280–287.

Kitchen, W., Ford, G., Orgill, A., Rickards, A., Astbury, J., Lissenden, J., Bajuk, B., Yu, V., Drew, J., & Campbell, N. (1987). Outcome in infants of birth weight 500 to 900g: A continuing regional study of 5-year-old survivors. *The Journal of Pediatrics, 111*, 761–766.

Kitchen, W., Ford, G., Rickards, A.L., Lissenden, J.V., & Ryan, M.R. (1987). Children of birth weight <1000g: Changing outcome between ages 2 and 5 years. *The Journal of Pediatrics, 110*, 283–287.

Klein, N., Hack, M., Gallagher, J., & Fanaroff, A.A. (1985). Preschool performance of children with normal intelligence who were very low-birth-weight infants. *Pediatrics, 75*, 531–537.

Landry, S.H., Chapieski, L., Fletcher, J.M., & Denson, S. (1988). Three-year outcome for very low birth weight infants: Differential effects of early medical complications. *Journal of Pediatric Psychology, 13*, 317–327.

Landry, S.H., Fletcher, J.M., Zarling, C.L., Chapieski, L., & Francis, D.J. (1984). Differential outcomes associated with early medical complications in premature infants. *Journal of Pediatric Psychology, 9*, 385–401.

Levine, M., Oberklaid, F., & Meltzer, L. (1981). Developmental output failure: A study of low productivity in school-aged children. *Pediatrics, 67*, 18–25.

Lindgren, S.D., Harper, D.C., & Blackman, J.A. (1986). Environmental influences and perinatal risk factors in high-risk children. *Journal of Pediatric Psychology, 11*, 531–547.

Meisels, S.J., Plunkett, J.W., Roloff, D.W., Pasick, P.L., & Stiefel, G.S. (1986). Growth and development of preterm infants with respiratory distress syndrome and bronchopulmonary dysplasia. *Pediatrics, 77*, 345–352.

Molfese, V.J. (1989). *Perinatal risk and infant development: Assessment and prediction.* New York: The Guilford Press.

Nickel, R.E., Bennett, F.C., & Lamson, F.N. (1982). School performance of children with birth weights of 1000g or less. *American Journal of Diseases of Childhood, 136*, 105–110.

Parmelee, A.H., Sigman, M., Kopp, C.B., & Haber, A. (1975). The concept of a cumulative risk score for infants. In N.R. Ellis (Ed.), *Aberrant development in infancy: Human and animal studies* (pp. 113–121). Hillsdale, NJ: Erlbaum.

Rawlings, G., Reynolds, E.O.R., Stewart, A., & Strang, L.B. (1971). Changing prognosis for infants of very low birth weight. *Lancet, 1*, 516–519.

Ross, G. (1985). Use of the Bayley Scales to characterize abilities of premature infants. *Child Development, 56*, 835–842.

Ross, G., Lipper, E.G., & Auld, P.A.M. (1985). Consistency and change in the development of premature infants weighing less than 1500 grams at birth. *Pediatrics, 76*, 885–891.

Ross, G., Lipper, E.G., & Auld, P.A.M. (1986). Early predictors of neurodevelopmental outcome of very low-birthweight infants at three years. *Developmental Medicine and Child Neurology, 28*, 171–179.

Rourke, B.P., & Finlayson, M.A.J. (1978). Neuropsychological significance of variations in patterns of academic performance: Verbal and visual spatial abilities. *Journal of Abnormal Child Psychology, 6*, 121–133.

Sameroff, A.J., & Chandler, M.J. (1975). Reproductive risk and the continuum of caretaking causality. In F.D. Horowitz, E.M. Hetherington, J. Scarr-Salapatek, & G.M. Siegel (Eds.), *Child development research* (Vol. 4, pp. 187–244). Chicago: The University of Chicago Press.

Siegel, L.S. (1979). Infant perceptual, cognitive, and motor behaviors as predictors of subsequent cognitive and language development. *Canadian Journal of Psychology, 32*, 382–395.

Siegel, L.S. (1981). Infant tests as predictors of cognitive and language development at two years. *Child Development, 52*, 545–557.

Siegel, L.S. (1983). Predicting possible learning disabilities in preterm and fullterm infants. In T. Field & A. Sostek (Eds.), *Infants born at risk: Physiological, perceptual and cognitive processes* (pp. 295–315). New York: Grune & Stratton.

Siegel, L.S. (1984). Home environmental influences on cognitive development in preterm and full-term children during the first 5 years. In A.W. Gottsfried (Ed.), *Home environment and early cognitive development* (pp. 197–233). New York: Academic Press.

Siegel, L.S. (1985, April). *Linguistic, visual-spatial, and attentional processes in school age prematurely born children.* Paper presented at the meeting of the Society for Research in Child Development, Toronto, Canada.

Siegel, L.S. (1988a). A system for the early detection of learning disabilities. *Canadian Journal of Special Education, 4,* 115–122.

Siegel, L.S. (1988b). Evidence that IQ scores are irrelevant to the definition and analysis of reading disability. *Canadian Journal of Psychology, 42,* 201–215.

Siegel, L.S. (1989a). A reconceptualization of prediction from infant test scores. In M. Bornstein & N.A. Krasniger (Eds.), *Stability and continuity in development* (pp. 80–94). Hillsdale, NJ: Erlbaum.

Siegel, L.S. (1989b). IQ is irrelevant to the definition of learning disabilities. *Journal of Learning Disabilities, 22*(8), 469–478.

Siegel, L.S., & Cunningham, C.E. (1984). Social interactions: A transactional approach with illustrations from children with developmental problems. In A. Doyle & D.S. Markowitz (Eds.), *Children in families under stress* (pp. 85–98). San Francisco: Jossey Bass.

Siegel, L.S., & Feldman, W. (1983). Nondyslexic children with combined writing and arithmetic learning disabilities. *Clinical Pediatrics, 22,* 241–244.

Siegel, L.S., & Heaven, R. (1986). Defining and categorizing learning disabilities. In S. Ceci (Ed.), *Handbook of cognitive, social and neuropsychological aspects of learning disabilities* (Vol. 1, pp. 95–129). Hillsdale, NJ: Erlbaum.

Siegel, L.S., Saigal, S., Rosenbaum, P., Morton, R.A., Young, A., Berenbaum, & Stoskopf, B. (1982). Predictors of development in preterm and full-term infants: A model for detecting the at risk child. *Journal of Pediatric Psychology, 7,* 135–148.

Smith, A.C., Flick, G.L., Ferriss, G.S., & Sellman, A.H. (1972). Prediction of developmental outcome at seven years from prenatal, perinatal, and postnatal events. *Child Development, 43,* 495–507.

Stewart, A.L., Reynolds, E.O.R., & Lipscomb, A.P. (1981). Outcome for infants of very low birthweight: Survey of world literature. *Lancet, 1,* 1038–1040.

Taub, H.B., Goldstein, K.M., & Caputo, D.V. (1977). Indices of neonatal prematurity as discriminators of development in middle childhood. *Child Development, 48,* 797–805.

Vohr, B.R., & Garcia Coll, C.T. (1985). Neurodevelopmental and school performance of very low-birth-weight infants: A seven-year longitudinal study. *Pediatrics, 71,* 345–350.

Wallace, I.F. (1988). Socioenvironmental issues in longitudinal research of high-risk infants. In P.M. Vietze & H.G. Vaughan, Jr. (Eds.), *Early identification of infants with developmental disabilities* (pp. 356–382). Philadelphia: Grune & Stratton.

Wiener, G., Rider, R.V., Oppel, W.C., & Harper, P.A. (1968). Correlates of low birth weight. Psychological status at eight to ten years of age. *Pediatric Research, 2,* 110–118.

13

The Prediction of Cognitive Abilities at 8 and 12 Years of Age from Neonatal Assessments of Preterm Infants

Marian D. Sigman, Sarale E. Cohen, Leila Beckwith, Robert Asarnow, and Arthur H. Parmelee

In 1971, we began a longitudinal study of preterm infants. One aim of this study was to design a set of measures that would identify early in infancy those children at risk of developing cognitive difficulties later in life. We have found that performance on some of the infant measures is associated with childhood cognitive abilities. This documentation of continuity from infancy to childhood offers some hope that clinically predictive assessments could be designed.

If one were to develop such assessments, the earlier in the infant's life that they could be applied the more useful they would be. For this reason, a number of our assessment measures were designed and administered early in the first year of life. In fact, several of the newborn assessments do appear to be associated with later intelligence. Measures of the newborn's attention to visual stimuli and organization of sleep states in the laboratory were correlated with later cognitive abilities. About one-third of the variance in IQ at 8 years of age for the preterm infants from English-speaker families was predicted by a sleep state measure, the attention measure, and the total amount of time that the infant was talked to by the caregiver in the home (Sigman, Beckwith, Cohen, & Parmelee, 1989). Thus, characteristics of the neonate and the home environment were jointly associated with subsequent cognitive development.

The demonstration of stability between early infant measures and later cognitive measures is clearly just the first step in the process of developing early assessments or understanding developmental continuities. One would like to have a more precise understanding of the functions jointly tapped by the infant measures and childhood cognitive assessments. One way to approach this issue is through divergent validation. By including outcome measures that assess a variety of independent functions, the pattern of associations between the early infant measure and the outcome assessments may specify the particular functions underlying the observed continuity. Furthermore, one would expect that infant measures that were associated with each other would be tied to the same outcome measures while infant measures that were unrelated would be predictive of different childhood abilities.

We have attempted to carry out such divergent validation with assessments administered when the subjects reached 8 and 12 years of age. While our findings from the 8-year assessments have been discussed in a previous chapter (Sigman et al., 1989), these findings will be reviewed again here for two reasons. First, the findings from the two age periods complement each other and give a more complete picture of the results. Second, the results from the 8-year follow-up shaped the design of the longitudinal follow-up administered at 12 years of age. Many of the hypotheses tested with the 12-year data were based on the results of the 8-year testing. The following sections of this chapter will review the design of the study, sample characteristics, and neonatal methodology before elaborating on the results at 8 and 12 years of age.

DESCRIPTION OF THE STUDY

Sample

The subjects to be discussed in this chapter were a group of preterm infants who were born at UCLA Medical Center or transferred to the nursery shortly after birth between July 1972 and the end of 1974. Prematurity was defined by a gestational age at birth of 37 weeks or less based on maternal report of last menses and a birth weight of 2,500 grams or less. Infants with obvious congenital anomalies or syndromes were not enrolled in the study. This chapter will focus on the infants from families in which English and languages other than Spanish were used in the home. This is a slightly different sample than discussed in previous papers, since a small group of non-English-speaking immigrants is included. The mean gestational age for the 73 infants who were tested on the WISC-R at 12 year was 32.5 weeks (SD = 3.3) and the mean birthweight was 1830.79 gms (SD = 491.97). While this subsample was culturally more homogeneous than the entire sample, the group is quite varied in terms of socioeconomic status. The mean Hollingshead index is 43.98, with a standard deviation of 13.1. The sample size varies at different ages because children could not be tested or located; generally, about 60 to 70 children were tested at each age.

Design of the Study

Families were recruited into the study before the infant was discharged from the hospital. The family was contacted by a public health nurse after discharge, and a home visit was conducted. All infants were provided with free medical care through the Well-Baby Clinic at UCLA during the first 2 years of enrollment in the study. Age was computed from expected date of birth to correct for the variations in gestational age. Standardized developmental tests—the Gesell and Bayley—were administered on five occasions during infancy, the Stanford-Binet was administered at 5 years of age, and the WISC-R was administered at 8 years.

The sleep state and attention measures were conducted on the same day, at 40 weeks conceptional age. All infants had been discharged from the hospital at this time and had been home for about a month. The family brought the infant to the laboratory and testing began after a short physical and neurological examination. The visual attention assessment was conducted first, the infant was fed, electrodes attached, and was put down for a nap by the caregiver in a small crib.

Responsiveness to Visual Stimuli

The infant's responsiveness to a single 2×2 checkerboard was observed (Sigman, Kopp, Parmelee, & Jeffrey, 1973). In order to minimize the variations due to state differences, a standardized procedure preceded the observation. All infants were tested with a 10-minute neurological assessment, which tended to leave them in the awake, alert state. In order to calm the babies somewhat, the infants were then fed a small amount of milk. With the eyes still open, the infant was placed in an infant seat facing a white screen, and the 3-minute observation commenced. After the first 1-minute trial, the checkerboard was illuminated with a series of flashing lights during the second 1-minute trial. On the third trial, the checkerboard was not illuminated. The infant's eyes were observed through a peephole at the side of the stimulus, and fixations were recorded and decoded in half-second intervals.

A preliminary study indicated that preterm infants showed longer fixation durations at expected date of birth than full-term neonates (Sigman, Kopp, Littman, & Parmelee, 1977). We followed a small sample of full-term infants from birth to 2 weeks of age and found no change in total fixation time, although other studies have found a decline in fixation time to unchanging stimuli as full-term infants mature (Brennan, Ames, & Moore, 1966; Fantz, 1965; Lewis, Goldberg, & Campbell, 1969; Wetherford & Cohen, 1973).

Preterm infants appear to process visual stimuli somewhat more slowly than full-term infants (Caron & Caron, 1981; Friedman, Jacobs, & Werthman, 1981; Rose, Gottfried, & Bridger, 1976; Rose, 1980; Sigman, 1976; Sigman & Parmelee, 1974). The longer fixation durations shown by preterm infants at term may therefore reflect a similar slowness in the rate of visual processing. Alternatively, the preterm infant may be less able to modulate states of arousal so that he or she is not able to inhibit looking at the unchanging visual stimulus. Whatever the basis for the long fixation durations, preterm infants who look for long periods of time are expected to develop cognitively less well over time.

Sleep State Integration

For the study of sleep states, a single sleep polygraph recording was made for each subject at term, 40 weeks conceptional age, during a day nap in a sound-attenuated laboratory room (Beckwith & Parmelee, 1986). The recordings were bipolar from the frontal temporal, frontal central, temporal occipital, and central occipital positions over both hemispheres following the 10–20 system (Anders, Emde, & Parmelee, 1971). Respiration and heart rate were monitored electronically; eye movements and body movements were noted by direct observation.

The recording time was 90 minutes, with the final 60 minutes used for analysis and the first 30 minutes considered to be adaptation to the strange situation. Records were visually analyzed by 20-second epochs, with state and EEG codes determined independently, without knowledge of the subject's medical history or subsequent development. Data were coded for each 20-second epoch on the basis of observable behavior and physiological functioning: awake (eyes open); quiet sleep (eyes close, no eye movements, no body movements except for occasional body jerks, and regular respiration); active sleep (eyes closed, eye movements, body movements, irregular respirations); and, indeterminate sleep (eyes closed but not fitting either of the other two sleep states). Each 20-second epoch was coded in terms of the state that prevailed for most of the period.

The EEG was coded without knowledge of sleep states using a 3-digit numbering system, and the last digit in the code identified the general nature of the pattern, and the first two digits indicated the specific form of the pattern expected at 40 weeks conceptional age (Anders et al., 1971). At this age, the EEG patterns of preterm and full-term infants are very similar, with only a scattering of immature EEG patterns in the preterm infants that are not found in the full-term infants (Parmelee & Sigman, 1983). In our previous studies and in studies by others (Parmelee et al., 1967), four patterns have been readily identified in the sleep of the infants at term. These patterns are as follows: (a) 402-LVF, low voltage fast activity; (b) 403-M, mixed low voltage, fast and slow waves; (c) 405-HVS, high voltage, slow waves; and (d) 407-TA, alternating burst of high voltage, slow waves with attenuated periods, known as *trace alternant*.

We initially focused on quiet sleep as a marker of neurophysiological variation in the newborn period (Beckwith & Parmelee, 1986). This is a state that requires a high level of cybernetic control to suppress body and eye movements and maintain regular respiration concordant with each other for sustained periods of time along with specific EEG patterns. In the first months of life, quiet sleep rapidly increases in amount and in the strength of concordance of the determining parameters (Parmelee & Stern, 1972; Parmelee & Garbanati, 1987). Further, this developmental process seems to be more a function of brain maturation than environmental circumstance in the early period (Anders, Keener, & Kraemer, 1985). In the analyses of quiet sleep it is particularly important to include the specific EEG pattern, 407-TA (trace alternant), as a criterion of normal development, since lethargic infants secondary to illness or neurological problems can have long periods of no movement and regular respiration and appear to be in quiet sleep. Such infants, however, generally lack the expected EEG pattern, trace alternant. Therefore, the total amount of quiet sleep independent of the specific EEG pattern is not an adequate marker of normal brain development whereas that with the trace alternant EEG pattern is.

Active sleep rapidly decreases in amount in the first months of life as the amount of quiet sleep and waking increase. Neurophysiologically and behaviorally, active sleep appears to be a disorganized state in that it is characterized by irregular respirations and heart rate, frequent body movements often of a twitching nature, and rapid eye movements. This state, however, does have an underlying distinctive neurophysiological organization and, even though it decreases in amount with maturation, it also develops increasing concordance and organization of the determining parameters (Parmelee & Stern, 1972; Parmelee & Garbanati, 1987). In the infants in our study, the expected EEG patterns 402-LVF and 403-M were so consistently present in active sleep that we have used the total amount of active sleep independent of EEG for our analyses. Active sleep is considered to be influenced by environmental circumstances (Anders et al., 1985) and related to the neurophysiological mechanism involved in wakefulness, particularly, to the alert awake state (Denneberg & Thoman, 1981) and, specifically to the alert orienting awake state in animals (Morrison, 1983).

On the average, the infants were asleep 93% of the observed time. About half the sleep time ($M = 56\%$) was coded as indeterminate sleep and half as more organized states of quiet and active sleep. Active sleep (26% of the sleep time) exceeded quiet sleep (18%) as expected at this age. The EEG pattern of 407-TA was predominant in quiet sleep, but the range of individual variability was wide. For example, infants had from 0% to 100% of quiet sleep with 407-TA as the associated EEG pattern. This EEG pattern was only manifested in quiet and indeterminate sleep, almost never in active sleep. The distribution of time that the infant was in various sleep states was unrelated to performance on the visual attention measure.

Infant–Caregiver Interaction

Assessments of the rearing environment were derived from naturalistic home observations made when the infants were 1, 8, and 24 months (Beckwith, Cohen, Kopp, Parmelee, & Marcy, 1976; Beckwith & Cohen, 1984). At the 1-month visit, the infants were observed on an average for 73 minutes of awake time; at 8 month, 1½ hours of awake time; and at 24 months, 50 minutes of play time. The observer used a precoded check list, and every 15 seconds recorded presence of a set of infant behaviors, caregiver behaviors, and events defined as contingent or reciprocal interactions between caregiver and child, as well as behaviors of other persons towards the infant.

Certain interactive events were selected a priori for study as indicators of responsive caregiving. At 1 month, these were maternal positive attentiveness to the infant, face-to-face talk, mutual visual regard, maternal contingency to distress, and infant held upright; at 8 months, contingency to distress was omitted and contingency to nondistress vocalization and floor freedom were added, at 24 months, positive attentiveness, reciprocal interaction, and time spent in intellectual tasks (dramatic play, books, puzzles, and blocks) were used. The codes of each of these indices were converted to standardized scores at each age that assessed the degree to which the infant–caregiver interaction was facilitative.

ASSOCIATIONS OF THE NEONATAL MEASURES AND 8-YEAR INTELLIGENCE

Relations with WISC-R IQ

Correlations were computed between the measures of visual attention, sleep states, and home interactions with IQ as determined by the WISC-R. A significant negative association was found between fixation duration and WISC-R IQ at 8 years (Cohen & Parmelee, 1983; Cohen, Parmelee, Beckwith, & Sigman, 1986; Sigman, 1983; Sigman, Cohen, Beckwith, & Parmelee, 1986). The particular measures showing correlations were the length of the first fixation to each new stimulus, the total fixation time in the first trial, and the total fixation time over all trials. Infants who showed longer fixations were less developmentally competent later in life.

The proportion of sleep time that the infant spent in quiet sleep without the specific EEG criterion was unrelated to IQ at 8 years, but the percentage of quiet sleep with the 407-TA EEG pattern was significantly correlated with 8-year IQ (Beckwith & Parmelee, 1986). This was the only EEG pattern in all the different states to show an associations with intelligence. Thus, the findings supported the expectation that the degree of state control in sleep, as manifested in the amount of this highly organized quiet sleep pattern, was positively associated with later intelligence in childhood.

The proportion of sleep time that the infant spent in indeterminate sleep was also associated with IQ, although, in this case, the correlation was negative. Infants whose sleep was difficult to classify were likely to have lower developmental and cognitive scores at every testing period from 4 months to 8 years than infants whose sleep was more classifiable. Indeterminate sleep appeared to indicate a lack of neurological integration. While the disorganized sleep states were only present for a short period of time, the central disorganization did not appear to be outgrown.

Correlations were also computed between the home summary scores and IQ at age 8 years. Generally, the individual summary scores obtained at 1 month had little association with later cognitive development. However, the frequency of total talking to the 1-month-old infant was significantly related to 8-year IQ. The 8-month caregiver–infant interaction summary score was predictive of later competence in childhood for the female infants but not the male infants. The 24-

month summary score was associated with childhood intelligence scores for both males and females (Beckwith & Cohen, 1984).

Relations with WISC-R Factor Scores

One way to specify the processes captured by each of these infant measures is to compare predictions to different cognitive functions. Intelligence tests can be considered to measure a variety of intellectual processes. Performance on the WISC-R is often viewed in terms of the child's abilities on three factors, verbal comprehension, perceptual organization, and freedom from distractibility (Kaufman, 1975). In order to determine whether the attention and sleep measures tapped different processes, correlations were computed between the measures of the newborn and the three WISC-R factors (see Table 1).

Both the attention measures and the proportion of time that the infant spent in indeterminate sleep were associated with all three factors. These measures, then, seem to be tapping a precursor of general intellectual capacities. On the other hand, the percentage of time that the infant was in active sleep was significantly correlated with the freedom from distractibility factor and neither of the other two factors. Freedom from distractibility is thought to reflect the child's capacity to sustain attention. In line with this finding, children with school learning problems had showed less active sleep as neonates than children without learning problems (Cohen, Parmelee, Sigman, & Beckwith, 1988). Thus, there were some differential relation between the state regulation and attention measures with cognitive outcomes in the school years.

Contribution of Laboratory and Home Interaction Measures to Prediction of Later Outcomes

We have previously shown that a consistently responsive relationship between the caregiver and infant can buffer the child's development against problems in neurological integration (Beckwith & Parmelee, 1986). Another way to address

Table 1. Correlations between Neonatal Measures with Factor Scores on the 8-Year WISC-R

WISC-R Factors	Sleep States Quiet with			Fixation Time		
	Active	407 TA	Indeterminate	First	Trial 1	Total
Verbal Comprehension	—	−.28[a]	−.26	−.37	−.30	−.29
Perceptual Organization	—	.32	−.26	−.28	−.27	—
Freedom from Distractibility	.26	—	−.39	—	—	−.27

[a]All correlations shown are significant, $p < .05$, df range from 59 to 63.

this issue is to examine the relative contribution of early neurobehavioral functioning and home interaction to later development across the entire range of relations rather than comparing an optimal group to all others. A multiple regression was calculated with WISC-R Full Scale IQ measured when the children were 8 years old. The total frequency that the caregiver talked to the 1-month-old, percentage of 407-TA in quiet sleep, proportion of time in active and in indeterminate sleep, total fixation time, and Hollingshead Index were entered into a multiple regressions with WISC-R Full-Scale IQ as the dependent variable. Three variables predicted the 8-year IQ (Adjusted R^2 = .30), total talking by the caregiver, proportion of time in quiet sleep with the 407-TA EEG code, and total fixation time. Thus, measures from all three domains contributed independently to the variance in intelligence at 8 years of age.

DESIGN OF THE 12-YEAR FOLLOW-UP

The follow-up study at 12 years of age had several objectives. First, we wished to determine whether the neonatal assessments and observations continued to predict general intelligence. Another aim was to utilize measures that captured different types of cognitive and attentional abilities. Based on the findings at age 8 years, we hypothesized that the attention and active sleep measures would be associated with different types of cognitive skills at 12 years of age. The final aim was to determine whether the characteristics of the infant and the caregiving environment continued to have additive influences on later cognitive development.

Theoretical Considerations

The nature of the continuity between infant attention and later intelligence has been discussed in considerable detail in recent years (Bornstein & Sigman, 1986; Columbo & Mitchell, 1990). An entire volume of the *European Bulletin of Cognitive Psychology* (1988) was devoted to consideration of whether early measures of infant attention and habituation reliably and validly reflect information processing. As an alternative, some theorists consider that the visual orientation of the infant may be seen as an operant procedure involving a synchronous reinforcement schedule (Malcuit, Pomerleau, & Lamarre, 1988). Lécuyer (1988) emphasizes the importance of the infant's *control* of processing rather than *speed* of processing. In his view, variations in fixation time and rate of habituation stem from individual differences in the ability to marshall attention. He sees the fast habituator as the infant who spends less time in blank looking. This viewpoint is not unlike the argument we have presented in terms of arousal control. The infant who looks more briefly or habituates more rapidly may be less buffeted by endogenous stimulation and more able to focus attention to exogenous stimuli.

Several other explanations for the association between fixation measures and later cognitive abilities have been proposed. One theory suggests that early preference for novel stimuli may continue so the child will show similar interests in novel tasks and situations (Berg & Sternberg, 1985). This interest in, and comfort with, novelty will promote learning. Thus, the link between early attention and later cognitive skills is seen as reflecting the child's attraction to and ability to use novel information.

Selection of Measures

Guided by these theories, we selected a number of measures at 12 years of age designed to reflect the underlying processes that might account for the continuity between the infant attention and sleep measures and later cognitive abilities. The measures were selected to reflect accuracy of speeded information processing, capacity for sustained attention, and ability to reason with novel information.

Information-Processing Ability

The span of apprehension is a measure of information processing on which subjects have to report which of two predesignated target letters are present in arrays of tachistoscopically presented stimuli (Asarnow, Granholm, & Sherman, 1991). A series of matrices of capital letters was flashed on a computer screen for 50 msec. Each matrix contained a random array of letters including either a T or an F, but not both. The subject's task was to determine whether the predesignated target letter was present on each trial. The total number identified correctly was calculated on two sets, one with 3 items and one with 12 items. There were 16 matrices randomly presented over 96 trials for each task. The dependent measure was the number of trials on which the child was correct.

Capacity to Sustain and Shift Attention

While the span of apprehension measures the accuracy of information processing with brief presentations of stimuli, the continuous performance task assesses capacity to sustain attention to a monotonous task over repeated trials (Neuchterlein, 1983). The subject was required to monitor a screen while a long sequence of rapidly presented random target stimuli were displayed. This paradigm involved the brief (50 msec), rapid (every 1.0 sec) presentation of randomly generated digits from 0 through 9 on the center of a viewing screen. The subject's task was to attend and press a button when, and only when, a target digit (the number 8) appeared. The task was continued for 400 trials. A rest interval occurred during which the child was instructed to alter his or her response by pressing when 0 was present and not pressing when 8 was flashed.

An additional 100 trials were then presented. This condition provided a measure of the ability to shift attention and to inhibit an overlearned response. The number of correct responses on both sets was calculated.

Interest and Ability to Use Novelty

In order to measure the adolescent's ability to reason with novel information, an experimental analogies problem designed by Marr and Sternberg (1986) was administered to the adolescents. The adolescent was required to pick the correct verbal solution to an analogy such as "Bread is to Food as Water is to _____." In this case, the alternative solutions were "Beverage (clearly correct), Medicine, Rinse, and Thirst." Each verbal analogy was preceded by a bit of novel information which was either relevant or irrelevant to completion of the analogy. In the current example, the irrelevant precue was "Water runs uphill." In the case of a relevant precue such as "Lakes are dry" followed by "Trail is to Hike as Lake is to _____ , the precue had to be attended to for the correct solution. In this case, the alternatives were "Swim, Walk, Water, and Dust." The correct solution given the precue was Walk rather than Swim as it would have been without the precue. For half the 40 items, the novel information was relevant to the solution and had to be used for a correct solution, while the novel information was irrelevant for the other 20 items and could be ignored. The subject had to judge whether the precue was relevant or irrelevant and incorporate the novel information into the solution when the precue was relevant.

In order to ensure that the subjects understood the procedure, a training period was provided. The subject was first requested to complete a simple verbal analogy, "Apple is to red as lemon is to _____ ." All the children responded with "yellow." Then, the experimenter said, "But suppose I told you that all lemons are blue. Now if I said "Apple is to red as lemon is to _____ , what would you say?" All the subjects responded "Blue." Two more examples of relevant precues and one example of an irrelevant precue were given and explanations were also provided although all the children were successful during this procedure. For the first 5 items on the actual test, errors were corrected and explained. For the 2 items where the precue was relevant, the precue was repeated an additional time with an exhortation that this information be remembered. The next 35 items were then administered with no corrections. Following this oral presentation of the test which was done in case some of the children could not read well, the child was given the 20 items where the precue was relevant. The child was told that in all cases the precue was important and to respond again knowing this information. Children did this last section on their own. Number of correct responses was calculated separately for each administration of the relevant precued items as well as for the single administerion of the irrelevant precued items.

Hypothesized Relations between Infant Measures and 12-Year Cognitive Assessments

Our expectations of relations between infant measures and outcomes were based partly on the associations found at 8 years with the factor scores and partly on theoretical rationales. Because the infant attention measure has seemed to tap information processing skills, we hypothesized that the attention measure would be associated with scores on the span of apprehension task. The infant attention measure was not expected to be related to performance on the continuous performance task because the attention measure did not seem to reflect sustained attention. On the other hand, it seemed likely that the amount of time that the infant spent in active sleep might be associated with the continuous performance task. Both the continuous performance task and freedom from distractibility on the WISC-R appear to tap the capacity for the child to sustain attention. Since active sleep was associated with freedom from distractibility on the WISC-R at 8 years, we hypothesized that it should be associated with accuracy on the continuous performance task at 12 years.

RESULTS OF THE 12-YEAR FOLLOW-UP

Performance on the Cognitive Measures

The children continued to show generally good cognitive abilities as had been true at earlier ages. Mean IQ on the WISC-R was 111 with a SD of 14.9 and a range from 77 to 139 (see Table 2).

The attention measures were quite easy, and the verbal analogies were quite difficult for children in this sample. The mean number correct on the 20 verbal analogies where the precue was irrelevant was 13.4 with a range from 6 to 20. When the novel information was relevant, this fell to a mean number correct of 8.2 of the 20 items. Part of this difficulty may have stemmed from the necessity to decide whether the novel information was correct. The mean for correct solution rose to 11.4 when the children were told that the information was relevant and they only had to apply the novel information to their solutions.

Associations between the 12-Year Cognitive Measures

Correlations were computed between scores on the various cognitive measures administered at 12 years of age. The span of apprehension measures were unrelated to any of the other cognitive assessments with one exception. The number correct on the more complicated span was associated with the total correct on the continuous performance task ($r(58) = .29, p < .05$). Performance on the attention measures was generally unrelated to intelligence except that

Table 2.   Number Correct on Cognitive and Attention Measures Administered at 12 Years of Age

	N	$\bar{X}$	SD	Minimum	Maximum
Span 3	60	90.93	3.65	76	96
Span 12	60	69.70	7.63	53	83
CPT	60	126.38	8.57	87	132
CPT-Shift	54	30.15	3.01	20	33
Analogies-Precue Relevant	56	8.20	4.35	1	16
Analogies-Precue Irrelevant	56	13.43	3.64	6	20
Analogies-Precue Relevant 2	55	11.39	4.49	2	18
WISC-R IQ	73	111.04	14.91	77	139

more intelligent children were better able to shift cues on the CPT ($r(52) = .32$, $p < .05$). Intelligence was associated with higher scores on all the analogies problems.

Relations between the Infant Measures and 12-Year Cognitive Assessments

Correlations were computed between the infant attention and sleep state measures with the 12-year cognitive measures. As can be seen from Table 3, some of our hypotheses were confirmed while others were disconfirmed. Some of the visual attention measures were associated with scores on the span of apprehension problem (Sigman, Cohen, Beckwith, Asarnow, & Parmelee, 1991). Thus, there did seem to be some association between early control of attention mea-

Table 3.   Correlations between Scores on Infant Measures and 12-Year Cognitive and Attention Measures

WISC-R Factors	Sleep States Quiet with			Fixation Time		
	Active	407 TA	Indeterminate	First	Trial 1	Total
Span 3	—	—	$-.25$[a]	—	$-.33$	—
Span 12	—	—	—	$-.27$	—	—
CPT	.30	—	—	—	—	—
CPT-Shift	.32	.33	—	—	—	—
Relevant Precue Analogy	—	.28	$-.33$	—	—	—
Irrelevant Precue Analogy	—	.30	—	$-.38$	$-.36$	$-.37$
Relevant Precue Analogy 2	—	—	$-.31$	—	—	—
WISC-R	—	.24	$-.25$	$-.31$	$-.32$	$-.31$

[a]All correlations shown are significant, $p < .05$, df range from 51 to 71.

sures and later accuracy of information processing. Moreover, in line with our expectations, infant attention was unrelated to scores on the continuous performance test.

The only infant measure associated with sustained attention on the continuous performance task was the percentage of time that the infant was in active sleep. We had predicted that there would be continuity between active sleep and later sustained attention because of the findings at 8 years of age. Infants who engaged in more active sleep at term continued to have higher factor scores on freedom from distractibility at 12 years (r (71) = .26, $p < .05$). Moreover, freedom from distractibility on the 12 year WISC-R was associated with both the overall score on the CPT ($r(58) = .27$, $p < .05$), and the score in the shift condition ($r(52) = .43$, $p < .05$), but not with scores on the span of apprehension.

Relations between the Early Measures and Intelligence at 12 Years

Another question addressed by the 12-year follow-up was whether the early measures continued to be associated with overall intelligence. In order to address this issue, correlations were computed between the infant measures and Full Scale IQ on the WISC-R administered at 12 years of age. The attention measures associated with 8-year intelligence continued to be associated at 12 years of age (see Table 3). The percentage of time that the infant spent in quiet sleep with 407, indeterminate sleep, and total amount of time that the caregiver talked to the neonate were also correlated with IQ as had been true at 8 years (Cohen, Parmelee, Beckwith, & Sigman, 1992).

We calculated a multiple regression of the attention, sleep state, and caregiver measures with IQ at age 12 years like the one calculated at 8 years of age. Twenty-nine percent of the variance in intelligence at 12 years of age was accounted for by total talking by the caregiver, total fixation time, proportion of time in quiet sleep with the 407-TA EEG code, and Hollingshead index. Thus, the same characteristics of the infant and of the caregiving environment continued to contribute independently to the prediction of intelligence at 12 years.

DISCUSSION

To summarize the aims and results briefly, the follow-up study attempted to define more precisely the nature of processes that were continuous from infancy to adolescence. In line with our hypotheses, the infant attention measure did seem to tap accuracy of speeded information intake and not to reflect the capacity for sustained attention. There was also no evidence that infants who were more efficient visual processors were any more comfortable or skillful in including novel information into their reasoning than infants who were not so efficient.

These results support the notion that infant attention measures assess either infant information processing or something about the infant that will be a precursor of such processing. Because the infants in this study were neonates, their capacity for information processing may be quite limited. The attention measure may be assessing the infant's capacity to focus efficiently rather than information processing directly. However, the nature of the continuity appears to be not so much in terms of attention modulation as in the capacity to encode and retrieve information when it has been encoded. This is in contrast to the infant's capacity to maintain active sleep, which does appear to be related to later ability to sustain attention.

The group differences in intelligence as a function of early infant and home characteristics are startling. Infants who are efficient lookers and are talked to in the home in the first month have far greater intellectual abilities (M IQ = 121.8) than infants who show long fixations and are less well cared for (M IQ = 100.4). The process by which frequent talking to the neonate influences development needs to be defined. In general, we have thought of this variable as telling us something about the caregiver emotional involvement with the neonate and the kind of caregiving that will be provided in the infant's future. However, Eckerman and Oehler (this volume) suggest that talking to the preterm infant may have very dramatic effects on the infant's state, which, in turn, influence the caregiver's perception of infant responsiveness. Thus, talking to the infant in the first month of life may start a positive cycle which has consequences for later cognitive development.

In summary, certain infant and caregiver characteristics do seem to have potential as predictors of cognitive development. While none of the individual variables account for large amounts of the variance in outcome at school age, sets of variables do account for about 30% of the variance and mean scores and the extremes of the groups are quite different as noted in the previous paragraph. This is surprising, given that all these measures were made during the neonatal period. The infant's distribution of attention continues to be important for adolescent cognitive skills as it was for childhood cognitive skills. The integration of states manifested in sleep also seems related to later cognitive and attentional functions. The kind of environment provided by the caregiver adds to the potential that the infant manifests in attention and state control. The findings of this study do suggest that the infant develops separate abilities and characteristics in early life which follow independent but continuous paths with later cognitive and attentional capacities.

REFERENCES

Anders, T., Emde, R., & Parmelee, A. (Eds.). (1971). *A manual of standardized terminology, techniques and criteria for scoring of sleep and wakefulness in newborn infants.* Los Angeles: UCLA, Brain Information Service, NINDS Neurological Information Network.
Anders, T.F., Keener, M.K., & Kraemer, H. (1985). Sleep-wake state organization, neonatal assessment and development in premature infants during the first year of life. II. *Sleep, 8,* 193–206.

Asarnow, R., Granholm, E., & Sherman, T. (1991). Span of apprehension in schizophrenia. In S. Steinhauer, J.H. Gruzelier, & J. Zubin (Eds.), *Handbook of schizophrenia: Neuropsychology, psychophysiology, and information processing* (Vol. 4). North Holland: Elsevier.

Beckwith, L., & Cohen, S.E. (1984). Home environment and cognitive competence in preterm children in the first five years. In A.W. Gottfried (Ed.), *Home environment and early mental development*. New York: Academic Press.

Beckwith, L., Cohen, S.E., Kopp, C.B., Parmelee, A.H., & Marcy, T.G. (1976). Caregiver-infant interaction and early cognitive development in preterm infants. *Child Development, 47,* 579–587.

Beckwith, L., & Parmelee, A.H. (1986). EEG patterns of preterm infants, home environment, and later IQ. *Child Development, 57,* 777–789.

Berg, C.A., & Sternberg, R.J. (1985). Response to novelty: Continuity vs. discontinuity in the developmental course of intelligence. In H.W. Reese (Ed.), *Advances in child development and behavior, 19,* 1–47.

Bornstein, M., & Sigman, M.D. (1986). Continuity in mental development from infancy. *Child Development, 57,* 251–274.

Brennan, W.N., Ames, E.W., & Moore, R.W. (1966). Age differences in infant's attention to patterns of different complexities. *Science, 151,* 354–356.

Caron, R., & Caron, A. (1981). Processing of relational information as an index of infant risk. In S.L. Friedman & M. Sigman (Eds.), *Preterm birth and psychological development*. New York: Academic Press.

Cohen, S.E., & Parmelee, A.H. (1983). Prediction of five-year Stanford-Binet scores in preterm infants. *Child Development, 54,* 1242–1253.

Cohen, S.E., Parmelee, A.H., Beckwith, L., & Sigman, M. (1986). Cognitive development in preterm infants: Birth to 8 years. *Journal of Developmental and Behavioral Pediatrics, 7,* 102–110.

Cohen, S.E., Parmelee, A.H., Beckwith, L., & Sigman, M. (1992). Biological and social precursors of 12-year competence in children born preterm. In C. Greenbaum & J. Auerbach (Eds.), *Cross-national perspectives in children born at risk* (pp. 65-78). Norwood, NJ: Ablex Publishing Corp.

Cohen, S.E., Parmelee, A.H., Sigman, M., & Beckwith, L. (1988). Antecedents of school problems in children born preterm. *Journal of Pediatric Psychology, 13,* 493–508.

Colombo, J., & Mitchell, D.W. (1990). Individual differences in early visual attention: Fixation time and information processing. In J. Colombo & J. Fagen (Eds.), *Individual differences in infancy*. Hillsdale, NJ: Erlbaum.

Denenberg, V.H., & Thoman, E.B. (1981). Evidence for a functional role for active (REM) sleep in infancy. *Sleep, 41,* 185–191.

European Bulletin of Cognitive Psychology. (1988). 8, No. 5.

Fantz, R. (1965). Visual experience in infants: Decreased attention to familiar patterns relative to novel ones. *Science, 146,* 668–670.

Friedman, S.L., Jacobs, B.S., & Werthmann, M.W. (1981). Sensory processing in pre- and full-term infants in the neonatal period. In S.L. Friedman & M. Sigman (Eds.), *Preterm birth and psychological development*. San Francisco: Academic Press.

Kaufman, A.S. (1975). Factor analysis of the WISC-R at 11 age levels between 6½ and 16½ years. *Journal of Consulting & Clinical Psychology, 43,* 135–147.

Lécuyer, R. (1988). Please infant, can you tell me exactly what you are doing during a habituation experiment? *European Bulletin of Cognitive Psychology/Cahiers de Psychologie Cognitive, 8,* 476–481.

Lewis, M., Goldberg, S., & Campbell, S. (1969). A developmental study of information processing within the first three years of life: Response decrement to a redundant signal. *Monographs of the Society for Research in Child Development, 34.*

Malcuit, G., Pomerleau, A., & Lamarre, G. (1988). Habituation, visual fixation, and cognitive activity in infants: A critical analysis and attempt at a new formulation. *European Bulletin of Cognitive Psychology, 8,* 415–440.

Marr, D., & Sternberg, R.J. (1986). Analogical reasoning with nonentrenched concepts: Effects of conceptual novelty on gifted and non-gifted students. *Cognitive Development, 1,* 53–72.

Morrison, A.R. (1983). Paradoxical sleep and alert wakefullness: Variations on a theme. In M. Chase & E. Weitzman (Eds.), *Sleep disorders: basic and clinical research.* New York: Spectrum.

Neuchterlein, K.H. (1983). Signal detection in vigilance tasks and behavioral attributes among offspring of schizophrenic mothers and among hyperactive children. *Journal of Abnormal Psychology, 92,* 4–28.

Parmelee, A.H., Jr., & Garbanati, J.A. (1987). Clinical neurobehavioral aspects of state organization in newborn infants. In H. Yabuuchi, K. Watanabe, & S. Okada (Eds.), *Neonatal brain and behavior.* Nagoya, Japan: University of Nagoya Press.

Parmelee, A.H., Jr., Schulte, F.J., Akiyama, Y., Wenner, W.H., Schultz, M., & Stern, E. (1968). Maturation of EEG activity during sleep in premature infants. *EEG and Clinical Neurophysiology, 24,* 319–329.

Parmelee, A.H., & Sigman, M. (1983). Perinatal brain development and behavior. In M.M. Haith & J.J. Campos (Eds.), *Handbook of child psychology; Vol. II. Infancy and developmental psychology.* New York: Wiley.

Parmelee, A.H., & Stern, E. (1972). Development of states in infants. In C. Clemente, D. Purpura, & F. Meyers (Eds.), *Sleep and the maturing nervous system.* New York: Academic Press.

Rose, S.A. (1980). Enhancing visual recognition memory in preterm infants. *Development Psychology, 16,* 85–92.

Rose, S.A., Gottfried, A.W., & Bridger, W.H. (1979). Effects of haptic cues on visual recognition memory in full-term and preterm infants. *Infant Behavior and Development, 2,* 55–67.

Sigman, M. (1976). Early development of preterm and full-term infants: Exploratory behavior in eight-month olds. *Child Development, 47,* 606–612.

Sigman, M. (1983). Individual differences in infant attention: Relations to birth and intelligence at five years. In T. Field & A. Sostek (Eds.), *Infants born at risk: Physiological, perceptual and cognitive processes.* New York: Grune & Straton.

Sigman, M., Beckwith, L., Cohen, S.E., & Parmelee, A.H. (1989). Stability in the biosocial development of the child born preterm. In M. Bornstein & N. Krasnegor (Eds.), *Stability and continuity in mental development.* Hillsdale, NJ: Erlbaum.

Sigman, M., Cohen, S.E., Beckwith, L., & Parmelee, A.H. (1986). Infant attention in relation to intellectual abilities in childhood. *Developmental Psychology, 22,* 788–792.

Sigman, M., Cohen, S.E., Beckwith, L., Asarnow, R., & Parmelee, A.H. (in press). Continuity in cognitive abilities from infancy to 12 years of age. *Cognitive Development.*

Sigman, M., Kopp, C.B., Littman, B., & Parmelee, A.H. (1977). Infant visual attentiveness in relation to birth condition. *Developmental Psychology, 13,* 431–437.

Sigman, M., Kopp, C.B., Parmelee, A.H., & Jeffrey, W.E. (1973). Visual attention and neurological organization in neonates. *Child Development, 44,* 461–466.

Sigman, M., & Parmelee, A.H. (1974). Visual preferences of four-month-old premature and full-term infants. *Child Development, 45,* 959–965.

Wetherford, M., & Cohen, L. (1973). Developmental changes in infant visual preferences for novelty and familiarity. *Child Development, 74,* 418–424.

14
Further Investigations of Intellectual Status at Age 8 Years: I. Long-Term Consequences Into Adulthood. II. Neonatal Predictors.*

Jane V. Hunt, William H. Tooley, and Bruce A.B. Cooper

INTRODUCTION

Our longitudinal study of infants with birth weights less than 1,500 grams began in 1964, along with the introduction of neonatal intensive care. There were relatively few survivors during the first few years, but additional infants were enrolled continuously throughout the next two decades. By the time children reached 8 years of age they were well studied. Efforts were made to bring them in for medical examinations and developmental evaluations at least twice during the first year and annually thereafter to age 6 years. They were seen again, when possible, at 8, 11, and 14 years.

The follow-up of the very low-birthweight infants was considered important, not only to judge specific innovations in medical care of the newborn and the effects on later development, but also, in a more general way, to monitor the status of a new group of survivors with unknown potential. The increasing survival rate for those receiving neonatal intensive care created a population considered to be at risk for developmental problems, surviving only after a precarious start in life that may have resulted in brain damage.

Expectations from Earlier Studies

Prematurity, and especially extreme prematurity, was linked to intellectual disabilities and learning disorders long before the advent of modern neonatal care. One important investigator was Mary Shirley (1938), who, more than 50 years ago, described the intellectual, social, and personality attributes of preterm infants and young children compared with full-term counterparts. Shirley was aware of intellectual problems. In her paper she cited 12 earlier studies focusing on intellectual development. One study (Brander, 1937) examined 376 school

* This chapter is dedicated to the memory of Donya Harvin. She assessed the children's psychological development, and many of her insights found their way into the research.

Research reported in this chapter was supported in part by Pediatric Pulmonary SCOR, HL 27356.

age children and Shirley noted a direct relationship between birth weight and intelligence: "Below 1500 grams birth weight no case of normal intelligence" (p. 116, Table 1).

Shirley was interested in pursuing reports of incidental findings that ascribed special attributes to preterm infants and children. Preterm infants had been included in the longitudinal studies conducted at the Center for Child Health and Development, Harvard School of Public Health. She examined records for 65 younger children, ages 6 to 30 months and for 30 older children, ages 3½ to 6 years. She noted, "a constellation of traits that has crystallized more or less of its own accord out of incidental notes and cumulative observations made on premature babies and young children" (p. 116). She characterized her findings as a behavior syndrome of prematurity, and described it thus:

> Keen auditory and visual sensitivity or interest; lingual-motor, manual, and locomotor difficulties manifested by speech difficulties, choppy, slap-dash manipulation, and lunging, clumsy gait or overcaution in motor pursuits; hyperactivity or sluggishness and occasional tremor; difficulties in sphincter control. Emotional and social features of the syndrome are: short, flitting attention; high susceptibility to distractions; high irascibility; stubbornness and negativism; shyness and overdependence on the mother; and possibly high and versatile aesthetic interests. Boys manifest the syndrome somewhat more completely than girls. (p. 126)

Many of the characteristics described by Shirley are familiar today and have been documented repeatedly. Motor awkwardness, speech problems, attention deficit disorder, and hyperactivity are problems reported for low birthweight and other categories of high-risk infants and young children. Research efforts during the past decades have focused on determining the problems that occur frequently in high risk populations, and on finding remediating or preventative intervention programs.

Shirley anticipated contemporary interests by her observations about the probable importance of the postnatal environment for some of the characteristics she noted for preterm children. Remarking on the dual events of social deprivation of the newborn and subsequent maternal overprotection, she suggested that the family environment could account for most of the social and emotional differences of prematures. The interaction of special deficits and environment was noted in the following example: "Poor motor capacity combined with high maternal solicitude may explain the premature's greater tendency to seek help from adults in minor difficulties and to give up readily in the face of slight adversity." She evoked the image of the vulnerable young child.

Cecil Drillien was another early investigator of the long-term status of preterm infants. She examined Edinburg infants with birth weights of 3 lbs (1,360 gm) or less (Drillien, 1958) and found a high incidence of developmental problems. When these children were evaluated at school age (Drillien, 1961), she found that 50% of those located were ineducable in normal school because of physical and/or mental handicap, 25% required special education within the normal school, and the remaining 25% ranged from low-average to superior in ability. She reported a high incidence of physical defects (53%), and 78% were reported to have behavior problems. She found an increasing incidence of severe handicap in the later born children, associated with the increased survival rate, "which, in turn has probably resulted from improved techniques in premature baby care, more adequate antenatal care of mothers, and possibly from modern methods of treating infertility" (1961, p. 463). Drillien's reports were well known to neonatologists introducing intensive care to newborn nurseries. The spectre of latent disabilities (Francis-Williams, 1970; Fitzhardinge & Ramsay, 1973; Francis-Williams & Davies, 1974) gave impetus to the establishment of longitudinal "follow-up" studies of very-low-birthweight infants.

Early Reports of Outcome

fIn 1974 we reported the outcome of 63 children, 40 of whom had been born before 1969 (Hunt, Harvin, Kennedy, & Tooley, 1974). Outcome at ages 3 through 7 years was reported: 39% were normal, 32% had normal IQs but some evidence for mild to moderate intellectual problems, 29% had scores in the borderline or retarded range. No child in the low IQ categories had an infant IQ above 90 at 12 months; based on group comparisons at 12 months we predicted that 15% of the infants born in 1969–1972 would have low IQ scores in early childhood. We concluded that the incidence of serious developmental problems might be declining, even though new treatments for neonatal respiratory disease, instituted in 1969, had clearly improved survival rates for very low birthweight infants (Tooley, 1979). The evidence for a decline in the incidence of serious handicaps was not supported by additional enrollments of new infants into the study, but survival rates continued to improve.We found that the incidence of handicap stayed approximately the same, even though the survivors included more of the very small and very sick infants (Hunt, Tooley, & Harvin, 1982).

In 1972–1975 we studied 65 infants by monthly visits to the home for repeated assessments during the first year of life. All but 2 appeared to be developing normally by the end of the first year if full allowance was made for the degree of prematurity. Apparent differences in development among groups differing in gestational age were eliminated when test scores were corrected for prematurity (Hunt & Rhodes, 1977). However, as noted, we had determined that the full range of handicaps was considerably greater when evaluations were made in childhood than when infant data were the basis for a report.

Concerns for the quality of life of the recipients of neonatal intensive care were being raised in medical journals and in the popular press, and the costs of providing such care on a broad basis were being questioned. In 1974 we participated in the deliberations of a conference organized to explore the ethical issues and some of the policy implications of neonatal intensive care (Jonsen &

Garland, 1976). Our contribution to the deliberations was to present evidence that most handicaps were not detected at birth, or even during the first year of life, so decisions to provide or withhold special care could not be made on the basis of behavioral criteria. We also noted that some of the most serious medical problems were not always associated with poor outcome; some of the older children in the study who were developing normally at school age had been among the sickest and smallest at birth. We took the position that no basis yet existed for reasonable predictions about individual infants during the first weeks of life.

An interest in issues related to individual differences guided our research designs and analyses. Figure 1 (from Hunt, 1979) illustrates the difficulty in predicting any but the most severe childhood problems from infant developmental test scores. At 6 and 12 months most of the infants who went on to have intellectual difficulties at 4 to 6 years of age could not be distinguished from those infants who were destined to be entirely normal at the older ages. By age 2 years the developmental test score (IQ from the Cattell Infant Test) was beginning to differentiate between the two groups of children, but individual prediction remained difficult in most instances. Not until the children reached age 3 years did the IQs (Stanford-Binet, L-M) closely approximate those that would be achieved at 4 to 6 years of age. (Scores shown in Figure 1 were adjusted for prematurity at all ages.)

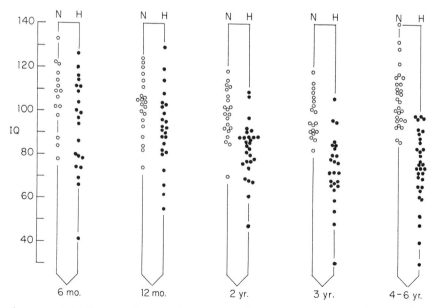

Figure 1.   Distribution of mental test scores at four younger ages for children also tested at 4–6 years; comparisons at each age between groups that were normal (N) or handicapped (H) at 4–6 years. (From Hunt, 1979, reprinted by permission.)

I. LONG TERM CONSEQUENCES INTO ADULTHOOD

Intellectual problems in childhood can be defined at two levels of reality. The first is the demonstration of a disability, usually by standardized testing of mental abilities; the second is the determination of the academic and social significance of the problem that has been identified. The long-term importance of the disability is of consequence, and on both levels. Disabilities may be transient or may persist. However, a transient disability may affect a child's attitude towards academic work long after the skills in question have reached acceptable levels. For example, immaturity in visual-motor integration skills may delay the acquisition of reading and writing; the child may experience considerable frustration and withdraw effort.

We have been interested in determining the kinds of intellectual and academic disabilities evident at age 8 years in our group of very low-birthweight preterm infants, and in following the educational experiences of the children into adolescence and young adulthood. We wondered what special educational interventions had been encountered during the early school years and what significance the problems determined by test scores at 8 years of age have had on subsequent educational progress and special educational needs. Further, we were interested in obtaining the opinions of our study members and their parents regarding problems, interventions, and outcomes. In this section of the chapter we will describe the investigation of 8-year-old outcomes and report the findings gathered by questionnaire from study members at ages 11 through 24 years. The children came, on average, from fairly advantaged environments, with parents who had received some education beyond high school. Therefore, their educational histories generally reflect middle class, "mainstream" experiences.

Outcome at 8 Years

We were interested in determining how the vulnerability of high-risk infants and preschool children translates into intellectual and educational problems during the school years. Originally we had included varied groups of high-risk infants who were followed longitudinally to determine developmental progress. These groups included very low birth weight infants (at or below 1,500 g), low-birthweight infants (1,501–1,750 g), larger birthweight preterm infants with hyaline membrane disease, and infants who had received intrauterine transfusions. The problems noted at preschool ages were reminiscent of those described by Shirley. The kinds of problems noted did not vary according to specific high risk group, but the incidence of all problems at 4 to 6 years was greatest for the group of children who had birth weights at or below 1,500 grams.

At 8 years of age the children were administered tests of mental abilities and academic achievement, along with other assessments, ratings, and information generated from parent interviews. Our study of intellectual outcomes focused initially on the evidence that could be derived from 8-year test scores. Although we knew the children and their families well by that age, the clinical notes and ratings were difficult to present in a manner that could readily be replicated by others.

The detailed description of the determination of specific outcomes from test scores has been reported (Hunt, Cooper, & Tooley, 1988). Test scores available were those from the Wechsler Intelligence Scale for Children—Revised (WISC-R), the Bender Gestalt Test of Visual-Motor Integration (Bender), and the Wide Range Achievement Test (WRAT). We reported the outcomes for 108 very low birth weight children (BW ≤ 1500g). Approximately 80% of the children had full-scale WISC-R IQs at or above 85 (normal range or above). Three disability groups were determined within this normal IQ category: Low Visual-Motor (Bender score 15 or more points below IQ), Low Performance (WISC-R Performance IQ 15 or more points below Verbal IQ), and Low Verbal (WISC-R Verbal IQ 15 or more points below Performance IQ). Children with IQs below 85 were categorized by IQ into Low (IQ 70–84) and Very Low (IQ below 70). The proportions in each group were: No Disability, 36.1%; Low Visual-Motor, 21.4%; Low Performance, 12.0%; Low Verbal, 12.0%; Low IQ, 13.9%; Very Low IQ, 4.6%.

Learning disabilities also were defined by test scores. A learning disability was determined when one or more of the WRAT scores was at least 1½ standard deviations below the child's IQ (in this instance, 22 points). Such problems were defined for 16.7% of the children, including 10.3% of the No Disabilities group, 34.8% of the Low Visual-Motor group, 30.8% of the Low Performance group, 7.7% of the Low Verbal group, and 6.7% of the Low IQ group. The higher proportions in the Low Visual-Motor and Low Performance groups added some external validity to the importance of those outcome categories. The Low Verbal group had a lower average IQ than the other groups with normal scores, perhaps reducing the likelihood of having as great a proportion of individuals with the large discrepancy between IQ and achievement.

Evidence for Continuity in Specific Disabilities

Because the disabilities defined at 8 years were based on test scores and score differences, the possibility remained that these disabilities were age or test specific and not necessarily indicative of genuine functional problems. However, some evidence for continuity at younger ages was determined (Hunt & Cooper, 1989). When the Low Verbal and Low Performance groups were compared with the No Disability outcome group for specific performance on the Stanford-Binet Intelligence Test at younger ages, problems with verbal items were found for the Low Verbal group and problems with performance items for the Low Performance group at all ages from 3 through 6 years. The score discrepancies between Verbal and Performance IQ on the WISC-R at 8 years appeared to identify genuine and deeply rooted differences, at least when comparing the disability groups with the group with no such score discrepancies. The selected discrepancy of 15 points was chosen because the probability of such a score difference is less than 5%. As noted, the incidence was 24% in the very low-birthweight group.

Educational Histories

Questionnaires were sent to study members who were in the age range 11 to 24 years to determine past and present educational experiences, including any remedial assistance that had been given. Efforts were made to contact all very low-birthweight study members who had been tested at age 8 years, including the 108 whose data comprised the analysis of outcomes described previously (all of whom had been born at the same hospital where they received neonatal care) and an additional 37 children who were born elsewhere and transferred to the same hospital during the first hours of life. Study members were encouraged to consult with their parents in providing the information, and many did. In fact, some of the questionnaires were completed by parents. When questionnaires were not returned, telephone calls were used to obtain information and responses were gathered for 101 of the 145 children. The proportions responding in each outcome group varied from 50% (4 of 8) in the Very low IQ group to 93% (14 of 15) in the Low Performance group.

Questions were asked about grade retention and about special educational assistance or placements. The information is summarized in Table 1. Delayed school entry or repeated kindergarten was reported from 16 children, attesting to the early recognition of immaturity or special needs in many instances. Thirty-two children experienced some grade retention, including 17 (35.42%) in the No Disabilities outcome group of whom 5 repeated more than one grade. Proportions with grade retention were approximately the same for all outcome groups, with the exception of the Low Performance group. That group, perhaps because of normal or better than normal language ability, reported a lower retention rate (1 child in 14).

Special educational assistance also is summarized in Table 1. Overall, 42 children received some special assistance and 20 of those had a special teacher or class. Fifteen children (31.25%) in the No Disabilities group had some special assistance, although three of those received only speech therapy. Proportions were comparable for the Low Visual-Motor outcome group and slightly higher for all others. Noteworthy was the high proportion of children in the Low Performance group who received special educational assistance (50%), in contrast to the low proportion with grade retention (7%).

A small proportion of children (14.85%) reported both grade retention and special educational assistance, and 58.42% reported some intervention of one or both kinds. The proportion was higher for children in outcome categories with greatest problems, as would be expected. However, the outcome categories,

Table 1. Special Educational Interventions Recollected at Ages 11–24 Years

	Outcome Groups (8 Years)						
	No[1] Disab. (N = 48)	Low[2] V-M (N = 9)	Low[3] Perf. (N = 14)	Low[4] Verb. (N = 9)	Low[5] IQ (N = 17)	V. Low[6] IQ (N = 4)	Total (N = 101)
RETENTION							
Delayed Entry/Repeated Kg.	7	2	1	2	4	—	16
Repeated Primary (1st-3rd)	10	1	—	—	—	1	12
Repeated Intermediate or Above	5	1	—	—	2	1	9
Repeated More than 1 level	5	—	1	—	—	—	5
Total Children	17	4	1	2	6	2	32
Group %	35.42	44.44	7.14	22.22	35.29	50.00	31.68
SPECIAL EDUCATION							
Mathematics	2	2	1	—	1	—	6
Language Arts	7	2	1	—	1	—	11
Special Teacher/Class	5	—	3	3	7	2	20
Speech	4	1	2	2	2	—	11
More than one	3	2	—	—	1	—	6
Total Children	15	3	7	5	10	2	42
Group %	31.25	33.33	50.00	55.56	58.82	50.00	41.58
Retention and Special Education	7	2	—	1	4	1	15
Group %	14.58	22.22	—	11.11	23.53	16.67	14.85
SOME INTERVENTION							
(Retention and/or Special Ed.)	25	5	8	6	12	3	59
Group %	52.08	55.56	57.14	66.67	70.59	75.00	58.42

Outcome Groups (see text):
1. No Disabilities
2. Low Visual-Motor
3. Low Performance
4. Low Verbal
5. Low IQ
6. Very Low IQ

defined by test scores are obviously not closely associated with school problems, given that over half of the No Disabilities group reported some intervention. Conversely, one individual in the Very Low IQ outcome group at age 8 years reported no interventions and average grades of C in high school.

Because the study members reported directly in most cases, there remains the possibility that some interventions were not reported. For example, delayed school entry and early grade retentions or special education might not have been remembered or even known. We cannot be sure that all respondents consulted their parents as requested. Therefore, the amount of educational intervention may be underreported. In any event, by report a high proportion of the very low-birthweight group found its way into special educational circumstances. The 42 children (41.58%) who reported no interventions had varied comments. Some reported attendance in gifted programs; two parents with children in the low IQ outcome category regretted that no special intervention programs had been available (children received schooling in a wide geographic area, including both urban and rural settings).

We asked about the value of the interventions that the study members reported. The children themselves (some now young adults) overwhelmingly endorsed the special teachers, and one study member commented, "repeating the fourth grade was the smartest thing I ever did." Parents were mixed in their reactions, some suggesting that the child felt stigmatized by the special educational attention. The contrast between parents and children in retrospective memories of special education and grade retention is only suggested in our data, but raises an interesting possibility regarding differences in the perception of social problems associated with special education.

Adult Outcome

The most compelling information gleaned from the questionnaires was the current circumstances of those who were 18 years of age or older and who were taking their place in adult society. We had 20 respondents in the adult category, 10 males and 10 females. Their reports were extremely interesting, particularly in light of the high incidence of educational interventions reported.

The 20 young adults, ages 18 to 24 years, were distributed among the 8-year outcome groups as follows: No Disabilities, 12; Low Visual-Motor, 2; Low Performance, 4; Low Verbal, 1; Low IQ, 1; Very Low IQ, 0.

We compared the level of educational attainment for the young adult group with that of their own parents (see Table 2). For the parents, education levels used were (a) less than high school graduate, (b) high school graduate, (c) high school graduate plus some college or technical education (high school plus), and (d) college graduate or higher. Values were derived by averaging the educational levels of both parents, or in the case of a single mother by using her educational level. The mean rating for the parents of the young adults was 2.6, comparable to

Table 2.   Education Comparisons Between 20 High Risk Young Adults & Their Parents

Parents (average per pair)			Children		
Rating	Description	Number	Rating	Description	Number
1	Less than High School Graduate	2	1	Less than High School Graduate	3
2	High School Graduate	9	2	High School Graduate	4
3	High School Plus	4	3	Attending or Attended Community College	7
4	College Graduate or Higher	5	4	Attending or Graduate from a Major University	6
	Average Rating:	2.6		Average Rating:	2.8

that determined for the entire sample at 8 years and indicating that, when averaged, parents had some education beyond high school graduation.

Analogous levels were determined for the young adult group as follows: (a) less than high school graduate, (b) high school graduate, (c) attending or dropped community college, and (d) attending or graduated from a major university. As shown in Table 2, three individuals had not graduated from high school; one was still in school at age 18 and two girls were out of school and raising children (one hoped to return to school). Four high school graduates were noted, all of whom had jobs. Seven of the young adults were attending or had attended a community college and 6 others were attending or were graduated from a major university. The average educational rating of 2.8 was comparable to that of the parent group.

An inspection of individual cases was equally encouraging. The study member in the Low-IQ category at 8 years had graduated from high school and was successfully running a small business; the individual in the Low-Verbal category at 8 years was attending a community college and taking business and computer courses; neither of the aforementioned had reported any educational intervention. The Low Performance group was divided between three individuals who were and had been doing very well academically—two had been in honors programs and attending major universities and one was on the honor roll in high school; the fourth individual had considerable difficulty with mathematics but persevered and graduated from a two-year college program. The special ability in verbal tests at 8 years may have predicted advantage for three and possibly a compensatory factor for the fourth individual. Two young women in the Low Verbal category at 8 years reported no educational interventions, average grades in high school and, currently, office jobs and marriage.

The No Disabilities group of 12 individuals included 6 who reported educational interventions and 6 who did not. Those with interventions included some who had severe learning disabilities. One woman who had significant hearing loss was successfully completing university studies; three others had graduated from high school, not without difficulties, and were employed in semiskilled jobs; and two had not graduated from high school.

The remaining six individuals in the No Disabilities outcome group did not report any educational interventions. One was still completing high school, getting average grades; one was a student at a 2-year college with plans to transfer and continue his education; two were students at major universities, and one had graduated from a major university and was employed in a highly skilled occupation. The sixth individual was taking time off to prepare for "the world's toughest triatholon." One of the university students, with a major in Environmental Studies, reported he was about to begin field work in the South Chinese rainforest.

The individual histories appear to corroborate the objective evidence in Table 2 that these study members, despite their extreme prematurity at birth were in many ways typical young adults in American middle-class society. They were born from 1964 to 1971, an era that saw many changes in neonatal intensive care but still an era in which the very-low-birthweight infant was at high risk for developmental problems. And, in fact, 8 of the 20 young adults (40%) did report some special educational intervention such as grade retention or special programs. However, most had successfully pursued their educational and occupational goals. Persistent handicaps that may well have been the result of extreme prematurity and its complications included one incidence of deafness (with good intellectual abilities) and one incidence of learning disabilities that were so disabling that they have continued to present difficulties beyond the period of formal education. There were no surprises in the permanence of the disabilities of these two individuals. What is surprising is the discovery that, of those reporting, the incidence of special difficulties dropped from 40% during school years to 10% upon completion of formal education.

Some Comments about the Nonparticipants

As noted, questionnaires were completed for 101 of 145 study members tested at age 8 years. Twenty-nine individuals were lost to the study and could not be contacted regarding the survey. They came from all 8-year outcome groups and across all birth years included, and no trend or pattern was discernible. Fifteen individuals either directly refused to participate (three instances) or failed to return the questionnaire, even though, in some cases they agreed to do so over the telephone. A number of individuals were interviewed directly by telephone, either the study member or, in his or her absence a parent. The 15 who refused, either actively or passively, had a distribution by outcome groups and by year of birth similar to that of the lost group, and again no trend was noted. Of the three outright refusals, two were made by parents of study members and the third by a 12-year-old girl who protested that we were always expecting something to be wrong with her. It would be interesting to know how many of the other study members shared her point of view. There was no indication, based on outcome categories at 8 years, that the refusers had any greater likelihood of educational problems.

II. NEONATAL PREDICTORS

The importance of illness and treatment effects on outcome was a continuing research theme in our longitudinal study. Early comparisons between infants with very low birth weights who did or did not have neonatal hyaline membrane disease revealed significant IQ differences, particularly when infants who were *small for gestational age* (SGA) were excluded from analysis. The SGA infants tended to have less illness at birth, but the underlying conditions leading to the SGA condition appeared to leave that group equally vulnerable to developmental problems. Because our major research interest was to identify neonatal physiological states that led to handicap we usually eliminated the SGA infants from prediction analyses.

Figure 2 shows a typical comparison of infants with and without neonatal hyaline membrane disease, in this instance with IQ at 8 years of age. The difference in the two distributions as shown was not significant, but the average IQ difference between the groups was. Extreme scores, shown in Figure 2, accounted for the mean score difference. The broad overlap in outcomes between groups indicated that more precise definitions of neonatal illness were needed.

In an effort to refine our study of the effects of hyaline membrane disease on mental development, we next examined some of the specific physiological complications common to that illness that might be expected to impact directly

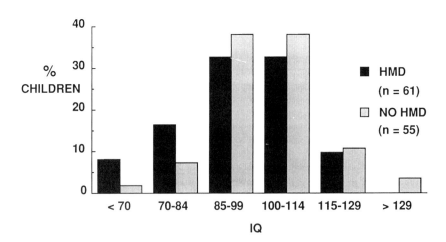

Figure 2.   IQ comparisons at 8 years of age for very low birthweight children who did or did not have neonatal hyaline membrane disease; each IQ category represents one standard deviation of scores from the WISC-R.

on brain function. Variables selected were those that were available from infants' hospital records and that had been found to have major effects on central nervous system structures in animal models of asphyxia and sustained hypoxia (Myers, 1977).

We examined blood values of acid/base balance (pH), oxygen levels, and carbon dioxide levels (Hunt, 1976). Absolute values were not expected to be as important as the duration of time at the abnormal levels, and so we generated minutes per level as variables. When infant developmental test scores at 12 months were examined, duration of very high blood levels of carbon dioxide was found to be more closely related to test scores than was duration of very high blood levels of oxygen (induced during therapy) for infants who had some minutes in both states. Generating reliable physiological variables from available data was extremely difficult and costly, and the number of possible variables to be examined was very large. The method was put aside, awaiting some evidence that might justify investigating other specific physiological variables.

The Illness Rating

Our next approach was an attempt to capture the clinical knowledge of physicians regarding the seriousness of each infant's neonatal illnesses. The neonatologist who knew the children best and had attended most of them during neonatal life reviewed all medical records, then rated each infant according to the overall severity of illness. A 7-point scale was used, with a rating of 1 indicating no illness and a rating of 7 indicating illness so severe that the infant barely survived. The reliability of the rating was assessed by comparison with ratings by another neonatologist who had no information about any of the infants prior to reviewing the medical records. The correlation between the two sets of ratings was .91, suggesting a common universe of clinical agreement about the relative severity of neonatal illness.

We examined the association of the illness rating and our measure of family functioning, the averaged parent education rating, with the intellectual outcomes determined at 8 years of age (Hunt et al., 1988). We had anticipated that some outcomes might be more closely associated with the level of neonatal illness than others. However, we found that the level of neonatal illness predicted whether or not the infant was likely to have *any* of the intellectual problems determined at age 8 years, but whether those problems would be moderate, with IQ in the normal range, or severe, with IQ below normal was predominantly a function of the level of parent education (see Figure 3). In the figure, both the illness ratings and parent education ratings were dichotomized into low and high values. The illness rating was associated with the proportion of children with any problems at 8 years; a larger proportion of children in the group with low illness (none to mild) had normal IQs and no other problems. However, for those with moderate to severe neonatal illness, the extent of the intellectual problem at 8 years—

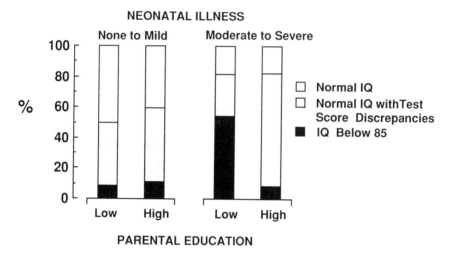

Figure 3. Comparisons between ratings of neonatal illness and of parent education on intellectual outcomes at 8 years of age.

normal IQ with score discrepancies (low verbal, low performance, low visual-motor), or with IQ below normal—appeared to be associated with the parent education rating.

The influence of the child's family on intellectual status at 8 years of age was not surprising, but the association of neonatal illness with outcome at 8 years was noteworthy. The implication of these findings is that remediation through environmental experience is not only possible but very likely a major determinant of the long-term effects of severe neonatal stress to the central nervous system. However, the caveat remains that the likelihood of having no intellectual problem at 8 years was greatly improved when there had been a less stressful neonatal course. Prevention of neonatal complications is still of paramount importance in improving the outcome of the very low-birthweight infant.

Specific Neonatal Predictors

The success of the illness rating in predicting outcome at 8 years resulted in renewed interest in finding and testing those neonatal variables that were bound up in the more general rating. Our approach to this effort was to list those neonatal conditions that had the most serious clinical implications, and then to determine what evidence we had from neonatal records that pertained to such conditions. No effort was made to be comprehensive in listing all possible available neonatal variables because such composite risk scales had proven to be ineffective in predicting subsequent mental ability (Sigman & Parmelee, 1979;

Stave & Ruvalo, 1980; Vohr, Oh, Rosenfield, & Cowett, 1979; Rose & Wallace, 1985).

We further elected not to attempt to predict the specific 8-year outcomes described previously (Hunt et al., 1988) because of restrictions in sample size and the large number of predictor variables. Predicting with such specificity appeared to be unlikely, given the broad variability within and among neonatal factors and the subsequent broad range of social and educational experiences. The nonspecific association between IQ at 8 years and overall severity of neonatal illness was siginficant and independent of the highly significant correlation between parent education level and IQ. Therefore, we selected IQ at 8 years as the outcome measure for subsequent prediction studies.

Fifty-four variables were derived from pertinent neonatal data. Six were measurements of respiratory physiology, 13 were related to treatment regimens for respiratory disease, 5 represented the numbers of blood gases and x-rays taken, 2 were for Apgar scores, 13 pertained to nutritional status (8 associated with calories and weight gain, 5 with protein intake), 4 variables were related to fluid balance, and 11 indicated the presence of specific complications during neonatal life (intracranial hemorrhage, infection, patent dectus arteriosis, etc.).

Selection of Predictors

Of the 54 variables, 19 had simple correlations with IQ at 8 years of .20 or greater and were considered potential predictors. The variables are listed in Table 3. Some were essentially redundant and/or highly intercorrelated. To reduce the number of predictors, we selected representative variables from the domains of illness and nutrition. The variables chosen for illness were, *lowest pH overall*, *total number of blood gases*, *total number of x-rays*, *maximum inspiratory pressure on mechanical ventilation (cm H₂O)*, and *maximum expiratory pressure on mechanical ventilation (cm H₂O) (correlation with IQ = .19)*. To represent nutritional status we selected *percent of birth weight on day 14*, *days to reach 1.5 g protein/kg*, and *days to reach 75 calories/Kg*.

Selection of Sample

The sample from which we obtained the initial correlations (N = 124) included infants who were born outside of our hospital and transferred for neonatal intensive care.[1] In addition, the infants were born over a period of 14 years (1965–1978), during which time treatment of lung disease improved. Important treatment changes were introduced in 1969. Therefore, we excluded infants from

---

[1] We used our complete sample to obtain the best estimate of the correlations between IQ and our neonatal variables for purposes of variable selection only.

Table 3. Correlations of Neonatal Variables with WISC-R
Full-Scale IQ at Age 8 Years

Neonatal Variable Set	r
RESPIRATORY PHYSIOLOGY	
Lowest pH overall	.23
Total hours $FIO_2 > 60\%$	−.21
TREATMENT FOR RESPIRATORY DISEASE	
Maximum inspiratory pressure, cm H_2O	−.22
BLOOD GASES AND X-RAYS	
Total number of x-rays	−.25
Total number of blood gases	−.25
Total number of blood gases, week 1	−.23
Total number of blood gases, month 1	−.23
NUTRITION: CALORIES	
Days to reach 50 cal/Kg	−.30
Percent of birth weight on day 14	.29
Days to reach 75 cal/Kg	−.29
Days to reach birth weight	−.25
Mean calories, week 2 (g/Kg/day)	.23
Mean calories, week 1 (g/Kg/day)	.22
Days to reach 100 cal/Kg	−.20
NUTRITION: PROTEIN	
Days to reach 1.5 g protein/Kg	−.32
Days to reach 1 g protein/Kg	−.23
Mean protein, week 1 (g/Kg/day)	.20
FLUID BALANCE	
Mean urine for days 2 & 3 (cc/Kg/day)	.24
APGAR AT 5 MINUTES	.22

our predictive analyses who were outborn or born prior to 1969, and those who were small for gestational age (birthweight by gestational age < 3% by California standards; Williams, 1976). These deletions left 65 infants, born between 1969 and 1978.

We next added 51 infants for our predictive analyses who had also been tested at age 8 years, and who were followed under our revised protocol that began midyear 1978. The addition of this second group allowed us to examine the replicability of our prediction. (All had birthweights at or below 1,500 grams, were born between 1978 and 1981 at our hospital, and were not small for gestational age.)

Simple Correlations

Pearson correlations of the selected predictors with IQ for the earlier born group of 65 children, the later born group of 51 children, and the total group of 116 are presented in Table 4. Values are given for simple correlations of the predictors

Table 4. Pearson Correlations (r) and Semipartial Correlations (sr) between WISC-R IQ at age 8 Years and Parent Education, Illness and Nutrition Predictors; Correlations are for 2 Cohorts, 1969–78 (original) and 1978–81 (replication), and for combined samples (1969–1981)

	Year of Birth					
	1969–1978		1978–1981		1969–1981	
	(N = 65)		(N = 51)		(N = 116)	
	r	sr	r	sr	r	sr
EDUC	.46[a]		.33[d]		.39[a]	
TXRAYS	− .25[d]	− .30[c]	− .35[c]	− .37[c]	− .30[b]	− .35[a]
TOTBG	− .21[e]	− .28[d]	− .34[d]	− .41[c]	− .27[c]	− .34[b]
PIPMV	− .18	− .21[e]	− .27[d]	− .31[d]	− .21[d]	− .24[c]
PEEPMV	− .12	− .15	− .27[d]	− .36[c]	− .16[e]	− .20[d]
LOPHALL	.12	.22[e]	.12	.15	.11	.18[e]
PCTWT14	.33[c]	.27[d]	.16	.30[d]	.26[c]	.30[b]
DTO75C	− .33[c]	− .30[c]	− .19	− .24[c]	− .27[d]	− .29[c]
DTO15P	− .30[d]	− .30[c]	− .15	− .24[e]	− .24[c]	− .29[c]

Family functioning:
EDUC: average of parents' education level

Illness variables:
TXRAYS: total number of x-rays
TOTBG: total number of blood gases
PIPMV: maximum inspiratory pressure on mechanical ventilation (cm H_2O)
PEEPMV: maximum expiratory pressure on mechanical ventilation (cm H_2O)
LOPHALL: lowest pH overall

Nutrition variables:
PCTWT14:   percent of birth weight on day 14
DTO75C: days to reach 75 g calories/Kg
DTO15P: days to reach 1.5 g protein/Kg

[a]$p < .0001$, [b]$p < .001$, [c]$p < .01$, [d]$p < .05$, [e]$p < .10$

with WISC-R Full Scale IQ at age 8 years and for the semipartial correlations of the predictors with IQ, with the parent education variable partialed out of IQ only.

The Role of Parent Education as a Predictor

It may be noted in Table 4 that the semipartial correlations between the predictors and IQ (when the variance shared with parents' education is removed) were generally larger than the simple correlations. This indicates that education acted as a suppressor variable in the relation between the neonatal predictors and IQ. That is, direct effects of neonatal illness on IQ were modified by the Parent Education variable in an independent manner. The Parent Education variable was uncorrelated with all the neonatal predictors, and so the variance in IQ that was predicted by parents' education was basically irrelevant to the relations between

IQ and the illness and nutrition variables. Removing the variance in IQ that was predicted by education provided a more accurate estimate of the true relationships between IQ at age 8 years and the illness and nutrition predictors, as shown by the semipartial correlations.

Factor Analysis

We submitted the 8 variables selected as illness and nutrition predictors for the total group ($N = 116$) to principal factor analysis with varimax rotation.[2] This analysis produced two principal factors representing illness and nutrition. (Squared multiple correlations were used as prior communality estimates, resulting in two principal factors. The highest structure coefficients for two factors were clearly consistent with the illness and nutrition variable sets, thus validating our ad hoc classifications.)

Prediction Analyses

We used multiple regression analysis to predict 8-year IQs of the 65 infants from our original sample. We regressed IQ scores on parents' education level, the illness and nutrition factors, and the interaction of the illness and nutrition factors. The result was a multiple $R = .57$, $F (4,60) = 7.39$, $p < .0001$. After controlling for parents' education, which predicted 22% of the variance in IQ scores in this reduced sample, illness and nutrition factors predicted an additional 9% of the total variance in IQ scores, and the interaction contributed an additional 3% of the variance. The adjusted R-squared $= .29$.

Interpretation of the results indicated that higher IQ was predicted by parents' higher education, less neonatal illness, more rapid nutritional gains, and a lower interaction component (of the illness and nutrition factors).

We examined the replicability of our prediction by regressing 8-year IQs for our more recent group of 51 children who were born between 1978 and 1981. For this group, the result was a multiple $R = .52$, $F (3, 47) = 5.71$, $p < .002$. Parent education predicted 11% of the variance in IQ, and the illness and nutrition principal factors predicted an additional 16% variance in IQ. The interaction between illness and nutrition factors was not significant for this group. The adjusted R-squared was .22.

The replication of the prediction analysis with a separate group of children provided strong evidence that the neonatal variables selected have important long-term implications for IQ in the very low birth weight population. The bivariate plot for IQ vs. predicted IQ (from the composite of parent education,

---

[2] Again, the use of the larger group provided the best estimates for the factors to be used in the predictive analyses. Although this analysis included both the earlier born and later born children, note that this analysis did *not* involve our criterion variable, IQ at 8 years.

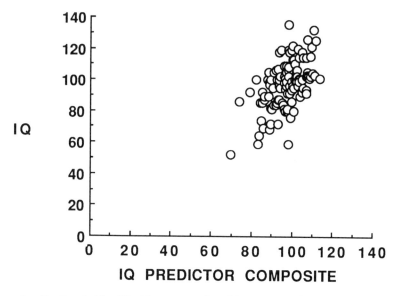

Figure 4. Scatterplot for IQ at 8 years predicted by a composite of neonatal illness and nutrition factors and parent education rating.

nutrition, and illness variables) is shown in Figure 4 for the combined group of 116 children ($R = .54$, $F (4,111) = 11.32$, $p < .0001$).

DISCUSSION

In the two sections of this chapter we have set forth a sampling from more than two decades of research with very low-birthweight preterm infants who received neonatal intensive care in our University hospital. Our focus has been on the long-term effects of neonatal events and the further definition of those events into medically useful predictors of later status. Our bias has always been to under-stand individual differences, and to study development in all aspects—not only mental development, but health, physical growth, educational progress, social and emotional development, and family functioning. However, the most press-ing question, and the one that has received most support over the years has been around the issues of long-term handicaps in mental abilities.

We have examined the intellectual status of very low birth weight infants at 8 years of age, when the children were already enrolled in school and beginning to move through the educational systems in their communities. In this chapter we have examined the relations between the kinds of intellectual problems defined at 8 years and educational experiences, including grade retention and special educational assistance of all kinds that were reported by the children when they were 11 to 24 years old. Our definitions of intellectual problems at age 8 were based strictly on test scores and score discrepancies, a tactic that encourages replication by others but necessarily omits an important body of information gathered at annual evaluations. Issues of social and emotional development, family functioning, and detailed information on learning disabilities were not addressed here.

The high proportion of special educational attention reported by our study members and their parents is noteworthy. Surprisingly, half the children who appeared intellectually normal by test score criteria (the No Disabilities outcome group at 8 years) reported some educational intervention, and the proportions were even greater for those who had been defined as having problems at 8 years. As noted, our children came from predominantly middle-class families and attended typical schools throughout northern California. We can assume with some confidence that the very-low-birthweight population did have an impact on the educational system, often requiring special interventions in school.

The status of those study members who had reached at least 18 years of age gave a different, and more hopeful picture of the very long-term outcome of the high-risk population. Here we began to see that either educational interventions had provided much that was required for ultimate academic success, or that, once the educational process was completed the individuals blended into society without incident. The exceptions were few. The young adults appeared to be at least equalling the educational attainments of their parents. This evidence for growth and resiliency even beyond age 8 years sounds a cautious note for investigators who base predictions on behavioral evidence determined very early in life.

Our data also testify to the importance of the child's family circumstances in guiding ultimate development. We were very fortunate, given our special interest in predicting the effects of neonatal events, that our children were reared predominantly in nurturing family environments. Even so, the most salient predictor of IQ at 8 years was our marker variable for the family milieu, averaged parent education. The correlation (.39) for the whole group of 116 children was comparable to that expected for low-risk middle-class populations.

The most important result to date from our study is the demonstration that specific variables associated with neonatal illness and with medical treatment during the period of neonatal intensive care are predictors of IQ at 8 years of age. The assumption that such neonatal influences existed has dominated our research strategies, despite the lack of success reported for neonatal scales as predictors. The assumption was based on the consistent finding from our own and other longitudinal studies that very-low-birthweight infants with hyaline membrane disease had poorer outcome, as a group, than did those without this major illness complication. The success of our clinical rating of illness in predicting outcome redirected our efforts to identify discrete predictor variables, first for clinical relevance and then for statistical validation of ad hoc categories and the generation of factor scores from those categories.

Given the demonstration that neonatal illness and treatment influenced intellectual outcome, there remains compelling evidence in our studies and others' that familial factors modify the effects of neonatal damage (Bendersky, 1989; Leonard, Clyman, Piecuch, Juster, Ballard, & Behle, 1990), presumably through a combination of genetic and environmental effects (Plomin & Bergeman, 1990). Identifying salient indicators of damage may be useful in investigating the critical elements of developmental resiliency or the interaction between neonatal damage and environmental deficits. The implications of our findings may be important for those who look for predictors in infant behaviors because our results suggest that infants might be categorized according to individual risk factors *known* to be associated with long-term effects, rather than categorizing infants by general risk status. Short-term differences between high-risk and low-risk infant groups are frequently significant, whether one studies behavior (Caron & Caron, 1981; Rose & Wallace, 1985), electrophysiology (Salamy, Mendelson, Tooley, & Chaplin, 1980), or clinical neurology (Kurtzberg et al., 1979). Often these differences between groups are subtle and not clinically impressive, but they demonstrate delays and deviancies in development that suggest stress to the central nervous system. Whether these differences determined in infancy have implications for long-term development or merely represent transient response to stress cannot be determined without further follow-up. However, the logistics and expense of long-term follow-up are formidable. If long-term predictors were used to distinguish infant groups, differences determined in infancy would then have important implications. The fact that our set of neonatal predictors replicated for a second group of children suggests that the predictors may prove useful for other studies. Some of the individual predictors are highly derived and not directly representative of any specific physiological state. *Total blood gases* and *total x-rays* are marker variables of the same genre as *parent education*; the former must be associated with important aspects of illness, just as the latter must tap into important aspects of the family milieu. In contrast, some of the variables identified in the separate nutrition factor, such as days to reach 75 calories/Kg, may be closer to reflecting direct effects. In general, the nutrition factor was the better predictor in regression analyses whether it was entered before or after the illness factor. Both factors may be indicators of illness, but the nutrition variables may have a more direct association with threats to the integrity of the central nervous system.

As noted, our consistent goal has been to determine specific aspects of neonatal physiology that relate to long-term problems, rather than to generate a set of predictors per se. Further refinements are obviously in order for the variables defined to date. However, considering that all children included in these analyses were sufficiently intact to be testable on the WISC-R at age 8 years (thus excluding approximately 3% with the most severe development problems), it is encouraging to find that the neonatal variables predicted such a considerable amount of the variance in school-age IQ.

REFERENCES

Brander, T. (1937). Uber die Bedeutung des Partus praematurus fur die Entstehung gewisser zerebraler Affectionen, mit besonder Berucksichtigung schwerer und lichtere Grade exogen bedingter Uterbegabung. *Acta Psychiatrica* (Kbh.), *12*, 313–332. (*Psych Abstracts*, 1938, #1902).

Bendersky, L.M. (1989). Cognitive and motor differences among low birth weight infants; impact of intraventricular hemorrhage, medical risk, and social class. *Pediatrics*, *83*, 187–192.

Caron, A.J., & Caron, R.F. (1981). Processing of relational information as an index of infant risk. In S. Friedman & S. Sigman (Eds.), *Pre-term birth and psychological development* (pp. 219–240). New York: Academic Press.

Drillien, C.M. (1958). Growth and development in a group of children of very low birth weight. *Archives of Diseases in Childhood*, *33*, 10–18.

Drillien, C.M. (1961). The incidence of Mental and physical handicaps in school-age children of very low birth weight. *Pediatrics*, *27*, 452–464.

Fitzhardinge, P.M., & Ramsay, M. (1973). The improving outlook for the small prematurely born infant. *Developmental Medicine and Child Neurology*, *15*, 447–459.

Francis-Williams, J. (1970). *Children with specific learning difficulties*. New York: Pergamon Press.

Francis-Williams, J., & Davies, P.A. (1974). Very low Birthweight and later intelligence. *Developmental Medicine and Child Neurology*, *16*, 709–728.

Hunt, J.V. (1976). Environmental risk in fetal and neonatal life and measured infant intelligence. In M. Lewis (Ed.), *Origins of intelligence* (pp. 223–258). New York: Plenum Press.

Hunt, J.V. (1979). Longitudinal research: A method for studying the intellectual development of high risk infants. In T.M. Field, A.M. Sostek, S. Goldberg, & H.H. Shuman (Eds.), *Infants born at risk. Behavior and development* (pp. 443–459). New York: Spectrum.

Hunt, J.V., & Cooper, B.A.B. (1989). Differentiating the risk for high-risk preterm infants. In M.C. Bornstein & N.A. Krasnegor (Eds.), *Stability and continuity in mental development* (pp. 105–122). Hillsdale, NJ: Erlbaum.

Hunt, J.V., Cooper, B.A.B., & Tooley, W.H. (1988). Very low birth weight infants at 8 and 11 years of age: Role of neonatal illness and family status. *Pediatrics*, *82*, 596–603.

Hunt, J.V., Harvin, D., Kennedy, D., & Tooley, W.H. (1974). Mental development of children with birthweights ≤ 1500 g. *Clinical Research*, *22*, 240-A (Abstract).

Hunt, J.V., & Rhodes, L. (1977). Mental development of preterm infants during the first year. *Child Development*, *48*, 204–210.

Hunt, J.V., Tooley, W.H., & Harvin, D. (1982). Learning disabilities in children with birth weights ≤ 1500 grams. *Seminars in Perinatology*, *6*, 280–287.

Jonsen, A.R., & Garland, M.J. (1976). *Ethics of newborn intensive care*. Berkeley, CA: Institute of Governmental Studies, University of California.

Kurtzberg, D., Vaughan, H.G., Jr., Daum, C., Grellong, B.A., Albin, S., & Rotkin, L. (1989). Neurobehavioural performance of low-birth-weight infants at 40 weeks conceptional age: Comparison with normal fullterm infants. *Developmental Medicine and Child Neurology*, *21*, 590–607.

Leonard, C.H., Clyman, R.I., Piecuch, R.E., Juster, R.P., Ballard, R.A., & Behle, R.N. (1990). Effect of medical and social risk factors on outcome of prematurity and very low birth weight. *Journal of Pediatrics*, *116*, 620–626.

Myers, R.E. (1977). Experimental models of perinatal brain damage: relevance to human pathology. In L. Gluck (Ed.), *Intrauterine asphyxia and the developing fetal brain* (pp. 37–98). Chicago: Year Book Medical Publishers.

Plomin, R., & Bergeman, C.S. (1990). The nature of nurture: Genetic influence on "environmental" measures. *Behavioral and Brain Sciences, 13,* 3–28.

Rose, S.A., & Wallace, I.F. (1985). Cross-modal and intra-modal transfer as predictors of mental development in fullterm and preterm infants. *Developmental Psychology, 21,* 949–962.

Salamy, A., Mendelson, T., Tooley, W.H., & Chaplin, E.R. (1980). Differential development of brainstem potentials in healthy and high-risk infants. *Science, 210,* 553–555.

Shirley, M. (1939). A behavioral syndrome characterizing prematurely-born children. *Child Development, 10,* 115–128.

Sigman, M., & Parmelee, A.H. (1979). Longitudinal evaluation of the pre-term infant. In T.M. Field, A.M. Sostek, S. Goldberg, & H.H. Shuman (Eds.), *Infants born at risk.* New York: SP Medical & Scientific Books.

Stave U., & Ruvalo, C. (1980). Neurological development in very-low-birthweight infants. Application of a standardized examination and Prechtl's optimality concept in routine evaluations. *Early Human Development, 4,* 229–241.

Tooley, W.H. (1979). Epidemiology of bronchopulmonary dysplasia. *Journal of Pediatrics, 95,* 851–855.

Vohr, B.R., Oh, W., Rosenfield, A.G., & Cowett, R.M. (1979). The preterm small-for-gestational age infant: A two-year follow-up study. *American Journal of Obstetrics and Gynecology, 133,* 425–431.

Williams, R.L. (1976). Appendix: Final report from the Community and Organization Research Institute to the California Department of Health. In G.C. Cunningham, W.E. Hawes, C. Madore, F.D. Norris, & R.L. Williams (Eds.), *Intrauterine growth and neonatal risk in California.* Sacramento, CA: Infant Health Section, Maternal and Child Health, State of California Department of Health.

V
Interventions and Their Effects

15

Individualized, Family-Focused Developmental Care for the Very Low-Birthweight Preterm Infant in the NICU*

Heidelise Als

A NEW ERA OF NEWBORN INTENSIVE CARE

Over the past two decades there has been a marked increase in the survival of low-birthweight (LBW) infants, both in this country and abroad (Behrman, 1985; Hack, Fanaroff, & Merkatz, 1979). As described in earlier chapters, this is especially true for very low-birthweight (VLBW, i.e., less than 1,500g) infants. Of the 3.7 million live births annually in the U.S., approximately 250,000 (6.8%) are LBW and 41,000 (1.1%) are VLBW (Behrman, 1985; Bernbaum & Hoffman-Williamson, 1986). For infants with birthweights greater than 750g, survival is now likely, that is, better than 50%, and, for infants with birthweights greater than 1,000g, it is now probable. Of high-risk pregnancy identification and neonatal intensive care units (NICU) in perinatal referral centers, fewer than 5% of moderately premature infants will die. With these advances, the emphasis is gradually shifting from issues of survival to the prevention and amelioration of the complications, which are increasingly evident in the newly surviving populations (Bachner, Brown, & Peskin, 1988). Developmental outcomes of VLBW infants are not entirely encouraging. Although overall preterm infants develop surprisingly well (see other chapters, this volume), milder attentional organizational sequelae are increasingly emerging. Even if infants are raised in supportive social milieus, and even if they have been spared the major medical complications often associated with prematurity, as Hunt and her associates recently showed (Hunt, Cooper, & Tooley, 1988), almost 50% of such children at age 8 and 11 years have mild disabilities, and almost 11% have moderate to severe problems. When infants with high neonatal illness were followed who in addition came from homes of low parent education and a poor social milieu, 82% of the infants showed some problem and almost 55% had moderate to severe problems. Escalona (1984) and others have concluded that infants born with biological

* This work was supported by grants GO-08720110 from NIDRR and HO24590003 from EEPCD, U.S. Department of Education, as well as by a grant from the J.P. Hood Foundation and the Merck Family Fund.

Special thanks go to the families who participated in the research, and to the Departments of Nursing (NICU) and of Newborn Medicine at the Brigham and Women's Hospital, as well as to the research staff of the Neurobehavioral Infant and Child Studies Group at Children's Hospital, Boston.

interference such as prematurity *and* environmental interference such as a poor social milieu are at ''double hazard'' for poor developmental outcome. The Hunt et al. (1988) data furthermore show that, even in homes with high parent education, complicated neonatal illness takes a major long-term toll, with 81% of infants showing mild problems and almost 10% showing moderate to severe problems.

In some cases, the developmental outcome of preterm infants can be compounded by various exacerbating factors. These include: (a) the treatment required for the medical conditions most typically associated with poor outcome after prematurity, that is, the by-products of neonatal intensive care (Taeusch & Ware, 1987), the very care that ensures the survival of these infants yet may put the infant in long-term developmental jeopardy; (b) the environmental conditions of the NICU setting, which by necessity must focus on survival, yet may disrupt and disturb the developmental progression of the infants; (c) the trauma that may be engendered to the emotional and physical functioning of the family of such an infant, the very system of support the infant's lifelong development most depends on; (d) the barriers often inherent in the organizational structures designed with acute short-term organ care as focus yet impacting on long-term family and child development and family system functioning; and (e) in a number of cases, the inadequacy of resources available to infant and family after discharge from the NICU environment.

Medical Conditions

The developmentally most feared medical conditions of the very low-birthweight preterm infant are *chronic lung disease,* specifically, *bronchopulmonary dysplasia* (BPD), *intraventricular hemorrhage* (IVH), and *retinopathy of prematurity* (ROP).

BPD is a complex syndrome, and specific subtypes continue to be defined. A recent review by O'Brodovich and Mellins (1985) defines the criteria for diagnosis of BPD as acute lung injury in the first 2 weeks of life; followed by clinical findings of retraction, tachypnea, and wheezing; radiographic evidence of hyperinflated areas and fibrotic strands; and abnormalities of gas exchange requiring oxygen treatment and often prolonged ventilator support. The more immature the infant, the greater the risk of BPD. For infants <1,000g birthweight, the incidence is as high as 50%; for infants <900g, it is virtually 100% (Gerdes, Abbasi, Bhutani, & Bowen, 1986). Truog, Jackson, Badura, Sorensen, Murphy, and Woodrum (1985) show population figures of 24/1000 live births with a birthweight of <2.5kg and 140/1,000 live births with birthweight of <1.5kg. For the general population the incidence is estimated at 1.3 for 1,000 births. In high-risk referral settings, the rate is much higher.

The major reasons for BPD appear to be lung immaturity (Hyers & Fowler, 1986), oxygen toxicity (DeLemos, Wolfsdorf, & Nachman, 1969; Holm, Notter, Siegle, & Matalon, 1985) and high ventilator pressure with subsequent pressure or baro-trauma of inflammation damage to the small airways (Avery et al., 1987; Gerdes et al., 1986; Hyers & Fowler, 1986; Reynolds & Taghizadeh, 1974; Taeusch & Ware, 1987). Thus, the very treatments necessary, namely, mechanical ventilation and oxygen therapy, appear to be the major contributing factors. Current medical therapies include efforts at prevention by enhancing prenatal lung development by treatment of the mother with glucocorticoids, thyroid, catechols, and mesenchymal peptides; and treatment of the infant after birth with exogenous surfactant for prevention and/or amelioration of respiratory distress syndrome (RDS) (Merritt & Kraybill, 1986). These efforts so far are at least partially successful. Once BPD is established, medical management appears very difficult. The lung pathology involves damaged ciliary function leading to continuous accumulation of secretions in terminal and respiratory bronchioles, ulceration and necrosis of bronchiolar membranes, and often widespread fibrosis (Bonikos, Bensch, Northway, & Edwards, 1976). The infants may show chronic secretions with frequent episodes of coughing and vomiting, a tendency to wheeze, low threshold to respiratory infection, reactive airway disease, and chronic hypoxemia, as well as high risk for the cardiac condition of cor pulmonale, i.e., an overworking of the heart because of poor lung function. Chronic aspiration occurs in 80% of infants and may further aggravate chronic lung disease (Goodwin, Graven, & Haberkern, 1985). The infants' growth is usually significantly impaired. They have an increased caloric requirement because of the increased oxygen consumption and the increased work of breathing (Weinstein & Oh, 1981). The difficulty with increased caloric intake is the simultaneous need for fluid restriction to prevent fluid overload. Diuretics, although used therapeutically, and showing short-term benefits (Kao, Durand, Phillips, & Nickerson, 1987; Kao, Warburton, Platzker, & Keens, 1984; Kao, Warburton, Sargent, Platzker, & Keens, 1983) are controversial if used chronically because of their potentially negative effects on pulmonary function and growth (Bauchner, et al., 1988). BPD infants must be provided with continuous increased oxygen to prevent damaging hypoxic vasoconstriction and to decrease the work of breathing. Yet weaning from oxygen is a constant goal. However, too early weaning will result in diminished growth and therefore poorer recovery. Ultimately, improvement in lung function depends on increased lung size and therefore on adequate growth (Bauchner et al., 1988). Aside from all these very difficult to balance factors, lower respiratory tract infections are a major risk for mortality and for rehospitalization. Up to 80% of infants will develop pneumonia in the first year of life, often requiring reintubation (Sauve & Singhai, 1985; Vohr, Bell, & Oh, 1982). Prevention of infection at all cost is critical. A host of additional complications is unfortunately more the rule than the exception, such as trachael stenosis, subglottic cysts obstructing the upper airway, partial or complete vocal chord paralysis leading to hoarseness, and wheezing. The medical compromise of BPD, it appears, does not ever resolve completely. Studies in late childhood show obstructive airway disease, ventilation/profusion imbalances, and persistent bronchial hyperactivity (Bauchner et al., 1988; Smyth, Tabachnik, Duncan, Reilly, & Levison, 1981; Tepper, Morgan, Cota, & Taussig, 1986; Wheeler, Castile, Brown, & Wohl, 1984). Thus, from a purely medical perspective, a number of these infants are prolongedly and acutely severely ill. Furthermore, each of the medical factors involved has a major impact on the developmental and social interactive function of the infant and, therewith, on the parents and other caregivers.

Intraventricular hemorrhage is the second major threat to the early-born preterm infant and appears to be often, but not necessarily, associated with BPD. Each of the millions of cells in the cerebral cortex originates in the germinal layers lining the ventricular system. At 26–28 weeks, the germinal matrix is still full of tiny blood vessels needed to supply oxygen to produce the mass of cortical cells (Volpe, 1981). Since many of these cells are migrating to form the outer cortical mantle, this leaves the tissue lax, unsupported, and very susceptible to hemorrhage. It is thought that any event contributing to sudden blood flow velocity changes, such as intubation, hypoxemia, suctioning (Lamont, Dunlop, Crowley, Levene, & Elder, 1983; Volpe, 1981), chest physical therapy (Gorski, Hole, Leonard, & Martin, 1983; Perlman & Volpe, 1983), and adverse handling is apt to cause rupture of these fragile vessels at this time (Goldson, 1983; Lou, Lassen, & Friis-Hansen, 1979a, b; Milligan, 1980; Volpe, 1981). A small hemorrhage will be contained within the germinal layer. A larger hemorrhage may rupture into the ventricular system and cause hydrocephalus, or it can erupt into the surrounding brain matter. Since the motor fibers to the legs pass close to the germinal matrix, a moderate hemorrhage may yield spastic diplegia. Massive hemorrhage may rupture far enough into brain matter to cause quadriplegia and severe retardation. Up to 50% of newborns born before 32 weeks gestational age have some degree of hemorrhage and the incidence increases with the reduction of gestational age (Volpe, 1981).

Retinopathy of prematurity occurs if the retina is not vascularized, as is the case in early-born preterms. It is thought to result from hyperoxic vasoconstriction in the most immature part of the retina, followed by hyperoxic injury after the hyperoxia ends. Neovascularization then proceeds with abnormal results. Other causes appear to include hypoxia, hypercapnia, intraventricular hemorrhage, seizures, apnea, and exchange transfusions which alter oxygen delivery to the tissues, all events the infant with BPD is subject to (Brown, Milley, Ripepi, & Biglan, 1987; Procianoy, Garcia-Prats, Hittner, Adams, & Rudolph, 1981; Purohit, Ellison, Zierler, Miettinen, & Nadas, 1985; Sacks, Shaffer, Anday, Peckham, & Delivoria-Papadopoulos, 1981; Shohat, Reisner, Krikler, Nissenkorn, Yassur, & Ben-Sira, 1983). Exposure to bright light, a frequent event in most NICUs, has recently been implicated as a possible exacerbating factor (Glass, Avery, Kolinjavadi, Subramanian, Keys, Sostek, & Friendly, 1985). The current overall incidence of ROP is estimated at 20% for prematures <2,500g; it is as high as 59.5% for infants <1,000g (Merritt & Kraybill, 1986). Approximately 2% of all infants with ROP will become blind due to stage IV disease with retinal detachment. Infants with scarring require lifelong follow-up.

Mild scarring may lead to myopia which can be corrected with glasses. Strabismus is frequent. More severe scarring can lead to retinal detachment. Secondary glaucoma has also been reported in infants with severe scarring (Bauchner et al., 1988; Pollard, 1980).

Given the extremely complicated medical picture of the VLBW infant, developmental handicap is not surprising. The presence of BPD has been shown to be an acute indicator of a high incidence of not only prolonged and arduous hospital courses (Goldson, 1984) but also of pronounced later neurodevelopment problems (Goldson, 1984; Meisels, Plunkett, Roloff, Pasik, & Stiefel, 1986; Vohr et al., 1982), some of which appear to be of a progressively deteriorating nature (Campbell, McAlister, & Volpe, 1988). The specific behavioral and developmental characteristics of the infant with BPD may at least to some extent result from and interact with the medical condition leading early on to a vicious cycle in which some infants and caregivers are caught. In some infants, the chronic hypoxemic state appears to lead to a hypervigilant, pervasive state of panic and oversensitivity to environmental stimuli, such as lights, noises and especially touch. Such infants, may become chronically agitated, squirming and restless, cycling from episodes of listless lethargy with obligatory respirations to periods of intense frantic agitation with arching, drowning-like struggle for air, the build-up of mucous secretions, and resulting in coughing and bronchospasms for which such an infant may need to be sedated. Feeding may become difficult, with back arching, gagging, vomiting, and at times further increased agitation. Burping may be spasmodic, and gas passing and bowel movement strain may be triggered by even mild forms of stimulation and input. Social interaction and even gentle caregiving manipulation may increase rather than reduce stress. In such infants, physiological changes resulting in and further contributed to by agitation may be frequent and rapid, and at times life threatening. Typically successful methods of interacting with, giving care to, and consoling a preterm infant appear ineffective and at times counterproductive for these infants. Their continued struggle for calm functioning and relaxation may eventually leave them depleted. They appear functionally resigned and give the behavioral impression of emotional depression, as if giving up on their own developmental progress and recovery. The behavioral patterns observed seem costly, maladaptive, and at times physiologically counterproductive. In their caregivers, such infants appear to trigger feelings of resignation, helplessness, and often outright anger in the face of ineffectual management efforts, despite best intention. Prevention of the infants' unsuccessful self-regulation efforts and in turn the unsuccessful regulation efforts by the caregivers seems of foremost importance for this population.

Environmental Conditions in the NICU

The VLBW infant is typically hospitalized in an NICU for 4 or more months, the infant with BPD sometimes for a year or more. Studies are increasingly documenting that the NICU environment in and of itself may contribute adversely to the problems of the VLBW infant. Bright overhead lighting, constancy of noise, crowding, and noncontingency of various forms of stimulation (Gottfried & Gaiter, 1985; Lawson, Daum, & Turkewitz, 1977), frequent interruption of sleep and rest states (Korones, 1976), and adversity of effect of even the most well-intentioned social approaches (Gorski et al., 1983) and of various care-giving procedures (Long, Philip, & Lucey, 1980) have been documented to have deleterious effects on the infant. (For a review of studies, see Als, 1986.) Since these infants are only intermittently yet for a prolonged period in need of episodic acute intensive care, yet find themselves continuously in a highly intensive care setting staffed with personnel attuned to the rapid changes in needs of those infants with short-term acute disease, they often receive unnecessary and harmful "spill-over" intensive care (Taeusch & Ware, 1987), involving often frequent, routine blood drawing, blood transfusions, chest physical therapy, suctioning, handling, and changes in management plans that may not be optimally appropri-ate for their ongoing disease status but that derive from short-term acute manage-ment. Thus, again, the very treatment intended to help them may become their enemy. A new perspective and reevaluation of current, active, crisis-oriented NICU care may be necessary for such infants. This may require an increased awareness and sensitivity on the part of the staff members who often are, by virtue of their professional preparation, action, and intensivist oriented rather than long-term developmentally oriented.

Family Conditions

Much has been written about the emotional trauma to parents who give birth prematurely (Cupoli, Gagan, Watkins, & Bell, 1986; Klaus & Kennel, 1982; Klaus, 1982; Minde, Whitelaw, Brown, & Fitzhardinge, 1983; Minde, Morton, Manning, & Hines, 1980; Minde, Trehub, Carter, Boukydis, Celhoffer, & Morton, 1978). (For a review, see Als, 1986.) The normal progression and emotional preparation for parenting has been abruptly interrupted, and the parents are as premature as the infant. The desynchronization of emotional unpreparedness compounded by fear for the life of the child often leads to helplessness, anger, grief, and often prolonged depression in the parent. These experiences pose significant barriers to regaining confidence in oneself and daring to become invested and committed to the infant. The roller-coaster of emotional upheaval is described vividly by many parents who have undergone this experience. Parental discord, misunderstanding, and isolation are frequent. The spillover costs to other children in the family and other family members also needs to be considered.

The parents' emotional helplessness and injury is often compounded by physical problems for the mother which may be concomitant to the prematurity such as toxemia, a ruptured uterus with severe blood loss, need for caesarean section, and often a threat to the mother's life. It appears that the mother and the infant's father often are reluctant to consciously emotionally acknowledge the impact of these factors in the face of a very ill child. All available emotional energy appears to be directed towards worry about the child, in turn leaving the parents increasingly depleted and exhausted and the necessary grief resolution unaccomplished (Cupoli et al., 1986). The physical set up and highly technological aspects of the NICU environment, may then inadvertently add to the stress of the parent, at times further exacerbated by the attitude of the professionals in the medical setting, who project this environment to be matter-of-course for the infant. Parents report feelings of ongoing inadequacy increased by feeling continuously observed for "appropriate parenting behavior." Cultural difference may further add to the sense of isolation. Crowded, often noisy conditions, and multiple other barriers to privacy and to emotional support, can become further hindrances in the recovery of the parents. These typically occurring traumatic components of preterm parenting are further increased for the parent of the VLBW infant with BPD. The physical appearance and behavioral functioning of the infant, who may show considerable colour changes, at times puffiness from fluid overload, who may be hyperreactive and hypersensitive to approach; the continuous, brittle health status, the irritability, disorganized behavioral pattern, and diffuseness in regulation and responsiveness, may make the parents feel helpless and rejected by their own infant. At times such parents appear to become chronically depressed, mirroring the infant's spiral of deterioration. For the professional in the NICU setting the challenge in reaching the parent may be increased, when the emotional state of the parent is camouflaged by exemplary behavior in the NICU, regular visiting patterns, attentive courtesy to the staff, resulting in an overintellectualized defense pattern, while the detachment and distance between infant and parent increases in the simultaneous yearning to come closer and to develop trust in the infant's survival and competence. Such parents make evident the inadequacy of NICU professionals' training and preparation in providing both better care and support.

NICU Organizational Structures

Not only does the physical environment and the focus on acute care in the NICU appear to be geared to acute biomedical trauma and crisis intervention, but this focus, furthermore, appears to carry and determine the interrelatedness and dynamics of the institutional structure of the medical system (Gilkerson, Gorski, & Panitz, 1989). The early-born preterm infant in such an environment, however, is foremost a displaced fetus which abruptly finds itself in a high-technology intensive care unit instead of in the econiche of the maternal womb for which its evolutionary history over the millenia has adapted it and where it expects to support and nurture its neurodevelopmental progress for another 12 to 16 weeks. While the displaced fetus is in need of crisis intervention in order to manage the physiological disruption from in utero to extrautero existence, such a fetus is first of all an organism in development, and in very rapid development, at that. Thus, it appears that the conceptualization of the econiche provided for the fetal child may need to shift in focus beyond an acute organ care perspective which conceptualizes the preterm infant as a collection of inadequate organs in need to be "fixed" or made more adequate by technological devices and chemical treatments such as the respirator, intravenous feedings, pulmonary, cardiac, and other metabolism supplementing drugs. The conceptualization of the NICU setting may need to be expanded by the realization of its important, transition-facilitating nature of support to the normal natural econiche of the developing fetal infant, namely, the parent. Such an expanded perspective of an actively developing infant rather than an acutely, statically impaired infant would, by necessity, shift the focus of care in an NICU beyond the organs of an infant body, to include the functioning and developmental process of a pre-maturely extrauterine child in an actively evolving family context.

This perspective moves into focus some of the aspects of the organizational structure of the NICU medical settings which may be exacerbating rather than supporting of the developmental process (Gilkerson et al., in press; Kaluzny, 1982; Turnbull & Turnbull, 1986). NICUs appear to be modeled on adult intensive care units (ICU), with many of the aspects of intensive care perhaps even more medicalized because of the fragility, smallness, and immaturity of the newborn organism. They represent the apex of the acute care model. Patients are delivered in, or transported to, specially designated hospitals with highly trained staff and with the most advanced technological equipment. Neonatology and neonatal nursing are emergency medicine specialties. Physicians and nurses appear to be attracted to this field because of the critical nature of the care they dispense. Perhaps because the patients are so small, perhaps because they are preverbal, and perhaps because they do not yet have life histories and, therewith, a stature and identity of their own, the ICU care afforded them appears often more intense than that afforded to an older child or an adult. Isolettes close together in small spaces, operating-room like conditions on a 24-hour basis, with nude, exposed patients, bright lights, equipment present at all times, open discussion of the "patient" in the presence, not only of the patient discussed, but of many other patients, are just a few of the signs indicating the groundedness of NICUs in a medical pathology model, in contrast to a developmental model.

NICUs especially in hospitals that are regional centers for the high-risk deliveries typically draw patients from a wide geographical area. Parents and infants are often not only physically, but geographically separated. Diverse family and community systems, at times reflecting the full population cross-section of a region or a state come together in an NICU, represented by the fragile extrauterine infants lying side by side in their isolettes and the family members who attempt to visit them. NICUs tend to function in isolation from the communities their patients come from, nor does NICU staff typically have first-hand knowledge of community resources, training, and background in infant and family development, or in family and community functioning. Thus, organiza-tional structures within the NICU itself and within the hospital structure the NICU is part of may need to become more cognizant of their developmental opportunity, become more system supportive rather than organ repair oriented, expand the medical science focus to include a broader social science base, and open themselves to larger social community interaction.

As Gilkerson (Gilkerson et al., in press) points out, hospitals typically function as self contained and self sufficient communities. They "duplicate most of the basic services of the communities in which they exist: they have a library, power plant, police department, plumbers, electricians, town government (administration), restaurants (hospital staff rarely go into the community to eat on work days), shops, and different neighborhoods with different personalities (e.g., newborn nursery versus adult oncology); they even have a local newspaper!" . . . "The extent to which hospitals succeed in creating a total institution is the extent to which they become isolated from the community." Isolation and exclusiveness appears further increased by hospitals' strong regulation of the professionals who can enter and have the privilege of practicing there. Legitimacy of authority is granted by formal means such as licensing, publications and membership in professional societies. In-house referrals are similarly strongly regulated, for example, who can refer to a follow-up clinic or a gastrointestinal work-up, and so on. While the medical profession appears to monitor closely who can participate in the system, the organizational structure appears highly decentralized and characterized by a great deal of medical professional autonomy and self-regulation (Konner, 1987). Hospitals have been described as incompletely integrated institutions (Gilkerson et al., in press; Starr, 1982), lacking a single, clear line of authority. This is an anomaly by the standard model of bureaucratic organizations. Hospitals typically have been described to have three or four separate centers of authority—the trustees, the physicians, the nurses, and the administration—which appear to be held together in a fluid alliance. While intrainstitutional coordination of a loose confederation of independent departments and programs is described to pose an enormous challenge to a hospital, it is also speculated that this kind of structure poses difficulties for the interface with community resources and programs, let alone for the individual infant and family in need of care and support in the hospital as well as in the community. Change towards a developmental, life-span system perspective advocated, therefore will need to be adaptive change, that is, change not so much in adding to existing services, that is, change in the means used to reach the ends, but change in the ends themselves, change which modifies overall direction and reflects change in goals as well as means (Kaluzny, 1982; Gilkerson et al., in press). Such change, which requires a paradigm shift in conceptualization, may well be the most difficult to achieve, but may be the most promising in the face of the challenge of support for VLBW high-risk infants and their families.

Discharge from the NICU

The emotional, financial, and developmental cost infants with BPD engender in the NICU makes them also difficult in terms of discharge planning. Since by the nature of their condition they appear unpredictable, discharge planning is often unsuccessful. Carefully targeted dates and accomplishments fall by the wayside, further increasing the sense of failure in staff, parents, and no doubt the infant. Infants stable enough on oxygen by nasal cannula are often sent home, only to be readmitted to a pediatric ward after a course of vomiting, weight loss, fluid overload, and eventual hypoxemia. Once readmitted, the risk for nosocomial infection, especially respiratory syncytial virus, is very high. The unfamiliarity of the staff with the multiple problems of the infant, and the environmental and caregiving patterns of the acute care medical ward, make less than optimal care likely. Diagnostic overtesting is a usual concomitant of such an admission, at times perhaps camouflaging the helplessness of the medical staff. Frequently, feeding may cease altogether during such admissions, and at times a gastrostomy tube may be placed surgically, circumventing normalized oral-feeding activities. Repeated hospitalizations of this kind seem not unusual. A third option is the transfer of the infant to a "long-term care facility," with the goal for rehabilitation, or to a community hospital with a special care nursery, depending on the severity of the infant's illness. In some cases neither setting nor staff are necessarily equipped to do well by such an infant. Intermittent back and forth shuttling to a pediatric ICU may result, at times with increasing developmental cost to infant and family. A fourth alternative may be home care of the infant. Management at home of an infant on oxygen with feeding and breathing difficulties who may be in need of multiple medications can be a daunting experience for many parents (Taeusch & Ware, 1987), especially if realistic preparation is not given, and community agencies, for example, visiting and home care nurse associations and early intervention programs, are not experienced with such a highly sensitive, complicated infant. Parents then may struggle for services and support, at times exhausting their resources, financially, physically, and emotionally, as the cycle of rehospitalization takes its toll.

DEVELOPMENTAL INTERVENTIONS IN THE NICU

There is increasing suggestion that high technological care of the early-born preterm, delivered within a developmentally informed framework, may significantly and positively influence immediate and long-term outcomes for VLBW babies. Research studies to date have demonstrated the possibly positive effects of reduction in light (Glass et al., 1985), noise (Bess, Peek, & Chapman, 1979; Long et al., 1980; Newman, 1981; Perlman & Volpe, 1983), as well as of supplying carefully instituted positions (Martin, Herrell, Rubin, & Fanaroff, 1979), tactile and vestibular stimulation (Barnard, 1973, 1981; Barnard & Bee, 1983; Burns, Deddish, Burns, & Hatcher, 1983; Field, 1980; Field et al., 1982; Korner, 1981, 1986; Korner, Guilleminault, Vanden Hoed, & Baldwin, 1978; Korner, Kraemer, Haffner, & Cosper, 1975; Korner, Ruppel, & Rho, 1982;

Korner, Schneider, & Forrest, 1983; Kramer & Pierpoint, 1976; Long et al., 1980; Moltz, 1960; Phibbs, Williams, & Phibbs, 1981; Rausch, 1981; Rice, 1977; Scafidi et al., 1986; Schanberg & Field, 1987; Scott, Cole, Lucas, & Richards, 1983; Scott & Richards, 1979; Solkoff & Matuszak, 1975; White & Labarba, 1976), feeding modes and nonnutritive sucking (Anderson, Burroughs, & Measel, 1983; Bernbaum, Pereira, Watkins, & Peckham, 1983; Burroughs, Asonye, Anderson-Shanklin, & Vidyasagar, 1978; Collinge, Bradley, Perks, Rezny, & Topping, 1982; Field et al., 1982; Hansen & Okken, 1979; Horton, Lubchenco, & Gordon, 1952). The importance of carefully instituted supplemental social contact and sensory stimulation has been demonstrated (Leib, Benfield, & Guidubaldi, 1980; Masi, 1979; Scarr-Salapatek & Williams, 1972), as has the great physiological sensitivity of the VLBW infant even to very mild forms of social input (Gorski, 1980; Gorski et al., 1983; Gorski, Huntington, & Lewkowicz, 1987), interruptions of restfulness (Korones, 1976, 1985), routine environments (Gaiter, 1985; Gottfried, 1985; Linn, Horowitz, Buddin, Leake, & Fox, 1985) and routinely performed therapeutic interventions such as suctioning and chest physical therapy (Gorski et al., 1983; Hasselmeyer, 1964; Perlman & Volpe, 1983). Recent work by Thoman (Thoman, 1987a, b; Thoman & Graham, 1986; Thoman & Ingersoll, 1988) is exploring the opportunity for infant initiated seeking of co-regulation of respiration via provisioning of a mechanically activated "breathing bear" in the isolette. Other investigators (Alfonso, Wahlberg, & Persson, 1989; Anderson, Marks, & Wahlberg, 1986; Schmidt & Wittreich, 1986; Wahlberg, 1987; Whitelaw, 1986; Whitelaw et al., in press) are evaluating the increasing inclusion of the mother as an optimal co-regulator and co-breather, based on clinical work in South America with the so-called kangaroo-care method (Whitelaw & Sleath, 1985). Skin-to-skin contact per se has been variously explored by researchers in full-term development (Klaus & Kennel, 1982; Montagu, 1978) and is gaining increasing attention from findings of physiological studies, which point to potentially quite basic feedback dynamics with a variety of beneficial hormonal production and regulation loops implicated in digestion and feeding behavior and in emotional and arousal regulation (Marchini, Winberg, & Uvnas-Moberg, 1988; Stock & Uvnas-Moberg, 1988; Uvnas-Moberg, 1989). Thus, these studies have tested the effects of specific visual, auditory, tactile, vestibular, or multimodal stimulations for varying periods of time during hospitalization. Other studies have begun efforts to evaluate the increasing inclusion of at least the mother into a more active holding and feeding role (Anderson et al., 1986; Schmidt & Wittreich, 1986; Wahlberg, 1987; Whitelaw, 1986; Whitelaw et al., in press; Whitelaw & Sleath, 1985). A few studies, in addition, have attempted to teach parents how to provide appropriate stimulation and interaction for their infants during hospitalization (Nurcombe, Rauh, Howell, Teti, Ruoff, Murphy, & Brennan, 1984). Little is known at this point about the practical and psychological dynamics involved in supporting parents to be the primary caregivers and psychological nurturers of their NICU infants.

Much of the literature concerning parenting in the NICU has discussed the difficulties such an experience provides for families (Field, 1970, 1980; Minde et al., 1978, 1980, 1983). The need for support to help a family during hospitalization of their infant, transition to home, and care following discharge is well recognized. Families whose infants are cared for in the NICU are reported to experience feelings of loss and lack of confidence in their own skills when medical support systems are terminated on discharge of the infant. High family stress levels result from added responsibilities, restricted freedom and uncertainty. Appropriate support extends from within the nursery into the community through the transition process as well as in the early home management and care of the infant (Shelton, Jeppson, & Johnson, 1987).

An assumption underlying traditional intervention approaches is that something is "dysfunctional" in the infant, the family, or the infant–family interaction process (Turnbull & Turnbull, 1986). Any dysfunction in the NICU infant is not likely to be identified until the dysfunction is of significant enough deviance to be labeled. "Deviance" in one area, by the time of diagnosis, may already have impacted on other areas, extending the original dysfunction and creating secondary areas of difficulty (Beckman-Bell, 1981). Most infants with subtle central nervous system dysfunctions exhibited in mental and emotional processing disorders such as hypersensitivity, irritability, hyperactivity, attentional and state disorganization, depression, and/or in dysfunction of the motor system such as dystonia typically are not identified by medical specialties until a significant delay or disturbance in development has been demonstrated (Coleman, 1981; Field, 1982; Gorski, 1980). These problems may not be attended to by professionals until as late as 6–12 months, even in infants with eventually severe or multiple handicaps (Gorski, 1980) yet these infants will have evidenced these issues since birth, thus engendering great insecurity and confusion in their caregiving parents.

Even if the original or initial damage or disorder can not be prevented or significantly altered, secondary disabilities often associated with and derived from such disorders can be alleviated or prevented through appropriate supports to family and infant (Guralnick & Bennett, 1987). Factors known to result in significant stress in families include delayed development, difficult temperament and behavioral disorganization, and policy regulated social emotional responsiveness and self-image (Beckman-Bell, 1980; Gallagher, Beckman-Bell, & Cross, 1983). Each of these factors are thought to be alterable through facilitation of positive and healthy family–infant interaction patterns, thereby enhancing infant development while reducing family stress levels. All these investigations demonstrate the importance of attending to the developmental needs of preterm infants and their families, and have implications for the care provided in the NICU. A major difficulty for the clinical implementation of the implications of these research efforts is the lack of an integrated and unifying framework of development (Als, Lester, Tronick, & Brazelton, 1982; Meisels, Jones, &

Stiefel, 1983) and, therewith, of an approach to individualized comprehensively organized developmentally supportive care for infant and family in the NICU.

A unifying approach which orients the formulation within a theoretically sound model of development extending to the functioning of the infant, the family, the institution and the community is needed. Such a developmental approach must account for the infant's often prolonged needs for simultaneously appropriate medical and developmental experiences. It must provide opportunities for facilitation of social functioning and development while supporting the infant's physiologic and motor systems and the infant's state regulation. It must support parents in understanding and using their infant's cues as a basis for interaction. Support and intervention cannot end when the infant is discharged from the NICU, but must systematically link families and infants to sound models of community-based supports that build on the care and intervention provided in the NICU, assist and facilitate families in early intervention services access, and in the coordination of those services. Such an approach supports the family's capacities to care for and facilitate continued growth and development of their infant. It seeks to enhance intra- and interinstitutional self-awareness and, therewith, to facilitate organizational structure change towards increasingly open and coordinated interfacing and mutual support towards the common goal of long-term enhancement of infant and family functioning. Our research into developmental NICU caregiving for the VLBW preterm infant derives from this viewpoint.

A THEORETICAL FRAMEWORK FOR INDIVIDUALIZED, COMPREHENSIVE, FAMILY-FOCUSED, DEVELOPMENTAL NICU CARE

The conceptualization underlying our NICU work is based in the synactive theory of development (Als, 1982a). This theory draws upon several widely accepted principles of development, such as (a) the principle of species adaptedness, which sees the organism at any stage in its development as having evolved to competency at that stage, rather than as an imperfect precursor model of later stages (Blurton Jones, 1974, 1976; Hinde, 1970; Hinde & Spencer-Booth, 1967; Towen, 1984); (b) the principle of continuous organism–environment interaction from the unicellular stage of development throughout the lifespan and applicable to such domains of human functioning as neuroembryological, motor, cognitive, and emotional social development (Bunge, Johnson, & Ross, 1978; Fowler & Swenson, 1979; Hunt, 1963; Palay, 1979; Patterson, 1979; Patterson, Potter & Furshpan, 1978; Piaget, 1952; Sherrington, 1940); (c) the principle of orthogenesis and syncresis, which postulates that, wherever development occurs, it proceeds from a state of relative globality to a state of increasing differentiation, articulation, and hierarchic integration (Bruner, 1968, 1974; Coghill, 1962; Gesell, 1946; Gesell & Armatruda, 1945; Hooker, 1936, 1942; McGraw, 1945;

Piaget, 1952; Werner, 1957); and (d) the principle of dual antagonist integration, which postulates that organisms always strive for smoothness of integration, and that underlying this striving is a tension between two basically antagonistic physiological types of responses, the exploratory or reaching-out response, and the avoiding or withdrawing response. These responses are differentially called upon, depending on the current regulation and stimulation threshold of the organism (Denny-Brown, 1962, 1966; Schneirla, 1959, 1965; Schneirla & Rosenblatt, 1961, 1963). If stimulation is currently appropriate for the organism in terms of complexity, intensity, and timing, it is thought that the organism has strategies available to actively move towards that stimulation, take it in and make it productive for its own development. If stimulation, on the other hand, is currently inappropriate for the organism, the organism is thought to employ strategies to actively avoid, move away from and defend itself against that stimulation.

A synthesis of the four principles of development outlined results in the principle of synaction (Als, 1982a, 1986), which proposes that development proceeds through the continuous balancing of approach and avoidance, yielding a spiral potentiation of continuous intraorganism subsystem interaction and differentiation and organism-environment interaction aimed at bringing about the realization of hierarchically ordered species-unique developmental agenda.

The Parenting Process

The synactive formulation, applied to the individual infant, focuses on the internal subsystems of functioning: the autonomic system, the motor system, the state organizational system, and, within it, specifically, the attentional interactive system, which are in mutual support and regulation with each other at all times and, in turn, with the environment, fostering or hampering the synaction of systems leading to increasing differentiation and modulation, that is, functional competence, or to disorganization and disturbance (Als, 1982a, 1986, 1989; Als, Lester, Tronick, & Brazelton, 1982a, b). This formulation may also be helpful in application to the parents and family of the developing child in the NICU, to each of the partners individually in terms of his or her internal subsystem functioning, and to the family system as a whole. In this model, the process of normal parenting is seen as a continuous letting go, launching, and supporting the infant towards increasing autonomy and self-regulation (Als, 1986). The mother's womb is seen as stimulus barrier, affording nurturing protection and regulation for the development of the fetus (Als, 1989; Freud, 1955). The mother, in turn, is regulated and supported by her spouse and partner, the extended family unit, and the community at large with its respective cultural social context. With delivery of the infant at birth, the stimulus barrier increasingly thins. The infant moves from being held in the parent's arms to gradually sitting in an infant chair, to moving to the floor, becoming increasingly independently mobile, and expanding the interfaces and connections with increasingly many others, adults and children, familiar and unfamiliar, until eventually the infant becomes an adult and a parent him or herself, ever expanding the cycle of differentiation. Figure 1 depicts schematically this process of increasing letting go.

The infant is fuelled internally towards accomplishment of developmental trajectories and goals and is continuously striving to regulate the internal systems to do so. The infant, in turn, is regulating and eliciting the caregivers' systems to aid the infant in doing so. Failure to accomplish the goals set for the self and set for the other person leads to disorganization, frustration, anger, ineffectiveness, sadness and helplessness, and, over time, to maladaptive, restricted, canalized functioning and costly adaptation, such as seen in self-stimulatory and self-destructive behavior, or in withdrawal and depression (Als, 1982a). Simply stated, the developing infant is part of a continuous interactive communication and regulation system in which the infant's goal-directed strivings are aided and supported by the capacities of the infant's partners and caregivers (Gianino & Tronick, 1988; Tronick, 1989). The infant's behavior serves as route of communication, specifying whether the infant is currently succeeding in achieving self-set goals, whether the world around the infant is currently working for the infant, or whether the infant is becoming increasingly disorganized in his efforts towards the self-set goals. The caregiver's goal is the simultaneous transformation of the infant's disorganization into modulation and further differentiation of organization. Thus, there is a continuous interplay of self-directed and other-directed regulatory behavior of all partners involved in a family system. These mutual regulation processes and mutual interactive organizational modulation reparation, leading to increasing differentiation, competence, and effectiveness are seen as lifespan issues (Als, 1986; Stern, 1985). The commitment to mutual organizational success and affective balance is the driving force behind supportive relationships. Stress and disorganizations and system desynchronizations are

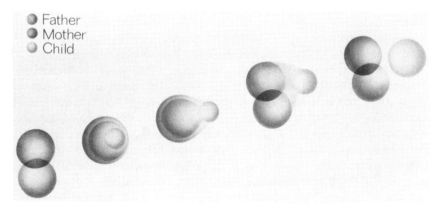

● Father
● Mother
● Child

Figure 1.   Parenting, a Process of Letting Go

necessary concomitants of opening up when reaching for the next goal to be accomplished. The bigger the step attempted or more difficult the goal, the more disorganization and opening up of previously well-regulated balances can usually be expected. Intensity of disorganization and stress in this model is an index of energy available to be brought to bear towards the goal. Apparent disorganizations are seen as adaptive momentary pauses and opportunities for reflection, reassessment and restructuring of the self-regulatory and other-regulatory process, and for refinement of the goal.

The NICU Infant

This synactive formulation puts into perspective the task and opportunity of the NICU. The preterm infant is removed abruptly from the protective stimulus barrier of the mother's womb and the family econiche, at times up to 16 weeks too early. In the model depicted in Figure 1, the gradual progression of letting go, with its naturally built-in touch points, has been interrupted and moved from a very early phase of intrauterine enclosure to a much later phase. The infant finds himself or herself in need of care by highly technically skilled adult strangers with whom neither the infant nor the infant's parents have had any previously established emotional and co-regulatory relationship. The infant's developmental progression, as well as the parents' developmental progression in the framework of increasingly autonomous and confident self-regulatory differentiation, are abruptly disrupted and transposed forward to a stage more akin in its demand characteristics to that of a much older child or adult who has developed to maintain self-balance and profit from the inputs of adult strangers. From this psychodynamic perspective, as well as from a purely neurobiological perspective, given the rapid development of the brain from the 24th to the 40th week of fetal life, and the emergence and differentiation especially of association cortical areas in this period, the impact of the ontogenetically unexpected experience the NICU provides is not surprising. Animal models have given substantial evidence of the fine-tuned specificity of environmental inputs necessary in the course of sensitive periods of brain development to support normal cortical ontogenesis (Bourgeois, Jastreboff & Rakic, 1989; Duffy, Burchfiel, & Snodgrass, 1978; Duffy, Mower, Jensen & Als, 1984; Mower, Burchfiel, & Duffy, 1982; Spinelli, Jensen, & DePrisco, 1980). The mechanism implicated is largely active inhibition and suppression of normal pathways through overactivation of currently functional pathways, leading to less differentiated and less modulated overall later functioning. The suppressions appear to be at least in part mediated by endorphin mechanisms, which may help explain the differential vulnerability of frontal cortical areas in early-born preterms (Duffy, Als, & McAnulty, 1990) given the hierarchical ordering of endorphin receptor sites in primates, with substantial increase in evolutionarily and ontogenetically later, that is, more recent, association cortical areas, culminating in frontal cortex (Lewis, Mishkin, Bragin, Brown, Pert, & Pert, 1981).

Passage of impulses or messages from cell to cell is accomplished by chemical neurotransmitters, which often are released only if up to four or five different regulatory systems concur in a proper, specific configuration. Endorphins probably play an important but only small part. More than two dozen neurotransmitters have so far been identified, and no doubt there are many more. The sensitivities and densities of receptors for certain neurotransmitters vary widely from region to region in the brain and are influenced by experience, since the brain and the sensory organs are continuously mutually dependent on each other for normal structural and functional development.

All parts of the brain are complexly interdependent with each other. Areas that are neuroarchitectonically and temporally remote from the original focus of impact, insult, or scar formation can show difference, damage, or malfunction much later, when certain connections become important in the course of the ontogenesis and evolution of complex integrative motor, cognitive, and affective functions. All regions of brain development are intimately interrelated, and damage in one region may have ripple effects into other regions. Yet compensatory strategies can also be developed, with appropriate developmental support, especially in the very young brain, as has been demonstrated with animal models (Goldman, 1976; Goldman-Rakic, 1980). The burden and opportunity in the NICU, then, is on the identification and provision of individually, brain developmentally appropriate and supportive environments and care in order to ensure normal developmental functioning and progression for the NICU infant, and the regaining of the infant into the psychological, if not the physical, protective family econiche.

The synactive formulation, thus, puts into perspective, not only the NICU parent infant relationship, but also the interaction between disciplines in the NICU, and between organizational structures and institutions geared to support the NICU infant. It is important to articulate the shared goals that each partner is currently working towards. The behavior engaged in and the affect displayed by those involved in the goal realization become the avenues for identification of the current arenas of competence and success for the respective professional and, from there, the opportunity to identify the next step possible, by engaging the dynamic fuelling power via the regulating energy of others engaged towards the mutually shared goal. Support and fuelling requires, first of all, recognition of already existing competence and strength in the person or system to be supported and fuelled. It also requires trust in the growth potential of the competence and strength. Furthermore, it requires commitment towards the shared goal and commitment to provide regulatory positive energy towards the other person or system on behalf of the aimed for goal. Development in this model is a process of mutual self- and other-regulation in a multisystem dynamic matrix towards mutually shared goals. Improved developmental functioning comes about by the identification of open valences of energy available in interfacing individuals, and the engagement of that energy in a mutual positive regulation process towards increasingly differentiated, mutually supported and supportive autonomy.

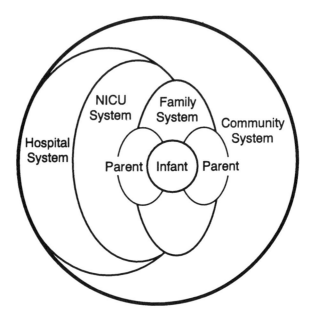

Figure 2.   Synactive Model of Family-Focused NICU Care

Figure 2 conceptualizes this model by identifying the interfacing valence surfaces towards supportive care and intervention on behalf of optimal development of infant and family in the NICU.

SUGGESTIONS FOR THE PRACTICAL STRUCTURING
OF DEVELOPMENTAL CARE IN THE NICU

The sensitivity of the very young nervous system provides a unique opportunity to make the NICU an appropriate, developmentally supportive environment, rather than a hazardous place of increased stress. Improvement of the environmental structure and timing, input, and experience provided needs to be based on better understanding of the functioning of the individual infant.

The overriding principle for family-focused, individualized developmental care and intervention is its developmental process orientation. The nature of the developing infant in a developing family system requires such a developmental process orientation. Prescriptive approaches and "cook-book care," although taught more readily, is not sensitive to the goals of enhancing and supporting development and of supporting infant and parents onto a mutually enhancing developmental path, but rather interferes with this goal, moving and maintaining parent and infant in a dependent role, to "be done to" rather than to be supported to be and do themselves. The developmental care plan is always based on observation and evaluation of the infant and considers the needs and desire of the parents. Its formulation always involves the collaboration of the parents, and the primary care team, including the primary nurse, primary physician, and relevant therapist(s), supported by the developmental specialists as indicated. It considers always the comprehensive functioning of infant and parents, specifying the following goals:

infant behavioral goals in terms of increasingly robust and well-modulated autonomic functioning (respiration, color, visceral stability), motoric functioning (tone, position, movement patterns); state organization (range of states, robustness of state; state regulation) and improvement in competent self-regulation;

infant developmental goals in terms of increasingly developmentally appropriate (a) sleep cycles, (b) feeding ability, (c) increasing fine and gross motor ability, (d) increasing interactive and social emotional development, and (e) increasing cognitive development;

parent goals in terms of (a) feeling of being supported in the NICU as an active partner and participant; (b) courage in observing the infant and trusting own observation; (c) recognizing stress and comfort signals; (d) valuing own efforts and competence in comforting, regulating, and organizing the infant, and in giving care to the infant; (e) experiencing pride and joy in the infant and in own competence with the infant; (f) trusting own importance and effectiveness in parenting the infant;

environmental goals in terms of (a) reduction of interference from noise, light, traffic and so on; (b) provision of private, individualized and personalized living space for infant and family; (c) integration of medical apparatus and equipment into normalized living; (d) provision of special aids such as hammocks, buntings, suckles, and so on, to facilitate regulation and development;

nursing and medical goals in terms of (a) integration and delivery of necessary medical procedures in developmentally facilitative and appropriate ways; (b) preparation for support during and facilitation after all medical procedures; (c) review of necessity in frequency, mode and kind of medical procedures, elimination of all unnecessary medical procedures and change of developmentally modifiable procedures; (d) communication to infant and parent about value and purpose of all medical procedures including problems encountered; (e) identifying strategies in how difficult procedures will be implemented; (f) realistically preparing infant, parent and staff for stress experienced through and after a procedure or event, and providing anticipatory guidance for the emotional mechanisms to deal with it without minimizing or suppressing stress, yet rather acknowledging stress and exploring ways of integrating it.

Specific care plan principles specify that:

1. Care and intervention modifications must always be appropriate to each individual infant's current and changing needs and be based on the infant's individual cues.
2. Care and intervention must always seek to reduce the infant's stress behaviors and enhance self-regulatory and competence behavior.
3. Care and intervention must be appropriate to the infant's integrated subsystem functioning and must take into account the infant's autonomic, motoric, state organizational and alert-interactive capacities and thresholds to stress.
4. If stress is inflicted due to necessary medical procedures, developmental care and intervention must be planned to prepare the infant, contain the infant during the stressful procedure, and restabilize the infant behaviorally after the stressful procedure, making the stress experience a strengthening accomplishment of competence rather than a further weakening and depleting event the infant is at the mercy of.
5. Care and intervention must not be short sighted and single-shift oriented, but must take the 24-hour course of the infant into consideration as well as the developmental goals appropriate and aimed for in the course of the current developmental phase. This is important in terms of the development of appropriate sleep cycles, feeding ability, and especially emotional development. Only the infant who sees himself or herself as effective and successful in accomplishing reliable and predictable interactions with the world will sustain effectance motivation, and a growing sense of competence and pride, critically necessary for all development, especially in the face of severe illness.
6. Care and intervention must always seek creatively to normalize the NICU environment to allow for such emotional development. The necessary medical care needs must be integrated and viewed from an overall developmentally appropriate framework.
7. Care and intervention must be consistent with the gestational age and the illness of the infant and avoid the pitfalls of seeing the preterm infant as an inadequate fullterm infant who needs to be "fixed". Viewing him or her as a displaced fetus who is grappling to resynchronize disrupted systems of functioning into an effective developmental course affords a developmentally appropriate perspective, emphasizing and supporting the infant's strengths.

8. Care and intervention must always focus on the parents' needs and strengths as well as the infant's. The resynchronization of a normal developmental course intimately involves the parents as primary caregivers.

9. Care and intervention must be provided by the primary caregivers, the parents, supplemented and supported by the NICU primary care team of the infant. The family unit is the unit of care.

Specific caregiving considerations regarding the physical environment might include, for instance, consideration of the location of the infant's crib or isolette and the use of a special triage nursery or area for acute procedures, with the goal of avoidance of noise due to faucets and sinks, refuse receptacle lids, doors opening and closing, telephone, overhead pagers, and radios, avoidance of overhead bright and all direct lighting, and avoidance of traffic and activity level; consideration of bedding and clothing, for instance, by provision of a water mattress or sheepskin of boundaries, "nesting," shielding, and covering of an isolette or crib with a thick blanket, and clothing in soft garments without binding seams, use of hats and of swaddling, inclusion of specific aids to self-regulation, for instance, provision of an opportunity to suck during and between feedings including gavage feedings, to hold on to caregiver's hand or finger during manipulations, to use finger rolls to grasp, footrolls, hammocks, and buntings; reduction of stress on the initial warming table by covering and shielding; consideration of an optimal position for the infant such as prone or side-lying; provision of sufficient space around each infant's isolette and/or crib with the availability of a reclining chair or bed to allow for parent caregiving, privacy for feeding, and for resting with the infant.

Specific considerations regarding direct caregiving to the infant might include, for instance, organization and implementation of all procedures through two or three key primary nurses rather than multiple and changing caregivers; timing and sequencing of manipulation, for example, bathing and feeding in one or two separate sessions; review of the advisability of suctioning and chest physical therapy schedules, of vital sign taking and weighing schedules, review of need for and timing of blood drawing, x-rays, ultrasounds, spinal taps; as well as, support and positioning of the infant for, during, and after procedures deemed necessary; consideration of gavage feeding while held close on the parent's chest or contained inside the shielded isolette, supported by holding on and with opportunity to suck; breast or bottle feeding in a quiet, shielded space, without simultaneously talking to or looking at infant; positioning with shoulder and trunkal support, foot bracing and provision of hand holding; timing of feeding with natural sleep cycle without interruption of deep sleep and without periods of exhausting crying preceding feeding; consideration of demand feeding as soon as possible; provision of opportunity for sucking at all times; consideration of the soothing effect of emersion in deep, warm water versus sponge bathing with lukewarm water; attention to temperature maintenance of the water, the infant's position during bathing, and consideration of transition facilitation.

Some manipulations by definition are painful and stressful to the infant, e.g., spinal tap, suctioning, and so on, yet may have to be administered. Facilitation might consist of the preparation of the infant's state and calmness plus support to flexor positioning with a facilitating caregiver present to give inhibition to hands and feet by tucking the infant into flexion, letting the infant hold on, and providing an opportunity for sucking while shielding the infant from unnecessary interruptions and stresses; the efficient execution of the necessary manipulation while supporting the infant's behavioral regulation during the manipulation; and the unhurried reorganization and stabilization of the infant's regulation, with provision of prone placement, opportunity for holding onto caregiver's finger and for sucking, encasement of trunk and back of head in caregiver's hand, while held close in on the caregiver's (parent's) chest, inhibition provided to soles of feet, and removal of extraneous stimulation such as stroking, talking, and position shifts, in order to institute calm restabilization securely. Only then, gradual removal of one aid at a time may assure continued maintenance of stabilization. This may initially take up to 15 to 20 minutes after a manipulation, but over time will improve the infant's self-regulatory abilities, making the caregiver's facilitation increasingly less necessary.

Specific state regulatory suggestions might include, for instance, attention to sleep cycle of the infant, with prevention of interruption, especially of deep sleep; structuring of transitions into sleep and structuring of sleep maintenance by avoidance of peaks of frenzy and overexhaustion; continuous maintenance of a calm, predictable environment and schedule; and establishment of a reliable, repeatable pattern of gradual transition into sleep in prone or side-lying in the isolette or crib. For many infants, calming may best be initiated and maintained on the parent's body. Transition to the crib may be accomplished with provision of steady boundaries and encasing without any additional stimulation. Review of 24-hour sleep patterns and establishment of increasingly mature sleep cycle may need continuous attention. Critical review of the use of the automatic swing for the irritable infant is indicated. For some infants it appears to lead to momentary quieting, but not necessarily to increased internal regulatory controls over time. Soothing, gentle instrumental music or the parent's voice may be comforting for some infants for transition into sleep. A nonstimulating sleep space with removal of exacting visual targets, removal of social inputs, and so on, may need to be available in preparation to relaxing into sleep on the parent's body or in the isolette. A regularly implemented sleep routine may be helpful for many infants.

Organization of alertness may be facilitated by prevention of bright lighting, shielding of the infant's eyes and of the isolette or crib; prevention of an active bustling environment around the infant; development of familiarity with the environment through predictability of the visual, auditory, and social aspects of the surroundings; a home-like atmosphere geared to a very sensitive newborn infant; as well as prevention of over-stimulation when in the isolette and when outside of the isolette. A cluttered visual environment can be too stimulating. Screens can be used to provide protected spaces where only an open nursery room is available.

Social input modalities such as looking, talking, and touching may need to be titrated carefully. Low, animated facial expression with quiet looking without movement, while providing firm containment to limbs and trunk may be optimal for maintenance of alertness. Talking while looking is often overstimulating, as may be patting, stroking, rocking, and so on. Containment is usually facilitating. Once upset, tactile vestibular inputs may be soothing, yet only with simultaneous removal of visual and auditory inputs. Some infants apparently cannot tolerate any input once upset and may do best when held quietly in close contact with the provision of steady extremity and mouth containment. Social inputs may need to be carefully titered during and after activities, for example, feeding, when they may easily lead to hiccoughing, gagging, spitting, aspiration, and so on.

Development of familiarity with the professional caregivers seems also important with the goal of providing continuity in the direct contact care persons providing for care by as few different caregivers as possible. Primary care nursing with small, highly consistent teams may be desirable. All contact with other medical and paramedical personnel might be mediated by the primary nurse so that for the infant he or she remains the reference person at all times when the parents are not there.

Parent and family involvement from day one on of hospitalization appears to be very important ingredient of developmental support and is discussed in more detail elsewhere (Als, 1986). It has to be kept in mind that continuous soothing, quiet containment provided by the parent's steady hands and/or body for the hands, feet, and mouth of the infant may be more productive for the very small infant's organization, and therewith assuring to the parent, than touching, stroking and talking to the infant, which may induce agitation, apnea, and/or other withdrawal behaviors. Individualized careful timing of inputs in concurrence with the increasing self-regulatory stability and differentiation of the infant is the goal at all times.

In a developmental model of NICU care, the behavioral stability and reactivity of the infant, sleep and wake cycle organization and internal regulatory capacities are considered from day one on. Discharge planning starts on day one. Systematic development of assessment throughout the hospital course is seen as a necessity. A poorly regulated, hypersensitive, and reactive infant who does not have a well-developed sleep pattern places a very different demand on the caregiving parents than a well-regulated infant. Depending on the parent's confidence, emotional make-up, and resourcefulness, a sensitive infant may do better at home in establishing regulatory abilities. This requires much anticipatory guidance, support, and follow-up provided for the parents, as well as astute appreciation of the parents' emotional make-up and overall internal and external resources and supports. Otherwise, it is seen as the task of the nursery to support the infant to the level of successful behavioral self-regulation by a carefully structured approach towards regulatory improvement. If these issues are taken into account systematically from the very beginning of the hospitalization, then usually a quite successful pattern of self-regulation including effective sleeping and feeding is developed by discharge.

RESEARCH ON THE INDIVIDUALIZED, FAMILY-FOCUSED, DEVELOPMENTAL APPROACH TO NICU CAREGIVING

In order to test the hypothesis that attention to the individual infant's behavioral cues and respect for the infant's family as primary caregivers can bring about increase in specific self-regulatory behaviors and will improve the medical and developmental outcome of the infant, we have so far conducted two studies. We have focussed on the <1,250g, respirator-dependent infant at high risk for bronchopulmonary dysplasia and intraventricular hemorrhage (Als, Lawhon, Gibes, Duffy, McAnulty, & Blickman, 1986, 1988). The first study was conducted in two phases: Phase I, the control phase, and Phase II, the experimental phase. A behavioral observation method based on the synactive theory of development was used. The model attempts to document the thresholds from balanced modulated functioning to stressed and disorganized functioning in various behaviorally observable subsystems of infant functioning, thus yielding a profile of current behavioral developmental instability and fragility and current developmental strengths. Documentation of specific purported stress behaviors, specific purported regulatory and organizational stabilization behaviors, and specific initiating and approach behaviors is seen as the basis of assessment of current fragility, sensitivity or deviance vs. robustness, modulation, and well functioning. Table 1 gives a list of purported stress and defense behaviors; Table 2 gives a list of purported self-regulatory and approach behaviors readily observed in the preterm infant (Als, 1982b, 1984).

Behavioral observation of the individual infant during any of the medical and caregiving interventions necessary for the infant provides the basis for identification of supportive individualized modifications of care. Implementation is tailored to each individual infant on the basis of current behavioral organization and in the framework of medical and developmental progression. Each infant was observed on days 10, 20, 30, and so on, throughout nursery stay. There were 8 control group and 8 intervention group infants. The second study consisted of random assignment of infants into control and experimental groups. There were 18 control group and 20 experimental group infants. In the second study, intervention started on day 1. Observations were conducted every tenth day, and

Table 1. Purported Disorganization Signals

1. Autonomic and Visceral Disorganization Signals
   a. seizures.
   b. respiratory pauses, irregular respirations, tachypneic bursts
   c. gasping
   d. color changes to mottled, webbed, pale, cyanotic, dusky, or grey
   e. gagging, choking
   f. spitting up
   g. hiccoughing
   h. straining as if or actually producing a bowel movement
   i. gas passing, urinating, defacating
   j. twitching
   k. tremoring and startling
   l. coughing
   m. sneezing
   n. yawning
   o. sighing

2. Motoric Disorganization Signals
   a. motoric flaccidity, or "tuning out"
      1) trunkal flaccidity
      2) extremity flaccidity
      3) facial flaccidity
      4) gaping mouth; tongue protrusion
   b. motoric hypertonicity
      1) with hyperextensions
         of legs and feet: sitting on air, leg bracing, leg extensions, toe splaying
         of arms and hands: airplaning, saluting, finger splaying
         of trunk and head: arching, opisthotonus, head extension
         of face: facial grimacing, tongue extensions
      2) with hyperflexions
         of trunk and extremities: fetal tuck, fisting, high-guard arm position
   c. frantic, diffuse activity, squirming, flailing
   d. motoric drowning-like struggles (stretch drown: trunkal extend–flex alternations)

3. State-Related Disorganization Signals
   a. diffuse sleep, awake or aroused states with whimper-like sounds, facial twitches and discharge smiling
   b. floating and roving or darting eye movements
   c. strained fussing or crying; silent crying
   d. staring
   e. active averting
   f. panicked or worried alertness; hyperalertness
   g. glassy-eyed, strained alertness; lidded, diffuse alertness
   h. rapid state oscillations; frequent abrupt buildup to arousal
   i. irritability and prolonged diffuse arousal and shift to diffuse sleep
   j. crying
   k. frenzy and inconsolability
   l. sleeplessness and restlessness

Adapted from Als (1986).

Table 2.   Purported Behavioral Goals and Self-Regulatory Strategies Toward These Goals

1. Autonomic Stability
   a. smooth respiration
   b. pink, stable color
   c. stable viscera

2. Motoric Stability
   a. smooth, well-modulated posture
   b. well regulated tone throughout trunk, extremities and face
   c. synchronous, smooth movements with efficient modulated motoric strategies, such as hand clasping, foot clasping, finger folding, hand-to-mouth maneuvers, grasping, holding on, searching to suck and suckling, handholding, and tucking together

3. State Stability and Attentional Regulation
   a. clear, robust sleep states
   b. rhythmical robust crying
   c. effective self-quieting
   d. reliable consolability
   e. robust, focused, shiny-eyed alertness with modulatedly intent and/or animated facial expression: frowning, cheek softening, mouth pursing to ooh-face, cooing, smiling

Adapted from Als (1986).

experimental group infants were cared for by nurses who had been specially trained in behavioral observation and individualized caregiving.

The behavioral observations conducted were based on the assumption that the behavior of the infant is the primary route of communicating thresholds to stress relative functional stability and goal strivings towards the next step. An observation began with the recording of a minimum of 20 minutes of baseline observation before the infant under study received the medical or nursing caregiving manipulations to be observed. It continued throughout a caregiving manipulation (e.g., IV line placement, suctioning, spinal tap, vital sign taking, feeding, bathing, diaper changing, and so on, or any combination of these), and was followed by an additional 20 minutes of postmanipulation observation in order to assess the infant's return to baseline or continued stress. An observation typically lasted from 1½ to 3 hours. The behavioral observation sheet used (see Figure 3) is structured for the tabulation in continuous time sampling recording of a series of reliably observable behaviors thought to indicate disorganization and behaviors thought to indicate self-regulatory efforts and maintenance (see Tables 1 and 2). Each observation sheet is segmented into five two-minute columns, thus, each covering a total of 10 minutes. Digital readouts of the transcutaneous oxygen level (TcPO2 or oxymetry reading) and heart rate recording were also

OBSERVATION SHEET   Name _____   Date _____   Sheet Number _____

Time:	0-2	3-4	5-6	7-8	9-10		Time:	0-2	3-4	5-6	7-8	9-10
Resp: Regular						**State:** 1A						
Irregular						1B						
Slow						2A						
Fast						2B						
Pause						3A						
Color: Jaundice						3B						
Pink						4A						
Pale						4B						
Webb						5A						
Red						5B						
Dusky						6A						
Blue						6B						
Tremor						AA						
Startle						**Face** Mouthing						
Twitch Face						**(cont.):** Suck Search						
Twitch Body						Sucking						
Twitch Extremities						**Extrem.:** Finger Splay						
Visceral/ Resp: Spit up						Airplane						
Gag						Salute						
Burp						Sitting On Air						
Hiccough						Hand Clasp						
BM Grunt						Foot Clasp						
Sounds						Hand to Mouth						
Sigh						Grasping						
Gasp						Holding On						
Motor: Flaccid Arm(s)						Fisting						
Flaccid leg(s)						**Attention:** Fuss						
Flexed/Tucked Arms Act. Post.						Yawn						
Flexed/Tucked Legs Act. Post.						Sneeze						
Extend Arms Act. Post.						Face Open						
Extend Legs Act. Post.						Eye Floating						
Smooth Mvmt Arms						Avert						
Smooth Mvmt Legs						Frown						
Smooth Mvmt Trunk						Ooh Face						
Stretch/Drown						Locking						
Diffuse Squirm						Cooing						
Arch						Speech Mvmt						
Tuck Trunk						**Posture:** (Prone, Supine, Side)						
Leg Brace						**Head:** (Right, Left, Middle)						
Face: Tongue Extension						**Location:** (Crib, Isolette, Held)						
Hand on Face						**Manipulation:**						
Gape Face						Heart Rate						
Grimace						Respiration Rate						
Smile						TcPO$_2$						

2002 02 1M (12/83)   H Als, 1981

Figure 3.   NIDCAP Behavioral Observation Sheet. (from Als et al., 1986, reprinted with permission.)

sampled and recorded every two minutes. Ongoing respiratory rate was collected by counting chest wall expansions every two minutes for 30 seconds, multiplying the figure by two and recording it in the respective box. Behavioral categories were checked as to their presence in the course of any given two-minute epoch. A manual of definitions of all behavioral categories is available (Als, 1984).

For the intervention group infants, the observation record formed the basis for a narrative description of the infant's behavior before, during, and after the respective caregiving procedure observed. On the basis of this description, suggestions for the reduction of stress behaviors and the increase of self-regulatory behaviors were made yielding specific inputs for an individualized developmental care plan, in accordance with the general guidelines discussed above. The developmental care plans were formulated in collaboration with the infant's parents and primary caregiving teams.

Results of the first study showed, as Figure 4 depicts, that the experimental infants experienced significantly briefer stays on the respirator (18 days vs. 43 days; $p<.01$) and in increased oxygen (32 days vs. 66 days; $p<.05$), and showed significantly earlier breast or bottle feeding (50 days vs. 79 days; $p<.01$).

Developmental outcome after discharge from the NICU was assessed at 1, 3, 6, and 9 months post-EDC. Assessments included, at 1 month, the APIB (Als et al., 1982a, b); and at 3, 6, and 9 months, assessments with the Bayley Scales of Infant Development (Bayley, 1969). In addition, at 9 months post EDC, the infants were observed and videotaped in a 15-minute play observation with one of their parents (Kangaroo-Box Paradigm; Als, 1983, 1984, and 1985; Als & Brazelton, 1981). Developmental outcome after discharge from the NICU showed significantly better behavioral regulation scores at 1 month post-EDC, as measured with the APIB, significantly better Mental and Psychomotor Developmental Indices at 3, 6, and 9 months post-EDC, as measured with the Bayley Scale of Infant Development, and significantly better behavioral regulation

	No. of Days on Respirator		No. of Days on 02		No. of Days Before Bottle Fed	
Group	I	II	I	II	I	II
Mean	42.88	18.38	66.38	32.00	79.25	49.63
SD	18.92	10.97	35.60	14.65	21.89	13.54
	df = 14 t = 3.168 p < .01**		df = 14 t = 2.526 p < .05*		df = 14 t = 3.255 p < .01**	

all values 2-tailed

Figure 4.   Medical Outcome Variables
Group I: Control Group; Group II: Experimental Group
(Adapted from Als et al., 1986).

scores at 9 months post-EDC, as measured in a videotaped Kangaroo-Box Paradigm observation. The APIB, as Figure 5 depicts, showed the experimental infants as more well modulated, with higher thresholds to disorganization in terms of motor system ($p<.05$), state maintenance ($p<.1$), attentional competence ($p<.1$), and self-regulation ability ($p<.02$).

Figure 6 shows additional behavioral differences, as assessed with the APIB.

Of the 18 summary variables, 4 favored the intervention group. These included the ability to cuddle and to inhibit crawling motion when placed in supine ($p<.02$), a motor capacity measure including the assessment of tone, motor maturity, and balance of postures ($p<.05$), a measure of alertness ($p<.1$), and of overall behavioral organization and interactive attractiveness ($p<.05$). Of the five body signal parameters measured, the intervention group showed a significantly lower incidence of motoric extension behaviors such as grimacing, arching, fingersplays and salutes, considered indicators of stress ($p<.02$). They also showed a higher number of normal reflexes ($p<.05$). The MDI from the Bayley Scale at 3, 6, and 9 months, as Figure 7 depicts, showed a highly significant group difference at all three age points favoring the experimental infants ($p<.00001$).

The experimental infants showed mean scores between 110 and 124, the control infants between 91 and 78. Moreover, there was a significant time effect, with the control infants declining significantly over time ($p<.03$). The psychomotor developmental index (PDI) also showed a significant group effect, again favoring the experimental infants at all three age points ($p<.04$).

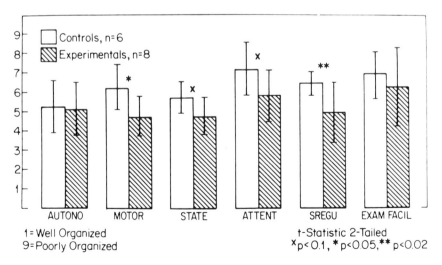

Figure 5.   APIB System Scores, means and standard deviations, at 44 weeks post-EDC. (From Als, 1989, reprinted with permission.)

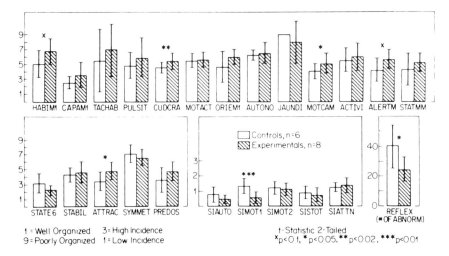

Figure 6.   APIB Summary Scores, body signal parameters and reflex score, means and standard deviations, at 44 weeks post-EDC. (From Als, 1989, reprinted with permission.)

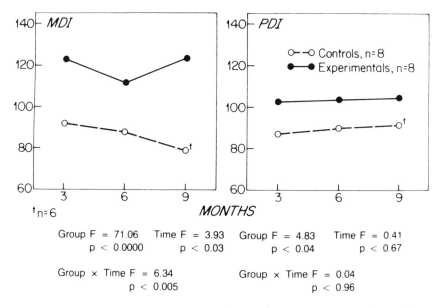

Figure 7.   Bayley Scale Scores at 3, 6, and 9 months post-EDC—Mental Developmental Index (MDI) and Psychomotor Developmental Index (PDI). (From Als, 1989, reprinted with permission.)

Figure 8A shows the comparison results for the 20 parameters measured by videotape analysis from the Kangaroo-Box Paradigm. This paradigm involves first a 6-minute play episode of parent and child focused on the kangaroo box.

Six parameters showed group differences favoring the intervention group infants and ranging in significance level from $<.1$ to $<.001$. They involved fine motor fluidity and modulation (FMOTOP, $p<.05$), degree of differentiation, range and appropriateness of affective functioning (AFFECP, $p<.001$), highest affective phase achieved in the course of the interaction (HIPOTP, $p<.05$), social interactive competence (SOCIAP, $p<.1$), modulation and speed of movement (TEMPOP, $p<.02$), and the overall summary rating of performance (SUM-MAP, $p<.05$). In the Stillface Episode (Figure 8B), in which the parent is instructed to no longer help and/or interact with the child in any way, nine parameters out of 19 showed significant differences, ranging in significance level from $<.05$ to $<.01$, and again favoring the experimental group infants over the control group infants. The parameters involved, again, fine motor modulation (FMOTOS, $p<.01$), apparent understanding of the task without the mother's help (COGNIS, $p<.02$), highest affective level achieved in the Stillface Episode (HIPOS, $p<.05$), ability to elicit the parent by socially positive measures in order to resume play with the child (SOCIAS, $p<.01$), ability to combine object play with social elicitation (OBSOCS, $p<.01$), ability to stay engaged in the task and break it down into manageable components (ATTENS, $p<.01$), modulation of speed of movement (TEMPOS, $p<.05$), the ability to show pleasure and pride in an accomplishment (PLESPS, $p<.01$), and the overall summary competence rating (SUMMAS, $p<.05$). It is of interest that the control group infants showed poorer performance than the experimental group infants on many more parameters when studied under increased stress, i.e., the Stillface Episode, when the parent no longer could be of assistance, than when they were helped by the parent.

Figure 8C shows the 12 parent parameters in play, the parent's ability to maintain the still face (PSTILF), and the parent's ability to reengage the infant during the reunion episode (REPLAY). Only one parent parameter showed a significant group difference, namely, Degree of Parent's Facilitation of Play (DPFACL, $p<.05$), indicating that control and experimental group infants' parents were overall equally adept and invested in making the play successful and enjoyable for the infant, yet the intervention group parents were more sensitive to the specific needs of their infants, although this may be a chance finding. The last three parameters graphed involve interaction parameters, and all three showed significant group differences. The parameters measured are Degree of Turn-Taking Ability (DTURNT, $p<.01$), Degree of Overall Synchrony of the Interaction (OSYNCH, $p<.05$), and Overall Quality of the Interaction (OQUALI, $p<.001$). Again, the experimental group parent-infant pairs showed the better scores in free play at 9 months. The experimental group infants appeared, again, significantly more well organized, well differentiated, and well

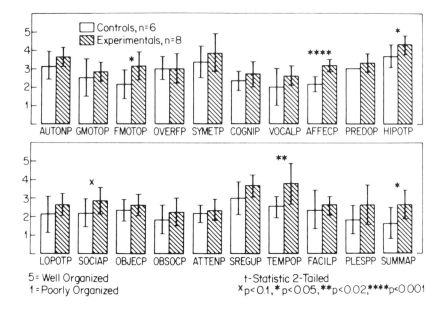

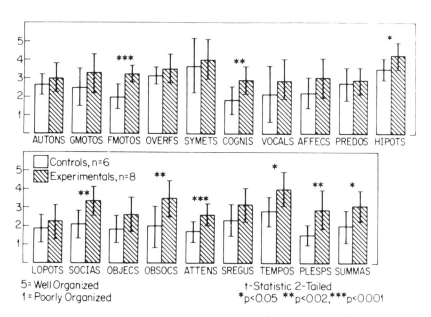

Figures 8.   (a) Kangaroo-Box Paradigm at 9 months post-EDC: Play Episode.
(b) Kangaroo-Box Paradigm at 9 months post-EDC: Still-Face Episode.
(c) Kangaroo-Box Paradigm at 9 months post-EDC: Parent and Interaction Parameters. (From Als, 1989, reprinted with permission.)

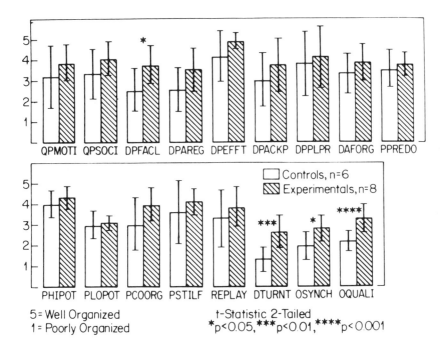

5 = Well Organized
1 = Poorly Organized

t-Statistic 2-Tailed
*p<0.05, ***p<0.01, ****p<0.001

modulated than the intervention infants. These results are taken to support the hypothesis that the synactive formulation of development provides a specific framework for the design of appropriate social and sensory contexts for the high-risk preterm infant in the NICU, from which the infant may profit significantly not only medically, but also developmentally (Als, 1989). Recently, the infants from this study have been retested at age three years with an extensive neuropsychological battery. Preliminary analyses indicate that overall cognitive functioning and, in particular, verbal expressive performance, quantitative performance and attentional performance are significantly higher for the children in the experimental group than those in the control group (Als, Lawhon, Duffy, McAnulty, & Gibes, in preparation).

In the second, larger study (Als, Lawhon, Duffy, McAnulty, Gibes, & Blickman, in preparation), which started on day 1 instead of day 10, the experimental group infants, again, showed significantly shorter stays on the respirator ($p<.05$), fewer days on supplemental oxygen ($p<.025$), and earlier establishment of breast/bottle feeding ($p<.01$). Furthermore, they showed improved average daily weight gain from birth to 42 weeks PCA ($p<.05$), younger postconceptional age at discharge ($p<.025$), shorter hospital stay ($p<.025$), and lower incidence of IVH ($p<.001$). The incidence of bronchopulmonary dysplasia (BPD) was not different; however, the severity score for BPD (stage 0–3) appeared significantly lower in the experimental group ($p<.02$) (Als, Lawhon,

Gibes, Duffy, McAnulty, & Blickman, 1988). These findings seem to support further the hypothesis that VLBW infants in the NICU may benefit in their medical outcome from developmentally individualized behavioral care. The infants in this study are currently also followed for more long-term outcome.

The clinical implications of the studies to date have had an impact on overall caregiving in the NICU, especially the care of long-term hospitalized, chronically ill newborns with severe lung disease who typically suffer from pronounced hypersensitivity to stimulation often accompanied by increasingly distorted motor system development with shoulder retraction, head and trunkal arching and extension, poor trunkal tone, and increased leg extensor tone. Promotion of flexor tone and calm relaxation together with structuring of a developmentally supportive environment in order to maximally facilitate normal social-emotional, cognitive, and motor development in the face of chronic severe illness and prolonged hospitalization is the goal. Developmentally focused normalization of the hospital environment with the integration of the infant's care by his or her own family, affording space, respect and nurturance and the ongoing opportunity for increasing developmental differentiation is aimed for.

Figures 9 through 16 show some of the caregiving modifications currently successfully implementable in a developmentally oriented NICU.

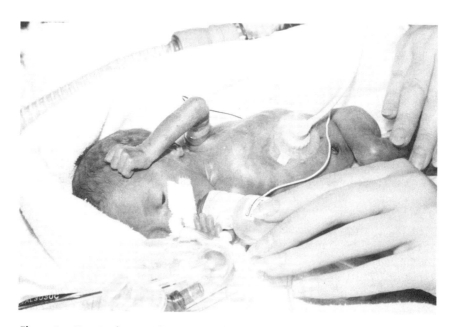

Figure 9.   Day 2 of 27-week preterm infant intubated on warming table, sidelying in "nest": facilitation by caregiver to help legs into soft flexion; opportunity for sucking; gradual relaxation of arms into midline flexion while actively sucking (From Als, 1986, reprinted with permission.)

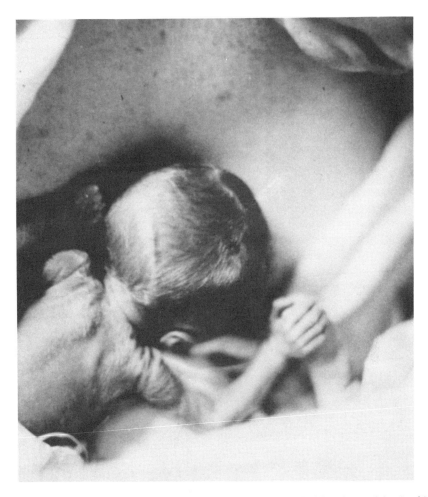

Figure 10.   Day 3 of 25-week preterm intubated infant held and cared for in skin to skin contact with the mother.

Figures 11a, b, and c.   Day 3 of 26-week preterm infant in isolette, orally intubated; in bunting, in nest of sheepskin-covered waterbed, quietly sleeping; beginning to awaken, with eyebrow and forehead raising when given small nipple to suckle in preparation for feeding; shielded gavage feeding by the mother.

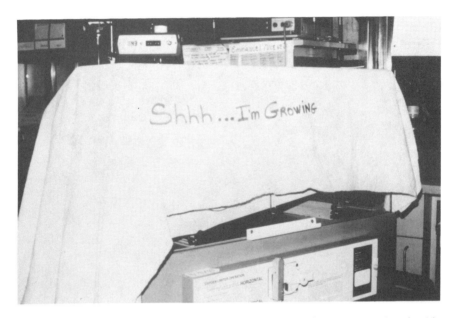

Figure 12.   Shielding of isolette with blanket. (From Als, 1986, reprinted with permission.)

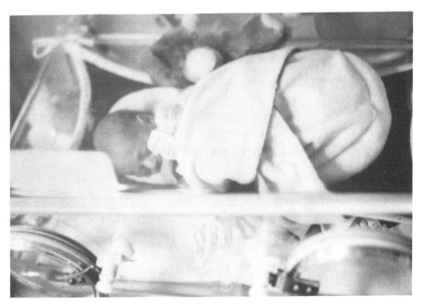

Figure 13.   Very sensitive former 26-week preterm now 29 weeks in bunting on hammock in isolette, sidelying with arms in flexion, in relaxed sleep. (From Als, 1989, reprinted with permission.)

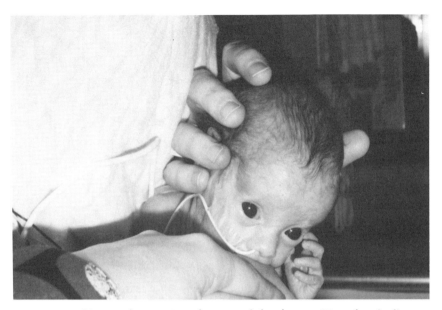

Figure 14.   Shiny-eyed, now 30-week preterm infant born at 25 weeks, nippling on the breast while gavage feeding.

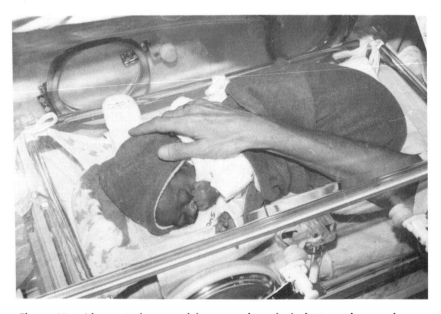

Figure 15.   After a taxing caregiving procedure, in isolette on hammock, supported by special frame; facilitation by containment in bunting, sidelying position, aided by caregiver's encasing arm and hand, and by opportunity to suck on special "suckle" (nipple in soft cloth strip). (From Als, 1986, reprinted with permission.)

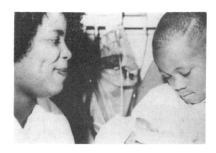
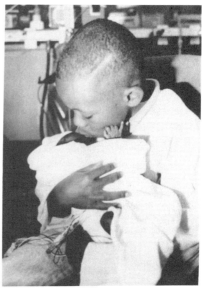

Figures 16a and b. 27-week preterm infant now 30 weeks, held and kissed by older brother with mother smiling gently at both children.

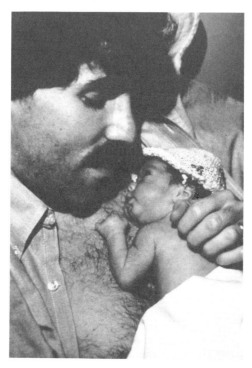

Figure 17. Former 25-week preterm infant, now 32 weeks, cared for and relaxing in skin to skin contact with the father.

378

SUMMARY

The VLBW preterm infant is a product of advances in neonatal medical technology. Now that survival even of very early-born and very small infants is increasingly assured, our attention is shifting to the quality of survival. The brain of the immature fetal infant is the critical organ that orchestrates and influences all aspects of development. The protection and support of the immature yet rapidly differentiating brain in NICU environments is becoming a foremost priority for all those giving care to the infant and the infant's family. The synactive model of development outlines access avenues for the observation of that brain's function via the behavior displayed by the infant and for the support of parents and professional caregivers. Autonomic, motoric, state organizational, attentional, and self-regulatory capacities of the infant can be observed productively in order to identify succinctly and specifically what the infant's own current developmental goals are and where the infant's thresholds to disorganization and ability for self-maintenance and increasing self-regulation and self-differentiation lie. Disorganization is a necessary concomitant of all development. In order to take the next step to differentiation, previously integrated and synchronized connections have to be opened up which necessitates the disorganization and dysynchronization of subsystems in their interplay. When the newly in-reach agendum becomes gradually mastered and disorganization diminishes, then the subsystems realign and support each other again, now at a higher level of more differentiated functioning. If disorganization is too massive and more differentiated new alignment of subsystems is not possible, then a maladaptive, costly realignment may occur at a more rigid, canalized level of functioning, forcing the infant over time to practice and fall back onto maladaptive strategies and precluding flexible differentiation and goal attainment. The synactive framework of development provides an approach to identify on an individual basis for each child and with each family the opportunities currently available to support optimal differentiations and modulation without overtaxing the child and while respecting and supporting the family. Respect for the child's behavioral communications as meaningful expression of the child's active participation in and shaping of his or her own developmental trajectory engenders in the caregiver confidence in the child and the caregiver's own ability to jointly negotiate the next step in the developmental process.

The social context evolved over thousands of generations of human phylogenesis is surprisingly fine-tuned in its specificity to provide a good enough environment for the normal fullterm nervous system to unfold, initially intrauterinely, then extrauterinely, adequate to assure the continuation of human evolution. With the advances in medical technology, that is, material culture, even the very immature nervous system can exist and develop outside the womb. However, the social context of the traditional special care nursery brings with it less than adequate support for that immature nervous system and its neurobiologically necessary nurturance by its family system, leading at times to maladaptations, disability, and perhaps death. Detailed observation of the behavior of the fetus displaced from the womb into the NICU, interacting without reacting to the onslaught of unexpected sensory experiences, can be the opportunity to estimate and infer how appropriate environmental and social context can be provided sufficiently astutely in order to support that highly sensitive and highly vulnerable being's developmental progression, regained and supported in its family niche.

The studies reported to date indicate that, for the very low-birthweight, initially critically ill, and premature infant in the experimental groups, the family-focused, individualized, behavioral-developmental approach to care, emphasizing from early on the infant's own strengths and apparent developmental goals and instituting supports for self-regulatory competence and achievement of these goals improves outcome not only medically, as shown in reduced respirator and oxygen dependency, improved feedings, decrease in severe BPD and IVH, and shorter hospital stays, but also behaviorally and developmentally, as shown in significantly better mental and motor performance as well as overall better differentiation and modulation of functioning postterm. The results indicate that reduction in disorganization and increase in support to behavioral self-regulation improves developmental outcome, perhaps by preventing active inhibition of CNS pathways due to inappropriate inputs during a highly sensitive period of brain development. Developmentally appropriate input may, thus, well be associated with improved cortical development. It appears that, in order to improve medical and developmental outcome for the high-risk, very low-birthweight preterm infants, environmental structuring as well as timing and kind of input provided for the infant can be productively based on the astute observation of the individual infant's current behavioral cues. The interpretation of the infant's behaviors in a framework of regulatory efforts towards self-set goals appears productive in forming a base for individualized behavioral structuring and care, leading not only to improved medical status but also to improved developmental outcome and perhaps improved family and professional functioning.

REFERENCES

Affonso, D.D., Wahlberg, V., & Persson, B. (1989). Exploration of mothers' reactions to the kangaroo method of prematurity care. *Neonatal Network, 7*, 43–51.

Als, H. (1982a). Towards a synactive theory of development: Promise for the assessment of infant individuality. *Infant Mental Health Journal, 3*, 229–243.

Als, H. (1982b). The unfolding of behavioral organization in the face of a biological violation. In E. Tronick (Ed.), *Human communication and the joint regulation of behavior* (pp. 125–160). Baltimore: University Park Press.

Als, H. (1983). Infant individuality: Assessing patterns of very early development. In F. Call, E. Galenson, & R.L. Tyson (Eds.), *Frontiers in infant psychiatry* (pp. 363–378). New York: Basic Books.

Als, H. (1984). *Manual for the naturalistic observation of newborn behavior (preterm and fullterm infants).* Unpublished manuscript, The Children's Hospital, Boston, MA.

Als, H. (1985). Patterns of infant behavior: Analogs of later organizational difficulties. In F.H.

Duffy & N. Geschwind (Eds.), *Dyslexia: A neuroscientific approach to clinical evaluation* (pp. 67–92). Boston: Little Brown and Co.

Als, H. (1986). Synactive model of neonatal behavioral organization: Framework for the assessment and support of the neurobehavioral development of the premature infant and his parents in the environment of the neonatal intensive care unit. In J.K. Sweeney (Ed.), *The high-risk neonate: Developmental therapy perspectives* (pp. 3–55). New York: The Haworth Press.

Als, H. (1989). Self-regulation and motor development in preterm infants. In J. Lockman & N. Hazen (Eds.), *Action in social context. Perspectives on early development* (pp. 65–97). New York, London: Plenum Press.

Als, H., & Brazelton, T.B. (1981). A new model of assessing the behavioral organization in preterm and fullterm infants: Two case studies. *Journal of American Academy of Child Psychiatry, 20,* 239–269.

Als, H., Lawhon, G., Duffy, F.H., McAnulty, G.B., & Gibes, R. (in preparation). *Individualized behavioral and environmental care for the VLBW preterm at high risk for BPD and IVH: Outcome to age 3 years.*

Als, H., Lawhon, G., Brown, E., Gibes, R., Duffy, F.H., McAnulty, G.B., & Blickman, J.G. (1986). Individualized behavioral and environmental care for the very low birth weight preterm infant at high risk for bronchopulmonary dysplasia: Neonatal intensive care unit and developmental outcome. *Pediatrics, 78* (6), 1123–1132.

Als, H., Lawhon, G., Gibes, R., Duffy, F.H., McAnulty, G.B., & Blickman, J.G. (1988, February). *Individualized behavioral and developmental care for the VLBW preterm infant at high risk for bronchopulmonary dysplasia and intraventricular hemorrhage. Study II NICU outcome.* Paper presented at the New England Perinatal Association Annual Meeting, Woodstock VT.

Als, H., Lawhon, G., Duffy, F.H., McAnulty, G.B., Gibes, R., & Blickman, J.G. (in preparation). *Individualized developmental care for the very low birth weight preterm infant at high risk for chronic lung disease and intraventricular hemorrhage: Medical and neurofunctional effects.*

Als, H., Lester, B.M., Tronick, E.Z., & Brazelton, T.B. (1982a). Towards a research instrument for the assessment of preterm infants' behavior. In H.E. Fitzgerald, B.M. Lester, & M.W. Yogman (Eds.), *Theory and research in behavioral pediatrics* (Vol. 1, pp. 35–63). New York: Plenum Press.

Als, H., Lester, B.M., Tronick, E.Z., & Brazelton, T.B. (1982b). Manual for the assessment of preterm infants' behavior (APIB). In H.E. Fitzgerald, B.M. Lester, & M.W. Yogman (Eds.), *Theory and research in behavioral pediatrics* (Vol. 1, pp. 65–132). New York: Plenum Press.

Anderson, G.C., Burroughs, A.K., & Measel, C.P. (1983). Non-nutritive sucking opportunities: A safe and effective treatment for preterm neonates. In T. Field & A. Sostek (Eds.), *Infants born at risk* (pp. 129–147). New York: Grune and Stratton.

Anderson, G.C., Marks, E.A. & Wahlberg, V. (1986). Kangaroo care for premature infants. *American Journal of Nursing, 86,* 807–809.

Avery, M.E., Tooley, W.H., Keller, J.B., Hurd, S.S., Bryan, H., Cotton, R.B., Epstein, M.F., Fitzhardinge, P.M., Hansen, C.B., Hansen, T.N., Hodson, A., James, L.S., Kitterman, J.A., Nielsen, H.C., Poirier, T.A., Truog, W.E., & Wiung, J.T. (1987). Is chronic lung disease in low birth weight infants preventable? A survey of eight centers. *Pediatrics, 79,* 26–30.

Barnard, K.E. (1973). The effect of stimulation on the sleep behavior of the premature infant. *Communicating Nursing Research, 6,* 12–40.

Barnard, K.E. (1981). A program for temporally patterned movement and sound stimulation for premature infants. In V.L. Smeriglio (Ed.), *Newborns and parents.* Hillsdale, NJ: Erlbaum.

Barnard, K.E., & Bee, H.L. (1983). The impact of temporally patterned stimulation on the development of preterm infants. *Child Development, 54,* 1167.

Bauchner, H., Brown, E., & Peskin, J. (1988). Premature graduates of the newborn intensive care unit: A guide to followup. *Pediatric Clinics of North America, 36,* 1207–1226.

Bayley, N. (1969). *Manual for the Bayley Scales of Infant Development.* New York: The Psychological Corporation.

Beckman-Bell, P. (1980). *Characteristics of handicapped infants: A study of the relationship between child characteristics and stress as reported by mothers.* Unpublished doctoral dissertation, University of Arizona.

Beckman-Bell, P. (1981). Child-related stress in families of handicapped children. *Topics in Early Childhood Special Education, 1*(3), 45–54.

Behrman, R. (1985). Preventing low birth weight: A pediatric perspective. *Journal of Pediatrics, 107,* 842–854.

Bernbaum, J., & Hoffman-Williamson, M. (1986). Following the NICU graduate. *Contemporary Pediatrics, 3,* 22–37.

Bernbaum, J., Pereira, G.R., Watkins, J.B., & Peckham, G.J. (1983). Non-nutritive sucking during gavage feeding enhances growth and maturation in premature infants. *Pediatrics, 71,* 41–45.

Bess, F.H., Peek, B.F., & Chapman, J.J. (1979). Further observations on noise levels in infant incubators. *Pediatrics, 63,* 100–106.

Blurton Jones, N. (1974). Ethology and early socialization. In M.P.M. Richards (Ed.), *The integration of a child into a social world* (pp. 263–295). Cambridge, MA: Cambridge University Press.

Blurton Jones, N. (1976). Growing points in human ethology: Another link between ethology and the social sciences. In P.P.G. Bateson & R.A. Hinde (Eds.), *Growing points in ethology* (pp. 427–451). Cambridge, MA: Cambridge University Press.

Bonikos, S., Bensch, K., Northway, W., & Edwards, D. (1976). Bronchopulmonary dysplasia: The pulmonary pathologic sequel of necrotizing bronchiolitis and pulmonary fibrosis. *Human Pathology, 7,* 643–666.

Bourgeois, J., Jastreboff, P.J., & Rakic, P. (1989). Synaptogenesis in visual cortex of normal and preterm monkeys: Evidence for intrinsic regulation of synaptic overproduction. *Proceedings of the National Academy of Sciences, United States of America, 86,* 4297–4301.

Brown, D., Milley, R., Ripepi, U., & Biglan, A. (1987). Retinopathy of prematurity: Risk factors in a five-year cohort of critically ill premature neonates. *American Journal of Diseases of Children, 141,* 154–160.

Bruner, J.S. (1968). *Processes of cognitive growth in infancy.* Worcester, MA: Clark University Press.

Bruner, J.S. (1974). Nature and uses of immaturity. In K. Connolly & J. Bruner (Eds.), *Growth of competence* (pp. 11–49). New York: Academic Press.

Bunge, R., Johnson, M., & Ross, C.D. (1978). Nature and nurture in development of the autonomic neuron. *Science, 199,* 1409–1416.

Burns, K.A., Deddish, R.B., Burns, W.J., & Hatcher, R.P. (1983). Use of oscillating waterbeds and rhythmic sounds for premature infant stimulation. *Developmental Psychology, 19,* 746–752.

Burroughs, A.K., Asonye, U.O., Anderson-Shanklin, G.C., & Vidyasagar, D. (1978). The effect of non-nutritive sucking on transcutaneous oxygen tension in non-crying preterm neonates. *Research in Nursing and Health, 1,* 69–75.

Campbell, L.R., McAlister, W., & Volpe, J.J. (1988). Neurologic aspects of bronchopulmonary dysplasia. *Clinical Pediatrics, 27,* 7–13.

Coghill, G.E. (1962). *Anatomy and the problem of behavior.* New York: Macmillan.

Coleman, M. (1981). *Neonatal neurology.* Baltimore: University Park Press.

Collinge, J.M., Bradley, K., Perks, C., Rezny, A., & Topping, P. (1982). Demand vs. scheduled feedings for premature infants. *Journal of Obstetric Gynecologic, and Neonatal Nursing, 90,* 362–367.

Cupoli, J.M., Gagan, R.J., Watkins, A.H., & Bell, S.F. (1986). The shapes of grief. *Journal of Perinatology, 6*(2), 123–126.

DeLemos, R., Wolfsdorf, J., & Nachman, R. (1969). Lung injury from oxygen in lambs. *Anesthesiology, 30*, 609–611.

Denny-Brown, D. (1962). *The basal ganglia and their relation to disorders of movement.* Oxford: Oxford University Press.

Denny-Brown, D. (1966). *The cerebral control of movement.* Springfield, IL: Charles C. Thomas.

Duffy, F.H., Als, H., & McAnulty, G.B. (1990). Behavioral and electrophysiological evidence for gestational age effects in healthy preterm and fullterm infants studied two weeks after expected due date. *Child Development, 61*, 1271–1286.

Duffy, F.H., Burchfiel, J.L., & Snodgrass, S.R. (1978). The pharmacology of amblyopia. *Archives of Ophthalmology, 85*, 489–495.

Duffy, F.H., Mower, G.D., Jensen, F., & Als, H. (1984). Neural plasticity: A new frontier for infant development. In H.E. Fitzgerald, B.M. Lester & M.W. Yogman (Eds.), *Theory and research in behavioral pediatrics* (Vol. 2, pp. 67–96). New York: Plenum Press.

Escalona, S. (1984). Social and other environmental influences on the cognitive and personality development of low birthweight infants. *American Journal of Mental Deficiency, 88*, 508–512.

Field, T. (1982). Affective displays of high-risk infants during early interactions. In T.M. Field & A. Fogel (Eds.), *Emotion and early interaction.* Hillsdale, NJ: Erlbaum.

Field, T.M. (1979). *Infants born at risk: Behavior and development.* New York: Spectrum Publications.

Field, T.M. (1980). *High-risk infants and children: Adult and peer interactions.* New York: Academic Press.

Field, T.M., Ignatoff, E., Stringer, S., Brennan, J., Greenberg, R., Widmayer, S., & Anderson, G.C. (1982). Effects of non-nutritive sucking during tube feeding of I.C.U. preterm neonates. *Pediatrics, 70*, 381–384.

Fowler, W., & Swenson, A. (1979). The influence of early language stimulation on development: Four Studies. *Genetic Psychology Monographs, 100*, 73–109.

Freud, S. (1955). Beyond the pleasure principle. In J. Strachey (Ed.), *The standard edition of the complete psychological works of Sigmund Freud* (Vol. 18). London: Hogarth.

Gaiter, J.L. (1985). The behavior and caregiving experiences of term and preterm newborns. In A.W. Gottfried & J.L. Gaiter (Ed.), *Infant stress under intensive care* (pp. 55–82). Baltimore: University Park Press.

Gallagher, J.J., Beckman-Bell, P., & Cross, A. (1983). Families of handicapped children: Sources of stress and its amelioration. *Exceptional Children, 50*(1), 10–19.

Gerdes, J., Abbasi, S., Bhutani, V., & Bowen, F. (1986). Improved survival and short term outcome of urban ''micro preemies.'' *Clinical Pediatrics, 25*, 391.

Gesell, A. (1946). *The ontogenesis of infant behavior.* New York: Wiley & Sons.

Gesell, A., & Armatruda, C. (1945). *The embryology of behavior.* Westport, CT: Connecticut Greenwood Press.

Gianino, A., & Tronick, E.Z. (1988). The mutual regulation model: The infant's self and interactive regulation, coping and defense. In T. Field, P. McCabe, & N. Schneiderman (Eds.), *Stress and coping* (pp. 47–68). Hillsdale, NJ: Erlbaum.

Gilkerson, K., Gorski, P.A., & Panitz, P. (1989). Hospital-based intervention for preterm infants and their families. In S.J. Meisels & J.P. Shonkoff (Eds.), *Handbook of early intervention: Theory, practice and analysis.* Cambridge, MA: Cambridge University Press.

Glass, P., Avery, G.B., Kolinjavadi, N., Subramanian, S., Keys, M.P., Sostek, A.M., & Friendly, D.S. (1985). Effect of bright light in the hospital nursery on the incidence of retinopathy of prematurity. *New England Journal of Medicine, 313*(7), 401–404.

Goldman, P.S. (1976). The role of experience in recovery of function following orbital prefrontal lesions in infant monkeys. *Neuropsychologia, 14*, 401–412.

Goldman-Rakic, P.S. (1980). Development and plasticity of primate frontal association cortex. In

F.O. Schmitt Worden (Ed.), *The cerebral cortex* (pp. 198–218). Cambridge, MA: MIT Press.

Goldson, E. (1983). Bronchopulmonary dysplasia: Its relation to two-year developmental functioning in the very low birthweight infant. In T. Field & A. Sostek (Eds.), *Infants born at risk* (pp. 243–250). New York: Grune and Stratton.

Goldson, E. (1984). Severe bronchopulmonary dysplasia in the very low birth weight infant: Its relationship to developmental outcome. *Journal of Developmental and Behavioral Pediatrics, 5,* 165–168.

Goodwin, S.R., Graven, S.A., & Haberkern, C.M. (1985). Aspiration in intubated premature infants. *Pediatrics, 75,* 85–88.

Gorski, P.A. (1980). Infants at risk. In M.J. Hanson (Ed.), *Atypical infant development* (pp. 57–80).

Gorski, P.A., Hole, W.T., Leonard, C.H., & Martin, J.A. (1983). Direct computer recording of premature infants and nursery care: Distress following two interventions. *Pediatrics, 72,* 198–202.

Gorski, P.A., Huntington, L., & Lewkowicz, D.J. (1987). Handling preterm infants in hospitals: Stimulating controversy about timing stimulation. In N. Gunzenhauser (Ed.), *Infant stimulation: For whom, what kind, and how much?* (pp. 43–51). Skillman, NJ: Johnson & Johnson.

Gottfried, A.W. (1985). Environment of newborn infants in special care units. In A.W. Gottfried & J.L. Gaiter (Ed.), *Infant stress under intensive care* (pp. 23–54). Baltimore: University Park Press.

Gottfried, A.W., & Gaiter, J.L. (1985). *Infant stress under intensive care.* Baltimore: University Park Press.

Guralnick, M.J., & Bennett, F.C. (1987). *The effectiveness of early intervention for at-risk and handicapped children.* New York: Academic Press.

Hack, M., Fanaroff, A., & Merkatz, I. (1979). The low-birth weight infant—evolution of a changing outlook. *New England Journal of Medicine, 301,* 1162–1165.

Hansen, N., & Okken, A. (1979). Continuous TcPO2 monitoring in healthy and sick newborn infants during and after feeding. *Birth defects: Original Article Series, XV*(4), 503–508.

Hasselmeyer, E.G. (1964). The premature neonate's response to handling. *American Nurses Association, 1,* 15–24.

Hinde, R.A. (1970). *Animal behavior.* London, New York: McGraw-Hill.

Hinde, R.A., & Spencer-Booth, Y. (1967). The behavior of the socially living rhesus monkeys in their first two and a half years. *Animal Behavior, 15,* 169–196.

Holm, B., Notter, R., Siegle, J., & Matalon, S. (1985). Pulmonary physiological and surfactant changes during injury and recovery from hyperoxia. *Journal of Applied Physiology, 59,* 5–8.

Hooker, D. (1936). Early fetal activity in mammals. *Yale Journal of Biology and Medicine, 8,* 579–602.

Hooker, D. (1942). Fetal reflexes and instinctual processes. *Psychosomatic Medicine, 4,* 199–205.

Horton, F.H., Lubchenco, L.O., & Gordon, H.H. (1952). Self-regulatory feeding in a premature nursery. *Yale Journal of Biology and Medicine, 24,* 263–272.

Hunt, J. (1963). Motivation inherent in information processing and action. In O.J. Harvey (Ed.), *Motivation and social interaction: The cognitive determinants* (pp. 35–94). New York: Ronald Press.

Hunt, J.V., Cooper, B.A.B., & Tooley, W.H. (1988). Very low birth weight infants at 8 and 11 years of age: Role of neonatal illness and family status. *Pediatrics, 82,* 596–603.

Hyers, T., & Fowler, A. (1986). Adult respiratory distress syndrome. *Federation Proceedings, 45,* 1–10.

Kaluzny, A.D. (1982). Change in health-care settings. In P.L. Trohanis (Ed.), *Strategies for change* (pp. 43–65). Chapel Hill, NC: University of North Carolina, Technical Assistance Development System (TADS).

Kao, L., Durand, D., Phillips, B., & Nickerson, B. (1987). Oral theophylline and diuretics improve pulmonary mechanics in infants with bronchopulmonary dysplasia. *Journal of Pediatrics, 111,* 439–444.

Kao, L., Warburton, D., Platzker, A., & Keens, T. (1984). Effect of isoproterenol inhalation on airway resistance in chronic bronchopulmonary dysplasia. *Pediatrics, 73*, 509–514.

Kao, L., Warburton, D., Sargent, C., Platzker, A., & Keens, T. (1983). Furosemide acutely decreases airway resistance in chronic bronchopulmonary dysplasia. *Journal of Pediatrics, 103*, 624–629.

Klaus, M., & Kennel, J.H. (1982). *Parent-infant bonding.* St. Louis: Mosby.

Klaus, M.H. (1982). Application of recent findings to clinical care. In M.H. Klaus & M.O. Robertson (Eds.), *Birth, interaction, and attachment* (pp. 129–134). Johnson and Johnson Pediatric Roundtable Series No. 6.

Konner, M. (1987). *Becoming a doctor: A journey of initiation into medical school.* New York: Viking Press.

Korner, A.F. (1981). What we don't know about waterbed and apneic preterm infants. *Pediatrics, 68*, 306.

Korner, A.F. (1986). The use of waterbeds in the care of preterm infants. *Journal of Perinatology, 6*(2), 142–147.

Korner, A.F., Guilleminault, C., Vanden Hoed, J., & Baldwin, R.B. (1978). Reduction of sleep apnea and bradycardia in preterm infants on oscillating waterbeds: A controlled polygraphic study. *Pediatrics, 61*, 525.

Korner, A.F., Kraemer, H.C., Haffner, M.E., & Cosper, L. (1975). Effects of waterbed flotation on premature infants: A pilot study. *Pediatrics, 56*, 361.

Korner, A.F., Ruppel, E.M., & Rho, J.M. (1982). Effects of waterbeds on sleep and motility of theophylline-treated preterm infants. *Pediatrics, 70*, 864–869.

Korner, A.F., Schneider, P., & Forrest, T. (1983). Effects of vestibular proprioceptive stimulation on the neurobehavioral development of preterm infants: A pilot study. *Neuropediatrics, 14*, 170–175.

Korones, S.B. (1976). Iatrogenic problems in intensive care. In T. Moor (Ed.), *Report of 1969 Ross Conference on Pediatric Research.* Columbus, OH: Ross Laboratories.

Korones, S.B. (1985). Physical structure and functional organization of neonatal intensive care units. In A.W. Gottfried & J.L. Gaiter (Ed.), *Infant stress under intensive care* (pp. 7–22). Baltimore: University Park Press.

Kramer, L.I., & Pierpoint, M.E. (1976). Rocking waterbeds and auditory stimuli to enhance growth of the preterm infants. *Journal of Pediatrics, 88*, 297–299.

Lamont, R.G., Dunlop, P.D., Crowley, P., Levene, M.I., & Elder, M.G. (1983). Comparative mortality and morbidity of infants transferred in utero or postnatally. *Journal of Perinatal Medicine, 11*, 200–203.

Lawson, K., Daum, C., & Turkewitz, G. (1977). Environmental characteristics of a neonatal intensive care unit. *Child Development, 48*, 1633–1639.

Leib, S.A., Benfield, D.G., & Guidubaldi, J. (1980). Effects of early intervention and stimulation on the preterm infant. *Pediatrics, 66*, 83.

Lewis, M.E., Mishkin, M., Bragin, E., Brown, R.M., Pert, C.B., & Pert, A. (1981). Opiate receptor gradients in monkey cerebral cortex: Correspondence with sensory processing hierarchies. *Science 211*, 1166–1169.

Linn, P.L., Horowitz, F.D., Buddin, B.J., Leake, J.C., & Fox, H.A. (1985). An ecological description of a neonatal intensive care unit. In A.W. Gottfried & J.L. Gaiter (Ed.), *Infant stress under intensive care* (pp. 83–112). Baltimore: University Park Press.

Long, J.G., Philip, A.G.S., & Lucey, J.F. (1980). Excessive handling as a cause of hypoxemia. *Pediatrics, 65*, 203–207.

Lou, H.C., Lassen, N.A., & Friis-Hansen, B. (1979a). Impaired autoregulation of cerebral blood flow in the distressed newborn infant. *Journal of Pediatrics, 94*, 118–121.

Lou, H.C., Lassen, N.A., & Friis-Hansen, B. (1979b). Is arterial hypertension crucial for the development of cerebral hemorrhage in premature infants? *Lancet, 1*, 1215–1217.

McGraw, M.B. (1945). *The neuromuscular maturation of the human infant.* New York: Haffner Press.

Marchini, G., Winberg, J., & Uvnas-Moberg, K. (1988). Plasma concentrations of gastrin and somatostatin after breast feeding in four-day-old infants. *Archives of Disease in Childhood, 63,*(10), 1218–1221.

Martin, R.J., Herrell, N., Rubin, D., & Fanaroff, A. (1979). Effect of supine and prone positions on arterial oxygen tension in the preterm infant. *Pediatrics, 63,* 528–531.

Masi,W. (1979). Supplemental stimulation of the premature infant. In T.M. Field (Ed.), *Infants born at risk: Behavior and development* (pp. 367–388). New York: Spectrum Publications.

Meisels, S.J., Jones, S.N., & Stiefel, G.S. (1983). Neonatal intervention: Problem, purpose, and prospects. *Topics in Early Childhood Special Education: Infants at Risk, 3*(1), 1–13.

Meisels, S.J., Plunkett, J.W., Roloff, D.W., Pasik, P.L., & Stiefel, G.S. (1986). Growth and development of preterm infants with respiratory distress syndrome and broncho-pulmonary dysplasia. *Pediatrics, 77,* 345–352.

Merritt, J., & Kraybill, E. (1986). Retrolental fibroplasia: A five-year experience in a tertiary perinatal center. *Annals of Ophthalmology, 18,* 65–67.

Milligan, D.W.A. (1980). Failure of autoregulation and intraventricular hemorrhage in preterm infants. *Lancet, 1,* 896–898.

Minde, K., Whitelaw, A., Brown, J., & Fitzhardinge, P. (1983). Effect of neonatal complications in premature infants on early parent–child interactions. *Developmental Medicine and Child Neurology, 25,* 763–777.

Minde, K.K., Morton, P., Manning, D., & Hines, B. (1980). Some determinants of mother-infant interaction in the premature nursery. *Journal of American Association of Child Psychiatry, 19,* 1–21.

Minde, K.K., Trehub, S., Carter, C., Boukydis, C., Celhoffer, L., & Morton, P. (1978). Mother-child relationships in the premature nursery: An observation study. *Pediatrics, 61,* 373–379.

Moltz, H. (1960). Imprinting: Empirical basis and theoretical significance. *Psychological Bulletin, 57,* 291–314.

Montagu, A. (1978). *Touching, the human significance of the skin.* New York: Harper & Row.

Mower, G.D., Burchfiel, J.L., & Duffy, F.H. (1982). Animal models of strabismic amblyopia: Physiological studies of visual cortex and the lateral geniculate nucleus. *Developmental Brain Research, 5,* 311–327.

Newman, L.F. (1981). Social and sensory environment: Low birthweight infants in a special care nursery. *Journal of Nervous Mental Disease, 169,* 448–455.

Nurcombe, B., Rauh, V., Howell, D.C., Teti, D.M., Ruoff, P., Murphy, B., & Brennan, J. (1984). An intervention program for mothers of low-birthweight babies: Outcome at six and twelve months. In J.D. Call Galenson (Ed.), *Frontiers of infant psychiatry* (Vol. II, pp. 201–210). New York: Basic Books.

O'Brodovich, H., & Mellins, R. (1985). Bronchopulmonary dysplasia. *American Review of Respiratory Disease, 132,* 694.

Palay, S.L. (1979, October). *Introduction to the nervous system: Basic neuroanatomy.* Lecture delivered at the Harvard Medical School, Boston.

Patterson, P.H. (1979). Epigenetic influences in neuronal development. In S.O. Schmitt & F.G. Worden (Eds.), *Neurosciences fourth study program* (pp. 929–936). Cambridge, MA: MIT Press.

Patterson, P.H., Potter, D.D., & Furshpan, E.J. (1978). The chemical differentiation of the nerve cells. *Scientific American, 239,* 50–59.

Perlman, J.M., & Volpe, J.J. (1983). Suctioning in the preterm infant: Effects on cerebral blood flow velocity, intracranial pressure and arterial blood pressure. *Pediatrics, 72,* 329–334.

Phibbs, C.S., Williams, R.L., & Phibbs, R.H. (1981). Newborn risk factors and costs of neonatal intensive care. *Pediatrics, 68,* 313–321.

Piaget, J. (1952). *The origins of intelligence in children.* New York: International Universities Press.

Pollard, Z. (1980). Secondary angle-closure glaucoma in cicatricial retrolental fibroplasia. *American Journal of Ophthalmology, 89,* 651–653.

Procianoy, R., Garcia-Prats, J., Hittner, H., Adams, J., & Rudolph, A. (1981). An association between retinopathy of prematurity and intraventricular hemorrhage in very low birth weight infants. *Acta Pediatrica Scandinavica, 70,* 473–477.

Purohit, D., Ellison, R., Zierler, S., Miettinen, O., & Nadas, A. (1985). Risk factors for retrolental fibroplasia: Experience with 3025 premature infants. *Pediatrics, 76,* 339–344.

Rausch, P.B. (1981). Effects of tactile and kinesthetic stimulation on premature infants. *Journal of Obstetrical, Gynecological and Neonatal Nursing,* pp. 34–37.

Reynolds, E., & Taghizadeh, A. (1974). Improved prognosis of infants mechanically ventilated for hyaline membrane disease. *Archives of Disease in Childhood, 49,* 505–509.

Rice, R.D. (1977). Neurophysiological development in premature infants following stimulation. *Developmental Psychology, 13,* 69.

Sacks, L., Shaffer, D., Anday, E., Peckham, G., & Delivoria-Papadopoulos, M. (1981). Retrolental fibroplasia and blood transfusion in very low birth weight infants. *Pediatrics, 68,* 770–774.

Sauve, R., & Singhai, N. (1985). Long-term morbidity of infants with BPD. *Pediatrics, 76,* 725.

Scafidi, F.A., Field, T.M., Schanberg, S.M., Bauer, C.R., Bega-Lahr, N., Garcia, R., Poirier, J., Nystrom, G., & Kuhn, C.M. (1986). Effects of tactile/kinesthetic stimulation on the clinical course and sleep/wake behavior of preterm neonates. *Infant Behavior and Development, 9,* 91–105.

Scarr-Salapatek, S., & Williams, M.L. (1972). A stimulation program for low birth weight infants. *American Journal of Public Health, 62,* 662–667.

Schanberg, S.M., & Field, T.M. (1987). Sensory deprivation stress and supplemental stimulation in the rat pup and preterm human neonate. *Child Development, 58,* 1431–1488.

Schmidt, E., & Wittreich, G. (1986, October). *Care of the abnormal newborn: A random controlled clinical trial study of the "Kangaroo method of care for the low birth-weight newborns."* Paper presented at the Interregional Conference on Appropriate Technology Following Birth, World Health Organization, Italy.

Schneirla, T.C. (1959). An evolutionary and developmental theory of biphasic processes underlying approach and withdrawal. In M.R. Jones (Ed.), *Nebraska Symposium on Motivation* (pp. 1–42). Lincoln: University of Nebraska Press.

Schneirla, T.C. (1965). Aspects of stimulation and organization in approach and withdrawal processes underlying vertebrate development. *Advances in Study of Behavior, 1,* 1–74.

Schneirla, T.C., & Rosenblatt, J.S. (1961). Behavioral organization and genesis of the social bond in insects and mammals. *American Journal of Orthopsychiatry, 31,* 223–253.

Schneirla, T.C., & Rosenblatt, J.S. (1963). "Critical periods" in the development of behavior. *Science, 139,* 1110–1115.

Scott, S., Cole, T., Lucas, P., & Richards, M. (1983). Weight gain and movement patterns of very low birthweight babies nursed on lambswool. *Lancet, 2,* 1014–1016.

Scott, S., & Richards, M. (1979). Nursing low-birthweight babies on lambswool. *Lancet, 2,* 1028.

Shelton, T.L., Jeppson, E.S., & Johnson, B.H. (1987). *Family-centered care for children with special health care needs* (2nd ed.). Washington, DC: Association for the Care of Children's Health.

Sherrington, C.S. (1940). *Man on his nature.* Cambridge, MA: Cambridge University Press.

Shohat, M., Reisner, S., Krikler, R., Nissenkorn, I., Yassur, Y., & Ben-Sira, I. (1983). Retinopathy of prematurity: Incidence and risk factors. *Pediatrics, 72,* 159–163.

Smyth, J., Tabachnik, E., Duncan, W.J., Reilly, B.J., & Levison, H. (1981). Pulmonary function and bronchial hyperreactivity in longterm survivors of bronchopulmonary dysplasia. *Pediatrics, 68,* 336–340.

Solkoff, N., & Matuszak, D. (1975). Tactile stimulation and behavioral development among low birthweight infants. *Child Psychiatry and Human Development, 6,* 33–37.

Spinelli, D.N., Jensen, F.E., & DePrisco, G.V. (1980). Early experience effect on dendritic branchings in normally reared kittens. *Experimental Neurology, 68,* 1–11.

Starr, P. (1982). *The social transformation of American medicine.* New York: Basic Books.

Stern, D.N. (1985). *The interpersonal world of the infant. A view from psychoanalysis and developmental psychology.* New York: Basic Books.

Stock, S., & Uvnas-Moberg, K. (1988). Increased plasma levels of oxytocin in response to afferent electrical stimulation of the sciatic and vagal nerves and in response to touch and pinch in anesthetized rats. *Acta Physiologica Scandinavica, 132*(1), 29–34.

Taeusch, H.W., & Ware, J. (1987). Chronic lung disease of prematurity—is the veil lifting. *Perinatal Medicine, 7*, 133–140.

Tepper, R., Morgan, W., Cota, K., & Taussig, L. (1986). Expiratory flow limitation in infants with bronchopulmonary dysplasia. *Journal of Pediatrics, 109*, 1040–1046.

Thoman, E.B. (1987a). Intervention for premature infants: A new perspective. In G. Casto Ascione (Ed.), *Current perspectives in infancy & early childhood research* (pp. 11–20). Logan, UT: Early Intervention Research Institute.

Thoman, E.B. (1987b). Self-regulation by prematures with a breathing blue bear. In J.J. Gallagher (Ed.), *The malleability of children* (pp. 51–69). Baltimore: Brookes Publishing.

Thoman, E.B., & Graham, S.E. (1986). Self-regulation of stimulation by premature infants. *Pediatrics, 78*(5), 855–860.

Thoman, E.B., & Ingersoll, E.W. (1988). *Self-regulation of stimulation by prematures—a replication and evidence for learning* (Abstract). International Society for Developmental Psychobiology.

Towen, B.C.L. (1984). Primitive reflexes—conceptional or semantic problem? In H.F.R. Prechtl (Ed.), *Clinics in developmental medicine, #94: Continuity of neural functions from prenatal to postnatal life* (pp. 115–126). Philadelphia: Lippincott.

Tronick, E.Z. (1989). Emotions and emotional communication in infants. *American Psychologist, 44*, 112–119.

Truog, W., Jackson, C., Badura, R., Sorensen, G., Murphy, J., & Woodrum, D. (1985). BPD and pulmonary insufficiency of prematurity. *American Journal of Diseases of Children, 139*, 351–355.

Turnbull, A.P., & Turnbull, H.R. (1986). Stepping back from early intervention: An ethical perspective. *Journal of the Division of Early Childhood, 10*(2), 106–117.

Uvnas-Moberg, K. (1989). The gastrointestinal tract in growth and reproduction. *Scientific American, 26*(1), 78–83.

Vohr, B., Bell, E., & Oh, W. (1982). Infants with bronchopulmonary dysplasia: Growth pattern and neurologic development outcome. *American Journal of Diseases of Children, 136*, 443–447.

Volpe, J.J. (1987). *Neurology of the newborn*. Philadelphia: W.B. Saunders.

Wahlberg, V. (1987). Alternative care for premature infants—the "kangaroo method:" Advantages, risks, and ethical questions. *Neonatologica, 1*(4), 363–367.

Weinstein, M., & Oh, W. (1981). Oxygen consumption in infants with bronchopulmonary dysplasia. *Journal of Pediatrics, 99*, 959.

Werner, H. (1957). The concept of development from a comparative organismic point of view. In D.B. Harris (Ed.), *The concepts of development* (pp. 125–148). Minneapolis: University of Minnesota Press.

Wheeler, W., Castile, R., Brown, E., & Wohl, M. (1984). Pulmonary function in survivors of prematurity. *American Review of Respiratory Disease, 129*, 218–219.

White, J.L., & Labarba, R.C. (1976). The effects of tactile and kinesthetic stimulation on neonatal development in the premature infant. *Developmental Psychobiology, 9*, 569–577.

Whitelaw, A. (1986). Skin-to-skin contact in the care of very low birth weight babies. *Maternal and Child Health, 7*, 242–246.

Whitelaw, A., Heisterkamp, G., Sleath, K., Acolet, D., & Richards, M. (1988). Skin to skin contact for very low birth weight infants and their mothers. *Archives of Disease in Childhood, 63*, 1377–1380.

Whitelaw, A., & Sleath, K. (1985). Myth of the marsupial mother: Home care of very low birth weight babies in Bogota, Columbia. *Lancet, 1*, 1206–1208.

16
Evaluating Effects of Intervention with Parents of Preterm Infants*

Leila Beckwith
Carol Rodning

Sophisticated medical technology is increasing the rate of survival for infants born very tiny and very early (Hack, Caron, Rivers, & Fanaroff, 1983; Saigal, Rosenbaum, & Stoskopf, 1984). The infants, however, show a greater proportion of neurological, health, and developmental problems than their heavier preterm peers, who in turn show more developmental sequelae than do healthy full-term infants (Fitzhardinge, 1985; McCormick, 1985). Preterm birth is both the cause and the result of multiple biologic risks. The risks may exist prenatally, perinatally, and continue into postnatal life with consequences for development. Although most preterm infants will develop normally, many will have mild to moderate dysfunctions.

Children's development, however, is dependent, not only on their early biologic risks, but on their life experiences as well (Sameroff & Chandler, 1975). Supportive and responsive family environments can buffer children against biologic vulnerabilities whereas less optimal environments compound the problems, thereby causing the double jeopardy of exposing children to a combination of biologic and social adversity (Beckwith & Parmelee, 1986; Escalona, 1982).

Premature birth, and its associated perinatal problems, are experienced by most parents as an acute emotional crisis characterized by anxiety, grief, depression, stress, and for some parents rage and blame, which interfere with the parents' confidence in themselves and their infant (Blacher, 1984; Kaplan & Mason, 1960; Minde, 1984; Seashore, Leifer, & Barnett, 1973). The stress begins immediately after the birth, continues through the infant's hospitalization, and into the child's early years. For parents with fewer resources psychologically, emotionally, and economically, the additional stresses of prematurity may overburden the parents to the extent that sensitivity and responsiveness are reduced.

* Funds for the support of this work were provided by the Center for Prevention Research, National Institute for Mental Health, Grant #MH36902. An earlier version of this work was presented in R. Pianta (Chr.), *Relationship based interventions with infants/young children and their parents*. Symposium presented at the meeting of the American Psychological Association, August 12, 1989, New Orleans.

In addition to the added pressures on parents, preterm infants are often less active, less responsive, and less content social partners than full-term infants (Field, 1987; Goldberg, Brachfield, & DiVitto, 1980). They are likely to be more unpredictable, more fussy during social interaction, have less eye contact, smile less, show less positive affect, and vocalize less (Crnic, Ragozin, Greenberg, Robinson, & Basham, 1983; Field, 1982; Lester, Hoffman, & Brazelton, 1985). The premature infant's biological rhythms of sleep, wake, and feeding are less organized and stable. Parents of preterm infants often need to compensate for their child's interactional deficiencies by increased initiating activity, skill sensitivity, and monitoring of the child's thresholds and needs (Bakeman & Brown, 1980; Crnic et al., 1983). In the initial months, parents of premature infants often do not get the positive feedback from their children that is reassuring about their child's development, affirming about their own effectiveness as parents, and facilitating of pleasure in the parenting role (Goldberg, 1978).

Since it has been shown that the presence of multiple risk factors greatly increases poor developmental outcomes (Rutter, 1987; Sameroff, Seifer, Barocas, Zax, & Greenspan, 1987; Werner & Smith, 1982), interventions that foster supportive and responsive relationships within the child's family are of importance. By lessening potential risk within the family environment, the biological risk can be mitigated (Sameroff & Fiese, 1990; Werner, 1990). The question is to what degree and for how long do professional interventions directed toward support of the parents foster more positive developmental paths for the infants.

In general, intervention programs with parents of preterm infants have consistently shown positive effects (Seitz & Provence, 1990). Minde and his associates (Minde, Shosenberg, & Thompson, 1983; Minde, Whitelaw, Brown, & Fitzhardinge, 1983), found that self-help groups for parents of preterm infants resulted in greater parental confidence in themselves and their children. They had fewer concerns about their infant's health, were more attentive, more interactive during the first year of infancy and as the children became toddlers permitted more autonomy. Another program, by Nurcombe and his associates (1984; Rauh, Achenbach, Nurcombe, Howell, & Teti, 1988), found that as few as 11 sessions with a pediatric intensive care nurse effectively increased parental role satisfaction and confidence, and that the children, at ages 3 and 4, had higher cognitive scores. Two models of intervention were compared to a nonintervention control group by Barrera, Rosenbaum, and Cunningham (1986). One intervention taught parents a specific, developmentally enhancing curriculum, and the other emphasized sensitivity in parent–infant interaction. Both intervention strategies were found to have beneficial effects. Mothers in intervention provided more materials, a greater variety of stimulation, and were more responsive to their infants than the mothers of preterm infants in the control group. The children in both intervention groups had higher developmental scores and more verbal independent play as toddlers than the preterm children in the control group. Remarkably, Widmayer and Field (1981) demonstrated that even short-term intervention during only the first postnatal month was effective. The intervention was designed to promote the mother's understanding of her own infant, and was associated with mothers talking more to their infants, increased responsiveness of the infants during face-to-face interaction at 4 months, and higher developmental scores in the children at 1 year corrected age.

The study discussed in this chapter focuses on children in double jeopardy—sick preterm infants being reared by low-income parents. This investigation differs from others in its evaluation of the power of intervention to influence security in the children's attachment relationships and the mothers' relationships to their own families of origin. We reasoned that intervention would promote more sensitive interactions of mothers to their infants which would in turn foster more secure attachments in the children.

The most extensively developed and empirically supported theory of parent–child relationships is the concept of attachment (Ainsworth, 1973; Ainsworth, Blehar, Waters, & Wall, 1978; Bowlby, 1969; Bretherton & Waters, 1985; Sroufe, 1985). Multiple studies now support that secure early attachment relationships foster positive personality and social development (Bretherton, Bates, Benigni, Camaioni, & Volterra, 1979; Londerville & Main, 1981; Sroufe & Fleeson, 1986; Waters, Wippman, & Sroufe, 1979).

Since there is increasing evidence to support the hypothesis that childhood relationships with the family of origin affect maternal parenting behaviors (Fraiberg, 1980; Main, Kaplan, & Cassidy, 1985; Ricks, 1985; Rutter, 1987; Stevenson-Hinde, 1990) assessments of the mothers understanding of their childhood relationships with their own parents were included in this research. The data now available indicate that serious disruptions in the parent's own family of origin, due to death, separation, or discord, are related to later difficulties in parenting (Rutter, 1987). In addition, maternal reconstruction of childhood relationships are related both to the quality of current parental behavior and to the child's security of attachment (Grossman, Fremmer-Bombik, Rudolph, & Grossman, 1988; Main et al., 1985; Ricks, 1985). It has been argued that parental history and personality are the most influential determinants of parental behavior, because they affect parenting directly as well as indirectly through mediating the extent and satisfaction of social support (Belsky, 1984). That proposition and the evidence for cross-generational transmission of attachment led to our inclusion of maternal history as an important framework for understanding intervention.

METHOD

Subjects

Ninety-one infants at double jeopardy, small preterm infants who had experienced respiratory distress and who were from less economically advantaged families, were identified before hospital discharge from the neonatal intensive care units of four hospitals in the Los Angeles area. Criteria for recruitment for the infants were birthweight less than 2,000 grams, gestational age by maternal report less than 35 weeks, and at least 3 days of respiratory assistance in the neonatal intensive care unit. Criteria for the families were parents who were English speaking without a college degree and neither parent working in more than a semiskilled job. Ninety-one families were recruited and randomly assigned to one of two groups. One group received intervention services, the other did not. Table 1 reports the descriptive information about the infants and their families at recruitment.

There were no significant differences between the groups on maternal age, education, social class, ethnic membership, gender, parity, gestational age, or birthweight. The families in both groups were unemployed, working class, or lower middle class, with a high school education. A large percentage of the sample was single mothers and represented ethnic minorities. The infants were on the average, of very low birthweight ($M = 1,440.9$ g); almost all had experienced respiratory distress that required ventilatory assistance.

Thirty-seven subjects were assigned to the intervention group and 54 to the comparison group. More subjects were enrolled in the comparison group as a higher rate of attrition was observed in this group during the course of recruitment.

Attrition was minimal within the intervention group with only 2 of the 37, 5%, not completing at least one of the two laboratory testings at 13 and 20 months. One family refused to continue in the study when their child was diagnosed with cerebral palsy, and one family could not be located. In contrast, the attrition rate was high within the control group, 35%; 19 did not continue,

Table 1.   Description of Parents and Infants at Intake

	Intervention n = 37		Control n = 53	
	M	SD	M	SD
Parents				
Maternal age	25.1	5.7	24.7	5.9
Maternal education	12.2	2.2	12.1	2.2
Hollingshead	32.8	9.8	31.8	10.8
% Ethnic minority	63%		64%	
% Single	51%		43%	
% Welfare or supported by extended family	49%		50%	
Infants				
Birthweight	1540.4g	417.8	1372.7g	392.3
Gestational age	31.2wk	2.7	30.2wk	2.9
% Females	43%		54%	
% First born	49%		53%	

with 35 participating in at least one of the two laboratory testings at 13 and 20 months. Of those who did not continue, two control families moved out of state, one family refused to continue when their child was diagnosed with cerebral palsy, and the rest could not be located. At the time the infants were 1 year old corrected age; the intervention group contained 35 families, and the control group 35.

INTERVENTION

The intervention was the provision of a home visitor with specialized training in child development. The home visitors were two highly educated professionals, one a pediatric nurse and the other an early childhood educator, both of whom were remarkable personally for their dedication, stability, empathy, and caring. They made themselves available on a weekly basis to the parents, and, if necessary, on evenings and weekends. While the primary emphasis was on the relationship of the intervenor and parent, which was expected in turn to influence the parent–child relationship, the intervenors had a dual focus. They set out to be supportive emotionally, to listen empathically, and to nurture the parents. At the same time, the intervenors worked to involve the parents in observing and interpreting their child's needs and preferences; understanding and responding to their child as a social partner; and affirming their child's strengths and competencies.

During their visits they provided basic services that supported the mother as an individual and as a parent in any way that was appropriately helpful. Services were diverse, including: Transportation to medical appointments and social service appointments, help with household chores that were overwhelming to the mother at the moment, whether doing the dishes or organizing furniture in order to set up a quiet place for the baby. The intervenors were flexible about meeting places and times, and, if they sensed that the mother was feeling depressed or dejected, they would take the mother to lunch and on outings, and facilitate respite child care arrangements.

Intervention began at hospital discharge and lasted until the children were 13 months corrected age. Intervention dramatically reduced attrition to less than 5%, and as reported in the results section, the mothers in intervention were found to be more open and expressive about themselves and their life circumstances than the comparison group when interviewed by an outside evaluator at the end of their first year in the study.

Measures

Assessments of the infant, the mother, and the mother–infant relationship took place at recruitment, and when the infants were 1, 9, and 13 months corrected age, during the period of intervention. Continued assessments were then made

Table 2. Measures

	Recruitment	1	9	13	20
			Months		
Medical					
Obstetrical Complications Scale	X				
Postnatal Complications Scale	X				
Maternal Interview					
Family background	X				
Current relationships to family of origin	X			X	
Relationship to father of baby	X			X	
Friendship/social supports	X			X	
Emotional stability	X			X	
Planfulness in life decisions	X			X	
Role of the baby in mother's life	X			X	
Responsiveness to interview	X			X	
Interest in study	X			X	
Developmental expectations				X	
Mother–Infant Interaction					
Home observations		X	X		
Laboratory Play					X
Infant					
Bayley MDI				X	X
Functional and symbolic play				X	X
Security Attachment				X	X

after intervention ceased, when the infants were 20 and 36 months corrected age. Assessed were medical complications of the mother and the infant, maternal attitudes about significant past and present relationships, quality of the mother–infant interaction, and infant functioning socially and developmentally. Table 2 lists the specific measures.

Medical

Obstetrical Complications Scale. (Littman & Parmelee, 1978). The Obstetrical Complications Scale consists of 41 items defined as optimal or nonoptimal. These include maternal characteristics such as mother's age, health, and prior obstetrical history, pregnancy events such as illness, bleeding and hypertension, and infant items related to birth events, onset of respiration, and the Apgar score.

Postnatal Complications Scale. (Littman & Parmelee, 1978). The Postnatal Complications Scale notes hazardous perinatal events. The items denote the presence or absence of respiratory difficulties, metabolic disturbances, infections, seizures, surgery, and so on.

Maternal

Intake and Exit Interviews. An independent clinician, the second author, naive to all other assessments of the mothers and children and unaware of intervention or control group membership, used the pre- and postintervention maternal interviews, done at recruitment and when the infants were 13 months of age, to rate what in her judgment were significant dimensions of the mothers' lives. These dimensions included: (a) their histories with their family of origin; (b) their present relationships to other adults, including their family of origin, the father of the baby, and friends; (c) personality characteristics within the mothers of emotional maturity, and the ability to plan life decisions; (d) the function of the baby in the mothers' lives; and (e) interest in the study and openness in the interview.

Scores for the rating of stability of *Family Background*, generated by questions from the initial interview with the mother, were assigned as follows: *a(1)* was assigned when the mother indicated that she had been exposed to physical abuse, sexual abuse, or substance abuse by the parent(s); *a(2)* was assigned if her description indicated a discordant household characterized by divorce, remarriage, and/or multiple changes in living circumstances with the mother not living continuously with at least one parent; *a(3)* was assigned for living stably with a single parent; and *a(4)* was assigned for stability in living with two parents whether original or through remarriage.

Scores for *Current Relationship to Family of Origin* ranged from *a(1)*, assigned when the mother was isolated from family of origin; *a(2)* when her description indicated being enmeshed in unsatisfying, discordant, and dependent relationships; *a(3)* when she was judged to be autonomous with limited support from her family; and *a(4)* when she was judged to be autonomous with satisfying support.

Scores for *Relationship to Father of Baby* ranged from *1)* no ongoing relationship; *2)* erratic and unstable; *3)* stable but less satisfying; *4)* stable and satisfying.

Emotional Stability was conceptualized as the way in which the mother discussed the past and present circumstances of her life. It was scored on a 4-point scale ranging from *1)* scattered, fragmented, contradictory statements; *2)* unrealistic, denying, irrelevant statements; *3)* rational, but depressed, anxious, angry, distressed statements; *4)* balanced, accepting, integrated statements.

Scores for *Planfulness in Life Decisions* ranged from *1)* fatalistic and passive; *2)* impulsive decisions and actions without regard to long-term consequences; *3)* goals but unsure of strategies for attainment; and *4)* goals with realistic strategies for attainment.

Scores on *Role of the Baby in the Mother's Life* ranged from *1)* never referred to directly or indirectly; *2)* mother's need for someone to love her; *3)* to solidify the relationship with the father; *4)* generative desire of mother and father to be a family.

Responsiveness to Interview was scored with a range from *1)* concrete and limited responses without elaboration to *4)* open, expansive responses by subjects who took advantage of the opportunity offered by the questions to talk freely with the interviewer.

Interest in the study ranged from *1)* defensive and suspicious; *2)* cautious and reserved; *3)* cooperative and open; and *4)* appreciative of participation.

Scores for *Developmental Expectations*, rated at 13 months but not at intake, ranged from *1)* no expression of awareness of child's development; *2)* unrealistic expectations; *3)* some developmental awareness; *4)* realistic and balanced sense of child's development.

Mother–Infant Interaction

Home observations. Mother–infant interaction was observed both in the home and in a laboratory procedure.

The social transactions and the caretaking that occurred between the mother and the child were observed in *naturalistic observations in the home* when the infants were 1 and 9 months, corrected for degree of prematurity. The independent observer was unaware of all other information about the mothers and children, including intervention or control group membership. Behaviors of each member of the dyad and reciprocal interactions involving both members of the dyads were time-sampled every 15 seconds using a precoded checklist. The frequency scores were then converted to percentages of observed time except for contingency to distress, which was defined as the percentage of fuss/cry episodes which were responded to in less than 45″ (Beckwith, Cohen, Kopp, Parmelee, & Marcy, 1976; Beckwith & Cohen, 1984).

Laboratory play. Observations were made of mother–child interaction in the laboratory in two free play contexts when the infants were 20 months of age, corrected for prematurity. One situation provided miniature representational toys, such as dolls, cars, and dishes, for joint play. The other provided books. Both contexts were videotaped and later scored by an independent rater, naive to the home observations, the interview data with the mothers, and the intervention or control group designation. Two Q-sorts of 40 items for the mothers and 40 items for the children, developed by Richters (1987) to describe mother–child interaction in structured problem-solving tasks in the laboratory, were adapted for the free play situations. Items that related to specific aspects of problem solving were deleted from both Q-sorts, resulting in 23 items for the mothers, and 20 items for the children, which were arrayed by the judge in five-point rectangular distributions with *1* being least characteristic and *5* most characteristic. In order to reduce the data, principal component factor analyses were done for the childrens' and mothers' behaviors. Five factors were generated for each, which cumulatively accounted for greater than 70% of the variance in each set of items. The five factors for the children and mothers are produced in Tables 3 and

Table 3. Mother–Child Interaction at 20 Months:
Item Loadings on Child Factors

Item	Positive Affect	Dependency	On Task	Self Control	Passive
Relaxed in task	.81				
Promotes relationship	.66				
Pays attention to mother		.88			
Enjoys task	.89				
Restless			− .64		
Controls session	− .63				
Reserved				.77	
Indifferent to praise	− .65				
Eager to please mother	.62				
Easily frustrated	− .80				
Distracted			− .59		
Reflective					.63
Tests limits				− .64	
Responsive to mother		.87			
Maintains interest		.59			
Uses instructions		.87			
Spontaneously talks					− .70
Positive mood	.86				
Avoids physical contact	− .61				
Curiosity			.73		

Note. Items are from Q-Sort (Richters, 1987).

4 in terms of the factor on which each item loaded most heavily. The first five factors produced eigenvalues greater than 1.

Infant

Bayley scales of mental development. (Bayley, 1969). The Bayley scales were administered at 13 and 20 months by an examiner who had no knowledge of the mothers, the home observation data, or the intervention or control group designation.

Spontaneous play. Functional and symbolic play was assessed in the laboratory during 16 minutes of spontaneous play with the mother present but not involved. The child's play was recorded live by an observer seated in the playroom using a time-sampling procedure and checklist. Play was categorized as: Simple manipulation, relational play, functional play, and symbolic play. The duration of play by categories was measured by the total number of 10-second intervals in which each category of play was recorded (Ungerer & Sigman, 1983).

Security of attachment. The Strange Situation was used at 13 and 20 months to assess the quality of the infant's attachment to the mother (Ainsworth et al.,

Table 4. Mother–Child Interaction at 20 Months:
Item Loadings on Child Factors

	Factor				
Item	Responsive	Positive Affect	In- Effective	Physical Affection	Engages Child
Over controlling	− .81				
Laughs		.83			
Relaxed	.79				
Engages child					− .69
Unexpressive		− .79			
Cues child to task			− .71		
Creates fun atmosphere			− .41		
Indiscriminate praise			.76		
Patient	.88				
Questions, not directs	.44				
Irritable	− .70				
Smooth transitions	.71				
Adjusts child's posture		− .59			
Uses child's name		.56			
Hugs child				.67	
Intrusive	− .85				
Structures appropriately				− .73	
Self-conscious				.59	
Interrupts	− .86				
Timid			.52		
Promotes relationship	.76				
Cooperative	.80				

Note. Items are from Q-sort (Richters, 1987).

1978). The procedure is a controlled-observation technique consisting of successive episodes in which the infant is exposed in standard order to a novel environment, a female stranger, the departure of the mother, the return of the mother, the departure of the mother again, the return of the stranger, and subsequent return of mother. The procedure was videotaped, and the videotapes for each age were sent to an independent judge, nationally recognized as an expert in attachment theory. The judges, with no other information about the mothers or children, classified the children as to their quality of attachment to their mothers.

RESULTS

Attrition within the Control Group

Since only two members assigned to the intervention group did not complete the study, attrition could not be considered a selective bias in the intervention group.

The high attrition rate in the control group, however, raised the possibility of a selective bias in the controls that were retained. Therefore, analyses were done to identify potential differences between the control subjects who dropped out of the study before the 13-month assessments and the control subjects who remained, and to determine if the retained control group was still equivalent to the intervention group. The three groups were compared by a series of one-way analyses of variance on the subject recruitment criteria of maternal age, maternal education, social class, ethnic membership, marital status, as well as infant gestational age, birthweight, gender and parity. No significant differences were found on these variables.

We considered however, that the group might differ in other subtle, but significant, psychological variables not reflected in demographic characteristics. To test this possibility, an independent judge, the second author, blind to the study design, individual group assignment of the subjects, and whether the family remained or dropped out of the study, was asked to read the interviews done with the mothers at recruitment and to determine whether or not the initial interviews revealed differences between the mothers in any consistent manner.

The judge read the transcripts and identified significant psychological issues that were then scored on a four point scale for each subject, as described in the measures section. A series of one-way analyses of variance were used to determine if the control subjects that left the study differed in meaningful ways from the control and intervention subjects that stayed. Table 5 lists the rating scales and the mean scores for the three groups.

Table 5. Mean Scores at Initial Interview for Intervention and Control Groups

| | Group | | | | | |
| | Intervention Stayed in Study | | Controls Stayed in Study | | Controls Left Study | |
Rating	M	SD	M	SD	M	SD
Family background	2.7[a]	1.1	3.4[a]	1.0	3.1	1.1
Current relationship to family of origin	2.1	1.3	2.7	1.2	2.0	1.2
Relationship to father of baby	2.9	1.1	2.8	1.2	3.1	1.1
Emotional stability	2.4	1.0	2.8[a]	.9	2.1[a]	1.1
Planfulness in life decisions	2.4	1.2	2.7	1.2	2.4	1.2
Role of the baby in mother's life	2.7	1.2	2.8	1.2	2.8	1.2
Responsiveness to interview	2.0	.6	2.5[a]	1.0	1.8[a]	.9
Interest in the study	2.4	.9	2.7[a]	.6	2.2[a]	.5

[a]$p < .05$
Note. Means with same superscripts differed significantly at $p < .05$

As shown in Table 5, this qualitative analysis revealed differences that the demographic variables did not.

The control subjects who stayed in the study came from more stable families of origin than the intervention group. The mean score for the intervention group indicated that, as children, they were more likely to be exposed to familial discord, instability, and disruption, whereas the control group that stayed in the study tended to come from more stable, less chaotic home environments. The control subjects who stayed were also more emotionally stable, less defensive in the interview, and more interested in participating in the study than the control subjects who left. The groups did not differ, however, in (a) their current relationships to their families of origin, (b) the stability of relationship to the father of the child, (c) maternal ability to plan major life decisions, and (d) attitudes toward their children.

In summary, differential attrition created a selection bias that resulted in the intervention group being composed of more defensive women from less stable family backgrounds, and the retained control group composed of mothers who were more open, less defensive, and from more stable family backgrounds.

Results During Intervention

Maternal behavior with the child. Since intervention began at birth, pre- and posttest analyses of maternal behavior with the child were not possible. Therefore, comparisons were made between the intervention and control groups during the course of intervention and after intervention ended. Since the intervention and control groups were determined by random assignment and selected on the basis of the same recruitment criteria, it was considered that systematic differences between the groups would show the influence of intervention. Because attrition acted to potentially bias the control group toward more confidence, and less ambivalence in their parenting relationship with their child, two-way analyses of variance were carried out to test for the influence of intervention, with both stability of family of origin and group assignment as independent factors. Thus, controls from dysfunctional and stable families of origin were compared to intervention mothers from dysfunctional and stable families of origin. Subjects were designated as having dysfunctional families of origin if they had been assigned a rating of either 1 or 2, whereas ratings of 3 or 4 constituted stability.

Naturalistic observations of the infants and their mothers at home when the infants' were at corrected ages of 1 and 9 months were analyzed by a series of 2 (intervention/control) × 2 (dysfunctional/stable families of origin) analyses of variance with the percentage of observed time of each maternal behavior as dependent variables. Analyses included all subjects that were observed at each period, with the exception of four subjects, three from the control group and one from the intervention group, who were excluded from all further analyses because of overt sensory or mental handicap in the child.

At 1 month, there were significant interactions between intervention and family of origin. As can be seen from Table 6, mothers receiving intervention from stable families of origin and control mothers from stable families of origin did not differ in frequencies of maternal behaviors when their infants were one month corrected age. The mothers receiving intervention from dysfunctional or unstable families of origin, however, were significantly different from control mothers from unstable backgrounds. As shown by significant interaction terms on the analyses of variance, and by post-hoc Bonferroni tests, women from unstable backgrounds receiving intervention talked more to their infants, $F(1,62) = 4.2$, $p < .05$; engaged in more mutual visual regard, $F(1,62) = 4.6$, $p < .05$; and spoke more to their infants in an en face position, $F(1,62) = 4.9$, $p < .05$. In fact, mothers from unstable families, who received intervention, were as responsive and attentive to their infants as the women from stable backgrounds in both the intervention and control groups.

By 9 months, there was a main effect of intervention. Women receiving intervention, regardless of family background, talked more to their children than did women who were not in intervention, $F(1,65) = 5.2$, $p < .03$.

Table 6. Mean Mother–Infant Interaction Scores at 1 and 9 Months for Intervention and Control Groups from Stable and Chaotic Families of Origin

	Group							
	Intervention				Control			
	Stable		Chaotic		Stable		Chaotic	
Maternal Behavior	M	SD	M	SD	M	SD	M	SD
1-Month:								
Talks	36%	27	48%[a]	17	34%	22	23%[a]	16
Holds	60	20	56	14	57	21	68	16
Mutual Gaze	09	05	13[a]	07	11	09	05[a]	06
Contingency to Distress	92	16	91	16	93	13	79	22
Face to Face Talks	06	04	10[a]	06	08	08	04[a]	06
9-Month:								
Talks	32	16	29	09*	28	16	20	06
Holds	11	16	08	07	11	09	09	09
Mutual Gaze	09	04	08	05	09	05	08	04
Contingency to Distress	96	11	98	05	92	20	97	06
Face to Face Talks	07	05	06	04	05	04	06	06

Note. Means with same superscripts differed significantly at $p < .05$.
*Intervention and control groups differed at $p < .05$
[a]$p < .05$.

Results at End of Intervention

Maternal attitudes. To determine whether intervention fostered maternal stability and positive attitudes about the maternal role, rating scales used at entrance into the study, were also used to evaluate the exit interviews with the addition of one scale about the children's development and impact on the mother's life. Since the chaos and disruption in the family of origin differentiated intervention and control mothers at entry into the study, two-way analyses of variance were done comparing control mothers from dysfunctional and stable families of origin to intervention mothers from dysfunctional and stable families. Table 7 compares the interview ratings of mothers from more and less dysfunctional families of origin, and who did and did not receive intervention.

As can be seen from Table 7, women receiving intervention in comparison to those who did not, regardless of family background, were more likely to be in more autonomous, less isolated and angrily enmeshed relationships with their own families of origin, $F(1,59) = 3.8$, $p<.05$; were more likely to be in more stable, satisfying relationship with the father of their baby, $F(1,59) = 4.5$, $p<.05$; and were judged to be more emotionally stable, $F(1,59) = 4.7$, $p<.05$. The intervention group was also rated as having significantly more awareness than control mothers of issues in their own child's development, $F(1,60) = 8.3$, $p<.01$; and the impact of their child in their lives, $F(1,60) = 4.4$, $p<.05$. This

Table 7. Mean Scores at Exit Interview for Intervention and Control Groups from Stable and Chaotic Families of Origin

	Group							
	Intervention				Control			
	Stable		Chaotic		Stable		Chaotic	
Rating	M	SD	M	SD	M	SD	M	SD
Current relationship with family of origin	3.4	1.1	2.5	1.5*	2.8	1.3	1.7	1.1
Relationship to father of baby	3.5	.9	2.7	1.2*	2.5	1.4	2.3	1.4
Emotional stability	3.1	.7	3.0	1.0*	2.8	.8	2.1	.9
Planfulness in life decisions	2.4	.7	2.3	.8	2.2	.6	1.7	.8
Role of the baby in mother's life	3.1	.9	2.9	1.0*	2.5	1.0	2.3	1.3
Responsiveness in interview	2.6	.9	2.8	.9*	2.4	.8	2.0	.8
Interest in the study	3.2	.7	3.2	.9	2.7	.6	2.9	.9
Developmental expectations	2.4	1.5	2.5	1.5*	1.7	1.1	1.1	.4

*Intervention and control groups differed at $p < .05$.

was true even for psychologically disadvantaged mothers from unstable families of origin in the intervention group. Women receiving intervention were also judged to be more open and expressive in the interview, $F(1,60) = 4.1$, $p < .05$. Moreover, in comparing the initial and 13-month interviews, by repeated measures analyses of variance, the mothers receiving intervention significantly increased in involvement with their families of origin, whereas the control group remained the same.

Children's development. The children were assessed in the laboratory, at 13 months corrected age, at the conclusion of intervention, on the Bayley Scale of Mental Development, number of functional and symbolic play events, and security of attachment. Two-way analyses of variance with the scores for the Bayley Scale and the play events as dependent variables, and a Chi-Square test with security of attachment as the dependent variable, indicated that the children from the intervention and control groups did not differ on any of the assessments. Similarly, there were no differences associated with the stability of the mother's family of origin.

Despite changes in maternal attitudes and behaviors, there were virtually no apparent differences in the infants at 13 months, at the end of intervention. They did not differ on Bayley MDI scores; infants in both the control and intervention groups performed competently, with the intervention infants gaining an average score of 108, and the control infants 107. Children whose parents did and did not receive intervention also did not differ in security of attachment; there was a high percentage, 49% of insecure attachments in both groups, relative to the original sample of Ainsworth and her associates (1978).

Results 7 Months Postintervention

Children's development. In the 13-month assessments no differences were found between the children in the intervention and control groups. Since maternal attitudes and life circumstances had changed positively in the intervention group, it was hoped that these changes would be transmitted in some discernible way to the children. Table 8 compares the children in the intervention and control groups at 20 months corrected age.

Significant differences in Bayley MDI scores were evident by 20 months, with the children whose mothers had been in intervention achieving higher scores than those whose mothers had been in the control group, $F(1,60) = 4.1$, $p < .05$.

The scoring of attachment at 20 months included classification for D (disorganization), which was not done at 13 months, and therefore used more rigorous criteria for security in attachment (Main & Solomon, 1986).

Maternal–child interaction. Although there were no significant differences in the distribution of classification of security in attachment, it was thought that the impact of intervention would result in increases in attachment behaviors associated with security, that is more positive mutuality, more responsiveness and cooperativeness in the relationship between the mothers and their children.

Table 8.   Mean Scores for Infants at 20 Months in the Intervention and Control Groups from Stable and Chaotic Families of Origin

	Group							
	Intervention				Control			
	Stable		Chaotic		Stable		Chaotic	
Measure	M	SD	M	SD	M	SD	M	SD
Bayley MDI	103.1	12.3	98.2	15.5[a]	94.8	15.3	92.7	15.9
Functional and Symbolic Play Events	51.1	17.3	41.1	19.4	38.4	16.3	42.5	18.6
% Secure Attachment	28%		31%		50%		67%	

[a]$p < .05$

A series of two-way analyses of variance were done with the factor scores as dependent variables, and intervention/control and security/insecurity at 20 months as grouping criteria. Attachment security at 20 months was used as a grouping criteria in order to ascertain whether there were shifts in attachment behaviors even though there had not been shifts in attachment classifications. Positive shifts in attachment behaviors in the insecurely attached intervention groups were anticipated. Tables 9 and 10 compare the intervention and control groups by security of attachment on the factors generated from the Richters Q-sort for mother–child interaction.

There was a significant interaction between intervention and security of attachment for child factor 1, positive affect, $F(1,50) = 4.6$, $p<.05$. Children who showed secure attachments to mothers who had received intervention showed significantly more positive affect in play with them than did children in secure attachment relationships with mothers who had not received intervention, as well as children in insecure relationships with mothers in intervention. The differences in the factor scores between the securely attached intervention and securely attached control groups suggested that the secure classification did not

Table 9.   Mean Child Factor Scores at 20 Months for Intervention and Control Groups Whose Children Did and Did Not Show Security of Attachment

	Group			
	Intervention		Control	
Factor	Secure	Insecure	Secure	Insecure
1. Positive Affect	.69[a]	− .24[b]	− .24[b]	− .03
2. Dependency	− .09	− .30	.42	− .07
3. Task behavior	− .18	.06	.01	.17
4. Self-control	.51	− .15	− .03	.35
5. Passive	− .11	.06	.49	− .03

Note. Factor score with different superscripts differ significantly from each other, $p < .05$.

Table 10.   Mean Maternal Factor Scores at 20 Months for Intervention and Control Groups Whose Children Did and Did Not Show Secure Attachment

| | Group | | | |
| | Intervention | | Control | |
Factor	Secure	Insecure	Secure	Insecure
1. Responsiveness	.25	− .07	.28	− .23
2. Positive Affect	.76[a]	− .19[b]	− .27[b]	.06
3. Ineffective	− .11	− .07	.16	.22
4. Physical Affection	.09	− .37	.26	− .13
5. Engages Child	.27	.11	− .27	− .01

Note. Factor score with different superscripts differ significantly from each other, $p < .05$.

represent a single profile of characteristic behaviors in nonstressful free play interaction with their mothers. Security in the intervention group was characterized by more positive affect, whereas securely attached children in the control group were less affectively positive.

There was also a significant interaction found between intervention and security of attachment for maternal factor 2, positive affect, $F(1,50) = 5.2$, $p<.05$. The differences in the factor scores, as shown by posthoc Bonferroni tests, suggested that the mothers in intervention who established a secure attachment relationship with their children, were able in a nonstressful situation to be more affectively positive, i.e., more humorous and playful. In contrast, the mothers in the control group who established a secure attachment relationship with their children were more serious, as were mothers in the intervention group with children with insecure attachments.

A comparable series of two-way analyses of variance were conducted with the five maternal and child factors as dependent variables, and intervention/control and stable/unstable family of origin as grouping criteria. One maternal factor, factor 3: Ineffectiveness in the mother–child relationship, significantly discriminated between mothers from chaotic and stable families of origin, $F(1,50) = 5.00$, $p<.05$. Mothers from chaotic families of origin in the intervention group had a mean factor score of .22, similar mothers in the control group had a mean factor score of .45, whereas mothers from stable families of origin in the intervention group had a mean score of − .42 and the control group counterparts had a mean score of − .04. This finding points to the powerful influence of experience in the family of origin on the next generation's ability to be positively effective in their relationships with their own children.

DISCUSSION

The subjects for this study were intentionally chosen for both biological and social vulnerability in the infant and family. Previous studies that investigated issues of prematurity in more psychologically and economically advantaged samples likely had subjects that were motivated to participate by interest in the issue, interest in their child, or a sense of social obligation. In contrast, in the present study the provision of services and an ongoing supportive relationship with the intervenor provided strong motivation for many of the families in the intervention group to participate. The absence of services for control subjects created an unexpected bias toward retaining families that were more stable and organized with functioning social support systems. Qualitative, clinical analyses of the initial interviews in which mothers retrospectively reported their family experiences as children revealed significantly more dysfunction, abuse, and instability in the lives of the mothers in the intervention group.

While all groups were comparable on recruitment criteria, the shift toward more personal resources in the control group, as the result of attrition, necessitated larger gains in the intervention group for intervention effects to become evident. Demonstrating differences between the intervention and control groups then, required more change from the most vulnerable group.

In the study, despite the need for extraordinary gains in the group with the most risk factors, intervention was associated with positive changes in maternal behavior and attitudes. The impact of intervention on the mother was consistent with many other intervention studies of parents with preterm infants (Heinicke, Beckwith, & Thompson, 1988; Seitz & Provence, 1990). More specifically, the mothers in intervention in this study became more emotionally stable themselves over the course of intervention and were able to form more autonomous and supportive relationships to their own families of origin. With their preterm infants, the mothers in intervention were more responsive during the infant's first year of life. During the course of intervention, it was the mothers from the unstable families of origin who showed the most noticeable changes in their attitudes and behaviors.

While it was hoped that the number of children with secure attachments would be higher in the intervention group, this was not the case at either 13 or 20 months. However, the children did differ significantly on developmental quotients at 20 months. As expected for children from low-SES homes, DQ scores declined in both the intervention and control groups during the second year of life. However, the scores declined less for children in the intervention group and remained above 100 for the children in intervention whose mothers came from stable families of origin.

While the maternal changes from intervention were not directly transmitted to security of attachment of the child, 7 months postintervention showed that children with secure attachments in the intervention group had more positive affect and a greater sense of autonomy while interacting with their mothers than all other children including their secure counterparts in the control group. Similarly, the mothers in invention with secure attachment relationships to their children were more humorous, more effective, and permitted more independence in their children's activity than all other mothers.

It is interesting that the effects of intervention during the first year of life were evident in increased involvement between the mother and infant, and in the second year of life in increased positive affect and autonomy. It appears that intervention facilitated the mothers' developmentally age-appropriate responses to their children, as also noted by Minde and his associates (1983) in their intervention project.

The more evident changes associated with intervention, when it was occurring, were with the mothers at higher parenting risk, from unstable families of origin, whereas the evident differences seven months following intervention were with the mothers and infants at lower risk, those with secure attachment relationships. It appears that in this stressed parental group, the effects of intervention were more transitory and short lived for the women at higher risk, and the effects were more durable for those at lower risk.

The powerful influence of experience in the family of origin on the next generation's ability to be positively effective in their relationships with their own children, was evident in the mothers' involvement with their infants, and effective parenting with their toddlers. Cross-generational transmission was apparent even though the measurement of dysfunction, abuse, and stability in the family of origin was grossly measured by the mother's response to a limited number of questions and her intimations about traumatic events experienced in her family. It is interesting to note, however, that this cross-generational impact on the mother was not transmitted directly to the child in the organization of the attachment relationship in infancy and toddlerhood. The fact that the clinical interview did not evaluate the meaning the mother had created out of her childhood and family experiences may have obscured evidence for direct cross-generational transmission of attachment organization (Main et al., 1985; Ricks, 1985).

The effectiveness of intervention was mediated by preexisting factors in the mothers' own lives and relationship histories. Although it was expected that the relationship of the intervenors to the mothers would influence the infants through the mothers, it turned out that it was the mothers' relationship histories that mediated the impact of intervention.

REFERENCES

Ainsworth, M.D.S. (1973). The development of infant-mother attachment. In B.M. Caldwell & H.N. Ricciuti (Eds.), *Review of child development research* (Vol. 3, pp. 1–94). Chicago: University of Chicago Press.

Ainsworth, M., Blehar, M., Waters, E., & Wall, S. (1978). *Patterns of attachment*. Hillsdale, NJ: Erlbaum.

Bakeman, R., & Brown, J.V. (1980). Early interaction: Consequences for social and mental development at three years. *Child Development, 51*, 437–447.

Barrera, M., Rosenbaum, P., & Cunningham, C. (1986). Early home intervention with low birth weight infants and their parents. *Child Development, 57*, 20–33.

Bayley, N. (1969). *Bayley Scales of Infant Development*. New York: Psychological Corporation.

Beckwith, L., Cohen, S.E., Kopp, C.B., Parmelee, A.H., & Marcy, T.G. (1976). Caregiver-infant interaction and early cognitive development in preterm infants. *Child Development, 45,* 579–587.

Beckwith, L., & Cohen, S.E. (1984). Home environment and cognitive competence in preterm children in the first five years. In A.W. Gottfried (Ed.), *Home environment and early mental development.* New York; Academic Press.

Beckwith, L., & Parmelee, A.H., Jr. (1986). EEG patterns of preterm infants, home environment and later IQ. *Child Development, 57,* 777–789.

Belsky, J. (1984). The determinants of parenting, A process model. *Child Development, 55,* 83–96.

Blacher, J. (1984). Sequential stages of parental adjustment to the birth of a child with handicaps: Fact or artifacts? *Mental Retardation, 22,* 55.

Bowlby, J. (1969). *Attachment and loss: Vol 1. Attachment.* New York: Basic Books.

Bretherton, I., Bates, E., Benigni, L., Camaioni, L., & Volterra, V. (1979). Relationships between cognition, communication, and quality of attachment. In E. Bates, L. Benigni, I. Bretherton, L. Camaion, & V. Volterra (Eds.), *The emergence of symbols: Cognition and communication in infancy* (pp. 223–269). New York: Academic Press.

Bretherton, I., & Waters, E. (Eds.). (1985). Growing points of attachment theory and research. *Monographs of the Society for Research in Child Development, 50* (1-2, Serial No. 209).

Crnic, K.A., Ragozin, A.S., Greenberg, M.T., Robinson, N.M., & Basham, R.B. (1983). Social interaction and developmental competence of preterm and full-term infants during the first year of life. *Child Development, 54,* 119–121.

Escalona, S.K. (1982). Babies at double hazard: Early development of infants at biologic and social risk. *Pediatrics, 70,* 670–676.

Field, T.M. (1982). Individual differences in the expressivity of neonates and young infants. In R. Feldman (Ed.), *Development of nonverbal behavior in children.* New York: Springer-Verlag.

Field, T. (1987). Affective and interactive disturbances in infants. In J.D. Osofsky (Ed.), *Handbook of infant development.* New York: John Wiley.

Fitzhardinge, P.M. (1985). Follow-up studies on infants. In H. Winick (Ed.), *Mother and infant.* New York: John Wiley.

Fraiberg, S. (Ed.). (1980). *Clinical studies in infant mental health: The first year of life.* New York: Basic Books.

Goldberg, S. (1978). Prematurity: Effects on parent-infant interaction. *Journal of Pediatric Psychology, 3,* 137–144.

Goldberg, S., Brachfield, S., & Divitto, B. (1980). Feeding, fussing and play: Parent-infant interaction in the first year as a function of prematurity and perinatal medical problems. In T. Field, S. Goldberg, & D. Stern (Eds.), *High-risk infants and children: Adult and peer interactions.* New York: Academic Press.

Grossman, K., Fremmer-Bombik, E., Rudolph, J., & Grossman, K.E. (1988). Maternal attachment representations as related to patterns of infant-mother attachment and maternal care during the first year. In R.A. Hinde & J. Stevenson-Hinde (Eds.), *Relationships within families: Mutual influences* (pp. 241–260). Oxford: Clarendon Press.

Hack, M., Caron, B., Rivers, A., & Fanaroff, A.A. (1983). The very low birth weight infant: The broader spectrum of morbidity during infancy and early childhood. *Journal of Developmental and Behavioral Pediatrics, 4,* 243.

Heinicke, C.H., Beckwith, L., & Thompson, A. (1988). Early intervention in the family system: A framework and review. *Infant Mental Health Journal, 9* (2), 111–141.

Kaplan, D.N., & Mason, E.H. (1960). Maternal reactions to premature birth viewed as an acute emotional disorder. *American Journal of Orthopsychiatry, 30,* 539–552.

Lester, B.M., Hoffman, J., & Brazelton, T.B. (1985). The rhythmic structure of mother-infant interaction in term and preterm infants. *Child Development, 56,* 15–27.

Littman, B., & Parmelee, A.H. (1978). Medical correlates of infant development. *Pediatrics, 61*, 470–474.

Londerville, S., & Main, M. (1981). Security of attachment, compliance and maternal training methods in the second year of life. *Developmental Psychology, 17*, 289–299.

Main, M., Kaplan, N., & Cassidy, J. (1985). Security in infancy, childhood and adulthood: A move to the level of representation. In I. Bretherton & E. Waters (Eds), *Growing points of attachment theory and research. Monographs of the Society for Research in Child Development, 50*, 1-2 (Serial No. 209).

Main, M., & Solomon, J. (1986). Discovery of an insecure disorganized/disoriented attachment pattern: Procedures, findings and implications for the classification of behavior. In M. Yogman & T.B. Brazelton (Eds.), *Affective development in infancy*. Norwood, NJ: Ablex Publishing Corp.

McCormick, M.C. (1985). The contribution of low birth weight to infant mortality and childhood morbidity. *New England Journal of Medicine, 312*, 82–90.

Minde, K. (1984). The impact of prematurity on the later behavior of children and on their families. *Perinatology, 11*, 227.

Minde, K., Shosenberg, N., & Thompson, J. (1983). Self-help groups in a premature nursery-infant behavior and parental competence one year later. In E. Galenson & J. Call (Eds.), *Frontiers of infant psychiatry* (pp. 264–271). New York: Basic Books.

Minde, K., Whitelaw, A., Brown, J., & Fitzhardinge, P. (1983). Effects of neonatal complications in premature infants on early parent-infant interactions. *Developmental Medicine & Child Neurology, 25*, 763–777.

Nurcombe, B., Howell, D.C., Rauh, V.A., Teti, D.M., Ruoff, P., & Brennan, J. (1984). An intervention program for mother of low-birthweight infants: Preliminary results. *Journal of the American Academy of Child Psychiatry, 23*, 319–325.

Rauh, V.A., Achenbach, T.M., Nurcombe, B., Howell, C.T., & Teti, D.M. (1988). Minimizing adverse effects of low birthweight: Four-year results of an early intervention program. *Child Development, 59*, 544–553.

Richters, J.E. (1987, April). Trading places: Varying attachment status in mother-child interactions. In K. McCartney (Chr.), *Bi-direction of effects in parent-child interaction*. Symposium conducted at the Society for Research in Child Development, Baltimore.

Ricks, M.H. (1985). The social transmission of parental behaviors: Attachment across generations. In E. Bretherton & E. Waters (Eds.), *Growing points of attachment and research. Monographs of the Society for Research in Child Development, 50*, 1-2 (Serial No. 209).

Rutter, M. (1987). Continuities and discontinuities from infancy. In J.D. Ososfsky (Ed.), *Handbook of infant development*. New York: Wiley.

Saigal, S., Rosenbaum, P., & Stoskopf, F. (1984). Outcome in infants 501–1000 grams birthweight delivered to residents of the McMaster Health Region. *Journal of Pediatrics, 105*, 969–976.

Sameroff, A.J., & Chandler, M.J. (1975). Reproductive risk and continuum of caretaking causality. In F.D. Horowitz, E.M. Hetherington, S. Scarr-Salapatek, & M. Siegel (Eds.), *Review of child development research* (pp. 187–244). Chicago: University of Chicago Press.

Sameroff, A.J. & Fiese, B.H. (1990). Protective factors in individual resilience. In S.J. Meisels & J.P. Shonkoff (Eds.), *Handbook of early childhood intervention*. New York: Cambridge University Press.

Sameroff, A.J., Seifer, R., Barocas, B., Zax, M., & Greenspan, S. (1987). IQ scores of 4-year-old children: Social-environment risk factors. *Pediatrics, 79* (3), 343–350.

Seashore, M.L., Leifer, A.D., & Barnett, C.T. (1973). The effects of denial of early mother-infant interaction on maternal self-confidence. *Journal Personality & Social Psychology, 26*, 269–378.

Seitz, V., & Provence, S. (1990). Protective factors in individual resilience. In S.J. Meisels & J.P. Shonkoff (Eds.), *Handbook of early childhood intervention*. Cambridge University Press.

Sroufe, L.A. (1985). Attachment classification from the perspective of infant-caregiver of infant-caregiver relationships and infant temperament. *Child Development, 56* 1-14.

Sroufe, L.A., & Fleeson, J. (1986). Attachment and the construction of relationships. In W. Hartup & Z. Rubin (Eds.), *The nature and development of relationships* (pp. 51–71). Hillsdale, NJ: Erlbaum.

Stevenson-Hinde, J. (1990). Attachment within family systems: An overview. *Infant Mental Health Journal, 11,* 218–227.

Ungerer, J., & Sigman, M. (1983). Developmental lags in preterm infants from one to three years. *Child Development, 54,* 1217–1228.

Waters, E., Wippman, J., & Sroufe, L.A. (1979). Attachment, positive affect, and competence in the peer groups: Two studies in construct validation. *Child Development, 50,* 821–829.

Werner, E.E. (1990). Protective factors in individual resilience. In S.J. Meisels & J.P. Shonkoff (Eds.), *Handbook of early childhood intervention.* New York: Cambridge University Press.

Werner, E.E., & Smith, R.S. (1982). *Vulnerable but invincible: A longitudinal study of resilient children and youths.* New York: McGraw-Hill.

Widmayer, S., & Field, T. (1981). Effects of Brazelton demonstrations for mothers on the development of preterm infants. *Pediatrics, 67,* 711–714.

17

Efficacy of Comprehensive Early Intervention for Low-Birthweight Premature Infants and Their Families: The Infant Health and Development Program*

Ruth T. Gross
Jeanne Brooks-Gunn
Donna Spiker

Biological and environmental circumstances render young children vulnerable to deficits in developmental well-being, including physical and emotional health, cognitive and verbal abilities, and social competence (Brooks-Gunn, 1990a).

Low-birthweight (LBW) premature infants may be at risk from both biological and environmental factors since socioeconomic deprivation is a risk factor for prematurity. The Infant Health and Development Program (IHDP) was therefore undertaken to test the efficacy of a comprehensive intervention in the first 3 years of life in improving the health and developmental outcome of these vulnerable infants. This multicenter randomized controlled trial has the potential to provide pertinent information on national policy matters, particularly with regard to the efficacy of early intervention programs in enhancing the school-relevant outcomes of such children (IHDP, 1990).

---

* The Infant Health and Development Program was funded by grants to the Department of Pediatrics, Stanford University; the Frank Porter Graham Child Development Center, University of North Carolina at Chapel Hill; and the eight participating universities by the Robert Wood Johnson Foundation. Additional support was provided from the Pew Charitable Trusts; the Bureau of Maternal and Child Health and Resources Development and the National Institute of Child Health and Human Development, HRSA, PHS, DHHS (MCH-060515); and the Stanford Center for the Study of Families, Children, and Youth. The second author was also supported by grants to the Follow-up of the Infant Health and Development Program from the Pew Charitable Trusts and the Bureau of Maternal and Child Health and Resources Development.

Dr. Gross was National Study Director of the Infant Health and Development Program (IHDP). Dr. Spiker was Deputy Director of the IHDP. Dr. Brooks-Gunn is Co-Director of the IHDP Follow-up Program.

We would like to express our gratitude to all the participants in the IHDP and to Dr. Ruby Hearn, Vice President of the Robert Wood Johnson Foundation. Rosemary Deibler, Jamie Traeger, and Diane McIntosh are to be thanked for their help in manuscript preparation.

411

IMPACT OF LBW

Incidence of LBW

Approximately 250,000 LBW infants ($\leq$ 2,500 grams) are born each year in the United States, constituting 6% to 7% of all births in 1986 (National Center for Health Statistics, 1989). LBW incidence has remained discouragingly stable for the past decade. However, substantially more LBW infants than before are surviving to be discharged home (Lee, Paneth, Gartner, Pearlman, & Gruss, 1980; Hack, Fanaroff, & Merkatz, 1975; McCormick, 1985). The success in achieving improved survival rates for LBW infants raises concerns about their subsequent health and development.

Morbidity Associated with LBW

While a decrease in LBW infant mortality has occurred as a result of the technological advances in perinatal care, health and developmental problems are seen in many survivors (Hagberg, 1979; McCormick, 1990; Paneth et al., 1981). Such problems include intellectual and cognitive delays, major neurosensory handicapping conditions, minor neurodevelopmental deficits, psychosocial problems, school failure, and a variety of health problems (Hoy, Bill, & Sykes, 1988; Kopp, 1983; McCormick, 1989; various chapters, this volume).

Intellectual deficits are more common in LBW than in full birthweight (FBW) children (Hoy et al., 1988; McCormick, 1989). Studying a sample of approximately 600 children born in two Edinburgh hospitals in 1953–1955, Drillien (1964) demonstrated that IQ scores decline with decreasing birthweight in the first four years of life. The percentage of children with IQ scores below 80 at 4 years was 29% for those under 4.8 pounds, 13% for those between 4.9 and 5.8 pounds, and 4% for those above 5.9 pounds. In a more recent study of 501 LBW and 203 FBW children born in 1958–1965 (McBurney & Eaves, 1986), the difference in scores of the LBW and FBW groups on the Stanford-Binet Intelligence Scale was nine points at 30 months and 15 points at 48 months, even after excluding children with major cerebral deficits or significant learning or visual problems, and those with IQs under 50. In a more recent small-sample study of very low-birthweight infants ($\leq$ 1,500 grams) and matched controls, all born in 1976, IQ scores were lower for LBW than FBW 9-year-olds (Klein, Hack, & Breslau, 1989).

As the LBW survivors reach school years, there is an increased incidence of school dysfunction (Caputo, Goldstein, & Taub, 1979; Drillien, Thompson, & Burgoyne, 1980; Dunn, 1986; Grunau, 1986; Nickel, Bennett, & Lamson, 1982). When compared on a group basis with FBW children, their performance is lower on some measures of language development, school success, and academic achievement through middle childhood (Breslau, Klein, & Allen, 1987; Dunn, 1986). For example, in the Vancouver Study (Grunau, 1986), 22% of the LBW cohort was below grade level in the first year of school, and an additional 15% had been placed in special classes, schools or institutions (see Klein et al., 1989, and McCormick et al., 1989, for similar results). In summary, the biological vulnerability of LBW infants is seen in higher rates of health and developmental dysfunction than FBW infants.

This vulnerability is compounded by the association between socioeconomic status and psychosocial development such that lower developmental scores and poor health are seen among disadvantaged children when controlling for elements of neonatal status (Collaborative Group, 1984; Eaves, Nattall, Klonoff, & Dunn, 1970; Escalona, 1982; Frisch, Belek, Meller, & Eugel, 1975; McCormick, Shapiro, & Starfield, 1984; Shapiro, McCormick, Starfield, Krischer, & Bross, 1980). Adverse outcomes are not only seen in infancy, but persist through early and middle childhood. In fact, the effects of neuromotor, perceptual and behavioral problems may become more pronounced with age, given the increased demands (both academic and social) placed upon children in elementary school, and may become especially pronounced for LBW disadvantaged children (Levine, 1990; McCormick & Brooks-Gunn, 1989).

RATIONALE FOR EARLY INTERVENTION PROGRAMS FOR LBW INFANTS

Both the results of previous intervention programs for LBW infants and for socioeconomically disadvantaged children informed our decision to mount the Infant Health and Development Program.

Programs for LBW Children

The extent to which neonatal and later early interventions can prevent or ameliorate the adverse outcomes in LBW, premature infants is uncertain but is suggested by results of several types of studies. There is some evidence that visual and kinesthetic stimulation in the newborn nursery can lead to short-term gains in physical and cognitive development (Ramey, Bryant, Sparling, & Wasik, 1984; Bennett, 1987). Other studies have sought to enhance the quality of the mother–newborn relationship through teaching the mother about the neonate's behavior and/or providing parent supports groups (Brown et al., 1980; Klaus & Kennell, 1982; Minde et al., 1980). The outcomes of such interventions have been mixed, with few data on long-term effects.

There are also a number of single site, small-sample studies of home visiting interventions for LBW infants that have reported significant improvements in the developmental status of the participants (Scarr-Salapatek & Williams, 1973; Ross, 1984; Bromwich & Parmelee, 1979; Resnick, Eyler, Nelson, Eitzman, & Bucciarelli, 1987; Field, Field, Goldberg, Stern, & Sostek, 1980;). Once again, the long-term effects of such programs are unknown. Furthermore, even less is known about the effects of center-based programs that directly target LBW infants, who may be vulnerable to participation in a group care component which increases exposure to acute infectious conditions (Haskins & Kotch, 1986; Child Day Care Infectious Disease Study Group, 1984).

Programs for Socioeconomically Disadvantaged Children

The most persuasive evidence that early intervention might avert negative adverse childhood outcomes is found in studies of primarily FBW children from socioeconomically deprived families. In particular early educational services have led to improvements in cognitive functioning and school performance for full-term disadvantaged children, although these have been primarily preschool programs. The results from 11 separate programs were summarized by Lazar, Darlington, Murray, Royce, and Snipper (1982). Most of the children in these programs were low-income black children. When compared to controls (some randomized and some matched samples), children who had attended the preschool intervention programs demonstrated higher intelligence scores at age 6, were less likely to have been held back a grade or to be in special classes by middle childhood, and were more likely to have higher math achievement scores in the early grades. These findings are particularly impressive given that the study samples comprised children with preschool Stanford-Binet IQ scores of 70 to 85. Results from the Abecedarian Project and Project CARE, two early interventions begun in infancy, providing home-based and center-based care, and using a curriculum upon which the IHDP curriculum was based, report similar positive findings (Ramey, Bryant, , & Wasik, 1985; Ramey & Campbell, 1987). The Parent–Child Development Centers, which also provided early center-based intervention, report sustained effects as well (Blumenthal, 1989).

In contrast to data on cognitive and school outcomes, little information is available about the efficacy of such early programs in promoting behavioral competence (reductions in behavior problems, increases in prosocial behavior) (Benasich, Brooks-Gunn, & Clewell, 1990). Likewise, only a few studies have investigated and reported enhanced maternal employment, maternal education, and parenting skills (Benasich et al., 1990; Clewell, Brooks-Gunn, & Benasich, 1989).

The success of early educational interventions for socioeconomically disadvantaged children provided a rationale for investigating the effectiveness of such interventions for LBW premature children, many of whom would have the additional problem of socioeconomic disadvantage.

THE INFANT HEALTH AND DEVELOPMENT PROGRAM

Design of the Study

The IHDP is a multicenter, randomized, controlled trial to evaluate the efficacy of an intervention consisting of pediatric follow-up, early child development programs and family support services in reducing the prevalence of health and developmental problems among LBW, premature infants (in this study, defined as $\leq$ 2,500 grams and $\leq$ 37 weeks gestational age) (IHDP, 1990). Infants were randomized by the National Study Office (NSO) to either intervention (INT) or follow-up (FU) immediately after hospital discharge, using a procedure that involved close monitoring for balance and for absence of bias on initial characteristics associated with their outcomes (Efron, 1971; Pocock & Simon, 1975). The characteristics for which balance was sought were birthweight, gender, maternal age, maternal education, maternal race (black, Hispanic, white and other), primary language in the home, and infant participation in another study. For full details of the randomization procedure, see Kraemer and Fendt (1990). See Table 1 for the distribution of these characteristics.

Organization

Medical schools in eight demographically diverse geographical locations were selected by competitive review to participate in the IHDP: University of Arkansas for Medical Sciences; Albert Einstein College of Medicine of Yeshiva University; Harvard Medical School; University of Miami School of Medicine; University of Pennsylvania School of Medicine; University of Texas Health Science Center at Dallas; University of Washington School of Medicine; and Yale University School of Medicine. The coordinating center for the program, the National Study Office, was located at Stanford University. It was responsible for the management of the study and for the collection, analyses, and dissemination of the data. The development and implementation of the specific program for the children receiving the intervention was the responsibility of the Program Development Office at the Frank Porter Graham Child Development Center at the University of North Carolina. A Research Steering Committee was charged with producing the research plan and making decisions related to the research issues. A National Advisory Committee served in an oversight capacity.

Choice of LBW Groups

The rationale for choosing LBW premature infants was that, as a group, they exhibit cognitive, scholastic, and behavioral deficits, when compared to FBW infants from comparable socioeconomic backgrounds. Such deficits are seen

Table 1. Baseline Characteristics (Prerandomization) of the Primary Analysis Group

Baseline Characteristics	ARK Mean	(SD)	EIN Mean	(SD)	HAR Mean	(SD)	MIA Mean	(SD)	PEN Mean	(SD)	TEX Mean	(SD)	WAS Mean	(SD)	YAL Mean	(SD)
Birthweight (grams):																
Intervention Group	1861.0	(429.1)	1785.3	(427.6)	1741.2	(455.0)	1727.1	(492.7)	1920.9	(422.3)	1754.3	(395.4)	1810.6	(432.5)	1947.8	(434.2)
Follow-Up Group	1817.0	(437.1)	1837.9	(420.9)	1761.7	(466.0)	1682.4	(586.3)	1810.4	(466.8)	1746.3	(440.9)	1842.6	(455.8)	1719.9	(504.3)
Gestational Age (weeks):																
Intervention Group	33.1	(2.3)	32.6	(2.5)	33.1	(2.8)	32.6	(2.3)	33.6	(2.7)	32.8	(2.8)	33.1	(2.5)	33.3	(2.2)
Follow-Up Group	33.0	(2.5)	32.8	(2.5)	32.7	(2.9)	32.7	(2.6)	33.7	(2.7)	33.2	(2.8)	33.5	(3.1)	32.7	(3.0)
Neonatal Health Index:*																
Intervention Group	100.5	(16.4)	104.2	(14.1)	100.9	(14.2)	103.0	(15.0)	99.8	(15.8)	98.4	(19.2)	101.4	(15.9)	97.3	(16.4)
Follow-Up Group	99.7	(15.7)	97.8	(16.5)	99.6	(16.7)	97.7	(16.3)	100.1	(16.1)	100.9	(13.9)	99.2	(16.1)	101.8	(15.4)
Maternal Age (years):																
Intervention Group	23.3	(4.5)	24.8	(6.1)	26.4	(5.9)	22.7	(6.1)	24.3	(5.8)	22.0	(6.0)	26.3	(5.4)	26.9	(5.9)
Follow-Up Group	24.5	(5.9)	25.7	(6.5)	27.7	(5.7)	22.7	(5.2)	22.8	(5.7)	21.4	(5.0)	27.3	(5.7)	25.7	(5.8)
Maternal Education:**																
Intervention Group	1.8	(0.8)	1.7	(0.9)	2.2	(0.8)	1.5	(0.7)	1.7	(0.8)	1.6	(0.6)	2.1	(0.9)	2.3	(0.8)
Follow-Up Group	2.0	(0.8)	1.8	(0.9)	2.5	(0.7)	1.5	(0.7)	1.9	(0.8)	1.4	(0.6)	2.2	(0.8)	2.3	(0.8)
	%		%		%		%		%		%		%		%	
Gender:																
Male:																
Intervention Group	47.9		50.0		48.9		52.3		47.9		49.0		49.0		54.3	
Follow-Up Group	47.5		50.0		48.4		50.0		41.5		40.9		50.0		62.1	
Maternal Race:																
Black:																
Intervention Group	54.2		41.3		40.0		77.3		95.8		69.4		23.5		26.1	
Follow-Up Group	52.5		47.8		31.2		80.4		94.3		71.6		16.3		45.5	
Hispanic:																
Intervention Group	2.1		39.1		6.7		11.4		0.0		14.3		2.0		4.3	
Follow-Up Group	0.0		40.2		6.5		14.3		1.9		14.8		2.5		1.5	
White/Other:																
Intervention Group	43.7		19.6		53.3		11.4		4.2		16.3		74.5		69.6	
Follow-Up Group	47.5		12.0		62.4		5.4		3.8		13.6		81.3		53.0	

*Neonatal Health Index: score standardized to mean of 100 with high scores signifying better health. (55)
**Maternal Education: 3-point scale where 1 = less than high school graduate; 2 = high school graduate; 3 = some college or more.
From *The Journal of the American Medical Association* (June 13, 1990) 263:3035–3042. Copyright 1990, American Medical Association. Reprinted with permission.

across all birthweights. For example, McCormick, Shapiro, and Starfield (1980) looked at the rehospitalization of premature survivors in the first year of life. A continuum of risk was demonstrated in terms of infants who were re-hospitalized more than once during the first year: 38.2% ≤ 1,500 gms, 21% 1,501–2,000 gms, 16.2% 2,001–2,500 gms, and 8.4% for < 2,500 gms at birth. Even though the infants ≤ 1,500 gms had a greater degree of rehospitalization, infants 2,001–2,500 gms still remained at risk in comparison to the FBW cohort.

Both heavier born and lighter born LBW infants have more school problems. Using the 1981 National Health Interview Survey of over 10,000 children, 34% of children born < 2,000 gms, 20% of children born at 2,001–2,500 gms, and 14% of FBW children were experiencing school difficulties as defined by repeating a grade, placement in a special education class or receiving remediation (McCormick et al., 1989).

In a large study in Finland, at age 14 years, 75% of children weighing < 1,500 gms., 80.3% weighing 1,500–1,999 gms, 86.9% weighing 2,000–2,499 gms, and 94.4% weighing 2,500 grams or more at birth were in a regular classroom at or above grade level (Rantakallio & Von Wendt, 1985). Almost three times as many children with a 2,000–2,499 gm birthweight (5.6%) attended no school, or a school for the mentally retarded as compared to FBW children (2.0%).

Even though deficits are seen across the LBW continuum, lighter born LBW infants are more likely to exhibit deficits than are heavier born LBW infants. However, since the heavier born LBW infants as a group exhibit some deficits (and therefore might benefit from intervention) and since this particular intervention had not been tested on heavier born or lighter born LBW infants, we chose to include both groups of LBW infants in the IHDP. Additionally, from a policy perspective, we felt it was important to include all LBW infants. And, finally, from a statistical perspective, as the range of variation on birthweight becomes more restricted, it is harder to assess the effects of birthweight upon outcome. Consequently, we adopted a sampling procedure that stratified on birthweight so that two-thirds of the subjects would be ≤2,000 gms and one-third 2,001–2,500 gms.

Choice of Environmental Risk Groups

Although biologically vulnerable infants are often environmentally vulnerable as well, LBW infants are born into families across the socioeconomic and ethnic spectra. Thus, we chose to include diverse sites in the study in order to render our results more generalizable (keeping in mind that our sample is specific to 8 sites and is not a national representative sample). Since the efficacy of this type of comprehensive early intervention for LBW infants was uncertain, the sample diversity would allow for the examination of the effects of socioeconomic and ethnic variability on intervention efficacy. We feel this is one of the strengths of the IHDP.

Projected Sample Size

The research design included stratification by eight sites and two birth weight groups (infants weighing 2,001 to 2,500 gms, designated *heavier*, and those weighing ≤ 2,000 gms, designated *lighter*). One third of the sample came from the *heavier* and two thirds from the *lighter* group. To minimize the cost of the study, subjects within each weight group were allocated such that one third were randomized to the intervention group and two thirds to the follow-up group. The targeted overall sample size was based on an estimated effect size (ES = difference between treatment group means, expressed in SDs) of 0.5. For a single outcome, a power of 99% (p = .05, two tailed) was required in the total group and the *lighter* group alone.

Based on our research design, the targeted number of subjects at each of the eight sites was 135. The targeted and actual numbers of enrolled subjects are shown in Table 2. The differences between these numbers reflect the effects of randomization allocation and the shortfall of subjects at some sites. The actual enrollment remained adequate for a power of at least 99%.

Recruitment and Randomization

A total of 4,551 hospital-born LBW infants were screened for eligibility to participate in the study. The majority of infants who were excluded before randomization (N = 3,249) were ineligible due to protocol criteria related to: (a) residence, (b) gestational age greater than 37 weeks, or (c) hospital discharge

Table 2.   Targeted and Actual Enrollment for Primary Analysis Group

Study and Weight Group	Enrollment Targets (Per Site)	Actual Enrollment By Site								
		ARK	EIN	HAR	MIA	PEN	TEX	WAS	YAL	Total
Follow-Up	90	80	92	93	56	53	88	80	66	608
Heavier	30	30	32	31	20	23	30	31	23	220
Lighter	60	50	60	62	36	30	58	49	43	388
Intervention	45	48	46	45	44	48	49	51	46	377
Heavier	15	21	15	14	15	22	17	16	22	142
Lighter	30	27	31	31	29	26	32	35	24	235
Total	135	128	138	138	100	101	137	131	112	985
Heavier	45	51	47	45	35	45	47	47	45	362
Lighter	90	77ˎ	91	93	65	56	90	84	67	623

Follow-Up: The group receiving the pediatric follow-up services but not the intervention services.
Intervention: The group receiving both the pediatric follow-up services and the intervention services.
Heavier: Infants weighing 2001 to 2500 g at birth.
Lighter: Infants weighing ≤2000 g at birth.
From *The Journal of the American Medical Association* (June 13, 1990) 263:3035–3042. Copyright 1990, American Medical Association. Reprinted with permission.

before or after the designated recruitment period. In terms of health, only those unhealthy infants who had an illness or neurological deficit so severe as to preclude participation in the intervention program (N = 61) were excluded. Thus, the vast majority of LBW premature infants who survived the neonatal hospitalization and who lived in the site's catchment area (i.e., within 45 minutes transportation time from each center) were included in the study.

Of the group of 1,302 who met the eligibility criteria, the parents of 274 (21%) refused consent. Of the 1,028 infants who were randomized, 43 were withdrawn before participating in the study primarily because the parents refused to accept the group assignment or families could not be located immediately after randomization. The remaining 985 infants (designated the Primary Analysis Group) constitute the cohort for the trial.

Program Delivered to Both Treatment Groups

The program began upon discharge from the neonatal nursery and continued until 36 months corrected age (age corrected for prematurity). Infants in both groups participated in the same pediatric follow-up, comprised of medical, developmental, and social assessments, with referrals to existing pediatric care and other community services as needed. These took place at eight clinic visits at 40 weeks conceptional age, 4, 8, 12, 18, 24, 30, and 36 months corrected age. Site personnel assisted families to obtain access to health care; three sites chose to provide primary care for their subjects.

Program Delivered to the Intervention Group

In addition to the above, the subjects in the INT Group only were offered a structured educational curriculum with family support, which was delivered via three modalities: home visits (Wasik, Bryant, & Lyons, 1990); children's attendance at a special Child Development Center; and parent-group meetings. The protocol specified four home visits per month in Year 1, and two visits per month in Years 2 and 3. On average across all sites, families received about three visits per month in Year 1 and one and a half per month in Year 2 (Ramey, Bryant, Wasik, Sparling, Fendt, & LaVange, 1992). The home visitor provided information and support, and implemented two specific curricula: *Partners for Learning* (Sparling & Lewis, 1985), a program of learning activities for the parent to use with the child which emphasizes cognitive, linguistic and social development; and *Problem Solving for Parents* (Wasik, 1984), a systematic approach to help parents learn to deal with child-rearing and personal problems.

The Child Development Centers (CDC) provided the INT children with an enriched, extrafamilial, educational experience beginning at 12 months corrected age and continuing until the last child at the site reached 36 months corrected age. The CDCs used the same curriculum as in the home visits. The children were scheduled to attend the center at least 4 hours daily, 5 days per week. The mean number of hours attended per day was about 5; the mean number of days attended in each year was 130 to 135. For most children, transportation was provided by the program. Adult–child ratios were 1:3 for children ages 12 to 24 months and 1:4 for children ages 24 to 36 months. Class sizes were 6 and 8 children, respectively. Teaching staff and home visitors met educational entry criteria of a B.A. or higher degree and received initial and ongoing training.

The curriculum was altered for LBW infants in several ways (Sparling, Lewis & Neuwirth, 1990). First, new curriculum items age-tailored to LBW infants were developed. *Early Partners*, a subset of *Partners for Learning*, was designed to be used soon after birth, with the infant who does not yet have the capabilities of the FBW child. The activities are designed to support the early development of premature and low-birthweight babies through mutually responsive interactions between the parent and her child. There is a focus on parenting skills that include the ability to calm the baby, provide appropriate levels of stimulation, recognize signals of discomfort or overstimulation, and provide opportunities for self-motivated, nonrepetitious actions and exploration.

Second, parents, home visitors, and teachers were trained to recognize the different behavioral and motor responses often associated with LBW. Techniques to reduce environmental stress (loud noises, bright lights) to help babies self-regulate, to promote consistency in handling and to foster and enhance the mother–child relationship, especially after the neonatal intensive care unit experience, were emphasized.

Third, stringent health surveillance procedures were in place in the Child Development Centers and were stressed in the home visits. All CDC staff received special training about health issues, and health consultation was provided to the CDC and home visit staff by the pediatric staff.

Data Collection

As mentioned above, all children were seen in eight clinic visits at 40 weeks conceptional age and at 4, 8, 12, 18, 24, 30, and 36 months corrected age. Children in both the INT and the FU groups received the same schedule of pediatric follow-up visits, which included health, developmental, and social assessments, some of which comprised the outcome measures. Specifically, at these visits, data were collected on child health and health services, neurodevelopmental status, family demographic information, use of non-IHDP community services and day care. At selected, prespecified visits, data also were collected on life stress, social support, and childrearing attitudes.

Cognitive assessments were performed in the clinic at corrected ages 12, 24, and 36 months by qualified staff "blinded" to the child's treatment group status. Behavioral data were obtained at ages 24 and 36 months by blinded interviewers. The quality of each family's home environemnt was assessed at 12 and 36 months by blinded staff. Morbidity and health-status data were gathered by the clinic staff (aware of treatment status) in an interview with the mother at all assessment points.

All assessors received special training and ongoing monitoring by the staff at the National Study Office to insure standardization of data collection. Detailed instruction manuals for all data forms were provided to the nurses and social workers who conducted the clinical interviews and exams; they participated in national training meetings and periodically submitted audiotaped interviews for review and feedback. A separate team of developmental supervisors and assessors who conducted the blinded cognitive, behavioral, and home environment assessments participated in a rigorous training program. Detailed instruction manuals and videotaped assessments were reviewed at national training meetings with the site supervisors. The supervisors conducted an on-site training program with the blinded assessors, whose assessments were closely monitored throughout the entire data collection period with a protocol for periodic reliability checks and site visits by NSO staff.

Prerandomization Variables

Several prerandomization variables were examined, including site, maternal education, maternal age, ethnicity (black, Hispanic, white and other), initial health status, birthweight and gender (see Table 1). Initial health status was assessed with the Neonatal Health Index, a measure that standardizes length of stay of the neonatal hospitalization for birthweight (Scott, Bauer, Kraemer, & Tyson, 1989). These variables were selected because they were associated with primary outcomes in other studies (Egbuonu & Starfield, 1982; Field, 1980, 1987; Kleinman & Kessell, 1987; McCormick et al., 1987, 1988; McCormick & Brooks-Gunn, 1988).

Outcome Measures at Age 3

Primary outcome measures included cognitive competence, behavioral competence, and health status. Secondary outcomes included maternal functioning—HOME Inventory scores, employment and education history, childrearing beliefs, maternal problem solving, and actual behavioral interactions with the child.

The Stanford-Binet Intelligence Scale, Form L-M, 3rd edition (1972 norms) was used because of the amount of experience that has been accumulated with it—more than 1,800 references are listed in *Tests in Print* and in the *Mental Measurements Yearbook* for this instrument. It has substantial validity at this age level. It was used in almost all of the previous LBW follow-up studies and the FBW early intervention studies. The 4th edition could not be used in this study since the psychometric evaluation was not available in time for the age-3 assessments.

A maternal report scale, the *Child Behavior Checklist* (Achenbach, Edelbrock, & Howell, 1987), was chosen as the measure of behavior problems at 3 years because it is currently the most commonly used measure for older children (aged 4 upwards); it allows for measurement of two dimensions of behavior problems—internalizing and externalizing; it has published data on reliability and validity; it has been used with LBW infants; and a version for 2-to 3-year-old children was developed in 1986 (Achenbach et al., 1987). In addition, the *Behavior Checklist* (Richman, 1977; Richman & Graham, 1971) was obtained at 24 and 36 months. A new prosocial measure, the Adaptive Social Behavior Inventory, also was obtained at 36 months; three scales have been identified— expressive, disruptive, and compliant behavior (Scott & Hogan, 1990).

Health status was operationalized in a multidimensional manner as follows: *morbidity*, defined as the presence or absence of specific symptoms or conditions over the 3 years (serious morbidity and total morbidity indices were derived); *functional status*, defined by limitations in the activities of daily living due to health problems based on the *Functional Status II(R) Scale* (Stein & Jessop, 1986); *alterations in physical growth* (length, and body mass index); *and maternal rating of her child's health* (Eisen, Donald, Ware, & Brook, 1980).

Data Analytic Procedures

The data analytic procedures to test the efficacy of the intervention are described in detail in Document 04773 archived in NAPS (see IHDP, 1990). Briefly, two procedures were used. In the primary analysis, effect sizes (ES) were estimated by first testing for hetereogeneity across the weight and site groups and then estimating an averaged ES if there was significant heterogeneity or a pooled ES if not. To protect against false-positive results in testing efficacy with eight primary outcome measures, a Bonferroni correction was applied, and the .006 (.05/8) significance level was used for each outcome. When a significant effect of the intervention was found in the primary analysis, a secondary analysis using multiple linear regression was employed to test whether certain initial status variables had an effect on outcome. The prerandomization initial status variables and the treatment variable were entered, as well as the treatment by initial status variable interactions.

Results and Discussion

Sample retention. A very intense degree of activity was required to maintain the study population. A recent survey taken at the eight sites indicates that 30% of the IHDP sample had no telephone; 32% have moved four or more times over the past 4 years, and approximately 25% require three or more appointments before they come in for their scheduled evaluation. These figures indicate the degree of mobility and difficulty in contacting and maintaining the cohort for an extended number of years.

Overall, 93% of the randomized infants participated in the age-3 assessment. The low rate of 7% lost to follow-up is gratifying, since rates as high as 30% were expected at the time the study was being planned, given past experience with populations like those served by the IHDP clinics. This small dropout rate did not change the comparability between the groups. The drop-out rates in the INT and the FU groups and in the *heavier* and *lighter* groups were essentially identical. Only one factor, maternal education, showed a significant difference ($p = 0.02$), with a greater loss of low-education mothers than higher educated mothers.

Cognitive competence. The INT Group had significantly higher mean IQ scores at 36 months than did the FU Group (9 points, or more than half of a standard deviation). Further, more than twice as many infants in the FU Group had very low IQs (under 70) and IQs in the mildly delayed range (under 85) than did infants in the INT Group. A significant effect also was found at 24 months on the Bayley Mental Scores, but not at 12 months (see Figure 1).

The mean IQ of the FU group was low (just under 85), suggesting that this LBW sample is indeed at-risk for developmental and school problems. Very low-mean IQs were found at the five sites that had the most environmentally disadvantaged families (the exceptions are Washington, Yale, and Harvard, where mean IQ scores for the FU Group were between 91 and 97) (see Figure 2, Tables 1 and 4).

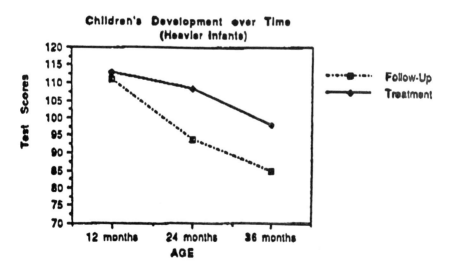

Figure 1.   Mean IQ Scores of Treatment and Follow-Up Groups by Age for Heavier Born Children (Birthweight = 2,001–2,500 gms.)

The tests at 12 months and 24 months were the Mental Scale of the Bayley Scales of Infant Development, and at 36 months, the Stanford-Binet IQ Scale (from Brooks-Gunn, Liaw, & Kato, unpublished data).

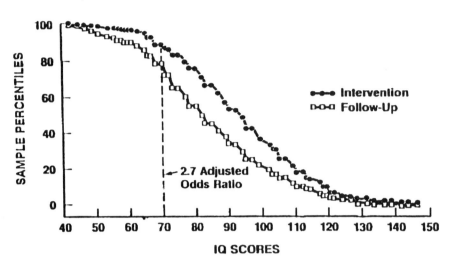

Figure 2. Possibilities for Information on Cumulative Distributions of Stanford-Binet IQ Scores at 36 Months Corrected Age: The Percentage in the Intervention and Follow-Up Groups with IQ Scores Greater Than Each Value

Note: The cut point of 70 is the IQ level below which the scores fall into the mental retardation range according to the Stanford-Binet manual. As shown the adjusted odds for having a score <70 were 2.7 times greater in the FU Group. The 95% confidence interval for the adjusted odds ratio at an IQ score of 70 is 1.6–4.8. The odds ratio and the confidence interval were obtained, controlling for site and initial status variables, using multiple logistic regression. (Reprinted with permission from "A Multisite Randomized Intervention Trial for Premature Low Birthweight Infants: The Infant Health and Development Program," in Rogers and Ginzberg, 1990.)

Although the treatment effect was significant for both birth weight groups, it was larger for the *heavier* LBW infants, 13.2 IQ points, ES of .83 for the *heavier* and 6.6 IQ points, ES .41 for the *lighter* LBW groups. We are currently conducting analysis to elucidate this treatment by birth weight interaction. We are examining the association between maternal education and the two birth-weight groups vis-á-vis treatment effect sizes (in essence, a possible three-way interaction among treatment, birthweight group, and maternal education).

Another current approach to elucidating the cognitive findings more fully involves the effects of the intervention for various aspects of cognitive ability (based on factor analyses of the Bayley and Stanford-Binet Scales) to see for which cognitive abilities the treatment effects are found. Initial results suggest that treatment effects are found in all of the domains of cognitive functioning assessed by these tests at 24 and 36 months and that larger effects are found for visual-motor-spatial abilities than language abilities (Brooks-Gunn, Liaw, & Kato, 1991). Additionally, the effect sizes are larger at 36 months than at 24 months for overall IQ scores, and no differences are seen at 12 months (see Figure 1).

Table 3.   Cumulative Stanford-Binet IQ Scores By Birth Weight
and Study Group

Cumulative Stanford-Binet IQ Scores At 36 Months	Birth Weight Group					
	≤1,500 g		1,501–2,000 g		2,001–2,500 g	
	N	(%)	N	(%)	N	(%)
<70:						
Intervention Group	22	(26.8)	11	(7.9)	6	(4.8)
Follow-Up Group	43	(28.7)	39	(18.8)	37	(18.2)
<85:						
Intervention Group	39	(47.6)	44	(31.4)	32	(25.6)
Follow-Up Group	95	(63.3)	97	(46.6)	111	(54.7)
<90:						
Intervention Group	48	(58.5)	58	(41.4)	43	(34.4)
Follow-Up Group	104	(69.3)	119	(57.2)	124	(61.1)
<100:						
Intervention Group	64	(78.0)	87	(62.1)	69	(55.2)
Follow-Up Group	123	(82.0)	152	(73.1)	158	(77.8)
Total Sample:						
Intervention Group	82	(100.0)	140	(100.0)	125	(100.0)
Follow-Up Group	150	(100.0)	208	(100.0)	203	(100.0)

Note. The cut point of 70 is the IQ level below which the scores fall into the mental retardation range, according to the Stanford-Binet manual. The groups with scores <85 also include children with scores that are one standard deviation below the mean, which we refer to as subaverage. The groups <90 include 23.2% of the distribution which approximates the lowest quartile. The groups <100 include those below the mean.
From The Journal of the American Medication Association (June 13, 1990) 263:3035–3042. Copyright 1990, American Medical Association. Reprinted with permission.

Finally, a study has been conducted (Ramey et al., 1992) in which the unweighted sum of participation frequencies in each of the intervention program modalities (home visits, attendance at the CDCs and parent group meetings) constituted a Family Participation Index. The Index scores did not vary systematically with mother's ethnicity, age, or education, or with child's birthweight, gender, or neonatal health status, but were positively related to child's IQ score at 36 months. These findings are consistent with other studies linking intensity of intervention with degree of positive cognitive outcomes for high-risk children.

Behavioral competence. The INT Group had significantly lower maternally reproted behavior problem scores than the FU Group (means of 43.7 vs. 47.2) (see Table 4). The percentage of children reported by their mothers in the "clinically significant range" (score of 63 or higher) (McConaughy & Achenbach, 1988) was 1.5 times lower in the INT than the FU Group (see Figure 3). This finding is important in that LBW infants may have a relatively high incidence of behavior problems, and other studies report that moderate to severe problems at this age predict problems in school-age children (Dunn et al., 1986; Chazan & Jackson, 1974; Escalona, 1982; Stevenson, Richman & Graham,

Table 4.   Site Variations in Three Primary Outcome Measures*

Site By Study Group	Stanford-Binet Intelligence Scale			Child Behavior Checklist Ages 2–3			Mother's Report: Morbidity Index		
	N	M	SD	N	M	SD	N	M	SD
ARK:									
FU	77	85.2	16.8	76	47.8	22.7	77	7.0	3.2
INT	42	99.5	18.0	42	39.3	16.7	41	6.9	2.7
EIN:									
FU	78	74.2	15.7	77	47.1	20.5	77	6.2	2.6
INT	43	84.7	18.4	43	49.0	22.6	43	6.5	3.3
HAR:									
FU	88	96.7	22.4	87	44.6	20.2	88	8.8	3.5
INT	43	97.1	21.5	40	41.1	18.4	43	9.1	4.1
MIA:									
FU	51	68.0	14.2	49	53.8	21.3	49	5.5	2.4
INT	40	81.0	12.0	39	49.1	16.0	40	6.1	2.6
PEN:									
FU	51	82.5	16.2	51	45.6	19.9	51	6.6	3.0
INT	43	95.1	12.6	43	43.9	24.2	43	6.9	2.4
TEX:									
FU	79	80.4	12.9	75	48.1	20.6	77	5.7	2.4
INT	47	87.1	17.6	47	42.7	17.2	47	7.8	3.5
WAS:									
FU	76	92.0	21.6	73	49.1	18.7	75	7.8	3.1
INT	47	100.5	21.3	46	45.7	17.9	47	8.8	3.6
YAL:									
FU	61	91.1	20.0	59	42.6	18.9	57	7.1	3.2
INT	42	102.5	17.3	38	38.7	16.6	41	8.7	3.0
Total:									
FU	561	84.5	19.9	547	47.2	20.5	551	6.9	3.1
INT	347	93.5	19.1	338	43.7	19.1	345	7.6	3.3
Total N	908			885			896		

*These are the three outcome measures that showed significant treatment effects.
FU = Follow-Up Group; INT = Intervention Group
For full names of sites, see list of participating universities.
From The Journal of the American Medical Association (June 13, 1990) 263:3035–3042.
Copyright 1990, American Medical Association. Reprinted with permission.

1983). A significant maternal education by treatment interaction indicated that the treatment effect was found primarily in the infants whose mothers had a high school education or less.

Health Status

The two groups had similar scores on activities of daily living, growth, and maternal ratings of health and serious illness (as measured by the Mother's

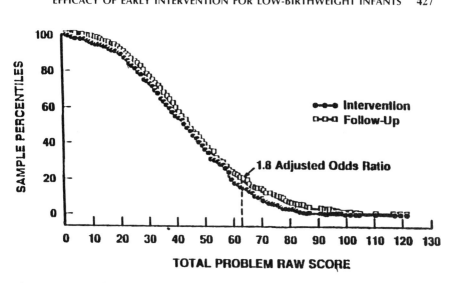

Figure 3. Cumulative Distributions of the "Total Problem Raw Score" from the Child Behavior Checklist Ages 203 at 36 Months Corrected Age: The Percentage in the Intervention and Follow-Up Groups with Scores Greater than Each Value.

Note: According to the authors of the scale, 64 is the cut point at or above which scores are indicative of clinically evident behavior problems. As shown, the adjusted odds for having a score above 64 were 1.8 times greater in the FU Group. The 95% confidence interval for the adjusted odds ratio at the cut point is 1.2–2.9. The odds ratio and the confidence interval were obtained, controlling for site and initial status variables, using multiple logistic regression. (Reprinted with permission from "A Multisite Randomized Intervention Trial for Premature Low Birthweight Infants: The Infant Health and Development Program" in Rogers and Ginzberg 1990.)

Report: Serious Morbidity Index). However, the INT mothers, reported higher total morbidity index scores (Mother's Report Morbidity Index) than did the FU mothers for the *lighter* group only. The difference was small and due to a higher frequency of brief illnesses reported in the INT group. This finding may reflect a real increase in acute conditions as a result of group care, or it may reflect the more intense health surveillance and health education in the INT compared to the FU Group. In an additional study (McCormick, Brooks-Gunn, Shapiro, Ben-asich, Black, & Gross, 1990) no major increases in medical care resulted from the intervention, a validation of the lack of difference in the mother's report of serious morbidity. Of considerable importance to the feasibility of this intervention is the fact that not a single serious infectious epidemic or serious major accident occurred during a 2-year period at eight different rigorously controlled CDCs.

Maternal effects. In terms of secondary effects to the mothers, mothers in the INT group were more likely to be employed, to be employed more months, and to enter the work force sooner than were mothers in the FU group (Brooks-

Gunn, McCormick, & Shapiro, 1990). Results from analyses of videotaped mother–child interactions made at 30 months indicated positive effects of the INT for ratings of the mothers' interactive behavior related to the affective and teaching quality of the interactions (Spiker & Ferguson, 1990). Finally, significantly higher scores on the HOME Inventory, a measure of the quality of the home environment, were found for the INT group at 36 months (Casey, Bradley, & Caldwell, 1990). These secondary effects of the INT suggest that this comprehensive early intervention program served to enhance certain important aspects of maternal functioning that might possibly translate into lasting benefits.

CONCLUSIONS

The IHDP provided an educational family support and pediatric follow-up intervention to LBW premature children across a spectrum of socioeconomic status and ethnicity. The results indicate real promise of decreasing the number of LBW premature infants at risk for later developmental disability. As such, the IHDP may provide a starting point for the development of subsequent intervention programs related to implementation of P.L. 99-457, particularly since little information is available on the type of special services needed and received by LBW children and on the efficacy of providing comprehensive intervention services to LBW children (Richmond, 1990). The IHDP, because of its sample size, the involvement of eight diverse clinical sites across the country, the availability of a comparable group who did not receive the intervention, and high retention in both treatment groups, is in a position to help develop generalizable conclusions about the long-term effects of educational interventions in the first years of life.

The trial also has implications for the closely related issue of the provision of services to biologically and, for a significant number of children in this trial, environmentally vulnerable infants and preschoolers. Infants with both biological and environmental risk factors have been termed to be at "double jeopardy" (Parker, Greer, & Zuckerman, 1988), and likely to exhibit significant developmental delays (Brooks-Gunn, 1990b; McCormick & Brooks-Gunn, 1989). Additionally, the environmentally vulnerable children are less likely to receive health and educational services at an early age than their more advantaged agemates, compounding the problems conferred by their biological vulnerability (McCormick & Brooks-Gunn, 1989).

The long-term significance of these findings is being addressed in the continued follow-up of the study cohort. Although IQ effects may attenuate, as seen in other studies, there are important advantages to be anticipated as the children enter school, particularly in the inner cities. These may include higher academic achievement, fewer placements in remedial classes or retention in grades and fewer school drop-outs. Such results would amply justify the cost of the program.

REFERENCES

Achenbach, T.M., Edelbrock, C.S., & Howell, C.T. (1987). Empirically-based assessment of the behavioral/emotional problems of 2- and 3-year-old children.

Benasich, A.A., Brooks-Gunn, J., & Clewell, B.C. (1990). Who benefits from intervention programs begun in infancy? A review of maternal and child outcomes. *Journal of Applied Developmental Psychology.*

Bennett, F.C. (1987). The effectiveness of early intervention for infants at increased biologic risk. In F.C. Bennett, & M.J. Guralnick (Eds.), *The effectiveness of early intervention for at-risk and handicapped children* (pp. 79–112). Orlando, FL: Academic Press.

Blumenthal, J.B. (1989, April). *Results from a long-term follow-up of the Parent-child Development Centers.* Paper presented in a symposium on "Long-Term Effects from Early Intervention? More Fuel for the Fire" at the Society for Research in Child Development meetings, Kansas City, MO.

Breslau, N., Klein, N., & Allen, L. (1987). *Very low birthweight: Behavior sequelae at nine years of age.* Unpublished manuscript. Henry Ford Hospital, Department of Biostatistics and Research Epidemiology and the Department of Psychiatry.

Bromwich, R., & Parmelee, A. (1979). An intervention program for pre-term infants. In T. Field, A. Sosek, S. Goldberg, & H. Schuman (Eds.), *Infants born at risk: Behavior and development* (pp. 389–411). New York: S.P. Medical & Scientific Books.

Brooks-Gunn, J. (1990a). Identifying the vulnerable child. In D.E. Rogers & E. Ginzberg (Eds.), *Improving the life chances of children at risk.* Boulder, CO: Westview Press.

Brooks-Gunn,J. (1990b). Promoting healthy development in young children: What educational interventions work? In D.E. Rogers & E. Ginzberg (Eds.), *Improving the life chances of children at risk.* Boulder, CO: Westview Press.

Brooks-Gunn, J., Liaw, T., & Kato, P. (1991, April). *The efficacy of the Infant Health and Development Program in altering cognitive abilities at 12, 24, and 36 months of age.* Paper presented in an invited symposium on the Infant Health and Development Program at The Society for Research in Child Development Meeting, Seattle, WA.

Brooks-Gunn, J., McCormick, H., & Shapiro, S. (1990). Are the mothers' lives affected? *Infant Behavior and Development* (Special ICIS Issue), *13*, 100.

Brown, J., LaRossa, M., Aylward, G., Davis, D., Rutherford, P., & Bakeman, R. (1980). Nursery-based intervention with prematurely born babies and their mothers: Are there effects? *Journal of Pediatrics, 97,* 487.

Caputo, D. V., Goldstein, K.M., & Taub, H.B. (1979). The development of prematurely born children through middle childhood. In T.M. Field (Ed.), *Infants born at risk* (p. 219). New York: Spectrum.

Casey, P., Bradley, R., & Caldwell, B. (1990). Was the home environment enhanced? *Infant Behavior and Development* (Special ICIS Issue), *13*, 99.

Chazan, M., & Jackson, S. (1974). Behavior problems in the infant school: Changes over two years. *Journal of Child Psychology and Psychiatry, 15,* 33–46.

Child Day Care Infectious Disease Study Group, Centers for Disease Control. (1984). Public health considerations of infectious diseases in child day care centers. *Journal of Pediatrics, 105,* 683–701.

Clewell, B.C., Brooks-Gunn, J., & Benasich, A.A. (1989). Evaluating child-related outcomes of teenage parenting programs. *Family Relations,* pp. 201–209.

Collaborative Group. (1984). Antenatal steroid therapy: Effects of antenatal dexamethasone administration in the infant: Long-term follow-up. *Journal of Pediatrics, 104,* 259–267.

Drillien, C.M. (1964). *The growth and development of the prematurely born infant.* Edinburgh: Livingstone.

Drillien, C.M., Thompson, A.J.M., & Burgoyne, K. (1980). Low-birthweight children at early school age: A longitudinal study. *Developmental Medicine and Child Neurology, 22,* 26–47.

Dunn, L.M. (1986). *Bilingual Hispanic children on the U.S. mainland: A review of research on their cognitive, linguistic and scholastic development.* Circle Pines, MN: American Guidance Service.

Dunn, H.G., H., H.H., Crichton, J.U. Robertson, A.M., McBurney, A.K., Grunau, R.V.E., & Penfold, P.S. (1986). Evolution of minimal brain dysfunctions to the age of 12 to 15 years. In H.G. Dunn (Ed.), *Sequelae of low birthweight: The Vancouver study* (pp. 249–272). Philadelphia: Lippincott Co.

Eaves, L.C., Nattall, J.C., Klonoff, H., & Dunn, H.G. (1970). Developmental and psychological test scores in children of low birthweight. *Pediatrics, 45*(9–20), 10.

Efron, B. (1971). Forcing a sequential experiment to be balanced. *Biometrika, 58,* 403–417.

Egbuonu, L., & Starfield, B. (1982). Child health and social status. *Pediatrics, 69,* 550–557.

Eisen, M., Donald, C.A., Ware, J.E., & Brook, R.H. (1980). *Conceptualization and measurement of health for children in the health insurance study* (R-2313 HEW). Santa Monica, CA: The Rand Corporation.

Escalona, S.K. (1982). Babies at double hazard: Early development of infants at biologic and social risk. *Pediatrics, 70*(5), 670–676.

Escalona, S.K. (1984). Social and other environmental influences on the cognitive and personality development of low birthweight infants. *American Journal of Mental Deficiency, 88*(5), 508–512.

Field, T.M. (1980). Interaction of high risk infants: Quantitative and qualitative differences. In D.B. Sawin, R.C. Hawkins, L.D. Walker (Eds.), *The exceptional infant* (Vol. 4). New York: Brunner Mazel.

Field, T., Goldberg, S., Stern, D., & Sostek, A.M. (Eds.). (1980). *High-risk infants and children: Adult and peer interactions.* New York: Academic Press.

Fowler, M.G., & Cross, A.W. (1986). Preschool risk factors as predictors of early school performance. *Developmental Behavioral Pediatrics, 7*(4), 237–241.

Frisch, R.O., Belek, M.K., Meller, L.D., & Eugel, R.R. (1975). Physical and mental status at 4 years of age of survivors of respiratory distress syndrome. *Journal of Pediatrics, 86,* 497–503.

Grunau, R.V.E. (1986). Educational achievement. In H.G. Dunn (Ed.), *Sequelae of low birthweight: The Vancouver study* (pp. 179–204). Philadelphia: Lippincott Co.

Hack, M., Fanaroff, A.A., & Merkatz, I.R. (1975). The low birthweight infant-evolution of a changing outlook. *New England Journal of Medicine, 301,* 1162.

Hagberg, B. (1979). Epidemiological and preventive aspects of cerebral palsy and severe mental retardation in Sweden. *European Journal of Pediatrics, 130,* 71.

Haskins, R., & Kotch, J. (1986). Day care and illness: evidence, costs and public policy. *Pediatrics, 77*(part 2), 951–982.

Hoy, E.A., Bill, J.M., & Sykes, D.H. (1988). Very low birthweight: A long-term developmental impairment? *International Journal of Behavioral Development, 11,* 37–67.

Infant Health and Development Program (IHDP), (1990). Enhancing the outcomes of low birthweight, premature infants: A multisite, randomized trial. *Journal of the American Medical Association, 263,* 3035–3042.

Klaus, M.H., & Kennell, J. (1982). Interventions in the premature nursery: Impact on development. *Pediatrics Clinics of North America, 29,* 1263.

Klein, N.K., Hack, M., & Breslau, N. (1989). Children who were very low birthweight: Development and academic achievement at nine years of age. *Developmental and Behavioral Pediatrics, 10*(1), 32–37.

Kleinman, J.C., & Kessel, S.S. (1987). Racial differences in low birthweight: Trends and risk factors. *New England Journal of Medicine, 317*(12), 749–753.

Kopp, C.B. (1983). Risk factors in development. In J.J. Campos & M. Haith (Eds.), *Handbook of Child Psychology: II* (pp. 1081–1188). New York: Wiley.

Kraemer, H.C., & Fendt, K. (1990). Randomization in clinical trials: Issues in planning. *Journal of Clinical Epidemiology, 43*, 1157-1167.

Lazar, I., Darlington, R., Murray, H., Royce, J., & Snipper, A. (1982). Lasting effects of early education: A report from the Consortium for Longitudinal Studies. *Monographs of the Society for Research in Child Development, 47*(2-3, Serial No. 195).

Lee, K.S., Paneth, N., Gartner, L.M., Pearlman, M.A., & Gruss, L. (1980). Neonatal mortality: An analysis of the recent improvement in the United States. ASPH Vol. 70, No. 1 and U.S. Department of Health and Human Services Public Health Service. National Center for Health Statistics.

Levine, M.D. (1990). Neurodevelopmental dysfunction during childhood: The high impacts and policy implications of insidious handicaps. In D.E. Rogers & E. Ginzberg (Eds.), *Improving the life chances of children at risk*. Boulder, CO: Westview Press.

Lerner, J.A., Inui, T.S., Trupin, E.W., Douglas, E. (1985). Preschool behavior can predict future psychiatric disorders. *Journal of the American Academy of Child Psychiatry, 24*,(1), 42–48.

McBurney, A.K., & Eaves, L.C. (1986). Evolution of developmental and psychological test scores. In H.G. Dunn (Ed.), *Sequelae of low birthweight: The Vancouver study* (pp. 54–67). Philadelphia: Lippincott Co.

McConaughy, S.H., & Achenbach, T.M. (1988). *Practical guide for the Child Behavior Checklist and related materials*. Burlington, VT: University of Vermont, Department of Psychiatry.

McCormick, M.C. (1985). The contribution of low birth weight to infant mortality and childhood morbidity. *The New England Journal of Medicine, 312*, 82–90.

McCormick, M.C. (1989). Long-term follow-up of infants discharged from neonatal intensive care units. *Journal of the American Medical Association, 261*(12), 1767–1772.

McCormick, M.C. (1990). Neonatology: Where are we and what more could we do? In D.E. Rogers & E. Ginzberg (Eds.), *Improving the life chances of children at risk*. Boulder, CO: Westview Press.

McCormick, M.C., Brooks-Gunn, J. (1989). The health of children and adolescents. In H.E. Freeman & S. Levine (Eds.), *Handbook of medical sociology*. Englewood Cliffs, NJ: Prentice Hall.

McCormick, M.C., Brooks-Gunn, J., Shapiro, S., Benasich, A.A., Black, G., & Gross, R.T. (1990). Health care use among young children in day-care: Result seen in a randomized trial of early intervention. *Pediatric Research, 27*(4), 249A.

McCormick, M.C., Brooks-Gunn, J., Shorter, T., Holmes, J., Wallace, C.Y., & Heagarty, M.E. (1987). *Health in the year following delivery among low-income women*. Paper presented at the Society for Pediatric Research.

McCormick, M.C., Brooks-Gunn, J., Shorter, T., Holmes, J.H., Wallace, C.Y. & Heagarty, M.C. (1989). Outreach as casefinding: Its effect on enrollment in prenatal care. *Medical Care, 27*(2), 103–111.

McCormick, M.C., Shapiro, S., & Starfield, B.H. (1980). Rehospitalization in the first year of life for high-risk survivors. *Pediatrics, 66*(6), 991–999.

McCormick, M.C., Shapiro, S., & Starfield, B.H. (1984). High-risk young mothers: Infant mortality and morbidity in four areas in the United States, 1973–1978. *American Journal of Public Health, 74*(1), 18–23.

Minde, K., Shosenberg, N., Marton, P., Thompson, J., Ripley, J., & Burns, S. (1980). Self-help groups in a premature nursery: A controlled evaluation. *The Journal of Pediatrics, 96*(5), 933–940.

National Center for Health Statistics. (1989). *Health, United States, 1988. Public Health Service*. Washington, DC: U.S. Government Printing Office. (DHHS publicaton no. (PHS) 89-1232).

Nickel, R.E., Bennett, F.C., & Lamson, F.N. (1982). School performance of children with birthweights of 1,000 g or less. *American Journal of the Diseases of Childhood, 136*, 105–110.

Paneth, N., Kiely, J.L., & Stein, A. (1981). Cerebral palsy and newborn care, III. Estimated prevalence rates of cerebral palsy under differing rates of mortality and impairment of low birthweight infants. *Developmental Medicine and Child Neurology, 23*, 801.

Parker, S., Greer, S., & Zuckerman, B. (1988). Double jeopardy: The impact of poverty on early child development. *Pediatrics Clinics of North America, 35*(6), 1227–1240.

Pocock, S.J., & Simon, R. (1975). Sequential treatment assignment with balancing for prognostic factors in the controlled clinical trial. *Biometrics, 31*, 103–115.

Ramey, C.T. (1990). The Infant Health and Development Program for LBW, premature infants: The intervention. *Pediatric Research, 27*(4), 253A.

Ramey, C.T., Bryant, D.M., Campbell, F.A., Sparling, J.J., & Wasik, B.H. (1989). Early intervention for high-risk children: The Carolina early intervention program. *Journal of Prevention and Human Services, 7*, 33–57.

Ramey, C.T., Bryant, D.B., Wasik, B.H., Sparling, J.J., Fendt, K.H., & LaVange, L.M. (1992). The Infant Health and Development Program for low-birthweight, premature infants: Program elements, family participation, and child intelligence. *Pediatrics, 89*, 454-465.

Ramey, C.T.,& Campbell, F.A. (1987). The Carolina Abecedarian Project: An educational experiment concerning human malleability. In J.J. Gallagher & C.T. Ramey (Eds.), *The malleability of children* (pp. 127–139). Baltimore, MD: PH Brookes Publishing Co.

Ramey, C.T., Bryant, D.M., Sparling, J.J., & Wasik, B.H. (1985). Educational interventions to enhance intellectual development: Comprehensive daycare versus family education. In S. Harel & N. Anastasiow (Eds.), *The 'at-risk' infant: Psycho/socio/medical aspects* (pp. 75–85). Baltimore: PH Brookes Publishing Co.

Ramey, C.T., Bryant, D.M., Sparling, J.J., & Wasik, B.H. (1984). A biosocial systems perspective on environmental interventions for low birth weight infants. *Clinical Obstetrics & Gynecology, 27*, 672–692.

Rantakallio, P., & Von Wendt, L. (1985). Prognosis for low-birthweight infants up to the age of 14: A population study. *Developmental Medicine and Child Neurology, 7*, 655–663.

Resnick, M.B., Eyler, F.D., Nelson, R.M., Eitzman, D.V., & Bucciarelli, R.L. (1987). Developmental intervention for low birth weight infants: Improved early developmental outcome. *Pediatrics, 80*, 68–74.

Richman, N. (1977). Is a behavior checklist for preschool children useful? In P.J. Graham (Ed.), *Epidemiological approaches in child psychiatry* (pp. 125–137). London: Academic Press.

Richman, N., & Graham, P.J. (1971). A behavioural screening questionnaire for use with three-year old-children. Preliminary findings. *Journal of child Psychology and Psychiatry, 12*, 5–33.

Richmond, J. (1990). Low-birth-weight babies: Can we enhance their development? *Journal of the American Medical Association, 263*, 3069–3070.

Rogers, D.E., & Ginzberg, E. (Eds.). (1990). *Improving the life chances of children at risk*. Boulder, CO: Westview Press.

Ross, B.S. (1984). Home intervention for premature infants of low-income families. *American Journal of Orthopsychiatry, 54*, 263–270.

Scarr-Salapatek, S., & Williams, M.L. (1973). The effects of early stimulation on low-birth-weight infants. *Child Development, 44*, 94–101.

Scott, D.T., Bauer, C.R., Kraemer, H.C., & Tyson, J. (1989). Neonatal health index for preterm infants. *Pediatric Research, 25*,(4), 263.

Scott, K., & Hogan, A. (1990). *Adaptive Social Behavior Inventory*. Coral Gables, FL: University of Miami.

Shapiro, S., McCormick, M.C., Starfield, B.H., Krischer, J.P., & Bross, D. (1980). Relevance of correlates of infant deaths for significant morbidity at one year of age. *American Journal of Obstetrics and Gynecology, 136*, 363–373.

Sparling, J.J., Lewis, I.S., & Neuwirth, S. (1990). *Early partners*. Lewisville, NC: Kaplan Press.

Sparling, J.J., & Lewis, I.S. (1985). *Partners for learning*. Winston-Salem, NC: Kaplan Press.

Spiker, D., & Ferguson, J. (1990). The effects of early intervention in the IHDP on maternal interactive behavior. *Infant Behavior and Development* (Special ICIS Issue), 13, 98.

Stein, R.E., & Jessop, D.J. (1986). *Tables documenting the psychometric properties of the functional status II (R) measures.* Pact papers/AECOM, Department of Pediatrics, Albert Einstein College of Medicine, New York.

Stevenson, J., Richman, N., & Graham, P. (1983). Behavior problems and language abilities at three years and behavior deviance at eight years. *Child Psychology and Psychiatry, 16*(2), 215–230.

Wasik, B.H., Bryant, D.M., & Lyons, C.M. (1990). *Home visiting: Procedures for helping families.* Newbury Park, CA: Sage Publications.

Wasik, B.H. (1984). *Coping with parenting through effective problem solving: A handbook for professionals.* Chapel Hill, NC: Frank Porter Graham Child Development Center, CB# 8180, UNC-CH.

18

An Interactionist Perspective on Interventions with Low-Birthweight Infants

Virginia A. Rauh
John Brennan

INTRODUCTION

In 1981, Ramey, Zeskind, and Hunter provided a framework for the design and evaluation of early interventions for preterm infants, with particular attention to developmental processes. In the near decade since that review, much has been learned about risk research and the science of intervention with high-risk populations. While contributions have come from many quarters, two lines of research, one theoretical and the other applied, have been largely responsible for progress in the field. The first involves the dynamic modeling of complex developmental processes. The ideas of Sameroff (1982a), Belsky (1984), Crnic, Greenberg, Ragozin, Robinson, and Basham (1983), Dunst (1985), Garbarino (1982, 1983), and Sroufe (1983), among others, have generated new hypotheses about how parenting capacity and child development are influenced,directly and indirectly, by individual and contextual factors. Such models provide a theoretical framework for explicit tests of hypothesized development paths in normal as well as high-risk populations. The second line of research comprises experimental work that addresses those child, family, and contextual attributes that shape the intervention experience and determine program success. A decade of progress in intervention research has thus profited from both improved models of child development and empirical studies that address the effects of within-group variability on factors likely to modify the outcome of intervention. As portended by Ramey et al. in their 1981 review, the theme underlying these advances is interactional.

Interactional approaches to understanding child development have predominated since the mid-1970s (Magnusson & Endler, 1977). "Transactional" models (e.g., Sameroff & Chandler, 1975) refer to a special case of interaction where the interplay between variables is reciprocal and the process dynamic, a concept derived from the early works of Thomas, Chess, Birch, Hertzig, and Korn (1963) and Bell (1968). Strictly speaking, transactional models presume that independent variables do more than modify the effects of other variables on outcome, but rather act to change each other (Rutter, 1983a). According to this model, developmental continuities as well as discontinuities depend upon the shifting organism–environment relationship. Indeed, longitudinal studies have demonstrated that powerful self-righting tendencies of the caregiving environment can potentially compensate for a host of biological/constitutional disadvantages (Sameroff, 1982; Werner & Smith, 1982; Breitmayer & Ramey, 1986).

Historically, interventions for low-birthweight children evolved relatively independently of the longitudinal literature, so it is not surprising that intervention studies have been slow to adopt interactional models in their rationale and design. In 1982, Bell and Pearl stated,

> A new perspective in risk research is emerging out of a transactional approach to development, one that considers the many developmental and contextual changes that occur over major developmental periods in the lives of children. The task of risk research for all but the disorders with a short incubation time will be to reconstruct, segment by segment, the developmental and contextual processes by which pathology develops. Once the pathways by which the disorder emerges become clear, an optimal time and mode of screening and intervention can be devised for each disorder. (p. 57)

In practice, incorporating interactional principles into intervention research has not been so easy. First of all, environments that are sensitive to, and can compensate for, early deficiencies, so that they are not transformed into later deficits are difficult to construct. To do so requires adequate resources and a good understanding of what constitutes a beneficial environment for different subgroups of high-risk infants. Secondly, traditional analyses of differences between group means obscure the fact that some children improve with intervention while others do not. In most intervention studies, sample sizes are simply too small to model the complex interactions of variables that impinge upon the intervention experience. Finally, there is considerable confusion in the developmental literature regarding the interpretation of interaction effects. Although the debate has centered around the application of appropriate statistical methods to detect the presence of interaction, the controversy may be more a function of what is actually meant by interactions that statistical techniques per se (Rutter, 1983a). Rutter goes on to caution us that unless specific hypotheses on particular types of interactions can be translated into testable operationalized predictions, "the interactionist perspective will not lead to a better understanding of developmental processes" (p. 315).

Interventions for low-birthweight infants have been well reviewed elsewhere with regard to traditional program parameters (e.g., content, duration, and intensity of treatment) and experimental rigor (e.g., characteristics of the sample method of assignment to groups, adequacy of controls, psychometric properties of measures, length of follow-up, and magnitude of main treatment effects). The reader is referred to reviews by Heinicke, Beckwith, and Thompson (1988), Field (1986), White and Casto (1985), Barnard (1984), Ramey, Bryant, and

Suarez (1985), and Lamb (1983); and metaanalyses by Heverly, Neuman, and Forquer (1982), Ottenbacher and Petersen (1985), Castro and Mastropieri (1986), and Ottenbacher, Muller, Brandt, Heintzelman, Hojem, and Sharpe (1987). Without a cogent framework for conceptualizing various types of interactional (and transactional) processes, however, the results of many studies remain difficult to interpret. We continue to be plagued by inconsistent findings and unexplained treatment effects (or lack thereof) (e.g., Casto & Lewis, 1984; Halpern, 1984; Bennett, 1987). This is especially frustrating because, as the preterm and low-birthweight cohorts of the 1970s mature, early intervention studies are beginning to yield longer term results in the areas of school achievement, learning disabilities, and behavioral adjustment of low-birthweight children.

Although we cannot assume the presence of interaction effects, it is often possible to increase the explanatory power of interventions or maximize intervention effects by addressing interactions. Explicit tests of hypotheses regarding the interaction effects of treatment X subject (or family) attributes require appropriate study design that randomly assign subjects, on the basis of the attributes of interest, to treatment and control conditions. In the absence of such design, large sample sizes may permit the testing of interaction effects, provided the distributions of the variables of interest are suitable. Experience with some of the most visible early intervention programs of the 1970s, targeting socially rather than biologically disadvantaged children, has taught us that programs certainly do not affect all participating children and their families in the same way (e.g., Kessen & Fein, 1975; Bryk, Wohlleb, Malson, & Mathis, 1975; Love, Nauta, Cohen, Hewlett, & Ruopp, 1976), although interaction effects were not formally tested in most evaluations. Most recently, the Infant Health and Development Program has demonstrated the success of a comprehensive early intervention in reducing the health and developmental problems of LBW infants across eight different sites (Gross et al., 1990). Because of the large sample size (958 subjects were randomly assigned to treatment and control conditions), the investigators were able to explore interaction effects of treatment with maternal demographic and infant birthweight variables.

Additional evidence for the presence of interaction effects comes from smaller studies which have identified, often on a post hoc basis, factors that seem to modify program success. These factors include family and social systems (Dunst, 1985; Guralnick & Bennett, 1987; Parke & Tinsley, 1982), maternal psychosocial characteristics (Osofsky, Culp, & Ware, 1988; Beckwith, 1988), attributes of the subject–intervenor relationship (Emde, 1988b), and other sources of within-group variability that shape the intervention process (Widmayer & Field, 1981; Belsky, 1986; Worobey & Brazelton, 1986).

Inspired by Rutter's (1983a) thoughtful discussion of statistical and personal interactions, the present chapter examines the evidence for interactive processes that influence the responses of low-birthweight children and their families to various kinds of early interventions. The evidence is gathered from observational as well as experimental work with infants thought to be at risk for aberrant development because of perinatal adversity, primarily low birthweight. Where empirical data are not available for biologically high-risk infants, we have included relevant studies of healthy, term infants. The literature is reviewed in four sections, each relating to a class of variables that have potential modifying effects on the intervention process or its outcome: demographic, social-contextual, psychological and infant constitutional/biomedical. Each section is accompanied by an analytic example, based on data from the Vermont Infant Studies Project, a longitudinal study to assess the effects of an early intervention for LBW infants (Rauh, 1982; Nurcombe, Howell, Rauh, Teti, Ruoff, & Brennan, 1984a; Rauh, Achenbach, Nurcombe, Howell, & Teti, 1988; Achenbach, Phares, Howell, Rauh, & Nurcombe, 1990). A brief description of the Vermont project and summary of findings to date are included below.

THE VERMONT INFANT STUDIES PROJECT

The Vermont Infant Studies Project is a longitudinal study of the effects of an intervention for low-birthweight, preterm infants (Rauh, 1982; Nurcombe et al.,1984; Rauh et al., 1988; Achenbach et al., 1990). Briefly, the intervention program consisted of 11 1-hour sessions, 7 prior to the infant's hospital discharge and 4 home visits extending into the fourth month following discharge. Each session was conducted by a neonatal intensive care nurse, and included the infant, mother, and father (when available). The purpose of the intervention was to acquaint the parent(s) with the infant's functioning, and to facilitate adjustment to the care of a low-birthweight infant (Rauh, Nurcombe, Ruoff, Teti, & Howell, 1982). A demonstration of the infant's behavioral capabilities, using the Brazelton Neonatal Behavioral Assessment Scale, provided an introduction to the intervention program. Additional techniques included modeling, demonstration, verbal instruction, and practical experience handling the infant (Rauh et al., 1990). By promoting sensitive and responsive caretaking, the intervention aimed, indirectly, to foster child development. All infants born between April 1980 and December 1981 whose birthweight was below 2,250 grams and gestational age under 37 weeks, and who were in intensive care for at least 10 days, were screened for inclusion in the LBW group. Infants resulting from multiple births, with congenital anomalies and/or severe neurological defects, or born to single mothers were excluded because of the possible confounding effects of such factors on later development. Seventy-eight of the 86 mothers whose infants met the selection criteria agreed to participate in the study. Following recruitment, each dyad was randomly assigned to the experimental ($N = 38$) or control ($N = 40$) group. A comparison group of normal birthweight infants (over 2,800 grams and more than 37 weeks gestation) was recruited sequentially from the regular nursery ($N = 41$).

Assessments of maternal adjustment and child development were made at 6, 12, and 24 months, and annual assessments of child behavioral adjustment and cognitive development have continued into the early school years. It was hypothesized that, as a result of intervention, (a) mothers would experience more favorable adjustment (as measured by confidence and satisfaction in the mothering role, and perception of ease/difficulty of the infant's temperament); and (b) low-birthweight intervention infants would be cognitively advanced relative to low-birthweight controls, but not significantly different from normal birthweight controls.

Results

Significant positive intervention effects on Satisfaction with the Mothering Role (a scale derived from a semistructured interview designed for the present study), and maternal perception of Ease/Difficulty of Infant Temperament (a 4-point scale derived from the Carey Infant Temperament Scale) were found at six months (Nurcombe et al., 1984). No intervention effects on cognitive development (as measured by the Bayley Scales of Infant Development) were present at 6 and 12 months, although the cognitive advantage of the intervention group increased over time. After controlling for the effects of social class, significant positive intervention effects were found on 3- and 4-year cognitive development scores (as measured by the McCarthy General Cognitive Index), such that the magnitude of the treatment effect at four years (12.9 points) represented .86 SD in terms of the McCarthy's standardized norms (Rauh et al., 1988). These positive effects on child cognitive development have been sustained through 7 years of age (Achenbach et al., 1990). At age 7, after adjusting for SES, the LBW intervention group scored significantly higher than the LBW control group on three of the four scales of the Kaufman Assessment Battery for Children (Mental Processing Composite, $p = .001$; Sequential, $p = .04$; and Simultaneous, $p < .001$). There were no significant differences between LBW intervention and normal birthweight control groups on any measure. Although SES was significantly associated with the cognitive performance of the LBW children, intervention had a significant additional effect on cognitive performance, over and above that accounted for by SES. Using the z-transformations of the cognitive scores for subjects with complete data from 6 months to 7 years (21 LBW intervention, 28 LBW control, and 28 NBW control), the mean z scores were plotted and adjusted for SES by ANCOVA. Figure 1 shows the progressive divergence between LBW intervention and LBW control scores over the 7-year follow-up period (Achenbach et al., 1990).

Beyond these group differences in mean cognitive development scores, inter-

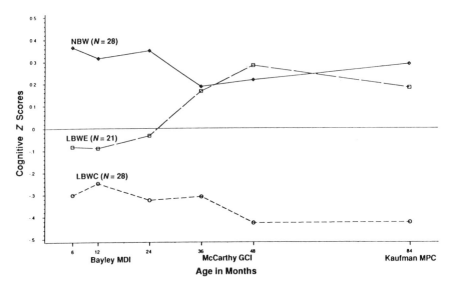

Figure 1. Cognitive Developmental Outcome Over Time Among Low-Birthweight Experimental, Low-Birthweight Control, and Normal Birthweight Control Infants

vention also seems to have prevented major developmental lags in individual children.

PATTERNS OF INFLUENCE ON THE INTERVENTION PROCESS

Figure 2 provides a conceptual schema to guide the present discussion.

Potential program effect modifiers can be grouped into at least four categories: demographic factors, social-contextual factors, parental psychological characteristics, and characteristics of the infant. The diagram encompasses many of the components present in Belsky's (1984) process model of the determinants of parenting. As will be seen, certain parts of the present "model" can be fairly well specified as to the underlying constructs and the direction of effects. Other paths of influence are more speculative; in some cases, we cannot even be certain whether the impact is positive or negative. As in Belsky's model of influences on parenting, attributes of the parent(s), the child, and the social context are not equally influential in supporting or undermining the success of various interventions.

Figure 2 represents a slice in time, and does not capture the dynamic nature of person–environment transactions over time. The effect of each component might be expected to change over time as a result of reciprocal influences within the system, as well as the impact of unmeasured external factors. Effective intervention requires a kind of fit between the target(s) of the program, the explicit goals

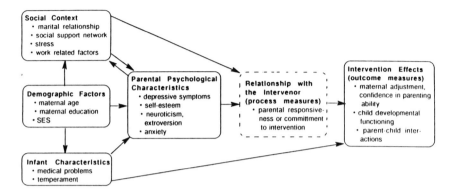

Figure 2. Conceptual Model of the Relationships Among Potential Program Effect Modifiers

of treatment, and the existing resources and constraints of the total system. The purpose here is to provide interventionists with the knowledge to improve the fit, and hence the success, of their programs.

Before taking a look at the evidence for interaction effects, it is useful to clarify what is meant by interaction effects of this context. Basically, we wish to identify factors or conditions that enhance (or reduce) the likelihood that intervention will have a beneficial effect for the families of high risk infants. Interaction, or effect modification, exists when a condition facilitates the intervention process so that the effects in the presence of this condition is greater than that of either the intervention or the condition alone. Alternatively, intervention in the presence of some condition may be less effective than intervention or the condition alone (a kind of antagonism). Higher order interactions are also possible in which one condition (e.g., psychological well-being) either potentiates or hinders intervention in the presence of a second condition (e.g., social support or stress). Such interactions are more difficult to test because they require larger samples and appropriate distributions of the independent variables so that all possible cross-product terms can be considered.

Baron and Kenny (1986) have distinguished the moderator from the mediator function of variables. The moderator function (mathematically expressed as an interaction) partitions an independent variable into subgroups that "establish its domains of maximal effectiveness in regard to a given dependent variable," while the mediator function represents the "generative mechanism through which the focal independent variable is able to influence the dependent variable of interest" (p. 1173). Both kinds of processes might be considered in the study of intervention effects.

The measure of interaction for a set of data may be a calculated index, a sample regression coefficient, or an analysis of variance contrast (a special case of regression analysis where all independent variables are nominal). Clues to the presence of interaction effects in a set of data may often be obtained by subgrouping or stratifying within samples, a frequent strategy in clinical epidemiologic research, but one that requires appropriate distributions of variables and sufficient sample sizes. Further analysis of the nature of interactions will depend upon the model employed, since interaction effects may be additive (as quantified by linear regression analysis) or multiplicative (as quantified as logistic regression analysis). Much has been written in the epidemiological literature about the meaning of different kinds of interactions and their applicability (e.g., biological, public health, individual decision making). The reader is referred to Rothman, Greenland, and Walker (1980) for a further discussion of this issue. In reviewing the early intervention literature, it is clear that few studies have been designed to address interaction effects. The present discussion is intended to encourage interventionists to consider possible interaction effects during the design phase of their work, so that explicit tests of such interactions may further inform our understanding of intervention effects.

DEMOGRAPHIC CHARACTERISTICS

Demographic or status variables, such as maternal age, educational level, and socioeconomic status (SES), have been rather routinely assessed in intervention studies to establish group comparability prior to treatment. Because of their potential confounding effect on the association between intervention and outcome (especially in the case of cognitive development), maternal educational level and SES have generally been used as control variables. Few studies have considered the interactive effects of demographic factors on the outcomes of interest.

Young maternal age has been associated with more strict, angry or punitive attitudes toward the young child in normal samples (Osofsky & Osofsky, 1970; Jones, Green, & Krauss, 1980), and with inappropriate expectations about child development among preterm and term infants (Field, Widmayer, Stringer, & Ignatoff, 1980), and with inappropriate expectations about child development among preterm and term infants (Field, Widmayer, Stringer, & Ignatoff, 1980). In a sample including preterm infants, maternal age effects on parenting style were still present after controlling for the effect of demographic factors and the degree of life stress (Ragozin, Basham, Crnic, Greenberg, & Robinson, 1982). The extensive literature on the risks of adolescent parenthood deals largely with full term infants (e.g., Zuckerman, Walker, Frank, Chase, & Hamburg, 1984; Zuckerman, Winsmore, & Alpert, 1979), and most intervention programs have been designed for this population. Osofsky et al. (1988) found that an intervention for adolescent mothers of term infants was significantly less effective (in terms of 6-month maternal interactive behaviors and 13-month child cognitive development) for the youngest adolescent girls (less than 16 years) and for those whose infants were at higher risk (on the basis of birthweight, gestational age, and apgar scores).

In one of the few intervention studies targeting teenage mothers of preterm infants, Field (1986) compared the effects of two different interventions on maternal interactional style and child development at 1, 4, and 12 months. All participating young mothers were from impoverished families, so that the children were at both environmental and biological risk. Intervention was based on the MABI, a modification of the Brazelton Neonatal Behavioral Assessment Scale, in which mothers assess their own infants. Two different forms of the program, differing in intensity, had approximately equivalent beneficial effects on 1-month mother–infant interactions, maternal perception of infant temperament, and 12-month Bayley Mental Development Scores. The possible modifying effect of maternal age within the intervention group was not addressed.

Additional work with normal samples suggests that young maternal age alone is a rather poor predictor of child cognitive outcome, once SES is controlled (e.g., Zuckerman et al., 1984; Belmont, Cohen, Dryfoos, Stein, & Zayacs, 1981; Oppel & Royston, 1971). Furthermore, once the effects of obstetric complications and cultural group were controlled, Lester, Coll, and Sepkoski (1983) found that maternal age had no main effect on neonatal behavior, but maternal age interacted with or potentiated the effects of the other risk factors such as medical complications. The apparent contribution of maternal age to child behavior and development is more likely explained by the effects of the correlates of age, including family structure and living arrangements (Kellam, Ensminger, & Turner, 1977), and other psychosocial factors.

In normal samples, socioeconomic status (SES) has been shown to predict about 20% of the variance in IQ scores of school-age children (e.g., White, 1982). As with maternal age, the evidence suggests that the correlates of SES may be the functional predictors. For example, within SES strata, Sameroff, Seifer, Barocas, Zax, and Greenspan (1987) found that psychosocial correlates of SES were associated with child cognitive functioning, accounting for an additional 16% of the variance in 4-year verbal IQ scores. Those correlates included, among others, measures of maternal mental health, anxiety, attitudes, and social supports. Similarly, Parmelee, Beckwith, Cohen, and Sigman (1983), in their intensive longitudinal study of preterm infants, found that intervention was less effective for families of lower SES. In addition to economic problems, such families were characterized by larger size, more marital problems, and less consistent child care arrangements, suggesting that the socioeconomic marker variable is associated with a whole set of social and psychological stressors that all contribute to the low priority of the infant in the family.

For the most part, intervention studies have lacked the statistical power needed to address the effects of demographic variability within the intervention group. The one exception is the Infant Health and Development Program, which found interaction effects of treatment with maternal age and education (Gross et al., 1990). Specifically, younger mothers in the intervention group reported higher child morbidity scores than younger mothers in the control group at adjusted age 3 years ($p = .003$). Since higher morbidity scores were also associated with higher maternal education, it is possible that the higher scores reflected increased vigilance and health education in the intervention group. Secondly, intervention had a differential effect on mothers' reports of child behavior problems depending on the mothers' level of education. For college-educated mothers, there was no intervention effect on child behavior problems, while for those with less education, the intervention group reported fewer behavior problems ($p = .009$.

An Illustration of the Modifying Effects of Demographic Factors

In the Vermont study, there were no significant maternal age effects or age X intervention effects on child development. There were, however, significant main maternal age effects on the 6-month maternal measure of Role Satisfaction ($F = 9.00$, $p = 0004$), such that younger mothers had less favorable Role Satisfaction scores than older mothers regardless of intervention. Furthermore, age accounted for an additional 16.6% of the variance in Role Satisfaction, over and above that accounted for by intervention alone (F value of the change in $R = 13.31$, $p = 0005$).

Within the intervention group, there was a significant age effect on the process measure, Maternal Receptivity to Intervention, such that the youngest mothers were least receptive to intervention, as reported by the nurse-intervenor at the completion of the program (ANOVA $F = 3.30$, $p = .036$). The mean ages of mothers for each of the four increasing levels of Receptivity were 23.5, 27.4, 28.6, and 31.0 years, respectively. Maternal Receptivity was not associated with SES or maternal educational level, but the association with cognitive development remained throughout the follow-up period.

Interaction effects of treatment X maternal educational level on child cognitive development were not addressed in the original analyses because maternal educational level (or the marker variable, socioeconomic status) was considered as a covariate, rather than a main effect, for all tests of mean group differences in cognitive development. In order to examine interaction effects here, we divided the sample into two groups according to maternal educational level: less than or equal to 12 years ($n = 60$), and greater than 12 years ($n = 50$). The classification variable, maternal education, served to define strata consisting of relatively similar women between whom the effects of intervention could be evaluated. We selected 4-year McCarthy scores as the outcome because intervention effects, sustained through this age, seemed likely to have implications for early school performance. Table 1 shows the layout of data for a stratified comparison of the treatment and control conditions. Inspection of the means reveals that the intervention group out-performed the control group overall (by ANOVA, $F = 12.16$, $p = .001$), but that the treatment effects were not uniform across strata. To further explore the significance of the interaction, we dichotomized the outcome variable (using the McCarthy national mean of 100 as the cut point), and computed the risk of falling below the national mean for children in each maternal educational stratum.

Using the odds ratio as the measure of program impact, Table 2 demonstrates the magnitude of the difference in stratum-specific effects. Among the less educated mothers, the risk of an LBW control child scoring below the national mean was 3.8 times that of a child who had received intervention. Among more highly educated mothers, the risk of a LBW control child scoring below the national mean was 13 times that of a child who received intervention.

In light of the Infant Health and Development Program finding of a maternal education X treatment effect on 3-year child behavior problems, we tested the significance of this interaction effect in the Vermont data set. Children were assessed annually on the Child Behavior Checklist (Achenbach & Edelbrock, 1981; Achenbach, Edelbrock, & Howell, 1987). Although there were no intervention effects on child behavior problems (t-scores, mother-report), we were interested to know if behavior problems were sensitive to the modifying effects of maternal education on response to intervention. No such education X treatment effects on behavior problems were found at any assessment from 2 through 6 years, but mothers with less than college education consistently reported more behavior problems than college-educated mothers, regardless of intervention or birthweight.

Typically, a stratified analysis is followed by a multivariate modeling technique to determine the type of interaction observed. This involves the fitting of a regression model (linear or logistic) that contains a cross-product term. If the estimated regression coefficient is significantly different from zero, interaction is considered to be present. For the purpose of this illustration, small sample size precludes such techniques. A proper test of age or education X treatment interaction effects requires the formulation of a priori hypotheses and appropriate sample selection to ensure adequate distribution of cases and controls at each factor level.

Table 1. Group Means on 4-yr McCarthy Scores, Stratified by Maternal Educational Level ($\leq$ 12 years versus > 12 years)

Stratum	Intervention			Control			Significance
	n	$\bar{x}$	SD	n	$\bar{x}$	SD	(t-test)
1 (Low Ed)	12	103.7	6.6	23	94.9	16.9	$p = .04$
2 (High Ed)	15	119.7	19.3	9	95.1	17.4	$p = .005$

Table 2. Comparison of Intervention Effects on 4-year McCarthy Scores between Two Maternal Educational Levels

| | Stratum 1: Low ED | | | | Stratum 2: High Ed | | |
	Control	Intervention	Total		Control	Intervention	Total
<100	15	4	19	≤100	6	2	8
≥100	8	8	16	≥100	3	13	16
	ODDS RATIO = 3.8				ODDS RATIO = 13.0		
	$X^2 = 2.07, p = .08$				$X^2 = 5, p < .05$		

Conclusions Regarding the Modifying Effects of Demographic Factors

The bulk of the evidence suggests that demographic factors do interact with intervention to affect the experience as well as the outcome, so that individuals with specific demographic profiles are more or less likely to benefit from specific programs. However, identification of such interaction effects may do little to further our understanding of the intervention process. Indeed, the longitudinal literature suggests that such global variables alone are rather poor predictors of outcome, once we control for the effects of a range of psychosocial correlates. As posited in Figure 2, the influence of demographic factors on response to intervention may be mediated or explained by components of the social context, infant characteristics, and parental psychological attributes. For example, a teenage mother, with good self-esteem and a supportive family, who delivers a LBW infant may be an excellent candidate for intervention. Likewise, a well-educated adult mother with a very unresponsive infant may be so incapacitated by depressive symptoms as to be unresponsive to many types of intervention. In either case, some knowledge of the social context, the condition of the infant, or the parent's personal disposition, and how these factors are likely to affect the outcome of intervention would be helpful in selecting the mode and/or timing of intervention.

SOCIAL-CONTEXTUAL FACTORS

The importance of the social context for child development is well-recognized (e.g., Bronfenbrenner, 1986), with most research focused on intrafamilial aspects of the parent–child relationships (Maccoby & Jacklin, 1983). Sameroff and Chandler's notion of a "continuum of caretaking casualty" hypothesizes that, at one end of the continuum, the caretaking environment is sufficiently adaptive (or resourceful) to compensate for biological risk, whereas, at the other end of the continuum, the environment has insufficient resources (or too many stresses) to overcome even minor perinatal problems (Sameroff & Chandler, 1975). In such a transactional model, the child's resiliency depends upon the degree of *contextual plasticity*, or the ability of the immediate environment to adapt to the needs of the developing child (Sameroff, 1982). This phenomenon has particular relevance to the high-risk infant whose needs may elicit and/or require rather different responses by parents and the wider social environment (e.g., Goldberg, Corter, Ojkasek, & Minde, 1990).

There is recent evidence from the correlational literature that preterm infants are more vulnerable or sensitive to their environments than term infants, suggesting that social factors may have a heightened impact on development in high-risk samples (Crnic & Greenberg, 1987; Greenberg & Crnic,1988). Specifically, measures of family relationship, autonomy within the family, and family organization/control were more frequently and more strongly related to maternal–child behaviors among preterm than term infants at 24 months (Crnic & Greenberg, 1987). In the same study, earlier measures of maternal attitudes, social support and mother–infant behavioral factors were also more frequently related to subsequent 24-month family structure, style, and functioning among preterms. For example, mothers' intimate support at 1 month was significantly related to 24-month family dimensions among pretern but not term children. Pascoe, Loda, Jeffries, and Earp (1981) also reported that social supports were predictive of mothers' provision of child stimulation in a sample of 3-year-olds who had been hospitalized in the neonatal intensive care nursery. These findings suggest concurrent ordinal person–environment interactions, as well as transactional processes over time. That is, the family context appears to affect, differentially, children with biological vulnerability. Those biologically vulnerable children also appear to influence their own family environments over time. The process is not only bidirectional but also truly transactional in that one independent variable (i.e., intimate support) actually changes another independent variable (some other dimension of the family system, such as parenting style), perhaps by virtue of opening or closing social opportunities (Rutter, 1983b).

Additional support for the power of social-contextual influences on development in high-risk samples comes from a longitudinal study of preterm, very low-birthweight infants by Goldberg et al. (1990). The authors found that measures of the family environment predicted teachers' ratings of child behavioral problems at four years. Furthermore, as demonstrated by Crnic and Greenberg, the effects were bidirectional, so that the family environment at four years was a function of early infant characteristics (in this case, temperament). Siegel (1982, 1984) also found preterm infants to be highly responsive to environmental influences. Compared to a group of term infants, the association of environmental factors with 3-year developmental outcome was stronger for preterm infants.

These longitudinal findings demonstrate that the biologically high-risk infant is not only susceptible to social-contextual influences but also capable of shaping this context over time. Such plasticity on the part of the infant as well as the immediate environment provided a rationale for a whole generation of early intervention studies targeting the family systems of low-birthweight and preterm infants (see review by Heinicke et al., 1988). Among other factors, these interventions focused on the parents' social network (Barnard, Booth, Mitchell, & Telzrow, 1983), quality of parent–infant interaction (Barrera, Cunningham, & Rosenbaum, 1986; Field et al., 1980; Widmayer & Field, 1981; Minde, Shosenberg, Morton, Thompson, Ripley, & Burns, 1980; Minde, Shosenberg, Thompson, & Morton, 1983; Rauh et al., 1988), and attachment (Siegel, Bauman, Schaefer, Saunders, & Ingram, 1980). Although this body of work implicitly assumes a transactional model of development, the predominant approach to study design and analysis reflected a *process-context* model in which the impact of a particular environmental condition (in this case, an intervention program) is more or less the same irrespective of characteristics of the family (Bronfenbrenner, 1986). Only a handful of studies have addressed the possible modifying effects of social-familial context on program success, and very few of these have considered such effects in the design phase of the study.

Affleck, Tennen, Rowe, Roscher, and Walker (1989) reported a modifying effect of social support on the success of an early intervention for preterm, largely very-low-birthweight infants, such that mothers who expressed greater "need" for support showed more optimal 6-month maternal adaptation than those with less "need" for support. Furthermore, for those mothers who expressed a low "need" for support, intervention had a negative effect. It is of interest that program participation had no significant effects on 6-month outcomes independent of mother's "need" for support. We will return to this example in the next section, when we consider the possibility that expressed "need" for support is more reflective of maternal psychological well-being than the actual amount of resources in the environment.

Using post hoc analyses, other intervention researchers have examined the social circumstances of successful and unsuccessful participants. For example, in a sample of disadvantaged preterm, low-birthweight infants, Beckwith (1988) found a differential drop-out rate between intervention and control groups such that women who dropped out of the control group were more likely to have a history of family instability and less likely to be connected to a medical support system, as indicated by their lack of prenatal care. Of those who received intervention, those with unstable family histories and lack of prenatal care actually benefitted most from the intervention, as measured by responsiveness to the infant. Intervention effects became apparent only when those interactions were examined.

Minde et al. (1980) found that the quality of the husband–wife relationship (an indicator of intimate support) seemed to moderate the mother's response to a self-help intervention group for parents of preterm infants. Mothers who participated in a self-help group visited their infants more in the hospital, stimulated their infants more, and expressed more confidence in their caretaking abilities. Frequency of maternal visitation (an outcome measure) was also found to be a function of the quality of the marital relationship. Furthermore, intervention mothers reported that their relationships with one or more significant persons in their life had improved since participating in the intervention program (Minde et al., 1983). The complex relationships among the informal support system (e.g., the marriage), the formal support system (e.g., the intervention group), and response to intervention (e.g., maternal visitation, quality or relationship with significant others, and aspects of the mother–child relationship) thus seem to be bidirectional, and the effects on outcome interactive.

An Illustration of Social Context x Treatment Effects

In the Vermont Infant Studies Project, mothers were interviewed in the home six to eight months after delivery using a measure of social support, the Interview Schedule for Social Interaction (ISSI) (Henderson, 1980). This instrument assesses (a) the availability of people to whom the respondant is attached, (b) the adequacy of these attachments, (c) the availability of the major provisions of social relationships (e.g., social integration, nurturance reassurance of self-worth, sense of reliable alliance, and guidance), and (d) the adequacy of these provisions.

To examine the possible modifying effects of the social support subscales on intervention outcome, we again used stratified analyses. The scores on the measures of social support do not follow the normal distribution (the distributions are bimodal, with most respondants scoring at the high end and a subgroup clustering around a lower mode), so that mothers were classified into "high" or "low" level. Table 3 shows the mean group differences on developmental scores, stratified by availability of attachment figures.

Inspection of the means reveals that the intervention group out-performed the control group within each stratum, but the significant effect was confined to

Table 3. Group Means on 4-yr McCarthy Scores, Stratified by Maternal Availability of Attachment* (AVAT)

Stratum	Intervention			Control			Significance (t-test)
	n	x̄	SD	n	x̄	SD	
1 (Low)	7	107.9	20.5	11	94.6	20.1	$p = .19$
2 (High)	20	114.3	15.7	21	95.2	15.3	$p < .001$

*Interview Schedule for Social Support, Subscale (Henderson, 1980)

Table 4. Comparison of Intervention Effects on 4-year McCarthy Scores between Two Levels of Maternal Availability of Attachment (AVAT)

	Stratum 1: Low AVAT				Stratum 2: High AVAT		
	Control	Intervention	Total		Control	Intervention	Total
<100	6	2	8	≤100	15	4	19
≥100	5	5	10	≥100	6	16	22
	ODDS RATIO = 3				ODDS RATIO = 10		
	$X^2 = .35, p > .5$				$X^2 = 8.9, p < .01$		

those children whose mothers reported available attachments. Using the odds ratio as the measure of program impact, Table 4 shows that the odds of a LBW control child scoring below the mean were three times those of an intervention child, for children whose mothers reported low availability of attachment figures.

Among high availability mothers, the odds of a LBW control child falling below the mean were 10 times those of an intervention child. Reliance on the overall effect measure would be somewhat misleading since it suggests that all LBW infants who participated in the program were equally likely to score above the mean.

Tables 5 and 6 show a similar finding for perceived adequacy of attachments. Again, the intervention program appears to have been relatively more effective for mothers who reported more adequate attachment. As is the case with availability of attachments, the low adequacy group did not benefit from intervention to the same degree as the high adequacy group (odds = 2.8 versus odds = 11.7).

Using the same method, we also evaluated the contribution of availability and adequacy of social integration. Again, there was a similar differential effect of intervention for "high" and "low" support mothers on the availability as well as the adequacy measure, such that the program was relatively more effective for the high adequacy/availability women. Again, the magnitudes of the effects were similar to those for the two attachment measures.

Table 5. Group Means on 4-yr McCarthy Scores, Stratified by Maternal Adequacy of Attachment* (ADAT)

	Intervention			Control			Significance
Stratum	n	$\bar{x}$	SD	n	$\bar{x}$	SD	(t-test)
1 (Low)	9	105.0	11.5	12	95.9	20.1	$p = .21$
2 (High)	18	116.5	18.7	20	94.4	14.9	$p = .001$

*Interview Schedule for Social Support, Subscale (Henderson, 1980)

Table 6. Comparison of Intervention Effects on 4-year McCarthy Scores between Two Levels of Maternal Adequacy of Attachment (ADAT)

	Stratum 1: Low ADAT				Stratum 2: High ADAT		
	Control	Intervention	Total		Control	Intervention	Total
<100	7	3	10	≤100	14	3	17
≥100	5	6	11	≥100	6	15	21
	ODDS RATIO = 2.8				ODDS RATIO = 11.7		
	$X^2 = .48, p > .3$				$X^2 = 8.8, p < .01$		

Conclusions Regarding the Modifying Effects of the Social Context

Although the above-described studies involve variously defined biologically high-risk samples and different measures of social conditions, results suggest that social-contextual factors affect intervention outcomes, as measured by maternal confidence and adaptation (Affleck et al., 1989; Minde et al., 1980, 1983), and infant cognitive development (Rauh et al., 1988). Returning to Figure 2, it is not clear whether the effects of social contextual factors on maternal and child outcomes are direct, indirect or both. Those intervention studies originally designed to evaluate "process" measures (e.g., maternal commitment/resistence to intervention) did not tend to include assessments of longer term maternal and child outcomes. Other studies employed process measures only after failing to find significant intervention effects on outcome. As a result, virtually no studies included all the measures needed to explore the associations among measures. Furthermore, the evidence is unclear regarding both the size and the direction of effects. Different components of the social context (e.g., quality of the marital relationship, social network, medical support system, etc.) seem to be associated with both the process and the outcomes of intervention, but we do not know whether the social context influences the intervention process and outcomes, whether the intervention process and outcomes affect the social context, or both (as suggested by Minde's findings). The results of our own analyses do not answer this question since the measure of social support was administered after the completion of the intervention program. Although it is unlikely that intervention significantly altered families' total social support networks (there were no group differences on the social support measure), some mothers did name the nurse intervenor as a member of their social network. In addition, it is not clear which components of the social context are most influential. On the basis of previous findings regarding the determinants of parenting competence (e.g., Belsky, 1981; Crnic et al., 1983), we might expect intimate support (or degree of attachment) to exert a more powerful effect than social network support (i.e., degree of social integration) on a mother's ability to utilize intervention. This question deserves further study.

Finally, the evidence suggests that some forms of intervention may have a negative impact on outcome when delivered in the context of certain social support conditions (i.e., low "need" for support). One possible explanation for the confusion is that social support, like many social-contextual variables, is partly a function of maternal personality and long-standing psychological characteristics that predate the intervention experience. Indeed, the positive association between family resources/supports and personal well-being of the parents has been frequently reported in the intervention literature (e.g., Trivette, Deal, & Dunst, 1986; Dunst, Leet, & Trivette, 1988) as well as the observational literature (e.g., Henderson, Duncan-Jones, Byrne, Adcock, & Scott, 1979; Cutrona & Troutman, 1986). Affleck's finding that mothers with low "need" for support responded negatively to intervention may be accounted for by socially isolated women with problematic psychological dispositions who are unable to take advantage of the intervention experience because they cannot form a relationship with the intervenor. In other words, these women may express a low "need" for support, not because they already have sufficient support, but rather because they are somehow personally unable to use support in a healthy manner. This interpretation of such apparently discrepant findings would make them consistent with the bulk of the evidence, suggesting that most interventions for the families of LBW infants are not very successful in reaching socially isolated, hard-to-help families. As suggested by Parmelee et al. (1983), such multiproblem families cannot afford to make the new infant a priority.

Well-controlled studies are now needed in which both the formal and the informal social support system are manipulated so that the nature of the interplay between the two can be more fully understood, as suggested by Tinsley and Parke (1983). If, for example, the quality of intimate support or attachment (e.g., the marriage) has a more powerful impact on the success of the intervention program than the quality of the friendship network, we might choose to include a marital support component in the treatment plan for certain families. Another future area of investigation involves the impact of the employment context on response to intervention. Influences on the intervention process may involve the availability of concrete resources (such as money, transportation, child care arrangements), the level of social strain (Crouter, Belsky, & Spanier, 1983), and dual role conflict (e.g., Stuckey, McGhee, & Bell, 1982).

Whether the social context functions as a resource or a hindrance to the intervention process is partly a function of the mother's (father's) psychological profile. The social context may influence the intervention process through its impact on the mother's psychological well-being. For example, the social support system (including work conditions) may set the stage for responsiveness to intervention by means of its effect on the mother's self-esteem or affective state. Similarly, maternal psychological disposition may influence the intervention process or outcome either directly or indirectly via its impact on the social environment.

PARENTAL PSYCHOLOGICAL CHARACTERISTICS

The importance of parental psychological well-being for the developmental competence of the normal child is widely accepted. In samples of full-term children, maternal depression is perhaps the most widely studied psychological factor that has been related to parenting (Belsky & Pensky, 1988), among clinically depressed (Field, et al., 1988; Weissman, Paykel, & Klerman, 1972) as well as subclinically depressed women (Conger, McCarthy, Yang, Lahey, & Kropp, 1984; Colletta, 1983). Maternal depressive symptoms have been associated with hostility (Bromet & Cornely), 1984; Lyons-Ruth, Cornell, Grynebool, Botein, & Zoll, 1984), and unfavorable self-perceptions of mothering capacity (Weissman et al., 1972). Studies of the effects of maternal depression on infant outcome suggest an adverse effect on early attachment and emotional development (e.g., Wolkind, Coleman, & Ghodsian, 1980; Radke-Yarrow, Cummings, Kuczynski, & Chapman, 1985), and interactive behaviors with their mothers (Cox, Puckering, Pound, & Mills, 1987; Field, Healy, Goldstein, & Guthertz, 1990). Depressive symptoms are likely to disturb those components of the child's physical (Bradley & Caldwell, 1976; Siegel, 1981) and interactive environments (Clarke-Stewart, 1973) that are strongly associated with early developmental competency. Older children of depressed mothers have been shown to exhibit a range of psychopathology, intellectual and attentional difficulties (Hammen, Gordon, Burge, Adrian, Jaenicke, & Hiroto, 1987; Weissman et al., 1984; Triad, 1987; Breznitz & Friedman, 1988).

In a socially heterogeneous sample of 215 children (half of whose mothers were originally selected because of maternal emotional problems), Sameroff et al. (1987) found that a cumulative maternal psychosocial risk index was highly predictive of 4-year verbal IQ scores. Psychological components of the risk index and their associations with cognitive development included maternal anxiety ($r = -.16$, $p<.05$), overall mental health ($r = -.24$, $p<.01$), and attitudes toward child-rearing ($r = .50$, $p<.01$). A cluster analysis revealed that parental attitudes shared variance with maternal educational level and minority status (demographic variables), while mental health and anxiety measures were more closely related to social support.

Among the other maternal psychological characteristics that have been linked to childcare practices are parental neuroticism, maternal self-esteem and self-efficacy (Unger & Wandersman, 1985). In mothers of healthy infants, Cutrona and Troutman (1986) found that parenting self-efficacy mediated the association between social support and maternal postpartum depression, in the presence of high stress (in this case, a temperamentally difficult infant). Similarly, in a sample of clinically depressed and nondepressed mothers, Teti and Gelfand (1990) found that maternal depression, social support, and infant temperament influenced mothers' behaviors with their infants primarily through their influence on maternal self-efficacy. We will return to the role of infant temperament as a possible modifier of intervention effects in a later section, but would emphasize here that a LBW infant, regardless of temperament, is likely to be a stressor. As suggested by Teti and Gelfand, a mother with low self-efficacy might be expected to withdraw from the challenges of a difficult baby and have more trouble establishing a sensitive relationship with the child. Such a mother would seem to be a candidate for an intervention aimed at improving sensitivity and responsivity to the infant, especially in the case of low birthweight. It is not clear, however, whether mothers with low self-efficacy are likely to be as receptive to the intervention process as mothers who feel better about themselves.

The notion of receptivity or responsiveness to intervention as a determinant of program success has only recently been addressed (e.g., Woroby & Brazelton, 1986; Belsky, 1986). Belsky has shown that positive intervention effects with normal, full-term infants were a function of the degree of parental engagement or involvement with the intervention (1986). In a sample of preterm, low-birthweight infants, Rauh et al. (1988) similarly found that maternal receptivity to intervention (as judged by the nurse-intervenor at the completion of the intervention program) was predictive of subsequent maternal and infant outcomes. Specifically, maternal receptively was significantly associated with maternal role satisfaction 6 months later, and with infant cognitive development 6, 12, 24, 36, and 48 months later. Further, the measure of maternal receptivity was not a function of socioeconomic status or maternal education.

Involvement in the intervention process can be conceptualized as a "mediating" variable; that is, an internal process or mechanism that may partly account for or explain the success or failure of a program (see Figure 2). An important aspect of parental engagement is the quality of the parent–intervenor relationship (Emde, 1988a), or, in some instances, the parent–staff relationship, which may continue long after the completion of the formal program. This aspect of intervention may be at least as important as the content of the treatment. As noted by Rutter (1983b), the reciprocity and degree of active involvement in the relationship may define the meaning and quality of the experience for the parents. One example comes from the work of Affleck et al. (1989), in which mothers who said they "needed" more support used the nurse-intervenor largely to ventilate feelings and solve problems, while those "needing" less support sought more information about medical conditions and child development.

According to Hinde (1979) and Hinde and Stevenson-Hinde (1987), each relationship is influenced by the social nexus of the relationships in which it is embedded, so that social-contextual factors, as well as psychological factors, may influence a parent's response to intervention. For example, Minde et al. (1980) reported that the quality of the current marital relationship moderated mothers' response to a self-help intensive care nursery intervention group. In the same study, mothers who recalled poor childhood relationships with their own mother interacted less sensitively with their preterm infant. In a sample of developmentally delayed infants and toddlers, Dunst et al. (1988) hypothesized that mothers' commitment to intervention would depend upon family needs. They found that the adequacy of family resources (both intra- and extrafamilial supports) accounted for a significant proportion of the variance in maternal well-being (47%, $p<.01$) and commitment to intervention (48%, $p<.01$). In a sample of high-risk infants, Barnard et al (1985) found that mothers with low social support were more resistant to intervention than those with higher levels of support.

At present, there are few good process measures to assess the quality of the participant's relationship with the intervenor and/or the whole intervention experience. Furthermore, it is not clear to what degree a given program's success depends upon a "halo" or even a true Hawthorne effect (Als, 1984). As noted by Nurcombe, Rauh, Howell, Teti, Ruoff, Murphy, & Brennan (1984), virtually no interventions with low-birthweight children have included a dummy intervention to assess the Hawthorne contribution.

An Illustration of Psychological Characteristics x Treatment Effects

Using data from the Vermont Infant Studies Project, the present authors explored the possible modifying effects of maternal psychological functioning on the success of intervention. Measures of Neuroticism and Extraversion (Eysenck & Eysenck, 1968) were administered to the mother during the first 6–8 months of the infant's life. Neuroticism and Extraversion are thought to be two stable, emotionally based dimensions of personality that account for much of the variation in individual differences (depression is considered to be a component of neuroticism/negative affectivity). Belsky and Pensky (1988) have suggested that such dimensions may have implications for childrearing behavior and, hence, child developmental outcomes. Since Neuroticism and Extraversion are thought to have strong interpersonal consequences, these traits might be expected to modify the intervention experience.

We first examined the effects of Neuroticism on 6-month maternal Role Satisfaction, since intervention was found to have a beneficial effect on this area of functioning. We categorized Neuroticism into two levels, using the mean value as the cut-point (Low Neuroticism < 9, high Neuroticism ≥ 9). Using two-way ANOVA, there was a significant main effect of maternal Neuroticism on Role Satisfaction ($F(1,65) = 11.68$, $p<.001$), but the effect was uniform across groups, suggesting that Neuroticism did not modify the effects of treatment on maternal Role Satisfaction (i.e., no interaction). There were no significant main effects of Neuroticism or Neuroticism X treatment effects on 4-year McCarthy Scores, nor were there any effects on cognitive development at any other assessment through the age of 6 years.

We next examined the effect of Extraversion on 6-month maternal Role Satisfaction, by dividing Extraversion into two levels at the mean value (low

Extraversion < 10, high Extraversion ≥ 10), and found no main effect (F(1,65 = .55, p = .46). There was, however, a significant Extraversion X treatment effect (F(1,65) = 6.20, p = .02). Table 7 shows the data layout for the test of mean group differences. Among high Extraversion mothers (who might be described as warm, friendly, compassionate, and sociable), intervention appeared to have a beneficial impact, whereas among low Extraversion mothers (who might be described as cool, formal and impersonal), there was no significant treatment effect. There were no main or interaction effects on 4-year cognitive development. Although Extraversion was not significantly associated with Maternal Role Satisfaction overall, inspection of the control group means shows that mothers scoring low on Extraversion actually appeared to have better adjustments than high Extraversion mothers 6 months later. This finding may suggest that the birth of a low-birthweight infant, in the absence of a formal support program, can be an especially stressful and frustrating experience for warm, expressive mothers. Low extraversion mothers, on the other hand, may have lower expectations or more psychological defenses than their highly Extraverted counterparts, although such findings should be interpreted with caution due to the small size of the sample.

We were also interested to know if child behavior problems were more sensitive than cognitive development to the possible modifying effects of maternal psychological factors on response to intervention. That is, although we might not expect early intervention to influence later child behavior problems directly, there may be some indirect or interactive effects of maternal personality X treatment on child behavioral functioning. Zero-order correlations of Neuroticism with behavior problems were significant at 3 ($r = .31$, $p = .002$), 4 ($r.27$, $p = .007$), 5 ($r = .26$, $p = .008$), and 6 years ($r = .29$, $p = .004$). Using ANOVA, there were no significant main or Neuroticism X treatment interaction effects at any assessment point.

There were no significant associations between Extraversion and behavior problems at any assessment. Table 8 shows the data layout for the comparison of group means of 4-year child behavior problems, stratified by extraversion. Two-way ANOVAS showed no significant main effects of Extraversion on behavior problems at any point of assessment, but significant interaction effects with

Table 7. Group Means on Maternal Role Satisfaction* Stratified by Maternal Extraversion**

Stratum	Intervention			Control			Significance
	n	x̄	SD	n	x̄	SD	(t-test)
1 (Low)	9	16.8	6.2	13	15.2	4.6	$p = .54$
2 (High)	21	14.2	3.9	23	18.8	4.7	$p < .001$

*low scores are optimal
**Eysenck Personality Inventory (Eysenck & Eysenck, 1968)

Table 8.   Group Means on 4-yr Child Behavior Problems*, Stratified by Maternal Extraversion**

| Stratum | Intervention | | | Control | | | Significance |
	n	x̄	SD	n	x̄	SD	(t-test)
1 (Low)	8	57.4	8.6	8	46.4	8.5	$p = .02$
2 (High)	15	52.5	10.3	15	56.5	7.1	$p = .23$

*Child Behavior Checklist (Achenbach & Edelbrock, 1981)
**Eysenck Personality Inventory (Eysenck & Eysenck, 1968)

treatment at 3, 4, and 5 years (3 years: $F(1, 54) = 15.95$, $p < .0001$; 4 years: $F(1,45) = 7.67$, $p = .008$; 5 years: $F(1,49) = 7.49$, $p = .009$), but not at 6 years ($F(1,49) = .47$, $p = .50$). There were no significant differences between intervention and control groups for high extraversion mothers, while among low-extraverted mothers, intervention was associated with reports of more behavior problems. The apparent negative effect of intervention on child behavior problems among low-extraverted mothers may be due to an increased willingness to report problems, rather than a true disordinal interaction effect. However, it is important to consider the possibility that intervention might have a negative effect on certain subjects under certain conditions. The relatively low number of behavior problems reported by mothers of LBW controls raises additional questions. Analysis of the Teacher's Report of child behavior problems in grades 1 and 2 may clarify the issue, and remains to be explored.

Conclusions Regarding the Modifying Effects of Psychological Factors

It is clear from the observational literature that some parental psychological factors, such as maternal depression, have a direct impact on child care practices and the mother–child relationship. This association is present in samples of clinically disturbed and nondisturbed mothers, as well as samples of high risk and normal infants. The direction of effects, however, is less well-established. Although the birth of a high-risk infant and the behavioral style of that infant may be sufficiently stressful to impede caregiving and disrupt the emerging parent–child relationship, such a stressful event may affect parental psychological functioning seriously, only transiently, or not at all. This may depend upon the initial level of functioning and the nature of the resources available to the parents. Furthermore, if it can be shown that parents with particular profiles are excessively vulnerable to stresses accompanying the birth of a LBW infant, interventions might be designed to monitor and treat such special situations. To date, intervention research offers little empirical data on the effects of intervening with clinically (or subclinically) disturbed parents of LBW infants. Teti and his colleagues are currently examining the effects of an intervention program designed specifically for depressed mothers of infants. Results may provide further insights into the effects of maternal depression on the process of intervention, and the importance of self-efficacy as a mediating factor. Our own data suggest that positive intervention effects on maternal Role Satisfaction may depend upon enduring psychological traits in the mother (e.g., Extraversion). Maternal Role Satisfaction is likely to be related to self-efficacy, at least within the parenting realm, so this whole area of maternal psychological functioning would seem to offer promise for future research.

Regarding the possible interaction effects of maternal psychological factors with intervention on child developmental outcomes, the observational literature suggests that maternal psychological factors have a stronger impact on child behavioral functioning than child cognitive development. Again, the construct of maternal self-efficacy may have some explanatory power, but it is not clear the extent to which maternal self-efficacy plays a role in the development of child behavioral competence and child cognitive abilities. Nor is it clear whether positive intervention effects on maternal social role functioning will necessarily translate into beneficial child effects.

CHARACTERISTICS OF THE INFANT

Biomedical Factors

Interventionists have long been concerned with infant biomedical attributes that predict or increase the probability of adverse outcomes. Birthweight, gestational age, and severity of medical problems have been frequently used to define target populations. Assigned to treatment (and control) conditions on the basis of one or more biomedical factors, groups were generally considered to be homogeneous with respect to risk status.

Recent longitudinal work suggests, however, that low-birthweight children are not at equal risk for developmental problems (e.g., Sostek, this volume). Landry, Chapieski, Fleicher, and Denson (1988) have shown that low-birthweight (<1,801 grams) preterm infants with bronchopulmonary dysplasia and those with intraventricular hemorrhage (grades III and IV) with associated hydrocephalus are at higher risk for cognitive and motor deficits over the first 3 years of life than those infants with intraventricular hemorrhage (grades I and II) and respiratory distress syndrome. Other findings suggest that it may not be the sickest or the smallest infants who are at highest risk, and hence the most appropriate targets for intervention. In a recent historical prospective study of low-income low-birthweight children, Carran, Scott, Shaw, and Beydouin (1989) found that infants between 1,500 and 2,500 grams were at very elevated risk for mild educational handicaps when compared to their normal birthweight peers. In a cohort of children who had reached the ages of 11 to 12 years, the low-birthweight children had a risk 2.48 times that of normal birthweight children, higher than that of the very low-birthweight children, whose risk ratio was 1.2. The authors also note that infants between 1,500 and 2,500 grams are a very large group (about five times the size of the very low-birthweight group), and, potentially, a very costly group for the educational system, particularly in light of recent legislation for the handicapped (i.e., Public Laws 94–142 and 99–457).

Few intervention studies have explored the possible modifying effects of biomedical conditions on intervention outcomes. Barrera et al. (1986) reported that intervention effects depended upon infant birthweight and perinatal complications. After participating in either a developmental or parent–infant intervention, mothers of very low-birthweight infants were significantly more responsive to and involved with their children than mothers of infants weighing between 1,500 and 2,500 grams, as well as normal control mothers. In addition, a very low-birthweight group who participated in an educational/therapeutic home intervention showed greater gains than the low-birthweight group as measured by the Bayley MDI and the HOME Inventory, although it is likely that the very low-birthweight group had greater room for improvement. The Infant Health & Development Program (Gross et al. 1991) found a significant treatment X birthweight interaction effect on 3-year Stanford-Binet IQ scores, such that the intervention was more effective for higher birthweight infants ($p = .014$). Among 3-year-olds with birthweights $\leq 1,500$ grams, there was no significant difference in the proportion of intervention vs. control children with IQ scores <70, so that the intervention did not appear to be effective for the lighter group.

In theory, different interventions could be designed for subgroups of high-risk infants with different biomedical needs, although the possibilities are infinite even within the population of low-birthweight infants. The specification of infant biomedical factors that potentially modify developmental outcome is difficult, because such factors are embedded in a complex system of direct and indirect psychosocial influences on development. A range of infant biological conditions may elicit a fixed set of parental (or environmental) responses (depending on social/contextual conditions), so that variability in response to intervention is actually constrained by the options in the caretaking environment rather than biomedical attributes of the infant. Similarly, the compensatory nature of some caretaking environments may overshadow a range of infant biomedical problems, so as to render those biomedical conditions less predictive of developmental outcomes.

Infant Temperament

Variously defined, temperament is thought to be a property of the organism that organizes interactions with the environment over a wide range of situations. The reader is referred to several recent volumes for in-depth treatment of theory, measurement, and clinical applications (e.g., Plomin & Dunn, 1986; Kohnstamm, Bates, & Rothbart, 1989). For the most part, temperament research has focused on normal samples of children, with the exception of a few studies that have explored temperament among physically ill or developmentally disabled children (e.g., Carey, 1985; Goldberg & Marcovitch, 1989). Thomas and Chess (1977) have suggested that difficult temperament in a child who has other problems requiring special care may be more stressful to parents than difficult temperament in an otherwise normal child. It is this aspect of temperament—its impact on the caregiver(s) and the parent–child relationship—that is especially relevant to our discussion of possible modifying effects on response to intervention.

The effects of maternal (paternal) psychological factors on parental "report" or "perception" of infant temperament must be considered, since some researchers have noted a significant association of maternal reports of temperament with psychological characteristics of the mother assessed before the birth of the infant (e.g., Vaughn, 1986). The parental reporting bias is quite evident in the perception of the "ease" or "difficulty" of the infant's temperament, which understandably reflects the goodness of fit between parent and child. Furthermore, such perceptions have been shown to be modifiable by intervention in the case of our own work with LBW infants (Nurcombe et al., 1984; Rauh et al., 1988). Specifically, overall group differences on maternal perception of infant difficulty at 6 months were significant, $F(2, 67) = 7.38$, $p = .001$, and the a priori contrast showed that LBW intervention mothers perceived their infant to be less difficult than LBW control mothers, $F(1,67) = 14.01$, $p < .01$. This index (derived from the Carey Infant Temperament Scale) was not associated with socioeconomic status. The implications of more favorable maternal perceptions of ease of caretaking are, however, unclear.

As pointed out by Stevenson-Hinde and Hinde (1988), temperamental differences cannot be regarded as invariant features of a child's behavioral style, independent of the child's relationships. Recent studies of normal infants examining the associations between infant temperamental characteristics and differences in caregiving suggest that temperament does indeed influence maternal responsiveness and other maternal interactive behaviors (see review by Crockenberg, 1986). Most importantly, these effects appear to be mediated by maternal self-efficacy (e.g., Cutrona & Troutman, 1986), so that, if one controls for self-efficacy, no significant association remains between infant temperament and maternal behavior (Teti & Gelfand, 1990). Among preterm, LBW infants, Goldberg et al. (1990) suggest that some mothers are unusually tolerant or well prepared, so that they are able to adjust to a wider range of infant characteristics, including difficult temperament. To the extent that temperament influences maternal responsiveness and maternal responsiveness affects child development, temperament could conceivably enhance or hinder beneficial intervention effects. Similarly, to the extent that maternal competence and tolerance are associated with positive temperamental traits by the end of the first year of life, such maternal behaviors may be an appropriate target for intervention.

Conclusions Regarding the Modifying Effects of Infant Factors

Evidence regarding the role of infant characteristics in the intervention experience remains inconclusive. The most convincing work suggests that, where modifying effects are likely to be present, they are mediated by or depend upon maternal psychological attributes and the quality of the mother–child relationship. Mothers high in self-efficacy may be so positive and persistent as to achieve a successful relationship with their infant, regardless of infant characteristics. Although there are limits to compensatory effects in the case of extremely damaged infants, achievement of reasonable intervention goals for both parent(s) and child would likely be influenced by certain parental characteristics. What remains to be shown is whether those characteristics themselves are feasible targets for the intervention process.

Regarding the role of temperament, the controversy over validity and reliability of the measures continues. Furthermore, it is not at all clear that maternal reports of temperament for LBW infants are stable over the first year of life.

CONCLUSION

The field of intervention research with high-risk infants has moved forward in fits and starts since the early 1970s. Just as important as the advances in complex data modeling and analytic strategies over the past decade are the small human victories gained in the field. As observed by Emde (1988a), we have perhaps learned more from the process of conducting the interventions themselves than from measuring differential outcomes in the child and family. In reviewing the literature, one cannot help but be impressed by the tireless efforts of interventionists to learn lessons from their experiences with families who have failed to be engaged by the intervention process. Early intervention researchers are a unique and hybrid group, comprising applied researchers and practitioners who share a long tradition of social concerns. Experimental "failures" have become opportunities for progress.

Referring to Figure 2, we can summarize the findings from each of the areas discussed. To begin with, demographic characteristics are likely to function as intervention effect modifiers, but such statistical interactions tell us very little about the processes involved. Additional analyses reveal that there are specific psychosocial correlates of the status variables that actually account for apparent effects on treatment success. These include components of the social context, infant characteristics, and parental psychological attributes that exert a more immediate or direct effect on response to intervention. We can be fairly certain of the direction of effects (demographic to psychosocial), although severe parental emotional disorder could conceivably exert a limiting effect on parental educational and economic status over time.

Regarding the modifying effects of social/contextual factors, the evidence is clear that measureable aspects of the environment exert a powerful effect on the likelihood of program success. Findings in the area of social support suggest that the resources and deficiencies of intimate relationships (i.e., marital) may be more important effect modifiers than other social supports, but this area deserves further study. Furthermore, evidence for the moderating role of parental psychological factors is convincing, so that it will be important to include both classes of variables in future intervention studies. This is all the more important in trying to sort out possible causal relationships, since influences between personal psychological and social contextual factors are often bidirectional. In addition, measures of current environmental conditions are good predictors of subsequent environmental conditions, and their effects are likely to be cumulative over time. It is not clear how maternal psychopathology will affect response to treatment over time, although both Sameroff and Rutter's findings suggest that it is the amount and degree of psychopathology, rather than the type that has the largest impact on child functioning. Results concerning the role of self-efficacy offer promising directions for future research for several reasons. First, maternal self-efficacy seems to mediate the effects of environmental as well as personal stressors (ranging from individual depression to the care of a difficult infant) on actual maternal–child interactive behaviors. Secondly, there is some evidence to suggest that maternal self-efficacy is modifiable, at least in the area of parenting competence, making it a promising focus for intervention.

The quality, affective characteristics, and nature of the parent–intervenor relationship deserve attention in future intervention studies (Emde, 1988b). In reviewing the evidence for possible intervention program effect modifiers in the areas of demographic, social-contextual, individual psychological, and infant constitutional factors, we are left with the impression that much of the influence of these factors is captured by the subject (in this case the mother)–intervenor relationship. That is, if we control for aspects of the subject–intervenor relationship (which may function as the final conduit in the path that determines the success or failure of the intervention), might the effects of all other variables be sharply reduced or disappear altogether? Or, are the potential effects of some factors (such as poverty or serious illness in the child) strong enough to wash out the beneficial effects of a positive relationship? These are questions that remain to be answered, and will depend to a large extent upon the goals of the intervention program.

Considerable confusion remains regarding the distinction between intervention process and outcome measures. We have tried to distinguish measures of maternal receptivity or commitment to intervention from the more traditional outcome measures of maternal adjustment and child developmental functioning, but we do not have enough data to draw conclusions about the associations between such measures and the impact of other variables on the whole process.

That is, we do not know if strong maternal commitment to an intervention program will foster program success, as measured by child outcome, in the presence of powerful environmental deterents (for example, unemployment). One might argue that maternal commitment or receptivity is unlikely to be high under such adverse circumstances, but, again, this may depend upon an individual's inner resources and psychological strengths. In addition, we do not know which aspects of the subject–intervenor relationship actually enhance commitment and longer term outcomes for the mother and the child.

In conclusion, interventionists can no longer conduct their work without considering the complex web of relationships within which the family functions. It is unlikely that a single intervention program will be uniformly effective for the heterogeneous group of children whom we refer to as *low birthweight*, although highly intensive, comprehensive programs may have some beneficial effects for many LBW children. Future intervention strategies and public health/educational policies will depend upon the cost and benefit of such efforts. The challenge, as formulated by Paneth (1990) in relation to the delivery of highly technical neonatal intensive care for LBW infants, is to balance the sensitivity and specificity of our services. That is, how do we ensure that the LBW infants who "need" early intervention receive it (i.e., sensitivity); while those who do not "need" intervention avoid it (i.e., specificity)? It is hoped that a better understanding of those factors that influence development and potentially modify a child and families' response to intervention will result in the design of more efficient services to these children.

REFERENCES

Achenbach, T.N., Phares, V., Howell, C.T., Rauh, V.A., & Nurcombe, B. (1990). Seven-year outcome of the Vermont Intervention Program for low-birthweight infants. *Child Development, 61*, 1672–1681.

Achenbach, T.N., & Edelbrock, C. (1981). Behavioral problems and competencies reported by parents of normal ad disturbed children aged 4 through 16. *Monographs of SRCD, 46* (1, Serial No., 188).

Achenbach, T.N., Edelbrock, C., & Howell C.T. (1987). Empirically based assessment of the behavioral/emotional problems of 2-3 year-old children. *Journal of Abnormal Child Psychology, 15*, 629–650.

Affleck, G., Tennen, H., Rowe, J., Roscher, B., & Walker, L. (1989). Effects of formal supports on mothers' adaptation to the hospital-to-home transition of high-risk infants: The benefits and cost of helping. *Child Development, 60*, 488–501.

Als, H. (1984). Discussion. In J.D. Call, E. Galenson, & R. Tyson (Eds.), *Frontiers of infant psychiatry* (pp. 211–217). New York: Basic Books.

Barnard, K. (1984). Nursing research related to infants and young children. In H.H. Werley & J.J. Fitzpatrick (Eds.), *Annual review of nursing research*. New York: Springer.

Barnard, K.E., Booth, C.L., Mitchell, S.K., & Telzrow, R.W. (1983). *Newborn nursing models final report* (Grant #RO-NV-00719). Division of Nursing Bureau of Health, Manpower, Health Resources Administration, Department of Human Services.

Barnard, K.E., Harrond, M., & Mitchell, S.K. (1985). Caring for high-risk infants and their families. In M. Green (Ed.), *The psychological aspects of the family.* Cambridge, MA: Lexington Books.

Baron, R.M., & Kenny, D.A. (1986). The moderator-mediator variable distinction in social psychological research: conceptual, strategic, and statistical considerations. *Journal of Personality and Social Psychology, 51*(6), 1173–1182.

Barrera, M.E., Cunningham, C.E., & Rosenbaum, P.L. (1986). Low birthweight and home intervention strategies: Preterm infants. *Journal of Development and Behavioral Pediatrics, 7,* 361–366.

Beckwith, L. (1988). Intervention with disadvantaged parents of sick preterm infants. *Psychiatry, 51,* 242–247.

Bell, R.Q. (1968). A reinterpretation of the direction of effects in studies of socialization. *Psychological Review, 75,* 81–95.

Bell, R.Q., & Pearl, D. (1982). Psychosocial change in risk groups: Implication for family identification. *Perspectives in Human Services, 1,*45–49.

Belmont, L., Cohen, P., Dryfoos, J., Stein, Z., & Zayacs, S. (1981). Maternal age and Children's intelligence. In K. Scott, T. Field, & E. Robertson (Eds.), *Teenage parents and their offspring.* New York: Grune & Stratton.

Belsky, J. (1981). Early human experience: A family perspective. *Developmental Psychology, 17,* 3–23.

Belsky, J. (1984). The determinants of parenting: A process model. *Child Development, 55,* 83–96.

Belsky, J. (1986). A tale of two variances: between and within. *Child Development, 57,* 1301–1305.

Belsky, J., & Pensky, E. (1988). Developmental history, personality, and family relationships: toward an emergent family system. In R.A. Hinde & J. Stevenson-Hinde (Eds.), *Relationships within families, mutual influences* (pp. 193-217). Oxford: Clarendon Press.

Bennett, F.C. (1987). The effectiveness of early intervention for infants at increased biologic risk. In M.J. Guralnick & F.C. Bennett (Eds.), *The effectiveness of early intervention for at risk and handicapped children* (pp. 79–112). New York: Academic Press.

Bradley, R., & Caldwell, B. (1976). Early home environment and changes in mental test performance in children 6 to 36 months. *Developmental Psychology, 12,* 93–97.

Breitmayer, B.J., & Ramey, C.T. (1986). Biological nonoptimality and quality of postnatal environment as codeterminants of intellectual development. *Child Development, 57,* 1151–1165.

Breznitz, A., & Friedman, S.L. (1988). Toddlers' ability to concentrate: The influence of maternal depression. *Journal of Child Psychology and Psychiatry, 29,* 267–279.

Bromet, E., & Cornely, P. (1984). Correlates of depression in mothers of young children. *Journal of American Academy of Child Psychiatry, 23,* 335–342.

Bronfenbrenner, U. (1979). *The ecology of human development.* Cambridge, MA: Harvard University Press.

Bronfenbrenner, U. (1986). Ecology of the family as a context for human development: Research perspectives. *Developmental Psychology, 22*(6), 723–742.

Bryk, A.S., Wohlleb C., Malson, N., & Mathis, M.E. (1975). *Evaluation primer, Brookline Early Education Project,* Brookline, MA.

Carey, W.B. (1985). Clinical use of temperament data in pediatrics. *Journal of Developmental and Behavioral Pediatrics, 6,* 137–142.

Carran, D.T., Scott, K.G., Shaw, K., & Beydouin, S. (1989). The relative risk of educational handicaps in two birth cohorts of normal low birthweight disadvantaged children. *Topics in Early Childhood Special Education, 9*(1), 14–31.

Casto, G., & Lewis, A.C. (1989). Parent involvement in infant and preschool programs. *Journal of the Division for Early Childhood, 9,* 49–56.

Casto, G., & Mastropieri, M.A. (1986). The efficacy of early intervention programs: A meta analysis. *Exceptional Child, 52,* 417–424.

Clarke-Stewart, K.A. (1973). Interaction between mothers and their young children: Characteristics and consequences. *SRCD Monographs, 38* (6-7 Serial No. 153).

Colletta, N.D. (1983). At risk for depression: A study of young mothers. *Journal of Genetic Psychology, 142,* 301–310.

Conger, R., McCarthy, J., Yang, R., Lahey, B., & Kropp, J. (1984). Perception of child, childbearing values, and emotional distress as mediating links between environmental stressors and observed maternal behavior. *Child Development, 55,* 2234–2247.

Cox, A.D., Puckering, C., Pound, A., & Mills, M. (1987). The impact of maternal depression in young children. *Journal of Child Psychology and Psychiatry, 28,* 917–928.

Crockenberg, S.B. (1986). Are temperamental differences in babies associated with predictable differences in care-giving? In J.V. Lerner & R.M. Lerner (Eds.), *Temperament and social interaction in infants and children. New directions for child development* (pp. 53-73). San Francisco: Jossey-Bass.

Crockenberg, S.B. (1981). Infant irritability, mother responsiveness and social support influences on the security of infant-mother attachment. *Child Development, 52,* 857–865.

Crnic, K.A., & Greenberg, M.T. (1987). Transactional relationships between perceived family style risk status and mother child interactions in two year-olds. *Journal of Pediatric Psychology, 12*(3), 343–362.

Crnic, K.A., Greenberg, M., Ragozin, A., Robinson, N., & Basham, R. (1983). Effects of stress and social supports on mothers of premature and full-term infants. *Child Development, 54,* 209–217.

Crouter, A., Belsky, J., & Spanier, G. (1984). The family context of child development. In G. Whitehurst (Ed.), *Animals of Child Development, 1,* Greenwich, CT: JAI.

Cutrona, C.E., & Troutman, B.R. (1986). Social support, infant temperament and parenting self-efficacy: A mediational model. *Child Development, 57,* 1507-1518.

Dunst, C.J. (1985). Rethinking early intervention. *Analysis and Intervention in Developmental Disabilities, 5,* 165–201.

Dunst, C.J., Leet, H.E., & Trivette, C.M. (1988). Family resources, personal well-being and early intervention. *The Journal of Special Education, 2*(1), 108–116.

Egeland, B., Jacobovitz, D., & Sroufe, L.A. (1988). Breaking the cycle of abuse. *Child Development, 59,* 1080–1088.

Emde, R.N. (1988a). Risk, intervention, and meaning. *Psychiatry, 51,* 254–259.

Emde, R.N. (1988b). The effect of relationships on relationships: A developmental approach to clinical intervention. In R.A. Hinde & J. Stevenson-Hinde (Eds.), *Relationships within families, mutual influences* (pp. 354–364). Oxford: Clarendon Press.

Eysenck, H.J., & Eysenck, S.B.G. (1968). *Manual for the Eysenck Personality Inventory,* San Diego: Educational and Industrial Testing Service.

Field, T.M. (1986, July). Interventions for premature infants. *The Journal of Pediatrics,* pp. 183–191.

Field, T., Healy, B., Goldstein, S., & Guthertz, M. (1990). Behavior-state matching and synchrony in mother-infant interactions of nondepressed versus depressed dyads. *Developmental Psychology, 26,* 7–14.

Field, T., Healy, B., Goldstein, S., Perry S., Bendell, D., Schanberg, S., Zimmerman, E.A., & Kuhn, C. (1988). Infants of depressed mothers show ''depressed'' behavior even with nondepressed adults. *Child Development, 59*(6), 1569–1579.

Field, T.M. Widmayer, S.M., Stringer, S., & Ignatoff, E. (1980). Teenage, lower-class, black mothers and their preterm infants: An intervention and developmental follow-up. *Child Development, 51,* 426–436.

Flaherty, J.A., & Richman, J.A. (1986). The effects of childhood relationships on the adult's capacity to form social supports. *American Journal of Psychiatry, 193*(7), 851–855.

Fraiberg, S., Adelson, E., & Shapiro, V. (1975). Ghosts in the nursery: A psychoanalytic approach to the problems of impaired infant-mother relationships. *Journal of the American Academy of Child Psychiatry, 14*, 387–421.

Garbarino, J. (1982). *Children and families in the social environment.* New York: Aldine.

Garbarino, J. (1983). Social support networks: Rx for the helping professions. In J. Whittaker & J. Garbarino (Eds.), *Social support networks informal helping in the human services* (pp. 3–28). New York: Aldine.

Goldberg, S., Corter, C., Ojkasek, M., & Minde, K. (1990). Prediction of behavior problems in 4-year-olds born prematurely. *Development and Psychopathology, 2*(1), 15–30.

Goldberg, S., & Marcovitch, S. (1989). Temperament in developmentally disabled children. In G.A. Kohnstamm, J.E. Bates, & M.K. Rothbart (Eds.), *Temperament in childhood* (pp. 387–403). John Wiley & Sons.

Goldberg, W., & Easterbrooks, M. (1984). Role of marital quality in toddler development. *Developmental Psychology, 20*, 504–514.

Gray, S.W., & Wandersam, C.P. (1980). The methodology of home-based intervention studies: Problems and promising strategies. *Child Development, 51*, 993–1009.

Greenberg, M.T., & Crnic, K.A. (1988). Longitudinal predictors of developmental status and social interactions in premature and full-term infants at age 2. *Child Development, 59*(3), 554–570.

Gross, R. et al. (1990). Enhancing the outcomes of low-birth-weight, premature infants: A multi-site, randomized trial. *JAMA, 263*(22), 3035–3042.

Guralnick, M.J., & Bennett, F.C. (1987). Early intervention for at-risk and handicapped children: Current and future perspectives. In M.J. Guralnick & F.C. Bennett (Eds.), *The effectiveness of early intervention for at-risk and handicapped children* (pp. 365–382). New York: Academic Press.

Halpern, R. (1984). Lack of effects for home-based early intervention? Some possible explanations. *American Journal of Orthpsychiatry, 59*, 33–42.

Hammen, C., Gordon, G. Burge, D., Adrian, C., Jaenicke, C., & Hiroto, G. (1987). Maternal affective disorders, illness and stress: Risk for children's psychopathology. *American Journal of Psychiatry, 144*, 763.

Heinicke, C.M., Beckwith, L., & Thompson, A. (1988). Early intervention in the family system: A framework and review. *Infant Mental Health Journal, 9*(2), 111–141.

Henderson, S. (1980). A development in social psychiatry the systematic study of social bonds. *Journal of Nervous & Mental Disorders, 168*(2), 63–69.

Henderson, S., Duncan-Jones, P., Byrne, D.C., Adcock, S., & Scott, R. (1979). Neurosis and social bonds in an urban population. *Australizan New Zealand Journal of Psychiatry, 13*(2), 121–126.

Heverly, M., Neuman, F., & Forquer, S. (1982). Meta-analysis and cost-analysis of preventive intervention programs. *Report to the National Center for Clinical Infant Programs.* Philadelphia: Systems Research Unit.

Hinde, R.A. (1979). *Towards understanding relationships.* London: Academic Press.

Hinde, R.A., & Stevenson-Hinde, J. (1987). Interpersonal relationships and child development. *Developmental Review, 7*, 1–21.

Jones, F.A., Green, V., & Krauss, D.R. (1980). Maternal responsiveness of primiparous mothers during the postpartum period. Age differences. *Pediatrics, 65*, 579–584.

Kellam, S.G., Adams, R.G., Brown, C.H., & Ensminger, N.E. (1982). The long-term evolution of the family structure of teenage and older mothers. *Journal of Marriage and the Family, 44*, 539–554.

Kellam, S.G., Ensminger, M.E., & Turner, R.R. (1977). Family structure and the mental health of children: Concurrent and longitudinal community-wide studies. *Archives of General Psychiatry, 34*, 1012–1022.

Kessen, W., & Fein, G. (1975). *Variations in home-based infant education: Language, play and social development.* New Haven, CT: Yale University Press.

Kohnstamm, G.A., Bates, J.E., & Rothbart, M.K. (Eds.). (1989). *Temperament in childhood.* New York: Wiley.

Korner, A.F. (1981). What we don't know about waterbeds and apneic preterm infants. *Pediatrics, 68*(2), 306.

Korner, A.F., Schneider, P., & Forrest, T. (1983). Effects of vestibular-proprioceptive stimulation on the neurobehavioral development of preterm infants: A pilot study. *Neuropediatrics, 14*(3), 170–175.

Lamb, N. (1983). Early mother-neonate contact and the mother-child relationship. *Journal of Child Psychological Psychiatry, 24,* 487–494.

Landry, S.N., Chapieski, L., Fleicher, J., & Denson, S. (1988). Three-year outcomes for low birthweight infants: Differential effects of early medical complications. *Journal of Pediatric Psychology, 13*(3), 317–327.

Lester, B.M., Coll, C.T., & Sepkoski, C. (1983). A "cross"-cultural study of teenage pregnancy and neonatal behavior. In T. Field & A. Sostek (Eds.), *Infants born at risk.* New York: Grune & Stratton.

Love, J.M, Nauta, M.J., Cohen, C.G., Hewlett, C., & Ruopp, R.R. (1976). *National home start evaluation final report, findings, implications* (HEW Grant No. 105-72-1100). Ypsilante, MI: High/Scope Educational Research Foundation.

Lyons-Ruth, K., Cornell, D. Gryneboom, N., Botein, M., & Zoll, D. (1984). Maternal family history, maternal caretaking, and infant attachment in multi problem families. *Journal of Preventive Psychiatry, 2,* 403–425.

Maccoby, E.E., Jacklin, C.N. (1983). The "person" characteristics of children and the family as an environment. In D. Magnusson & V.L. Allen (Eds.), *Human development: An interactional perspective.* Hillsdale, NJ: Erlbaum.

Magnusson, D., & Endler, N.S. (1977). Interactional psychology: Present status and future prospects. In D. Magnusson & N.S. Engler (Eds.), *Personality at the crossroads: Current issues in international psychology.* Hillsdale, NJ: Erlbaum.

Minde, K., Shosenberg, N., Morton, P., Thompson, I., Ripley, J., & Burns, S. (1980). Self-help groups in a premature nursing—a controlled evaluation. *Journal of Pediatrics, 96,* 933–940.

Minde, K., Shosenberg, N., Thompson, J., & Morton, P. (1983). Self-help groups in a premature nursery follow-up at one year. In J.D. Call, E. Galenson, & R.L. Tyson (Eds.), *Frontiers of infant psychiatry.* New York: Basic Books.

Nurcombe, B., Howell, D.C., Rauh, V.A., Teti, D.M., Ruoff, P., & Brennan, J. (1984). An intervention program for mothers of low birth-weight infants: Preliminary results. *Journal of the American Academy of Child Psychiatry, 23,* 319–325.

Nurcombe, B., Rauh, V., Howell, D., Teti, D., Ruoff, P., Murphy, B., & Brennan, J. (1984). An intervention program for mothers of low-birthweight babies: Outcome at six and twelve months. In J. Call, E. Galenson, & R.L. Tyson (Eds.), *Frontiers of infant psychiatry.* New York: Basic Books.

Oppel, W.C., & Royston, A.B. (1971). Teenage births: Some social psychological, and physical sequaelae. *American Journal of Public Health, 61,* 751–756.

Osofsky, J.D., Culp, A.M., & Ware, L.M. (1988). Intervention challenges with adolescent mothers and their infants. *Psychiatry, 51,* 236–241.

Osofsky, H., & Osofsky, J. (1970). Adolescent mothers: Results of a program for low income pregnant teenagers with some emphasis upon infant development. *American Journal of Orthopsychiatry, 40,* 825–34.

Ottenbacher, K.J., Muffer, L., Brandt, D., Heintzelman, A., Hojem, P., & Sharpe, P. (1987). The effectiveness of tactiles stimulation as a form of early intervention: A quantitative evaluation. *Journal of Developmental and Behavior Pediatrics, 8,* 68–76.

Ottenbacher, K., & Petersen, P. (1985). The efficacy of early intervention programs for children with organic impairment: A quantitative review. *Evaluation Program Planning, 8,* 185–196.

Paneth, N. (1990). Technology at birth. *American Journal of Public Health*, 80(7), 791–792.

Parke, R.D. Tinsley, B.R. (1982). The early environment of the at-risk infant. In D.F.D. Bricker (Ed.), *Intervention with at-risk and handicapped infants, from research to application* (pp. 153–177). Baltimore: University Park Press.

Parmelee, A.H., Beckwith, L., Cohen, S.E., & Sigman, N. (1983). Social influences at medical risk for behavioral difficulties. In J.D. Call, E. Galensen, & R.L. Tyson (Eds.), *Frontiers of infant psychiatry* (pp. 247–255). New York: Basic Books.

Pascoe, J.M., Loda, F.A., Jeffries, V., & Earp, J.A. (1981). The association between mothers social support and provision of stimulation to their children. *Development and Behavioral Pediatrics*, 2, 15–19.

Plomin, R., & Dunn, J. (1986). *The study of temperament, changes, continuities, and challenges*. Hillsdale, NJ: Erlbaum.

Radke-Yarrow, N., Cummings, E.M., Kuczynski, L., & Chapman, M. (1985). Patterns of attachment in two-and-three-year-olds in normal families and families with parental depression. *Child Development*, 56, 884–893.

Ragozin, A.S., Basham, R.B., Crnic, K.A., Greenberg, N.T., & Robinson, N.M. (1982). Effects of maternal age on parenting role. *Developmental Psychology*, 18, 627–634.

Ramey, C.T., Bryant, D.M., & Suarez, T.N. (1985). Preschool compensatory education and the modifiability of intelligence: A critical review. In D.K. Detterman (Ed.), *Current topics in human intelligence* (Vol. 1, pp. 247–296). Norwood, NJ: Ablex Publishing Corp.

Ramey, C.T., Zeskind, P.S., & Hunter, R. (1981). Biomedical psychosocial interventions for preterm infants. In S. Friedman & N. Sigman (Eds.), *Preterm birth and psychological development* (pp. 395–415) New York; Academic Press.

Rauh, V.A. (1982). *The mother-infant transaction study*. Unpublished doctoral dissertation, Harvard University.

Rauh, V.A., Achenbach, T.N., Nurcombe, B., Howell, C.T., & Teti, D.M. (1988). Minimizing adverse effects of low birthweight: Four-year results of an early intervention program. *Child Development*, 59, 544–553.

Rauh, V.A., Nurcombe, B., Ruoff, P., Tette, A., & Howell, D. (1982). The Vermont-Infant Studies Project: The rationale for a mother-infant transaction program. In L. Bond & J.M. Joffe (Eds.), *Facilitating infant and early childhood development* (pp. 259–280). Hanover & London: University Press of New England.

Rothman, K.J., Greenland, S., & Walker, A.N. (1980). Concepts of interaction. *American Journal of Epidemiology*, 112 (4), 467–470.

Rutter, M. (1983a). Statistical and personal interactions: Facets and perspectives. In D. Magnusson & V.L. Allen (Eds.), *Human development: An interactional perspective* (pp. 295–319). New York: Academic Press.

Rutter, M. (1983b). The developmental psychopathology of depression: Issues and perspectives. In M. Rutter, C.E. Izard, & P.B. Read (Eds.), *Depression in young people: Developmental and clinical perspectives*. New York: Guilford Press.

Sameroff, A.J., Seifer, R., Barocas, R., Zax, N., & Greenspan, S. (1987). Intelligence Quotient Scores of 4-year-old children: Social-environmental risk factors. *Pediatrics*, 79 (3), 343-350.

Sameroff, A.J. (1982a). Development and the dialactic. The need for a systems approach. In W.A. Collins (Ed.), *The concept of development*. Hillsdale, NJ: Erlbaum.

Sameroff, A.J. (1982b). The environmental context of developmental disabilities. In D.D. Bricker (Ed.), *Intervention with at-risk and handicapped infants: From research to application* (pp. 141–152). Baltimore: University Park Press.

Sameroff, A.J., & Chandler, M.J. (1975). Reproductive risk and the continuum of caretaking casuality. In F.D. Horowitz (Ed.), *Review of child development research* (Vol. 4). Chicago: University of Chicago Press.

Siegal, E., Bauman, K.E., Schaefer, E.S., Saunders, N.N., & Ingram, D.D. (1980). Hospital and home support during infancy: Impact on maternal attachment, child abuse and neglect, and health-care utilization. *Pediatrics*, *66*, 183–190.

Siegel, L.S. (1981). Infant tests as predictors of cognitive and language development at two years. *Child Development*, *52*, 545–557.

Siegel, L.S. (1982). Reproductive, perinatal, and environmental factors as predictors of the cognitive and language development of preterm and full-term infants. *Child Development*, *53*, 963–973.

Siegel, L.S. (1984). Home environment influences on cognitive development in preterm and full-term infants during the first five years. In A.W. Gottfried (Ed.), *Home environment and early cognitive development* (pp. 197–233). New York: Academic Press.

Simeonsson, R., Cooper, D., & Scheinar, A. (1982). A review and analysis of the effectiveness of early intervention programs. *Pediatrics*, *69*(5), 635–641.

Sroufe, L.A. (1983). Infant-caregiver attachment and patterns of adaptation in preschool: the roots of maladaptation and competence. In N. Perlmutter (Ed.), *The Minnesota Symposium on Child Psychology*, *16*. *Development and Policy Concerning Children with Special Needs* (pp. 41–83). Hillsdale, NJ: Erlbaum.

Stevenson-Hinde, & J. Hinde, R.A. (1988). Individuals in relationships. In R.A. Hinde & Stevenson-Hinde (Eds.), *Relationships within families, mutual influences* (pp. 354–364). Oxford: Clarendon Press.

Stevenson-Hinde, J., & Hinde, R.A. (1986). Changes in associations between characteristics and interactions. In R. Plomin & J. Dunn (Eds.), *The study of temperament: Changes, continuities and challenges*. Hillsdale, NJ: Erlbaum.

Stuckey, M., McGhee, P., & Bell, N. (1982). Parent-child interaction: The influences of maternal employment. *Developmental Psychology*, *18*, 635–644.

Teti, D.M., & Gelfand, D.M. (1990, April). *Maternal depression, parenting and maternal self-efficacy: A longitudinal study of mothers and infants*. Paper presented at the International Conference on Infant Studies, Montreal.

Teti, D.M., Gelfand, D.M., & Pompa, J. (1990). Depressed mothers' behavioral competence with their infants: Demographic and psychosocial correlates. *Development and Psychopathology*, *2*(3), 259–270.

Thomas, A., & Chess, S. (1977). *Temperament and Development*. New York: Brunner/Mazel.

Thomas, A., Chess S., Birch, H. Hertzig, N., & Korn, S. (1963). *Behavioral individuality in early childhood*. London: University of London.

Tinsley, B.R., & Parke, R.D. (1983). The person-environment relationship lessons from families with preterm infants. In D. Magnusson & V.L. Allen (Eds.), *Human development, an interactional perspective* (pp. 93–110). New York: Academic Press.

Triad, P.V. (1987). *Infant and childhood depression: developmental factors*. New York: Wiley.

Trivette, C.N., Deal, A., & Dunst, C.J. (1986). Family needs, sources of support, and professional roles: Critical elements of family systems assessment and intervention. *Diagnostique*, *11*, 246–267.

Tulkin, S.R., & Cohler, B.J. (1973). Child-rearing attitudes and mother-child interaction in the first year of life. *Merrill-Palmer Quarterly*, *19*, 95–106.

Unger, D.G., & Wandersman, L.P. (1985). Social Support and adolescent mothers: Action research contributions to theory and applications. *Journal of Social Issues*, *41*, 29–45.

Vaughn, B. (1986). The doubtful validity of infant temperament assessments by means of questionnaires like the ITQ. In G.A. Konnstamm (Ed.). *Temperament discussed, temperament and development in infancy and childhood*. Lisse: Swets & Zeitlinger B.V.

Weissman, M., Paykel, E., & Klerman, G., (1972). The depressed woman as a model. *Social Psychiatry*, *7*, 98–108.

Weissman, M.M., Prusoff, B.A., Gammon, G.D., Merikangas, K.R., Leckman, J.F., & Kidd, K.K. (1984). Psychopathology in the children (ages 6–18) of depressed and normal parents. *Journal of the American Academy of Child Psychiatry, 23*, 78–84.

Werner, E.Y., & Šmith, R.S. (1982) *Vulnerable but invincible: A longitudinal study of resilient children and youth.* New York: McGraw-Hill.

White, K.R. (1982). The relation between socioeconomic status and academic achievement. *Psychological Bulletin, 91*, 461–481.

White, K.R., & Casto, G. (1985). An integrative review of early intervention efficacy studies with at risk children: Implications for the handicapped. *Analysis and Intervention in Developmental Disabilities, 5*, 7–31.

Widmayer, S., & Field T. (1981). Effects of Breazelton demonstrations for mother on the development of preterm infants. *Pediatrics, 67*, 711–714.

Wolkind, S., Coleman, E.Z., & Ghodsian, M. (1980). Continuity in maternal depression. *International Journal of Family Psychiatry, 1*, 167–181.

Worobey, J., & Brazelton, T.B. (1986). Experimenting with the family in the newborn period: A commentary. *Child Development, 57*, 1298–1300.

Zuckerman, B.S., Walker, D.K., Frank, D.A., Chase, C., & Hamburg, B. (1984). Adolescent pregnancy: biobehavioral determinants of outcome. *Journal of Pediatrics, 105*, 857–83.

Zuckerman, B.S., Winsmore, G., & Alpert, J. (1979). A study of attitudes and support systems of inner city adolescent mothers. *Journal of Pediatrics, 95*, 122–125.

AUTHOR INDEX

Fowler, A., 343, *384*
Fowler, M.G., *430*
Fowler, R.S., 178, *182*, 223, *236*
Fowler, W., 353, *382*
Fox, A.M., 98, *123*, 126, 149, *154*
Fox, H.A., 351, *385*
Fox, N.A., 95, 101, *122*
Fox, W.W., 46, *57*
Fraiberg, S., *465*
Frailberg, S., 381, *408*
Francis, D.J., 126, *153*, 260, *273*, 283, 284, 294, 297
Francis, P.L., 67, *85*
Francis-Williams, J., 189, *212*, 317, *336*
Frank, D.A., 442, *470*
Frankel, D.G., 79, *86*
Fremmer-Bombik, E., 391, *408*
French, K.S., 202, 207, *213*
Freud, S., 354, *382*
Freund, D.A., 53, *57*
Friedman, S.L., *18*, 157, *182*, 296, 301, 453, *464*
Friel, J., *274*
Friendly, D.S., 344, 350, *383*
Friis-Hansen, B., 344, *385*
Frisch, R.O., 413, *430*
Fullard, W., 166, *182*
Furlough, R.R., 49, *59*
Furshpan, E.J., 353, *386*
Furstenberg, F.F., 81, *86*

G

Gaensbauer, T.J., 84, *85*
Gagan, R.J., 346, 347, *382*
Gaiter, J.L., 346, 351, *382, 383*
Gallagher, J., 126, 147, *153*, 285, 286, 288, 297, 352, *382*
Gammon, G.D., *470*
Gamsu, H., 196, 197, *213*
Garbanati, J.A., 302, 303, *314*
Garbarino, J., 435, *466*
Garcia, R., 351, *386*
Garcia Coll, C.T., 276, 277, 278, 287, 290, 298
Garcia-Prats, J., 344, *386*
Garland, M.J., 318, *336*
Garmezy, N., 63, 81, *86*
Garside, R.F., 198, 199, 209, *213*
Gartner, L.M., 41, *58*, 412, *431*
Gelfand, D.M., 453, 460, *469*
Gelman, R., 67, *86*
Gennaro, S., 159, *181, 182*

George, C., 168, *182*
Gerdes, J., 342, 343, *382*
Gerhardt, T., 44, *55*
Geronimus, A., 42, *57*
Gesell, A.L., 67, *86*, 353, *383*
Gesten, E.L., 133, *153*
Gewitz, M.H., 46, *57*
Ghodsian, M., 453, *470*
Gianino, A., 355, *383*
Gibbson, A., *56*, 159, *181*
Gibes, R., 92, *121*, 364, 373, 374, *380*
Gil, J., 54, *56*
Gilbert, A., 177, *182*
Giles, H.R., 42, *57*
Gilkerson, K., 347, 348, 349, *383*
Ginzberg, E., 424n, 427n, *432*
Gjerde, P.F., 242, *254*
Gladstone, I., 47, *56*
Glass, G., 46, 48, *57*
Glass, P., 260, 262, *273, 274*, 344, 350, *383*
Gleick, J., 103, *122*
Goebel, R., *274*
Goldberg, C., 132, *152*
Goldberg, R.N., 44, *55*
Goldberg, S., 99, 100, 101, *121, 122*, 125, 147, *153*, 161, 162, 163, 174, 175, 178, *182, 183, 185*, 301, *313*, 390, *408*, 414, *430*, 447, *466*
Goldberg, W., 459, *466*
Goldfield, D., 177, *182*
Goldman, P.S., 357, *383*
Goldman-Rakic, P.S., 357, *383*
Goldson, E., 344, 345, *383*
Goldstein, H., 198, *212*
Goldstein, K.M., 239, *254*, 259, 269, 272, *273, 274*, 286, 298, 412, *429*
Goldstein, M.J., 252, *254*
Goldstein, R.F., 101, *121*
Goldstein, S., 453, 454, *465*
Golinkoff, R.M., 68, *86*
Goodwin, S.R., 343, *383*
Gordon, G., 453, *466*
Gordon, H.H., 351, *384*
Gordon, M., 201, *213*
Goren, C.C., 95, *122*
Gorski, P.A., 344, 347, 348, 349, 351, 352, *383*
Gortmaker, S.L., 42, *57*, 200, *212*
Gottfried, A.W., 78, *85*, 301, *314*, 346, 351, *383*
Gough, H.G., 242, *254*
Goyette, C.H., 194, *211*

SUBJECT INDEX